A HISTORY OF FRANCE

By the same author

General

ARIEL

BYRON

DISRAELI

EDWARD VII AND HIS TIMES

LYAUTEY

DICKENS

VOLTAIRE

POETS AND PROPHETS

A HISTORY OF ENGLAND

CHATEAUBRIAND

CALL NO MAN HAPPY

THE QUEST FOR PROUST

LÉLIA

VICTOR HUGO

THE LIFE OF SIR ALEXANDER FLEMING

ADRIENNE DE LA FAYETTE

Fiction

COLONEL BRAMBLE

THE FAMILY CIRCLE

THE WEIGHER OF SOULS

BERNARD QUESNAY

RICOCHETS

THE THOUGHT-READING MACHINE

ETC.

A
HISTORY
OF
FRANCE

by

ANDRÉ MAUROIS

Translated from the French by
HENRY L. BINSSE

Additional Chapters translated by
GERARD HOPKINS

JONATHAN CAPE
THIRTY BEDFORD SQUARE
LONDON

FIRST PUBLISHED NOVEMBER 1949
SECOND IMPRESSION JULY 1950
THIRD IMPRESSION APRIL 1952
FOURTH IMPRESSION NOVEMBER 1953
SECOND (revised and enlarged) EDITION SEPTEMBER 1956
REPRINTED JULY 1957
THIRD (revised) EDITION NOVEMBER 1960
REPRINTED SEPTEMBER 1961
REPRINTED NOVEMBER 1964
REPRINTED 1969

SBN 224 60484 8

PRINTED IN GREAT BRITAIN BY
LOWE AND BRYDONE (PRINTERS) LIMITED, LONDON
ON PAPER MADE BY JOHN DICKINSON & CO. LTD
BOUND BY A. W. BAIN & CO. LTD, LONDON

CONTENTS

BOOK ONE

THE FIRST BEGINNINGS AND THE MIDDLE AGES

BOOK TWO

RENAISSANCE AND REFORMATION

CONTENTS

BOOK THREE
THE ABSOLUTE MONARCHY

BOOK FOUR
THE FRENCH REVOLUTION

CONTENTS

BOOK FIVE
YEARS OF WAVERING

BOOK SIX
THE THIRD REPUBLIC

BOOK SEVEN
THE FOURTH AND FIFTH REPUBLICS

PREFACE

I HAVE been asked to provide for this new edition a few chapters bringing the history of France up to date. This I have done, though the undertaking is not without danger.

It is easy to be impartial when one is dealing with events which occurred several centuries ago. The struggles of the past have been resolved, the controversies extinguished. Those who played their parts upon the stage of history are dead. Occasionally a flame which one had thought was long smothered bursts again into life for a brief moment. I have known aloof professors to blaze with anger because I preferred Disraeli to Gladstone. I have seen English Catholics wax indignant over the dissolution of the monasteries, and French Protestants at the memory of Saint Bartholomew. But the sincere historian, where such matters are concerned, can at least try to establish the facts from the study of such documentary material and evidence as are available. It is easy for him to avoid writing in a partisan spirit.

When, however, he has to handle events in which he himself has been involved, controversies in which he has been compelled to take sides, he must exercise great care if he is to arrive at the truth without letting himself be led astray by passion and prejudice. It is difficult for a Frenchman of today to speak of Mendès-France or Edgar Faure with the same degree of detachment which he would bring to the study of Thiers or Guizot. But that is precisely what the historian must do. I have tried to deal with recent years, years which have been filled, in France, with contests and rivalries, as though I had not lived through them. I can only hope that I have succeeded. The reader will find in these additional chapters a statement of facts, not a formulation of judgments. Only future generations can have the right to judge.

The other danger inherent in the study of recent history is that events, small in themselves, take on undue importance. No more than sixteen years have elapsed since the Liberation of France. For us, however, those sixteen years bulk infinitely larger than would a similar period of time in the reigns of Louis-Philippe or Louis XIV. Ought we, then, to think only in terms of time, and give to our own period no more space than to a similar stretch of years in the nineteenth century? I do not think so. It is only natural that the reader should want more details about the occurrences of which he has been a witness, which he has discussed, which have produced consequences which are still, for him, matters of daily and capital importance. Nor must we forget that the last sixteen years have witnessed in France something very closely resembling a revolution, and have been as rich in change as have any of the most dramatic moments of our history.

For all these reasons, it has seemed to me a legitimate undertaking to add to this book — which my English readers are kind enough still to regard with favour — two complementary chapters. But my general conclusions remain unmodified. They are, I believe, as true as ever they were.

A. M.

A HISTORY OF FRANCE

BOOK ONE

THE FIRST BEGINNINGS AND THE MIDDLE AGES

CHAPTER I

HOW GAUL BECAME ROMAN

FEW regions in the world are more rewarding to the visitor than the
Valley of the Vézère, in the French province of Périgord. The river's
murky waters flow between two walls of stone, and its high banks are
pierced by black openings, the mouths of caves or shelters. In ages long
past these caverns, as thick as rabbit warrens on the edge of a forest, formed
a sort of prehistoric city. In many of them stone weapons have been
found, as well as tools, animal bones and human skulls. About thirty
thousand years ago a people dwelt there, entering and leaving their homes
by means of narrow footpaths or vine ladders. Both fire and difficulty of
access protected them against wild animals. Fishing and hunting supplied
their needs and, on the stone surface of their caves, they drew, 'with the
ease and charm born of long acquaintance',[1] pictures of reindeer and
buffalo.

It cannot be said that the history of these men belongs to the history
of France, for nations had not yet taken shape. Yet French civilization,
like all others, rests on deep and mysterious foundations. In France villages
of cave-dwellers are still to be found. The mists of a primitive religion —
belief in fairies, in charms, in sorcerers — everywhere linger over French
fields. A popular art in which geometric patterns and animal life prevail
is instinctive with the shepherd carving a bit of wood, with the rural potter
modelling his clay. And, towards the end of the prehistoric era, one must
think in terms of a fairly homogeneous Mediterranean civilization, of
trade, of merchants going to and fro, of towns built beside lakes, of
primitive agriculture, of the first domesticated animals. The thin outer
skin of historic times encases many layers of prehistory, and successive
generations which seem to have left no trace of their passage through this
world other than shaped or polished bits of stone, bronze tools, dolmens,
menhirs, burial chambers, footpaths and water-holes have in fact
bequeathed man a legacy of words, institutions and recipes without which
the sequel to their story would have been past conceiving.

There has never been a French race. The area which today goes to make
up France, being near the end of the European continent, was the place

[1] HENRI FOÇILLON.

where invasions stopped short and invaders settled down. At the beginning of the first thousand years before our era, you would have found Ligurians inhabiting the Alps, and in the Pyrenees, Iberians, perhaps the ancestors of the present Basques. Over the Mediterranean came Phoenician sailors: thus *Monaco* is a Phoenician word signifying a place for *rest*: a place where one *stops*. Semitic traders exchanged pearls, pottery and brilliantly coloured fabrics for slaves. Later on, Greek navigators made settlements along the edge of the sea and brought with them the civilization of the East, religious ideas and mysteries, money, the cultivation of the olive and a highly developed language. Massila (Marseilles), their principal colony, founded about 600 B.C. by mariners from Phocaea in Ionia, the Greeks made into a commercial port through which passed the tin they obtained from Britain by way of Germany and the rivers. Marseilles founded new colonies and Greek cities came to dot the coast: Nicaea (Nice), Agathe Tukhe (Agde), Antipolis (Antibes). In such manner the Provençal countryside was transformed by the Greeks, who brought to it not only the olive but the cypress, the fig, the grape, the acanthus, the pomegranate. The Battle of Flowers, that annual rite in Nice and in other cities along the Riviera, dates back to Greek days and was surely linked in the beginning to the cult of Demeter, Adonis or Persephone. The rose, native of Persia, passed through Greece and was then brought to southern France by way of Italy. It is thanks to Greek sailors and Roman soldiers that today the perfume of the rose is distilled at Grasse.

Many centuries before Christ a new civilization, the Celtic, filtered into the valleys of the Rhine and the Rhône. These Celtic tribes of warriors and shepherds came from the Danube area; by language and customs they belonged to the Indo-European group. It is not at all certain that there existed a true Celtic people. Ancient Greek writers, by whom all 'hyperborean' (northern) Barbarians were vaguely lumped together, applied the name Celt to any tall, light-skinned, fair-haired foreigner dwelling beyond the mountains. Yet there were dark Celts, and triumphant Roman generals, in order to display in Rome captives in conformity with popular tradition, had often to dye their hair. What seems to have been the common element was not a Celtic race but a Celtic language and civilization. And these peoples knew the art of forging the two-edged iron sword, the finest weapon of their day. At La Tène (near the Lake of Neuchâtel) and at Hallstadt, excavations have brought to light nothing less than factories for the production of arms. The Celts had taste, were acquainted with Greek ornament and used it to embellish their jewellery and their swords. In the fourth century their superiority of armament and their prowess enabled them to conquer an empire. They penetrated into Asia Minor (Galatia), crossed the Rhine and the Alps, peopled north Italy, burned Rome but did not remain there, and became the overlords of the native populations in the lands which are now France and Spain. It would be utterly false to suppose that the Celts, having annihilated the Ligurians and Iberians, replaced them. Rather should we picture to ourselves a slow penetration, a warlike aristocracy enslaving the local people and gradually assimilating them, the speech of the conquerors little by little becoming that of all the tribes west of the Rhine and the Alps. In French veins is mingled the blood of the Iberians and the Ligurians as well as that of the Celts, Romans and many another race. As for the name Gaulois, it was the appellation given by the Romans to the Celts (Galli).

The Celtic empire did not last and, from the end of the fourth century, the Gauls of northern Italy (Cisalpine Gaul) were all firmly bound to Rome. The Romans described as Transalpine Gaul the lands beyond the Alps and included in this area the territory which makes up modern Belgium. They were well aware that Celts occupied Great Britain and Ireland and that the Gauls traded with these fog-bound islands. To Roman eyes during the second century before Christ, Gaul must have seemed much as Morocco did to an Algerian of 1880 — a contiguous country, barbarous and troublesome. Whereupon military needs led to political annexation: with Rome at war with Carthage, the generals said it was important to protect communications between Spain and Italy along the Mediterranean coast. Towards the end of the second century before Christ, this whole region including Marseilles became a Roman province, and indeed *the* province above all others, whence the name Provence (Provincia). Said Pliny, '*Italia verius quam provincia*' ('More like Italy than a province') and this because nature, vegetation and climate reminded him of Italy. Beautiful cities — Arles, Nîmes, Orange — with their public baths, their forums, their arenas, grew there apace. Very soon, in what remained of free Gaul, the inhabitants saw themselves threatened at once from the east by the Germans, who were greedily and belligerently massing on the other side of the Rhine, and from the south by the Romans. Two classes of Roman citizen, the speculators and the soldiers, demanded the conquest of Gaul. The speculators coveted the slaves it would yield, its landed estates, its mines; the soldiers thought they would find there glory and political prestige and pointed out that in order to assure Rome's security against the Germans, it would be necessary to cover Italy's flank in

Gaul. Thanks to a general, statesman and man of letters, Julius Caesar, we possess a graphic picture of Gaul about 50 B.C. In reading what Caesar wrote we must bear in mind a few mistakes inevitable in Intelligence Service reports on relatively little-known tribes. Caesar, however, had had as a teacher in his youth a man of Gallic origin, Antiphon, and his own later campaigns had allowed him to journey the length and breadth of the country. He was as well informed on Gaul as a Roman – and a general – could be.

Be it in Gaul or in Britain, Celtic societies were, Caesar tells us, divided into clans. A group of clans formed a tribe, several tribes a nation. At the time of the conquest it is estimated that there were about seventy-two nations and four to five hundred tribes. Many of the latter have lent their names to French towns: the Parisii (Paris), the Bituriges (Bourges), the Lexovii (Lisieux), the Ebrocii (Evreux). But in Caesar's day the Gauls had no real cities. The tribe's *oppidum* was scarcely more than a fortified enclosure, surrounded by a stockade within which the market was held and refuge might be sought in time of war. There forgathered the Senate, an assembly in which participated the great landlords. Certain tribes had a king, others a tyrant; most were oligarchies. A few tribes were leagued together; almost all, through fear of their neighbours, maintained around their lands an untilled strip of forest and wasteland. Historians are not agreed on the population of Gaul in Caesar's time; their estimates vary from five to thirteen millions. The villages, crudely built in the middle of clearings, must have resembled those of the present-day tribes in Central Africa. In mud-wattle huts thatched with straw the men, seated on bundles of reeds, talked together while they drank their local brew, barley mead. The climate was colder than in Italy; the toga was not worn, but rather breeches (or trousers) and a deerskin jacket. The Romans called Cisalpine Gaul *Gallia togata*, since its inhabitants were clad like the inhabitants of Rome; but Transalpine Gaul they called *Gallia comata*, or *Gallia bracata*, long-haired Gaul, breeched Gaul. Gallic wooden shoes also astounded the Romans, who dubbed them *Gallicae*, whence the French word *galoches* (a wooden-soled leather shoe) and the English *galoshes*. Hunters and shepherds, and the Gauls above all, ate venison, pork and honey – a diet entirely different from that of the Roman soldier who, during the Gallic wars, complained at the amount of meat the quartermaster inflicted upon him.

About the Gallic religion we know little. Here was a subject on which Caesar – a foreigner – must have had great difficulty in securing information. We do know that the Gauls worshipped local and rural divinities: Borvo, god of hot springs, who has bequeathed his name to numerous watering places (Bourbonne, Bourbon-Lancy, Bourbon l'Archambault) and to the royal House of Bourbon; Diva, goddess of rivers (la Dives, Divonne-les-Bains). They also practised a more secret cult, the mysteries of which were taught by the religious fraternity of Druids. It seems that the centre of Druidism was in Brittany, for it was there that young Druids went to be initiated. But there are obvious links between the beliefs of the Druids and the religions of the Orient. The Druids taught that man's spirit survives death and, in some vague Elysian Fields, dwells within a new body. As magicians they knew a little astronomy, a little medicine, and they presided over such symbolic ceremonies as the harvest of the mistletoe from the oak trees at the time of the winter solstice, and sacrifice by fire at the time of the summer solstice. Druidical rites have left their legacy in France: mistletoe still adorns French houses at the time of the new year ('*Au gui, l'an neuf!*'), and on June 23rd Saint John's fires burn upon the hill-sides of France. The Druids exercised a certain moral authority over their followers, but it was never enough to bring about the unity of Gaul. Throughout Caesar's *Commentaries*, never do we find an account of a single effective intervention by this priesthood in any negotiation.

Gallic society was barbarous but not savage. Intelligent, sensitive to the beauty of words, curious about Roman life, the Gauls proved themselves good craftsmen and brave soldiers. Yet at the beginning of the first century before Christ, any unbiased observer might have foreseen that they would not long remain free. Marius had had to intervene at the battle of Aix-en-Provence to stop the invasion of Gaul by the Cimbrians and the Teutons. A strong Power cannot endure the continuance along its borders of a weak State, left by anarchy at the mercy of foreign aggressors. The Gauls were capable of heroism, not of discipline or long-continued effort. Factional strife split not only clans and tribes but even families. Tribal hatreds were at times so violent that the aristocracy of one tribe would call in the Romans to help them against others of their own blood. Could the Romans feel scrupulous about seizing a country ravaged by private wars, the frontiers of which lay unprotected? With scorn Cicero spoke of the Gauls: 'What could be filthier than their towns? What cruder than their farms?' To civilize them became in his eyes a legitimate and even praiseworthy undertaking. It must have been obvious that on the day when some Roman general made up his mind to conquer Gaul public opinion would support him.

In 58 B.C. the proconsul of both Cisalpine and Transalpine Gaul was Julius Caesar, a forty-six-year-old politician, as ambitious as he was able. Cultivated, courteous, open-minded, but without scruple, as impervious to hatred as he was to pity, Caesar had long been watching the death of the Roman Republic. In his opinion the republican aristocracy was finished, and some day a strong man would seize the reins of Roman power. He wanted to be that man. But to carry out this great scheme, he needed prestige and an army. The proconsulate of the two Gauls could supply him with both. As early as 59, Gallic quarrels had paved the way for intervention. The tribe of the Sequanes, at war with the Eduans, had summoned to their aid a German führer, the Suevian Ariovistus, who had answered their call, but had then refused to go home. The Eduans in their turn called on the Romans for help. At the same time the Helvetians (Swiss), hard pressed by the Germans, were also threatening Gaul. Caesar came, saw, conquered; he halted the Barbarians and then set up a military barrier along the Rhine. His ultimate purpose was the conquest of the Gauls. At his disposal were only eleven legions of five thousand men each, besides auxiliaries, and the local warriors were far more numerous. But the Gallic army was divided and undisciplined; Caesar's, made up of well-trained veterans, was greatly superior in armaments – ballistas, onagers; it included Balearic slingers and Numidian cavalrymen. Roman camps, admirably built, were protected by triple ramparts – ditch, embankment and stockade. Caesar had already had some military experience in Spain. He was not a great tactician, but an excellent organizer. Moreover, he had traits of character suited to his purpose. His mind was quickly made up, his movements were secret and like lightning, his offensives sudden and headlong. Thanks to disunity among the Gauls and to the support of certain pro-Roman tribes, he had within a few years conquered the whole country.

Caesar treated the Gauls with a harshness he had never shown in Rome. Arresting their chosen representatives, pilfering their gold and silver objects, selling at auction thousands of prisoners, he seemed to them to be without scruples. By means of these vast spoils he made himself one of the richest and most powerful of Romans. 'With Roman arms he subjugated the Gauls; with Gallic money, the Romans.' These atrocities, however, ended by making rebellion inevitable. The aristocracy which had called in Roman help regretted its folly. Vercingetorix, son of the chieftain of the Arvernes, a hero young, handsome, proud and utterly dedicated to the freedom of his country, assumed leadership of the rebels and sought to cut the lines of communication of the northern Roman legions. He believed himself amply protected from Caesar by the Cévennes, then covered with snow. But Caesar, marching more than forty-eight miles in one day, led twenty thousand men to the threatened point. Vercingetorix had not the siege implements to assault the Roman camp. He tried to bring the Romans to terms by means of famine, destroying all the crops and villages within their reach. For several months, by a campaign of guerrilla and partisan warfare, he held in check the best army in the world, but his defeat was inevitable. Bourges (Avaricum), the most beautiful of the Gallic towns, was captured and its inhabitants put to the sword. Once more the disunity of the Gauls led to their downfall. In September 52, Vercingetorix, besieged in Alesia, was obliged to surrender and offered himself as an expiatory victim to Caesar, who after four years of captivity had him executed. The war of independence dragged on for another year or two. All uprisings were ferociously suppressed by Caesar. A million prisoners were deported and sold. Many of the rebels had their right hands cut off. Finally, slaughter brought peace. The Gallic war had lasted for ten years; it had changed the countenance and future of Europe. Had Rome not been Latinized, the Roman Empire would quickly have become an Oriental empire. Latin Gaul restored the equilibrium, to the advantage of the West.

For Gaul became Latin, and the harshness of Roman oppression did not prevent speedy assimilation. Caesar, whose ambition thenceforward looked to Rome itself, wished to leave a pacified Gaul behind him. He knew how to allure as well as how to overwhelm. The Gauls loved war; he opened his legions to them, and created specially for them the Legion of the Lark, well named, a first-class division, in personnel wholly Gallic. The nobility of Gaul eagerly sought the honours Rome could bestow; Caesar made use of the policy which nineteen centuries later was to be followed by Lyautey in Morocco — the policy of the 'great caïds' whereby the conqueror wins to his own purposes the natural leaders of the conquered country. Rome readily granted the rights of citizenship to the peoples she annexed: 'You command our armies,' she said to them, 'you administer our provinces; between you and us exists no distance, no barrier.' The Gauls were by nature eloquent; soon their sons shone in the Forum. The aristocracy became Romanized. Julia, Caesar, and later Augustus were soon fashionable names in Gaul. No longer did the old families boast of their Gallic ancestors, but claimed to be descendants of Venus or Hercules. In each town a municipal senate made it possible for them to assume titles and honours. Certain southern French names are in direct lineage from those of Roman colonists: Talatorius has yielded Taladoyre and Malamater, Malamaire.[1] Elegant senators prided themselves on speaking a pure Latin, and took pleasure, with provincial pedantry, in the games of the rhetoricians. At Vienne, Lyons, Lutetia (city of the Parisii) were erected mass-produced Roman cities, each with its theatre and basilica, the latter serving at once as city hall and meeting place. Roman aqueducts brought them their water. Women draped in the Roman fashion shopped in their white-marble markets. Even in Rome, Gallic trousers dared to mount the rostrum and Cicero sighed over them. Among the people assimilation was slower. Martial boasts of having been read even in Gaul, although in 1940 Valéry had his readers in Tunis, and that was no proof that the people of the Tunisian countryside spoke French. The change from one language to another is a labour of centuries; the Gallic peasant, all the same, had to learn Latin words in order to talk to Roman colonists, to argue with the tax collectors or to serve in the legions. Veterans spread Roman civilization in the rural districts. Strategic roads and easy communications created the unity of Gaul. Everyone became used to thinking that, above the community, there was a unifying power, the State, the agents of which had power over the local authorities. Annually, at the junction of the Rhône and the Saône, there took place a *Concilium Gallicanum*, a kind of national assembly, dedicated to celebrating the cult of Augustus. And thus everyone came to respect a new, a purely Roman idea, that of the Law.

For five centuries Gaul remained a Roman province. This is a period as long as that between the Hundred Years War and 1870. Obviously during these five centuries the machinery of imperial administration underwent changes. But its basic characteristics remained stable. At the outset there were three Gallic governments, the provinces of Aquitaine, Lyons and Belgium, with a governor-general resident at Lyons. Later the Praetorian prefect kept close to the frontiers threatened by the Barbarians, at Trèves or Aix-la-Chapelle. The Emperor Julian, friend of Gaul, made Lutetia his favourite abode. The Roman bureaucracy was numerous and attentive to detail. The Praetorian prefect had attached to his retinue a chief registrar (protonotary), a herald, a supervisor of prisons, a secretary (*curator epistolarum*), a treasurer and numerous clerks. The governor was paid in gold and in kind; he was entitled to a cook and, if not married, to a concubine — 'since without these a man cannot live . . .'

[1] DONALD C. PEATTIE.

(*quod sine his esse non possunt*). Administrative despotism was tempered by the existence of *curias*, or municipal councils, and a 'defender of the city' (*defensor civitatis*). But in later practice these municipal honours were eschewed by the Gauls and they viewed it a privilege to be exempt from them, for the *curiales* were, with their own fortunes as bond, responsible for the collection of taxes. These taxes were high, and a burdensome tax system was one of the causes of the decay of the Empire.

We must briefly examine the financial organization of the Empire in Gaul because its influence has been felt throughout the history of French taxation. In the fourth century Rome levied, in the first place, direct taxes – real taxes on the official registered value of properties, values revised every fifteen years, this being the *tributum soli* – and a personal tax, the *tributum capitis* (these two taxes finding their equivalents in France prior to the Revolution in the *taille* and the *capitation*). Then there were indirect taxes: tariffs (for revenue, not protection), tolls, the salt monopoly, sales taxes (1 per cent) and countless secondary imposts. This system had two grave failings: it was burdensome and the burden was inequitably apportioned. Owners of large holdings, through their connections, obtained unmerited relief. The curials, who were the responsible assessors, were not honest. 'Scratch a curial and you find a tyrant', said Salvienus, and Ausonius added: 'Assessors of taxes – web of frauds.' The penalties were appalling: the collectors used torture to verify the taxpayers' declarations. There was, indeed, a *defensor civitatis*, elected by the local inhabitants, but the wealthy countered by creating a 'defender of the Senate'. What this meant was that to obtain relief you had to have an influential 'patron', and thus we can trace the outlines, even in Roman days, of a feudal system in Gaul.

At the beginning of the conquest, however, Gallic prosperity had been great. It was then that there developed the taste for farming and the love of the soil which the Gallo-Romans were to bequeath to the French. We must try to understand the sheer *joie de vivre* of those first generations, freed from anarchy by the peace of Rome, the *Pax Romana*. At last the country had roads, frontiers, a military police. Everywhere along the Roman highways sprang up new dwellings, Mediterranean in type, villas adorned with columns and porticoes, marble or terra-cotta statuary. Town-dwellers rejoiced in novel luxuries, the gaiety of the public baths, the endless variety of entertainments. Only a few decades earlier the Gauls had dwelt in huts of mud wattle in the midst of wildernesses. Now the Gallo-Romans cleared the soil, tilled it, waxed rich by selling its fruits in Rome, ever eager to obtain from Gaul grain (the trade in which astounded Polybius) and dairy produce. Gaul became the 'Egypt of the North'.[1]

Yet the poorer townspeople and the agricultural workers did not accept some of the changes. In the country, men remained loyal to Celtic traditions. 'Pagan', 'peasant', the words are the same in Latin — *paganus*. The 'dogged mythology' of the people shied away from the gods of the conqueror. But a new faith, a faith more of the people, began to spread through the Mediterranean world. In Marseilles as early as the first century of our era, evangelists from the East spoke of the Christ. It took a hundred years for Christianity to reach Lyons. Rome was tolerant of all religions, provided that they in turn tolerated the cult of the Emperor. But the Christians might neither adore a false god nor sacrifice to Caesar. They preached the sharing of earthly goods and with sledge hammers destroyed the statues of Venus and Jupiter. The reign of Trajan saw the beginning of their persecution. The blood of martyrs — of Saint Irenaeus, Saint Blandina, Saint Denis — sowed the seed in men's hearts. Missionaries, whose names cathedral churches later hallowed — Martial at Limoges, Gatien at Tours, Saturninus at Toulouse — carried the Gospel to the towns. Later, the Empire having itself become Christian at the time of Constantine, the basilicas, which the Romans had never viewed as religious buildings, were transformed into churches. The importance of the bishops increased. At the beginning these officers had been elected by the faithful, but the elections became the occasion of so much strife that often the people asked some saintly man to select their pastor for them. And later, when the Empire weakened to a shadow, the Church remained the only organized power. In the eyes of the masses it embodied justice, while the *élite* were grateful that it preserved their culture.

For there was a culture in Gaul, mediocre, perhaps, but flourishing. In Bordeaux, in Autun, in Poitiers, in Marseilles, in Toulouse, in Lyons during the fourth century, thousands of young people took courses in the schools of grammar or rhetoric. Their professors were members of the imperial bureaucracy. 'We desire', wrote the Emperor Gratian to the Prefect of the Gauls, 'that thirty measures of wheat be granted to the rhetorician, twenty to the Latin grammarian, and twelve to the Greek grammarian, if a qualified one is to be found . . .' The Celtic temperament readily adapted itself to the traditions of Latin eloquence. Greek also was in favour. Ausonius, patrician and poet of Bordeaux.

[1] GUGLIELMO FERRERO.

24

wanted his grandson to begin his literary studies with Homer and Menander. Unhappily this culture remained more formal than real. 'Among the Gauls there were at the end of the fourth century a certain number of important and honoured men, long entrusted with major responsibilities of state, half pagan, half Christian, that is, without bias one way or the other and, truth to tell, little anxious to take any position in religious matters; people of wit, well read, philosophers, full of a taste for study and the intellectual pleasures, wealthy and living on a magnificent scale.'[1] These great lords of Roman Gaul led agreeable and carefree lives, occupying their time with intellectual and literary diversions. In the fifth century, Sidonius Apollinaris, a man of the world, a bishop and a rhetorician, described a religious ceremony after which clerics and laymen, stretched on the grass in the shade, talked with gusto about literature. Then the Bishop suggested handball and, after a long game, Sidonius wrote some teasing little verses. Other more austere Christians sought refuge in monasteries, the first of which were founded after the year 360 by Saint Martin, one at Ligugé (near Poitiers), the other at Marmoutier (near Tours). The monk in the Occident was very different from what he had been in the Orient. There, withdrawing into the Theban desert, men wished to escape temptation and dedicate themselves as single (monoi)[2] beings to the rigours of asceticism. In Gaul monasteries sought rather to gather together men who wished to flee the world in order to live a spiritual life in common. The monasteries of southern Gaul (especially that of Lérins, founded by Saint Honorat on the islands near Cannes) would prove to be homes of new ideas and nurseries of bishops. All matters of dogma or liturgy, then, became objects of active correspondence between the local bishop and Saint Augustine at Hippo or Saint Jerome at Bethlehem. And thus 'the doctors laboured, the priests travelled, writings circulated', and Christianity remained a living thing while the Empire withered away.

For the three centuries since the conquest, Rome had guaranteed the security of the Gauls. Along the Danube and the Rhine the marches, or demilitarized zones, made the Barbarians keep their distance. The limes, strategic roads edged by trenchworks and studded every six or nine miles with fortified towers (castelli), constituted a Maginot Line along which troops, especially Gallic troops, were constantly on watch. To the rear, to defend this line against some future aggressor, the Empire maintained a strategic reserve, eight legions strong in the first century, four

---

[1] FRANÇOIS GUIZOT. [2] Hence the French word moine.

in the second. In addition to this a flotilla patrolled the Rhine and veterans' colonies had been established at Colonia (Cologne) and at Augusti Burgus (Augsburg). About 275, the guard along the Rhine ceased to be Roman. The Empire was suffering from an acute shortage of troops. The soldier's trade held no attraction for citizens, who preferred to pay a fee to buy themselves a substitute. So the emperors enlisted Barbarians and installed them on the frontiers, granting them lands under the regulations on 'military hospitality'. Here was the seedground of the Barbarian kingdoms. But this new army had no patriotism. From time to time it created an emperor in order to benefit from the largesse attendant upon his joyful advent to power. Political disturbances gave birth to military anarchy. Germanic raids despoiled Gaul. Cities as far away as Bordeaux tore down their temples to build fortifications. Not only was Gaul visited with fire and blood by the Barbarians, it was made bankrupt by the exactions of a Roman bureaucracy enamoured of confiscatory taxation. Levies were so heavy that small landowners sold their holdings to escape the curials. The Roman administrative machinery had become so costly that it finally destroyed all taxable assets. By the time of Julian (363), 'Gaul is out of breath'.[1] For still another century the Empire cut an impressive figure, but it was at the end of its powers. Nevertheless, even after the breakdown of all imperial administration, Gaul remained an *island* of Latinity. As distinguished from German or Balkan peoples, the Gallo-Romans had truly been assimilated by Rome. It was Rome which had first given them a word to express their unity and had first named their country *Gallia*; it was Rome which, by its network of roads, made it possible for the tribes to know each other; it was Rome which opened to them the culture of the ancient world; it was to Rome that they owed respect for justice and law. They would long be homesick for the Empire. One day they would seek to re-establish it.

[1] AMMIANUS MARCELLINUS.

CHAPTER II

HOW THE BARBARIANS INTERMINGLED
WITH THE GALLO-ROMANS

BEYOND the Rhine, in Germany's forests, plains and mountains, lived numerous tribes which, though not forming a single nation, spoke similar languages and had customs in common. Tacitus described them in a famous book in which he contrasted their virtues with the vices of a corrupt civilization. Tacitus's Germans bear the same relation to the Germans of reality as would later be borne by Rousseau's 'good savages' to the cannibals of Africa. Because of his hatred for the Rome of his day, Tacitus idealized its bloodthirsty neighbours. Perhaps the latter did possess certain virtues—courage and loyalty to their chieftains — but they were violent, treacherous and cruel towards all foreigners. Above everything they loved war and the chase. Their warriors' councils chose a king and bore him aloft upon a shield, but this sovereign was only the first among his peers; he recalls to our minds those kings in the *Iliad* whose authority was so insolently defied by refractory warriors. In war the Germans followed a troop leader, a führer who might or might not be their chosen king, and whom, because of the common danger, they blindly obeyed. But the bond between leader and followers was personal and not, as in Rome, legal. Thus two vague concepts, that of the tribe and that of the warrior band, governed the Germans' political and military life. The idea of the tribe included the election of a king and the power of warriors assembled in council; the idea of the band had its roots in the mystical link between the warriors and their führer. In confused fashion the Germanic tribes were knit together in peoples of the same blood: Ostrogoths, Visigoths, Saxons, Teutons, Vandals. They tended constantly to move towards the west and the south in their search for new lands and pasturage (*lebensraum*), required by their numerous children and by their wasteful methods of agriculture, which quickly depleted the soil; they were as greedy for the wealth of the Empire as they were envious of its climate. Moreover, the Huns, a warlike, Mongoloid people pushing through from Asia, constantly exerted pressure upon them from the east.

The Barbarian invasions were in no sense large-scale movements into

Gaul and Italy on the part of organized armies. The Germans desired neither to conquer nor to destroy the Empire, which they deeply admired. Rome, suffering from a shortage of man-power, enlisted whole tribes in her service, made auxiliary soldiers out of them and entrusted them with guarding the frontiers. In these border regions the Barbarians, being Roman troops, had the right of *hospitalitas*, which meant that they could have their share of lands and dwellings. Little by little these warriors not unreasonably came to believe themselves indispensable. Those among them who formed the Emperor's personal guard acquired the habit of making and unmaking their sovereigns. From the third century onwards, as the props of the State became weaker, armed bands penetrated into Gaul. Most of them were of no great size, numbering at most five or six thousand adventurers. They would ravage an area, burning the crops, killing the men and seizing the women, and then they would go away, although they sometimes settled down, taking care not to scatter their forces. Little by little the bands that occupied a particular territory and belonged to the same tribal group fashioned a kingdom. In this way, the fifth century saw the Visigoths occupy Aquitania, the Burgundians the valleys of the Saône and the Rhône, the Alamans Alsace, the Franks northern Gaul. In none of these regions did they meet with much organized resistance.

Where the Barbarians settled, the Gallo-Romans remained more numerous than the invaders. But the internal divisions among the latter and the weakening of the Empire made them easy prey. Often they took refuge in the cities and there surrounded themselves with ramparts, while the Germans pitched their camps in the ruined villas of the countryside. For a time, the two peoples lived side by side, each speaking its own language, but 'fraternization' was inevitable. There were business dealings, there was concubinage, there was intermarriage. When a Barbarian had married a Gallo-Roman woman, the children spoke the language of their mother. Gradually Latin grew dominant over German, which contributed little more than military words to the popular speech: *heaume* (helm), *trêve* (truce), *bourg* (fortress), *brèche* (breach). And later, in the face of new invasions, the Franks and the Gallo-Romans were to join forces. When in 437 the Huns attacked the Burgundians and engaged them in battles (the subject matter of the *Nibelungen*), Gallo-Roman areas welcomed Burgundian refugees as their 'guests', and in 451 Gauls, Franks and Romans, under the command of Aetius, last of the Romans, as well as with the spiritual support of Christian saints (among them Geneviève, patron of Paris), together defied Attila's Huns in the Battle of the Catalaunian Fields (Châlons-sur-Marne). Their victory saved the West. For the Burgundians, Goths and Franks, unlike the Huns, retained a sincere respect for Rome. In their minds marriage to a Roman woman of patrician family was an honour. They knew well that if they were to govern Romanized peoples, they must speak Latin and understand Roman law. During the fifth century, despite the presence of the Barbarians, life in Gaul, especially south of the Loire, was in no sense intolerable. Men of cultivation, such as Sidonius Apollinaris, did not believe that the Empire was on the point of disappearing. They sought to come to terms with the Goths and the Franks, who attended council meetings clad in the skins of wild animals or in short tunics, their hair smelling of rancid butter, their bodies of garlic. They tried to civilize these wild men. To the very end the Roman administrative machinery functioned after a fashion. Riding fast, Sidonius Apollinaris could still travel fairly quickly from Lyons to Rome. Later, however, even communications were interrupted. Orders ceased to arrive from the capital. Nothing continued to operate except municipal life which long remained Gallo-Roman. Finally, in 476, the Western Roman Empire ceased to exist although the Eastern Roman Emperor clung to the fiction of his authority in the West. He delegated his powers there to Theodoric, King of the Ostrogoths and, it was claimed, to the Bishop of Rome (which, later, seemed to legitimize the temporal claims of the Papacy).

After the fall of the Empire, Gaul became a mosaic of Barbarian kingdoms. There was no organized State, but there were warrior bands whose leaders governed, delegating authority locally to their military subordinates: *comites* (counts), *duces* (dukes). At first, following the German custom, a freemen's assembly gathered to take counsel and mete out justice, but when the original band spread out over the domains awarded to its chief warriors out of gratitude and for safekeeping, the king in normal times began to consult only those with whom he lived – his court, that is the persons dwelling in the courtyard of his farm or domain. Quickly enough the chieftain of the Franks, Clovis, dominated the other Barbarians throughout Gaul. And throughout the land the Catholic Church became more and more powerful. A study of the map of France shows that four thousand four hundred villages 'are named after saints. There are seven hundred Saint Martins, four hundred and sixty-one Saint Peters, four hundred and forty-four Saint Johns, two hundred and seventy-four Saint Germains, one hundred and eighty-five

Saint Pauls and one hundred and forty-eight Saint Aubins ...'[1] The Christian faith made certain the continuance of some sort of unity in Gaul. Clovis remained a pagan, but that very fact made it easier for him to come to terms with the Church than it was for the Burgundian or Visigothic kings, who were Christians but had embraced the teachings of Arius and believed that within the Trinity, the Father and the Son had two distinct natures. For the Arians, Christ was not altogether man or altogether God, a very dangerous heresy, since it made Christ into a demigod and, pleading unitarianism, actually encouraged a kind of polytheism. Clovis, who had married Clotilda, a Catholic, fell under his wife's influence and was baptized, thus guaranteeing himself the all-powerful support of the Trinitarian bishops. To the latter the essential thing was to rid Gaul of Arianism and to see to it that the Son should finally be universally recognized as co-substantial with the Father; to Clovis 'the identity of the three persons of the Trinity was a military and political operation'[2] and an operation which he carried out with constant success.

A pitiless cynic, Clovis bettered his portion by trickery and assassination as much as by prowess in arms. 'Thus every day', wrote Gregory of Tours naively, 'God caused Clovis's enemies to fall under his hand and increased his kingdom, because he walked before the Lord with a righteous heart and did what was pleasing in His eyes.' By slaughtering friends and enemies, Clovis extended his kingdom to the Pyrenees. 'Woe is me', he said, 'who have remained like a wayfarer among strangers, and who have no more kin to succour me in adversity!' His saying this was a device, remarks the simple-minded Gregory of Tours, to discover whether there remained anyone for him to kill. But this royal gangster did his country great service. After the collapse of the Empire, he re-established the territorial unity of Gaul, soon to be named France (land of the Franks); he sanctioned the union of the crown and the Church, a prerequisite for the country's spiritual unity; and finally, by proudly accepting from the Emperor Anastasius the title of Roman Consul, he affirmed the continuity of power.

According to German custom, the warriors had the right of choosing their king, but only from a certain family; thus what gave the king his prestige was his descent from a race of heroes, his military leadership and his consecration by the Church. The symbol of his power was his long hair (a survival of the sun-hero myth, the lengthy locks calling to mind the solar rays). He dwelt with his men-at-arms on vast farms, the produce of which kept him victualled. The royal residence constituted an entire village, where lived families plying all trades from that of the jeweller to that of the weaver. The Frankish king journeyed from farm to farm, with his *leudes* or officials, bearing with him in great triple-sealed coffers his treasure of money, precious vessels and gems; hunting and fishing, and recruiting his many concubines among the daughters of his servants. If a new mistress had the knack of pleasing him, she might be promoted to the status of wife and queen; in which case the preceding queen, cast aside, found herself locked up in some monastery. Family wars were the favourite sport of the Frankish kings. They came very near to ruining the country which the *Pax Romana* had previously made so prosperous. Little by little schools were closed and Latin culture was forgotten save by the Church or by an occasional eccentric king, such as Chilperic, who prided himself on being a Latinist and theologian and wished to add letters to the Roman alphabet in order to represent certain sounds characteristic of the Germanic languages. At first the cities continued to survive under the protection of their bishops, but then even they fell into ruin. The sole remaining authority was a warrior aristocracy of landed proprietors. These gentlemen farmers, half brigands, half policemen, protected their peasants against other brigands. A church was a place of asylum, inviolable, and a fugitive therein had the right to be supplied with the necessities of life. Religion remained powerful because the king and his great vassals feared everlasting punishment. When Merovius, a fugitive taking refuge in Tours near the tomb of Saint Martin, opened the Book of Kings to seek an omen, he read: 'Because you have abandoned the Lord your God, the Lord has delivered you into the hands of your enemies', and for a long time he wept bitterly. Thus by virtue of the Church, Roman law still sought to temper the ferocity of the Barbarians, but a whole new civilization had to take shape before the human animal could be held in check.

The dynasty of the Merovingian kings ruled France for three hundred years, longer than the Valois or the Bourbons. Their history is known to us through the Gallo-Roman Bishop, Gregory of Tours, and through the more recent narratives of Augustin Thierry (1840), written with talent but, like Tacitus's *Germania*, full of political passion. Augustin Thierry, a liberal, contrasts the French people 'Jacques Bonhomme', which he likes to think is of Gallo-Roman origin, with a selfish nobility of Frankish stock. This contrast is wholly artificial; big Gallo-Roman landowners were included among the great vassals, and especially among the bishops who surrounded the Merovingian kings. But the brutality of those sovereigns was scarcely tempered by their presence. Gregory of Tours paints a frightful picture in which the violence of these half-savage despots was wreaked upon their own sons, their wives and even on ecclesiastical dignitaries. The war between Queens Fredegunde and Brunhilde lasted for thirty years. Here was a tragedy comparable to that of the Atrides. Fredegunde, the beautiful serving-woman who won the heart of the King, forced him to marry her, strangled her rivals and hounded them even in the persons of their children, is one of history's most appalling characters. Brunhilde, daughter of the Spanish Visigothic king, enemy and sister-in-law of this upstart, lived sixteen years after Fredegunde's death, but the latter won her posthumous triumph through the agency of her son, Clotaire II. Brunhilde, betrayed by her vassals, was handed over to Clotaire, who had the old woman lashed to the tail of a horse, and its frantic hoofs tore her to pieces.

Such was life in these Merovingian palaces, which remind us at once of the seraglio and the slave market. A whole population of concubines schemed to win marriage 'with the ring'. The miserable custom of portioning out the kingdom among the sons of the deceased monarch turned every succession into a national catastrophe, followed by fratricidal wars. Sons conspired against their fathers, brothers against brothers, and the vanquished, shorn as a mark of their forfeiture, ended their lives in a cloister when they were not slain on the spot. Warriors broke into a church in the midst of a council, bellowing at the top of their voices. A bishop was assassinated at the foot of the altar. And yet Dagobert (628-639) was still a powerful sovereign, strong enough to intervene in Italian, Spanish and German affairs. After him the Merovingians fell into utter decay.

This age was one of the blackest in history, as are all those when an old order disappears, leaving men at the mercy of their own passions. The Gallo-Romans were no longer governed by an administration of the Roman variety. The Barbarians had wrecked the idea of the law, and everyone pleaded the customs of his tribe; they had wrecked the idea of State finances and the Merovingian kings had squandered the kingdom through gifts bestowed on their boon companions; they had wrecked the idea of a State justice, and the nobles, like the Church, thenceforth claimed the administration of their own justice. What did the Barbarians offer in return for what they had done? A taste for freedom? Not at all. Had the Germans formerly possessed the virtues ascribed to them by Tacitus, these had melted away in contact with a rich and sensual civilization. What had become of their much vaunted loyalty? In Gregory of Tours we find nothing but treachery. 'The Merovingian court is a house of prostitution, Fredegunde a shrew.'[1] Every king causes his wife and sons to be murdered; every man is for sale at the price of a little gold. Debauchery had worn the race out. Even Dagobert, 'prematurely exhausted by his numerous spouses, died *of old age* at the age of thirty-four'.[2] A society of this sort could not last.

But when one civilization dies, another is born. German royalty, hitherto elective, tended on Gallo-Roman soil to become hereditary. It was haunted by its recollections of the Empire. However rude the Merovingian kings may have been, they had memory of and respect for a culture. They sought to procure Byzantine works of art, mosaics, Oriental materials. Around them took shape a territorial and military aristocracy. It was made up in part of Gallo-Romans who had rallied to the conqueror and thus preserved their property, in part of German officers under whose protection the affrighted tillers of the soil were happy to place themselves. To speak of feudalism would be premature, because the *senior*, the 'old man', the landowner and protector had no thought of interposing between sovereign and subjects, but the partitioning of the kingdom among the sons of the king tended to weaken the power of the crown. The country was cut up by these inheritances. Burgundy and Aquitaine, Neustria and Austrasia (the eastern and western portions of northern France) acquired strong local feeling. Yet the remembrance of the united Gauls survived. Pressure along the borders exerted by new hordes (Huns and Saracens) reawakened it. The unity of the Church sustained it.

The unity of the Church was a remarkable phenomenon. In the midst of the most terrible period of political confusion, the Christian Church by and large maintained 'the unity of its teaching and the universality of its law'. From the fourth to the eighth century, six oecumenical (or general) councils were held, all in the East, but the West accepted their decisions. Fifty-four councils were held in Gaul in the sixth century. The ecclesiastical hierarchy was firmly established by that time and the territories of the various kingdoms had been divided into dioceses administered by their bishops. An attempt was made to make the Archbishop of Lyons, Primate of the Gauls, into a kind of independent patriarch like those in

[1] PIRENNE.   [2] FUNCK-BRENTANO.

the East, but the project failed through the jealousy of other cities (Arles, Sens). The bishops administered the property of the Church, which grew endlessly through the benefactions of the faithful and through the tithe (the gift of a tenth of their income made by Christians to the Church), a Jewish institution which the Catholic clergy sought to revive. 'We summarily warn you that, following the example of Abraham, you do not fail to offer to God the tithe of all your goods, in order to preserve the rest.' Respected by the people whose defenders they made themselves, the bishops were feared by lords and kings because of the powerful weapons at their disposal: excommunication and the interdict. An excommunicated prince, a kingdom under interdict were outcasts for all mankind. Very strong reasons were required for running the risk of such a penalty.

A great role was also played by the monks. At the beginning of the sixth century, monasticism had been reformed by Saint Benedict, who founded the monastery of Monte Cassino in Italy and published his celebrated *Rule of the Monastic Life*. Therein he inculcated abnegation, obedience and, above all, work. That was the novelty. The monks of the East, solitary contemplatives, did substantially no work; the Benedictines cleared the land of Europe. Benedict's rule is extraordinary for its mildness, its good sense and its moderation. It was introduced into France by Saint Maur and became the discipline usual in the French monasteries. In the beginning the monks were not priests; when they became such, they found themselves subject to the authority of the bishops and turned for relief first to the King and then to the Pope. During the Middle Ages, the great religious orders were responsible only to the Papacy and entered into conflict with the national churches. But during the confused and gloomy days I am now describing, the monks, like the bishops, helped to restore a little humanity within a savage society. The downfall of the Empire and the disappearance of its officials had left a terrifying void; the institutions of the episcopacy, of feudalism and the monarchy were to fill it.

CHAPTER III

HOW THE CAROLINGIANS SOUGHT TO
REBUILD THE EMPIRE

AFTER Dagobert's death, Merovingian decay was past mending and no great ruler made any further attempt to arrest it. Moral depravity had first produced debauchery in these kings; then it led to madness. Worn out by their excesses, they died even before they came of age. Their mothers, serving-girls forced into their fathers' beds, ruled in their stead. And all the while the kingdom's treasury dwindled, in part because of immunity from taxation granted in weakness to the more powerful lords, partly because the advance of Islam interrupted all trade with the East, the source of wealth. All through the Mediterranean world the Arab invasion moved forward with frightful speed. Mahomet had died in 632; by 635 the Moslem armies were at Damascus, by 641 at Alexandria, by 713 at Toledo. In 725 Arab bands crept up the Rhône valley as far as Autun. Nor were these new conquerors assimilable as had been the Germans. The Franks had admired Rome and accepted Christianity, but the Mohammedans remained loyal to their own customs and religion. At the beginning of the eighth century they were practically masters of the Mediterranean. They occupied all Spain and a part of Languedoc. Throughout southern France they slaughtered the men and violated and kidnapped the women. And thus dwellers in that region took refuge in eyries perched on rocky summits (Grimaldi, Èze). Then the Saracens settled down throughout the countryside, bringing with them buckwheat (in French still called *sarrasino*), the Damascus rose, porous earthenware jars to keep water cool, the date palm and saffron, a herb without which *bouillabaisse* would have been impossible. To the Saracens southern France likewise owes Moorish architecture, local dance forms and, to a certain extent, the poetic and scientific cultivation of its petty courts. But thanks to this curtain of infidels, the kingdom of France was divided from the Christian world of the East, the heir of classic civilization. Crass ignorance spread far and wide. Latin gave place to rustic dialects. Its sovereigns were so weak that all they possessed were the title, the curly locks and the long beards of kings. And the real chieftain of the kingdom was a high official called the Mayor of the Palace.

The mayor of the palace, at first merely chief steward of the King's household, later became an intermediary between the King and his other companions. When a whole sequence of kings showed great weakness and inability to govern, the palace mayors of Austrasia found themselves leaders of an independent aristocracy. For a century this high office passed from father to son in a family originally coming from the banks of the Meuse whose name was Pepin (a name still preserved in the Belgian town of Pepinster). In succession Pepin of Landen, called the Old, Pepin of Herstal and Charles Martel were the heads of this family and of the kingdom. Charles Martel reigned *de facto* over Austrasia and Neustria for twenty-six years. He had shaped a body of rugged Frankish infantry, with which, near Poitiers, he stopped in its tracks a raiding party sent out by the Arab Governor of Spain (732). This victory did not put an end to Saracen incursions; France's southern coast, lacking a fleet for its defence, remained open to their attack for two more centuries, but Europe and Christendom had been saved. Pope Gregory III, under threat in Rome from the Lombards, sent Charles Martel the keys to the tomb of Saint Peter and asked him to replace, as protector of the Roman Church, the all-too-remote Byzantine emperor. Here was a clever diplomatic move on the pontiff's part, for the Roman Church could hope for nothing from the iconoclast emperors of Constantinople and had everything to fear from the Lombards, whose capital, Pavia, was too close to Rome for comfort. Charles Martel, a loyal Catholic, lived on the other side of the Alps, which made him a desirable protector. He refused this honour because he already had heavy military burdens, but Rome would never again forget that only the Franks thenceforth had the strength to defend the Church.

Thus, in the chaos of the eighth century, two Powers continued to exist in western Europe: the Frankish army of the Pepins and the Papacy. The power of the Bishop of Rome was on the increase; he had the prestige of being Saint Peter's successor; he owned great domains and, since the fall of the Western Empire, was no longer dependent, like other bishops, on a territorial sovereign. The authority of the Roman pontiffs had been widened by the conversion of Great Britain, for although Italy, Spain and Gaul had been evangelized by independent missions, Rome herself had converted England and then had drawn upon the religious communities across the Channel in order to obtain apostles to bring the faith to the Germans. One of these missionaries, Saint Boniface, friend of Charles Martel's son, Pepin the Short, negotiated an agreement between this mayor of the palace, who wished to be king, and the Pope, who had need of military support against his neighbours. The Church agreed to legitimize a dynastic change and to recognize Pepin. The latter locked up Childeric III, last of the Merovingians, in a monastery, and had himself crowned, together with his wife, Bertha Broadfoot, by Saint Boniface – a skilful manœuvre since the sons born of their union were thus doubly hallowed. Better yet, in 754 Pope Stephen II crossed the Alps and anointed Pepin in the Basilica of Saint Denis, proclaimed the new king and his two sons 'Patricians of the Romans' and ordered the Franks never again to choose their sovereigns outside this family. In this fashion the kings of France took on the religious character which had marked the kings of the Bible. In return for this noteworthy service, Pepin drove the Lombards from the Pope's domains and handed over these reconquered territories not to the Byzantine emperor, their legitimate sovereign, but to a Roman Republic. The Papal States had been born.

In Charles, son of Pepin (later surnamed Carolus Magnus, or Charlemagne), the family produced the most illustrious of its leaders. Not that he was a creator. He inherited from his father the kingdom of the Franks and a tradition of alliance with Rome. But he had the luck to reign for forty-three years, and to be able to govern himself; a long reign is a great opportunity, and his character was equal to his good fortune. 'The Merovingian dynasty had lost all moral sense; Charlemagne took it as his task to better souls and to make virtue prevail.'[1] He elicited respect through his dignity of bearing, and affection through his friendliness of manner. Naturally we must not believe all the good things written about him by Einhard, his official biographer, who had read attentively the *Lives of the Caesars* and attributed to his hero everything he found worthy of praise in the Roman emperors.[2] Charlemagne had five legitimate wives (Himiltrude, Désirée, Hildegarde, Fastrade and Luitgarde) and four supplementary spouses whom the Church looked upon as 'evidences of intemperance'. He was of so dominant a disposition that he even forbade his daughters to marry, which became a cause of palace scandal. But he was pious, well-meaning and a hard worker. His imposing bulk, his long beard, his vitality, his endless capacity for work have taken on legendary proportions. His wonderful health and the vigour of all his appetites kept him in good spirits. He loved the language and the songs of his Franks. He wore their style of clothing: a linen tunic, scarlet breeches,

[1] FUSTEL DE COULANGES.   [2] LOUIS HALPHEN.

leathern bands around his legs, a vest made of otter skins, a white or blue cape. Only on ceremonial occasions did he allow himself to be decked in gold and jewels. The conversion of the pagans was the avowed purpose of his conquests, but his alliance with the Church paid him additional political dividends, the ecclesiastical hierarchy being in those days of anarchy the only possible administrative organ. In 773 Pope Adrian summoned him against the Lombards, who had recaptured the towns subdued by Pepin. Charlemagne came with a formidable army, defeated the Lombards, at Pavia put on his own head the famous iron crown and, in 774, visited Rome. He was dazzled. There were preserved the blood of Christ, His vesture and the table from the Last Supper. There the churches were the most beautiful, religious music the purest, ceremonies the most noble. There were still to be seen monuments of imperial splendour. Charlemagne was enchanted and conceived the plan of making his kingdom into a centre of culture and beauty. The Pope consecrated him King of the Franks and King of the Lombards and made him a Roman patrician. From that day he looked upon himself as the protector of Christendom and styled himself 'King by the grace of God', a new formula among the Franks.

For forty-three years Charlemagne waged war. But his campaigns, unlike those of the Merovingian kings, were not civil strife among jealous relatives. He was following out a vast scheme: the defence against the pagans of the former Roman Empire. The first stage in this operation was the conquest of the kingdoms which had been parts of the Empire (Lombardy and Aquitaine); the second, the struggle against the Barbarian invaders of the Empire: Saxons, Slavs, Avars, Saracens and, later, the Norse pirates who were establishing themselves along the coasts of the English Channel. Charlemagne wanted to add Spain to his conquests, and in 778 marched on Pamplona and Saragossa, but, having to retreat because of a Saxon attack in the north, he lost, in the vale of Roncesvalles, his rearguard and his nephew Roland. This episode of little military importance remains famous because it is the subject matter of the *Song of Roland* — thus demonstrating the superiority of poetry over history. Like such Roman emperors as Diocletian and Julian, Charlemagne most frequently had his headquarters on the Rhine because the most threatening danger came from Germany. Long did he struggle against the Saxons; he forbade them under pain of death to sacrifice men to the devil, that is, to the ancient Germanic gods; he deported ten thousand Saxon families to forced labour in Flanders; by such unwinning ways he finally converted these pagans. It was 'Christianity or death'.[1] He extended his kingdom from the Rhine to the Vistula. Pope Leo III, having been waylaid, accused, condemned and wounded by his enemies, came to beg Charlemagne's support, as master of Europe. The Frankish king was moved and accepted this role of arbiter of Christendom. In the year 800, in the Church of Saint Peter, he declared the Pope innocent. Leo III, to re-establish the Papacy's prestige, made a brilliant gesture. On Christmas Day, in Saint Peter's, he crowned Charlemagne Emperor of the Romans under the name of Charles Augustus. 'To Charles Augustus, crowned by God, great and pacific Emperor of the Romans, life and victory!' cried the people. At a stroke the Western Empire was revived and the Roman pontiff was ensured the right to make an emperor out of the soldier of the Church. Charlemagne's biographer, Einhard, says that the imperial title was displeasing to his hero, yet it is altogether unlikely that the ceremony had not been rehearsed. Truly he must have asked himself what would be the reaction in Byzantium, which viewed itself as the seat of the Empire. Nevertheless, he accepted and styled himself 'Emperor governing the Roman Empire', though he sought rather to create a Christian empire than to restore that of the Caesars. This new dignity added nothing to Charlemagne's power, but it reawakened in the consciousness of peoples the idea of the unity of the civilized world, which the Roman Empire had of old begun to propagate in Europe. At first, Constantinople was irritated; then, in 812, an agreement was reached and there were once more two emperors, one of the East and one of the West.

The idea of empire was Roman, but Charlemagne's administration never resembled that of Rome. In the days of the Roman emperors, power had been exercised by a hierarchy of officials and financed by the assessment of taxes. Charlemagne had neither a bureaucracy nor large revenues, for his empire had been impoverished by the Moham-medan blockade. Only the Jews could still deal with the infidels. Hence, at the court of Aix-la-Chapelle, place was set aside for them to dwell in. In case of any injury to their persons, a fine had to be paid to the Emperor. And it was through their agency that Charlemagne entered into corre-spondence with the Caliph Harun-al-Rashid, who made him the magnifi-cent gift of an elephant and a clock. Still, for the most part, the East, cut off by Islam, was by then no more than a mirage. For lack of gold, silver became the sole money in the West.

[1] LOUIS HALPHEN

39

Charlemagne had at his disposal only the revenues of his own domains and lacked officials to administer his empire. At his court, his personal servants – the seneschal, the cupbearer, the constable (*comes stabuli*, count of the stable) – were at the same time his collaborators. For correspondence and other writing tasks he had an ecclesiastical chancellor. Throughout the land there were two organizations available to him, one clerical and the other military. The lord of a manor, the warrior who had received some estate as a recompense, was dependent upon a duke, a count or a 'marquis' (chieftain of a *march*, or borderland), and these in turn derived from the Emperor. In fact local administrators, highly independent as they were, levied their own taxes and paid their own expenses. In order to have some check on them, the Emperor sent out inspectors, the celebrated *missi dominici*, who most frequently travelled in pairs – a bishop and a count. Upon their return, the inspectors gave an account of their mission to the Emperor, a busy master who wanted to be acquainted with everything that transpired. In order to deal with the difficulties brought to his attention, Charlemagne, 'under God's inspiration', dictated articles of law called 'Capitularies', which he then submitted to the assembly of the people.

There were two assemblies each year, one in the autumn, for which the Emperor and his counsellors determined the agenda, and the other a general meeting held in the spring. One of the chroniclers has left us a description of these general assemblies or 'Fields of May'. They gathered around the palace at Aix-la-Chapelle, Ratisbon or some other city. Only notables engaged in the actual debate, but before the sessions these notables met with their loyal followers, each great man in his own tent, in order to determine the line of action to be taken. Numerous messengers shuttled back and forth between the Emperor and the assembly. If the assembly expressed the wish to discuss some question with the Emperor, the latter willingly put in an appearance and everyone present said what he thought with complete frankness. Charlemagne liked to mingle with the crowd during the Fields of May and question people from every province of the Empire. He wanted to know in which regions people were dissatisfied and what were the causes of their uneasiness. In the Capitularies submitted to these assemblies were to be found not only laws but questions: 'How does it happen that, be it in the marches or in the army, when something must be done for the defence of the Empire, one will not give support to another? . . . Ask the bishops and the abbots what is the meaning of those words which they use without ceasing: *Forsake the world*. Inquire whether a certain one has forsaken the world when he labours daily to increase his possessions . . .' This goes to prove that Charlemagne took delight in mixing irony with his moralizing. The Capitularies do not show us an administrative genius – circumstances would not have afforded such a genius an opportunity to function – but they do betray common sense, curiosity and a wise regard for local custom, even the custom of conquered peoples.

After the Merovingian intellectual decadence, Charlemagne also encouraged a groping intellectual renaissance. He was inclined towards such things and during his meals had Saint Augustine and Saint Jerome read aloud to him. In Italy and even more in England he found learned men, because England, sheltered by the sea, had suffered relatively less since her conversion to Christianity from the invasions which had disrupted the Continent. On that island, monastic houses had been able to preserve both sacred and profane books, among the latter a portion of the works of Aristotle. The schools of York, where the celebrated Alcuin taught, were better than those of the Continent, and Charlemagne, who had met Alcuin in Italy, did everything he could to attract this scholar to his own court. When he had finally succeeded, he established a palace school, in which he himself, his beautiful and brilliant daughters and his counsellors were the pupils, as well as an 'Academy' wherein Charlemagne was called David and Alcuin Flaccus. Einhard gives us a picture of the Emperor placing his writing tablets under his bed pillows in order to write when he could not sleep. Alcuin's task, as a sort of minister of public education, was to revive the study of books, to set up monastic and episcopal schools, to restore manuscripts and to infuse culture with new life. The Emperor helped him and supplied him with messengers who went out searching for manuscripts with which to enrich the monastic libraries. In those days the copying of a book was a 'holy work'. We read in the Capitularies: 'We cannot suffer that in the sacred readings, in the midst of the holy offices, discordant solecisms should slip in, and it is our plan to reform these same readings . . .' To one abbot, Charlemagne wrote: 'Several monasteries having addressed to us writings wherein it was told us that the brethren were praying for us, we have noticed that in the greater part of these writings the sentiments were good but the words grossly uncultivated . . . Hence we exhort you not to neglect the study of letters . . .' Naturally this half-barbarous renaissance had much that was naive about it. The subjects discussed seem to us rather empty. Alcuin's writings are at once pedantic and puerile. Apart from

Einhard's *Life of Charlemagne*, the age has left us no important literature. But its activities constituted a return from a very low level. Alcuin himself was aware of these weaknesses; he wrote to the Emperor: 'During the morning of my life I sowed in Britain the seeds of knowledge; now, towards its evening, and although my blood may be chilled, I ceaselessly sow them in France and I hope that, with the grace of God, they will prosper in both countries . . .' Shakespeare and Montaigne were one day to be the fruits of these sowings.

During Charlemagne's last days, the pious scholar in him triumphed over the warrior and the emperor. He busied himself only with prayers, alms-giving and the revision of the Gospels. In 814 he died, and his empire did not long survive him. Invasions by pirates and Barbarians, fratricidal strife, successive dismemberment — it was to be the Merovingian story all over again for the Carolingians. Did this come from a lack of ability among Charlemagne's descendants? To tell the truth, this empire was not capable of maintaining its own life. Too extended for the available means of communication, ill defended through lack of ships and troops, it was also carved up as a result of family partitionings. Charlemagne's son, Louis the Pious, had three sons, and these three, after having long fought each other, came to an agreement on the division of their inheritance at Verdun in 843. Charles the Bald received Neustria, Aquitaine and the Spanish Marches — that is, the part of France west of the Rhône and the Saône. Louis the German united Austrasia, Bavaria, Swabia and Saxony. Finally, Lothaire accepted a bizarre strip of land, very long and narrow, which ran from the North Sea to Calabria, extending along the valleys of the Meuse, the Rhine and the Rhône. It was to this prince that Lotharingia (hence Lorraine) owes its name. The partition of Verdun had created two of the States of modern Europe: France and Germany. And it opened the road to the long-continued violence between the two countries by creating between them that Lotharingian corridor which both of these civilizations would continue to claim. Nevertheless, and despite the rapid break-up of his empire, it can be said that Charlemagne had created the West, by reawakening Latin culture there and by giving the West a feeling of its own unity.

Islam had helped in the process. As long as the Mediterranean had been an open sea, the Barbarian and Christian kingdoms had looked to the East, cradle of their religion, and towards Constantinople, trustee of the Roman tradition. Cut off from the East by the Mohammedan armies and fleets, they sought a new centre: they found it in the union of the Pope and the Emperor, of the Bishop of Rome and the King of the Franks. Thus there was a complete break with the political past. With Charlemagne's death began a new epoch which was (very much later) to be called the Middle Ages. Its essential characteristics were: first, the political power of the Church. Popes and bishops would crown kings. And these kings henceforth reigned, not as leaders of a warrior band, but as the anointed of the Lord. Ignorance among the laity assured civil power to churchmen, who were the guardians of all culture. Its second mark was a permanent military and landed aristocracy. In Merovingian days there had been great landowners, and they had exercised political power, but before Charlemagne, local posts of command were shifted about from individual to individual and from family to family according to the whim of royal favour. The Emperor's long reign consolidated the ducal, county and marchional houses. Local magistracies had become hereditary. The moment the central power weakened, these houses made themselves independent, and the kings became nothing more than the first among lords. Yet a longing for Christian unity was to survive Charlemagne. A Church hierarchy and a landed oligarchy governing divided peoples, while deep in all hearts there remained confused recollections of Roman greatness and of the greatness of the Frankish Empire — such was the Carolingian legacy. 'Of course, thirty years after Charlemagne's death this unity would break up. But its impress had been so strong that within the bosom of each of the new States there would remain, in its institutions, in its law and in its ecclesiastical organization, enough common elements for a European civilization to survive into the Middle Ages.'[1]

[1] FERDINAND LOT.

CHAPTER IV

HOW THE FEUDAL SYSTEM DEVELOPED – HOW THE CAPETIANS SUCCEEDED THE CAROLINGIANS

AFTER the treaty of 843, the dismemberment of Charlemagne's empire continued. As early as 888, seven different kingdoms could be counted: France, Navarre, Provence, Burgundy, Lorraine, Germany and Italy. Those rare literate individuals who still remembered a little history thought they were witnessing a new fall of the Roman Empire: 'The Frankish nation had shone in the eyes of the whole world', wrote the Deacon Florus. 'Now sunk low, this great Power has lost at once its brilliance and the name of Empire ... There are no more assemblies of the people, no more laws; in vain would an embassy arrive at a place where no court is held. What will become of the peoples bordering on the Danube, the Rhine, the Rhône, the Loire and the Po? All formerly united by the bonds of concord, now that the alliance is broken they will be afflicted by sad quarrels. What end will God's wrath cause to follow upon all these evils? Scarcely is there a man to be found who thinks of all this with fear, who reflects upon what goes on and is sorry: rather do men rejoice at the rending apart of the Empire and call peaceful an order of things affording us none of the goods of peace.'[1] Thus did the chosen few lament the dismemberment of the Frankish Empire; the mass of the people accepted it and even hoped for it. Why? For one thing, national characters were taking shape, and the union – under a single State – of nations already different was hard to bear. Of course Franks and Saxons had both of them formerly been Germans, but for four centuries the Franks, west of the Rhine, had mixed with the Gallo-Romans. By the ninth century the fusion was complete. Already one could properly speak of Frenchmen and of Germans; it was not a matter of race, but of customs, of language, of the ways men felt. In the second place, the peoples could see that the Empire was incapable of protecting them. New invasions cast terror over the countrysides. Even Charlemagne had been appalled by the incursions of the Men of the North, the Normans, who had come from Denmark or

[1] *Recueil des Historiens des Gaules et de la France*, Vol. VII.

Norway in vessels with complements of forty to sixty men, had sailed up the rivers of the West and had established, in the valley of the Seine and in Calvados, an independent State, the Duchy of Normandy. In the south, Saracen raids continued, leaving nothing but towns stripped of their people, young girls carried off into slavery, monasteries burned to the ground, farm lands abandoned. Everywhere for lack of people the forests were creeping back over the clearings. Wild animals threatened the villages. Small landholders, peasants, observing that administration of a great empire after the Roman fashion was no longer feasible, asked local governments to ensure the defence of the land against brigands and pirates.

The skeleton of such governments already existed. It was built of counts, marquises and dukes, all the warriors who had been granted domains or given commands. These soldiers, at least, were able to defend the regions they governed against the invaders. And to help them they had their vassals to whom they had given fiefs or lands held in *faith*. Then the vassal in turn had vassals of his own, the *vassi vassorum*, the vavasours. 'Those who were not sufficiently rich to equip themselves and to surround themselves with the necessary number of servants and horses contributed by groups of three, four or six to the support of a horseman. From top to bottom of the system, as each lord summoned his vassals and hastened to the aid of his suzerain, armies took shape which, at least theoretically, gathered together all the vital forces of the nation ...'[1] In short, the procedure is comparable with what would happen if, in a modern army, the President of the United States were to set up the general commanding an Army Corps as Governor of Austria, with rights of succession vested in the general's son, and if the general were to apportion the land among his colonels, who in turn would divide their domains among the captains, the local inhabitants accepting this regime out of fear of anarchy. And so the feudal system built itself up, slowly and unconsciously, throughout the West, and continued so to do as long as disorder moved the weak to wish to secure for themselves the protection of the strong. This system took on very different forms. Inheritance of a fief was never automatic, but neither the king nor the suzerain ever refused investiture to the child of a loyal vassal.

Little by little feudal property everywhere acquired the same essential characteristics. The owner obtained within his domains rights which had formerly been those of the State: the right of dispensing justice, of levying

[1] GABRIEL HANOTAUX.

45

taxes, of collecting quit-rents. The *taille* (poll tax, similar to the Roman *tributum soli*) was an impost paid by tenants to assure the defence of their persons and of their lands. Since all land needed defence, all land had to have a lord. But this lord himself held his land from a suzerain, to whom he owed help and service. What help? Above all help in war. The vassal must serve in person, on horseback. The garrison of the stronghold must be ensured by a rotational arrangement. The king has the right to demand lodging from his vassals. In times of peace, the vassals must come to court for assemblies and councils, must be present at their own expense at any festivals given by their lord, must supply him with a gift of money when his son is knighted or his daughter married, and must pay his ransom if he is made prisoner. Ownership of land dependent on no one is called an *allodium*, but these allodial fees tended very quickly to disappear. An independent farmer felt so weak that he voluntarily 'gave himself' to a lord who would protect him in return for quit-rent or service. Thus feudalism was the sequel to the Roman and Gallo-Roman system of patronage. The villein is none other than a dweller in a villa (*villanus*). The *manant* (peasant, from the Latin verb *manere*) is 'he who stays', but he is not, as has so often been said, 'bound to the glebe'. He can depart if he gives up all claim to his land. Can we say that he then would be without belongings? The answer is complex. In the ninth or even in the twelfth century no one accepted the idea of unencumbered property which you would have a right to sell. Moreover, customs were neither fixed nor always clearly defined. 'A society is not a figure in geometry',[1] and feudalism, rather than being a coherent system, was the sum total of millions of human beings, lords and villeins, forming, as it were, a great network of scattered bands.

For of the two Germanic conceptions — the tribe and the armed band — the band survived. In the tribe the freemen settled their affairs in an assembly. In the band, subject to warrior discipline, loyalty to the leader (*fidelity* is the same as *fealty*) became essential. Feudalism amounted to an armed band settled permanently on a domain around a chieftain and constantly ready to leave the labour of the fields for battle. The general had portioned the land out to his soldiers but retained the right to recall the soldiers to duty whenever that land was threatened. The system was accepted by all the peoples of the West because it represented an improvement over anarchy. In earlier days the villa of a Gallo-Roman had been a lovely dwelling with colonnades, pleasant to look at, impossible to

[1] MARC BLOCH.

46

defend. The feudal lord built a stronghold, at first of wood, later of stone either on a hill or on an artificial mound. Villages clung close to these keeps, protected by them — just as a flock of lambs clustered at the feet of the shepherd — and in case of danger the villagers took shelter behind these massive walls. In certain parts of France even churches were fortified and became places of refuge, as, for example, the cathedral at Albi. A class of landowning soldiers began to take shape — the nobility of the following centuries. The characteristics of these people were scorn for every activity other than war, laziness and a family spirit intensified by their common pride. Isolated in its châteaux, the nobility sought to liven these gloomy strongholds by festivities and ceremonials. A whole miniature court dwelt around the lord. His vassals sent him their sons as pages and these young men devotedly respected the Dame (lady, from Latin *domina*) of the house. When the lord died, his son (or, if he had none, his daughter) fell heir to the property, but had to receive investiture from the suzerain and swear fealty to him. During the investiture ceremony, the vassal knelt down, his joined hands between the hands of his suzerain, and said: 'From this day forward I become your man, for life and for limb.' The word homage, used to designate this act, reminds us that he who swore homage became the 'man' (*homme*) of another in the same sense as an officer still speaks of 'my men'. The whole system was based, somewhat as is the family, on a personal bond of moral obligation, and no longer, as in Roman law, on an impersonal code. To betray that bond was the most horrible of sins.

The feudal order had its faults and they were bad ones, but at least it was an order. In the tenth and eleventh centuries it afforded a remedy for anarchy and it quieted fears. Yet the brutality of this military police itself quickly became a danger. In the absence of any central power, the local soldier felt he could do as he pleased. And this was the moment when the Church undertook to tame the tamers and when the feudal lord, held in check by religion, became the knight. At its outset, the ceremonies of chivalry principally consisted of the investiture of new warriors. All primitive societies have had and still have such initiations. The Church was able to impose upon them a moral character. Purified by a bath and clad in a white tunic, the young man fasted, spent the night in prayer, confessed his sins, received Communion and finally was given his armour and his sword by his suzerain. 'In the name of God, of Saint Michael and of Saint George, I make thee knight', said the sponsor. Then the newly initiated had to swear an oath the precise text of which varied between the eleventh and the fourteenth centuries, but of which the general sense was: 'I shall serve God and my sovereign; I shall support the rights of the weakest; I shall not do battle for reward, gain or profit, but for glory and virtue alone.' Finally, new knights had to promise that 'in all things they would be faithful, courteous, humble and that they would never fail their given word, whatever harm or loss might spring therefrom'. Naturally so noble a rule was observed to the letter only by those who were worthy of it. The habits of the average knight were very different from the ideal of chivalry. But principles have their effect even when they remain only principles. Chivalry's influence was civilizing, and the Church even succeeded in imposing, during several of the days of each week, a Truce of God, during which it was forbidden to fight. This was a great relief for the poor people whose lands were the fields of battle.

The feudal hierarchy was never set up according to a plan. It grew, 'like the branches of a great tree'. The suzerain lords might themselves be dependent upon a sovereign lord, be it of Périgord, Champagne or Aquitaine. At the beginning these sovereign lords in their turn derived from the Carolingian King, the dispenser of justice, but by the tenth century the Frankish monarchy was in tatters and it was precisely from this 'paralysis of sovereignty' that feudalism was born. All the attributes of the State shifted into the hands of the local lord. The King retained only his personal domain. Moreover, the monarchy was then weakened in France by strife between two houses: the traditional Carolingian and a 'Robertian' (later Capetian) house, sprung from Robert the Strong, Count of Anjou and Blois, one of the greatest landowners in the country lying between the Seine and the Loire which is the heart of France. For one hundred and fifty years, during the ninth and tenth centuries, the Robertians had leaders of the first rank, great soldiers, adroit politicians. Several among them had been elected king – Eudes, Robert I, Raoul – and had alternated with Carolingian sovereigns. Eudes had defended Paris against the Normans, a great source of glory for the family. Others had been satisfied with the title Duke of the Franks, but had possessed estates greater than those of the Carolingian kings. The French clergy supported the Robertians against the Carolingians because the latter no longer had enough power to be the Church's effective protectors.

It is thus inaccurate to date, as was long the custom, the third French dynasty from Hugh Capet's election to the throne. Other Robertians had reigned before him. The central location of their domain, between

Orleans, Blois and Paris, operated in their favour. When in 987 the lords of France met to elect a king, they had a choice between Charles of France, Duke of Lower Lorraine, a Carolingian, and Hugh Capet.[1] The Archbishop of Rouen spoke in favour of Hugh: 'The throne', said he, 'is not acquired by hereditary right; only such a man should be elected to it as is distinguished not merely by the nobility of his birth but by the wisdom of his mind. Hence give the crown to the Duke ...' Hugh Capet's election was not a usurpation; it was an election and the recognition of a fact. But the first Capets had to play a difficult part. Their kingdom was reduced to their family domain. All around them great rival lords, the counts of Flanders and Blois, the dukes of Normandy, Anjou and Aquitaine felt themselves to be as powerful as the King. Were they to unite, the crown could do nothing against them. In the south, the crown was unknown. Who would build the unity of the kingdom? The Capetian Île-de-France or the Aquitaine of the counts of Toulouse? No man in those days could have foretold the outcome. The elected king was dependent upon his electors. He was so weak that such lesser lords, as the counts of Corbeil and Melun, worried him. The tower of Montlhéry, perched on a hillock, was enough to frighten him when he had to travel from Orleans to Paris. 'Charlemagne's successor did not dare leave home.' The only revenues he had were those from his own lands, and in order to live he had to move around from farm to farm, like the Barbarian kings of old. All about him, from their powerful stone castles, the very men who had selected him defied him. France had become a tissue of feudal cells, each of which had a fortress for its nucleus. Neither brain nor vital organs had yet taken shape.

Yet the dynasty held in its hands a number of trump cards. The Capetian King stood at the country's centre and his rivals were geographically divided. The Church supported him. In the most solemn ceremony of consecration, she had anointed him with chrism (mixture of oil and balsam) both on his head and on various parts of his body. It was said that the chrism in the consecration phial had been borne to Saint Remi by a dove for Clovis's baptism, and this origin, divinely winged, had its prestige. After having been consecrated, the King attended Mass and took Communion in both kinds, which emphasized his almost priestly character — whence the certainty among the people, who were deeply religious, that God had granted the King powers possessed by no other

---

[1] The wholly personal surname of Capatus, which had been bestowed upon this man, meant that he was clothed in a cape or cloak.

prince. Later it was thought that he could even perform miracles and cure scrofula, 'the king's evil'. (As late as the days of Louis XV, at the time of his consecration thousands of sick people came from all portions of the kingdom to be 'touched' by the King.) The King was not a cleric; 'his wife and his sword prevent him from being taken for a monk', but neither was he altogether a layman.[1] The King by divine right, the wonder-working King, the King of France was likewise in popular tradition the heir of the Emperor. In those years of discord, when the approach of the end of the first Christian millennium — the end of time according to the Apocalypse — caused 'waves of fear' to pass through the multitude, which nostalgically conjured up a Golden Age, a 'Sweet France', on which great rulers had imposed peace, Charlemagne's legend carried with it a feeling for national unity. 'Under a pine, near a dog-rose, a throne was set up, of pure gold; there sits the king who manages Sweet France. White is his beard and flowing are his locks.' He is wise, courtly to women, hard upon the infidels. God loves him and protects him. Such was the sovereign still fresh in the memory and still desired by the people of France. For a time the country found itself chopped up into fiefs, but the remembrance of unity had merely fallen asleep.

Not only were the first Capetians poor, their domain small, their vassals powerful, but linguistic anarchy added to the sovereign's weakness. Norman was spoken at Rouen and at Caen, Celtic in Brittany, the *langue d'oc* in Provence and Aquitaine. The feudal nature of the kingship eternally endangered it, for the royal domain was at the mercy of inheritances and dowries. To gather together the pieces of France was thus a labour of Sisyphus, and each generation had to accomplish anew the work of its predecessor. Another danger lay in the elective system which, each time a sovereign died, opened to question what had been achieved. The Capetians successfully sought to ward off this threat by having the King's eldest son consecrated during his father's lifetime. Thus on Christmas Day, 987, Hugh Capet had his son Robert the Pious anointed. The following year he had him married with great political effect to the widow of the Count of Flanders. And here we come to a romantic episode, revealing in the light it casts on the customs of that age. Robert was in love with his cousin Bertha, daughter of the King of Burgundy. He detested the wife, older than himself, who had been forced upon him. He renounced her and, as soon as he became king, married Bertha. The Pope ordered them to separate because their consanguinity prohibited

[1] MARC BLOCH.

their being man and wife. Robert persisted, and his kingdom was placed under interdict. In 1001 anathema triumphed over love. Robert left Bertha but, in 1011, unable to live without the woman he loved, he journeyed to Rome to beseech the Pope. But the Pontiff would not be swayed and Robert yielded. The story is interesting because it proves the weakness of the first Capetian kings who, tolerated rather than respected by the barons who only yesterday had been their equals, could retain power only through the support of the Church.

CHAPTER V

HOW THE CAPETIANS, IN ROUNDING OUT THEIR DOMAIN, FORMED THE KINGDOM OF FRANCE

THREE major facts dominate the eleventh century. The first is the conquest of England by the Normans. The Men of the North, Danes or Norwegians, who ruled at Caen, Bayeux and Rouen, had steeped themselves with startling speed in the Latin spirit. The mixture of Roman tradition and the youthful energy of the Vikings had produced tremendous results. Clear-minded, stubborn rulers, the dukes of Normandy were much more 'modern' than the kings of France. They levied taxes, administered their financial affairs with reasonable skill, built the beautiful churches of Caen and Bayeux and summoned learned clerics from all over the world to come and dwell in their monasteries. In 1066, Duke William the Bastard, later to be surnamed the Conqueror, seized England through combined diplomatic, military and religious action. He dominated the native population of that island, granted its lands to his knights, organized the Church, imposed his own tongue on the ruling class and proclaimed himself King of England while remaining Duke of Normandy. Henceforth the presence, on the soil of his kingdom, of a great vassal who was himself a powerful sovereign was a constant threat to the King of France. The problem would be resolved only on the day when the King of France became master of Normandy — or the King of England master of France.

The second important fact is the part played by the Crusades, by means of which the Church endeavoured to put the courage of the feudal warrior at the service of Christendom. Pilgrimages were then, as they had been in earlier times, one of the usual forms of religious devotion. By the thousands pilgrims went to Rome, to Saint James of Compostela, to Jerusalem. Ever since 637, the Holy Sepulchre had been in the hands of the infidels, but for a long time the Mohammedans in their tolerance had welcomed pilgrims. Harun-al-Rashid had even granted Charlemagne the right to protect the Holy Places. However, in 1071 Jerusalem passed into the hands of the Seljuk Turks, who almost totally forbade access to the Holy City. From this arose the plan to drive them out. Great popes conceived the notion that a holy war would increase the prestige of the Church and at the same time would discipline the knighthood. It is easier to direct warlike instincts than to suppress them, and a combination of penance and battle should prove pleasing to the knights, who loved valiant strokes of the sword and feared eternal torments. Less religious motives likewise played a part: Italian merchants wished to re-establish their trade with the Orient and great lords hoped to carve out fresh principalities for themselves. The First Crusade was primarily a French operation. Pope Urban II was a Frenchman; France was the cradle of chivalry; her nobles asked for nothing better than to embark upon this sublime adventure.

The First Crusade was preached by Urban II at the Council of Clermont in 1095. Peter the Hermit, astride his mule, wandered all over France enlisting men of the people under the banner of the cross. This poor men's Crusade was touching and ill fated. The greater part of its forces perished before reaching Jerusalem. The Crusade of the knights, better organized, was supplied by sea, thanks to the merchants of Italy. Three armies crossed Europe by three different routes. But their discipline was not equal to their enthusiasm. Each soldier, pilgrim and adventurer in one, changed leaders the moment he thought he had a ground for complaint. The great princes sought kingdoms for themselves just as much as they sought the glory of God. Alexius Comnenus, Emperor of Constantinople, was appalled at the arrival of these hordes. Yet in the end he came to an agreement with their leaders and lent them aid. Asia Minor was occupied and Jerusalem taken in 1099. A kingdom of Jerusalem was set up as a feudal State, the sovereign and barons of which were French. Thus the French tongue and civilization in the Near East acquired a privileged position.

Relations between the Crusaders and the infidels became better than one would readily have imagined. Friendships were sealed. The two cultures interpenetrated to the great profit of both, one of many occasions on which, through contact with the East, the Western mind has become aware of its own essential nature and reserves of strength. Just as the Persian wars coincided with the finest period of Greek thought, so too the Crusades were to mark the beginning of a European rebirth. For three centuries they fixed the world's commercial and maritime centres. Marseilles, Genoa and Venice, embarkation points for the Crusaders, became great cities, where inns were erected for the use of pilgrims. The policing of the Mediterranean was guaranteed by the military orders of knighthood, the Templars and the Knights of Saint John of Jerusalem, who constructed great Christian fleets and established the first international armed forces. Starting in the twelfth century, the Templars defended Provence against the Saracens, and in that land you can still find the ruins of their fortified castles. The immediate effect of the Crusades upon France was to strengthen the monarchy at the expense of the feudal lords. For many of the latter impoverished themselves in order to go to the Holy Land, and many of them died there. This weakening of the military class worked to the benefit not only of the kings but of the urban population.

In addition to the Crusades and the conquering of England another important fact of the eleventh century was the rebirth of the cities and the formation in France of a third estate. The towns of Roman days had not wholly disappeared during the period of anarchy, but they had lost their importance and their independence. The municipal system had ceased to operate. Only a few bishops had saved their ancient cities, of which they had become temporal lords. Now in the eleventh century new fortified towns had grown up to protect market-places, and the inhabitants of these boroughs (*burgs*) were called bourgeois. Under the shelter of their castle strongholds, former villas had become small towns (*villes*) where merchants dwelt. At the outset, the latter were villeins, like all the rest, in the eyes of their lord. But as they dwelt in groups, they had more opportunity for united action than had the tillers of the soil. They organized in religious confraternities and trade guilds. In such strenuous times, knowing themselves impotent if they were not united, they travelled in flotillas and caravans for defence against pirates and robbers, the caravan spirit necessarily being a spirit of co-operation. A town made itself rules, selected its own leaders, sought to obtain a charter and freedoms, that is, privileges. During that period, this was a movement characteristic of all Europe. German and Italian cities were in the forefront because they were the richest and most prosperous. In the south of France, the towns breathed new life into ancient administrative forms; those of the north formed communes on the basis of sworn association of the merchants against the bishops and feudal lords. Occasionally (as at Laon) the communes' movement towards freedom took on a revolutionary aspect; but this was an exception. The urban merchant accepted the feudal order; he only asked that he might participate in it and that his city might itself become a collective liege lord. The King encouraged this development because marketing privileges were for him a source of revenue. The rebirth of European trade began at Venice and in Flanders, where were to be found centres of maritime commerce with the Orient in one direction and Scandinavia and England in the other. Then, half-way between Venice and Flanders, there began for purposes of exchange, the Fair of Champagne, which enriched other French towns. Many a bishop and feudal lord amicably granted privileges to the bourgeois in order to further the gathering together on their lands of persons who would pay quit-rents and man militia bands.

In other lands the communes were to have more distinguished destinies. In Germany the Hanseatic cities became independent republics, as was the case with Florence, Milan and Venice in Italy. In England the bourgeois joined forces with the knights to form the House of Commons, and soon they ruled the land side by side with the barons. In France the bourgeois increased in wealth and in real power; they gave advisers to princes, judges to the law courts, geniuses to literature; but they remained a class apart, looked down on as inferiors by the nobility and the Church, and it was the discontent of this 'Third Estate' which in 1789 was to produce the Revolution. But in the tenth and twelfth centuries, the new bourgeois class leaned on the King and supported him against the feudatories.

Louis VI, the Fat (1108-37), king and judge, sought above all to maintain free communications between the royal and episcopal cities. He razed the strongholds which commanded passage along the roads and routed those petty tyrants of the Île-de-France who plundered merchants and pillaged monasteries. As against seignorial usurpations, Louis VI made himself the defender of the 'custom of the French'. Abbot Suger, his minister, praised him for defending churches, succouring the poor and the unfortunate, watching over the peace of the realm: 'It is a commonplace', said Suger, 'that kings have long hands ...' A novel idea, since no one would have thought of saying that the power of the early Capetians stretched very far. The new kingship respected the independence of the feudal lords within their domains, but placed itself above all these local powers in the maintenance of order, justice and peace. 'It is shameful for a king to transgress the law, because king and law draw their authority from the same source', said Suger. Thus throughout the country the King of France began to play the part of a righter of wrongs. He remained the first among the feudal lords, the suzerain of suzerains; he was also the anointed of the Lord, king by the grace of God; very soon he would not even have to invoke this sacred character in order to justify his power in the eyes of the French people. The very basis of the new monarchy

THE FIRST BEGINNINGS AND THE MIDDLE AGES

was the defence of law. There were cities which, in order to escape the
tyranny of their own magistrates, asked to be governed directly by the
King. Thus, whether he granted charters, intervened as a mediator
between cities and their feudal masters, or installed his own provosts, the
King worked hand in hand with the bourgeoisie.

Sensual and gluttonous, Louis VI died young, 'so devoured by his
belly that fat brought about his downfall'.[1] By a master stroke he had
married his son to Eleanor of Aquitaine, who brought the King of France
as her dowry the whole of the south-west as far as the Pyrenees. Unfortunately this was an ephemeral union. Louis VII was gallant, pious and
naively likeable. He charmingly remarked to one Englishman: 'To your
prince nothing is lacking. Gold and silver, precious stones, silken stuffs
– all these he has in abundance. We in France have only bread, wine
and well-being . . .' But his queen, Eleanor, did not share in the well-
being. She missed the troubadors of Aquitaine and said of her husband:
'I have married a monk, not a king.' He made the mistake of taking
her with him to the Holy Land when he went on the Second Crusade.
On this journey she acted in a most unsaintly manner, became infatuated
with a handsome Saracen slave and had to be hustled away from Antioch.
Abbot Suger wisely counselled the King to be patient: 'With regard to
the Queen your wife, I am of the opinion that you should dissemble the
displeasures she causes you until such time as you have come back to your
kingdom and can quietly consider this matter and various others . . .'
After Suger's death, however, divorce was unavoidable. Eleanor, a woman
of overweening temperament, had become enamoured of the Count of
Anjou, Henry Plantagenet, a heavy-set young man with the neck of a
bull, close-cropped red hair, volcanic energy and winning manners. She
married him and brought him Limousin, Gascony, Périgord and the
whole Duchy of Aquitaine. Such were the absurd results of the feudal
and personal relationship; the whim of a pretty woman could carve up
empires. From his mother, Matilda, Henry already possessed the Duchy
of Normandy; from his father, Maine and Anjou. After his marriage he
was much more powerful in France than the King of France. When, in
1154, he also became King of England, the Angevin Empire threatened
to swallow France.

Louis VII (1137-80) and the son, Philip Augustus, born of his third
marriage (with Alix de Champagne), each reigned for forty-three years.
Philip Augustus put his long term of power to good use. He became king

[1] Quoted by LUCHAIRE.

at the age of fifteen as heir to a heart-rending situation. Between the Angevin Empire of the Plantagenets and the German Empire of Louis the German, which likewise included a portion of Italy (in the old tradition that the Emperor was also King of the Lombards), the King of France in the twelfth century looked like a second-class sovereign. Yet Philip Augustus conquered the Emperor and drove the Plantagenets from France. Energetic, ruddy, as healthy and thick-set as a peasant, bushy-haired, violent but cunning, self-centred but reasonable, he was the very opposite of a feudal king. His ideal was not that of a knight but of a patient and crafty politician. Skilfully he played his game. Severe with the powerful, astute in making use of lesser men, the cities sided with him against the feudality, and from the beginning of his reign he kept in check a coalition of the more important lords. In his struggle against England, he was helped by the rancour of the Church, which had not forgiven Henry II for his murder of Archbishop Thomas à Becket, and by the family quarrels between Henry and his appalling sons. Had they been united, the Plantagenets would easily have conquered him. But they imprudently allowed him to play the sons off against the father, then later, brothers against brothers. With Richard Cœur de Lion, who succeeded Henry II, Philip Augustus was at first on good terms. Together they went on a crusade, then they fell at odds, and upon his return, Philip undertook the conquest of Richard's lands. It was lucky for him that the English king died (1199), leaving him with John Lackland as his opponent – a madman suspected of several murders, whose misdeeds made it possible to place his domains under confiscation. In this way feudal law played into the hands of Philip Augustus, enabling him to recapture, almost without fighting, Normandy, Maine, Anjou, Touraine and Poitou. For France here was a miraculous draught of fishes. The ease with which all these provinces changed hands proves that French unity existed in men's hearts before it existed in deeds. Yet the danger was not exorcized. The King of France's enemies joined forces; the King of England (John Lackland), the Emperor of Germany (Otto IV), Ferrand, Count of Flanders, together with other great lords massed their strength in Flanders. Against this coalition Philip Augustus had the support of the Church and the people. In 1214 at Bouvines, with the help of twenty thousand bourgeois infantrymen – a great novelty – he overcame the reactionary feudal forces and the foreign invaders. This victory consolidated the work of the Capetians. It was greeted by France with that extraordinary joy which goes with the liberation of a country aware of its unity. Everywhere the people danced, clerks sang, churches were hung with tapestries, the streets were strewn with flowers, grasses and leafy branches. For seven days and seven nights the students of Paris revelled with songs and dancing. The King had forgiven even those who had been leagued against him. The national community was born.

Philip Augustus was a modern king, a good organizer, a good diplomat, a good technician. He was not only lord of lords, but a governmental head. He realized the importance of economic matters and helped French merchants to recover their credit abroad. 'Our people must not be allowed to suffer', he would say. Moreover, he also took under his protection merchants from other countries who came to visit the fairs. To the French monarchy he gave 'the three instruments of rule which it lacked: tractable officials, money and soldiers'. In order to progress from a feudal to a national regime, the central power had to be rebuilt. Philip Augustus set up provincial bailiffs who three times a year were required to come to Paris to report on happenings in their bailiwicks and to render their accounts. During his reign the crown revenues went up from one hundred and twenty-eight thousand *livres* to four hundred and thirty-eight thousand. Under the feudal regime, taxes, like all other services, had a personal character. The royal policy in future would be to reconstitute the notion of the State. Under Philip Augustus this policy remained embryonic. The King pocketed certain receipts as a feudal lord: the revenues from his domain, the poll-tax, rights to trade and monopoly, feudal taxes. His royal receipts were still merely expedients: the substitution of taxes for duty services, the right of embossment (transfer duties) when a feudal property changed hands; periodical persecution of the unfortunate Jews, so profitable that in 1198 the King and the Count of Champagne 'assured themselves the sum total of all the property of their Jews'; imposts on the clergy, which was conspicuous for its wealth. Under Philip Augustus, the Templars, warrior and banker monks, fulfilled the function of king's treasurers. Their Commander for France, Brother Aimard, played the part of controller of the currency.

Philip Augustus was one of the first lovers of the city. He bestowed great care upon Paris, his capital, paving the two streets adjoining his palace, 'La Cité', streets which before his time had been malodorous mud paths. He set up a police force, the royal watch, made up of twenty men on horse and forty on foot. Facing the Cité on the right bank, the city of Paris was growing up as a business centre; on the left bank was the Latin Quarter, where dwelt the university students. The King built ramparts round this triple agglomeration, and for its defence erected 'Our Tower of the Louvre' to the west of this enclosure. When he went off on a crusade, it was to six Paris merchants that he handed over the keys of his Treasury and the guardianship of the seals. Until that time, whenever the King of France had gone on a journey, he had carried his meagre archives with him; because he had lost valuable account books in the course of an ambush, Philip Augustus set up the Royal Archives. Although a devout man, he well knew how to maintain the rights of the State against the claims of the Church. Pope Innocent III looked upon all kings as his vassals; Philip Augustus never subscribed to this view. He allowed a crusade to be organized against the Albigensian heretics by Simon de Montfort, but he refused to associate himself with it and only intervened, after the defeat of the Albigenses, in order to reunite to the crown the domains of Raymond VII, Count of Toulouse, and those of his vassals, the Viscount of Béziers and the Count of Foix. Thus the Church was responsible for the atrocities of this crusade and the monarchy took the spoils.

If one compares maps of the royal domain in 987 with those of 1223, one realizes that in the course of these two centuries the Duke of Île-de-France had become the King of France. The Capetians had so closely linked the crown and the national welfare that none but a few jealous great vassals questioned any longer the legitimacy of their power. The notion that the King could be elected by an assembly had been completely forgotten. Philip Augustus was the first of the Capetians who could without recklessness omit having his son consecrated during his own lifetime. Despite this omission, his son, Louis VIII, succeeded to the throne without any difficulty. After his coronation at Reims, he made a solemn entry into Paris; it was the occasion of popular rejoicing which recalled the days after Bouvines. Schools and courts were closed. At street corners orchestras of guitars, psalteries and kettledrums played while young people danced. Nothing unites a people as effectively as festivities. The convulsions of anarchy were succeeded by the traditions of the monarchy.

CHAPTER VI

HOW LOUIS IX MADE THE MONARCHY HOLY AND PHILIP THE FAIR MADE IT STRONG

COLD, ambitious, hard-headed, as his father, Philip Augustus, and ably supported by Blanche of Castile, his energetic and pious Spanish wife, Louis VIII seemed set to be a great king, but he died after reigning for three years, leaving four youthful sons and the regency to his widow. In his will he had left as 'appanages' for his younger sons French provinces — Artois, Anjou, Maine, Poitou and Auvergne. A dangerous precedent, for what did it serve to wrest the kingdom from the great vassals if the only result was to reconstruct an appanaged feudalism of the princes of the blood? However, Louis VIII probably thought that a prince stripped of all rights would be a jealous rival to the King and that the prestige of the royal family would suffer from such a deprivation.

Despite such great and imprudent generosity, as soon as Louis VIII died, a Capetian of the junior branch of the family, Pierre Mauclerc, Duke of Brittany, formed a coalition against the Queen Regent. The barons, hitherto subdued by strong kings and now confronted only by an unpopular foreign woman and a child, threw France into an upheaval which lasted for five years. They insisted that the right of election be restored to them. In other words, they wanted to revert from the national to the feudal monarchy. At first Blanche, knowing how weak she was, did not dare carry the child king from Montlhéry to his capital unless 'those of Paris came armed to fetch him'. None the less she saved the throne for this son and fashioned him in the image she had conceived of a knightly king. She laboured on his behalf as a passionately devoted mother, jealous unto madness. When the King married Marguerite of Provence, the Queen Mother so strangely interfered in the conjugal life of the household that Louis IX and his young wife, whose rooms were situated one above the other, had to meet on the stairway in order to outwit Blanche's supervision, a thing which did not prevent their having eleven children. Yet the King loved this tyrannical mother; he respected her until her death and 'for her made great mourning'.

Louis IX (who was later canonized and became Saint Louis) was endowed by his parents with deep piety and a violent temperament. In no sense was he a bigot, but a handsome knight with a laughing countenance who loved to jest with his intimates after having caused them to be seated at the foot of his bedstead. Despite his religious humility, he did not hesitate to dress himself royally, in a vermilion surcoat edged with ermine: 'In such fashion must one dress', he said, 'that wise men may not say one overdoes, nor young people of the world that one does too little.' Every morning he went to Mass and, after his siesta, heard the office of the dead. He used to ask his friend and seneschal, Joinville, 'Would you like better to be a leper or to have committed a mortal sin?' and reprimanded Joinville if Joinville preferred the sin. Yearly on 'Great Thursday' Louis washed the feet of poor men. 'Sire', Joinville candidly said to him, 'I shall never wash the feet of these villeins.' 'Indeed?' remarked the King. 'That is ill said', and he begged his friend to bring himself to wash them. His son he counselled to love God, to help the poor and wretched, to uphold the good customs of the kingdom, to flee the company of bad men, to surround himself with wise men free of envy, not to make judgment without knowing the facts, to have good provosts and bailiffs, 'to incur only reasonable expenses'. Here was a perfect *Manual for the King of France*. The meetings at the oak tree of Vincennes, under the shadow of which he meted out justice, seated upon a carpet among his companions, have remained famous. In his decisions he never took the rank of pleaders into account and, devout as he was, did not hesitate to defend the rights of his subjects against the Church.

Saint Louis, a valorous soldier, took part in two crusades: the Seventh in 1248, which lasted six years and was a long series of disasters, and the Eighth in 1270, which ended with the King's death in Tunis from an attack of the plague. The Sire de Joinville, who accompanied his royal master, has left us an account of these expeditions. They were much better organized than the earlier crusades. Horses were loaded on vessels the sides of which were let down for the operation. When they set sail, all hands sang the *Veni Creator* on the bridge, and the Crusaders 'drew away from the country where they had been born ... Bold indeed unto folly, for you go to sleep at night without knowing whether on the morrow you will be at the bottom of the sea ... ' More than one ship was lost; yet Louis, once finding himself at Cyprus aboard a vessel which was leaking, refused his companions' plea to transfer to another ship, lest it cause worry to the other passengers. Upon his return from the Seventh Crusade, he found a new coalition of the barons and the King of England arrayed against him. He overwhelmed it and then, to the great surprise of everyone, handed Poitou, Gascony and Guienne to the conquered English. 'For we have two sisters to wife and our children are first cousins, wherefore it is surely fitting that peace be between us.' In return he stipulated only that the King of England swear him homage for these provinces and that all other English claims on the Continent be abandoned. He thus gave proof of astounding moderation. But above all Louis sought to be just. To preserve peace among Christians and to fight the infidel was the sum total of his foreign policy. Thus he was always ready to negotiate and come to terms with other courts. In order to keep peace with Spain, he was eager to give up Catalonia. He intervened between the Pope and the Emperor suggesting that they should discuss their differences. Through this policy of moderation, 'he placed the crown of France at the highest level of prestige'. He won his greatest moral triumph on that day in 1264 when King Henry III and the English barons asked him to arbitrate their dispute. In a world where violence had been so powerful, here was an entirely new thing: respect paid to moderation. Never had a united Christendom come closer to realization.

Internally, Louis IX continued the work of Philip Augustus. He respected feudal legitimacy but suppressed its abuses. Specifically, he forbade private wars, that scourge of the poor. The centre for the administration of justice remained the king's dwelling, the *Curia Regis*, and it was as first judge of the kingdom that Saint Louis heard cases under the Vincennes oak, or at any other place where his court might be sojourning. But just as animals, when they move up the ladder of development, develop new organs, so as the kingdom evolved, the cells of the royal court split and became specialized as the Great Council, charged with political matters, the Chamber of Accounts, and the *Parlement*, or permanent court of justice. France's higher nervous system was taking shape. The *Parlement*, which sat at Paris, had nothing in common with the English Parliament, born at about the same time. It was a court of appeals, a supreme court for the entire kingdom, but not a representative assembly. In the provinces, Saint Louis subjected his bailiffs to new rules which served as safeguards for those under their administration, and he required them to remain in their bailiwicks forty days after the end of their terms of office, so that they might feel responsible for their actions. Throughout his reign, finances were healthy and receipts exceeded expenditure.

When, in 1270, Louis IX died, he bequeathed his son a prestige greater than that which he himself had inherited from his ancestors. From that time on the Capetian king would not only be accepted as a legitimate sovereign by birthright, but would be considered God's direct representative, who could do without other counsel whenever he felt himself inspired. Thus Louis IX's saintly purity had caused his family and the kingdom to move towards an absolute monarchy wholly foreign to the Frankish kings. Also thanks to him France had acquired a new prestige among the nations, the prestige of moral authority. It was natural that he should have been canonized (in 1297) and should have become Saint Louis. From the very moment of his death, France's poets sang of him:

> Good King Louis, you held the land under yoke
> To the profit of barons and of the little folk ...
> To whom may poor men cry now in their woe
> Since the good king is dead who loved them so?

It is hard to be the son of a saint. Philip III, the Bold, was pious, stout-hearted and a typical knight, but France's admiration for his father paralysed him and made him a spiritless sovereign. During his reign and that of his successor, Philip IV, the Fair, it was no longer the king's person who was dominant, but the 'king's people', whom we should today call the government departments. Philip III wound up his father's Crusade, announced that he would undertake another, and never set forth. His evil genius was Charles d'Anjou, his uncle, to whom the Papacy had offered the kingdom of the Two Sicilies, in the mistaken hope that Charles would be as good a king as Louis IX. Charles involved his nephew in a perfectly futile conflict with Aragon, for which Philip III had no desire. In the Instructions left him by the King, his father, he read: 'I teach thee that thou beware of thine own power, that thou have war with no Christian, and, if someone has done thee wrong, try thou several roads to recover what is thy due before thou makest war ... And take care that thou be well advised before starting any war, even though the cause be greatly reasonable, and thou hast thoroughly summoned the evil-doers and waited as long as thou shouldest ...' In 1282, however, Charles d'Anjou's French garrison was massacred at Palermo at the hour of Vespers (whence the name Sicilian Vespers by which this incident is still known) and Sicily yielded itself to Aragon, against the wishes of the Pope. The Holy Father then told Philip that here was a holy cause and that war against Aragon would be a crusade. This campaign turned into a miserable rout.

Yet under this reign the consolidation of the French domain continued. The vast county of Toulouse had come as a legacy to the King of France; he married his son to the heiress of the kingdom of Navarre and the county of Champagne, a good match for the crown of France. Little by little the king's men also took under their jurisdiction that mass of tonsured folk, 'clerics by law and ribald by life', who until then had wandered all over France with impunity, claiming the privileges of the clergy. Thus the work of the dynasty had gone on uninterrupted and effectively under Philip III, but the sovereign who, after Philip Augustus and Saint Louis, completes the trinity of great Capetians, was his successor, Philip IV, the Fair. In the list of kings, the Saint is bracketed between two politicians.

Philip the Fair, a figure of mystery, taciturn and retiring, who wore a belt of haircloth yet defied a pope, raises a question: was he himself a great sovereign, or rather a weak king made to serve the uses of bold advisers? It matters little. For what took place was of great import. He fell heir to a strong government and he made it stronger. During his reign the king's men were lawyers from the south or from Normandy, whose very sustenance had been the imperial and Roman law. Their ideal was less Saint Louis's Christian monarchy than Charlemagne's or Caesar's empire. The unity of the kingdom was their most cherished concern and lawsuits their favourite method. 'We who desire always to remain reasonable', wrote Philip the Fair to the King of England, Edward I. But this reasonableness needed only a legal precedent to justify any demand. Feudal law, Roman law, everything was grist to the French lawyers' mill as long as the King's interests were well served thereby. They had the Paris Palais de Justice built and staffed with permanent, salaried officials. Nothing helped to ruin feudalism as much as the growing prestige of royal justice. Any dissatisfied litigant appealed from his liege lord's court to the bailiffs and *parlements* of the king. In every village the local magistrate felt himself supervised and his power threatened. The King's domain grew even larger through marriage, inheritance and treaties: it included fifty-nine of the departments of modern France, administered by thirty-nine bailiffs and seneschals. All this machinery was expensive, six times more so than under Philip Augustus.

Philip the Fair, 'the most spendthrift of our kings', had only one financial principle, to get hold of money by any and every means. He tried new taxes: the *maltôte*, a levy on aggregate business; an income tax (a fiftieth or a hundredth) for 'the defence of the realm'; certified loans, guaranteed by liens on specific treasury receipts; confiscations. In 1306 all the

Jews were arrested and their goods seized. Then came the turn of the Lombard bankers. 'Our subjects are devoured by their usuries.' Such was the excuse. They were stripped, driven out, then summoned to return in order that more money might be extracted from them. Little did it matter whether his subjects were devoured as long as the King shared in the feast. Finally came devaluation through a debasing of the currency. 'We have been forced to have pieces coined which perhaps lack some of the weight and alloy of those struck by our predecessors . . .' There were also private counterfeiters, but these the King caused to be boiled alive, for a crime must be committed by the State in order to be permissible. This constant need for money, caused by the expansion of the royal administrative machinery, had political consequences: disagreements with the Papacy, the enfranchisement of serfs against a payment of cash, venality among office-holders, the frequent convoking of consultative assemblies to which the clergy, the nobility and the bourgeoisie were summoned in order to agree to and apportion taxes. Thus finances governed policy. It was under Philip the Fair that we see appear, for the first time in French history, the dilemma of administrative despotism or financial soundness. A strong government is expensive; a government which is too expensive ceases to be strong.

The Anglo-French problem had not been settled, and could not be as long as the King of England remained master of Guienne. 'The English then thought it just as natural to be at Bordeaux as they today find it natural to be in Bombay; the people of Bordeaux thought it as little natural as do today the people of Bombay.'[1] Numerous incidents led finally to war. France had Scotland as her ally; England, the Count of Flanders. At Rouen, Philip the Fair caused a squadron to be built to control the Channel. In the end Edward kept Guienne, admitted that he was a vassal of the French throne, married Marguerite (Philip the Fair's sister) and married his son (later Edward II) to Isabel, the daughter of the King of France. This was a serious mistake on Philip's part and was one of the causes of the Hundred Years War, for the claim which Edward III, Isabel's son, was to lay to the crown of France sprang from this marriage. Flanders wavered, as she would continue to do for centuries, between France and England. She was wealthy, proud and independent; the Flemish middle class resisted the pretensions of the counts of Flanders, thus encouraging foreign intrigue. Philip the Fair long struggled against Flanders, with alternate success and failure, for this people of weavers

[1] H. A. L. FISHER, *History of Europe*, 1930.

was more than once able to put to flight the knighthood of France, and the Matins of Bruges were as bloody as the Sicilian Vespers. At last, in 1305, a treaty was drawn up. Philip had acquired Lille, Douai and Orchies, today one of the richest of French provinces.

But the most serious struggle of this reign was that between the King of France and the Papacy. For three centuries Rome had fought the German Empire and the English monarchy to obtain recognition for the privileges of the clergy. Were investiture granted to bishops by lay sovereigns, were the latter to have the right to tax the property of the Church, were ecclesiastical offices to be obtained by intrigues and corruption, then the independence and purity of the Church would cease to exist. Making a divine institution subject to human powers was to abdicate and disown the faith. And in this cause a whole lineage of great popes had striven, with excommunication and the interdict as their weapons. They had been victorious over the Empire, but nationalism was growing. It was questionable whether the popes would succeed in preserving a clergy wholly dependent on the Holy See in strongly organized kingdoms. Especially the Capetian monarchy, jealous of its rights, was sooner or later bound to fall out with Rome. No man can serve two masters. Boniface VIII, a militant and victorious Pope, held that every human creature was subject to the Roman Pontiff. In 1296 he published a bull, *Clericis laicos*, wherein he forbade laymen to tax the clergy and punished by excommunication any cleric paying such taxes as well as the layman imposing them. Philip the Fair replied by forbidding the exportation of currency, which drained the revenues of the Vatican. The Pope yielded, but in 1300 celebrated at Rome a jubilee to mark the new century to which journeyed, from throughout Christendom, some two million pilgrims. Dazzled by the spectacle of his own power, Boniface VIII raged against the King of France and by means of the bull *Ausculta fili* (Hear, my son), invited Philip to clear himself of the charges of counterfeiting which had been lodged against him. By thus taking on the semblance of a dispenser of justice on a temporal question, the Pope seemed to arrogate to himself the government of the universe. In 1302, Philip called together an assembly of his barons and cities and, feeling that he had their support, resisted. The bull *Unam sanctam* set forth the Pope's views: 'Men live on two levels, one spiritual, the other temporal. If the temporal power should go astray, it must be judged by the spiritual power.' Thereupon the King of France defied the Papacy. One of his councillors, Guillaume de Nogaret, journeyed to Italy and, precipitating a scene of unprecedented violence sought through threats to obtain the abdication of Boniface VIII. The Pope did not yield, vested himself in the insignia of his office, and said that he would rather die than abdicate. Nogaret's stroke had failed. But the Pope, advanced in years, died as a result of his emotional disturbance. His successor likewise died very shortly after his elevation – there were those who said he had been poisoned.

In 1305 French influence brought about the election of the Archbishop of Bordeaux, Bertrand de Got, who chose the name of Clement V. Feeling that Rome was no longer a safe abode, he wandered about for some time from city to city and then in 1309 settled himself in the convent of the Order of Preaching Brothers at Avignon. The county of Venaissin, in which Avignon was situated, belonged to the Holy See and later the popes purchased the city as well. They dwelt there from 1309 to 1377 utterly subject to the influence of the kings of France. Avignon was completely transformed. The bishop's palace was transformed by the popes into a magnificent residence, filled with works of art. A pontifical court and administrative and fiscal machineries developed. The Papacy levied 'annates' (a year's revenue from all ecclesiastical benefices whenever they changed hands) and other taxes, which made it extremely unpopular. At that time of rising nationalism and an expanding royal treasury, conflict was inevitable between the two powers which vied for the taxpayer's poor pennies. This 'Babylonian Captivity' ended in 1377 and the Pope returned to Rome. But then rivalry between two nationalisms, Italian and French, ended with the election of two popes. Avignon and Rome both had their claimants and Christendom was cleft in two by the Great Schism.

Under Philip the Fair the most painful episode in these quarrels between France and Rome was the suit against the Knights Templars. This great monastic warrior Order, wearing a white uniform with a red cross, had been founded at the time of the Crusades to defend the Holy Land. In this it did not succeed, and by 1291, even Syria had been reconquered by the Mamelukes. But the Templars had acquired great wealth in France. The Commanderies of the Temple were, in many provinces, the most prosperous of all domains. The knights had business dealings and had even lent money to the King himself. To get rid of them would be profitable, and there was no lack of incriminating gossip to use against them. Some accused them of treason and of having struck a bargain with the Saracens; others accused them of loose living and heretical views. They were called infamous and their orgies were described in detail. 'To drink like a Templar' became a commonplace expression. The truth would seem to have been that their rule was austere, but that certain among them might perhaps have had the vices of the chaste, and certainly the mystery with which they surrounded their initiations was a great help to their enemies. The populace believed everything, the good and the bad. Nogaret the Terrible, master of the seals, set out to ruin the Templars and succeeded. By means of torture they were forced to admit everything their foes desired them to. Fifty-four knights were condemned to death by fire. Pope Clement V, appalled at so much cruelty, long sought to refuse a general condemnation of the Order. But in the end he himself yielded to blackmail and to threats. The Order was stripped and dissolved; its Grand Master, Jacques de Molay, was burned to death; its goods were seized. It is said that on his pyre Molay had 'summoned the King to appear within a year before the court of God'. This took place on March 11th, 1314, and Philip IV died before the year's end. This frightful judicial tragedy had lasting and detestable effects. Through the business of the Templars, a criminal procedure was set up which, later applied to cases of witchcraft, gave free rein to the most terrible methods of torture.

In order to win public opinion in all these conflicts, Philip the Fair, in 1308, convoked the States General at Tours. Not only the clergy and the barons but two hundred and fifty cities were represented therein. Was this any indication that France, like England, was turning towards parliamentary institutions? Not at all. Whereas in England two chambers very quickly took shape, the Lords and the Commons, and English knights and merchants were willing to sit together in the House of Commons, in France the three estates remained separate, thus making impossible any idea of national representation. The States General did not debate or initiate anything; it listened and gave its approval. Calling its members together merely helped the King to levy taxes and to put an end to complaints against the debased currency. This support was sorely needed, for at that time there was much irritation throughout the country. When Philip the Fair died, he was hated. Was this just? He had strengthened royal absolutism, fought feudal and ecclesiastical power and substituted the public might for individual interest – all useful in itself. But his harsh lawyers had achieved these results only by iniquitous means. A Louis IX would have obtained the same effects without causing the same suffering.

The prestige of the throne was likewise weakened by the scandalous lives of Philip the Fair's three daughters-in-law: Marguerite of Burgundy (wife of Louis X, the Quarrelsome), Jeanne of Poitiers (wife of Philip V, the Tall) and Blanche of the Marche (wife of Charles IV, the Simple). All three were accused of adultery. Jeanne's innocence was admitted and proclaimed by the *Parlement*, but Blanche and Marguerite were convicted of having had as lovers two of their gentlemen-in-waiting, Philip and Gautier d'Aulnay, who were put to death. The two princesses, condemned to solitary confinement, were locked up in the Château Gaillard. Later Blanche took the veil in the Abbey of Maubuisson. As for Marguerite of Burgundy, when her husband Louis X mounted the throne, he desired to marry Clementia, daughter of the King of Hungary. Marguerite was still alive though confined. The annulment of any marriage, even a royal marriage, is difficult and slow. In order to avoid endless and complicated negotiations with Rome, Louis had recourse to a discreet execution of his adulterous wife: he had Marguerite smothered in her cell between two mattresses.

CHAPTER VII

HOW, DURING THE MIDDLE AGES, A FRENCH CIVILIZATION TOOK SHAPE

THE Middle Ages was not a dark and barbarous period between two shining ones, antiquity and the Renaissance. On the contrary, the civilization of the Middle Ages was a great civilization, one of those which bestowed upon a man a moral and social equilibrium, one of those which also gave birth to the greatest works of art of the West. Of course Athens, Rome, Byzantium and Alexandria had in earlier times achieved a standard of culture to which Paris of the twelfth century could lay no claim, but the old civilizations, in order to produce more fruit, needed to have fresh stock grafted on to them. The originality of French medieval civilization lay in melting and moulding Mediterranean and Barbarian elements. French civilization is a 'fringe' civilization. All the fresh flowerings of mankind have taken place in areas broadly open to differing influences. Classical Greece blossomed on the fringe of the European and Asiatic worlds. France on her Mediterranean coast was in intimate contact with the Greek, Roman and Byzantine worlds; on the Atlantic coast with the Scandinavian Vikings; along the Pyrenees with Islam; along the Rhine with the Barbarians. This mixture saved her, as Foçillon puts it, from the eternal provincialism of central Europe. As early as the tenth century, but especially in the twelfth, there began a French renaissance the ideas and the arts of which were to spread out over all Europe.

The diffusion of a culture throughout Europe was, then, all the easier because the Church constituted a sort of community of peoples, imposing Latin upon them as a universal language and bringing about the acceptance by all of beliefs substantially unchallenged. In France as in England or in Germany, as in Spain or in Italy, the Middle Ages were above all an age of faith. A Frenchman of the twelfth century had no doubts about the meaning of this life. He believed that God had created the world as it is recounted in the Bible; that men were put on earth in order to work out their salvation; that on the day of the Last Judgment, some would be damned, others would be saved. He had a great fear of eternal damnation; he was ready, in order to escape it, faithfully to practise his religion, to go on pilgrimages, and to give alms. The moment cities became wealthy, local pride and unity of faith spurred them on to dedicate their energies and their credit to the construction of churches worthy of God. The contrast between the small populations of these towns, the poverty of their private dwellings and the splendours of their cathedrals, proves the intensity of their faith.

None then dreamed that a philosopher might cast doubts upon revealed truth. Such a wretch would have run the risk of being excommunicated, laid under an interdict, subjected to torture. Putting yourself outside the Christian community would have meant condemning yourself to death. To this rule there was a single exception: the Jews, who were tolerated both as witnesses to the Scriptures and as useful intermediaries in trade with the infidels, not to speak of their capacity to lend money at interest. They were confined in ghettos, but remained free to worship in their synagogues and to cultivate rabbinical lore. Through them Arabic culture penetrated into France. The lives of all the rest were dominated by the influence of the Catholic Church. Processions studded with the rich banners of the confraternities marked the passage of the months and days. The churches were bedecked with tapestries by the guild merchants; they were enriched with treasures of jewellers' work and the vestments of the clergy were embroidered in gold. What a rich American of the twentieth century does for his university, a wealthy merchant of the thirteenth would have done for his cathedral.

It was the Church likewise which had organized education. In the villages the priest taught a few privileged children their Catechism, reading, writing and simple arithmetic. The bishop's school had the right to give a 'licence' to teach. When, under the Capetians, the royal administration expanded, secretaries and lawyers that were sought after had also to be theologians. From this need were born the universities, which at the outset were guilds or corporations of professors and students. They were offshoots of the cathedral schools, wherein were taught the seven liberal arts: grammar, logic, rhetoric, arithmetic, geometry, astronomy and music. As early as the twelfth century, Paris was a teaching centre celebrated throughout Europe. Abélard's dream, like that of every learned man, was to teach there, and when he was unable to do so within the city itself, he established himself on the other bank of the Seine, on the Mount of Saint Geneviève. Little by little the kings of France realized that this gathering together at the *stadium parisiense* of young men from every country who came to drink 'at this fount of the Catholic faith' lent great prestige to the country and its sovereign. 'Never at Athens or at Alexandria had there been seen such an influx of students.'[1] The popes made use of the University of Paris to spread sound doctrine. 'The learning of the schools of Paris in the Holy Church', said Alexander IV in 1255, 'is like resplendent lamps in the hands of the Lord.' Yet these young scholars were very ill behaved, 'ever ready to plague a tradesman and seduce his wife, devourers at table but far from devout at Mass'. Some of their letters home are still preserved: 'We pray you to send us by the bearer of these presents enough money to buy parchment, ink, a writing-desk, and other things of which we have need. You will not leave us embarrassed . . .' Panurge would continue this tradition.

The university possessed neither a place of assembly nor a budget. It was not an educational centre for the sons of the nobility, who were taught within their own family circles. (In this we see the status of culture as compared with ancient times: while the Roman and Greek élite had been at once warriors and cultivated men, the functions were kept separate during the Middle Ages. The clerk taught, prayed, governed; the knight fought.) In 1253 Robert de Sorbon founded the first college in the University of Paris: the Community of Poor Masters and Scholars. The universities granted diplomas indicating that the recipients were bachelors of arts, masters of arts, doctors of law, theology or medicine, and these medieval titles have been preserved today even in American universities which are the heirs, through England, of the French medieval tradition. The classical humanities had no important place in these schools, which were essentially ecclesiastical. The lesson was a lecture in commentary upon a text from the Bible or Aristotle (the words *lecture* and *lesson* in English have preserved the sense they then had; not so in French). Public disputations or discussions of a question set by the master lasted at times for several days. 'Scholastic' was at the outset everything relating to the school. In Alcuin's day the master was called *scholasticus*. Later the name *schola* was given to the philosophy of the medieval schools. The great study was that of logic, for, since God had created it, the human reason could not err, and a chain of correct reasoning must lay bare the secrets of the world. Hence it is clear that the respect for abstract reason and the taste for logical clarity, attributed by Taine to the classical spirit of the seventeenth and eighteenth centuries, were born in France as early as the Middle Ages.

When we read the dissertations and questions of the masters of those

[1] G. LE BRETON.

days, for example the *Sic et non* of Peter Abélard (1079-1142), we are surprised at the nature of their researches. 'Was Adam saved or not? . . . Did the Apostles have wives or not? . . .' Abélard sought to apply the Socratic method, to awaken minds by asking questions, but since truth had been revealed in the sacred writings, a learned man of the Middle Ages could only interpret texts. Nevertheless, since he was not in ignorance of profane writings, since he admired Plato and even more admired Aristotle, he must have been tempted to reconcile reason, which, in Aristotle's logic, dazzled him, with faith. The great debate among medieval philosophers was on the nature of general ideas. Is an idea a reality, the only reality, as Plato taught, or is it merely a word, and is not reality the particular, the fact? Realists and nominalists argued with much subtlety, and through these debates minds were sharpened and the vocabulary took on precision. Saint Bernard, who reproached Peter Abélard with denying the mysteries and the obscurity of the faith, thought that the true knowledge of God was acquired by intuition, and that he who had tasted this true food of the soul scorned the crusts of knowledge gnawed by the rationalist. But Abélard was not convinced: 'It is something ridiculous', said he, 'to expound to others what neither oneself nor anyone else can intelligibly understand.' In this he anticipated Descartes.

The object of Saint Thomas Aquinas's labours was to reassure the faithful by showing them that it was possible to reconcile Aristotle with the Scriptures, intelligence with faith. 'Truth', said Saint Thomas, 'is one, hence truth according to knowledge and truth according to faith must coincide.' Either Aristotle's logic is in error or else it must confirm revealed truth, or at least that portion of such truth as is subject to demonstration. 'For certain things which are true of God exceed the capacity of the human reason, for instance that God is one in three persons, whereas others are accessible even to the natural reason, for example that God is.' Thus was resolved the intellectual crisis which might have upset the equilibrium of the twelfth century. Thanks to Saint Thomas, faith was confirmed, but by the same token scientific research was legitimized. Since faith and knowledge, the mind and the world, the ideal and the real necessarily coincide, man has the right, outside the mysteries, to seek truth in the world as in the Scriptures. He may question the real by means of the senses and experience; the task of the reasoning process will thereupon be to bring into agreement the findings of experience and revealed tradition. Thus Saint Thomas opened the road to the modern world. But whereas the scientist of the twentieth century does not believe it possible to construct an image of the world and admits that he is ignorant of the plan of the building of which he has measured a few stones, Saint Thomas, thanks to revelation, sturdily built to the very pinnacle of divine truth the spire of his intellectual cathedral.

Philosophers and theologians wrote in Latin, but from as early as the eleventh century there existed in France minstrels or 'inventors' (*trouvères*) who journeyed from castle to castle and from public square to public square reciting historical songs in the vernacular, at first short poems, then longer *chansons de geste* (*gesta* being deeds). Although it was the time of the Crusades, and the knights were not lacking in real adventures, they took delight in evoking the past. They had a nostalgia for Charlemagne and even for Alexander. Many were the versions of the *Chanson de Roland*, with the monks furnishing the historical detail and each *trouvère* adding touches of his own. The influence on manners and customs of these endlessly repeated tales, imprinted on minds by the tricks of rhythm and assonance, was profound and, towards the end of the twelfth century, the knight in real life began to imitate the knight of the epics, just as later on lovers would imitate Saint-Preux or Werther. The *chansons de geste* exalt the warlike virtues; in them personal courage is so proud that it refuses all help, all succour; Roland refuses to blow the horn which would have called back Charlemagne and thus abandons his brave companions to their fate. It was this spirit, heroic to the point of absurdity, which was to lose the day at Crécy for the chivalry of France. A knight is faithful to his suzerain, and his great dramas lie in conflicting loyalties. He is generous with his possessions, but touchy, jealous of his honour; any affront he avenges by the death of him who gives it; he keeps his word, even when it be given to an enemy. Saint Louis, the knightly king, keeps faith with the Saracens and with the King of England, losing a province rather than break an agreement. If we recall the faithlessness of Gregory of Tours's Frankish kings, the morality of the *chansons de geste* reveals a remarkable advance. In the *Chanson de Roland* is also found for the first time a feeling of patriotism, of love for 'sweet France' (which perhaps referred only to the Île de France, but what matter?). This heroic literature contributed greatly to shaping the French soul, and certain reflexes of defiance or pride on the part of French heroes of our own day bring back to our minds the *Chanson de Roland*.

Alongside the *chansons de geste* another literature grew up in France, centred around woman and dealing with love. Why this new prestige for womanhood? During the first centuries of feudalism, women had been treated harshly enough. Customs were coarse. The young girl of the castle had not only to remove the knight's armour, make ready his bed and bathe him, but massage him to help him to sleep.[1] Feudal marriage was a matter of business or of policy, not of love. Often the spouses got along so badly with each other that, with the connivance of the clergy, they found excuses for annulments. This was easy enough, and many women thus remarried three or four times. Kings had little tenderness for their queens. Eleanor of Aquitaine, wife of Henry II, and Ingeborg of Denmark, wife of Philip Augustus, passed portions of their lives in prison. It was the Crusades which, because of the lengthy absence of the lord, gave more power to the 'lady'. The only men who remained in the castle were adolescent pages or clerics able to read and write. Among them desire was mingled with respect; the page or the clerk 'sublimated' in love poems that which they dared not declare. Moreover, a wealthier society possesses more leisure; there is more time to make music for the ladies. At the charming petty courts of the Limousin, Périgord, Poitou or Aquitaine, troubadours sang their verses to their own accompaniments. The love they expressed was that of a servant, a respectful, almost a religious love. They had read Ovid's Art of Love. 'Courtly marriages' of a rather equivocal nature were celebrated which at least in theory tied bonds only of the heart and the mind, but at which on occasion a priest officiated. Great ladies had a lover when at the same time they had a husband; here were the beginnings of a long tradition. 'Courts of love' were organized, where lords and ladies publicly discussed grave matters: 'Who is the better friend, clerk or knight?' Eleanor of Aquitaine brought these 'courtly' manners to the court of France, then to that of England. Chrétien de Troyes, the great poet of the day, dwelt at the court of Champagne, where reigned the Countess Marie, Eleanor's daughter, and this sovereign suggested to the poet the theme of Lancelot, that of the knight subject to his lady. In the Middle Ages, Frenchwomen were at the forefront of the movement for the emancipation of their sex. 'Courtliness' had other consequences, both widespread and happy. It produced not only songs of love and the Roman de la Rose, but a discipline of customs and manners which was a great step forward on the path to civilization. Thenceforward certain characteristics of the France of the future took shape: the influence of women, the importance attached to love.

[1] GERARD DE ROUSSILLON.

To sing can have little value if the song does not come from the very
heart
And song cannot come from the heart unless tender love is deeply
bedded there.

While in courts and castles 'courtesy' paved the way for an aristocratic
civilization which was to reach its zenith in the seventeenth century, in
the towns the bourgeois and the clerics were continually annoyed at the
often scornful airs of the knight. They also, students' and merchants' sons,
were capable of writing verses, but most often they wrote them in a
jeering and rebellious style. Women? Listen to the preachers: 'Between
Adam and God in Paradise there was only a single woman; she did not
rest until she had succeeded in having her husband banished from this
garden of delights and in condemning Christ to the torments of the
Cross.' Another pictured them running about the streets of Paris, 'their
dresses cut low, their bosoms bare'. An anonymous treatise, De ornatu
mulierum, depicts them for us with their eternal desire to please. Here
are some of the chapter headings: 'On the Adornment of the Hair; On
the Beautifying of the Face; On Depilatories; On the Whiteness of the
Teeth; How to Make Sweet the Breath; On Clearing the Complexion.'
Let woman's charms be sung, her sovereignty exalted, but 'in their shops
and stalls the husbands knew well what she was worth. In the inns they
exchanged confidences'. The poet to amuse them was he who mocked
woman and her pretensions, the knight and his insolence, even, indeed,
the Church — her ambitious prelates, her theologians who thought of their
benefices, her Christians who forgot the law of Jesus Christ. Thus
was born a whole literature described as 'moral', which is like a counterpart to the chanson de geste, revolutionary in its power, an equalitarian
satire fully as French as the heroic poem. Perhaps the mixing of these two
strands assured the country's equilibrium. And from this point of view,
nothing could be more curious than the Roman de la Rose, which is in two
parts, the first composed by Guillaume de Lorris, 'wherein the art of love
is all enclosed', the second by Jean de Meung, thoroughly didactic and
satiric. The second Roman de la Rose is revolutionary. The privileges of
the nobility? True nobility can come only from the heart. All men are
equal:

> For I make them to be like
> As it seems at their birth;
> By me they are born alike, naked,

Strong and weak, fat and skinny,
Everything puts them on an equal footing
As far as their human condition is concerned.

He who has no personal merits is a mere villein. The king himself? He is
merely a great villein elected to defend the country. Love? It is merely
a need natural to men as it is to beasts, a matter subject neither to blame
nor to praise:

For when a man eats
Is he glorified thereby?

Several aspects strike the reader in this moral literature of the Middle
Ages. The first is the essential identity of human beings in all ages. The
strangeness of happenings and of dress deceive us. Within his armour
dwells the same soldier as within our battle dress; within the tight-fitting
bodice the same woman as Ovid had known or as Balzac would know.
The moral treatises of the thirteenth century are still to the point. Glance
at the *Doctrinal Sauvage* and you will find: 'If you think well of a man,
take care not to be angry with him over a trifle. If you are given an evil
report of him, do not believe it and wait until you know the truth, for
many a man is slandered falsely ... If you see a fool whose mind is
deranged, avoid provoking him in public, for he will surely revile you...'
The wisdom of the ancient moralist, that of Solomon's proverbs, that of
the Gospels and that of the modern moralist, a Montaigne or an Alain,
are intermingled in these writings which are for all times and ages. The
second aspect is the easiness of the style. The language is still unsure, but
the intelligence of the authors, the sureness of their judgments make the
texts easy enough to understand. La Fontaine and La Rochefoucauld are
already potentially present in this France of the Middle Ages. The third
characteristic is that affable lack of ceremoniousness in such historians as
Joinville or Villehardouin, which in no way prevents their attaining
greatness. This trait we find duplicated in the cathedral sculptors, as we
shall later find it in Degas or Manet. The blending of homely realism
and an austere art is a very French mixture.

Because in the Middle Ages religion lay at the centre of every thought,
religious architecture and sculpture, conceived as a handmaiden of
architecture, were the pre-eminent arts of the period. Thus throughout
Europe cathedrals sprang up, white 'prayers in stone', and for them
France set the example. It is a fact that in England as in Germany, the

faithful copied the churches of France, *opus francigenum*. Why? Because the France of the Capetians had a huge prestige throughout Christendom. In part she owed this to the great French monastic Orders, Cluny and Cîteaux, which spread all over Europe; in part to the authority of Saint Louis and the French princes of the Near East; in part, perhaps, to the renown of the University of Paris. The Romanesque cathedrals, whose arched vaults caused them still to resemble the Roman basilica, had above all been the achievement of monasteries and princes. When the Norman spirit, so straightforward and orderly, had dictated the plan, as at Caen (Abbaye-aux-Hommes, Abbaye-aux-Dames) Romanesque structures attained the purest beauty. But beginning with the twelfth century, the cathedral became the achievement of everyone dwelling in a given town. It was 'the book of a people without books'. Upon its walls and portals, revealed truth was blazoned, while upon the columns of its capitals was depicted the morality of daily life or the suffering of the wicked. 'In the Middle Ages', said Victor Hugo, 'human genius had no important thought which it did not grave in stone.' Medieval art is not a sensual but a didactic art. The cathedral 'was a treatise in theology'. Music was made for the Church: Masses, requiems, alleluias; and it remained anonymous, as did the architects, for its only object was the furtherance of prayer to offer to God. Thus all art was a religious function, a mystical communion with God, and was obliged to represent the divine mysteries, the angels, the saints, the devils, or to recall dogmas expressed in symbolic terms. Such is the case with all essentially religious civilizations, as, for example, with Buddhist art which, like the Christian art of the twelfth century, is not of this world.

Gothic is an ill-chosen word to designate the architecture of the great cathedrals. The Middle Ages never spoke of the Gothic style; those who later invented the term wanted to push aside as barbarous the most beautiful buildings of the West. Should we call it *ogival* architecture? But *ogive* does not mean the broken arch, and what is more, the broken arch is not an absolute characteristic of Gothic. The truth is that under the inspiration of Romanesque, Arabic and Byzantine sources, the French architects little by little mastered the technical difficulties in the art of constructing vaults and thus created an art of religious construction which was archaic until the twelfth century, classic in the thirteenth and fourteenth, and flamboyant or decadent in the fifteenth, and which was wholly their own. Their technical discovery (the nervure, or rib) was what made it possible to have the pressure of the vaults borne by external columns and buttresses, which freed the walls of their usual function as supports, allowed them to be stripped of stonework and lightened by great areas of glass, thus giving the nave an upward thrust and making the whole church an aspiration of the soul towards heaven. In all the world there is no more purely spiritua temple than the Cathedral of Chartres. That of Amiens, no less beautiful, is more bourgeois. The French of the *fabliau* collaborated with the French of the Crusades in building it. At times means were lacking to finish the spires, and there remained at the tops of the towers only a platform, as was the case with Notre Dame of Paris. It is important to notice this name, Notre Dame. The cult of the Virgin was then especially in favour because it united devotion and courtesy, God and the Madonna. This cult, as well as that of the saints, lent religion a human character which touched souls and helped to unite enthusiasms in the erection of a cathedral. As for the modest sculptural geniuses of those days, their names are unknown. They were willing to subordinate themselves to the architect and to fill the niche or the portal which had been assigned to them. At times they etherealized bodies, lengthened them, making the faces and smiles divine; at times also they surrendered themselves to violent satiric imagination in their representations of the devils and their victims. But always they served the master builder. Only in the fourteenth century would sculpture be separated from building.

The cathedrals express the faith of a religious era and the local patriotism of the towns and the guilds. The merchant corporations bore the expense of the enterprise. In the Middle Ages trade and craftsmanship worked together. They had had to do so at the beginning of this rebirth of commerce because, in order to struggle with the lord or find protection against the brigand, merchants could count only on the strength of group action. This need helped the Church to make the merchants accept a brotherhood which subordinated the interests of the individual to the rules of the collective. Under the planned economy of the Middle Ages, cornering supplies and selling at less than certain fixed prices were forbidden. And these rules were accepted because they worked fairly well. The market being limited by the difficulty of communication, it was not difficult to control so narrow an economy. Saint Thomas taught that private property was given to man only for the good of the community. Every object had a 'just price' and it was sinful to make an excessive profit. Lending at interest was forbidden by the Church, because money is incapable of producing anything. Yet since the need for capital was ever present, it was necessary at first to have recourse to the Jews, who were not required to observe the laws of the Catholic Church, later to the Lombards, who avoided the difficulty by charging not interest but an 'indemnity' for any lateness in repaying an obligation. The medieval merchants and artisans had their moral and social obligations and constituted an order, in the same sense as did knighthood. For them the object of life was supposed to be not to make a fortune but to please God and respect the law. The Provost of the merchants of Paris was a great personage, with whom the King himself took council. The bourgeois of the guilds wore robes lined with fur as imposing as those of the royal officials. The hungry scholar envied the lot of the one as much as he did that of the other.

As for the agricultural labourer, his lot was becoming somewhat better. In the *chansons de geste*, the villein is an inferior being, by nature uncouth and stupid. But then the *trouvère* was singing for the castle. At the beginning of the feudal regime, the lord, for the tillage of his part of the domain, his 'reserve', had possessed slaves (a survival from Roman days) and had required duty service of his tenants, which could amount to as much as three days per man per week. In the Middle Ages the slave had disappeared because slavery was not Christian; because it was unproductive; and because such inventions as the harness collar had done away with the most toilsome drudgery. The villein was a free man, subject only to certain obligations which, moreover, were on the decrease. Towards the end of the twelfth century, duty service on certain domains had been reduced to ten days a year. The master's reserve had been diminished and the land thus freed had been leased to tenants. The sale of farm products being difficult, the lord preferred to receive his rent as cash income. The leader of the band, the protecting warrior, had become one living from his landed investment. The *villa* had now become a *village*, in which each family had its cottage where it lived, most often in a single room, together with its birds and beasts. The life of a peasant family was in many respects like it is today. The children went to school less; their parents went to church more. But fairs, held on dates still observed in many a village, brought with them minstrels and jugglers (in our day, merry-go-rounds and shooting galleries). Occasionally a preaching friar made his appearance. Apart from such occasions, contacts with the outside world were rare. Everything was produced upon the domain except ploughs and other tools, millstones and cutlery, which were bought from itinerant traders. From the twelfth century onwards, the son of a serf, if he were ambitious and enterprising, could free himself by going to the city or entering holy orders.

When we consider the twelfth and thirteenth centuries, we may legitimately speak of the French miracle. At that time in very fact, between the Alps and the Pyrenees, between the Atlantic and the Mediterranean, a typically new life had been created. This civilization owed much to the ancient civilizations, to the Judaeo-Christian and even to certain Barbarian cultures. But from these disparate elements medieval France had wrought a civilization entirely its own. The cathedrals, the *chansons de geste*, knighthood, courtesy — all these were new and admirable inventions. The human animal, tamed in the ancient world by the philosophers, and in the Oriental world by its religions, had once again been unleashed in all its cruelty after the fall of the Roman Empire. Hence the necessity of imposing upon that animal new rules, a faith, a political system, manners, taste. France, between the tenth and the thirteenth centuries, furnished in great part the elements of a civilization which set up as the end of life, of the family, of marriage, of trade, of art, not happiness but salvation, and the influence of this civilization has been great on the whole of Christendom.

CHAPTER VIII

THE HUNDRED YEARS WAR (I)

NATIONALIST feeling was in the process of being born. The art, the customs and the language of the French had acquired characteristics which were French alone. Yet there remained a confusion and a danger. It lay in the strange interdependence of the kingdoms of France and England. Ever since the Norman conquest — even more since the advent of the Plantagenets — the English upper class had been Gallicized. English poets wrote in French; Eleanor of Aquitaine had introduced courtly manners into the English royal household; English kings bore themselves before ladies (as Froissart shows) as though they were French knights. But all this did not justify their being, on French soil, the lords of Guienne and other places. Either the same crown must unite the two kingdoms, or a bold stroke must sever the bond. In 1328 the problem became urgent. Charles IV, the Fair, had died without an heir. He had neither son nor brother. Three candidates could lay claim to the throne: Edward III of England, son of Isabella of France and grandson of Philip the Fair; Philip of Évreux, husband of Jeanne of Navarre and son-in-law of Louis X, the Quarrelsome; and Philip of Valois, grandson of Philip III, the Bold. The latter, although he was only a first cousin of the late king, carried the day because he was 'born in the kingdom'. The estates were wary of the Navarrese and the Englishman. Later on, in justification of this choice, the lawyers appealed to an ancient law of the Salic Franks under which women could not succeed to the throne or transmit the succession. The truth was that the Salic Franks were merely an excuse; what was wanted was a French king.

Thus ended the direct line of the Capetians and began the Valois dynasty. France did not gain by the change. The Capetians, politic and prudent kings, enriched by an ancient inheritance of experience, had built and strengthened the kingdom. The first Valois, 'kings by chance', as they were scornfully called in their own day, upstart monarchs, above all busied themselves with feudal prestige. Philip VI, of Valois — brilliant, impulsive, ill advised — looked upon war as a tourney, in which the object was not to be the victor, but to show one's courage and follow the rules of the game. He found confronting him in England a young king, Edward III, who also prided himself on chivalric courtesy, but who acted with the hardest realism. His motto was, 'It is as it is', and he might well have inherited it from his Capetian ancestors. He was wise enough, however difficult the decision, to accept Philip of Valois's accession to the throne and even pledged him fealty for Guienne. His submission was more apparent than real. He knew he must let hot feelings cool, bide his time and prepare. These preparations, thoroughly up to date, concerned both fighting men and armaments. In order to break the charge of the feudal baron's cavalry, Edward III had recourse to catapults and, above all, to bowmen. Until that time the bows in use had had too short a range and too little penetrating power to stop the armoured knights. The cross-bow took too long to reload. But Edward I, in the course of his campaigns, had discovered the Welsh long bow, which, at a hundred and seventy yards, could pin to his saddle the thigh of a knight clad in a coat of mail. Edward I had decreed that archery should be the sole sport permitted to all his subjects who were not 'lame or decrepit' and had issued orders that all those possessed of landed revenues of forty shillings or more must own a bow and arrows. Thus it was easy for him to recruit an infantry. In 1340 Edward III, therefore, possessed the most modern armament in all Europe.

The basic cause of the war was Edward III's firm intention to lay claim to the crown of France. Its immediate causes were the incitement of rebel *émigrés*, the popularity of a campaign in which a rich country could be sacked, and above all the Flanders question, key to English-French relations. England's principal product was wool; Flanders' chief industry, the weaving of cloth. Pastoral England and industrial Flanders had need of one another. The Count of Flanders, Louis de Nevers, was supported by his suzerain the King of France; the Flemish townsmen showed themselves to be violently pro-English. When, in 1337, Edward III, having completed his military preparations, defied Philip VI, denied his legitimacy, and summoned him to yield the throne of France, the English king was backed by the City of London, which feared that indispensable Flanders would fall under French influence. 'The King was concerned over the French succession; the people, over freedom of trade. Gathered together around the Woolsack, the Commons gladly voted arms. The mixture of industrialism and chivalry gave this whole business a weird aspect ... The simple-mindedness of the Crusades did not belong to that generation; in point of fact, these knights were the travelling salesmen of the merchants of London and Ghent ...'[1] This description is

[1] JULES MICHELET.

83

sound enough as long as we do not forget that had the King of England not wished to unite the two crowns, the Hundred Years War would not have taken place. Nevertheless, it was the Flemish merchants who led Edward III to show his true colours. In declaring war against the King of France, their suzerain, they felt scruples which were all the stronger because they had pledged themselves to pay two million florins to the Pope if they defaulted. The Fleming Jacques d'Artevelde found a means to reconcile respect for treaties with their violation. He advised the King of England to join to his own arms the arms of France. Thus it would be the ally and no longer the enemy of the Flemish who would become the true King of France and the recipient of their oath.

Thus the Hundred Years War was a dynastic war, a feudal war, a national war, and above all an *imperialist* war. The purpose of the English merchants in making a gift to the King of twenty thousand sacks of wool to pay the expenses of a campaign was to assure themselves of the two areas indispensable for their trade: Flanders, the purchaser of their wool, and the Bordelais, producer of wine, the receipts they obtained in Bruges and Ghent paying for the casks which came from Bordeaux. And finally we must add that this war was popular in England because it would lead her armies into a wealthy countryside, western France, where the soldiers would find abundant spoils. Edward III and his barons were the 'flower of knighthood', but 'their emblazoned shields served as banners for a scheme of pillage' the deplorable progress of which may be followed in the pages of Froissart: 'And the English were, in the City of Caen, Lords for three days; and they sent out all their profit by the barge-load: cloth, jewellery, gold and silver services, and all other rich things, until they reached their vessels of heavier cargo ... No man can believe how great was the store of cloth which the English found in the town of Saint Lô ... Louviers was a city in Normandy where much cloth was woven; it was large, rich, and suited for trade, but it was not enclosed and it was stripped and pillaged ... All of England was stuffed with the booty of France, so that there was not a woman who did not wear some ornament or who did not hold in her hand some fine linen or some goblet, part of the spoils shipped out from Caen or Calais...'

It is interesting to note, even so early in the course of history, that the principal characteristics of English policy were already developing and were imposed upon that country by its geographical location. England needed mastery of the seas, without which she could neither continue her trade nor send troops to the Continent nor remain in contact with those already stationed there. From the very first days of this war, the English sailors had the upper hand and were the victors at the Battle of Sluys. As long as this naval supremacy was maintained, England readily triumphed. (Later, Edward III neglected his fleet, the French and the Spanish joined forces, and England's naval inferiority marked the beginning of her reverses.) Furthermore, England, being able to send to the Continent only relatively small armies, sought to erect against her adversaries Continental leagues which she furnished with subsidies. Thus at the outset of the Hundred Years War, Edward III tried to ally himself against France not only with the Flemish Commons, but with the Emperor. 'In this he spared neither gold nor silver, and gave rich presents to lords, ladies and damsels. . . .'

In Guienne, Edward III already had a bridgehead, but Frenchmen in revolt told him that Normandy was not defended. Hence the landing at La Hogue, with one thousand ships, four thousand knights and ten thousand English and Welsh archers (1346). Normandy had not known war for several generations and allowed herself to be devastated without opposition. At that moment the King of England's only plan was to make a raid into northern France to pillage as much as he could, and to withdraw through Flanders. But he found the Seine bridges destroyed and he had to move up that river as far as Poissy, which gave Philip time to gather together his vassals. The two armies met near Abbeville, at Crécy. The battle here is of great importance because it marks one of the great military changes which wholly upset the relationships between classes in Europe. The victory of the Barbarian cavalry had foretold the end of the Roman Empire and the birth of the feudal regime. Cavalry, chivalry — the words are the same and describe the same men. Crécy marked the defeat of the finest feudal cavalry, that of France, by the foot-soldiery of the Welsh bowmen. Philip VI's knights fought bravely. They were defeated because the weapons of their infantry were inferior, because they did not have a proper respect for the new foot-soldiery and approached it too hastily, and because they were more keen for fame than for victory, more devoted to individual exploits than to collective discipline. 'Through pride and jealousy, they launched a disordered attack upon the English, neatly and suitably arrayed in three lines of battle.'[1] It was a massacre.

Philip did not understand the deep meaning of this defeat, which

[1] JEAN LE BEL.

marked a revolution. The following year, Edward III having laid siege
to Calais, the King of France once again mobilized his knights and sent
a message to the King of England, who was altogether too well en-
trenched, asking him to select a place of battle where the two armies
would have equal chances. But Edward III wanted a battle and not a
tournament. He refused and took Calais, which England was to keep
until the days of Elizabeth, thus guaranteeing her control of the Channel,
and from which she drove out all the former inhabitants in order to
replace them with Englishmen.

The Pope obtained a truce. When warfare began anew, France had a
new king, John II, the Good, a man as mediocre as his predecessor, 'slow
to get an idea and hard to dissuade from an opinion'. Edward's eldest son,
the Black Prince, undertook to link Bordeaux with Normandy. He won
back Languedoc, then he moved towards Poitiers where he defeated a
French army four times as largé as his own. The knighthood still refused
to acknowledge that a new kind of war was necessary. The King of
France himself was taken prisoner and his son, the Dauphin Charles,
became regent (he was the first heir presumptive to bear this title,
Dauphiné having been sold by its Dauphin, Humbert II, to Philip VI in
1349 on condition that the title of Dauphin would be borne in France
by the sovereign or by his princely heir). Lost wars always have deep-
seated effects on internal policy. Even wars that are won are expensive;
resources must be found; in order to gather money, governments have
to make concessions to the governed; prices rise; inflation brings with it
devaluation, and this process displeases peoples. Revolts become inevitable; epidemics follow armies; the Black Death (or Spanish influenza) lays
waste the countryside; the population diminishes; the labour force becomes
insufficient; property changes hands. This whole traditional pattern
accompanied the English war in France. Defeat involved a loss of prestige
on the part of the monarchy. For several months there was reason to
believe that, as had happened in England when John Lackland had had to
accept Magna Carta, the French monarchy, under the regency of the
Dauphin, Charles the Wise, would be forced to submit to constitutional
limitations and that the French, taking advantage of the weakening of
the King, were going to force him to accept the principle of taxes by
free consent. But whereas in England limited monarchy had been invented
by the barons, in France, where the nobility had shown a total lack of
political sense, it was upon the shoulders of the Third Estate 'that the lily-
strewn mantle almost fell'. At the States General of 1356, two men,

Robert le Coq, Bishop of Laon, and Étienne Marcel, Provost of the merchants of Paris, proposed reforms which we should today describe as democratic. The Dauphin was to be surrounded by three councils formed from the three estates, and counsellors who should prove displeasing to the estates would be excluded from office. For two years the States General endlessly assembled, even without royal convocation, which was a new and very bold phenomenon, and voted taxes. But Robert le Coq's schemes ended in nothing, first of all because he was in the service of the King of Navarre, Charles of Evreux, called the Bad — a candidate for the throne of France — the bad faith of which was offensive; because, also, the extreme difficulties of travel in the end discouraged many of those named as deputies to the States General (France was larger in area than England); and finally because it is always a mistake to try to base a national revolution upon a defeat. The prisoner King was not a great King, but he was *the* King and he was a prisoner.

In the mind of Étienne Marcel, who was not afraid of new or extreme measures, there remained one solution. Could not the Commune of Paris govern the kingdom, relying, as had happened in Flanders, on a federation of communes? Marcel believed that it could, and founded in Paris a party to which he gave as distinctive insignia a hood dyed in the city's colours, red and blue, colours which, if joined to the white of the royal standard, would even at that early date have given birth to the tricolour. Other cities 'took on the hood'. But Étienne Marcel went too far and was lost. He permitted an invasion of the King's residence and allowed the slaughter of two marshals under the Dauphin's very eyes. The latter, 'abashed', quit Paris resolved to find support in the provinces. This move was identical with that made by Thiers in 1871, and the effect of such a move has always been to push Paris to extreme measures. Étienne Marcel linked himself yet more closely with Charles of Navarre, and even with the English who held all the area west of Paris. In the neighbourhood of the capital, peasants rose in rebellion; ever since the beginning of this war they had suffered too much misery, and companies, or armed bands, provoked 'alarms' throughout the countryside. This *Jacquerie* (uprising of the *Jacques Bonhomme*) was repressed and twenty thousand peasants were slaughtered. In Paris, right-thinking people began to be indignant at seeing English soldiers as allies of the Provost of the merchants, and he was 'hooted at and censured', then assassinated. Charles re-entered his capital and was wise enough to show clemency. At last he signed a peace at Brétigny. The King of England renounced all claims to the throne of France, but besides Guienne he received Poitou, Périgord, Limousin and other provinces. This was a truce, not a solution. The French thus handed over were too French to resign themselves. 'With our lips we shall acknowledge the English', they said, 'but our hearts will never be moved.' Already we have passed beyond the time when provinces might follow the leadership of an individual. The two kingdoms of France and of England had to be completely united or radically severed.

No one knew this better than the Dauphin who, in 1364, became king under the name of Charles V. He was resolved to revise the treaty of Brétigny, but first he had to reorganize the kingdom and rebuild an army. Charles was capable of this task. This small man, frail, pious, learned, was a great sovereign. He seemed to be cold because, like all persons lacking in energy, he husbanded his powers, but his heart was warm and his mind earnest. He sought out scholars, collected manuscripts and, in the realm of action, surrounded himself with technicians. He had thrust aside Étienne Marcel's constitutional ideas and he reigned as an absolute but reasonable king. He had no hesitation in withdrawing from obscurity the best-qualified expert he could find, whether noble or bourgeois. He entrusted the reorganization of the army to a minor Breton aristocrat, Bertrand Du Guesclin, who had called attention to himself as much in fighting the English as in fighting those 'great companies' of men-at-arms who were pillaging the country areas, and in fighting the Navarrese. He had freed Languedoc of highwaymen, soldier brigands, by leading them off into Spain. Since French weapons were inferior to English, Du Guesclin concluded that it was best to refuse battle, allow the enemy to exhaust himself, harry him and recapture towns one by one. Charles soon summoned him back to Paris and made him commander-in-chief. At the same time the King was building a fleet at Rouen, in the Clos des Galées, and was making ready a modern artillery force. When he died in 1380, he had almost swept the English out of the kingdom, and that with very little fighting.

But there is never a great man who does not make great mistakes. Charles V had a younger brother, Philip the Bold, to whom King John the Good, their father, had given as appanage the Duchy of Burgundy, one of the richest and most beautiful of French provinces. The very principle of appanages was odious, and it divided the kingdom all the more seriously when the feudal lords thus created were princes of the blood. For the gift of the Duchy of Burgundy, Charles V was not responsible, but he made the error of favouring the marriage between the Duke, his brother, and the heiress of the Count of Flanders, thus uniting under one house all the provinces which covered France's borders to the north and the east. The King believed that he acted wisely. Had Margaret of Flanders not married the Burgundian, Edward III of England would have sought this match for one of his own sons, which would have brought the English to the very gates of Paris. But Charles V had not foreseen that the attraction of Flanders and of its opulent cities would have its effect upon the Duke of Burgundy and that, instead of having a brotherly vassal at Dijon, he would henceforth face a hostile sovereign in Brussels. When Philip of Burgundy into the bargain allied himself (through the marriage of his children) with the Wittelsbach family, which ruled over Holland, the danger grew greater. The centre of gravity of the Duke of Burgundy's estates was moving northwards. Never did France, still very newly united, run a greater risk of splitting. The feudal system, because it involved a personal link between a family and a province, because it subordinated public right to private right, continued to be a source of civil war. France was to give evidence of it during the course of one of the saddest periods in her history.

CHAPTER IX

THE HUNDRED YEARS WAR (II)

ONE of the virtues of monarchy is that it supplies a people with an undisputed leader. If the legitimacy of the King is not certain, monarchy ceases to be a viable form of government. It was France's ill fortune, at the most difficult moment in her relationship with England, to have kings whose legitimacy or authority were open to question. Charles VI was only twelve years old when Charles V died. Any minority brings with it a regency, a tutorship, conflicts; the King's uncles, especially Philip of Burgundy, plundered the kingdom. Their demands provoked rebellions. When the King cáme of age, he showed good intentions and called back his father's senile advisers, who were dubbed the *marmousets*, a name applied to grotesque faces often carved on door-knockers. But he had married a sensual and dangerous foreigner, Isabeau of Bavaria. He loved her, made her live in an atmosphere of great festivity, probably had good reason to be jealous, grew worried and tired and, coming of an unstable lineage, lost his reason. To have a mad king is a disaster for a country; to have a king whose derangement is intermittent is the worst kind of disaster. For he can be neither replaced nor respected. Around the unfortunate Charles VI, his uncle, the Duke of Burgundy, and his brother, the Duke of Orleans, struggled for power. Louis of Orleans was young, cultivated, deeply soaked in the arts of Italy, since he had married Valentine, a Visconti of Milan. His orgies gave scandal and it is even said that he was the lover of Queen Isabeau, his sister-in-law. John the Fearless, who had become Duke of Burgundy on the death of Philip the Bold (1404), had his cousin of Orleans assassinated (1407). Thus was unleashed one of those passionate, extraordinary and vain civil wars which have so often divided France. An Orleans party and a Burgundy party confronted each other. Bernard of Armagnac took the leadership of the former, for his daughter had married the new duke, Charles of Orleans. John the Fearless ensured himself the support of Paris, where, in bizarre alliance, the university students and the butchers together declared themselves 'Burgundians'. The Sorbonne was grateful to the Duke of Burgundy because, in the matter of the Pontifical schism, he had assumed the same attitude as that institution of learning and had supported the Pope of Rome against the Pope of Avignon; as for the butchers, the Burgundian had attached himself to them by means of gifts and favours, but this sorcerer's apprentice soon regretted having started a popular agitation of which he was not long master. Excesses produced their usual effects: the middle class and the university, disgusted at their violent allies, went over to the Armagnacs. Yet by this time the problem was no longer an internal one.

Civil hatreds put a country at the mercy of its enemies. When Henry V of England, in 1415, saw France torn between the Orleans and Burgundy factions and governed in the name of a mad king by a young and friendless dauphin, he cynically revived Edward III's claims to the throne of France. He had no right thereto, being only a very distant heir of the Plantagenets, but he aspired to take in marriage Catherine of France, daughter of Charles VI, and with her the finest of the French provinces. Such demands were too absurd to be met even by a country as unfortunate as France then was. War became inevitable. One might have thought that some obsession forced Henry V to imitate the campaign of his great-grandfather. Like his ancestor, he landed in Normandy. He had only two thousand five hundred men-at-arms, their retainers, and eight thousand archers — in all, counting menservants and transport troops, not more than thirty thousand. He seized Harfleur, the great arsenal of the west, despite a courageous defence, then, having sent a challenge to the Dauphin, he decided to march on Calais, and to cross the Somme at Blanche-Tache, which was the ford nearest Crécy. It was a bold undertaking, but the French nobles were divided; surely they would give the English the week which they needed in which to reach Calais. 'The essential thing was not to arouse the inhabitants along his route of march. Thus the King caused to be enforced to the letter the admirable orders of Richard II regarding army discipline: rape and the pillage of churches were forbidden under pain of the gallows; it was forbidden to cry *Havoc!* under pain of being beheaded; the same penalty applied to him who stole from a merchant or sutler; one's captain must be obeyed; one must occupy the indicated billets or else suffer imprisonment and the loss of one's horse . . .' Finding the ford defended, Henry V moved higher up the river and met the army of the French nobility at Agincourt. A terrible battle ensued in which France's knighthood — courageous, but having learned nothing and taken no heed of what Du Guesclin had sought to teach it — found itself shot to pieces by the archers and butchered by the English king's men-at-arms. Ten thousand Frenchmen perished in this battle (1415), one of the bloodiest of the Middle Ages.

Despite this victory, Henry could not have succeeded in seizing France with his tiny army had there not been complicity on the French side. But when, in 1417, the English invaded Normandy and its inhabitants appealed to the King of France, the High Constable of Armagnac replied that he was busy fighting the Burgundians. As for John the Fearless, he urged the people of Rouen to come to an understanding with the English, with whom he had entered into partnership because of the interests of his Flemish subjects. In Paris, an uprising handed the city over to the Burgundians, but not without producing thousands of victims. The Dauphin had to flee, and at the very moment when it still seemed to be possible to hope for a French-Burgundian reconciliation, Tanneguy du Châtel, friend of the Dauphin, killed John the Fearless on the Montereau Bridge (1419). The Armagnac-Burgundian feud became even more savage. Many years later, a Dijon monk, showing Francis I the pierced skull of John the Fearless, said to him: 'Sire, here is the hole through which the English entered France . . .' Paris and the Burgundians now swore *never* to acknowledge the Dauphin. By the Treaty of Troyes (1420), Isabeau, an accomplice of the Burgundians, constrained her demented husband to give their daughter Catherine to Henry V of England in marriage and to make Henry regent of France and, eventually, heir of the kingdom. As for the Dauphin, cut off, banished, disowned, he was reduced to defending himself as best he could between the Seine and the Loire. France's destitution was frightful. Wolves wandered even into the streets of the cities. The whole countryside, Alain Chartier tells us, seemed to have become a sea, 'in which each man had lordship only in proportion to his strength'. And yet the French did not resign themselves to becoming English. When, in 1422, Henry V and Charles VI died within three months, the Herald of France cried out at St. Denis: 'God grant long life to Henry VI, by the grace of God King of France and of England!' But the people wept for the poor mad King who had symbolized, however badly, the national independence.

Never had the country's situation been more deplorable. France had almost ceased to exist as a free nation. An English regent, the Duke of Bedford, governed in Paris. Two loyalties split the country. On the one hand, there was a child ten months old who was not French, Henry VI; on the other hand there was the new king, Charles VII, who was still called the Dauphin, or 'the King of Bourges', because he had not been consecrated. Charles VII was deeply pious and irresolute. A tormenting doubt deprived him of courage to struggle for his inheritance: was he truly the heir of the house of France? The misconduct of his mother, Isabeau, justified this doubt. He had little money, few soldiers. But the will of the French people bore him up. When that people feels that a cause is just, it is ready to sacrifice everything in order to make it triumph. Then right finds obscure friends in the country's every hamlet. Vainly did Bedford labour to conquer the French by behaving 'correctly' and by proving his capacity as an administrator. Whatever he did, he was the Englishman. The French, with touching eagerness, wanted a French king. But what could they do? Bedford, master of the north of France, had undertaken the conquest of the centre, and had laid siege to Orleans. Nevertheless, that city defended itself even more heroically because its lord, Charles of Orleans, was a prisoner among the English and because in feudal law an attack against a fief deprived of its lord was a great crime. For this reason the people of Orleans hoped that God's judgment would be in their favour and that they would be delivered. But by whom? Then it was that Joan of Arc appeared.

In March 1429, a young girl who had come from Lorraine to Chinon asked to see the Dauphin. She was 'strong, a little dark of complexion, with uncommon physical powers, but of modest mien and feminine voice'. As a peasant's daughter, she had been a shepherd girl and had led her father's beasts to their pasture. All about her, in the village of Domrémy, everyone spoke of the tragedy which had befallen the kingdom of France, invaded as it was by the foreigner; despite defeat, men still wished to hope, and they said that France, lost through a woman (Queen Isabeau) would be saved by a maid. Joan, very devout had heard celestial voices while she was guarding her flock and had seen appear 'in a great light' the Archangel Michael, Saint Catherine and Saint Margaret, who had pledged her to go to seek the Dauphin and to deliver Orleans. 'Since God ordered it, it was fitting to do it.' And finally she had succeeded in persuading the nearest captain royal, him of Vaucouleurs, after he had equipped her with a man's armour, to have her conducted to Chinon, where Charles was residing. It was already an astounding thing that a girl from the fields should have convinced this captain, but the story of Joan of Arc is at once the most surprising succession of miracles and the most reasonable succession of political actions. The aims which this Lorraine shepherd girl proposed were practical and urgent. She wished to restore to the Dauphin faith in his birthright — this she could accomplish because he was himself very devout and would believe in voices coming from Heaven; to deliver Orleans, because this symbolic victory would give confidence to the French people; and to have the Dauphin consecrated at Reims because the oil of the holy vial would ensure, in the eyes of all believers, the legitimacy of his power.

Everyone knows how she was introduced into the castle and at once recognized the King who was hiding amidst his lords and saluted him with the title, 'Gentle Dauphin'. We must remember he knew about the prophecy and was highly moved when Joan reassured him about his birth: 'I tell thee, on behalf of the Great Lord, that thou art the true heir of France and son of the King ...' From that moment on, Charles believed in Joan's mission, 'because he had to believe in her in order to believe in himself'. As for Joan, she had never had the least doubt concerning her voices, and it was in full confidence that she – a paltry girl – called upon the powerful English army to quit France: 'King of England, and you, Duke of Bedford, who call yourself Regent of France, hand over to the Maid sent hither by God the keys of all the good towns you have taken and violated in France ... King of England, if indeed you do not do it, I am a chieftain of war and on whatever ground I may reach your people in France, I shall make them depart therefrom, will they or not ...' She won from the Dauphin a small army, entered Orleans and freed the city to the sound of the *Veni Creator*. She had caused a standard to be embroidered for her: the points of the oriflamme bore the words JESUS MARIA and the fleur-de-lys. The fleur-de-lys and Christianity: with a sure instinct Joan buttressed herself on the two powers which had wrought France's unity. Did she hate the English? No, she was too good a Christian for that: 'But I know well that they will be put out of France, except for those who will remain there and die.' Far from hating them, she urged them to ally themselves with the French for a crusade. But an English regent cannot allow the possibility of a saintly girl opposing England's plans. Bedford called her – and believed her – a witch. Yet, she acted the part of a wise Frenchwoman. Understanding that all the ills of the kingdom had arisen from unappeased ill feeling, she required full forgiveness of Frenchmen for Frenchmen: 'If it pleases you to wage war', she wrote to the Duke of Burgundy, 'go against the Saracens.' Then, to Charles, who continued hesitant and fearful: 'Our Dauphin, no longer take so many and such lengthy counsels: follow me, and come assume at Reims your worthy crown ... Why do you doubt?' But time was lost in making good cheer; La Trémoïlle, a professional soldier who was hostile to Joan of Arc, sought to turn Charles against her and thwarted all her plans. Nevertheless, the Maid went about repeating that she 'would last only for one year' and that they must hurry. Her march on Reims began with the taking of Troyes and was a mere military exercise. During the consecration (July 17th), she stood beside the King, with her standard in her hand. Within five months, she had fulfilled her mission. 'Gentle King', she said, 'from henceforward is fulfilled the pleasure of God who wished that you should come to Reims to receive your worthy anointing, by showing that you are truly king and him to whom the king-dom should belong.' In that day of triumph, Joan was deathly sad: 'I should wish', said she, 'that it might please God, my Creator, that I might now lay aside arms and go to serve my father and my mother by watch-ing their sheep, together with my sister and my brothers, who would be indeed joyful at seeing me. . . .'

In the eyes of the English and the Burgundians, Joan was a witch and a heretic. How, had she not had the devil in her body, could she have conquered so quickly, without military strength? Now she wished to bring the King back into his capital. In the assault of September 1429, however, she was wounded in the thigh. Then La Trémoïlle's counsels of delay stopped Charles VII, who was by nature hesitant and wary. Joan rejoined the armies and was captured below Compiègne, because the gate had been closed behind her, perhaps through treason. Taken by the Count of Luxemburg's Burgundians (May 23rd, 1430), she was sold to the English who handed her over to an ecclesiastical court. Although the Maid was condemned beforehand, the trial lasted five solid months. Pierre Cauchon, Bishop of Beauvais, who was in charge of the question-ings, had called upon the assistance of a vice-inquisitor, of prelates and priests from Rouen, plus a dozen lawyers in church courts. A certain number of masters from the University of Paris played the part of assessors. Seventy-five judges were gathered together to confound this young girl in chains. 'The English', said Coville, 'attached a great political importance thereto; once condemned by the Church, her con-quests would become sacrileges; the English cause would become one with the cause of the Church.' Priests and laymen, English and French, all agreed to send Joan to the stake. It was only too clear that, since reasons of state required a verdict of guilty, the verdict was sure even before the trial began. Unbiased judges would have been convinced of Joan of Arc's good faith and patriotism by her admirable replies — which make this interrogation a wonderful document. A girl without education, almost a child, found answers so noble and so pure that even this dour tribunal was at times troubled by them, but she was none the less condemned to the flames and burned alive at Rouen, in the old market place, on May 30th, 1431. She was nineteen years old. Charles VII had done nothing to save her. And he waited fifteen years before starting the process of her rehabilitation.

The great who have been put in some high place through the efforts of other men easily believe that their own merits alone have won the victory. Thanklessness is a royal virtue. After Joan's death, Charles VII, the Well-Served, found, for the deliverance of France, other good soldiers: Richemont, La Hire, Xaintrailles and Dunois, Bastard of Orleans. But never would they have come on the stage if Joan had not set them in motion. She had created France's moral unity. In 1435, Philip the Good, Duke of Burgundy, made his submission. The civil war was over. In 1436, Paris yielded to the King, who made his solemn entry into the capital, but did not remain there. He had no love for that city, 'which called to his mind unpleasant memories'. Province by province the kingdom was regained: Normandy in 1450; Guienne in 1453; there were no more Englishmen in Gascony. They had been 'put out of France'; only Calais remained to them.

For Frenchmen Joan of Arc has remained the purest symbol of patriotism. Everything combines to give her this character: her youth, her courage, her faith, the desperate state of the country at the time she set out to save it, the miracle of her success, the victory of a shepherdess over a triumphant enemy, and above all the stake and martyrdom. By this unmerited torment, she became associated in the popular consciousness with the saints of Christendom. Like them she had been sent by God; she was the most obvious sign of the protection granted by Christ to the oldest daughter of his Church. As Napoleon used to say, she had proved 'that there is no miracle which the French genius cannot perform given circumstances in which the national independence is threatened'. She was to become so completely the national heroine that on the day when fresh Armagnacs and fresh Burgundians would once more divide France, the two parties quarrelled over possession of her, those of the Left claiming her because she was a daughter of the people, those of the Right because her banner bore the fleur-de-lys. Anatole France, an anti-clerical freethinker, who saw in Joan of Arc a neurotic person subject to hallucinations, a simple-minded girl cleverly managed by the clergy, nevertheless wrote these words: 'The thought came to her to restore the Dauphin to his heritage. For this thought she gave her life. Thus it was that she survived her cause and that her devotion remains an everlasting example. Here was martyrdom, without which men have established nothing great or useful in the world. Cities, empires, republics rest upon sacrifice. Thus it was not unreasonable or unjust that Joan should have become the symbol of the fatherland in arms . . .' She is the most striking instance of the miracles which faith and will can accomplish.

CHAPTER X

HOW FRANCE, AFTER THE HUNDRED YEARS WAR, RECOVERED AND BECAME GREAT

THE Hundred Years War had bankrupted the country, weakened the King, and raised the hopes of the great landed vassals, who constituted States within the State. For the purposes of rebuilding France, Charles VII lacked character but not intelligence. He was well served, which at least proves that he knew how to choose his servants. Above all, it was necessary to reorganize the army and the treasury. Bands roaming the highways to pillage the countryside were suppressed. The King possessed 'ordered companies' under his own pay; the feudal chivalry remained only a reserve. For the infantry, each parish in the kingdom, following the English example, had to supply one archer for every fifty hearths. This man was exempt (or *free*) of the head tax, but was required periodically to report for military training. These 'free archers' constituted a second reserve. The artillery, belonging wholly to the King, gave him great power against the strongholds of the larger vassals. In order to support this standing army, Charles VII obtained from the States General of 1439 a perpetual head tax of twelve hundred thousand *livres*. And there parted the political roads of England and of France. England, jealous of her freedoms, safe behind her girdle of seas, had told her kings from the days of Magna Carta: 'No taxation without representation.' France, always in danger and fresh from the sight of the threat of destruction, yielded to her sovereigns the control of an army and permanent taxes. How could she refuse? Her first need was to be defended. Charles VII had his faults; he lived openly with a beautiful mistress, Agnes Sorel, Lady of Fromenteau and of Beauté, by whom he had four daughters; after Agnes's death, he afforded the unedifying spectacle of a lustful old man; he had proved ungrateful to some of his best advisers; but he left France happy and strong.

Nothing is more surprising than the speed with which the King of Bourges became not only King of France, but one of Europe's most powerful sovereigns. France's energy and vitality, the moment she was given a chance, astonished the world. A few years later, in Germany, in Savoy, in Italy, Charles VII appeared as the arbiter of Europe. Ladislas of Hungary wrote to him: 'You are the pillar of Christendom'; the Doge of Venice said: 'He is the King of Kings, nothing is possible without him.' Thanks to a merchant of Bourges, Jacques Cœur, who, starting with nothing, had enriched himself by trading in precious metals, and then had set up counting-houses throughout the Levant, there was no longer to be seen 'in the eastern [Mediterranean] sea any mast which did not bear the fleur-de-lys'. Where the knights' Crusade had not succeeded in giving France protection over the Holy Places, that of the merchants ensured it. Jacques Cœur, capitalist and speculator, became the financier, the ambassador of the reign, until the moment when slanderous accusations and his too brilliant fortune brought upon him his inevitable downfall. By means of foreign alliances, Charles strengthened himself for the struggle, now become necessary, against the 'sires of the fleur-de-lys', meaning the great vassals of royal blood. This second feudality (Burgundy, Anjou, Bourbon Brittany, Albret, etc.) did not respect the royal authority. The dukes of Burgundy, 'Grand Dukes of the West', lacked only the title of king, for they had the kingdom. Besides Burgundy, which Philip the Bold had received as an appanage from his father, John the Good, they possessed Flanders through marriage and governed all the Low Countries as far as the Somme. In their capital, Dijon, they held a court at which French culture was then better represented than in Paris; Burgundian art, particularly its sculpture, was admirable. A veritable country, a new Lotharingia, was there taking shape along France's flank. In 1429 the Duke of Burgundy had founded the Order of the Golden Fleece, a knightly brotherhood whose prestige became European. Summoned by Charles VII to take his seat as a peer of France, Philip the Good (of Burgundy) proudly replied: 'I shall go, with forty thousand men.' The King of France freed him of having to pay homage, because it was prudent to do so. Here was a dangerous neighbour. In 1440 the great vassals organized a rebellion against the King which was called the *Praguerie*, the reference being to the Hussite uprisings in Prague, and to which the Dauphin, the future Louis XI, adhered. In rebellion against both parental and royal authority, the Dauphin Louis sought asylum with Philip of Burgundy. 'My cousin of Burgundy knows not what he does', Charles VII said bitterly. 'He is suckling the fox who will eat his hens.' The father knew his son all too well; he suspected him of having had Agnes Sorel poisoned; he even thought him capable of parricide, but he left him his inheritance intact. The king within him controlled his rancour as a man.

Louis XI is famous for two reasons. The first is that he was a strange, abnormal person, who has aroused the curiosity of historians and inspired the imaginations of novelists and playwrights: Sir Walter Scott, Casimir Delavigne, Théodore de Banville. The second reason is that, despite his faults, he was a great king, effective and realistic. As little knightly and feudal as it is possible to conceive, he neither kept his own word, nor believed in the oaths of others. Having been a bad son, he distrusted his own children. He believed that 'every man has his price', and, were it necessary, he paid that price. He gave ten thousand *écus* a month to his physician so that the latter would have a real interest in keeping him alive. Knowing the English to be 'inclined towards war against this kingdom', and fearing the possibility of a new Anglo-Burgundian alliance, he promised what amounted to a tribute to the court of England, fifty thousand *écus* to the King, sixteen thousand to the Ministers, plus gifts of silver services. It was Louis XI who, through these bargainings, truly ended the Hundred Years War — still smouldering under the ashes — by the Treaty of Picquigny in 1475. He suffered the King of England, Edward IV, to call himself King of France, and when he wrote to him, he gave himself only the title of Prince Louis. Ever ready to humble himself whenever he felt that he was the weaker, he exacted harsh vengeance when he had regained strength. As a captive, he promised submission; once set free, he forced obedience. Yet he liked men of worth, sought to inform himself on all matters, and had common sense. Being fearful of the great, he surrounded himself with bourgeois and lesser folk (Olivier le Daim, Tristan l'Ermite). In the end he made himself an object of detestation both to the feudal lords with whom he fought and to the masses of the people whom he taxed 'with great and awful head taxes', for at the hour of his death he was annually levying four million, seven hundred thousand *livres* to support the artillery and to meet other, similar expenditures. He laid nothing aside in the treasury, 'took everything and spent everything and built vast edifices for the fortification and defence of the towns and places in his realm'. Even 'when he was resting, his mind was at work . . . When he had war, he wanted peace; when he had peace or a truce, he was scarcely able to endure it . . . But that was his nature and thus he lived . . .'[1] He has been compared to a spider, and indeed there he was, at the centre of his web, either at Paris or at Plessis-les-Tours, ready to scurry out along one of its strands in order to seize an unwary fly, then climbing back, execution having been done, to the centre of his gossamer.

From the moment of his accession to the throne, he made himself

[1] PHILIP DE COMMYNES.

enemies by brutally driving away his father's advisers. The great men
of the kingdom set themselves up against him in a league which they
called the League of the Public Weal, 'in order to restore everything
to order and to protect the unfortunate populace'. We all know what
such programmes are worth and what, in most instances, those protect who
call themselves the protectors of the people. United, the dukes of Burgundy, of Brittany and of Berry could have endangered the kingdom,
had the English mixed in the affair. But the English were involved in
civil war at home and Louis XI had inherited from his father the advantage of a permanent army. 'The King of France is always prepared',
scornfully said the rebels. Louis, however, having saved Paris merely by
a hair's breadth, decided to do some appeasing. He made promises to his
enemies and then divided those enemies so that he could break his
promises. The most dangerous of the great vassals was, as always, the
Duke of Burgundy, Charles the Bold. Louis XI agreed to meet him at
Péronne in order 'there to fight over his wool and his skin'. The fox was
caught in the trap and the King, prisoner of the Duke, promised everything the latter desired. The moment he was free, he denied what he had
done, threatened, bullied. I have already remarked that oaths did not bind
him. 'He who has success likewise has honour', he used to remark.

He had success, by guile and above all by good fortune. Charles the
Bold went to Switzerland to meet defeat at Granson and, the following year, was killed in battle before Nancy. His daughter, Marie of
Burgundy, who was twenty years old, inherited the personal fortune and
the lands which were part of the Empire. The French provinces, which
had formerly been given as an appanage, reverted to the crown for
lack of a male heir. Thus, in 1477, by this stroke of luck, Louis regained
Burgundy and Picardy. In order to get what was left, he tried to marry
his son, then seven years old, to Marie of Burgundy. The attempt was
vain. She married Maximilian of Austria, who brought her imperial
support. But at least Burgundy was to be a fine French province and
no longer a rival kingdom. France had escaped the terrible danger of
watching a new Lotharingia take shape along her flank. But of that
episode there remained one problem: the problem of Flanders. The dukes
of Burgundy had made Brussels their capital and had Gallicized a part
of Flanders. By bringing these lands as a dowry to Maximilian, Marie
began a long rivalry between France and the Empire. This northern
French frontier was to remain until our own days one of the nerve points
where European crises come into being. Along this frontier, France is

dangerously vulnerable; the Germanies covet its lands because the Rhine flows down towards them; England jealously watches them because Antwerp is so close to her own shores, and this meeting of conflicting interests sets up dangerous eddies. In 1482 Marie of Burgundy died from a fall while riding. She left a son (Philip the Fair) and a little two-year-old daughter, Margaret of Austria; Louis XI succeeded in having this girl betrothed to his son, the Dauphin Charles (later Charles VIII), and it was agreed that she should receive as her dowry the Franche-Comté and Artois. Here was a great triumph. Another bloodless victory: in 1480, upon the death of King René and of his nephew Charles of Anjou, Maine and Anjou had reverted to France. Louis XI was burying his rivals; that was the surest way to dispose of them for ever. Thus 'did he gather in his basket the fruits which had ripened in his garden'.

He died powerful and terrifying. The picture given by Commynes of his last years has in the eyes of history coloured all his life. Hence our portrait of him tends towards the lugubrious. The novelists have taken delight in showing him in his castle at Plessis-les-Tours, clad in coarse, heavy cloth, surrounded by cross-bow men and archers, wearing a fur-lined cap from which hung leaden medallions, while from the branches of trees the corpses of those he had caused to be hanged swung to and fro. 'King Louis's orchard.' He would go to visit the cages in which his enemies wasted away, but he himself was caged, a prisoner of his fears. Why so many suspicions?. Did he suffer from remorse? He had squeezed his people, but only the better to defend them. He had been harsh on the feudal lords, but he had rearranged the pattern of France. He had had a certain number of modern ideas, had wanted standardized weights and measures, had advised the suppression of internal tolls, had established postal relays every four leagues. He had encouraged trade and had even desired that this occupation, as in England, should not be considered beneath the nobility; in this he had failed through the pride of the feudal lords. In brief, he had greatness of spirit and pettiness in his means. 'A base soul, unworthy of royalty', said Bossuet. This is not the impression given by Commynes, who knew him better. 'Never did I see him', he said, 'when he was not preoccupied and worried', and he shows us the King making work for himself when perchance he had none, and coursing deer in all weathers only to come back worn out and always in a rage against someone. Such agitation is the sign of a troubled rather than a low soul. And why should he not have been divided against himself, this heir of knightly kings whose quarrels with his father, and then with the Duke of Burgundy, had taught him to distrust and to hate. A business king, with all the faults of the bourgeois, but also with their good qualities, who, in short, carried on the business of the country. He died virtuously, says Commynes, 'and better than any other whom I have ever seen die'. He had called his son king during his own lifetime and had ordered that the kingdom be kept at peace until the new king grew up.

This new king, Charles VIII, was thirteen years old. He was weak in body and ugly, with an oversized head, which was stuffed with chivalric romances. He had been brought up at Amboise, far from his father, whose favourite child was his daughter Anne, who had married Pierre de Beaujeu. It was to the Beaujeu couple that Louis XI left the regency. This created an outcry and even more so when Anne, under pressure of opinion, sought to 'purge' the advisers of the late king. Commynes himself then made the acquaintance of prisons. The League of the Public Weal was reconstituted, but on this occasion the public described the war of the nobles as 'the senseless war', which was a sign of the times — more than ever were the people tired of the feudal lords and favourable to the crown. Louis of Orleans and the Duke of Brittany, Francis II, directed this uprising. Anne de Beaujeu won two victories over the rebels, one military and the other political. She called together the States General in 1484 to show that the people were on her side. The States General supported her, but demanded the freedoms of Charles VII's day, since every period looks upon the past as a golden age. The States General received stipulations of grievances and before them a wise and revolutionary speech was made by the deputy Philip Pot, Lord of La Roche in Burgundy: 'The State is the thing of the people ... the sovereign people created kings by its suffrage ... they are such, not in order to draw a profit from the people and to enrich themselves at its expense, but, forgetting their own interests, to enrich it and make it happy. If sometimes they do the opposite, they are tyrants ...' The States General asked to be convoked every two years; the next day they found the tapestries stripped from the walls and the furniture carried away. The sovereign people bowed.

Upon the death of Francis II, Duke of Brittany, an urgent problem arose. His daughter Anne was the heir. Whoever married her would own Brittany. Among her suitors was Maximilian of Austria, widower of Marie of Burgundy; already master of Flanders through his daughter Marguerite, were he to gain Brittany, he would encircle France. Anne de Beaujeu acted promptly and proposed her brother to the Duchess, causing the offer of marriage to be presented by an army of forty thousand men. This form of courtship is irresistible. Anne objected that the King of France was already affianced to Marguerite of Austria; the Beaujeu replied that this childish betrothal had been broken off. The Duchess resigned herself, and, despite her husband's ugliness, soon loved him. Without beauty, she herself was thin and lame, but a sharp Bretonne, highly educated and a patroness of the arts. She dwelt at Amboise, surrounded by Bretons, and her native land remained faithful to her. For many long years Brittany would assert that it accepted the sovereignty of the kings of France only by virtue of their being heirs of 'the Good Duchess'. After this marriage, the task of the Beaujeu was completed and Anne withdrew. She left her brother master of a fine kingdom wherein he no longer had anyone to fear.

CHAPTER XI

HOW, DURING THE FOURTEENTH AND FIFTEENTH CENTURIES, THERE WAS A GRADUAL TRANSITION FROM THE MIDDLE AGES TO MODERN TIMES

NOTHING would be more false than to depict Western society as leaping from one social condition called the *Middle Ages* to another called the *Renaissance*. These names were not invented until much later, and then only for the convenience of lecturers. Real history is made up of individuals and of acts, not of periods. What is true is that during the fourteenth and fifteenth centuries a rationalist and richer civilization began gradually to invade Christendom and that in France the feudal lords little by little lost their mastery. We have seen Charles VII and Louis XI building up permanent armies; we have noted that the augmented part played by infantry and artillery was sure to weaken the political power of the feudal cavalry. Institutions follow inventions only after a considerable lag, but they always end by coming into step. From war to war, the King of France increased his internal power. He had become the defender of the country but also its master. The bowmen stopped the knights short, cannon made breaches in keeps. Firmly established upon personal, national and religious bases, the King — son of France, anointed of the Lord, miracle-worker and commander-in-chief — was supreme over all other powers. This supremacy had assumed various forms: St. Louis's spiritual authority, the enlightened despotism of Charles V and of Charles VII, the wily manœuvring of Louis XI. Thenceforth, however, it was almost beyond question. Neither the feudality nor the States General had been able to oppose its rise. Surely, slowly, the French monarchy moved towards absolutism. But the French were not fearful of it: they felt that they were well protected. 'Our King', said Commynes, 'is in all the world the lord who has least reason to avail himself of this saying: I am privileged to levy upon a subject whatever I please; for neither he nor any other man has such a privilege, and they do him no honour who say that he has in order to make him seem the greater; on the contrary, they make him hateful and fearful to the neighbours who for nothing in the world would want to be under his lordship ...' *For neither he nor any other man* ... This phrase is of supreme importance. Thus we see that the King, according to Commynes, imposed rules upon himself and recognized limits to his power, those limits being the customs of the country. Concerning the nature of their power, Louis XI and Charles VIII had ideas altogether different from those of Louis XIV.

The three estates of the kingdom remained distinct. The nobility kept its privileges: freedom from taxation, judgment by its peers, a matchless social position. But during the course of the Hundred Years War, it had shown itself unsuited to its military and political role. Steeped in the ideas of chivalry, it was not realistic; on the contrary, it thought realism dishonourable. With its childish vanity, its puerile concern for tournaments, banquets and passages at arms, obsessed by personal allegiances, it had shown very little national feeling. Its passions were violent; the vengeances at the court of Burgundy testified to this. Religious sentiment restrained it hardly at all. The historians (Froissart, Monstrelet) pay lip service to the ideas of chivalry, but who still protected the widow and the orphan? Courtly love had become a rite. The knight, in a tourney, paraded his lady, wore her colours, her veil, and sometimes even her bodice, which he returned to her covered with blood. But there was no true passion. There still existed true knights, such as the father of Bayard, who taught their sons the code of honour: 'Serve God. Be kindly and courteous to all men of gentle breeding. Be humble and serviceable to all people. Be neither a flatterer nor a teller of tales. Be faithful in deed and in speech. Keep your word ...' But Bayard would not have been so highly praised had he not been an exceptional creature. Bayard himself loved to break many a lance in tournament. But the time was coming when realistic soldiers would say: 'Do not break lances; keep your arms in good repair and kill your enemy.' The hero and the soldier.

During the Middle Ages the clergy had acquired feudal habits. The splendour of worship had corresponded to the splendour of the tourney. The people had loved ceremonial richness, but had condemned the private magnificence of the bishops. The Great Schism, during which two popes had quarrelled over Christendom, had weakened the Church's prestige. Why fear excommunication when the excommunicators excommunicated one another? The people of France remained believers, but found fault with the sale of ecclesiastical offices and of indulgences and the absence of Christian virtues among certain members of the clergy. The priests' concubines ('priestesses') were hated. Many thought that it had become necessary to reform the Church. In 1458, the French clergy and King Charles VII had persuaded the Pope to approve the Pragmatic Sanction of Bourges, an action which shattered Roman fiscal policy and transferred to the King and to the Church of France a portion of the revenues which until then had gone to the Papacy. On the spiritual level, a new mysticism filled the needs of truly Christian souls. The *Imitation of Christ*, written about 1430, foreshadowed a devotion founded on love and on charity. Without this renewal, the Catholic Church would not have been able, during the following century, to combat the Reformation.

The active third estate was made up in the main of the middle class. This was a group distinct from the general masses, having its own privileges. You could gain admission to it, but only by fulfilling certain conditions and at the cost of an initiation fee. In the large cities, the majesty of the municipal corporation seemed wholly feudal. Paris had almost three hundred thousand inhabitants; Reims was the second city of the kingdom. Many bourgeois had bought seignorial domains and, like the nobles, had farmers with a system of *métayage*. In their corporate bodies, the regulations were becoming more and more rigid. Artisans lived in their own special sections in each town, and trades were hereditary. Over the countryside, there were fewer serfs. Some traces remained of this ancient condition; for instance, a tenant, in order to get married, had to obtain the permission of his lord, which gave rise to the absurd legend of the *droit de jambage* (a right entitling the lord symbolically to place his leg in the marriage bed, showing his right to the first night of marriage), which the Church should never have tolerated. Hard-working and economical, the French peasant was prosperous as long as war and taxes spared him. But soldiers and mercenaries pillaged him, and the head tax was heavy.

French art, during these last days of the Middle Ages, was going through a transformation. During the Hundred Years War, destruction and destitution had been such that it was scarcely any longer possible to erect great buildings. The majority of artists had then taken refuge in areas which remained on the edge of the struggle: Burgundy, Italy, a part of Flanders. Religious themes still inspired them for the most part. The story of Joan of Arc allows us to grasp the intensity of faith during the fifteenth century; the criticisms levelled at the Church itself give evidence of this faith. Had men at that time not been so believing, they would not have been so concerned with religious reforms. But the new religious art was less didactic and more emotional than that of the twelfth and thirteenth centuries. Already the artist was leaving the City of God and fixing his eyes upon the kingdoms of this world. Details observed by the senses were taking the place of inventions of the spirit. In the sculpture adorning its portals, the Middle Ages had expressed its idealism by means of the dematerialized bodies of their angels; during the fifteenth century, the scenes of the Passion (especially under Flemish influence) became realistic. The miniaturist took delight in depicting martyrs with the sadism of a man who has himself suffered. He discovered 'the plastic virtue of suffering'. The idea of death haunted Villon as it did the sculptors of the *danse macabre*. Parisians paid visits to the charnel house of the Holy Innocents. In Burgundy a fine school specialized in the carving of tombs. Some of these monuments, wherein the dead person is borne by black penitents, are beyond praise. Claus Slutter executed the tomb of Philip the Bold; that of Philip Pot has been transferred from the Abbey of Cîteaux to the Louvre; that of Pons de Gontaut, from the Château of Biron to the Metropolitan Museum. 'During the twelfth century the French stone-master began to turn towards nature eyes long lifted to the heavens. The artist made himself into an observer.' In contrast to what was taking place in Italy, we find at this time in France few fresco painters, because the walls of the Gothic cathedral had given place to stained glass windows, with the result that surfaces to cover were lacking. But French illuminators and miniaturists retained their own special genius (Jean Fouquet) and were to inspire the painters of the Italian Renaissance. The miniature, as they handled it, became a picture; their backgrounds were fine landscapes; their hunting scenes and their processions of state were worthy of Carpaccio or of Benozzo Gozzoli.

As for lay or profane art, in the thirteenth century it had been patronized only by wealthy communities, which ordered the construction of bell towers or city halls. In the fourteenth and fifteenth centuries, a powerful and rich man had artists working directly for him. Charles V was a great builder of town houses and castles; it was during his reign that the Louvre of Philip Augustus, enlarged by the architect Raymond du Temple, officially became the royal residence. The sons of John the Good were patrons (Angers tapestries ordered by Louis, Duke of Anjou;

Grandes Heures executed for John, Duke of Berry). Rich merchants like Jacques Cœur had built for themselves palaces adorned with sculpture. This epoch had a taste for portraits, hunting scenes, processions. Objects of art were consigned no longer to cathedral treasuries, but to the collections of individuals. Great lords and great bankers wanted to have in their own homes precious things from all over the world. The collector encouraged an art of luxury and of rich sensory impression. Woman's body was unveiled. The profane was mixed with the sacred, and, in a 'Virgin and Child', Agnes Sorel, the King's mistress, was painted as a madonna laying bare a beautiful naked breast. The 'bourgeois' art of the architect was making great strides forward. Rooms were better lighted and better heated. Abbeville merchants took pleasure in having their staircases and windows adorned with wood carvings both grotesque and whimsical. The artists of the cathedrals had accepted anonymity and had found their reward in the Faith; from the fifteenth century on (above all in the sixteenth) the artist became famous, respectable, spoiled.

Literature showed the same characteristics. It likewise ceased to be anonymous and became personal. The *chanson de geste*, ceaselessly reworked and given new endings, had been composed by teams of poets. But Charles of Orleans and Villon were individuals whose lives are known to us and are reflected in their work. This is also true of Froissart and Commynes. Writers of memoirs as much as they were historians, these men lived through the scenes they described for us. Such recollections give their chronicles a charm which would no longer characterize the erudite but second-hand historians who succeeded them. The feelings expressed by François Villon are the same as those we have seen represented in the works of art of his time: a deep sadness, a sad faith, an obsession with death. Here was the end of thirteenth-century optimism, when men were building the City of God. The terrors of war, the disorder of civil strife had made people weary and sceptical. Villon still knew how to pray — and pray touchingly — to the 'Lady of Heaven, Regent of Earth', in the name of his mother, 'a humble Christian', but he asserted that society was ill made, that shame and cruelty were universal, and that death, the only release, would soon carry away both the thief and the executioner, the 'Queen white as a lily' and 'Joan the good girl from Lorraine whom the English burned at Rouen'. (Moreover he found inspiration for this *Ballade des Dames du Temps Jadis* in the Bible and Saint Bernard, in Isaiah and in Solomon. The theme of his address to the great of this world is as old as poetry itself. '*Ubi Helena Parisque* . . .?' asked a hymn of the eleventh century.) It was an age of pessimism:

> Day of sadness and of temptation,
> Age of tears, of anxiety and of torment,
> Time of weariness and of damnation. . . .[1]

One characteristic which seemingly belongs to all periods bereft of hope is that their poets seek refuge in difficult forms. 'Frivolity is a violent state.' What could be more frivolous than the complication of rhythms? The ballad, the rondeau, *rimes redoublées* (later it would be sonnets with Du Bellay in exile and Cassou in prison) have the double advantage of concealing life's horrors and of giving birth to masterpieces. In Guillaume de Machault (1300-77), one of France's greatest artists, author of ballades and motets, the virtuosity of the musician was joined to that of the poet.

The theatre had been the most complete expression of the Greek soul, and Latin comedy had carried on the tradition of Aristophanes and Menander. Then the Catholic Church had shown herself hostile, for moral reasons, to actors. Nevertheless, it was by the Church's agency that the drama, from the tenth century on, began to revive. The custom arose, at the Easter Mass, of staging conversations among the Holy Women at the sepulchre. Then true liturgical dramas were composed in Latin. Finally 'miracles' or 'mysteries' in the vulgar tongue, representing the lives of the saints or the Passion, as well as 'plays', were performed on certain feast days by the confraternities, either in the church porch or on trestles. Folk dramas like those of Oberammergau give us some idea of these entertainments, which sometimes lasted through several days, a whole town being gathered together to witness the Mystery of the Passion. The public was urged to maintain a 'loving silence'. The actors, very numerous, were amateurs. 'To God the Father, given a jar of wine worth five pennies . . .' says the expense account of the Passion of Mons.[2] Comic elements were not lacking in these sacred dramas. Herod, Pilate, Judas and the Jews were handed over to grinning devils who issued from the flames of Hell, and the public was delighted with their writhings. The continuity of France's theatrical history is revealed by the fact that in the seventeenth century the Hôtel de Bourgogne still belonged to the Con-

[1] EUSTACHE DESCHAMPS.   [2] GUSTAVE COHEN.

fraternity of the Passion. Today, harlequin's cape, or the red cloth which frames the proscenium, descends directly from Hallequin's mantle with which was draped the mouth of Hell.[1] When these mysteries and miracles were revived in our own time, either at the Sorbonne or before the Cathedral of Notre Dame, we ourselves were able to testify that they retained their naive beauty, heightened by the architectural stage setting.

The comic elements were the least successful parts of this drama and they ended by killing the religious theatre. In 1584 the *Parlement* of Paris decreed that the mysteries were disrespectful and forbade them. Two other theatrical forms, the morality and the farce, produced a few masterpieces; the *Farce of Master Pathelin* has the speedy dialogue and the quasi-mechanical comedy of Molière, but not his poetry. As for the satirical farce, played by 'idiots' or fools, it was a parody of society which, allowing for the necessary differences, corresponds to what we know as the revue. In literature as in art, what strikes us in these first French achievements is the clarity of their construction and the considered sureness of their touch. We must likewise note the theatrical influence on painting and on sculpture. When the artist went to performances of the mysteries, he found both models and ideas.[2]

It is usual to attribute to the fifteenth century the 'invention' of printing. But from the bricks of Egypt to Gutenberg, the process was continuous. As early as the late Roman Empire, the *codex*, our modern book, began to replace the parchment roll. The notion of *printing* several copies of a given text by making use of letters engraved on wooden blocks had long been known in China. A number of circumstances lent it, in the fifteenth century, a new importance: the discovery of numerous ancient manuscripts, the development of the universities, travel narratives. What is called the 'invention' of printing was merely the combination of two novelties: separate characters, assembled by a compositor, and then broken up for further use, and the employment of metal characters which could be cast in great number. Laurens Coster of Haarlem and Johann Gutenberg of Mainz are reputed first to have had these ideas. However this may be, handsome books had been set up as early as 1455, and the invention reached Paris in 1470. Printing slowly transformed political life by making easier the moulding and information of a public opinion.

The fifteenth century was basically a period of transition. Many of the nobles, while keeping their fortified castles in the country, had caused

[1] GUSTAVE COHEN   [2] ÉMILE MALE.

to be built in some town, be it Périgueux, Bordeaux, Rouen or Dijon, a city house adorned with sculpture. This double domicile might be interpreted as a symbol of the day. The Middle Ages continued (the keep); a new social life was beginning (the town house). For the successive layers of a civilization exist together. Even today the survivals of the Middle Ages are numerous. More than one feudal fortress still dominates the French landscape, sometimes inhabited by the same family which long ago caused it to be erected (La Rouchefoucauld, Luynes, Uzès, etc.). The peasant's cottage, in many a province, has changed little. The Catholic church remains the centre of every French village. As of old, the bishop comes on his pastoral visitations. Pilgrims travel by train, but they go to Lourdes as formerly they went to Saint James of Compostella. The feelings of Charles of Orleans in exile were those of many a Frenchman in 1945. Country families retain something of that respect for the sacrament, of that asceticism, of that contempt for happiness which even today makes divorces in France rarer than in the Anglo-Saxon countries.

If you want to know what were the worries and thoughts of a Frenchman of the fifteenth century, open at random Jehan de Troyes' chronicle. 1460: The wheat is 'prosperous and in good ear', but there will be little fruit. The grape harvest will be small, but the wine very good. It is 'a great year'. In Paris, for receiving stolen goods, a woman has been buried alive and the goods confiscated; in order to delay her punishment, she pretended to be with child, but the matrons said that she was not. The Seine and the Marne have overflowed their banks ... 1461: King Louis XI has made his entry into Paris. Upon his entry, the herald, Loyal Cœur, presented him with five noble ladies who represented the five letters of the name *Paris*, and each of them made a speech of welcome. The horses were caparisoned with cloth of gold lined with sable, with velvet lined with ermine, and with cloth of Damascus mounted with goldsmith's work. At the fountain of Ponceau, three handsome girls took the part of the Sirens, all naked, and you could see 'their lovely breasts, round and firm, which was a very pleasant thing', and they warbled little motets. A few paces off, there was 'a Passion represented by people in dumb show, God stretched upon the cross and the two thieves to right and left'. On the Pont au Change, the birdsellers, who had a monopoly in selling their birds on the Place du Châtelet (they still have it), set free two hundred of their wares, brilliant of plumage. Then the King went to his dwelling of the Tournelles, where he dismissed the great personages of his father's court and named others to take their place which caused sore dismays.

Thus the dough of French life had already been mixed: the wheat and grape harvest; political changes; the theatre; the poets; the realism of the artists. It remained only to knead it and to shape it.

HOW, AT THE END OF THE MIDDLE AGES, FRANCE ALREADY POSSESSED MANY OF HER PERMANENT CHARACTERISTICS

FOR that rich stretch of land which is embraced as though by two open arms, the Alps and the Pyrenees, three political and territorial solutions were possible during the course of Europe's formative years. It could belong to and form part of a larger unit; it could be split up into several independent communities; or it could achieve its own unity. France, in the early days of her history, passed several times through each of these three phases. She had constituted a part of the Roman Empire; she had been shattered into Barbarian kingdoms; she had herself created a new empire, that of Charlemagne; at the time of the dismemberment of this empire, she had split up into numerous fiefs; then, bit by bit, one of the feudal lords, the King, had pieced these bits together into one domain. In the fifteenth century, France's national unity had been consolidated round a monarch.

Now the national solution triumphed not only in France, but in England and in Spain. In all three countries, a king unified the nation. For some time one might have wondered whether the Holy Roman Empire or the Church would not come to dominate Europe. United, the Pope and the Emperor could have made Christendom into a political reality. But the rivalry between the Empire and the Church had weakened both together, and they had lost all opportunity to create a homogeneous Europe. The Hundred Years War had given to the French as well as to the English an awareness of their differences. In feudal times, institutions had been approximately alike in both countries. Then the English and the French monarchies had followed divergent roads. In the fifteenth century, the English monarchy, solidly upheld by an aristocracy of squires and wealthy merchants, governed by means of benevolent justices of the peace, and annually summoned Parliaments in order to obtain funds. The French monarchy, on the other hand, sought to resurrect the Roman tradition of a central bureaucracy; it governed by means of office holders, but it had popular support because it had protected the people against the foreigner and against the feudal lords.

What were France's special characteristics in the fifteenth century? She owed to Rome her instinct for centralization. With her, patriotism was perennial and was bound up with national heroes, such as Charlemagne, Saint Louis, Joan of Arc; she remained Christian and Catholic; religion had infused her daily life. It had been by means of her religious art and her religious philosophy that in the Middle Ages she had shone throughout all Europe. Cluny and Cîteaux had spread French culture far and wide. In England, the knight evolved and became the gentleman; in Italy, he was to give place to the politician; the ancestral instinct of the French would continue to push them towards chivalric 'gestures'. Courtesy had taken root. The vocabulary of the court of love in France resembled that of feudal loyalty. It was Joan of Arc who accomplished 'what no created man could have done'; it was Blanche of Castile who moulded Saint Louis and protected him during his minority; it was Anne de Beaujeu who saved the kingdom for her brother. From time to time, to be sure, men revolted against this womanly influence. 'The wisest woman in the world, as far as good sense is concerned, has about as much as I have gold in my eye', said a fifteenth-century writer. But courtesy and chivalry had left their deep marks, and the French knights, as they would do for centuries, 'trifled with arms, honour and love'.[1] The moralists of the seventeenth century and the novelists of the nineteenth were to share in an age-old heritage of sentimental analysis.

The barriers between classes were higher in France than in England or in Italy. In Florence, a merchant could become a prince; in London, the middle class participated, with the knights, in the House of Commons; marriages between nobles and commoners were frequent; bourgeoisie and nobility were equal on the score of taxes. In France, trade remained debasing; the third estate sat in a section separate from the others. Ennoblement remained possible, but the ennobled plebeian, in acquiring the privileges of his new class, broke with the old. In England, the strength of the aristocracy arose above all from its constituting a political and administrative governing class; in France, the aristocracy sought to remain the warrior class above all, and in a period of harquebuses and artillery, this was an anachronism. Faithful to the laws of chivalry, lacking in the practical spirit, this French nobility would have regarded as dishonourable the electoral manipulations whereby the English nobility preserved its influence. It attributed an inordinate importance to bearing, to etiquette, to a hierarchy. Such, likewise, was the case of the Spanish

[1] ALAIN CHARTIER.

nobility, but in Spain there was scarcely any middle class, and class conflict was not of like importance.

In the fifteenth century, Europe was already formed, at least along its major lines. Three kingdoms – France, England and Spain – had almost reached their full development. France still needed to settle her frontiers in the north and north-east; that was to be the task of the following centuries. The danger that threatened her did not then come from Germany, which was divided into tiny States and therefore powerless, but from Austria, which, through the circumstances of feudal inheritance, gave every sign of uniting itself to Spain and the Low Countries, thereby encircling France. Truly, the feudal concept, by virtue of which a given tract of land is linked to a given person, was not suitable to modern times. National feeling is too strong for whole provinces to be able and willing to change their allegiance in accordance with the chance family alliances of their lords. The feudal idea had served its purpose in days when the essential thing was to find a remedy for anarchy; then it was better to have a rule of personal allegiance than to have an absence of all rule. But the era of personal bonds was coming to an end and the era of nationalities was beginning; it also was useful for a time. During the fifteenth century the two types of institution were still intertwined. We shall see, as French history went on, that territorial inheritances played a great part therein – often an ill-fated part. But an irresistible instinct attracted the country towards nationalism, and towards absolutism.

Although the kingdom was unified and national feeling was vigorous, many recently annexed provinces retained their original traits. The King respected their customs. Especially were the north and the south of France very different, both in their habits and in their style of government. Romanized earlier than the north, the south retained a feeling for Roman law, a taste for eloquence, and a more Latin culture. In Provence and in Aquitaine, the Arab occupation had introduced elements of poetry and of history. Contact with the East had been less completely severed than in the remainder of the country. It was in the south that the Albigenses and the Cathari sought to purify the Church, and it was in the south that the Huguenots were later to find a fertile soil. Throughout the course of French history and even until our own times, without the national unity ever being threatened thereby, deep political divergencies have been visible between north and south.

Two further characteristics, which have played basic parts in the country's life, were evident even in the Middle Ages. The first is France's astonishing power of recuperation. During the course of the Hundred Years War she suffered utter disasters which might easily have discouraged her. Yet barely a few years after the end of these trials, she had once again become Europe's most powerful nation. This ability to recover arises in part from the fertility of her soil and the labours of her peasants; in part it springs from an instinctive faith in her destiny and from a deep-rooted certainty that a Frenchman can only be a Frenchman. The second characteristic is belief in France's universal mission. The French, perhaps because they belong to a border civilization, are inclined to believe that it is possible to convince all men of the truth of a system of ideas. In the Middle Ages the University of Paris felt that Europe and the Church of Rome acknowledged its pre-eminence. During the seventeenth and eighteenth centuries, we shall observe the same phenomenon manifest under different forms. If the notion of a universal society should some day prove victorious, the French ought to be among the first to exercise a spiritual influence therein. They had elaborated, as early as the twelfth century, the concept of a homogeneous Christendom. The idea of a Europe united, not by the power of legions but by truths unanimously accepted, was born on the hill of Saint Geneviève.

BOOK TWO

RENAISSANCE AND REFORMATION

CHAPTER I

HOW THERE TOOK PLACE IN EUROPE
A REVOLUTION WHICH MEN LATER
CALLED THE RENAISSANCE

NEVER did the writers of the sixteenth century speak of a renaissance. Culture required no rebirth because it had never ceased to be alive. Far more than with a renaissance, we are here dealing with a revolution. The Middle Ages had possessed certainties. It had discovered truth, all truths, in the Sacred Scriptures as interpreted by reason. In the temporal world, it had attributed to every man his place in a defined social framework: feudality, commons, corporations. Unity had remained the dream of the people; the Empire, that of the sovereigns; Christendom, that of the popes. Then, early in the fourteenth and, above all, in the fifteenth century, a new way of life had supplied inquiring minds with the leisure to observe and to criticize. The discoveries of the navigators and of the astronomers had shown that the world was vaster than the Jews or the Greeks had believed. It was no longer in texts but on the earth and in the stars that truth had to be sought. No one cast doubt (at least openly) upon Christian teachings, but reformers criticized the clergy and satirists made mock of the monks. As was the case later, in the eighteenth century, men thought they dwelt in an age of 'light' which delivered them from outworn superstitions. 'Freed from that heavy Gothic night', said Rabelais, 'our eyes were opened to the single torch of the sun.' The night had been neither heavy nor Gothic, but the brilliance of summer brought forgetfulness of the beauties of the spirit's springtime.

Why was the first flame of this new light lit in Italy? Because in its ruins, in its marbles, in its inscriptions, Italy preserved the tradition of the ancient world. Beginning with the time of Dante and of Petrarch, it had given birth to a new classical language. In its wealthy cities — Milan, Venice, Florence, Naples — rich traders gave encouragement to scholars and artists. Capitalism was then in its childhood: what better investment for the Medicis than to surround themselves with a retinue of artists able to assure at once the present fortune and the future glory of their protector? The Renaissance was wrought in the palaces of princes and of bankers far more than in the universities. The shaping of powerful, distinctive individuals was furthered in Italy by the rivalry between the states — Milan, Florence, Rome, Venice, Naples. There, nothing was rigid in the feudal pattern, or even in the ecclesiastical hierarchy. Humanist popes gave Rome a splendour beyond compare. The ideal Frenchman of the Middle Ages had been Saint Louis, a valiant and devout soldier; the Italian ideal of the Renaissance knew how to handle a brush and compass as well as he did a dagger or a sword. He was an engineer, a diplomat, a scholar. Trickery and violence united to constitute *virtù*, very different from the virtue of the knight. Machiavelli's *The Prince*, the Renaissance's favourite book, was a manual of realistic politics, and, through the Italian marriages entered into by the kings of France, Machiavellian cynicism was to penetrate the court of the Valois.

The individual of the Renaissance did not cease to profess the Christian faith, but he no longer practised it. Not content to prepare for his salvation in another world, he wanted pleasure on this earth. In fifteenth-century Italy, Christian morality suffered an eclipse. Sexual life there was free and even licentious; murder was easily forgiven, especially if the murderer was an artist. 'Virtuous young people', said Benvenuto Cellini, 'are those who give the most thrusts with the knife.' In the world of the thirteenth century, Cellini would have deserved the gallows and Hell; in that of the twentieth, the electric chair; in the sixteenth century princes befriended him and took delight in his follies. Popes Pius II (Piccolomini) and Paul III (Alexander Farnese) tried, although themselves humanists, to neutralize 'the pagan odour' of the Italian Renaissance, but Sixtus IV, a great patron of the arts and creator of the Sistine Chapel, showed himself more the Roman Maecenas than Saint Peter's vicar, and the Borgia Alexander VI made vice at home in the Vatican. Nevertheless, if they are sometimes forbidding, the men of the Italian Renaissance have their own special greatness. It was in their image that Elizabeth of England and Francis I of France formed themselves. Baldassare Castiglione, an athlete and an intellectual, reminds us in *The Courtier* of the Greeks in the days of Pericles. Benvenuto Cellini, taking supper with his friends and their mistresses in a palace adorned with jasmine, enjoyed conversations which call to mind those of the pupils of Socrates. There was in the men of that epoch a passion and an enthusiasm, a need for varied and bold action, a love of beauty, a respect for the arts, a *joie de vivre* which are intoxicating; yet they possessed a cynicism and a nihilism to which Europe was to owe many of its ills.

Those were the days of an insatiable desire to learn. The 'humanist' of the Italian Renaissance not only read the ancient authors, and studied all the aspects of classical life, but he knew new manuscripts, and thus broke down Christian prejudices. A new programme of study — history, poetry, literature — shaped the 'humanist'. Theology's share had been reduced. The poets of antiquity had become the 'classic texts'. Contact with pagan thought had weakened the intellectual grip of the Church. As it spread over Europe, this culture was first of all to be hurtful to the simplicity of the various national literatures. Shortly we shall see Rabelais poking fun at the Graeco-Latin vocabulary of the new pedants. A Ciceronian period, in which the grandeur of rhythm hid the emptiness of thought, was to invade for centuries French oratory both in pulpit and in palace. But this inoculation of ancient culture, starting with the seventeenth century, was to be swept away and absorbed by the current of French intellectual energy. It was to produce Pascal, Bossuet, Racine, and would inspire Frenchmen with respect for form, the only assurance of lasting quality. In the classical writers, the men of the Renaissance found a wise philosophy, proved by centuries of experience and less absolute than that of the Middle Ages. From Seneca and Aristotle and the Latin poets, Montaigne derived rules of behaviour which freed his readers from useless rigour and harsh certainty. The mingling of humanism and Christianity was to be the basis of Western civilization.

None the less, in the sixteenth century one essential element was still lacking: the scientific spirit. The culture of Greece and Rome could not take the place of methodical research into the laws of nature by means of experience and experiment. The vast majority of cultivated men in Montaigne's day were indifferent to such investigations. Yet from the time of the Middle Ages the Arabs led the way in science. Thanks to them, geometry, trigonometry and algebra had won a place among the studies. Great artists like Leonardo da Vinci and Michelangelo would be led, through the necessities of their work, to study mechanics, descriptive geometry and anatomy. In 1543 Andreas Vesalius taught that, if one was to learn the surgeon's trade, it was better to dissect a corpse than to read ancient manuals. At the beginning of the century, Copernicus showed where Ptolemy had been wrong and placed the sun at the centre of our system. The progress of astronomy, however, had the curious effect of increasing the prestige of mathematics and of deductive investigation at the expense of inductive and experimental research. Men's eyes saw the sun revolving around the earth; by his calculations Copernicus showed that the earth revolved around the sun. And Copernicus was right. Hence one should rely more on the mind than on the senses. This notion was to postpone until the nineteenth century the era of major scientific discovery.

A basic characteristic of the Renaissance was that its culture belonged to the *élite*. The civilization of the Middle Ages had been popular. The troubadour and the jongleur performed on the public square; mysteries were played for the benefit of the populace on the porch of the cathedral; and the cathedral itself had been built by an anonymous architect with the help of an entire community. The art of the Renaissance, on the contrary, was aristocratic. Villon had written ballades understandable by every man; the sonnets of Ronsard and of Shakespeare were beyond the reach of simple folk. Humanism dug even deeper the moat between classes. Private architecture took the place of public architecture. It was intended to display magnificence and to afford pleasure. Italian architects, painters and sculptors were to spread all over Europe. They brought with them the classical orders, colonnades, horizontal lines, which replaced the high Gothic vaults and the vertical upthrust of Gothic naves. In sculpture and in painting art remained nominally Christian. The painter still clung to religious subjects, but he humanized them. Tintoretto filled the churches of Venice with the bodies of women. Titian shows us upon the same canvas, 'Sacred and Profane Love', two blonde beauties, one clothed, proper and timorous, the other shameless, proud and naked. For the tradition of the medieval artist, who had given naive expression to his faith, the Renaissance artist was to substitute the 'search for effect'.

I have already said that what here confronts us is a revolution rather than rebirth; it would be more accurate to say an evolution, for the change was not sudden. Neither faith nor the feudal spirit disappeared in France during the sixteenth century — far from it — but the middle classes, closely joined to the monarchy, weakened the feudality. Humanism obliged the Church to broaden education; preoccupation with immediate happiness took the place of preoccupation with eternal salvation, and artists became divorced from the masses. Yet the new ideas crossed the Alps very slowly and they produced different results in Germany, in England and in France. In Italy, humanism had disposed the *élite* towards a return to paganism. France, however, was a country violently shaken for a hundred years, disinclined towards puritanism as it was towards paganism, but enriched and made fertile by these foreign contributions. The country in the seventeenth century reverted to her own line of development, and the ultimate explosion of the new ideas was postponed until the eighteenth century. The French Revolution was the daughter of the Renaissance.

CHAPTER II

HOW ITALY FIRST SUMMONED AND THEN DISMISSED THE FRENCH

WHEN Louis XI died, two questions of foreign policy could claim the attention of a King of France: that of Flanders, an area coveted at once by France, England and the Empire, because each of these three Powers feared to see it occupied by one of the others; that of Italy, because the old dream of empire still obsessed Europe's sovereigns and because each of the Italian cities, at odds among themselves, would summon to its assistance any available foreign army. In the mind of a clear-thinking Frenchman, with an eye to the future, the problem of the north-east should have seemed the more important. There lay the real danger to France's frontiers. But Charles VIII, in order to free himself of his first Austrian betrothal, had given up the Franche-Comté and Artois. In all decency he could no longer attack these provinces, and what was more, his own desires drew him towards Italy. All men talked of the beauty of the Italian cities, of their artists, of their poets. The tiny French King, thin, ugly, deformed, deeply in love with his Breton Queen, herself a delicate cripple with a great heart, had a knightly soul. The young royal pair had sought to make a thing of beauty out of their château at Amboise; Anne hung the finest of tapestries upon the walls and covered the stone floors with Oriental carpets. Charles displayed his collection of arms to visitors: Charlemagne's blade, Saint Louis's sword, Du Guesclin's axe, Joan of Arc's coat of mail, lined with red silk. He dreamed of adding thereto a blade made famous by his own exploits. France was full of *émigré* Italians, exiled and burning with hate against the factions which had driven them out. In each of the large cities of the south, and even in Paris, an Italian priest gave the cue to his Italian parish. Genoese, Lombard and Florentine bankers were opening branch offices in France. French noble families were marrying into those of Italy. Countless were the Italians who held positions at court or in the army, and all these refugees sought to put France at the service of their own passions.

Nor was it difficult to find an excuse for intervention. Under the law, the five major Italian principalities — Rome, Venice, Naples, Milan and Florence — were united by the Lodi agreement; in reality, they conspired against one another, and within each of them there were at least two political parties. The kingdom of Naples, especially, had for two centuries been a subject of dispute between the French House of Anjou and the Spanish House of Aragon. In the days of Charles VIII, the King of Naples was Ferdinand of Aragon, hated by the Pope and by Ludovico the Moor, Regent of Milan. Were France to lay claim to Naples, she thought she would surely have powerful allies. Charles VIII, surrounded 'by men of small estate experienced in nothing', allowed himself to be seduced 'by the phantoms and glories of Italy'. In order that he might have his hands free, he bought off the Empire and England in exchange for dangerous territorial and financial concessions. His Italian schemes were popular. France felt herself strong. With her astonishing power of recuperation, she had already repaired all the disasters of the Hundred Years War. Thanks to Charles VII and Louis XI, she possessed Europe's most powerful army, and it was of urgent necessity to employ these companies abroad, because they included more foreigners than Frenchmen and threatened to despoil the countryside. So the King mobilized his forces at Lyons, gloriously embraced his little Queen, and departed for the Alps with more than thirty thousand men in August 1494. At the outset there took place the splendid cavalcade of which he had dreamed. For the entrance into Florence, the residents of that town stationed themselves at their windows, bedecked with tapestries, and watched the procession of kettle-drummers, fife players, cross-bow men, archers, halberdiers, Swiss, all superbly clad in the King's colours, red and yellow. At last appeared the King's household, his standards, and Charles himself, grasping his lance, riding a black horse, and encased in golden armour and a king's long blue mantle, which covered his horse's crupper. The sight was worthy of the romances of chivalry, but the Florentines remained hostile and distrustful. This royal army did not have a good reputation; it was full of downright ruffians, 'with little discipline', who pillaged Italy more than they admired her. Savonarola, the great Dominican preacher, had proclaimed a cohort of angels who should come out of France to deliver Italy from the papal exactions. 'It was', said Guichardin, 'a conflagration and a plague.' In Rome, Pope Alexander VI, who indeed had fostered Charles VIII's expedition, now appalled at what he had unleashed, barricaded himself in the Castel Saint'Angelo and appealed for help to the Sultan! Only the Neapolitans kept to their promise and, when the French appeared, revolted, in accordance with the plans which had been formulated against the House of Aragon. In February

1495, Charles VIII entered Naples, having attained his objective. For some time he enjoyed this earthly paradise, admired Italian gardens and the rich ceilings and floors of the palaces, engaged workmen capable of adorning his new château at Amboise with similar beauties. But it would be a great exaggeration to attribute to him the introduction into France of the spirit of the Italian Renaissance, for he had admired scarcely at all the finest works of the Florentines and the Romans. A handful of Neapolitan gardeners and cabinet-makers did not constitute the Renaissance. While he was abandoning himself to the delights of Naples, his army drew upon itself the hearty hatred of the Neapolitans, in whose eyes these liberators became conquerors. Now all Italy forgot its internal differences in its hatred of the occupying forces. The Pope, Venice, Ludovico Sforza and Ferdinand the Catholic formed a league against Charles VIII. He was betrayed by the very people who had summoned him.

The new Italian league armed itself. Charles realized he must return to France with the utmost speed lest his road back be cut off by the enemy. He hastily organized an imperial entry into Naples (in a scarlet mantle with a globe in his hand) and then began to retreat. In order to cross the Apennines, he had to give battle at Fornovo and won the day. The French who had been left as a garrison in Naples were made prisoner there after his departure. The expedition had been fruitless, but the soldiers brought back with them rich booty, and popular feeling remained favourable to the Italian campaign. From this diplomatic and military mess there arose an aroma of glory. But the King did not long survive it. In 1498, when only twenty-eight years old, he knocked his forehead against the stone lintel of a low door in a state of disrepair at Amboise, and died within a few hours. Since the children he had had by Anne had been sickly and puny, and had not lived long after birth, his cousin Louis of Orleans succeeded to the throne. The son of the poet Charles of Orleans was a young man of thirty-six, a good horseman, charming and weak, lovable and well loved. Immediately upon his accession he announced that he would leave everything as it was, not even removing his personal enemies: 'It is not decent and in accordance with the honour of the King of France to avenge the quarrels of a Duke of Orleans.' He had long been silently in love with Anne of Brittany. Now that she was a widow, he hoped to marry her, as much for her sake as for the sake of Brittany. Unhappily he was already married to a daughter of Louis XI, 'slight, dark, and round shouldered', Jeanne of

France. Cesare Borgia, son of Pope Alexander VI, undertook, in return for a generous fee in money and in lands, to arrange an annulment. This was possible because the marriage had been forced by Louis XI. Thus it happened that Brittany remained French and that the 'gentle Breton woman' remained queen, as devoted to her second king as she had been to the first.

The Italian mirage attracted Louis XII just as it had seduced Charles VIII. The paradisal climate, the natural wealth, the beauty, beckoned to the foreigner. Louis XII's favourite minister, Cardinal Georges d'Amboise, plotted with Cesare Borgia and, dreaming of becoming Pope, looked for support in Italy. Were feudal pretexts needed to justify a conquest, Louis XII, who had a Visconti grandmother, could proclaim himself heir of the Duchy of Milan whence the Visconti had earlier been driven by the Sforzas. Thus began again the adventure of Charles VIII. All Louis XII's campaigns were easy at the beginning; later on Italian reversals of feeling took place and those who had been enemies before were reconciled for the purpose of opposing France; thus victories were followed by defeats. Milan, conquered at first, was then lost. To ensure himself possession of that Duchy, Louis XII went so far as to offer the Archduke Charles of Austria, grandson of the Emperor Maximilian, the hand of his daughter Claude of France, with Brittany and Burgundy as her dowry. This would have been the undoing of all of Louis XI's achievements. Most fortunately the States General opposed this folly and declared these provinces untransferable and inalienable. Italy's power of attraction, however, remained great. The question of the Neapolitan succession having once again become open, Louis XII offered to split this kingdom with Spain. The King of Spain accepted, and then attacked the French. 'He has twice betrayed me', said Louis XII. 'Ten times have I taken him in', replied Ferdinand. Pope Julius II, an artist and warrior, aroused against Venice by Machiavelli, swore to have all the princes of Christendom take arms against that republic. A league was formed, with France to serve as its soldier. But scarcely did Venice seem in danger, when the Pope changed his tune. 'If Venice did not exist, it would be necessary to make another Venice', he said, and he declared war against the Barbarians, meaning thereby the French whom he had himself importuned! Having 'cast into the Tiber the Keys of Saint Peter and taken into his hand the Sword of Saint Paul', he formed a new Holy League, this time directed against France, in conjunction with Henry VIII of England, the Spaniards, the Venetians and the Swiss.

Defeated at Novara (1513), forced to return to France in order to defend his country against the English, the Swiss and the forces of the Emperor, Louis XII finally made peace and renounced his claims to Milan. The Italian mirage was fading away.

The French had fought long and to no purpose. They did not hold it against Louis XII, whom they called the Father of the People and whom the States General acclaimed whenever he appeared, thin, pale and leaning upon his small queen. Why? In part because they were prosperous. Ever since the days of Charles VII they had busied themselves in clearing away ruins and rebuilding. Throughout Europe, at the beginning of the sixteenth century, prices were rising. This was the effect of a progressive devaluation of currencies, but the phenomenon produced the usual feeling of well-being. Louis XII took pains to protect the peasants against the landed nobility, to revise the rights of compulsory feudal service and forced labour, and to lower the head tax. The currency depreciation benefited the farmers and impoverished the aristocracy. Many of the latter sold their lands, as happened at the time of the Crusades, and newly-rich commoners acquired them. The Italian wars took place outside the country, and France rejoiced in a delightful and novel prosperity. In the Loire valley, châteaux multiplied, and in the Ile de France many cathedrals were built. Their style was still Gothic, but flamboyant, with sculptured roses, flowered 'cabbages', high dormers encased in stone lacework, and galleries open to the rays of the sun. Georges d'Amboise, Archbishop of Rouen, commissioned the building of the Town Hall of that city and his own graceful palace. The King completely remodelled his castle at Blois, 'dwelling place of his father and mother, scene of his own birth'. Anne of Brittany had brought there from Amboise her tapestries, representing landscapes and battles, her bed 'accoutred in cloth of gold', her 'gilt and diapered chairs brought from Italy'. There she wound wool on her distaff in the midst of her women, while a poet read his verses to her or a jester amused her with his quips. Here was a 'delightful moment which allowed for the dawning, among the languishing graces of a dying civilization, of the first warm rays of that which was to arise'.[1] France loved her Queen Anne just as she loved her King Louis XII. But Anne died in 1514, leaving only two daughters; the elder was promptly married to the heir to the kingdom, the young Count of Angoulême, her first cousin. The King was so distressed by his wife's death and so greatly wasted away that the court became anxious

[1] GABRIEL HANOTAUX.

and advised him to remarry. He was only fifty-five. Mary, sister of the King of England, a young, seventeen-year-old princess, was suggested to him. He took her and she killed him. She had, beneath a glacial exterior, the overabundant passion of the Tudors. The wraithlike Louis XII had to go from feast to feast and serve his wife as 'a pleasant consort'. He died on January 1st, 1515.

CHAPTER III

HOW FRANCE BEGAN HER STRIFE WITH THE GERMANIC WORLD—FRANCIS I AND CHARLES V

THE sickly and delicate Louis XII was succeeded by his robust son-in-law and cousin once removed,[1] Francis I. Nothing would have caused greater sorrow to Queen Anne had she survived her husband. Francis of Angoulême had been brought up, at Cognac and at Amboise, by his mother, Louise of Savoy, a taciturn and masterful widow, capable of the conniving and spitefulness which accompanies ill fortune, but of solid intelligence and a noble woman. Anne hated Louise; Blois kept an eye on Amboise. When Louis XII remarried, Louise anxiously watched this young English queen whose son, were she to produce one, would stand between Francis and the throne. Louis XII was so worn out that a son seemed unlikely, but Suffolk, the English ambassador, dangerously pleased his royal compatriot. (He so greatly pleased her that she married him, three months after Louis XII's death.) An adulterous heir would have been no less dangerous than a legitimate one. Louise and her daughter Marguerite took turns as 'curators of the womb'. Finally Louis XII died and Francis I succeeded to the throne. 'We busy ourselves in vain', Louis had remarked melancholically; 'that big young fellow will spoil everything.' The big young fellow had become a splendid, strapping youth, intense, with as sturdy a stance as his crony, Henry VIII of England. He liked lovemaking, hunting, war, life. 'Far removed was any reminder of Queen Anne and her stiff austerity . . . The King liked blonde women with Flemish complexions, the handsome girls of the north . . . Joyful and hearty laughter pealed through a world of young people.'[2] Dominated and sheltered by his mother, Francis had been spoiled and worshipped by his sister Marguerite. She liked poets and artists; she had made her brother into an amateur humanist, too much of a good fellow for serious studies, though he tried his hand 'at Florentine games and at verses, which he turned out with

---

[1] Charles of Angoulême, father of Francis I, was first cousin to Louis XII. The latter had made the heir presumptive his son-in-law by marrying him to Claude of France.
[2] LOUIS BATTIFOL.

middling facility'. Just as later on there would be people called the 'new rich' Francis I was a 'new king'[1] who possessed the prestige of youth, wealth and beauty and the rash optimism produced by success obtained without effort.

In search of adventure, made dizzy by his new power, he must at once seek to revive the quarrel over the Duchy of Milan. Why? For fun. 'The King found himself at peace on all his borders, young, wealthy and powerful, and with a high-born heart, and about him people who did not advise him against war, which is the most noble exercise available to a prince or to a man of breeding . . .' He enlisted twenty-six thousand mercenaries, 'of which six thousand, calling themselves the Black Company, were almost the finest company ever seen', and 'a kind of artillery, no more than two feet in length, which fired fifty bullets at a time and was most serviceable; and thereof he caused three hundred pieces to be made at Lyons, which were borne on the backs of mules . . .' With this well-equipped expeditionary force, he crossed the Alps, met the Swiss who were occupying the Milanese territories, and defeated them at Marignano (1515). On the very field of battle, Bayard conferred knighthood on his sovereign. It was a great day for the young king, and a fine beginning to his reign, which brought him Milan, a reconciliation with the Pope and perpetual peace with the Swiss cantons, to which he promised an annual subsidy in return for the right to recruit soldiers there. The Swiss Guard was to become a permanent feature of the French court.

Under Louis XII, France had been fighting the Vatican openly ever since the betrayal of Pope Julius II. Leo X, an affable and prudent Medici, who was called His Cautiousness, had an interview of vital importance with Francis I after Marignano. What the Pope wanted was to persuade the young king to do away with the Pragmatic Sanction of Bourges, the charter of the liberties of the Gallic Church. This conversation succeeded and a new concordat was signed in 1516, but one as much to the King's benefit as to the benefit of the Vatican. Henceforward, if the choice of bishops was left in the King's hands (a victory for the State), it was required that the Pope give them their investiture (a victory for Rome). The King had the right to apportion ecclesiastical benefices (a victory for the crown), in exchange for which the Pope had the right to the annates, consisting of the newly appointed beneficiary's revenues for the first year (a victory for the Vatican). Thus the Pope and the King each acquired vast revenues at the expense of the French Church. This

[1] LUCIEN FEBVRE.

concordat, which remained in force until the Revolution, partly explains why Luther's and Calvin's Reformation failed in France. Less than any matter of doctrine, it was a matter of finance. England's Henry VIII broke with Rome in order to despoil the monasteries; Francis I had despoiled them by previous agreement with Rome. The concordat aroused strong protests from the *Parlement* of Paris: 'Only a general council wherein the Gallic Church should be represented would have had the right to legislate on these matters', the *Parlement* asserted, and the University of Paris added that the concordat was offensive to God. But they had to yield to the King's will and record the action. Who was right in this controversy? The Pope or the Sorbonne? In fact, the concordat saved the Catholic Church in France, but it placed that Church at the mercy of the public power, and it began a spiritual abdication on the part of the clergy which in the seventeenth century led to royal absolutism and in the eighteenth to anti-clericalism.

Young, rich, victorious, Francis I on his return from Marignano indulged in the most ambitious of plans. And what could be the supreme ambition of a king were it not the Empire? The imperial throne was elective, Maximilian was already old, and the electors were venal. Francis felt that he had some chance of gaining this impressive crown. The election, in which seven persons participated (three archbishops, the King of Bohemia, the Duke of Saxony, the Count Palatine and the Margrave of Brandenburg), always took place during the lifetime of the outgoing emperor, in order to avoid an interregnum. He who was elected, the chosen successor, carried the title of King of the Romans. Francis I had a dangerous rival, the grandson of the Emperor Maximilian, Charles of Austria. By the absurd interplay of territorial inheritances, this young prince, son of Philip the Fair and of Joan the Mad, herself daughter of Ferdinand, King of Aragon, and of Isabella, Queen of Castile, had title to Spain, the Low Countries, the Archduchy of Austria, and the kingdom of Naples! Already he held France in a vice; were he in addition to become Emperor of Germany, he would encircle the kingdom. The inverse proposition was likewise true; were Francis to obtain the Empire, Charles's estates would be cut off from each other. Never were two opponents more unlike. Francis I seemed the very image of strength and liveliness; Charles's face was pale, his mouth was always open, and he had a weak chin. But the brilliance of his eyes belied the weakness of his features. He was a man of great intelligence and determination. As against Francis I's gold, he gained the support of the powerful bankers of Augsburg, who were anxious to retain the connection between the Empire and Antwerp. At the cost of five hundred and fourteen thousand florins, Maximilian bought five votes for his grandson – a majority – and demanded fifty thousand florins as commission. German-Flemish capitalism won the day and Charles V was elected. For France, here was a mortal danger. She could not willingly see imperial soldiers at her very gates in the Low Countries. From that day began, between France and the Germanic peoples, a struggle in which the most recent wars are still episodes.

Henry VIII of England found himself wooed by both camps. In France he possessed a permanent bridgehead at Calais; it was near this city that Francis I came to meet him. Quite similar in their tastes, the two monarchs outdid each other in magnificence. The meeting was called 'The Field of the Cloth of Gold', because the tents of the King of France were woven of gold thread. 'When they were pitched in the sunlight, they were a handsome thing to see.' The King of England had caused an actual house to be built for him, 'all of wood and of glass', before which three fountains poured forth hippocras, wine and water. The kings 'came to greet each other on horseback and treated each other with great kindness'. But confidence was none too hearty, and when Francis I, the lover of dangerous gestures, paid a visit to the King of England without his guard, his gentlemen remonstrated with him: 'My master, you are mad to have done what you have done . . .' Nevertheless, Cardinal Wolsey, who had been offered the papal tiara by Charles V were he to betray Francis I, secretly arranged for a second meeting, this time between his master and the King of Spain. The King? The Emperor? Henry VIII, having weighed matters carefully, chose the Emperor for his ally, because the latter was the master of Flanders and the English merchants demanded that he do so. Now sometimes commercial counsel is bad diplomatic counsel. In sacrificing France, England destroyed the balance of power to the advantage of Charles V. She was one day to regret it.

Francis I decided to attack. Charles V was having trouble in Spain and in Germany. The moment might be propitious. This aggressive move delighted Charles V, who knew himself to be the stronger: 'Oh! The King of France wants to make me greater than I am? In a short while, either I shall be a very poor emperor or he will be a poor king of France!' All Europe turned against Francis I: Henry VIII, the Pope, the Venetians. Even the Constable of the Kingdom of France, Charles de Bourbon, went over to the enemy, galled because the crown had contested one of his legacies. Under such conditions, it had become folly to cross the Alps. Francis I did it, with his rash courage, and suffered a total disaster at Pavia. The army was destroyed, the King was made prisoner. To his mother, Louise of Savoy, he wrote: 'Madame, of everything there remain to me only honour and life, which are unscathed.' Among the verses which he composed during his captivity, the following fine line is to be found: 'The body conquered, the heart remains the victor.' The knightly tradition remained perennial in France.

The King taken prisoner . . . A dreadful peril, had France been divided. But then was it seen how greatly she had become aware of her unity since the days of John II, the Good. The Regent, Louise of Savoy, worthy of respect, received the respect she deserved. There were no conspiracies, no turbulent States General. The only opposition came from the *Parlement* of Paris, which began to shift its judicial power into political power by virtue of this captivity. France displayed dignity in her misfortune. And this saved her. Unsuccessful in provoking strife within France, Charles V began to find his prisoner a burden. He hoped to force a shameful settlement upon him: Normandy and Guienne should revert to England; to Spain would go all the heritage of Charles the Bold; to the traitorous Constable of Bourbon would go Dauphiné and Provence. Francis refused, grew ill with listlessness, hoped to die:

> Seeing that to gain one good I die with longing,
> That good being death, which I esteem as living. . . .

Charles V took alarm. If the King died, someone else would succeed him. What purpose would it serve to possess a corpse? Marguerite, a devoted sister, rushed to her brother's bedside, had Masses said there, received Communion with him, restored hope to him, and saved him. Already fortune's wheel was turning. Henry VIII, who began to find Spain too powerful, accepted two million from Louise of Savoy in return for abandoning his ally. In this bargain there had been a gratuity for Cardinal Wolsey, who found in this new betrayal both personal advantage and the means to continue his balance of power policy. Francis I, seeing that escape was impossible, decided to yield on the subject of Burgundy, fully resolved not to keep his word. He informed his counsellors that he would hold as null and void the oath he would be obliged to take under duress. Nevertheless, he agreed to hand over his two sons as hostages in order to guarantee the fulfilment of the treaty. Thus did he sacrifice them to the welfare of the kingdom. When he reached home and the agreement was made public, indignation against Charles V was general. The Pope declared null and void a treaty which made the King of Spain master of Christendom. In France, the Estates of Burgundy emphatically stated that the King had no right to alienate without their consent a province of the kingdom. Personal feudalism had come to an end. The Lord of the Royal Domain was henceforward to give way to the King of France and such, indeed, was the King of France's desire.

The break between France and the Empire marked the end of any policy of Catholic and Christian unity. In order to destroy the House of Austria, Francis I could no longer quibble over the opponents he might incite against the Empire. To the north-south, Flanders-Spain, pincers, there must correspond east-west pincers, and France must find an ally in eastern Europe. On the very evening of the battle of Pavia, Francis I had sent a secret messenger to Suleiman the Magnificent. Later an Ottoman admiral came to Paris as an ambassador. Politics was carrying the day over ideology, and even over the Faith, but could France allow herself to be overwhelmed? Like her, Hungary and Bohemia seemed to prefer the Turk to the Austrian. Italy was in rebellion against Spanish tyranny. The Pope begged for French protection. Charles V had the Constable of Bourbon attack Rome, the latter meeting his death in the assault upon the walls. 'The stones of Christendom are rising up against Your Majesty', one Spaniard dared write to Charles V. In 1529, Louise of Savoy, an excellent trader, succeeded in arranging with the Archduchess Marguerite, the Emperor's aunt and the governor of the Low Countries, the Peace of Cambrai, called 'the Ladies Peace'. The King's sons were returned to their father after payment of a ransom of two million gold *écus*; they reported that they had been very badly treated in Spain, and the King's resentfulness grew even greater. However, one clause in the Treaty of Cambrai was to make Francis I the brother-in-law of Charles V. The Emperor had an older sister, Eleanor of Austria, widow of the King of Portugal and thirty-two years old. She was given orders to marry Francis I. This tractable, self-effacing and virtuous princess spent seventeen years at the court of France, completely unnoticed. When she was widowed for the second time, she went back to live near Charles V.

Never was France's foreign policy more confused. Contradictory elements criss-crossed each other. On the one hand there was the duel between France and Austria. In order to win against the Emperor, France needed the Turks and the Protestant princes of Germany. But through this alliance with heretics, the most Christian King laid himself open to the discontent of his people. In France, public sentiment, especially in Paris, was inimical to the reformers. We shall see later that the King, and especially his sister Marguerite, would have wished to grant Protestants broad toleration, partly through natural kindliness and partly because the new alliances required it. But the country did not follow them along this path. Hence internal policy pushed Francis I towards Catholic Spain whereas foreign policy made him oppose the House of Austria. From this arose a series of realistic compromises. The marriage of the Dauphin, Henry of France (later Henry II), to a relative of the Pope's, the daughter of Florentine bankers, Catherine de' Medici, showed that Francis I was anxious to maintain ties with Catholic Italy. In this he did not succeed; Spain became mistress of the peninsula, and the Jesuits made the free spirit of the Italian Renaissance subject to their harsh discipline. France's Italian venture had ended only by splitting Christendom. When Francis I died in 1547, every clear-seeing mind realized that the genuine French problem was not Italian but German.

The new king, Henry II, had the wit to be aware of this. This man who, through an accident, reigned only a short time, was one of France's greatest kings. Cold, clear-witted, silent, he had a secret hatred of Spain based upon recollections of his captivity in Madrid. He detested Charles V. 'He wished him all the ill that any man can wish the bitterest of his enemies.' But he fought him adroitly. Henry's policy was: to give up the dream of Italian conquest; to concentrate his efforts in the north-east and there to fortify the country's frontiers; and to sign a lasting peace. In order to fulfil this great and wise plan, he took his friends wherever he might find them. In England he sought support from the Catholics, who still had influence, and married his eldest son, Francis, heir to the throne, to Mary Stuart, the child Queen of Scotland. This he did to prevent a Scottish-English reunion. In Germany, he relied upon the Protestant princes. Charles V would have liked to transform the elective Empire into a hereditary monarchy, which would have meant the unification of Germany. Henry II strove in the defence of 'Germanic liberties', which meant a divided Germany. 'Underhandedly to keep Germany's business as troubled as it could be' was his programme. It would be that of Richelieu and of Poincaré. He clearly saw that France's essential interests lay along the Rhine, and that before everything else a solution must be found for the age-old question of Lotharingia.

The German princes helped him to find it. Charles V's authoritarianism annoyed them. They offered the King of France 'the three bishoprics':

Metz, Toul and Verdun (provisionally) if he were willing to support them. Here was security guaranteed for the French frontier. Henry II agreed, but when he sought to move forward as far as the Rhine and 'make his horses drink in that river', the Germans who had summoned him turned against him. Francis de Guise, besieged at Metz, saved that town and there founded his reputation as a hero. Charles V, held in check, ill, worn away by the gout, abdicated in 1555. He suffered so grievously from his various maladies that he could no longer even open a letter. He would have wished to bequeath the Empire to his son Philip II, but the German princes no longer wished to be involved in Spanish quarrels. Charles had to cause his brother Ferdinand to be elected emperor and, at a solemn abdication ceremony in Brussels, transferred the remainder of his estates to his son Philip. Thus, by a long-pondered and dramatic act, the all-powerful emperor despoiled himself and then retired to a monastery. His departure calmed private hatreds. Henry II had no reason to fight Philip of Spain and the condition of the French exchequer called for peace. Nevertheless, Francis de Guise, strengthened by his prestige as a national hero, was determined once again to undertake the conquest of Italy. The King was weak enough to agree to this, and the expedition proved disastrous. The army sent to Italy was crushed, and France was invaded from all directions – in the north by the Spaniards and the English and in the east by Savoy. But Henry II proved himself firm in misfortune. Even though Philip II had captured Saint-Quentin and the Spaniards were at Noyon, the King refused to evacuate Paris: 'It remains for us to be stout-hearted and to be astonished at nothing', he said. Francis de Guise, who had sinned through rashness, redeemed himself by being bold. Hastily returning from Italy, he took command of a small army at Compiègne and, attacked at every hand, he himself attacked. The enemy was threatening Noyon; Guise, temporarily leaving the capital unprotected, marched on Calais and took that city by surprise. It seemed a miracle. When Henry II and the Duke of Guise came back together from Calais, Paris gave them a vociferous welcome. Then the bargaining began.

This was one of those moments when, after weary campaigns, the adversaries desired peace at any price. In England, Elizabeth had just succeeded Mary Tudor, the passionately loving wife of Philip II. Hence England cut herself off from Spain, and Spain ceased supporting Elizabeth in the Calais business. Henry II asked only to keep the three bishoprics, Metz, Toul and Verdun, cities securing the French border.

The Emperor Ferdinand yielded; his peoples would not have supported him, and he had the Turks on his hands. Philip II was willing to give up Saint-Quentin provided that France would forswear all claims on Italy and Savoy. In order to save face, Savoy and Piedmont were given as a dowry to Marguerite of France, sister to Henry II, an old maid of thirty-six who married Emmanuel, Duke of Savoy, while Philip II took to wife Henry II's eldest daughter. Elizabeth of France had been betrothed to Philip II's own son, Don Carlos, but the King of Spain, having become a widower, reserved this child for himself (she was then fourteen). Such was the Treaty of Cateau-Cambrésis (1559).

This treaty was one of those which created modern France. It took much courage for the King to sign it. The soldiers were furious: 'Within an hour and by a stroke of the pen to yield and sully everything, and to blacken all our fine past victories with three or four drops of ink – this was to vex our spirits and to bedevil our souls', said Vieilleville. But the prudent gave their endorsement. At last France was resolutely turning her back on Italy, where she had no business and where she would always be regarded as a conqueror, an invader, an occupier and worthy of detestation; and she was holding fast to Metz, Toul and Verdun, which were so often to save her very existence. What was more, she was recapturing Calais, which, in English hands, had been a lasting threat. Indeed, it was an excellent treaty, and the French never lost by it. Great festivities took place in Paris to celebrate both the peace and the weddings of the two princesses. These festivities began with joyful magnificence. But Henry II, who was an athlete, wished to take part in a tournament and was mortally wounded by the spear of Montgomery, 'a tall and sturdy young man', son of Monsieur de Lorges, Captain of the Guards. The shaft pierced the King's eyeball and entered into his skull. For nine days the King remained in a coma, and died without having regained consciousness, in the flower of his years and his mind, at the age of forty-one. Here was a heavy loss for France, because the King, having made peace abroad, would have been able to turn his attention towards internal affairs which were becoming troublesome. And he left behind him only youthful sons[1] and a foreign widow, Catherine de' Medici.

[1] The new king, Francis II, was fifteen. The Duke of Orleans (later Charles IX) was nine; the Duke of Anjou (later Henry III) was seven; the Duke of Alençon was an infant of five. The youngest of the five daughters, Marguerite of Valois, was six when she lost her father. She was later to be the wife of Henry IV, 'Queen Margot'.

CHAPTER IV

HOW THE FRENCH LIVED AND THOUGHT IN THE DAYS OF FRANCIS I AND HENRY II

THE men of the Renaissance seemed to be saying: 'Our kingdom is of this world.' They liked luxury, the beauty of jewels, of fabrics, of dress, of palaces, of gardens and of women. Their world seemed to them huge and marvellous, and life was 'spacious'. These were the days of the great voyages of discovery, and the Normans of Dieppe together with the Bretons of Saint-Malo showed themselves as bold in this as the mariners of Cadiz or of Lisbon. The French explorers had reached Newfoundland and Guinea; Jacques Cartier had discovered Canada. In France, even commerce became an adventure, above all in the provinces close to Italy and to Flanders. In 1531 at Lyons the first exchange was opened; capitalists speculated, arbitrated, absorbed the savings of the lesser fry. Spain, swollen with precious metals, imported French goods for gold. This new wealth, these opportunities ready at hand, these virgin continents, awakened prodigious energy and curiosity. The French in those days were impatient of all rule, were sure of themselves, proud of their young king, who seemed the very embodiment of the Renaissance. Vigorous, sensual, generous, cultivated, Francis I lent the 'most illustrious' crown of France a brilliance it had not possessed since Charlemagne and Saint Louis. His mother, Louise of Savoy, called him, 'my son, my emperor . . .' Had not the Empire been transmitted by the Romans to the Byzantines, and by the Byzantines to the Franks? It even seemed that his subjects prided themselves on having in him an absolute master. A French poet addressed himself to Henry VIII of England with scorn:

> For obeyed thou art not in good array,
> As is the noble king of France,
> Who is under the sufferance neither of people, silver, nor gold.
> An emperor is he, not a regent alone,
> For he reigns over the earth and they that dwell thereon.

In those days the King's court was France's well-spring of ideas, fashions and arts. It followed the King wherever he went. It consisted of a train of twelve thousand horses, of tents, of baggage, of tapestries, of gold and silver plate. The capital was wherever the King might be. Better than his city of Paris, Francis loved his castles along the Loire. Everywhere he wanted to have near him not only his counsellors, but 'his Household', his 'company', his mistresses, and his sister Marguerite, his faithful confidante. 'A court without ladies is a springtime without roses', he said. We must picture in our mind's eye, at Chambord or at Fontainebleau, those unending revels, the beauty of the costumes, men clad in cloth-of-gold doublets, silken tights, feathered caps; the King in silver cloth; music, games, schemes of love. Manners and minds were free. Gallantry which carried an overture of sport had taken the place of solemn courtesy. The court was hospitable to poets and artists. Louis XI had thought that 'knowledge makes for melancholy'; Francis I had an unbounded curiosity and was a 'lover of good literature and learned men' to whom he took pleasure in supplying subjects on which to sharpen their wits. 'Whoever chanced to come was received, but he must needs not be a fool or stumbler',[1] for the King's table was a true school, at which all subjects were discussed, from warfare to painting, and the King was as much skilled in one as in the other.

Nothing could be more interesting than to examine, in Benvenuto Cellini's autobiography, the relationship between the Italian sculptor and the King of France. The two men treated each other as equals. The King was eager to keep Cellini at his court, since the artist created marvels for his delight. For this, the King put up with a great deal. There was no budget or limit set to expenditure. Francis I showered the kingdom's reserves of gold and silver upon artists exactly as he saw fit. In Paris, Cellini led a wild life, driving the King's tenants out of the Petit-Nesle, in his studio unmercifully beating naked young women who were at once his models and his mistresses, and heaping abuse on the judges of the Châtelet. But he got off scot free through the King's favour until the moment when he fell out with the Duchess of Étampes, Francis's favourite. There lay the boundary of forgiveness. In the sixteenth century, art had the upper hand over morals, but not over pleasure. When it came to religion, the age was so full of inconsistency that Marguerite, a virtuous and believing princess, could write licentious stories in the *Heptameron*, and the King, as he left his mistress's arms, could proceed to a chapel to pray. The men and women of the Renaissance had so much animal violence that the scruples of their minds never put a check on the motions of their bodies. They were good Catholics, but they did not go abroad

[1] BRANTÔME.

without a dagger in their belts. The marriage of Henry II to Catherine de' Medici was to introduce into France the intrigues of the Italian courts, unpunished murders, mysterious duels, poisoned gloves; and the consequent mixture of the *condottiere* and the knight was to produce strange fruit.

Catherine de' Medici — ten years sterile, thereafter for ever pregnant — long played a background part at a court which dismissed her father as a 'Florentine pill vendor'. Her husband the Dauphin (later Henry II) had since 1536 passionately loved a widow, the *Grande Sénéchale*, Diane de Poitiers, eighteen years older than he. Cold and ambitious, she had taken Diana's crescent moon as her emblem and had had herself painted as the lunar goddess trampling Eros underfoot, with the device: *Omnium victorem vici* (I have conquered the conqueror of all). In Rouen Cathedral she had erected a splendid monument to her husband the *Grand Sénéchal* and — a widow beyond reproach — always publicly appeared clad in black and white. This did not prevent her from having herself carved in the likeness of Diana with her stag by Jean Goujon, who knew how to make the most of her long legs, her high breasts, and her small head, nor did it stand in the way of her accepting from the King castles and even crown jewels. Henry II took her everywhere with him on his travels and wrote her ardent letters: 'I cannot live without you . . . I beg you to have in remembrance him who has served but one God and one love . . .' Catherine suffered over this passion, but with skilful obstinacy insisted that 'as for Madame de Valentinois everything was as it should be'. Henry's romantic attachment to Diane (whom he had created Duchess of Valentinois) lasted for twenty-three years, in fact until death. In 1558 he wrote her: 'I beg you always to keep in memory him who has never loved, nor shall love, other than you; I beg you, my darling, to wear this ring for love of me . . .' That same year, 1558, Henry II had passed his fortieth birthday. Artemis, a grandmother, was fifty-nine, but she remained in his mind the triumphant victory of Jean Goujon, glory of the Château of Écouen, the threefold Grace whom it had pleased him to have adorn the stairway at Blois. Catherine, despite her pretences, had not been taken in. Scarcely had Montgomery dealt the mortal blow to his sovereign when Catherine, from Henry's very bedside, sent Diane packing. 'The dying King belongs to the Queen', and the Duchess of Valentinois was ordered to 'withdraw to her town mansion, return the crown jewels at once and give back a thousand gifts of which the Queen has kept careful record'.

Catherine de' Medici was as ugly as Diane was beautiful, but she had the Medici taste and in her protection of artists continued the tradition of Francis I. She held revels, gave magnificent concerts, and gathered treasures about her (which today are in the Louvre, the property of the French people). Tapestries, Limoges enamels, jewellery, rare books, the earthenware of Bernard Palissy display a happy alliance between French and Italian art. The respective roles of these two influences in French sixteenth-century art constitute a highly controversial problem among historians and connoisseurs. It seems that the court and the Italian artists it summoned to its service clashed with the French master masons and artisans, who naturally preferred what they knew best how to do. The French simplified Italian ornament, imposing upon it their own sense of measure, but they added to their traditional façades now an exterior stairway, now an open hallway in the Italian manner. Even more than the Italians, they studied the ancients and read Vitruvius's treatises on architecture. Thus this artistic revolution 'was above all a restoration'. Pierre Lescot's Louvre is a fine specimen of classic art. Jean Goujon's nymphs hark back, beyond the mystical and unreal forms of the Middle Ages, to the rational beauty of ancient statues. And we should likewise note that the areas of France affected by the new style were of small extent. Paris was so affected, as well as the valley of the Loire, because it was the region of the royal residences. Lyons, likewise, because the court was frequently there, and Rouen because Cardinal Georges introduced the new fashion in architecture; but at Tours the studios of Fouquet and Colombe continued the pure French tradition, and the portrait artists of the Valois court have left us pencil drawings of a purity and simplicity all their own.

In literature, at the beginning of the century, charming Clément Marot remained closely allied to Villon. His quick, light style, his ease, his skill at turning an epigram and at sharpening its final thrust begin a whole lineage of French writers, among them La Fontaine and de Musset. Thoroughly characteristic of his day by virtue of his mixture of mocking elegance and religion, Marot translated the Psalms into French and was persecuted as a Protestant by the Sorbonne. Thereupon, fearing that he would be jailed, he took refuge in Geneva, where he found intolerance in the opposite direction. Again he had to flee and died at Turin, in poverty and obscurity. It is not easy to be a free spirit during a time of fanaticism: you find yourself, as Montaigne put it, 'flayed by all hands, Ghibelline by the Guelphs, Guelph by the Ghibellines'. After Marot, a return to the forms and the vocabulary of antiquity as well as imitation of Petrarch won over the French poets. But it is wonderful to see the advantage they drew from these foreign contributions for the 'defence and illustration of the French language'. The treatise bearing this title, which appeared in 1549, was written by Joachim du Bellay, but under the inspiration of Ronsard and his friends in the Pléiade. Its author explains why French and not Latin must be used, and how the French language can — and should be — enriched through recourse to the technical vocabularies of all kinds of workmen and mechanics, such as mariners, metal casters, painters, engravers and others; through making use of the good writers, meaning the Greek and the Latin; and by reviving the 'great forms' of antiquity, meaning odes, epistles and satires. An imitative art might have been dangerous without the prodigious vitality of the period, but the French tongue then possessed a freshness, a wealth of invention, a freedom in the use of words which it would never recapture. It assimilated much more than it imitated.

In prose Rabelais was the author who dominated the age (Montaigne, Montluc and Brantôme came later). This was the case because he wholly represented it. Like his age, he was drunk with knowledge, with new words, with reading. Excessively fond of quotations, of compilations, of dissertations, he was so passionate a lover of words that he composed lists of epithets several pages long for the sheer joy of arranging them in sequence and translated into every known language the sayings of his Limoges schoolboy. A Christian? Surely, but ready to laugh at monks and without the slightest taste for martyrdom, physican as much as canon, and more so. Immoral? No, but indecent, after the wanton, crude and in no sense lascivious fashion of medical students. Moreover, he knew his age completely, and, as was the case later with Balzac, was curious about everything. Nothing is more admirable than a writer who is a skilled technician of all the techniques. He was able to poke spirited fun at judges, sophists and soldiers because he had studied law, scholasticism and war — a Molière before Molière, a Swift before Swift. Finally, Rabelais expresses his age's philosophy: a predisposition to cheerfulness. 'Pantagruelism' is at once moral hygiene, a desire for justice, a contempt for the things about which we busy ourselves, a brotherly sympathy for human affairs and an awareness of their vanity. Here is no exalted rule of life, and the Abbey of Thélème is neither La Trappe nor Clairvaux, but it is a healthy rule, although one far too reasonable to have had a great influence on his times.

Like all reformers, Rabelais had ideas on education. Those he made Ponocrates implant in Gargantua were above all scientific. He was horrified by pedants and 'hangmen of youth', by those 'colleges of filth' which he thought should be consigned to the flames. Pierre de la Ramée (Ramus) agreed with Rabelais on the idleness of an instruction which teaches only how to argue according to the rules of Aristotle's logic, in which the sole purpose of the student is to prove that he is right even when he knows he is wrong, to hang on to the ball when it is in his hands and to grab it if it is in the hands of another. Rabelais, in Gargantua's schooling, portrays a solemn doctor of theology making his pupil more and more stupid by having him recite backwards for thirteen years, six months and two weeks, the worst of the medieval manuals. It was partly to reform such curricula that Francis I furthered the creation of a body of royal lecturers who would teach, besides Greek and Latin, Hebrew and Arabic. The humanists were not by any means revolutionaries in philosophy or theology; they were learned men who urged sound methods in the teaching of grammar and literature. But sound methods sometimes lead minds further than one would have thought, and certain of the humanists would be drawn, through their studies, closer to the reformed Churches. Hence, to complete the picture, we must examine the part played by the Reformation in France.

CHAPTER V

HOW THE REFORMATION IN FRANCE
BECAME A POLITICAL PARTY

THE Reformation did not begin in France with an open struggle between the Catholic and Protestant faiths. Heresies had more than once divided the Roman Catholic Church; reformers had often called upon her to cleanse herself, but those very reformers held in respect the principle which the Church represented. During the thirteenth century, great teachers like Saint Thomas had achieved the synthesis of Catholicism and Aristotelianism and had thus set the best minds of the day at rest. In the universities, fear of the Inquisition had sufficed to preserve doctrinal unity. Disaffection was rather to be found among the populace. The ultimate failure of the Crusades had led many an honest fellow to ask whether Mohammed were not mightier than Christ. The Black Death had cast doubts on the goodness of God. The Church's economic power had aroused great jealousy among lords and sovereigns, who bore it ill that the Pope should have so many temporal goods at his disposal, as well as among the lower clergy, who felt that the bishops and abbots were too grasping. The Church's political power was irksome the moment national States began to take shape, since that power insisted upon its own law courts and supervision of its own budget, thus functioning as a State within the State. In France the effects of this national insurgence had been obvious from the days when Philip the Fair had constrained the will of Pope Boniface VIII. The higher clergy had turned this feeling to its own ends and had thus preserved clerical privileges by transferring them to the use of the French Church alone through the Pragmatic Sanction of Bourges in 1438. Whereupon the State, in the person of Francis I, had intervened, and the 1516 concordat had taken the place of the Pragmatic Sanction, but this economic solution, favourable to the King and to his Treasury, had not solved the spiritual problem.

And yet in the early sixteenth century this problem was serious. The latent paganism of the Italian Renaissance had infected even the Papacy itself; a pope like Alexander VI (Borgia) was not respected because he was unworthy of respect; the sale of indulgences and the base superstitions inculcated by the monks offended religious souls. The humanists, who knew Greek and Hebrew, were no longer satisfied with the Vulgate, read the Scriptures in the most authentic available texts, and scorned the authority of ignorant clergymen. The French (or Gallican) Church was becoming reformist, many of its bishops being cultivated and tolerant men. From their reading of the Bible there emerged a religion rather different from what the rest of Catholicism had become. In the Gospels they found Christ and His divine charity, but not rites and devotions, Purgatory or the worship of the saints. Salvation, the Christian's only principal concern, was not, in what they found there, dependent upon practices based upon custom. As early as 1508 – nine years before Luther (1517) – an aged professor of the University of Paris, Jacques Lefèvre of Étaples, published an appeal for the reading of the original texts: 'It is for having abandoned them that the monasteries are wasted away, that piety is dead, and that men prefer the good things of this world to those of heaven.' With the greatest audacity Faber Stapulensis (as he latinized his name) taught salvation through faith and not through works, the exclusive authority of the scriptures, the symbolic nature of the Mass. He reprehended prayers in Latin, the celibacy of the priesthood and the veneration of the saints. 'Six years before Luther,' said Michelet, 'the venerable Lefèvre of Étaples was teaching Lutheranism in Paris.' Lefèvre was even bold enough to publish the Bible in French.

On October 31st, 1517, the German monk, Martin Luther, nailed his ninety-five theses on the door of the castle church in Wittenberg. In them he asserted that faith alone saves, that pilgrimages, the recitation of the rosary, the lighting of candles and the worship of relics turned men away from true faith. Gradually he became more and more violent, for he was by nature intemperate, and he proclaimed that Rome was Babylon and the Pope Antichrist; here was no longer a reform but a break, and in 1520 he was excommunicated. Thenceforth, Lefèvre of Étaples would have been in great danger had not King Francis I and, above all, his sister Marguerite, Duchess of Alençon, protected him. Marguerite had taken as her adviser and spiritual director a liberal prelate, Briçonnet, Bishop of Meaux. Neither Briçonnet nor Marguerite had any thought of opposing a new religion to Catholicism; they sought, rather, within the bosom of this faith, the best means to enter into mystical intercourse with God by means of prayer. Both passed through crises of scruples and doubt. It had been Briçonnet's wish to assemble around him in Meaux the boldest minds of the Church; he chose Lefèvre of Étaples as his vicar general in spiritual matters and made his bishopric one of the French centres of the new reforming doctrine. Through affection for his sister, Francis I shielded Lefèvre, whom he called his 'bonhomme Fabri'. 'The whole French court, attentive only to fashion, to the last novelty in literature, to the pleasure of understanding the Scriptures or of singing the Psalms in French, came very close to being Lutheran without knowing it.'[1] But Luther's condemnation came like a thunderclap. The Sorbonne in its turn became greatly zealous, condemned Lefèvre of Étaples; the stage was set for a shift from erudition to inquisition, from the pulpit to the stake.

From 1525 on, the King's bondage at Pavia made his patronage less effective. The Regent, Louise of Savoy, felt weak and did not dare withstand the Pope and the Sorbonne on matters of dogma. The debate grew more and more bitter. At the outset only humanism and mysticism had been at issue, but now men began to speak of a 'so-called reformed' religion. In her efforts to maintain order despite the affliction of a kingless kingdom, the Regent needed the Church's support and so she countenanced a policy of harshness. Even Bishop Briçonnet became alarmed. Almost every reformer sets in motion forces which later he no longer can control: in the diocese of Meaux, poor people, fullers, weavers, smashed statues of the Virgin, or tore down public announcements of indulgences. By order of the *Parlement*, they were whipped, branded, a few of them burned alive. Briçonnet was intimidated and withdrew his earlier episcopal instructions, now affirming the existence of Purgatory and asserting that men must 'call upon the name of the Most Holy Virgin and all the other Blessed'. When Marguerite journeyed to nurse her prisoner brother in Madrid, she obtained from him with high courage — perhaps because she had less to fear — a letter shielding at least 'bonhomme Fabri', but the *Parlement* continued to cause heretics to be burned to death.

The return of Francis I was to determine the direction in which France would go in religion. Torn between his sister, a Catholic but of evangelical tendency who appealed to the King's natural kindliness, and the *Parlement* which invoked reasons of State, for several years Francis vacillated between indulgence and harshness. Moderate reformers of Briçonnet's variety were no longer a problem for they had 'renounced their errors'; those who remained to be dealt with were of a violent nature, indulging

[1] SAINTE-BEUVE.

in absurd and sacrilegious acts. Some persons advised the King to pro-claim himself head of an independent Gallican Church: Henry VIII and the German princes offered him their support provided he determined on this course of action. But he did not think that such should be the role of the most Christian King, the descendant of Saint Louis. Through the marriage of his son into the Medici family, he gave a pledge to the Papacy and to orthodoxy. Yet after this marriage, Marguerite under-took to win over the Dauphin's wife, and there was hope for a new age of tolerance. Partisan asperity disheartened the King. Both sides plastered the walls with pamphlets; one day the King found one affixed to his own door: *True specifications on the horrible abuses of the Papal Mass*. He was appalled by this direct attack on the most holy of mysteries. This was no longer reform but pure and simple heresy. The King with-drew his protection, and everywhere fires began to lick at their victims. Human cruelty is cunning: martyrs were roasted over slow fires to make them suffer the longer; the King himself agreed to take part in a pro-cession around the stakes. The heretics' property was seized and informers were given their reward. From 1538 on, utterly discouraged by the fana-ticism of his subjects, the King resolutely espoused the Catholic, which also meant the Spanish, party.

Whenever moderate conservatism clashes with revolutionary fanaticism, it is transformed into reaction, through a mixture of fear and scorn. And all reaction is cruel. In certain villages of the Durance, Waldensian schismatics had survived the persecutions of the Middle Ages, still read the Scriptures, repudiated the Mass, the Pope and Purgatory. Attracted by a similarity of doctrine, they linked themselves to the new Protestants. In 1545 the *Parlement* decided that two villages convicted of heresy, Cabrières and Mérindol, were to be razed to the ground and their inhabi-tants burned or banished. Francis I several times refused to sanction this bloodthirsty and stupid edict. But at last in 1545, ill and befuddled, he allowed himself to be persuaded to give his signature. The Baron d'Oppède, Lieutenant-General of Provence, had twenty-four villages put to the flames and their inhabitants slaughtered; nine hundred houses were burned and three thousand people put to death. On his deathbed, Francis I begged his son 'not to postpone the punishment of those who, under his name and authority, had done this harsh and scandalous deed'. But the guilty were never brought to justice. In 1543 the Sorbonne forced all its members to sign 'articles of faith'. Those who refused were sent to the stake. The name of Étienne Dolet, a great humanist and friend of the King, condemned as an atheist because he had published a translation of Plato, is the saddest symbol of this abdication of the mind. Such were the depths to which had sunk the great rebirth of letters! *'Non dolet ipse Dolet, sed pia turba dolet'*, he remarked on his way to execution.[1] And this crowd, so piously criminal, was for many long years to suffer and to cause suffering.

Francis I and the 'flower of the Marguerites' had, to the extent of their power, put a check on intolerance. Henry II, of a more sombre temperament, was frightened by the spread of the Lutheran movement. Mysterious gatherings were taking place even within the city of Paris; ladies of quality and university professors took part in them despite the risk of execution. The economic situation favoured this intellectual revolt, since the abundant supply of precious metals drawn from Spain's new colonies caused a greater and greater increase in prices. During a period of rising prices, although the country may be prosperous, workers with fixed wages and owners of farm land under lease find themselves embarrassed, which gives rise to a twofold discontent on the part of the proletariat and the aristocracy. Now economics have their spiritual repercussions; discontented man is receptive to heresy. Anxious, Henry II in 1549 established a 'Burning Court' within the *Parlement* of Paris which was instructed to make inquiry against heresy, now become a 'common plague'. The decree was far-reaching: a third of a heretic's possessions went to those who informed against him (which put a bounty onslander); it was forbidden to sell or to own heretical books (which set a bounty on intolerance); every heretic was subject to the death penalty (which set a bounty on cruelty); and finally the bench was to be purged — that matchless weapon in the arsenal of tyranny. For the judges themselves had been tainted with the new ideas. The criminal chamber of the *Parlement* was no longer bringing convictions. Princes of the blood — Navarre, Bourbon, Condé — members of the Coligny, Châtillon, Andelot families had been won over. In 1559, during a solemn session of the *Parlement*, brave judges declared that no one could deny the existence of grave abuses in the Church. Henry II, enraged at discovering judges 'gone astray from the Faith', stated that he would 'go watch them burning with his own two eyes'. But into those eyes was to plunge Montgomery's lance, depriving him of this comforting spectacle.

Prior to this the heretics had merely been Catholic reformers; for an

---

[1] A Latin play on words: 'Dolet himself sorrows not, but the pious crowd metes out suffering.'

open rebellion, a doctrine and an organization were needed; Calvin supplied the former and, even more, the latter. Before allowing themselves to be won over by a new theology, the French would have insisted that it possess clarity, and Calvin urged upon them a doctrine as French as Luther's had been German. His father was an attorney in Noyon. In 1536 the son published his *Christian Institutes* and in that same year reached Geneva, a liberal imperial city which had adopted the Reformation together with its confederate towns, Fribourg and Berne (in German the word for confederate is *Eidgenossen*, whence comes the term Huguenot). In Geneva, Lutheranism had won over the majority and had at once begun persecuting the Catholics: beliefs change, but the passions dwell eternal. So Geneva became the asylum for reforming Frenchmen, Calvin among them. In time he graduated from being a refugee to being a minister of the Gospel, and then became the power behind the throne of a theocratic government. Luther rendered unto Caesar that which was Caesar's; Calvin sought to blend Caesar and Christ into one. He turned his Protestantism (or Presbyterianism) into a new Catholicism. Seemingly this theocratic government was democratic, since pastors and elders were elected, but in fact the election was not free. A Consistory, which amounted to a private inquisition, spied on every citizen; above the Consistory stood the Colloquy, and then, at the top, the Synod. The Consistory concerned itself with the reform of men's customs and even with censuring households; the Bible was the law, and Geneva's judges applied the Mosaic code. From that city Huguenot propaganda spread throughout France, and it has been aptly remarked that Geneva's role during the sixteenth century, as a source of example and encouragement, was analogous to that of Moscow for communists the world over during the twentieth.[1]

Calvin's tenets were harsh. Man was damned by the fall of Adam; the old Adam lives again in each of us and arouses within us our vices and our crimes. Jesus crucified has redeemed, not all men, but those who by their faith crucify within themselves the old Adam. To have this faith, however, grace is necessary. Every man is predestined either to salvation or to damnation, and he cannot redeem himself through works; on the contrary, good works are the proof that he already possesses grace. The worldly effect of this dogma is paradoxical: a Calvinist constantly tends to fall back on a life of action, for indeed why should he meditate on his own soul since he can do nothing to change God's judgment? But he

[1] J. E. NEALE.

can, by achieving success, prove to himself that he is one of the elect. This strangely practical aspect of Calvinism pleased a portion of the French middle class; and to Calvinism likewise were attracted men of cultivation: professors, doctors and lawyers; the lower clergy and the friars; and a section of the nobility which, stripped of its benefices by the 1516 concordat and full of resentment against Rome, constituted the 'assault troops' of the Huguenot movement. The new faith grew especially strong in Lyons, where there existed a traditional bond with Geneva, in Normandy, Languedoc and the valley of the Rhône. Paris to a large extent remained Catholic. Since a military organization matched the religious, the Huguenot party soon became a State within the State, and we can understand why the kings of France were worried.

For centuries these sovereigns had struggled to prevent the Catholic Church from assuming too much authority within their kingdom; they had put a stop to the dreams of leadership which had inspired the great popes of the Middle Ages; they had won their way in the matter of the investitures; they had imposed first the Pragmatic Sanction, then the Concordat; and they had possessed themselves of their own lion's share of the wealth of the Church. They could not allow an aristocratic party, alleging religious reform, to attempt a political division of the kingdom. For there soon sprang up a whole school of Huguenot publicists who denied the King's absolute power; staunch 'republicans' sought in Plutarch examples of holy uprisings against tyrants. Had it found popular support, this propaganda would have been dangerous indeed for the monarchy. But unlike his fellows in Germany, the French peasant remained loyal to his traditional Catholicism. In France, Protestantism was – and to a certain extent is yet – the religion of a liberal, semi-aristocratic *élite*.

CHAPTER VI

HOW THE WARS OF RELIGION DIVIDED AND RUINED FRANCE

Heresy, a deficit, and a king not yet old enough to reign make up a dangerous mixture. The situation which Henry II left behind him was indeed explosive. The Italian wars had burdened the kingdom with debt; France's obligations amounted to forty million *livres*, borrowed at excessive interest rates. In order to pay the fixed charges it was necessary to increase the poll-tax and to offer public offices for sale — two unpopular expedients. The country needed peace and a strong hand, yet who had the power to rule? The new king, Francis II, was a child of fifteen, ailing, pimply, adenoidal. The Queen Mother, Catherine de' Medici, a large, mannish woman, conciliatory and intelligent, had brains, but the brains of a politician, not a statesman. 'God has left me with three small children and a wholly divided kingdom', she wrote to her daughter the Queen of Spain. She meant to put up the best fight she could for her sons, yet her double disadvantage of being a commoner and a foreigner compelled her to be prudent. Three parties were struggling for control: first, the Bourbons, princes of the blood who would succeed to the throne were the Valois to die out, whose leaders were Antoine de Bourbon (King of Navarre through his marriage to Jeanne d'Albret) and his brother, the Prince of Condé; next, the Guises, princes of Lorraine whose star had been rising ever since they had given a queen to Scotland (Marie de Guise), a queen to France (Mary Stuart), and a hero to the armies (Francis de Guise); lastly the Montmorency family, loyal to the crown but rivals of the Guises. Anne de Montmorency, High Constable of the Kingdom, was a Catholic but had three Huguenot nephews, among them the sober and admirable Admiral de Coligny. The Guises represented fanatical and intransigeant Catholicism. Antoine de Bourbon welcomed Huguenots at his court in Nérac because, ever since the dismissal of the Constable Bourbon, that family had withdrawn into opposition, and also because he had inherited the tolerance of his mother-in-law, Marguerite of Navarre, the 'flower of the Marguerites'.

Since the young king had married their niece, Mary Stuart, the Guises seized the reins of power; they did so by admitting the majority of young Francis II, a convenient fiction which permitted him to summon whatever councillors he might choose. The French people embraced the Guises 'with that ardour which always pushes it towards those who represent its passions of the moment'.[1] At once they became 'providential men', called by God for the defence of the Catholic religion. Francis, the soldier, was the most popular; the Cardinal of Lorraine, the real leader, was at once 'dictator, pope and king'. Antoine de Bourbon, first prince of the blood, would have had a rightful claim to the regency, but seeing that the populace was wholly captivated by the Guises, he thought it wiser to lie low. During these early days of the reign, the Huguenots would have been inclined to act as dutiful subjects, 'provided God's sovereign empire remain untouched', but the Guises and their extremist friends wanted to purge the realm of heresy. Thanks to their violence, they forced the adherents of reform into rebellion. The Guises' 'openly tyrannical manner of acting, the threats employed against the greatest men in the kingdom, the withdrawal into silence of princes and great lords, the decay of the principles of justice brought under the discretion of the principal rulers [the Guises], the resources of the realm apportioned at their order to whomsoever they pleased, as was likewise the case with all offices and benefices, in short, their violent and manifestly illegitimate government aroused wonderful hatreds against them . . . And so every man was forced to think of his own business, and many began to consult with one other in order to discover some proper remedy which would give the upper hand to the ancient and legitimate government of the kingdom'.[2]

Thus it was that the 'Huguenots by policy' joined forces with the Huguenots by religion. Every variety of malcontent, suffering persecution, decided to get rid of the Guises. There was no lack of soldiers, since the Peace of Cateau-Cambrésis had increased the number of unemployed veterans, and the theologians of Reform approved the conspiracy provided it was backed by a prince of the blood. The Bible abounded in such plots. It was agreed that armed bands would converge towards Blois and Amboise and would capture the court; the Guises, however, were warned, the scheme was uncovered and the schemers were apprehended. Frightful repressive measures followed; all the pinnacles of the castle of Amboise bore the heads of those put to death. As he was passing by, Jean d'Aubigny

[1] GABRIEL HANOTAUX.   [2] THÉODORE DE BÈZE.

remarked to his eight-year-old son, Agrippa: 'They have beheaded France, those hangmen . . . My boy, after mine, your head must not be spared in avenging those most honourable heads . . .' The result was savage hatred, passed on from generation to generation. Even Condé himself became worried when a sudden and fateful situation arose: Francis II, who was sickly and prey to a chronic inflammation of the ear, was stricken with a high fever. What a blow to the Guises! The Cardinal outdid himself with processions imploring Heaven to heal the King; the General threatened the doctors with hanging were the King to die. But death respects neither powers nor persons. Francis II breathed his last. The Guises had lost the first round.

The new king, Charles IX, was ten years old. He was a Valois through and through, weak, likeable, an aesthete and lazy. This time there must be a regency, and Catherine de' Medici secured it for herself by threatening the Guises with the Bourbons and the Bourbons with the Guises, at the same time calling upon all the parties to make peace. Feeling herself without authority, she smiled on both enemy camps. Because she failed, she is considered a knave; had she succeeded, history would have bestowed upon her the honour it accords Henry IV. In 1560, for the first time since 1484, the States General of the realm assembled at Orleans. The Chancellor, Michel de l'Hôpital, in the noblest of terms urged them to reconciliation; he pictured the advantages of a national council which might bestow upon all Frenchmen a common faith: 'Kindness will profit more than severity . . . Let us do away with those devilish names, names of party, faction and sedition – Lutherans, Huguenots, Papists; let us leave only the name Christian!' Catherine allowed Coligny, Condé and their families to practise their religion in their private homes; the Catholics and the *Parlement* reproached her for her leniency, and the Pope forbade any national council. Catherine substituted for it a 'colloquy' which took place at Poissy in 1561. The notion that a matter of faith might be settled by a public debate seems bizarre, but l'Hôpital hoped for it in all sincerity. Reasonable men have always a tendency to believe that humanity is like them, in which point of view they are not reasonable; life itself undertakes to disillusion them. The Chancellor opened the colloquy with a speech in which he pointed out that a civil war would weaken the country, that consciences cannot be forced and that the reformation of the Church would make possible the reunion of all Christians: propositions all too obvious to be effective. Théodore de Bèze defended Calvin's teachings in moderate terms; to this the Cardinal

of Lorraine replied. After several days, it was decided to appoint a committee to find a compromise. None was found and the whole business
went no further.

But Catherine did not forsake the idea of a possible reconciliation between the two forms of the Christian faith. With courageous persistence
she retained Théodore de Bèze and Coligny at court and did everything
she could to assure the Huguenots relative toleration without at the same
time over-exciting the Catholics. Her 1562 edict allowed Reformed persons to hold their meetings on the outskirts of towns and prohibited both
parties from carrying arms. Yet 'matters of principle cannot be resolved
by mediators themselves without principle'. How compromise over
eternal salvation? How agree that that which is truth on the outskirts can
be untruth in the centre of a town? Moreover, the matter was not merely
national in scope. If Catherine by some miracle had brought together
Guise and Coligny, Rome and Geneva would still have been at loggerheads. The Catholic and Protestant masses regarded all tolerance as
sinful; in Paris, the Catholic crowds set fire to the dwellings of Protestants;
in the south, the fury of the Huguenots was wreaked on Catholic churches.
The Catholic nobility, incensed, sought ways and means to get rid of
Catherine; she, taking fright, turned towards Coligny and asked him
what forces the Huguenots had at their disposal for the defence of the
monarchy. It amounted to an appeal for civil war. At heart both parties
wanted this war; some saw in it an opportunity to satisfy their hatreds,
others an excuse for pillage. Everyone was polishing up his weapons.
In March 1562 the Duke of Guise, who happened to be passing with his
men-at-arms through the town of Vassy, came upon a Huguenot
prayer meeting. In the battle which soon was raging, twenty-three of
the faithful were slain and a hundred and thirty wounded. This episode,
which the Catholics called an 'incident' and the Huguenots 'the massacre
of Vassy', was the spark that started the fire: Condé summoned the
Huguenots to battle and Guise marched upon Paris, which received him
with the cry, 'Long live Guise!' since men no longer troubled to cry,
'Long live the King!' At the Saint-Denis Gate, the Provost of the
merchants greeted Guise, calling him 'defender of the faith'. The policy
of appeasement had come to naught.

So there remained civil war. It began with strong foreign support for
both sides: Philip II of Spain spurred on and helped the Catholics,
Elizabeth of England encouraged the Huguenots. For a long time the
best men on both sides hesitated to call upon foreign troops; then passions

carried them away and Swiss, Spaniards and Germans were enlisted in the struggle. Hardened veterans terrorized the countrysides; the highways were infested with robbers, more or less under military discipline. The Frenchmen who so bitterly fought one another were men of the same nation, of the same class, often of the same family. Occasionally they remembered this with despair: 'Each man', said La Noue, 'reflected in his own heart that those whom he saw advancing were French, among whom there were some who were his relatives and friends, and that within the hour they would have to kill each other, and this made the event something horrible . . .' Well-born prisoners were decently treated: Francis de Guise shared his bed with Condé. But this kindliness was strictly limited to the leaders; the forces on the fighting front, small though they were in number, since they never consisted of more than eight to ten thousand men, plundered, slaughtered and raped with all the cheerful fury of partisans. One must read Montluc to gather any idea of the age's ferocious cynicism. Perhaps at the outset men fought for their faith; very soon indeed they were fighting for the fun of it. Catherine saw the party leaders disappear quickly enough; Antoine de Bourbon (King of Navarre and husband of Jeanne d'Albret) was killed; Montmorency and Condé, captured; Guise, assassinated by a Huguenot gentleman named Poltrot de Méré, who was quartered on the Place de Grève — a happening of bad omen for the future because the Catholics held Coligny responsible for the murder. Like all innocent men, the Admiral was unskilful in his defence. He wrote to the Queen Mother to disclaim guilt, but ended his letter thus: 'Do not think, Madame, that what I say is in any way to regret the death of Monsieur de Guise; I view it as the greatest good that could happen to this realm, and to the Church of God, and especially to myself . . .' Brantôme remarked: 'Many men were astonished how he, who was most cold and spare in speech, ever came to write such words . . .' In 1563, universal fatigue led to a sort of limping peace in the permanence of which no one believed. The Catholics felt themselves the stronger; the Huguenots retained their places of refuge like La Rochelle; and the delights of hating were twice as powerful as war weariness.

There followed a period of confusion and ferocity. War after war; the kingdom was given over to fire and the sword; men lacked bread. 'Everyone had his gang.' In Paris the Huguenots were outlawed; in Normandy, the Catholics; in the south, cathedrals and monasteries were sacked. Everywhere families split up. Fanaticism made assassination legitimate; banditry found its sanction in faith, for all men insisted that they owed obedience only to their consciences, which meant their fancies. 'Thus did the people accustom itself to disrespect for the magistracy.' As soon as parties supersede the State, and vengeance supersedes the Law, civilization is dying. Catherine turned alternately to Spain and to England; she sought to please all men, which led to her being accused of betraying all men. When she rushed to Bayonne, there to meet the Duke of Alva, at once the Huguenots feared the establishment of a Paris-Madrid axis and Coligny prepared to kidnap the King. In her turn Catherine the Mother became alarmed and the struggle began anew. Henry of Béarn, son of Antoine, the King of Navarre, and the strongminded Jeanne d'Albret, and grandson of the 'flower of the Marguerites', had become the dynastic leader of the Huguenots, whose political chieftain was Coligny. After a long series of sanguinary Catholic victories, Coligny skilfully fell back to the south, recruited new forces, marched on Paris and dominated the court. The Peace of Saint-Germain (1570) was due to the influence of a new party, the Politiques, or Catholic moderates, 'who prefer', as the true fanatics scornfully put it, 'the salvation of the kingdom to that of their souls'. The Cardinal of Lorraine and the Guises quit the court; Admiral de Coligny came back. 'This is to end things', remarked Étienne Pasquier, 'the way they should have begun.' In order to cement the peace, Catherine considered bestowing her daughter Marguerite on Henry of Navarre and her son, the Duke of Anjou, on Elizabeth of England. Two Protestant marriages! 'We now hope', she said, 'for more quiet in this country than we have had until now.'

In these hopes she was deceived. Slaughter lurked behind the wedding feast. When, in 1572, the marriage of Marguerite to Henry of Navarre had been arranged — to the great wrath and horror of the Catholics — Coligny was imprudently triumphant; he now wanted a reversal of alliances: war against Spain, friendship with England. But Elizabeth was none too eager; Catherine feared the Spanish armies and felt that France, with a Catholic majority, would resent such a policy. Above all she dreaded the influence which the Admiral, thanks to his quiet seriousness, was beginning to exercise over the young King. Charles IX was even planning campaigns with Coligny without informing his mother. Catherine lost control of herself: this Admiral was stealing her son from her and preparing to hurl France into a hopeless war. For such a woman, who had been nurtured in the Florence of poisons and hired ruffians, the natural conclusion was: 'I must rid myself of this fellow.' With the assistance of the Guises, she made the necessary preparations, and on Friday, August 22nd, a harquebus was discharged at the Admiral from the shelter of a window. He was merely wounded in the arm and said, 'See how good men are treated in France!' Still alive, wounded and a victim, in Catholic eyes Coligny became more dangerous than ever. The indignant King promised an investigation of the matter, which would surely have led to the Guises and, eventually, to the Queen Mother. Catherine made a desperate decision.

At that moment the Huguenot leaders were gathered together in Paris for the wedding of Henry of Navarre. The attack on Coligny angered them — not unreasonably — and their violent talk exasperated the chief citizens of Paris. Merchants closed their shops; the militia sharpened its pikes. 'This marriage', said the Parisians, 'will have a ruddy livery.' On August 23rd, Catherine confessed to her son the part she had played and told him that she was lost — and he as well — if they did not now drive matters to an extreme, by which she meant a slaughter of the Huguenots. Charles IX hesitated, and then, wrote Monsieur de Tavannes: 'King Charles, who was most prudent and who had always been most obedient to the Queen his mother, seeing what was afoot, suddenly resolved to join with the Queen his mother . . . and insure his person against the Huguenots by means of the Catholics, yet not without the utmost regret that he could not spare Coligny. . . .' On the twenty-fourth, at one-thirty in the morning, the alarm bells of Saint-Germain-l'Auxerrois gave the signal for the massacre. Lists had been drawn up so that no one might escape. Guise himself went to the Admiral's dwelling, and Coligny died heroically. In Paris three or four thousand Huguenots perished amid scenes of horror; in the provinces there were thousands more, particularly at Lyons and Orleans. The greatest names — La Rochefoucauld, Caumont la Force — were not spared. 'Paris looked like a conquered city', said Tavannes. 'The thirst for blood being quenched, plundering began . . . Princes and lords, gentlemen, archers, and soldiers of the Guard equally with all sorts and kinds of people mingled together, plundered, ransacked and killed in the streets. . . .' Only the princes of the blood — Henry of Navarre and Condé — escaped death, but they were held prisoner in the Louvre and 'invited to change their religion'. Abroad, Elizabeth went into mourning; Philip II sent congratulations: 'This is one of the greatest joys of my whole life . . .' In Rome, Pope Gregory XIII had a *Te Deum* sung. Orthodoxy had won the day over charity.

A massacre is no solution, especially when the decapitated body has spare heads to take the place of the old. 'The Religion' could lose five or six thousand of its leaders and still possess resolute fighters. In the south, the faithful and their pastors organized resistance. At the Milhau Assembly (1573) a full-fledged administration was set up by the Protestants. Under oath the members of the union swore to obey the States General of the Cause, a deliberative and aristocratic chamber under the control of a protector. Soon Henry of Navarre was in a position to play this part. After his pretended abjuration, he had remained at court, amusing himself with dalliance. One evening behind drawn curtains, one of his faithful followers said to him: 'Sire, is it indeed true that the spirit of God still works and dwells in you? You sigh to God on account of the absence of your friends ... But you have only tears in your eyes whereas they bear weapons in their hands. They fight your enemies while you wait upon them ... They fear only God, while you fear a woman before whom you clasp your hands at the moment they are clenching their fists; they are in the saddle, you, on your knees ...' These reproaches stung him; finally, on a 'very dark and frosty night', he fled, forswore his recantation and, in his own Béarn, rejoined that new Huguenot republic, cut off from the rest of the State, which Catherine had found confronting her immediately after the massacre.

Already Fate had struck the Queen Mother in her son. Since Saint Bartholomew's Day, Charles IX had seemed overwhelmed with melancholy. He spat blood, and the doctors called him 'pulmonary'. In May 1574 he became so weak that he had to take to his bed. On the morning of the thirtieth he caused Henry of Navarre to be summoned in order to recommend to his care 'a little child he had had' (by his favourite, Marie Touchet). On the thirty-first he died, aged twenty-four, in the arms of Catherine de' Medici. Henry III, his brother and successor, was in Poland, of which country Catherine had had him elected king; the treasury was so empty that France had great difficulty in paying the expenses of his return journey as well as those of the obsequies of Charles IX.

The new king, Henry III, had a strange and disturbing charm. Tall, thin, fastidious, gracious, a wag, he showed intelligence and innate liberalism, but inspired no respect; his effeminate manners, his bracelets and necklaces, his liking for perfumes upset people, as did even more his suspect 'little darlings', gentlemen who were altogether too bedecked and beruffled. When it was learned that he dressed himself as a woman for certain court festivities, he began to be called 'Prince of Sodom'. Compared to him, the virile Henry de Guise, called 'the Scarred', seemed to the Catholics a desirable leader. This all the more because they were greatly annoyed at finding Henry III, after Henry of Navarre's flight, once again pursuing a policy of appeasement towards the Huguenots. Through the Peace of Monsieur (1576), members of 'the Religion' gained places of refuge, freedom of worship, the right to any employment. And Saint Bartholomew's Day had only been four years before! It passed understanding. The truth was that the Treasury had almost no funds, and that no one would have lent the King of France enough to pay for his supper, far less enough to wage a war. Since royalty lay in default, there sprang up the idea of a league which would re-establish the authority of the Church and be under the leadership of Henry de Guise. From 1577 to 1584, Catholics and Huguenots eyed each other with hatred and distrust.

In 1584 the Duke of Anjou, the King's last remaining brother and the great hope of the Catholics, died suddenly of an infection of the lungs. Since Henry III had no children and there was no likelihood that he would have any, the heir by primogeniture would thenceforth be Henry of Navarre, a heretic! An odd situation – a King of France who could not even be consecrated. Henry III, solid partisan of legitimacy, accepted his cousin of Navarre as heir presumptive while asking him to become converted to Catholicism, but Navarre replied that this was a matter of conscience. The Guises were already on the look-out for a king; why not one of themselves? Henry of Navarre (descended from a son of Saint Louis) was related to Henry de Valois only in the twenty-second degree. Fanciful genealogists stood ready to prove that the ducal House of Lorraine (of which the Guises were a junior branch) had had as its founder Lothair, grandson of Charlemagne. Others favoured the candidature of the aged Cardinal of Bourbon, Henry of Navarre's uncle. None the less, a whole section of French opinion rallied to the League; pamphlets abounded; foreigners, smelling profits, took a hand in this French quarrel. Philip II promised the League soldiers; Elizabeth laid claim to Calais and Le Havre. The court tacked back and forth, while Catherine begged her son-in-law, Navarre, once again to be a Catholic. He wisely put her off without an answer, for had he acquiesced, he would have lost his partisans and placed himself at the mercy of his enemies. Henry III, scorned and detested, had to yield to the League and the Guises; in 1585 he granted them everything. Ten years earlier he had tolerated

Protestantism, now he outlawed it; he had granted places of asylum, now he withdrew them. And all this he did against his inclination, for he knew that these measures would bring war, and he had no resources with which to wage it.

This war was called that 'of the three Henrys' (Henry III, Henry of Navarre, Henry de Guise), but in fact King Henry and his mother continued to play the thankless part of mediators, which won them the contempt of the members of the League. 'Hardly can this farce be played with so many characters without some one of them looking shabby', Catherine had earlier written to the French Ambassador in Spain. Now she said: 'For twenty or thirty years we have tried cauterizing in the belief that we could tear this contagion out from among us, and we have learned by experience that such violence has served only to multiply it ...' Paris, aroused by the preaching monks and by the Duchess of Montpensier, sister of the Guises and a League amazon, was ready to declare against the King. In May 1588, Henry III forbade Henry de Guise entrance to the capital. The Scarred One came alone, with a retinue of only eight or nine men. He was greeted with such joy that he was almost smothered. The crowd threw flowers at him; women on their knees kissed the hem of his garment; the cry was 'Long live Guise!' He lowered his huge hat (no one knows whether he was laughing behind it) and replied with feigned modesty: 'My friends, this is too much ... You should cry, "Long live the King!" ' Furious, Henry III had troops brought into Paris and wanted to resist; the town was bristling with barricades; the students were marching on the Louvre; women were hurling missiles out of windows upon the King's soldiers. Guise was master of the situation. 'We must not wait any longer', the League chieftains told him. 'Let us go seek Sire Henry in his Louvre!' Guise let the opportunity and the King slip out of his hand, and soon regretted it. 'One must be Caesar or nothing — a fact the Duke of Guise finally acknowledged, but too late.'[1]

King Henry succeeded in finding safe refuge at Blois, but he had lost Paris, where Guise reigned, and when he convoked the States General, he asserted that all France supported his enemies. He yielded, humbled himself, but astute observers felt that the 'day of daggers' was drawing nigh. The Forty-Five, a company of that number of brave young gentlemen ready for anything, protected the King and awaited his orders. The order came: the Duke of Guise, a rebellious subject who threatened

[1] Pierre de L'Estoile.

the throne and the life of his master, must be killed. Many of his friends told Guise of his danger, but he relied on the King's weakness. 'He would not dare', he said. The King dared, without even consulting his mother. Henry de Guise was assassinated in the Château of Blois, whither he had been summoned for a council; the Cardinal of Guise was arrested and killed next day by halberd blows. Catherine de' Medici was appalled: 'What have you done?' she exclaimed. 'Now I am the only King', was her son's reply. The Cardinal of Bourbon roundly scolded the old Queen: 'Ah, Madame, here are some more of your tricks! You'll be the death of us all!' After swearing that she had had no part in it, Catherine sighed: 'I am at the end of my tether; I must go to bed ...' She never left it and died three weeks later. 'It is not a woman,' said Jacques de Thou, 'it is royalty which has just expired.' Royalty, however, was not as sick as de Thou imagined.

Saint Bartholomew did not wipe out 'the Cause'; the Blois murders did not at once wreck the League. Quite the opposite; Paris rose against the 'tyrant' whom the preachers thereafter referred to only as 'Henry III, late King of France'. The League refused to deal with 'M. Henry de Valois'. The fury of the League's priest members rose to delirium; in Paris a procession of a hundred thousand persons at a given signal snuffed out their candles, crying: 'Thus does God extinguish the Valois race!' Yet however alarming these antics may have been, they were those of a monster mortally wounded. Without the Guises and their popularity, the League could only fade away and 'burden the kingdom with the weight of its impotent death-throes'.[1] Henry III settled down at Tours and, abandoned by the Catholics, resolutely summoned to himself his cousin of Navarre. A truce was arranged between the brothers-in-law and they jointly besieged Paris. Henry of Navarre knew how to wage war. Soon the kings were at Saint-Cloud, and the League realized it was lost; in desperation it also betook itself to crime: preachers publicly asked if no man would avenge the murders of Blois. The Dominican Jacques Clément heard these appeals and questioned theologians as to the eternal salvation of a regicide for religion's sake. They reassured him; he wormed his way to the King (August 1st, 1589) and stabbed him with a *poignard*. Henry III died better than he had lived, as a king who thought only of the fate of his realm, when he said to Henry of Navarre: 'I die happy at seeing you by my side. The crown is yours ... I order all officers to recognize you as their king after me ...' Then he urged

[1] Gabriel Hanotaux.

him to change his religion: 'You will suffer many a rebuff if you do not make up your mind to accept another faith. I exhort you to do it . . .' He breathed his last at three in the morning. The directing committee of the League announced through its propaganda agency that this murder was legitimate and that the excommunicated King of Navarre could not succeed to the throne.

CHAPTER VII

HOW HENRY IV REBUILT FRANCE'S UNITY

P ROTESTANT King of a Catholic country, Henry IV had to play
a difficult hand; however, he held many trumps, of which the
first was his own person, so well shaped to please the French.
They were grateful to him for saying: 'We are born not only for ourselves, but above all to serve the country.' He wanted to be king of a
whole nation, and not of a part of one: 'Those who honestly follow
their conscience are of my religion, and as for me, I belong to the faith
of all those who are gallant and good.' He believed that kindness and
mercy are a prince's primary virtues. Yet the role of the sovereign is
not to provoke partisan feeling: 'All men want me to string the bow
of my business with the cord of their passions.' Endlessly Henry called
the French to union: 'We are all Frenchmen and fellow-citizens of the
same fatherland; therefore we must be brought to agreement by reason
and kindness and not by strictness and cruelty which serve only to arouse
men.' He pleased also because he was brave and a good soldier: 'I have
leaped upon cities' ramparts; surely I shall gladly leap upon barricades.'
Just as briskly did he write, with a mixture of country warmth and
Gascon poetry. Always in love, he sent his mistresses beautiful and passionate letters: 'My true heart, my dear love . . .' Nevertheless, Henry
the king held Henry the lover in check: 'Regarding whatever may be the
actions of a soldier, I seek no advice from women.' His sparkling eyes, his
arched nose, his square beard, his Gascon accent, his delightful character
and even his love-affairs soon became popular.

On the morrow of Henry III's death, Henry IV was king, but who
recognized him? Many a Catholic said, 'So be it if he is converted', and
he knew that he would have to come to that, that Paris was utterly
Catholic, that 'if France is a man, Paris is his heart', and that, as he was
later to say, 'Surely Paris is worth a Mass'. Moreover, his religion, which
was one of feeling rather than dogma, could adjust itself to a conversion.
What mattered for him was to remain a good Christian and to preserve
his dignity; he would not reach a conclusion except in his own time:
'I have often been called upon to change faith. But in what circumstances? With a dagger at my throat. Had I had no respect for my

conscience, respect for my honour would have prevented me ... What would those most devoted to the Catholic religion have said about me if, having lived to the age of thirty in one condition, they saw me suddenly change my belief under the expectation of thereby winning a kingdom? ...' He promised to look into the matter, to seek light. Those who were unwilling to wait, he said, had the right to forsake him. 'Among the Catholics, I shall have with me those who love France and honour.' And indeed he had them, plus a small Protestant army. The League organized itself against him; the Duke of Mayenne (brother of the late Duke of Guise) proclaimed the aged Cardinal of Bourbon king under the style of Charles X, and made himself Lieutenant-General of the realm. In Paris, the sectarian demagogy of the Sixteen (district representatives) annoyed the Catholic aristocracy, which refused to follow; Henry IV believed that it was possible for him to conquer his kingdom, and with ten thousand men he undertook this great task.

He could have withdrawn into Languedoc, but that would have been to forsake Paris, so he marched on Normandy where he knew he would find friendly cities. Thither Mayenne followed him; at Arques, near Dieppe, by his own qualities of leadership Henry IV won a first victory which guaranteed him Frenchmen of all parties, who turned by instinct to the nation's king. On the League's side there were the King of Spain and the Duke of Savoy, all France's enemies; such ill-made alliances upset decent people. The Paris middle class, which had embraced a Catholic party, was astounded and weary to see this party turn revolutionary. Even Mayenne wrote: 'The merchants think of their business, will have nothing to do with war, and advise peace.' The members of the *Parlement*, persecuted by the Sixteen, were secretly partisans of Navarre; the *Satire Ménippée* describes the anger of the well-to-do: 'In olden times, each man had wheat in his attic and wine in his cellar', the authors kept repeating; 'each had his silver plate, his arras, and his furniture ... Now who can boast of having enough to live on for three weeks, apart from the thieves? ...' Everyone wanted order, everyone awaited an energetic and forgiving ruler; what was more, this ruler existed and he was the King. All that was told of him was delightful: 'If you are losing your standard-bearers, rally to my white plume; you will find it on the road to victory and honour.' Then, on the eve of a battle: 'Quarter for Frenchmen, death to foreigners.' When at last he came to lay siege to Paris, he had not the heart to maintain too harsh a blockade and allowed the entry of foodstuffs: 'I do not want to rule over a cemetery', he said.

In 1593, the States General of the realm had been summoned to Paris. The deputies were few in number, but the people seemed to expect a decision from them. Mayenne made a speech from the throne and said that France wanted a Catholic king: his candidate was Mayenne. Philip of Spain wanted to seat on the throne of France his daughter, Isabella-Clara, grand-daughter of Henry II, and make France a more or less autonomous Spanish province. Meanwhile, Henry IV bargained at Suresnes. He felt that the time had come for his conversion. Were the States General to choose a king other than he, his legitimacy would thenceforth be contested; if, on the other hand, the legitimate king were to become a Catholic, Paris and France, weary of these long wars, would yield to him. 'Instruct me', he said to the bishops. 'I am not stubborn . . . You will win God a fine advantage, a handsome conquest of conscience.' Was he acting in good faith? 'During his life he had been twice Protestant and twice Catholic . . . Experienced in abjuration, he had created for himself a kind of faith which was at once very broad and at the same time very sincere . . .'[1] It cost him nothing to surrender to the popular will and, as he put it in his own Gascon, 'to jump the ditch'. But he wanted to be given the necessary time. He led the bishops a rare dance by his questions and his remarks, going as far as to refer to the cult of the saints as a form of leg-pulling. Finally on July 25th, 1593, at Saint-Denis, Henry IV, clad in white, was 'received into the bosom of the Church'. The League had no further reason for existence. In March 1594, after he had promised a full amnesty, the King entered Paris, his great city, and went to Notre Dame to hear Mass. His amnesty was honestly fulfilled. When France saw that the King wished no reprisals, it followed Paris's suit.

Nothing could be more admirable than the patience with which Henry IV completed the pacification of France. It was no easy task; bad feeling ran high. Many were furious at his leniency: 'If there are those who have forgotten themselves', he said, 'I am satisfied if they come to their senses and people stop talking to me about it.' He even bought many a submission, saying that this cost him ten times less than the use of force. He paid the debts of his worst enemy, Mayenne, limiting his vengeance to making the big rheumatic fellow keep up with his quick strides for a time. He made peace with the Spaniards. There remained the necessity of reconciliation with the Holy See; in this negotiation, Henry was very firm, and the cardinals advised the Pope to yield because France's Gallican

[1] GABRIEL HANOTAUX.

clergy supported the King and there was risk of a schism. Agreement was reached on the basis of the concordat of 1516; the liberties of the Gallican Church were retained; the King was to select the bishops and have the benefices in his gift. The Church, however, kept its possessions: a quarter of France's area, a hundred millions in revenue plus tithes, in return for which it pledged itself to maintain the places of worship and the schools. This left open the question of the Prince of Condé who, a Protestant, remained heir presumptive to the throne as long as the King had no legitimate male child. It was agreed that this young prince should be reared in the Catholic religion, and the Pope thereupon lifted the excommunication. Thus the monarchy kept the benefice lists and its authority over the French Church. The matter of the Jesuits alone remained unresolved; this order, founded in 1540, a real spiritual militia in the service of the Papacy and removed from the authority of the national hierarchy, had played a major part in the wars of religion. In 1594, the Jesuits had been banished from France as enemies of the King and the State; in 1603, Henry IV called them back, despite the remonstrances of the *Parlement*. 'I hold them to be necessary to my State', he said. 'If they have not been such under tolerance, I want them to be such by edict.'

As for the Protestants, true tolerance for them did not yet dwell in men's hearts. A few worthy men such as Bodin had as early as 1577 conceived the idea of separating the Church from the State. 'The prince is the sovereign judge; if he takes sides, he becomes no more than a party leader and runs the risk of perishing in the struggle. Without trying to determine which of the religions is the better, let the prince forswear violence.' But the majority of Catholics and Protestants still wished for the annihilation of their adversaries. Henry IV had hoped that his conversion would lead to that of the mass of Protestants, but nothing of the sort happened; they held his abjuration against him and continued to call the Catholic Church the 'beast of Rome'. All the King was able to obtain from the Huguenots was the acceptance of a kind of armistice — the Edict of Nantes. This act contained wise provisions: the right of Protestants to all State employment; religious worship to take place in fixed places and under set conditions; the right to make wills; the organization of the Protestant clergy into a synod, colleges and consistories; the creation in the Paris *Parlement* of a Chamber of the Edict and of a bipartite chamber in the *Parlement* of Toulouse. Certain secret articles were dangerous: the Protestants retained one hundred and fifty strong places and castles and hence did not abandon the erection of a State within the

State. Their past sufferings and experiences were such that we cannot blame them for having insisted on these safeguards, but the continuance in the kingdom of a party with separatist tendencies was a danger to France.

Religious pacification was not the only problem — far from it. 'You know to your cost, as do I to mine', said Henry IV to the notables of Rouen, 'that when God called me to this crown, I found France not only half ruined, but almost entirely lost to the French . . . Through my care and toil I have saved the heritage; I shall now save it from ruin.' There was much to be done. 'Destruction everywhere', wrote the Venetian ambassador. 'A great part of the cattle has disappeared, so that ploughing is no longer possible . . . The people are not what they used to be, courteous and honest: war and the sight of blood have made them sly, coarse, and barbarous.' Peasants were to be seen who, for lack of beasts of burden, themselves drew the plough 'and served as animals, with ropes over their shoulders'. In the towns, the population had decreased, at times by two-thirds. Looms had stopped. The financial situation was deplorable. 'All my shirts are torn', wrote the King himself, 'my doublet is worn through at the elbow, I often can entertain no one, and for the last two days I have taken my meals now with one, now with another.' But Henry IV knew that this land and this people had hidden resources; he bravely undertook to rebuild France, to restore to the French confidence in themselves, and to set things to rights. For this purpose he relied above all on his friend and companion, Maximilian de Béthune, Baron of Rosny (whom, in 1606, he made Duke of Sully).

Sully had more than genius; he had good sense, integrity and a vast capacity for work. 'Here I am', he wrote, 'locked up in my office, where I examine minutely and with the greatest attention all the abuses which remain to be rooted out.' Like Napoleon, he enjoyed reading intelligence reports: 'I shall always maintain that without this guide, you can act only as a blind man or a rascal.' He arose at four, worked until six-thirty, breakfasted, worked until noon, dined, worked and went to bed at ten. He was crusty and obstinate; even after the conversion of the King, he kept portraits of Calvin and Luther hanging on his walls. His very frankness made him dear to Henry IV: 'That hour when you no longer contradict me, I shall believe that you no longer love me', the King told him. Industrious and diligent, economical and even mean, Sully carried on the business of the realm like a French peasant. 'It must not be known', he would say, 'that the King has a few pennies.' He felt that States were built upon 'prudence, order and gold'. Towards those tax collectors and paymasters who stole on a large scale, he was pitiless. He went over their accounts with a fine tooth-comb and made them disgorge — sometimes unjustly, which led to the saying that he was more a soldier than a master of finance. He was indeed a soldier, and was put in charge of the artillery at the same time as the King entrusted the finances to him. He liked to stroll, between the Louvre and the Arsenal, in great market places full of cannon. 'Never will the artillery have its day in the sun unless it is managed by a superintendent of finances', he used to remark. When he came into office, he found a debt of three hundred million *livres*, and twenty-three millions in annual income which, after the deduction of local charges, only supplied seven millions as the King's net revenue, all of which went straight into warfare, pensions and gifts. With the co-operation of the chief men of the kingdom, much harshness, much pushing and pulling, debt conversions and repudiations, Sully succeeded not only in restoring equilibrium, but in laying away a reserve of thirteen millions in the Bastille and in enlarging his beloved artillery.

'Tilling the soil and keeping flocks — these are France's paps, the real mines and treasures of Peru.' The words are Sully's, who believed that the land was the only form of wealth and that those who worked it were the only nursery for the army. He performed wonders to repair the damages of war, rebuilding France's roads, lining them with elms, repairing bridges (he built Paris's Pont-Neuf in 1604), laying out a net-work of canals, re-establishing peace in the countryside by disarming the partisans, making illegal the seizure of the peasants' cattle and tools, requiring that every three months the feudal lords should destroy 'the wolves, foxes, wildcats and other noisome beasts', creating breeding studs, reorganizing the administration of the forests, draining marshes. Modern France in part owes to him the beauty of her roads, her forests and her fields. Trade and colonies, however, did not interest him. Fruitlessly did men talk to him about Quebec (founded in 1604). 'Things which remain separated from our body by foreign lands or seas will be ours only at great expense and to little purpose.' Like him, Henry IV loved the peasants and hoped to see 'a chicken in their pots every Sunday', but he wanted also to reorganize industry. Sully had no faith in this. He opposed the King's efforts to encourage the raising of silkworms, he opposed Champlain's voyages, he opposed luxury trades, he opposed revenue-contractors, he opposed the marriage of nobles to the rich daughters of commoners, he opposed lazy, idle and pleasure-loving ways of life. Had the King allowed him to do it, Sully would have set up in each bailiwick an inspectorate of morals, 'three censors and reformers', who would have had the right to look into 'the conduct and management of families'. Here was Calvin turned artilleryman and financier. Henry IV, more progressive, had hoped that the kingdom would produce at least the manufactured articles it needed. At the beginning of the sixteenth century, this had not been an idle hope; France was then developing her industry much more rapidly than England. But in 1600, everything had changed. The Italian wars followed by the wars of religion had ruined individuals, and therefore no private capital was available. Reconstruction had to be carried out by the State; it could concern itself only with luxury trades because the great masses of the people, impoverished by the poll-tax, had no purchasing power. The King stimulated the establishment of factories for the making of cloth of gold and cloth of silver, rugs and crystal ware. The results were less astonishing than legend would have them, but at least Henry IV and Sully gave France ten years' truce, and the country remembered it as a golden age.

In the French monarchy the problem of the Dauphin was always serious. Now Marguerite of Valois, long separated from Henry IV, had never given him any children. Most certainly it was not because of his impotence, since he produced a flourishing crop of bastards. His amorous escapades were beyond number: history has dug up the names of more than fifty-six of his mistresses, and Clio knows not everything. His best-beloved was the beautiful Gabrielle d'Estrées, by whom he had three children and whom he hoped to marry. Yet if 'Queen Margot', who had never loved her spouse, was ready to agree to an annulment, she was unwilling that it be used to encourage a misalliance, to be followed by the coronation of a hated rival. Gabrielle died suddenly, some said by poison, although the official account described her as a victim of eclampsia. In order to wipe out his debt to the Grand Duke of Tuscany, in 1600 Henry married Marie de' Medici, the niece of this creditor. At twenty-eight the Florentine was heavy and fleshy; the whole court nicknamed her 'the fat banker'. Marguerite kept in the background, but lived in Paris, and was even friendly to the royal pair. Beginning in 1601, Marie de' Medici presented the King with a son who was to be Louis XIII ('by whom your economies will be squandered', grumbled Sully) and then asserted herself by an annual pregnancy. The King, however, never became attached to this rather foolish and very jealous consort. Henriette de Balzac d'Entragues (daughter of Marie Touchet, who had been Charles IX's mistress) inspired in him a violent passion.

For one hundred thousand *écus* and a promise of marriage written in his own hand — a promise Henry IV had not kept and which he would later redeem at great cost — this young girl had sold herself to him. The three children whom Henriette bore the King were, like those by Gabrielle d'Estrées, ennobled and acknowledged, and their mother was created Marquise de Verneuil. The pranks of the ageing King displeased his people as much as his wife; that which had been charming in a young hero was offensive in a greybeard. Towards the end of his reign, open complaints were to be heard. 'By God, I shall die in this city,' said Henry; 'they will do me to death!' At the age of fifty-six, he fell in love with a girl of fifteen, Charlotte de Montmorency, whom her husband, the Prince of Condé, rushed off to Brussels for safety's sake. Henry IV went as far as to lay claim to her and to threaten the Archduke Albert with his going to get her at the head of an army. Dissoluteness ages badly, and Henry was no longer the wise and lighthearted boy of his younger years.

In foreign policy he continued to the end his opposition to the House of Austria, not as a Protestant, but because he viewed that house as dangerous to France. In his book, *Économies Royales*, Sully attributed to his master a 'Great Design' which would have made Europe into a Christian Society of Nations governed by a council of sixty elected members. Later Saint-Simon wrote about this: 'We find a weak semblance of this in the Empire. The Aulic Council, the Imperial Chamber, the diets, sometimes the Emperor himself settled differences. The powerful, sometimes even the lesser fry, objected and disobeyed, and we see force determining the outcome . . . the sentence remained unenforced and the adjudicated matter unexecuted . . .' Whatever the merits of the idea, it was fathered by Sully and not by the King, who had little use for great designs and who, at the time of his death in 1610, was thinking, rather, of going to war with the Habsburgs over a silly quarrel relating to Cleves and Juliers. Before his departure to take command of the armies, he bestowed the regency on Marie de' Medici and had her consecrated at Saint-Denis. Amusingly enough, at the Regent's coronation, Marguerite of Valois, first wife of their common husband, held the train of the royal mantle. Marguerite, her heart undismayed, had affection for her 'cousin of Italy'; sterile and approaching sixty, she likewise cherished the King's children, whoever they were (three Vendômes, three Verneuils and five little princes born to Marie). On May 14th, 1610, as Henry IV's coach passed along the rue de la Ferronnerie, a man jumped upon the running-board and with a stroke of his knife severed the King's aorta. Henry had been occupied in reading a letter; he died instantly. His assassin, Ravaillac, seemed to be insane and without accomplices, but it has been proved that in 1610 several plots were in hand. Henry IV had been attacked by all the parties because he would not allow himself to be a partisan. A victim's death always restores some greatness of heart to those who have not defended him during his lifetime: Catholics and Protestants praised to the skies him whom they had so bitterly attacked: 'You cannot be a Frenchman', said Henri de Rohan, 'without regretting the loss to its well-being France has suffered.' Ten generations have confirmed this judgment, and Henry IV remains, together with Charlemagne, Joan of Arc and Saint Louis, one of France's heroes. He typifies not France's mystical aspect, but its aspects of courage, good sense and gaiety.

CHAPTER VIII

HOW FRANCE WAS GOVERNED AT THE TIME OF HENRY IV'S DEATH

Six months before his death, in conversation with the Marshal de Lesdiguières, Henry IV had said that 'he well knew that the foundation of all France is the prince's authority. That is why he wanted his son, the Dauphin, to be, as it were, the centre towards which led all the lines of public power ... that it was his intention to establish him as absolute king and to give him all the true, essential marks of royalty, to the end that there might be no one in the realm who would not have to obey him ...' *Absolute king*; he himself was that. After so much division, horror of civil war had united the French behind him. His charm had established the power of the crown on love as much as, and more than, on force. For a century France would be 'mad about the Bourbons'. From 1610 on, the country and the King were one, not through constraint but by instinct. The suffering occasioned by disorder and the skill of the peacemaker had together begotten a willing submission. The people accepted and even desired the substitution of a central power radiating throughout the land, for the multiplicity of local authorities.

All the same, monarchical absolutism was limited by privileges (or liberties) and by custom. We must recall the fashion in which the realm had been built up, by marriages, inheritances, acquisitions, annexations of provinces and towns which gave themselves over to the King. One of the last of these annexations, that of Brittany, had been freely elected by the States General of the duchy because 'the hope of peace which we may entertain through union is preferable to everything that can be said against it'. In return for their adherence, provinces, manors and towns had been granted by the King guarantees which were called privileges or liberties. The privilege, an intermediate stage between such divided authority as had existed in the Middle Ages and that which was to be the equalitarian total power of the great democratic States, had been the means for winning acceptance of centralization from those whom it despoiled. From the King's point of view, it was a legitimate survival. The crown respected its commitments and did not try to apply a uniform law to all France. Each province was judged according to its custom; some had their provincial States General.

The jurists had long maintained that the States General, the nation's assembly or committee, was the most aged and the most worthy of the respect of the nation's institutions. In the sixteenth century, it was possible that the States General, thanks to French internal discord, might assume an authority similar to that of the English Parliament. But the States, composed of the three orders — the people (third estate), the nobility and the clergy — had always been weakened by the absurd traditional rule of voting by orders. That is, each order voted as a unit, so that the privileged orders were assured a two to one majority. (In the British Parliament, on the contrary, the small landowners split the aristocratic order by voting with the third estate, and vote by heads became the rule.) In Henry IV's day, public opinion had lost faith in the States General. 'All that happens at the meetings is talking and bowing, once the Chancellor has assured the whole realm, supposedly there present, of the government's good intentions.' The moment the States General began to talk too much out of turn, the King ordered the tapestries to be taken down from the walls and had the halls locked up, leaving the deputies with nothing to do except go home, which they did without too much outcry.

Who, then, watched over the observance of the custom of the realm? In theory, the *Parlements*. We have seen how little by little the courts of justice separated themselves from the King's court. At the beginning of the seventeenth century, there were *Parlements* at Paris, Toulouse, Bordeaux, Rouen, Aix, Grenoble, Dijon and Rennes — powerful and respected companies. The First President of Paris, one of the greatest personages in the kingdom, gave precedence only to the princes of the blood and the chancellor. The councillors, clad in scarlet robes and mantles lined with ermine — insignia of royalty because they represented the King — judged all matters as a court of last resort. They registered the royal edicts and, if they considered them contrary to the fundamental laws of the realm, they had the right to make remonstrances. Under a strong king, indeed, remonstrances were ineffective, in the first place because no one knew clearly what the fundamental laws of the realm were, and secondly because the King had the right to hold a 'bed of justice' at which he himself presided over the *Parlement*, and that body had to submit to his wishes. Existing only by virtue of the King, the *Parlement* could do nothing against the King. Henry IV treated it cavalierly: 'You have told me the burden this edict places upon our finances; but you supply me with no remedy to escape it and even less to keep my armies alive. Were each of you to offer me two or three thousand *écus*, or to hint that I might take your salaries or those of the paymasters of France, this would be a means for not making edicts; but you want to be well paid and think that you have done a great deal when you have made me remonstrances full of fine sayings and handsome phrases, whereupon you go to warm your hands at your own hearths and do everything to your own convenience.'[1] The magistrates 'then' liked to think that the *Parlement*, as a kind of supreme court, was sufficient to guarantee France against tyranny. But a court which the executive had the power to constrain guaranteed neither persons nor things.

In the administration of the kingdom, the King in part made use of his judges. Until the time, later on, of the *intendants*, bailiffs and seneschals were as much administrators as magistrates. In case of need, the first president of a provincial *Parlement* took the place of the governor. Directives were given by the King in his council, in which sat the chancellor, the superintendent of finances, and the secretaries of State, whose duties, in Henry IV's day, were still rather ill defined. (The chancellor was the fountainhead of justice, irremovable, the keeper of the royal seals.) As for defence, ever since Charles VII, the King had possessed an army and was himself its commander-in-chief. It consisted of the nobility (younger sons, above all); the French troops, cavalry and infantry; and mercenaries Swiss, Scottish and German. 'The late King Henry IV said that there were in France three hundred thousand men who were excellent soldiers, veterans, who had learned military discipline at their own expense; and it is sure that at the first drumbeat, eighty thousand men could easily be assembled and armed . . . The King also has in store a great abundance of weapons and cannon in all his strongholds. We have ourselves seen a hundred pieces of artillery, at Paris, on the walls and before the gates . . . Apart from cannon, there are to be found in the Arsenal magazines of weapons for fifty thousand infantrymen and fifteen hundred horsemen; as for powder, balls and other necessaries, the King has as much of them as he wants . . .' These imposing figures drew the admiration of all Europe. 'The King has told me', wrote Carew, the English ambassador, 'that he could recruit in his kingdom fifty thousand cavalrymen and two hundred thousand foot soldiers without stopping a single plough or a single artisan in his work.' In France the army has always had great prestige because it alone ensures defence against invasions; it afforded the King tremendous authority.

Finances had been the great weakness of the French monarchy. Sully,

[1] *Lettres Missives*, Vol. IV, p. 415.

loathed as must be a good finance minister, re-established a temporary equilibrium. In 1610 receipts amounted to about thirty million *livres*, which corresponded roughly to the expenditure, and a war chest had been set up. Moreover, the tax system had been slightly improved. The King had remitted poll-taxes in arrears, 'being more desirous of gaining the name of father of the people by doing good than of leaving some remembrance to posterity in more dubious ways'. By contrast, indirect taxes had been made heavier. The most famous impost, which was to play a major part in France's consequent history, was the *paulette* (named after Charles Paulet, whose inspiration it was). It was an annual levy equal to 1 per cent of the purchase value of government posts, which judges and other officials were henceforward to pay, and in return for which they would have the right to bequeath their offices to their sons. The *paulette* made government jobs hereditary and created a genuine 'nobility of the robe'. The day on which this tax was inaugurated, the monarchy 'sold its power to the middle class', but it took two centuries for the monarchy to become aware of it. And finally, the clergy (ever since 1560) had annually to give the king a portion of the Church's revenues. This sum was known as the 'free gift'; there was nothing free about it except its name.

At the beginning of the seventeenth century, a cross-section of the pyramid of French society would have presented approximately the following picture. At the apex was the King, surrounded by a ceremonial which, under the last Valois, had become wholly Oriental, but to which Henry IV had restored some humanity. We may well wonder whether the King's mistresses, so damned by the historians, did not play an essential role by supplying next to an all-too-flattered sovereign women who dared speak to him as a human being. The privacy of the bedroom has a healthy levelling effect upon rank and dignity. A harem, to be sure, wipes out this good effect because the favourite is cut off from the rest of the world and knows nothing of what is going on, but Agnes Sorel, Diane de Poitiers, Marie Touchet and Gabrielle d'Estrées were intelligent and well-informed women. After the king came the Great Ones. The highest aristocracy was made up of the princes of the blood, without peer, too highly placed and corrupted with power. Dangerous likewise were the foreign princes, like those of the House of Lorraine, who were dependent on France but retained sovereign rights. Belonging also to the caste of the great were the provincial governors, in principle nominated for three-year terms, but in fact often irremovable, powerful in their domains and bargaining with the King for their support of his cause. It should be noted that this high aristocracy had power only by the King's will; it was he who created governors; they were no more than his officers. The medieval hierarchy had been broken and a rebellious prince of the blood no longer possessed a whole chain of vassals with which to build himself an army. The French would demonstrate that a rebellion was still something to be feared, but from 1560 on, the Great Ones were altogether domesticated.

The next lower level was that of the middling and small nobility, representing about seventy thousand holdings. The greater part of these nobles, half peasant, half warrior, still dwelt in castles with drawbridges and turrets. But they were beginning to discover that they had been ruined by the depreciation of the currency and that the sole means of rebuilding their family fortunes would be to live under the King's shadow, he being the dispenser of posts and benefices. The King encouraged the concentration of the nobility at court because it placed at his mercy a turbulent class which had afforded his ancestors much trouble. In short, everything took place as though he had said to his nobles: 'Give up the relics of a feudal past which no one can bring back to life; give up dispensing justice, collecting taxes; above all give up private wars and civil war. *In return for this, your wages will be many a scrap of every sort — chicken bones, pigeon bones, without mentioning many a warm caress.*'[1] At court the King gave them a friendly reception; all were his companions at arms. But life at court was costly; the stakes were high and one's clothes had to be splendid. Soon, farms and tenant lands, meadows and mills were eaten up; one must fall back on the King's bounty. Under Henry IV the crown spent a third of the budget on pensions. Such was the price for keeping the nobles loyal. When democracy took aristocracy's place, the beneficiaries as well as the nature of the benefices would change, but the list was no shorter. No government can exist without friends and support, and no government which grants neither sinecures nor favours will have friends. The French aristocracy had not the skill, like the English, to keep intact its prestige and its power. The reasons for its unpopularity were its dependence on the King, its neglect of its local duties, its refusal to concern itself with commercial matters, and its refusal to mingle with the other orders for the purpose of discussing the country's problems.

The clergy was dependent on the crown as much as on the Holy See. Bishops were appointed by the King. When a diocese was vacant, its

[1] LA FONTAINE.

revenues went to the King. He also kept the roll of benefices. In return for the support of the Gallican Church, the crown granted the clergy a preponderant status in the country; bishops and archbishops were entitled to great honours, and numerous seats were set aside for them in the various councils. Like the nobility, the clergy was exempt from the poll-tax, the salt excise and a number of other imposts. The Assembly of the Clergy met from time to time to vote the free gift, and it took advantage of the occasion energetically to defend the privileges of the Gallican Church. Intimate union between the Church and the monarchy remained in France one of the elements of stability. The same thing was to happen in England, and later in the United States, because of agreement between the Protestant churches and the State. Lasting conflict between the civil and the spiritual powers always weakens a regime.

It has often been asserted that the nobility in France was a closed caste; nothing could be less accurate. Every wealthy burgher could make his son into a noble by having him educated and by purchasing for him a public office. A judge's or counsellor's robe conferred nobility, and the *paulette* allowed this nobility to be made hereditary. A magistrate, like a noble, was exempt from the poll-tax and other imposts; he paid only his capitation. Every fortunate merchant, every well-to-do surgeon or physician had his son taught Latin, and then transformed him into an officer of the King. In order to satisfy the ambitions of the bourgeoisie, the King multiplied government posts. During the seventeenth century, even the tiniest village had more office-holders than today. No country in Europe had been, as much as France was, turned into a pasture for lawyers and financial agents. The upper middle class, comfortably wrapped in furs, 'spread its red or black robes on every seat bedecked with the fleur-de-lys'. In earlier days the nobility had chosen war for its speciality; the French middle class had taken advantage of this to capture administration and justice. For these tasks it had great aptitudes — a liking for order and economy, often great intelligence, sometimes courage, as was the case with Harlay, First President, who defied the League. But it had its faults — vanity, stinginess, jealousy — which we find depicted in Molière's bourgeois and later in Balzac's.

When reference is made to the third estate of that day, it would be mistaken to believe that the true people were represented therein. Posing as the third estate was a clever dodge of the upper middle class (actually, at the base of the pyramid lay the unprivileged, those who paid the poll-tax). In France's towns there then lived a whole people of small merchants

— prudent, hardworking, timorous. There was very little of that financial boldness common enough in Italy and England. The French merchant was satisfied with little, laid something aside, dreamed of becoming an alderman and retiring. If he could, he would push his son towards the King's service; if not, he would leave him his business. The habits of this class changed very little between the seventeenth and the nineteenth centuries. The artisans worked in small groups — a few apprentices and a master. They were joined together in corporations for their trade, in confraternities for their fun. Moreover, the workers in a given craft constituted a sort of freemasonry; they had special jargons and means of identification. Many a riot and uprising was blamed on these associations, and the government made efforts to discourage them. The mass of little people did not like corporations; like feudalism, they had had their usefulness in the Middle Ages because they had made it possible for merchants and craftsmen to defend themselves. Gradually the dangers which had given them birth disappeared, leaving behind burdensome, authoritarian organizations which secured the masters the fattest of unjust privileges. Hence in the seventeenth century the tendency of the majority of the people was to ask the King's intervention in order to lessen the power of the corporations.

It is difficult to give an account of peasant life with any accuracy. The legend built up about this period, perhaps by contrast with the horrors of the civil wars, is that of a Golden Age, of a chicken in every pot. Such was not the feeling of the English ambassadors, who considered the people of France crushed with burdens and exactions: 'Its spoils are portioned out between the clergy, the court nobility, the country nobility, and the officers of justice.' Even a Frenchman, Cardinal du Perron, wrote: 'In England they all drink sound beer, eat good beef, and not a man is to be seen who is not clad in decent cloth or has not a silver goblet. In France they are destitute, emaciated; the kings ought to have some feeling of compunction.'[1] Meanwhile the land was more and more split up and the population grew. Already France was famous for the products of her soil: wines, fruits, woad, butter and cheeses; she exported salt and oils. The French peasant is a steady worker; he is never discouraged; but he counted on the King to free him from feudal survivals. A lack of firmness towards the nobility on the part of the sovereigns of the seventeenth and eighteenth centuries was to be one of the causes of the Revolution.

[1] La Bruyère.

CHAPTER IX

HOW THE RENAISSANCE AND REFORMA-
TION CHANGED FRANCE

HAD the Renaissance and Reformation produced lasting effects in France? A superficial glance at the country's situation in 1610 would suggest doubts concerning the depth of these two revolutions. It would show the King, at the end of the sixteenth century, more powerful than ever, the movement towards centralization and absolutism more accelerated than in the days of Louis XI, and Catholic mastery re-established. It is true that the Protestants had won the Edict of Nantes, but repressive reaction was busy and the Edict of Nantes would one day be revoked. The Renaissance seemed to be having as bad a time of it as the Reformation. The first years of the seventeenth century were heralded as an age of Christian faith and morality; the freedom of earlier writers was already out of fashion. Between the *Heptameron* and the *Princesse de Clèves* there lay only three generations, but what a difference in tone and in manners! And how much closer are the heroes of Corneille to those of the *chansons de geste* than to Panurge and Friar John! Hence we are justified in asking whether the Renaissance in France was not merely an interlude, without effect on the main course of the drama.

It was nothing of the sort. Despite appearances, the ties with the Middle Ages had been severed. The faith of the cathedral builders had given place to an uneasy searching. In a world which the astronomers had expanded, God seemed greater than ever, but further away. Man had been given over into his own hands. In his *Essays*, Montaigne showed that the individual can emerge with honour from this struggle to reshape a philosophy for himself, and France was not to forget Montaigne. Those who were to oppose him, like Pascal, were to combat him within themselves, for he was to be thenceforth an essential part of every French mind. Montaigne did not deny God — far from it — but he mounted Him upon a 'magnificently isolated' throne and lived as though God did not exist. Montaigne, as Sainte-Beuve well stated it, was the fullness of nature without Grace. Already he foreshadowed Spinoza and his abstract God. For a man like Montaigne, neither Saint Augustine nor Saint Thomas were the masters of his thinking; his references are all pre-Christian, Latin and Greek. By name and baptism he was a Christian; he went to Mass as a matter of convention, but Christianity played no part in his inner life; if it had left any traces in him, they were mere habits of conduct and speech. Montaigne was no more Christian than Voltaire; he was far less Christian than André Gide.

Thus the Renaissance had indeed been a spiritual revolution. While it thought itself no more than a search for a compromise between the ideas of ancient philosophy and those of the scholastics, it bore within it the seeds of nationalism, the French Revolution, modern science and world wars. Sixteenth-century man imagined that nothing essential had changed because he saw the King upon his throne, the lord in his castle and the parish priest in his church. Yet he failed to observe that from then on the King would be dependent on the banker or the gold mine, allowing him to maintain an army and do without the feudal nobility; he failed to see that soon wars would be declared, no longer to ensure the triumph of the true faith, but to defend the independence first of the middle class, then of the masses; he failed to note that humanism leads to scientific agnosticism. The intellectual revolution of the Renaissance in no way coincided with the Reformation. The cardinal fact was the break with the notion of revealed truth. Protestantism by no means denied revelation; it only sought to limit itself to the authority of the Scriptures. In the twentieth century the humanist revolution was to threaten Protestantism fully as much as Catholicism. And so the wars of religion might be described as fratricidal. Renaissance and Reformation were in reality contrary forces; it is true that much later French Protestantism, become liberal, like all minorities, would rejoin the current of the Renaissance, but in the sixteenth century no Huguenot could have foreseen this transformation. Calvin was less liberal than Bishop Briçonnet.

On the political level, national had taken the place of feudal conflicts. Royal marriages were to remain important (and would be so as late as Louis-Philippe's day), but this personal bond was merely a survival. During the Middle Ages, when the economy was the narrow one of a manor house or village, at most that of a market town, economic wars were scarcely within the range of possibility (except, perhaps, over trade with the East). The national economy of modern times was to imply the conquest of colonies rich, first, in precious metals, later in raw materials. Patriotism had been born in France long before, and it had been sturdy ever since the Hundred Years War; since Henry IV, no other feeling would be strong enough to vie with it in French hearts. When the nobility, during the days of the Fronde, toyed with foreign alliances, there was instant popular revolt. The general admiration for good King Henry represented the triumph of patriotism over faction. Still disputed in the sixteenth century by such Huguenots as Duplessis-Mornay, and by the 'Jacobin' Catholics of the League, absolute monarchy won the day in the seventeenth because the King embodied the nation's unity.

The birth of a great literature and the maintenance and enriching of the French language were essential factors in this unity. The best French minds had absorbed the works of the humanists, and thereafter they were to devote themselves to imitating the formal perfection of antiquity. No modern people would attach a greater importance to style, to eloquence, to the choice of words; even the preacher would become a man of letters; and by the same token Francis I, Henry IV and their successors were to be classic writers. For a long while these shared glories, these victories of sword and spirit, would suffice to unite the French, who found so much contentment in rejoicing at the beauty and the greatness of their country that for two centuries they forgot the daring of the Renaissance. With Henry IV, the nation reached a stopping place, a landing. The republicanism of Plutarch's heroes, popularized in Amyot's translation, left its mark on Corneille, just as Rabelais's heartiness is reflected in La Fontaine, but the ordinary Frenchman during the seventeenth century went to church on Sundays, cried 'Long live the King!' with all his heart, and put up with the privileges of the nobility and the clergy. He would not understand that in his father's day one of the great revolutions of the human spirit had just been accomplished.

What had happened? Only this, that in the sixteenth century, in France and a great area of Europe, a civilization based on revealed truth had been replaced by one based on sensory experience. At the time of the fall of the Roman Empire, classical philosophy had gone to sleep; Christian philosophy had saved the Western world. The Renaissance took up the story of the mind where the Greek philosophers had left off. Nothing in France's external appearance, the style of monuments and poems apart, as yet displayed the change. But the blow had been telling: men of the modern time would consult nature more than the Bible. For good or evil, this revolution has not run its term in our own day. It can end either in universal disaster, or in a new form of world State, a scientific and humanitarian 'Christianity', a religion of reason or, finally, by a return to the City of God. The historian's part is not to judge, but to point out its extent and to uncover, as early as the sixteenth century, the symptoms of what was to follow.

BOOK THREE

THE ABSOLUTE MONARCHY

CHAPTER I

HOW LOUIS XIII AND RICHELIEU CON-SOLIDATED HENRY IV'S WORK

CHILD rulers are the plague of monarchies. Henry IV had bestowed the regency on Queen Marie de' Medici, the haughty Italian — a fat blonde, handsome enough when Rubens painted her, very well pleased with herself, an authoritarian without authority. The new king was only nine, a sullen, shy child who was left to the mercies of riding masters, manservants and cooks. It is possible that his mother, by neglecting his upbringing, hoped to prolong his minority. She herself was dominated by a childhood friend, Leonora Galigai, a swarthy and greedy sorceress suckled by the same wet nurse as herself, whom she had imported from Florence. Leonora had married an affected fop named Concini, and for some years this strange pair ruled over the Queen Mother and, through her, over France. Concini, made Marquis of Ancre, had himself named marshal. The Great Ones protested, for Henry IV's death had restored their hope of again making France into an oligarchy. 'The day of kings has passed', they said; 'that of the princes and Great Ones has dawned'. By a miracle of charm and adroitness, Henry IV, playing on everyone's weariness of civil strife, had imposed the royal authority; but personal charm is not a 'recipe for government', and this 'skill, untransmittable, passed away with the artist'.[1]

The Concinis had the wisdom to retain Henry IV's old ministers, 'the bearded fellows', except for Sully whom everyone detested, and these old fellows had the wisdom to understand that the weaknesses of a regency made any war undesirable. The campaign which the late king had begun against the Habsburgs was wound up and, to make peace sure, Marie de' Medici decided to marry her son the King to Anne of Austria, daughter of Philip III, King of Spain, and great-granddaughter of Charles V. This caused an outcry among the Protestants, who felt that this was a threat to them, and it did not placate the Catholic nobility; the Great Ones of both religions formed a league and denounced the abuses of the regency. As for the country, it was against the Great Ones and for the King; so it was a reasonable step in 1614 to convene the States

[1] JEAN CANU.

General. Louis XIII, who had just reached his majority, appeared before it, dressed in white, elegant and frail. He was highly applauded. The ordering of the retinues was magnificent, but these 'gentlemen of the States' showed little feeling for the national interest; each of the three estates argued in its own behalf. The nobility of the sword went after the nobility of the robe and called for the abolition of the *paulette*, that is, of hereditary office. The clergy was most energetically represented by the young Bishop of Luçon, Richelieu, whose artful eloquence aroused admiration. With his arched nose and thin lips, his 'goatee and moustache in cavalry style', his paleness and slenderness, he cut a distinguished figure. He asked that ecclesiastics be more closely linked to power: 'Indeed they are, as they have good reason to be, more divested than any others of those personal interests which so often ruin public affairs, seeing that, celibate as they are, nothing remains to them except their souls, which, since they cannot amass riches, oblige them to think in this world, in their service of their king and their country, only about acquiring for ever, up there in heaven, a glorious and all-sufficient reward . . .' This amounted to nominating himself, and Marie de' Medici, who had admired this pale, proud young prelate, took note of it. The States General, after bitter discussions, was adjourned by the usual means – by the removal of the tapestries – and the delegates went home without having accomplished anything. Its bequest to the country was Richelieu, whom the Queen soon summoned to the council and whom Concini made his friend. This great bishop, of a good noble family, burned with ambition; from his distant diocese he had watched the court and had drawn up for his own guidance maxims on the art of success. He urged the budding statesman to silence, dissimulation and careful answers, which are like 'those retreats that save lives and equipment'. From the moment when Henry IV died, he had guessed that the Regent could help him and had manœuvred to attract her attention. Now he had only to besiege 'a beauty on the wane and a burning heart'.[1] He fascinated her with that glance 'no one could withstand' and, without ever laying aside his prelate's dignity, dominated her.

Yet in the very terms of the problem there was an element which the Regent, Concini and Richelieu wrongly neglected – the young king himself. He had been left to servants and a single favourite companion, Charles d'Albert de Luynes, a handsome fellow who, like Louis XIII, loved riding and hunting. No one took note that the King had become

[1] FIDAO JUSTINIANI.

of age, and hence was master; no one knew that he was aware of his rights, hard and when necessary even cruel. Unsociable, a dreamer, he played at being bored. He loved Luynes, feared women and did not enter his own wife's bed until five years after their marriage, and only when he was led to it by his favourite. He knew, however, how to reach a decision, how to lead and how to hate. When he grew tired of seeing the Marshal of Ancre show off, he secretly gave an order to the captain of his bodyguard, and Concini was assassinated. Louis XIII was sixteen years old – 'Yes, now I am King!' said he. At court it was as though lightning had struck. The courtiers, by profession abject, turned towards the new star. Richelieu, compromised by his connection with Concini, went back to his diocese; Marie de' Medici was exiled to Blois; on the Place de Grève, Leonora Galigai was burned as a witch. Luynes would have been the master had he possessed any mastery, but he was a weak fellow, ignorant of public affairs at a moment when the situation in Europe required the most refined intelligence. Catholics and Protestants were still fighting in Germany; Bohemia and Hungary were in revolt against the Emperor. The latter appealed for French help in the name of Catholicism, while the German Protestants asked the same country to intervene in order to put a stop to the undertakings of Austria. To have a free hand in Europe, France's ruler needed internal peace, yet the Queen Mother's party, still powerful, was a source of anxiety to the adherents of the King. Richelieu, who had become Marie de' Medici's secretary of writs, several times tried to effect a reconciliation between mother and son, but fruitlessly. In 1621, during a campaign, Luynes died of 'the crimson fever'. The King did not weep for him; indeed he shed few tears. After this death, Richelieu, freed of an enemy, was given the Cardinal's red hat, but the red robes had no worth in his eyes were they not to become a prime minister's livery.

Up to this moment, Louis XIII had considered Richelieu a turbulent and dangerous prelate, 'ready to set fire to the four corners of the realm', and wanted to have 'no dealings with him'. 'Here is a man', he said, 'who would greatly like to be in my council, but I cannot reconcile myself to it after all the things he has done against me.' But in 1624, Marie de' Medici's pressure as well as the Cardinal's abilities – at a time when ability was rare in this council – led Louis to yield. A mysterious and powerful middleman intervened to arrange a secret meeting between the King and the Cardinal. He was Father Joseph, a Capuchin mystic wholly devoted to Richelieu, a practical and visionary genius, a trader in the shadows and secret places, to whom the Cardinal would say: 'You are the principal agent God has employed in leading me to the honours to which I have been raised.' No sooner had he entered the council than Richelieu, 'with indescribable joy', saw his part grow greater and greater; soon the King realized that in him he would find the 'chief minister' for whom he had hoped, and forgetting his prejudices he placed the Cardinal at the head of state affairs.

A stubborn legend has distorted the relations between these two men. Novelists, playwrights and historians have depicted Louis XIII as a poor sovereign 'having all the virtues of a gentleman's gentleman, and not one single virtue of a master', to whom Richelieu assigned the role of 'playing second fiddle in the realm and first in Europe',[1] making the Cardinal out to be a superman, a despotic genius, quite without pity. 'He debased the King and brought honour to the reign', said Montesquieu. The truth — as always — is less simple. Far from having the soul of a valet, Louis XIII was a harsh master who entertained the highest of notions concerning his rights and duties as king. Jealous of his authority, he even bestowed shocking humiliations on Richelieu himself. With the *Parlement* he was ruthless: 'You have been created only to judge between Master Peter and Master John', said he to the First President, Le Jay, 'and if you continue your schemes, I will clip your nails so close that your flesh will suffer from it.' On another occasion: 'I do not compromise with my subjects and my officers . . . I am master and want to be obeyed . . . I have seen the fellows in the Bordeaux *Parlement,* and I have scrubbed their polls . . . The more considerate you are with such people, the more they take advantage of you . . .' It was the King and not the Cardinal who insisted upon putting men to death. To Richelieu, who was inclined towards leniency, the King wrote: 'It is ordered that you be less easy and less moved by pity for the said lords, for they have valued too low what they owe the master of the shop.' Such was his manner of expression, commonplace and picturesque. Louis XIII stammered, but he knew what he wanted to say; his intelligence was obvious, his will inflexible. His health alone failed him, and in this he was like his minister; their ailments and their medicines drew them together.

For Richelieu likewise was a sick man, burning with fever, nervous, often on the edge of tears, variable in temper, distraught, impatient. 'He cries whenever he feels like it', said Marie de' Medici. And indeed he had need for tears; from childhood he had shown a most melancholy dis-

[1] MONTESQUIEU.

position. As chief minister, he took his frugal meals alone in his room and sought silence at Chaillot or Rueil. At times his fiery temper broke out in brief yet terrible rages; whenever he said, 'Sir, your most humble servant', every prudent visitor saw fit to flee. But this irritable man had succeeded in fashioning for himself a steadfast will. 'One must will strongly', he would say, and sometimes countered all critics with 'the unbending stubbornness of a man who stops his ears'. His was an obstinacy of principle, not one arising from narrowness; never was there a clearer mind. 'Reason must be the rule and guide of all things', he used to remark. He went straight to the point and at a glance penetrated to the bottom of matters. After clarity, he viewed secrecy as the greatest virtue of a statesman. The 'Most Eminent' was also the 'Most Secret'. 'He does not do what he says and he does not say what he does', whispered his enemies. He believed in severity, but not in rancour: 'If a man is slave to his own vengeances, placing him in authority is putting a sword in the hands of a madman.' Few have been more attacked and slandered; he learned to bear this abuse calmly: 'Pay no attention to insults; they are good training for him against whom they are directed and work for the glory of him you would injure.' But if the greatness of the minister and the man is beyond dispute, it is false to say that he 'created' a French policy. Before him, more than one king had done his best to humble the Great Ones, to give France her natural borders, and to keep the House of Austria within bounds. Richelieu himself constantly denied that he followed a set pattern; he had no great designs, only a method. 'In politics', he said, 'you are impelled far more by the necessity of things than by a pre-established will', which is the ultimate wisdom of almost all men of action.

'My first goal was the majesty of the King; the second was the greatness of the realm.' He could reach these objectives only by stages. One of the obstacles was the continuance in France of Protestant fortified places and Huguenot armies. Richelieu the cardinal was tolerant; Richelieu the statesman could not suffer anything which divided the State; concerning the Protestants, he said: 'They must be reduced to that condition which befits all subjects in a State, which means that they must not be in a position to set up any separate body and they must be dependent on the wishes of their master.' In other words, what he asked of a Protestant was that he be an obedient subject. He preferred a French Huguenot to a Spanish Catholic. The pity was that some Huguenots then preferred an English Protestant to a French Catholic. Whence the necessity to put a stop to the 'chronic blackmail' of La Rochelle and the other places of asylum. La Rochelle was like the Calais of old, an English bridgehead in France; in order to help with the Protestant fortress's defence, Buckingham, the King of England's favourite, went so far as to land with an army on the Island of Ré. The Cardinal besieged La Rochelle and vanquished it, and in 1628 Louis XIII made his entry into the town. Here Richelieu's moderation became apparent: as conqueror, he imposed a peace of reconciliation: general amnesty, freedom of worship, no confiscation of goods. A few months later the Peace of Alais, or Edict of Grace, put a stop to the religious wars. The Protestants, who gave up military security, were granted every moral safeguard. Richelieu had fought the party, not the cult, and the conversion of the heretics was 'a work for which we must look to Heaven, without our applying any violence'.

The intrigues of the Great Ones were no less dangerous than those of the Huguenots, but the King and the Cardinal clipped their claws too. There was a moment when the two Queens plotted against Richelieu, and with them, Gaston of Orleans, the King's brother and heir to the throne; handsome Marie de Rohan, Duchess of Chevreuse (Anne of Austria's favourite friend, who had been left a widow at twenty-one through the death of the Constable de Luynes, Louis XIII's favourite); and the bastards of Henry IV. It was difficult to punish the Queens and the Duke, but the lesser players paid for their masters. Chalais, Montmorency, Cinq-Mars and other distinguished heads fell: Marshal de Bassompierre, a national hero, was cast into the Bastille for having played a tiny role in one of Marie de' Medici's conspiracies, and he remained there until Richelieu's death in 1642, 'although wholly innocent of any crime, and never having done anything which did not rather deserve praise and reward than punishment'. Richelieu was of a noble family, but he regarded the nobility as dangerous in the State the moment it ceased waging war for it, since the nobles carried the warrior spirit into internal affairs. Here was the reason for the harsh edicts against duelling, which Richelieu punished with death, and it was at this time that the aristocracy 'turned to gallantry because it could no longer turn to tragedy'. As for the people, said the Cardinal, all political thinkers are agreed that, were they to be too prosperous, 'it would be impossible to keep them within the rules of their duty . . . By losing the mark of their subjection, they would also lose awareness of their condition. They must be likened to mules which, being accustomed to their burdens, are spoiled by long idleness rather than by labour . . .' In his eyes, the object of government was not the happiness of the people, but the security of the State without which there is neither happiness nor people.

It seemed to him that the first requirement for this security was a realistic foreign policy. Protestants and Catholics were still at swords' points in Europe; the leadership of the Counter-Reformation lay with the House of Austria and Spain. The Emperor sought to destroy Germanic liberties and to rebuild German unity to his advantage. The Protestant princes stood out against him. What part should France play? For a long time Richelieu's great and only friend, François du Tremblay, Father Joseph, tried to convince the Cardinal of the necessity of rebuilding, by means of a kind of crusade, a Christian and Roman Europe, but Richelieu's penetrating intelligence went beyond appearances. Austria was pretending to fight for the faith, but in fact fought only for Austria. Were the House of Habsburg to triumph over the German princes, were it to dominate Germany, Bohemia, the Low Countries, Spain and Italy, then it would hold all Europe, and French independence would come to an end. Now was it not French civilization which had given Catholicism its European character? Was it not fulfilling his duty both as a French minister and as a Roman prelate to keep alive and strong the country of the Crusades and cathedrals, of Joan of Arc and Saint Louis? In reasoning thus, was Richelieu in his turn perhaps unconsciously a sophist and more patriotic than religious? However this may be, in order to save France and 'unstring the Spanish rosary', he decided to ally himself to the Protestant princes, and he convinced Father Joseph. 'Better than any man in the world, he distinguished between the bad and the worse, between the good and the better.'[1]

From 1624 to 1635 he applied all his skill to arousing enemies against Austria without involving France in the war. First Denmark, then Sweden, urged by him flew to the help of the German princes. Gustavus Adolphus, Sweden's Lutheran King, received from Richelieu subsidies with which to continue the war; even Father Joseph approved: 'Such things must be used as we use venoms of which a small quantity serves as antidote while too much kills . . .' The *too much* would have been a Protestant empire replacing the Catholic. Already Richelieu was taking his precautions, moving towards Alsace, negotiating with Catholic Bavaria, when Gustavus Adolphus died in 1632, marking the end of Swedish hegemony. In 1633 the Emperor's armies seemed to be

---

[1] CARDINAL DE RETZ.

disorganized by General Wallenstein's rebellion; this gentleman dreamed of establishing (to his profit) an empire in which all religions would be free. By taking advantage of this uprising, Richelieu hoped to advance without opposition to the Rhine, the kingdom's natural frontier. His troops slipped into Alsace. But within two years, Wallenstein had been assassinated, the Swedes beaten and the Protestant princes crushed at Nördlingen; Spain was sending troops to Austria, which would win the day if France did not openly declare herself. Richelieu hesitated no longer. It was now necessary to intervene on the side of the German Protestants if Austrian domination was to be staved off.

The war was not without its dangers. For ten years Richelieu had been striving to rebuild France's army and navy, but had run into financial difficulties, while the Spanish infantry was becoming the most formidable in Europe. In 1636 France was invaded and the Spaniards penetrated as far as Corbie, their scouts reaching Pontoise; all would have been lost had not courage matched the extent of the danger. By his absolute confidence in the intervention of Providence, however, Father Joseph heartened the King and the Cardinal, who showed themselves in the streets of Paris. The country supplied soldiers and money. It was the year of the first production of *Le Cid*, and noble feelings inspired noble exploits. Spain was repulsed; France regained self-confidence; Richelieu's enemies were lost. One of Voiture's letters jeered at 'those who, through hatred of its ruler, hated their own country, and who, to ruin one man alone, wanted France to be ruined'. He ended: 'Stop hating a man who is so fortunate in avenging himself on his enemies ... Leave your game before it leaves you.' It is a fact that after 1636 Richelieu had practically nothing but successes. His armies moved forward in Picardy and Artois; in the south they occupied Roussillon (Catalonia, Savoy, Turin). In 1642 France extended almost to the Scheldt, the Rhine, the Alps and the Pyrenees — in other words, her natural boundaries.

And there was another matter for congratulation: on September 5th, 1638, twenty-three years after her marriage, Anne of Austria had at last given France a dauphin; Gaston, Duke of Orleans, the Cardinal's enemy, lost all hope of succeeding to the throne. Two years later another miracle: the forty-year-old Queen brought a second son into the world, and Louis XIII 'gave evidence of greater joy than at the birth of the first, because he had had no hope of so great a happiness as to find himself the father of two children — he who had feared to have none at all'.[1] But in .

[1] Mme de Motteville's *Mémoires*.

November 1642, the Cardinal, long ill, felt that he was dying. He was not to see the French peace for which he had so long laboured.

When the priest who was administering the last rites asked him, 'Do you forgive your enemies?' he replied, 'I have had none save those of state.' He believed what he said, since he had given up everything in the kingdom's interests. With Richelieu, nationalism triumphed. Saint Louis had been a man ready to sacrifice a province to an idea; in the eyes of Louis XIII and Richelieu, France's greatness—which, moreover, was at one with the King's — was the sole essential idea. Greatness, not domination. What they wanted was not to establish France's hegemony over Europe, but to assure France's survival while preventing some other power from making Europe its own. For this reason, and not for any special hatred, Richelieu strained to cut down 'the great tree of the House of Austria'; for this reason was he severe with dissidents of all sorts, since without inner unity, France could not hope for external security. Regarding his foreign policy, historians are in agreement; all praise it and acknowledge that it is still a model for French diplomats. After his death, his domestic policy was variously judged; some accuse him of having so thoroughly wiped out all France's local powers and provincial liberties that excessive centralization made the Revolution inevitable. 'The French monarchy', they argue, 'was based upon an agreement between the King and his nobility, his *Parlements*, and the States of his kingdom. Richelieu, by maintaining that sovereignty is no more divisible than a point in geometry, by asserting that the sovereign has as much the right to break the law as to make it, ruined the structure the kings had erected and created a new government which was not workable.' Others reply that Richelieu did not invent absolutism, and that Louis XIII's royalty differed very little from Henry IV's.

It is certain that Richelieu wanted absolute authority for the King as for himself. He had tasted the luxury of power and 'loved glory more than morality allows'. When in 1635 he founded the French Academy, he wanted even the Republic of Letters to recognize his authority — and it was a most reasonable authority — over language and the works of the mind. Someone said of him that he had been 'the schoolmaster of the French nation'.[1] He did indeed try to teach the French logic in conception and firmness in execution. He found his people difficult to govern, having 'more heart than head', at once impatient and dilatory. How often did he bewail the 'apathy of France!' (But he likewise became aware, at the

---

[1] FIDAO JUSTINIANI.

time of Corbie, that 'recoveries' in France are speedy and wonderful.) Why have historians attributed to him more than to others ideas which were traditional and simple? Because he invested them with form. Richelieu was not only a great minister; he was a good writer, and nothing lasts in France like the perfection of form. In his clarity of perception and the finish of his maxims, Richelieu was essentially French; after his death the French, who had detested him while he lived, discovered his virtues — and acknowledged his worth.

CHAPTER II

HOW THE FRONDE WAS A REVOLUTION
AND HOW IT MISCARRIED

Louis XIII did not long survive Richelieu, and this double death once again raised the question of the very nature of the French State and royal absolutism. The *Parlement*, which had been humbled by the Cardinal and which would have delighted publicly to condemn his memory, at once sought and found an opportunity to reassert itself. In his will, Louis XIII had retained in power 'the relics of the Cardinal', by which he meant a council of men selected by Richelieu, which, during the infant king's minority, was to watch over Anne of Austria, the Regent and Gaston of Orleans, the Lieutenant-General of the Realm. Anne of Austria was a proud Spaniard, long weaned of tenderness through her husband's indifference, not ill willed ('The Queen is so kind', people said), but, despite her placid manner, like that of a 'fat Swiss woman',[1] inclined to fits of wrath which turned her voice into a shrill noisy falsetto. She brought the child King before the *Parlement* to request that the will be broken and her regency made unconditional. The *Parlement* joyfully greeted this chance to show its power and declared that 'the restrictions placed on the Regent were derogatory of the principles and the unity of the monarchy'. Anne won the right to form her own council, and the magistrates believed that she would take advantage of this power to sweep away 'the relics of the Cardinal'. Instead she surprised everyone by choosing as principal minister one of Richelieu's creatures, Guilio Mazarini, called Mazarin.

He was an Italian, born of a family 'of small estate, but not lowly'. He had served as a captain of infantry and then, through the favour of an ecclesiastical friendship, having become a canon at Rome without ever having been ordained, was made a papal legate and nuncio to France. Richelieu had espied in him a clever fellow, 'of wonderful industry and astuteness in managing men and putting them off with doubtful and misleading hopes'. His strong point was wheedling people, buying them, imposing on their credulity. Richelieu had been firm, and even hard; Mazarin was flexible and remembered neither benefits nor insults.

[1] CARDINAL DE RETZ's *Mémoires*.

'Now we saw', wrote de Retz, 'standing on the steps before the throne, whence the harsh and forbidding Cardinal Richelieu had struck with lightning rather than governed human beings, a successor soft spoken and benign, who wished for nothing, who was in despair because his dignity as a Cardinal did not allow him to humble himself before everyone as much as he would have desired . . .' All this was only on the surface, but the *Parlement* and the Great Ones thought that their day had dawned: 'The *Parlement*, free of Cardinal Richelieu, who had treated it as an underling, imagined that the golden age would be the one in which a master daily informed them that the Queen wished to be guided by their counsel alone. The clergy, which ever presents the world with an example of servility, extolled this attitude under the name of obedience. And that is how everyone suddenly discovered himself to be pro-Mazarin . . .' Everyone, and especially the Queen Mother. So long saddled with a spouse who did not love her — a virtuous woman into the bargain, or at least a prudent one, 'but possessed to a sovereign degree of the coquetry of her nation' — Anne suddenly encountered in her maturity this very handsome man whose black eyes caressed her, whose respectful vivacity amused her, and whose subtle gallantry gave her reassurance. What was the nature of the bond? Did she unite herself to him in secret marriage? The letters demonstrate a more than tender feeling; the facts show that she soon could not do without him and lodged him near her both at the Palais Royal and during the court's state journeys. The sequence of events would show that her choice had been good. Mazarin had less style than Richelieu, and his methods were less direct, but he followed the same pattern with the same tenacity, and he would leave Louis XIV in 1661 a kingdom stronger than ever.

France was extremely lucky to have in charge of her business, at the hour of the negotiations which were to put a close to a long period of war, a master diplomat. For the military victory had been won. At Rocroi (1643), the young Duke of Enghien (later the Great Condé) had defeated the 'fearsome Spanish infantry'. Turenne, having won his marshal's baton in Italy, had moved into Germany. Now the task was to harvest the fruits of victory. The peace conference which was, perhaps for centuries, to settle Europe's fate began in 1644; not until 1648 were the two Treaties of Westphalia (Osnabrück and Münster) signed upon the same day by the Catholic and Protestant Powers, which had deliberated separately. These treaties constituted a triumph for France and for Richelieu's policies. They left the Empire more than weakened, actually impotent. Germany was cut up into three hundred and fifty independent States, each with its army and its foreign policy; 'German liberties' were restored, and so France's security was guaranteed. Not only would these numerous States never agree in order to make war against her, but she could even find allies among them. An imperial diet continued to exist, but it had to come to its decisions unanimously, which amounted to saying that it could never come to any. France obtained full sovereignty over Alsace. The principle, *cujus regio, ejus religio* (an individual's religion depends on that of his sovereign), was extended to Calvinism; every subject must adhere to the worship of his region or his prince. If the religion of his area was not that of his heart, he had the right to emigrate and take his belongings with him. Thus the Emperor retained real power only in Austria, Bohemia and Hungary. Switzerland and the Low Countries remained in fact independent. Spain ceased to be a European Power; Germany no longer was (or had not yet become) one. The Treaties of Westphalia made France the arbiter of Europe.

By someone unaware of the unbelievable and permanent ignorance of peoples concerning foreign affairs, it might be thought that this diplomatic triumph would make secure the glory of the minister who won it. Not at all; no man has ever been more slandered than Mazarin. The silliest and most shameful accusations were made against him, and he knew it: 'A Latin tome has been composed against me, the gist of which is that I am in agreement with the Turk, and that if I am allowed to, I will hand Europe over to him . . . This morning a merchant said that it was a shame . . . that at Vienna I received twenty-nine millions and that the *Parlement* had discovered it . . .' As early as 1648, Paris was in the process of rebellion. Why? Because two foreigners, a Spaniard and an Italian, were governing France; because no more cardinals were wanted as 'first ministers'; because finances were in a bad way, taxes increasing, the income from the government bonds unpaid; and finally because, during those days, revolution was in the air, because the Neapolitans had successfully risen against their king and the English were about to decapitate theirs. Imitation is a potent factor in the lives of nations, and there are fashions in uprisings just as there are in assassinations. Even words have their influence; the Paris *Parlement* had nothing in common with the Parliament of London — the latter was a representative assembly, the former a company of hereditary magistrates — but the two institutions bore the same name, and this alone was sufficient to give ideas to the Paris Parlementarians and their First President. These magistrates had their merits — honesty, courage, culture. Brought up on the classics, they talked glibly about republican liberties; but they clung to their posts, to their fortunes and to the impressive ritual of their ceremonies, all of which made them conservative revolutionaries. The same could be said for those who were nicknamed 'The Important Ones', great lords and ladies for whom romantic rebellion added spice to the irregularity of their passions. 'Monsieur de Beaufort took it into his head to govern', says Retz, 'a thing of which he was less capable than his own valet . . .' And La Rochefoucauld remarks: 'A cabal took shape . . . which was called that of the Important Ones . . . All agreed to be Cardinal Mazarin's enemies, to broadcast the Count de Beaufort's imaginary virtues, and to affect a false honour of which they made themselves the dispensers . . .' Far more determined was the attitude of the people of Paris, which thought itself strong, feared Mazarin less than Richelieu, and had found a leader in a demagogic prelate, Paul de Gondi (later Cardinal de Retz), an excellent writer, as we have seen, but an ambitious cynic bitterly opposed to Mazarin. 'Digging down among the small', said Gondi, 'is the surest way to make oneself the equal of the great.' As co-adjutor to his uncle, the Archbishop of Paris, who was in his dotage, Gondi was in an excellent position to push himself to the top.

These combined forces came very close to endangering the monarchy. Their successive uprisings, which are referred to as the 'Fronde' (the French word for a sling) because stones were shot into the windows of the Cardinal-Minister ('The whistling of a sling was heard this morning; I believe it is snarling at Cardinal Mazarin' — '*Un vent de fronde — A soufflé ce matin — Je crois qu'il gronde — Contre le Mazarin*') amounted to an advance version of the French Revolution. The royal family had to leave Paris, pamphlets defamed the Queen and the Cardinal, and the people stormed into the palace, forcing the Regent to show them the small King lying in his bed. Louis XIV would not forget these scenes, which so strangely resembled those during the course of which his family was to perish. There were several clashes followed by limping settlements. The two principal ones were the Parlementary Fronde (1648-49) and the Fronde of the Princes (1649-53). The first struggled for principles, *Parlement* rightly thinking that its constitutional duty lay in defending the independence of its magistrates. When one of these, the venerable Pierre Broussel, was arrested and taken off to Saint-Germain the people of Paris, given the cue by Mazarin's enemies, rose up. 'Men suddenly became angry, ran around, cried out, closed their shops.' Delighted, Gondi betook himself to the Palais Royal followed 'by an infinite number of people howling, "Broussel! Broussel!"' The Queen proved to be proud and very sharp; Mazarin was pliant, perplexed. 'Madame,' remarked a wit, 'Your Majesty is sick indeed; the Bishop-Co-adjutor is bringing you extreme unction.' The Co-adjutor (Gondi) indeed hoped to emerge as prime minister, but he soon regretted, as do all sorcerer's apprentices, the whirlwind he had unleashed. Neither he nor the First President, Matthew Molé, who certainly had displayed courage, was well received by the people. The insurgents had Paris in their hands. At last Broussel had to be turned over to them. The poor old fellow was so appalled by the ovation given him and by all the clamour around him that he himself suggested a proclamation urging the Parisians to lay down their arms.

But the people were not satisfied. They were insistent that Mazarin should disappear. The court fled to Rueil; it would have been in serious peril had its opponents been united. But what idea had they in common? The magistrates of the *Parlement* called for the kingdom's traditional liberties and the supervision of taxes; the noble 'Frondeurs' were on the march to regain their lost privileges and undo Richelieu's work; the people, stirred up at first by the princes and the magistrates, 'fathers of the people', no longer trusted those who had aroused them; Madame de Chevreuse 'knew no other duty than to please her lovers'. Among the military men, Condé supported the court; Turenne, led astray by the lovely eyes of Madame de Longueville, campaigned against the King and bargained with the Spaniards, whose intervention alarmed those still possessed of patriotism and common sense. Gondi himself noted that all 'this smelled of the League's processions'. Turenne's army abandoned its general; the *Parlement*, justly scandalized at the Spanish alliance, which stank of treason, decided to talk things over with the court. The people, however, still threatened to kill anyone who might favour negotiation 'before Mazarin should have left the kingdom'. First President Molé's firmness triumphed; he journeyed forth publicly, confronting the uprising: 'The court does not hide', he said. At the conference which began at Rueil, an agreement was reached. Mazarin could have dictated his own terms; he preferred to purchase support by granting concessions which he was fully determined to repudiate. This first Fronde had been no more than one long April Fools' Day.

The peace of Rueil settled nothing. Both parties remained strong; a 'leaven of discontent' remained among many of the magistrates and persons of means, out of all patience with 'that thief, that buffoon, that pedlar, that impostor of an Italian'. The people blamed Mazarin, who had nothing to do with it, for the high price of wheat; what was even more important, the Great Condé, bulwark of the court, suddenly turned against it. A man of vast pride, he thought that without him Mazarin would have been defeated and that the Cardinal did not treat him with sufficient respect. All the Amazons — Madame de Longueville, Madame de Chevreuse — were plotting anew. In order to link himself more closely to this group, Gondi had taken Mademoiselle de Chevreuse, by agreement with her mother, as his mistress. 'It is as true', said he, 'of ecclesiastics as it is of women, that they cannot preserve dignity in love affairs except through the high rank of their lovers.' Gondi and his women, the better to destroy Mazarin, pretended to become reconciled to him and urged him to have Condé and the princes arrested, their insolence having become unbearable. Now to place the victor of Rocroi and Lens under arrest was a rash move; it aroused the whole country. The *Parlement* took sides with Condé. Were the uniting of the two Frondes, that of the *Parlement* and that of the princes, to take place, Mazarin would be lost. In January 1651 he had to retire for a while, after having freed Condé. But Anne of Austria played her cards well; she won Gondi to the crown by offering him a cardinal's hat, and secured the support of Turenne, the only general to match Condé. Mademoiselle de Montpensier, the 'Grande Mademoiselle', a mannish girl who believed herself fated to become Queen of France (by marrying her cousin, Louis XIV), took command of an army, and, dressed in armour, determined to join Condé. She it was who opened Paris to the prince's forces. However, Mazarin knew that there was one man on whom he could always rely against Condé, namely Condé himself — who was so intolerable and vainglorious that Paris would end by preferring even Mazarin to him! The patriotic populace was aroused at seeing Spanish flags in the army of the Fronde; the mob was beginning to turn against those who had spurred it on. Blood flowed; the Hôtel de Ville was set on fire; during the battle of the Saint-Antoine suburb, the Grande Mademoiselle ordered the cannon of the Bastille to fire on the royal troops, in order to cover Condé's retreat. 'That cannon shot killed her a husband!' said Mazarin. The time was near when the middle party, 'that variety of people who can do nothing at the beginning of troubles, but can do everything at the end', would be coming into the game. Now merchants' deputations arrived with tears in their eyes begging the King to return to Paris. The celebrated Broussel who, in the days of his popularity, had been elected provost of the merchants, was bluntly dismissed without the crowd's even noticing it; short are the loves of the populace. In October 1652 Louis XIV, very manly and regal, made a military entrance into Paris, and everyone who counted came to pay him court in the corridors of the Palais Royal. The Fronde was finished.

Mazarin waited for several months before returning. 'This outcast, this troubler of the public peace, this scoundrel', this enemy of the people was received, 'not only without murmur or outcry, but in triumph and all bedecked with glory', wrote the bourgeois Vallier. At the Hôtel de Ville, the Syndic of the *rentiers*, who a little earlier had said that 'Mazarin was the greatest garbage of the century', bowed very low before the Cardinal-Minister. Those who had been the most eager in hurling abuse at disfavour, were the quickest to stoop before the return to fortune. As for the King, who had gone out to meet the Cardinal, to him the Fronde had taught its lasting lessons. He had seen his palace overrun by the mob with the aid of rebellious nobles and parlementarians drunk with their own importance; he had seen how the unpopularity of a too-powerful minister could cause the estrangement of a kingdom. From then on he resolved to govern by himself, without any principal minister, to keep his nobles tamed and to send the parlementarians back to their job of dispensing justice. Yet he retained Mazarin until the latter's death — 'He loved me and I loved him', he later said. Louis recognized the worth of this tight-mouthed and discreet 'stepfather' who showed him the principles of politics, and above everything else, he would never have discharged the minister whose return betokened the King's victory over the Fronde.

Why had this movement come to naught? Because it had been a bundle of selfish and contradictory interests, lacking fixed principles. It has often been described as a rehearsal of the 1789 Revolution: Broussel recalls Bailly, Paris's bourgeois mayor in 1789; de Retz recalls Talleyrand and the reviling of Mazarin gives a foretaste of the scurrilities of *Père Duchesne*, during the Terror. But in 1789 the nation would be consulted and represented; the Fronde had been merely a faction. Through the moral and material ruins which it left behind it, almost as regrettable as those of the wars of religion, it was to instil into Frenchmen's minds the desire to continue the monarchical and absolutist reaction begun by the first Bourbons. Revolt had discredited freedom.[1]

Mazarin lived until 1661, and during the last years of his life did good work for France. Spain had to be dealt with, once and for all; that country, though whittled down by the Treaties of Westphalia, none the less persisted in poisoning all France's domestic quarrels. Showing as few scruples as the enemy, Mazarin organized revolts in Catalonia, Portugal and Naples and, in order to beat Spain down, did not hesitate to ally himself with Cromwell's regicide and Protestant England. He was merely following Richelieu's tradition: no religion on the battle-field. Thanks to this alliance and Turenne's genius, he won the Battle of the Dunes. Militarily, Spain was thenceforth out of the picture. Yet to ensure peace an alliance was needed, and the King had to marry the daughter of the King of Spain. Now Louis was passionately in love with one of Mazarin's nieces, Marie Mancini, but in marriage a king must consider the interest of the crown rather than the leanings of his heart. Mazarin begged Louis XIV to master his passions: 'I implore you, for your glory, for your honour, for the service of God, for the good of the kingdom . . . generously to command yourself . . .' The King yielded. The Peace of the Pyrenees completed the re-establishment of France's borders, giving her the Roussillon, the Cerdagne and Artois; Catalonia remained Spanish, which was just, since this province formed a natural part of the Iberian Peninsula. Maria Theresa, eldest daughter of Philip IV and Elizabeth of France, married Louis XIV. In return for a dowry of five hundred thousand gold *écus*, she gave up her rights to her father's throne. Spain, however, was very poor; the dowry could never be paid; and all hopes remained legitimate, even that of one day seeing the two crowns united, since Philip IV had not at that moment any male heir.[2] Mazarin had more than completed Richelieu's work; in 1661 he died, after having discussed finances with one of his favourite assistants, Colbert, in the very midst of his death throes. Louis XIV's personal rule had begun.

[1] See LOUIS MADELIN, *La Fronde*.
[2] Widowed in 1646, he had just remarried. But the child who was to succeed him under the name of Charles II was not yet born when Louis XIV married Maria Theresa, in 1660. The future Charles II came into the world during the following year, 1661.

CHAPTER III

HOW THE GREAT KING DOMINATED
THE GREAT CENTURY

VOLTAIRE wrote that anyone who thinks and has taste, places real value on only four centuries in the world's history: that of Pericles, that of Augustus, that of the Medicis and that of Louis XIV. 'Europe', he said, 'has owed her manners and her feeling for social life to the court of Louis XIV.' This is true enough, even though Voltaire, like most of the men of his day, too much neglected France's civilizing influence during the Middle Ages. The politeness of the eighteenth century was no more than the grand-daughter of the courtesy of the thirteenth. The novelty of his reign was the King's success in making his tastes the country's tastes; he governed alone, and this personal government the French not only accepted but, for the first twenty years, loved. 'Everything was quiet during this reign', adds Voltaire: no more civil wars, no more Fronde; ceremonial majesty replaced the hubbub of uprisings. Inside the country, an astonishing splendour of literature and the arts; outside, despite reverses towards the end, a vast prestige. For all Europe the King of France was then 'the great King'; his century was to remain the Great Century.

Everything about it had indeed been great, and first of all Louis XIV himself. 'The King's calling', he wrote, 'is great, noble, and delightful when a man feels himself worthy to perform well everything he undertakes.' Having known Mazarin's tutelage, he had resolved to be his own minister and never wanted any churchmen on his council. He presided over it himself, worked six hours a day, tied himself down to signing the vouchers for the smallest State expenditure and to keeping a memorandum book which amounted to France's journal and ledger. Saint-Simon, who disliked him, said that he was born with a mind below the mediocre (an assertion belied by the King's letters), but 'a mind able to shape itself, to refine itself, and to borrow from others without imitating and without embarrassment', which, coming from a foe, is the handsomest of tributes. Louis had perfect manners, not allowing himself even the kindliest and most innocent chaffing, and never passing a woman without lifting his hat; 'I add that this was true of chambermaids and those he knew to be such', Saint-Simon naively adds. 'His most commonplace utterances were never lacking in natural and apparent majesty.' He had been born kind and patient; his weaknesses lay in loving flattery, in welcoming and encouraging the most clumsy praise, which quickly produced an unawareness of truth and a confusion of the State's interest with care for his own glory. Even though he was a pious and believing man, he was willing to have his court make of him a god; little by little he became majestically selfish, judging men solely by their devotion to his person. But for a long time all this seemed bearable and even pleasant, because after so much disquiet, France thirsted after authority.

The shifting of the court at this time from Paris to Versailles strengthened the monarch's despotism by withdrawing him from the controls of public opinion. Several factors led to this decision: the disturbance before he came of age, which had made a vivid impression on the young King; the impossibility at the Louvre, where people could come and go at will, of protecting the sovereign against the inquisitiveness of visitors; the nuisance of having mistresses there and the 'danger of parading such great scandals before so populous a capital'. It had been with Mademoiselle de la Vallière, when their love was still a secret, that Louis had gone on his first visits to Versailles, staying in a small castle built by Louis XIII. Gradually he erected there 'innumerable buildings', and finally, beginning in 1682, he made of it his principal residence. Five thousand people, the pick of the French aristocracy, then dwelt at the château, and five thousand others in its neighbourhood. By its absence, the French nobility lost its local prestige in the provinces, but on the other hand any great lord who failed to live at court cut himself off from favours, posts, pensions and benefices. 'He is a man whom I do not see', was a sentence without appeal, coming from the King's lips. Life at Versailles was ruinously expensive, and this was a deliberate part of the system. As a matter of policy, Louis forced magnificence upon all. 'He drained everyone by making luxury honourable', and thus reduced the courtiers to dependence upon his bounty for their existence, whence came the amazing prestige of all those who could get near him and beg favours: mistresses, bastards, doctors and serving men. The King prided himself on not listening to women, even to those he loved, 'the weakness which is naturally theirs often causing them to prefer trifling interests to the most weighty considerations'. But this was only partially put into practice, for he did all he could to change into princes of the blood the bastards he had had by Louise de la Vallière and those, doubly adulterous, by the Marquise de Montespan, and towards the end of his life he submitted to the pious wishes of Madame de Maintenon. At court he regulated with extreme care the least details of ceremonial and fell into almost unbelievable rages if the wife of a secretary of state dared be seated before a duchess. Saint-Simon thought that this arose from his having 'a mind by nature tending toward smallness', yet likewise admitted that, not having enough real favours to bestow, the King was clever in substituting imaginary privileges for those more substantial. He knew how to give worth to the tiniest dispensation: an invitation, a word, a glance. A solemn frivolity is one of the sound tools of despotism.

'*L'état, c'est moi.*' ('The State—I am the State!') Louis XIV never uttered these words, but the idea was in his mind. Under him the States General was never convened; ministers became chief clerks; the *Parlements* had been forced back to their narrow tasks as courts of justice; cabals were few and timid. However, the custom of the realm, the King's piety and his good sense prevented this absolutism (except in religious affairs) from degenerating into tyranny. The monarchy still acknowledged the rules of tradition. When Louis XIV sought to erect into a dukedom the lands of Chancellor Séguier, the *Parlement* returned the letters patent to him because a magistrate had no right to receive a reward at the hands of the court. The King's soldiers were forbidden entrance into the greater part of the principal cities. At the Bastille, a fortress lying in the heart of the capital, only disabled veterans might make up the garrison. By contrast it was true that any subject could be locked up there merely at the King's command, given in a letter sealed with his *cachet* (seal) and countersigned by a secretary of state. These *lettres de cachet* were employed, firstly, for matters of state, few in number, running to dozens, not to thousands; secondly, for family matters upon the request of a father or a husband, since in France each family was still regarded as a 'community which governed itself', and hence the royal power put its authority at the disposal of each father of a family; or lastly for police matters, in order to spare a guilty man the notoriety of the law courts, and a respectable family this same stigma. The *lettre de cachet* was an arbitrary instrument affording no guarantees to its object and victim. Nevertheless, in Louis XIV's time, the institution aroused few complaints; it was thought to ward off great evils and unnecessary scandals; only during the following century would opinion be aroused against it.

Louis XIV ruled France by means of councils on which, in theory, he alone made decisions. These were the High Council, that of dispatches, that of finance and, for religious affairs, the Council of Conscience. The ministers were few: the chancellor, the controller-general and the secretaries of state for war, the navy, and the King's household. The King rarely changed them; he employed only seventeen in fifty-four years of personal rule, and he selected men of lowly birth so as to have them entirely within his power. At the very outset of his reign, he brought about the arrest, trial and life imprisonment of the Superintendent of Finances, Nicholas Fouquet, a bountiful patron of the arts, who was worshipped by his friends, especially Madame de Sévigné and La Fontaine, but who had acquired the dangerous habit of confusing the credit of the State with his own. An overhandsome entertainment which Fouquet gave the King at his Château of Vaux-le-Vicomte (and perhaps his attentions to Louise de la Vallière) brought about his downfall, probably undeserved, for he was a finance officer 'like others', whose peculations respected the custom of the land, and whose intelligence and courage were above the average. The legal proceedings were irregular; no document of any sort was supplied to the accused; the presiding officer was changed in the court of first instance; the court was made up of the superintendent's foes. In a word, no shred of justice. Locked up at Pignerol in 1664, Fouquet died there in 1680; the whole business arouses our curiosity and does the regime small honour.

But the generation of ministers which followed was ably chosen. Colbert, Le Tellier and his son Louvois, fulfilled their tasks as 'chief clerks' as scrupulously as any men could. In the field of finance, Colbert's job was a hard one, for he had to deal with a lavish sovereign. 'I entreat your Majesty', he wrote to the King, 'to allow me to say that in war and in peace, Your Majesty has never consulted his finances to determine his expenditures . . .' In Colbert's view, endowed as he was with common sense, that rarest of qualities among technical men, there was no other means of balancing the budget than to increase receipts and diminish expenses: 'We must save five pennies on unnecessary things. I assure Your Majesty that, for my part, a useless meal costing two thousand francs brings me unbelievable pain . . .' He tried also to simplify public accounting, to lessen the number of exemptions from the poll-tax, to soften the harshness of the prosecution and the means of compulsion used against tax receivers. But his task remained ever incomplete because of the wars which endlessly caused new deficits. The King's solicitude for 'glory' outmatched his concern for straightening out his finances.

Colbert believed without reservations in a managed economy. 'We must resign ourselves', he said, 'to do people good despite themselves.' His aim was to draw gold and silver (which he believed to be the only real wealth) into France, first, by work, 'source of all spiritual and temporal goods'. For the first time in France, agricultural and industrial producers were glorified at the expense of office-holders, and especially those living on unearned incomes. Next, by economic warfare and protective tariffs, for Colbert, as a mercantilist, wanted to prevent the precious metals from leaving the kingdom, even in payment for useful articles. Finally, by regulation: 'The State must order the industry of a great people on the same basis as the divisions of a government department.' Colbert established state manufactures and monopolies which still exist (Gobelin tapestries, the striking of coins and medals, tobacco, the royal printing houses, gunpowder and saltpetre). In private industry, his subsidies and orders encouraged mines, glassworks and, above all, factories for working wool and silk. All this was supervised by regional committees of industrialists and merchants, and by the Inspectorate General of Manufactures. The corporative regime was strengthened, combines and strikes were forbidden, regulations were established governing raw materials, manufacturing methods and labour policy. Here was a wholly totalitarian organization. On the land he particularly encouraged industrial crops: madder, flax, hemp, mulberry. Regarding internal trade, he knew that he should abolish the divisions and customs duties cutting France in two; but he did not do so. Regarding external and colonial trade, he took an interest in Canada and established, without great success, the Company for the Commerce of the Western and Eastern Indies. The sum total of all this constituted a tremendous effort which should have and could have yielded great fruits; but Colbert died before the harvest was gathered; his successors did not continue his effort, and France was outstripped by England.

Louvois, son of Le Tellier and Colbert's rival, worked like the latter for the King's greatness. He was opinionated, arrogant and without scruples, but he created for France the first true standing army of modern times. Before him, regiments and companies belonged to their colonels and captains, who recruited them, paid them and had a personal interest in maintaining phantom units on paper. Louvois was unable to wipe out this system, but he made it less dangerous by placing alongside the honorary colonels and captains, lieutenant-colonels and lieutenants who held the effective command. As for general officers, the creation of a 'table of command', establishing each man's seniority, put a stop to scandalous conflicts of authority on the field of battle. The soldiers were volunteers, enlisting for four years; Louvois (1670) forced upon them a uniform and severe discipline and armed them better than any other troops in Europe. Soldiers armed with the bayonet, invented by Vauban in 1687, took the place of pikemen. Cavalrymen were given carbines; a regiment of bombardiers and twelve companies of cannoneers were established. For the management of supplies, Louvois inaugurated the army *intendants*, and in 1674 the Invalides was founded to serve as a home for old soldiers. This very considerable army (three or four hundred thousand men) included illustrious regiments: the Swiss Guards, the French Guards, the Regiment of the King's Household, the Great and Little Musketeers. But admirable organizer though he was, Louvois was a dangerous counsellor for Louis XIV; in order to make himself indispensable, he urged towards war a sovereign who was all too inclined to seek glory. Saint-Simon tells the terrible story of a war deliberately brought on by Louvois to re-establish his credit with the King after a stormy session during which the minister had been roundly abused.

At the moment when Louis XIV took over the management of affairs, however, a long peace seemed possible. Towards 1665, France was the strongest Power on the Continent. Spain had been made weak, and Louis XIV might hope — Maria Theresa's dowry having remained unpaid — to obtain some day either the reunion of the two kingdoms, or at least the Low Countries. Germany and Italy, parcelled out, were no longer dangerous forces; by a restoration England had put on the throne Charles II, who was a friend of the King of France and even accepted subsidies from him. Thus France seemed to be without enemies; her aim should have been to rectify her north-eastern frontier bit by bit and without armed conflict. Vauban, a great military engineer and architect, was building covering strongholds for her; the ramparts, curtain walls and demilunes of which protected and adorned the country for two centuries, and it was Vauban who indicated to the King the towns necessary to complete this belt of stone. Vauban did not like war, and no desire for vainglory or conquest inspired him. Nevertheless, France possessed neither Lille nor Douai nor Strasbourg nor Besançon and seemed still to lie open to the invader.

Upon the death of Philip IV in 1665, a conflict called the War of Devolution broke out in this wise: the Queen of France, Maria Theresas had been born of the marriage of this king to one of Henry IV', daughters; now her half-brother, only four years old, was to succeed to the throne of Spain under the name of Charles II. Louis XIV laid claim to a part of his territorial inheritance under the right of 'devolution', a purely private custom which favoured the children of the first bed. Turenne marched into Flanders, this being the only means to make sure of a royal inheritance. No military obstacle prevented him from going as far as the Scheldt and seizing Antwerp, but there were diplomatic reasons for being cautious — any French advance in the Low Countries alarmed Holland and England. Through the intercessions of his charming sister-in-law, Henrietta, Louis XIV had secured Charles II's neutrality; Holland, more dogged, called the Swedes and certain German princes to its assistance. Rather than yield, it opened its dykes and put in power William of Orange, the man who symbolized resistance to France, agreeing in order to survive that its middle-class republic be transformed into a military government. With heroic obstinacy, Holland fought on from 1672 to 1678 and, by raising coalitions, succeeded in putting France on the defensive. In 1677 a dynastic upset took place; Mary, niece of the King of England and his heir presumptive, married William of Orange, a concession on the part of Charles II to his Protestant subjects which powerfully strengthened and encouraged Holland. Louis XIV had to make peace; the treaty, signed at Nijmegen in 1678, gave France a portion of Flanders and the Franche-Comté. The frontiers of modern France had been approximately settled. Strasbourg was still lacking; by a judicial decree in 1681 Louis XIV annexed it without a blow, and other places were acquired in the same fashion, through consultations of jurists who 'interpreted' ancient treaties. Nothing better shows what was then France's strength than Europe's acceptance of these 'juridical' annexations.

Up to this time, Louis XIV's policy had at slight cost brought great and serviceable results, but in 1685 Catholic James II succeeded his brother Charles II, and in 1688 a Protestant Whig revolution placed on the throne the most constant of France's foes, William of Orange and his wife, Mary. Thenceforward England and Holland, acting jointly, would seek to beat down Louis XIV just as Elizabeth had formerly defeated Philip II. The Dutch and English merchants believed that Antwerp in French hands meant their certain ruin. William III continued England's traditional policy: the defence of Flanders, the mastery of the sea and the shaping of a coalition against the Continent's greatest Power. As a preventive measure, Louis XIV had occupied the left bank of the

Rhine, and Louvois, on the other side of that river, had laid waste the Palatinate in order to create a desert between the Empire and Alsace. The King reprehended this harshness, which was to be the starting-point of age-long resentment. Against him were then leagued England, the Empire, Holland, Spain and Sweden. The purpose of this league, called that of Augsburg, was to push France back into the frontiers which had been defined for her by the Treaties of Westphalia and the Pyrenees. Continental Europe was alarmed over France's military power; England and Holland had been aroused by Colbert's ideas and were fearful of a maritime and colonial France. At first the excellent French fleet, under the command of Tourville, won the day over the combined naval strength of England and Holland. It was impossible, however, at the same time to hold the Mediterranean and the ocean, the sea and the land, and Colbert was no longer there to equip the French flotillas. They were finally wiped out at La Hogue and Louis XIV wanted to come to terms. At the Congress of Ryswick he displayed canny moderation, agreeing to give up the Low Countries and to recognize the House of Orange in England. He thought it was better to do this than to allow Spain, with English help, to rebuild the empire of Charles V. For his part, William III thought he had succeeded in establishing a continental equilibrium between France and the Empire. After Ryswick (1697) it seemed that Europe's peace was assured.

Fate took it upon herself to trouble the waters, and the mischievousness of events triumphed over the relative wisdom of the sovereigns. The only matter which remained threatening was that of the Spanish succession. Charles II, Spain's slow-witted king, was soon to die without an heir (1700). Who would get his throne? A son of the Emperor? A French prince? The Elector of Bavaria? To have the Empire in Spain and in Italy would mean that France would again be encircled; anxious for peace, Louis XIV therefore suggested giving Spain to the Elector of Bavaria, while the Dauphin (son of Maria Theresa) would content himself with Naples, the two Sicilies, Tuscany and Guipúzcoa, while granting Milan to Austria. Here was a reasonable solution, but 'Death had not signed the treaty'. The Elector of Bavaria, a five-year-old boy, died; the French prince and the Archduke remained the sole contenders, and compromise was barred. Fresh negotiations began between Louis XIV and William III, both ready to dismember Spain in order to keep the peace. Believing that French support for a weakened Spain was the more valuable, because it was geographically closer at hand, the Spanish ministers had obtained from their dying king a will which appointed as his successors the Duke of Anjou or the Duke of Berry, grandsons of Louis XIV. Were they to refuse, the Austrian prince would be substituted for them. Thus was Louis XIV's hand forced; he could no longer refuse the kingdom of Spain on behalf of his grandsons without himself re-establishing Charles V's empire. He accepted the perilous honour and sent the Duke of Anjou, under the name of Philip V, to Madrid (1701). Great was William III's rage; he opened negotiations with the Emperor, while Louis XIV, in reprisal and contrary to the Peace of Ryswick, recognized as King of England the exiled Stuart pretender, James III.

The War of the Spanish Succession sadly filled the last days of the reign and lasted until 1713. The purpose of the English remained the same: to preserve the balance of power in Europe, to prevent Louis XIV from uniting the forces of Spain and France and to force him to evacuate the Rhine delta and Flanders. France had the advantage of occupying the land under dispute from the very beginning of the war, but she was worn out with fifty years of strife and, worst of all, she had not the mastery of the seas. The allied generals, Marlborough and Prince Eugène, taking advantage of the fact that the French armies had ventured beyond Vauban's fortified lines, hastened to replace siege warfare with a war of movement, to the great horror of orthodox military men. The flintlock and the bayonet in the infantries of both armies had replaced the pike and the musket; the losses on both sides were frightful. Marlborough crushed the French and the Bavarians at Blenheim (1704), then reconquered Flanders at Ramillies (1706). Yet the Whigs, who had known how to win the war, did not know how to make peace. As early as 1709 the English could have secured a treaty which would have freed them of all fears in Flanders; in France there was great discouragement. 'Everything has gone to pieces', wrote Fénelon, 'and will not be repaired during this war. My conclusion is that an armistice must be bought at whatever price may be required . . .' The pressure of taxes, fraud and extortion were wrecking the country. 'We are living like gipsies, and not like people who govern', Fénelon also said. But the English demands were such (they asked Louis XIV himself to drive his grandson from the Spanish throne) that the King refused. He sent a message to the governors of the provinces: 'Although my tenderness for my people is no less lively than that which I have for my own children, although I share all the evils which war can bring down upon such faithful subjects, and I have shown all Europe that I longed for the benefits of peace, I am convinced that my people would themselves object to obtaining peace on terms contrary equally to justice and to the honour of the French name . . .' Marshal de Villars encouraged the King not only to resist but to attack: 'Let us work out some aggressive schemes, for to rely always on fortified lines is a means never to win and to lose much every day.' And Louis XIV remarked: 'Since there must be war, it is better to wage it against my enemies than against my children.' The Battle of Malplaquet in Flanders was far from being as fortunate for the Allies as those which preceded it; the victors lost more than a third of their forces and Villars withdrew in such good order that pursuit was impossible.

In England public opinion was tired of the war. Swift found fault with those who wished to impose too harsh terms on France. 'After the Battle of Ramillies', he said, 'the French were so discouraged over their losses and so impatient for peace that their King was resolved to sign under no matter what reasonable conditions. But when his subjects were informed of our exorbitant demands, they became jealous of his honour and were unanimous in helping him to continue the war at any price rather than yield . . .' An unforeseen event confirmed the English in their desire to come to terms with France. The unexpected death of the Emperor of Austria threatened to join in the person of the Archduke the crowns of Spain and of Austria, were Philip V to abdicate; here again the balance of power would be broken and Spain would be in Flanders — all the things England had feared for a century. Turning a somersault — one of the features of its foreign policy — England made a separate peace with France. Mrs. Masham had replaced the Duchess of Marlborough in Queen Anne's favour and the Tories had succeeded the Whigs. The Dutch and the troops of the Empire still continued to fight. Louis XIV said to Villars: 'If some mischance should befall your army, what must I do? Withdraw to Blois, as I am advised by several? Yet my army could not possibly be so whipped that it could not hold along the Somme. If a mishap takes place, write to me. I shall gather together in Paris whatever men I may find; I shall proceed to Péronne or to Saint-Quentin to perish with you or save the whole State.' The Battle of Denain (1712) cooked the Dutch goose. 'Marshal de Villars saved France at Denain', Napoleon was later to write. This was true, but Louis XIV had royally supported Villars. In 1713 the Treaty of Utrecht put a stop to this long conflict. France retained Vauban's cities and approximately her present frontiers, but she was debarred from Belgium, and even England insisted that the Dunkirk fortifications be razed — a bungling insult. Besides this, the French lost Newfoundland and Acadia; the Empire gave up Spain; Holland and Portugal became tenders in the tow of the British man-of-war. England emerged mistress of the waters and at ease on the Continent. The days of British dominion were beginning.

HOW, DURING THE REIGN OF LOUIS XIV, THE MONARCHY'S GREATNESS PREPARED THE WAY FOR ITS DOWNFALL

THE medieval king had been half a priest; with Louis XIV he became literally a living idol. To him husbands sacrificed their wives: 'To share with Jupiter involves no slightest dishonour.' The monarch's personal life was like a function of the State; in an absolute monarchy, what takes place in the antechambers is fully as important as the events in the legislative halls of a constitutional regime. At the court of Versailles, good Queen Maria Theresa was never at her ease; the only part she played there was to supply the crown with a dauphin, who was addressed as Monseigneur and who died in 1711, a man of fifty. Monsieur, the King's brother, an effeminate fellow, belonged utterly to his darling Chevalier de Lorraine; his first wife, Henrietta of England, Charles II's sister, lively and charming, was a great favourite with her august brother-in-law and served as go-between in negotiations between France and her own country. When she died at a youthful age ('Madame is dying, Madame is dead . . .'), Monsieur married a hulking German, the Princess Palatine, so masculine that people said, 'Madame is the kingdom's stupidest man, just as Monsieur is its stupidest woman'. Together these two simpletons produced a man of talent, the Duke of Chartres, later Duke of Orleans and Regent of France. His tutor, the Abbé Dubois, had taught him history; he hated etiquette, exalted English freedom, had the boldness of an unbeliever, reading Rabelais during Mass and toiling with a chemist to discover the philosopher's stone or to distil perfumes. The court asserted that 'the Devil in person presided over his labours'. In order to join his illegitimate to his legitimate family, the King arranged for his nephew Chartres to marry one of his bastards, Mademoiselle de Blois, who was nicknamed 'Mrs. Lucifer'. Madame, who had a horror of bastards, slapped Monsieur her son when he informed her of this matrimonial event; yet what could she do? The King required it, and the King reigned, even over family life.

The first 'avowed mistress' was the touching Louise de la Vallière, a lady in waiting to Madame, blonde, gracious and sweet. 'That little violet hiding beneath the grass and ashamed to be a mistress, to be a mother, to be a duchess', as Madame de Sévigné put it. She loved the King for his own sake, gave him four children, blushed at the great rank he bestowed on her and, from 1667 on, saw herself supplanted by the haughty Marquise de Montespan, 'the Incomparable', as 'thundering and triumphant' as La Vallière was timid. For a time the King had both of them living at Versailles in an apartment dubbed that of 'the Ladies'; then in 1674, under Bossuet's influence, La Vallière entered a Carmelite monastery, there to do penance. She had dwelt thirteen years at court; she was to remain thirty-six in the convent. When she was informed in her cloister of the death of the Count of Vermandois (one of Louis XIV's natural sons) she burst into tears, and then remarked: 'This is bewailing too much the death of a son over whose birth I have not yet shed enough tears . . .' Madame de Montespan had eight children by the King, among them the Duke of Maine, his father's favourite, and the Count of Toulouse. A governess, Madame Scarron, was entrusted at Versailles with the up-bringing of these fruits of adultery. The King, who was a pious man, regretted the scandal, but felt that he gave enough to virtue 'if, when he allowed his heart free rein, he remained the master of his head', or, in other words, if his mistresses reigned but did not rule. No one could have foreseen that the 'widow Scarron', born Françoise d'Aubigné, preceptress of 'France's legitimized' children, would succeed her patroness, Madame de Montespan, in the King's bed. Daily seeing Louis XIV, she succeeded in pleasing him by her intelligence and discretion, was created by him Marquise de Maintenon, and then, after Maria Theresa's death, secretly became his wife (December 1684). She was then forty-nine; the King, forty-six — a handsome triumph for virtue! The King's Jesuit con-fessor had helped Madame Scarron, knowing that his society would find in her a pillar of strength. She was admired by the devout and respected by the poor daughters of noble families, for whom was built, under her supervision, the educational establishment at Saint-Cyr. Saint-Simon, who hated her and called her 'the dreadful and ignominious Maintenon', acknowledged in her a skill and tact which explained her power. The Duchess of Burgundy, whose husband, the King's grandson, had in 1711 become dauphin, paid court to Madame de Maintenon, whom she called 'my aunt'.

Never was there an heir to the throne more worthy to rule than the Duke of Burgundy; educated by Fénelon as a liberal and reformer, he would have knit the monarchy together. But suddenly in 1712 death

struck this whole family a series of blows. The kindly Duchess was the
first to go; then her husband the Duke; after them followed the little
Duke of Brittany, their eldest son; and in 1714 died the Duke of Berry,
Louis XIV's third grandson. The only survivor was a child of two, the
Duke of Anjou, later Louis XV. To the men of that day, this string of
sudden deaths looked suspicious; there was talk of poison; accusations
were made against the court of Austria and especially against the Duke
of Orleans, the Regent to be. In order to diminish the latter's chances for
the throne, the King declared his two legitimized bastards, 'and their
male posterity without end, true Princes of the Blood, entitled to assume
the quality, ranks, and full honours thereof, and qualified for succession
to the crown . . .' The charges against the Duke of Orleans were false;
as a matter of fact the Duke of Berry died from a fall while riding, and
the three others seem to have been victims of an epidemic ('purple
measles', meaning scarlet fever, a terribly contagious malady); poison had
played no part in events. But the slander clung to him and, as is always
the case, proved effective.

If the loveliness of Versailles today seems melancholy, how its gold, its
crystal, its stairways of rose marble, its fountains and its lawns must
have sparkled with gaiety when thousands of witty and charming men
and women there rejoiced in that permanent festival which constituted
life at court. The gowns studded with precious stones, the uniforms, the
servants' liveries, the chandeliers hung with brilliants, the carriages, the
green and flame-coloured velvet curtains, the brocades of the upholstery
made of every moment a fairy show of colour and light. There was always
being performed some air of Lully's, some comedy by Molière, one of
Benserade's ballets. 'At six we go riding in our barouches', wrote Madame
de Sévigné, 'then we go out on the canal in gondolas. There music is
being played; we return at ten and go to the play; midnight sounds and
we take supper.' At the beginning of his reign, the young King himself
took part in the ballets and masquerades; he always loved Corneille,
Racine and Molière. He keenly encouraged gambling for high stakes at
his court; debts gave him a hold over his courtiers. Devoted to 'the
shell of religion', he heard Mass daily and twice a week went to Bene-
diction of the Blessed Sacrament; on these occasions the ladies were careful to put in an appearance, for regular attendance won them merit.
Later, like its monarch, the court grew older. The King took his ease
in the room of Madame de Maintenon, his unavowed wife, where he
had his easy-chair and, on a little table, the *Imitation of Christ* and a

Psalter. For his amusement the young ladies of Saint-Cyr played *Esther*
and *Athalie*. When death came, he greeted it with his usual dignity.
'My child', he said to the little five-year-old Dauphin, 'you can be a
great king. Do not imitate me in the taste I have had for building, or
in my liking for war . . .' Massillon, who delivered the Great King's
funeral oration, began it with these words: 'God alone is great, my
brethren . . .' But the King was no longer there to hear him.

Religious matters had as great importance during Louis XIV's century
as in the days of Philip the Fair. Men's minds were seeking a new
equilibrium; Descartes had taught them to hold nothing true if it were
not clearly proved to be such; he had added that reason and method
lead back to faith. There were a few declared atheists, but they greatly
offended public opinion. 'Atheism does not exist', said La Bruyère. 'The
high personages who are most suspected of it are too lazy to make up
their minds that God does not exist; their indolence extends to the point
of making them cold and listless about this matter of such capital import,
just as it does regarding the nature of their souls and the deductions
to be drawn from a true religion; they do not deny these things, nor do
they agree to them; they don't think about them . . .' Yet Gassendi
and Saint-Évremond were freethinkers and, even among believers, the
Church met with political and intellectual difficulties. On the political
level, the old differences concerning the rights of the State and those of
Rome were rising anew; in 1682 the Gallican Church had issued a
forthright Declaration in which the French bishops recognized the Pope's
authority in matters of faith, but refused him the right to intervene in
temporal affairs. The Vatican protested, refusing canonical investiture
to the new French bishops, and the King had to yield in order to be able
to supply the dioceses with pastors. The Gallican policy, however —
that of the Declaration, that of Bossuet — remained the policy of the
French State until the time of the Third Republic, as may be seen in
Anatole France's *Anneau d'améthyste*.

The most serious spiritual controversy was that between the Jansenists
and the Jesuits. It recalls to our minds those of the medieval theologians;
faith was running into the same difficulties as in the age of heresies: the
problems of evil and free will. Jansenius, Bishop of Ypres, in *Augustinus*,
a treatise on Saint Augustine, had supported the inevitable efficacy of
divine grace and asserted that it placed man under the happy necessity
of not sinning. Here were ideas reminiscent of Calvin's; they were
attacked by the Jesuits, condemned by Rome and defended in France by

the Port Royal 'solitaries' and by Blaise Pascal in a masterpiece, his *Provincial Letters*. Pascal's thesis was that the propositions condemned in *Augustinus* were not to be found in that work and that in a question of fact no authority can intervene. The quarrel became unbelievably bitter; the King's Jesuit confessor hated the Jansenists, who constituted a powerful party in the *Parlement* and even at court. The Jesuits and their friends found little trouble in winning over the King, who 'thought himself an apostle' were he only to persecute Jansenism. In the end Port Royal was razed to the ground and its loyal inmates scattered. But the 'little society' secretly survived into the nineteenth century, and an unavowed Jansenism remained in France the Catholic aspect of the Reformation.

Ever since Henry IV had brought about religious peace by means of the Edict of Nantes, the Protestants had held their own, numbering nearly a million two hundred thousand souls. They dwelt principally in Languedoc, in Dauphiné and along the west coast. The Catholic clergy did its best to persecute the 'so-called reformed religion'. Urged on by his confessor, Louis XIV forbade the Protestants to build new churches, and then gave priests the right to enter the homes of dying members of the cult in order to exhort them to change their faith before breathing their last. In 1681 the King sanctioned the conversion of children to Catholicism starting at the age of seven. Saint Augustine was cited as an authority in the search for an excuse to use constraint in matters of faith. And then Protestants were barred from being notaries, bailiffs or even grocers! Under pressure from his confessor, Père La Chaise, and Madame de Maintenon, Louis thought he was doing his duty by authorizing the dragonnades, during the course of which the King's soldiers were to be seen torturing the King's subjects in order to force them to become Catholics. Such cruelty was employed that many of the reformed abjured their creed in dismay and proceeded from torture to Communion. At last, on October 17th, 1685, an ill-fated day for France, the King signed the Revocation of the Edict of Nantes; the public practice of their religion was forbidden to the Protestants. 'Unanimous' praises poured forth, a phenomenon which is always symptomatic of oppression. As many members of the Reformed Church as were able went into exile in England, Holland, Germany and even America, where they established respectable and respected Huguenot colonies; thus did France lose four hundred thousand of her finest subjects, in its army and navy, among its magistrates and businessmen. And this was the greatest mistake of the whole reign.

The transfer of the court to Versailles had severed court from city. The city, however, passionately aped the court. The nobility apart, Paris society was made up of the magistrates, doctors, men of letters and merchants. Molière's comedies show us the things which then deserved mockery: the avarice of the bourgeoisie, the pedantry of the doctors, ignorant, affected women, blue stockings, pious impostors. But, if the learned ladies had their shortcomings, they were useful in that they disseminated taste and unified the language. The *salons* — and this was true even of the days of Louis XIII — contributed to making French a classical and universal tongue. Thanks to the *précieuses* and their friends, France became a 'land of grammarians', and literature became there a part of the country's active life. 'Good manners', said Voltaire, 'penetrated even into the back rooms of petty merchants.' And the higher level of comfort helped in the process: a townsman in the seventeenth century got more for less money than a great lord in the days of Henry IV. No longer did people move about Paris on mule or horseback, but in coach or chaise, and the typical Parisian depicted by La Bruyère attentively read the *Gazette de Hollande* or the *Mercure Gallant*, spent a few hours closeted with the ladies, attended a military review or a comedy and knew how to sing all the dialogue in at least one opera. He was a professional spectator, idler, gossip; above all he was a confirmed townsman: 'Don't speak to most of your bourgeois about ploughing or saplings, about cuttings or second crops of hay if you want to be understood; for them such expressions form no part of the language. With some, discuss the various measures of cloth, prices, rates of interest; with others, appeal procedures, civil petitions, emoluments, removals. They know the world, and what is more they know it from its least handsome and least glittering side; of nature — its beginnings, its growth, its gifts, and its bounty — they know nothing.'[1]

In France it was an age of masterpieces. During the seventeenth century French literature set Europe a model; and to the eyes of Frenchmen in the twentieth it remains an example of perfection. Valéry was an admirer of Bossuet, La Fontaine and Racine; Proust drew his sustenance from Saint-Simon and Madame de Sévigné. Molière remains our greatest writer of comedy; Corneille, Pascal, La Rochefoucauld, La Bruyère — each of these names calls to mind so much that is splendid that their very mention suffices for their praise. Now what is the essence of this French classicism? The imitation of Greek and Roman writers? Such imitation

---

[1] La Bruyère, *Les Caractères ou les Mœurs de ce Siècle: De la Ville.*

had been much more narrowly required during the preceding century. The Cartesian method? 'Yet Descartes thought like his contemporaries; he did not teach them to think like him.'[1] Respect for reason? Who had had that more straitly than Saint Thomas? Corneille's heroes are not reasonable any more than those of Retz. The abstract and impersonal approach of this artistic flowering? But we find Pascal and Madame de Sévigné wholly personal. What makes a writer classical, said Valéry, is that he seeks not 'to make the new' but to 'make enduringly', which means fashioning a masterpiece which shall be independent of circumstance and of date. La Rochefoucauld observes himself, but analyses within himself the everlasting man; Racine transposes dramas of his own time into ancient or biblical tragedies. The classics have been rebuked for the respect they paid to rules; however, it was precisely that discipline, imposed upon writers passionately concerned with life at court, with the three unities, with taste, which yielded so much loveliness. The great classicist is a governed romanticist;[2] the pseudo-classicist was to appear only when the social amenities had too greatly lessened the force of passion. Another effect of court life was to develop to a degree never before attained the science of analysing human feelings. From Madame de La Fayette to Proust, there was to be an established and continuous tradition of analytical novels in which France excelled.

In art even more than in literature, French classicism ordered nature. All the works of this age possess their simple, intelligible unity. This is true of the landscapes of Poussin or Claude Lorrain, of Puget's or Coysevox's sculpture, of the Louvre's colonnade as much as of the dome of the Invalides. Indeed the whole reign is no more than one vast work of art fashioned about a centre, the *Roy Soleil*: buildings, paintings and gardens existed only for his glory; his will cut vast, noble perspectives through forest and marshland, at Paris and Versailles. The cathedral of the Middle Ages allowed the town to nestle about it; the classical masterpiece required that it be detached, alone, in unencumbered thought. The Place Vendôme and the Place des Vosges are examples of perfect city planning; but Versailles above all lays before us the unity of the age. There the landscape is made for the castle and the castle for the King. He it was who directed the labours of his architect Mansart, his gardener Le Nôtre, his painter Le Brun, the countless artists who wrought those door handles, those balusters, those candelabra. The French garden had replaced the Italian pleasure ground. Symmetrical, intellectual, regularly bestrewn

---

[1] DANIEL MORNET.   [2] On this point see FIDAO JUSTINIANI and HENRY PEYRE.

with statues and fountains, it satisfied the mind while preserving the illusion by virtue of the distant and hazy countryside which stretched beyond the Great Canal. During the eighteenth century it was fashionable to belittle Versailles, to prefer to it the no less artificial romanticism of English gardens; but in France the English garden tended to take on classical lines, and a Frenchman of our own day by national instinct still takes infinite pleasure in the regular and comprehensible beauties of the Great King's pleasances. 'Versailles must be ranked very high. It must be defended against all comers. We are on Versailles' side; what am I saying? we are *a part of it*',[1] as of the Place Vendôme, of the vistas of the Concorde and Corneille's tragedies.

In so centralized a regime, was it possible for any public opinion to take shape? Not only was there a very lively one, but it reverberated; not by means of the press — papers were infrequent and empty — but by means of the newsmongers who in those days created a word-of-mouth journalism. There were state, or political, newsmongers and newsmongers of Parnassus, of letters. 'It was they who gave reputations their first start in Paris.' Their great ambition was to be the first to convey a morsel of information, to explain events, to criticize them; they were strategists, diplomats, theologians.

> Alone they govern all the world,
> They take towns by assault;
> Without their fingers in a pie, the whole thing is at fault,
> And in wisdom they have no peers.[2]

Newsletters, common in English-speaking countries of the twentieth century, existed in France as early as the seventeenth, and weekly their writers, thanks to the Dutch bankers, received war news which the government had not yet made public. Certain groups gathered at designated points such as under the chestnuts of the Tuileries. Here was a stock exchange for news. Retired field-marshals took up their posts there to comment on military operations. Each garden went in for its speciality: at the Palais Royal, internal politics; foreign affairs at the Tuileries; literary news at the Luxembourg. Then private letter-writers spread the news throughout the provinces; Madame de Sévigné's letters were copied and circulated all over Provence. Indeed French public opinion was much more free in 1710 than in 1810.

Under Louis XIV, what were the conditions of rural life? Had the

---

[1] H. DE MONTHERLANT.   [2] JEAN DONNEAU DE VIZÉ.

people grown more miserable? The evidence is contradictory. In a letter to the King written during 1695, Fénelon compares France to a 'large desolate hospital, without sustenance'. Uprisings provoked by want were numerous and were pitilessly crushed. 'All this Breton soldiery', said Madame de Sévigné, 'does nothing but kill and steal.' Colbert, who for ten years had struggled to establish industries, discouraged farmers by forbidding the export of cereals. The celebrated description of the peasants by La Bruyère comes to mind: 'Sullen animals, male and female . . . blackened, pallid, and scorched by the sun', living 'in lairs . . . on black bread, water, and grapes.' Was this merely a purple passage? Perhaps, yet it remains true that during the seventeenth century the French peasant paid the taxes from which the privileged were exempt and which went for their support, and that the value of peasant property decreased by a half during this reign. In direct contradiction we have the testimony of Voltaire who, in his *Siècle de Louis XIV*, maintained that these vague complaints made no distinction between farmers and day labourers: 'The latter support themselves only by the labour of their hands; and so it is in all the countries of the world, where the greater part must live by the sweat of their brows. But scarcely is there a kingdom in the universe where the husbandman, the farmer, is better off than in certain French provinces, and England alone can compete in this respect. The proportional poll-tax, in some provinces taking the place of the fixed capitation, has played its part in making more substantial the fortunes of husbandmen who possess ploughs, vineyards and gardens. The labourer, the workman must be cut down to necessitousness in order to be willing to toil: such is man's nature . . .' Wealthy Voltaire easily made the best of things; those who suffered complained. One prayer went the rounds: 'Our Father who art in Versailles, thy name is no longer hallowed; thy kingdom is diminished; thy will is no longer done on earth or on the waves. Give us our bread, which is lacking to us . . .'[1] Many might well have added, 'And deliver us from the tax farmers', for the 'financiers' alone grew wealthier. It was said that each king had his statue among those he loved: Henry IV in the midst of his people, on the Pont-Neuf; Louis XIII among the tumultuous favourites of the Place Royale; Louis XIV with the tax collectors in the Place des Victoires. In 1690 and again in 1709, the destitution of the realm was so great that in order to replenish the treasury the King himself had to have his silver furnishings, his gold plate and even his throne melted into bullion.

[1] Quoted by A. BAYET.

A few courageous Frenchmen knew that the country stood in need of radical reforms. Vauban wrote to the Marquis de Torcy: 'I have long been obsessed with a folly on which I have often reflected without any intention of correcting it: having thus been unable to resist temptation, I have yielded to it . . .' This temptation was that of writing a book, the *Dîme royale* (*The Royal Tithe*), which Vauban rounded off with memoranda addressed to the King. Therein he showed that the poll-tax had fallen into such a state of corruption that the very angels of heaven could not have succeeded in straightening it out, and that not enough attention had been paid to the common people, 'the most bankrupt part of the kingdom', and that 'which has always suffered the most and is suffering the most'. Forty years of roving life and his engineering profession, which had put him in touch with men of all classes, had made him one of the best-informed of Frenchmen. Out of his experience he had come to believe that any privilege tending towards tax exemption is unjust and that every subject should contribute in proportion to his means. He proposed a new fiscal system with a tithe in kind on the products of the land, a tithe in money on other income, excise taxes, customs duties and revenues from royal property. The poll-tax he would have abolished altogether. This book was completed in 1700; Vauban read it to the King, then published it, without authorization, in 1706. He was condemned by decree of the council and, quite literally, died of a broken heart. His book, indeed, was more remarkable for its warmth of purpose than for the realism of what he proposed, but it has remained famous as an example of the interest which a great figure, a favourite of the King, could take, to his own disadvantage, in the sufferings of the 'common people'.

At the moment when Voltaire wrote his *Siècle de Louis XIV* it took courage to glorify the Grand Monarch. His reign had been unpopular and praises had faded away. When the King died, said Saint-Simon, 'the provinces, in despair at their own ruin and prostration, trembled with joy. The people, bankrupt, overwhelmed, disconsolate, thanked God with scandalous rejoicing for a release of which it had forsworn all hope even in its dearest dreams . . .' Voltaire did not deny the King's shortcomings, but he added: 'Although he has been blamed for meannesses, for harshness in his zeal against Jansenism, too great arrogance with foreigners in the days of his success, for his weakness regarding several women, too much severity in personal matters, for wars lightly undertaken, for ravaging the Palatinate with fire, for persecuting the

Protestants, nevertheless his great qualities and achievements, when ultimately weighed in the balance, are preponderant over his faults. Time, which ripens men's judgments, has put its seal upon his reputation; and despite everything which has been written against him, his name will not be uttered without respect and without associating with it the idea of a century eternally memorable.' And indeed if we take into account the sum total of beauty added to France's heritage, the intellectual order thanks to which were nurtured the very men who one day would transform the country, and the prestige which the French nation enjoyed throughout Europe, it is impossible to deny this age the title of great. Unfortunately greatness is not the same as stability; the regime bore within it the germs of the disease which would destroy it. By making his nobility live at Versailles and reducing it to a menial condition, Louis XIV ruined every element of local government in France. He reduced the French aristocracy to impotence. This would not have been perilous had he leaned upon the people for support, but the King wanted himself to be the sole source of power. 'This was to make a revolution not only desirable, but conceivable and possible. All our revolutions for the last hundred years have had as their necessary and sufficient condition the establishment of centralized power, thanks to which a minimum of imagination and a minimum of strength and continuous effort yield at a stroke a whole nation to him who will take the risk. From the day when it became clear that the seizure of two or three buildings or a handful of important persons was all you needed to gain mastery over the whole country, there began the era of political changes through short and sudden violence.'[1]

[1] PAUL VALÉRY.

CHAPTER V

HOW THE REGENCY WEAKENED THE MONARCHY

ALTHOUGH many of her kings were minors at the time of their accession, and France has therefore known many regents, the word *regency* always evokes the years following the death of the Grand Monarch, with their overtones of elegant debauchery, polite vice and scandalous dissoluteness. Is this association of ideas justified? Michelet, who greatly favoured the Regent, denies, not the scandals, but the idea that they were limited to the France of that day. Debauchery, yes — but it had already existed, he says, under Louis XIV, the difference being that, especially following the advent of Madame de Maintenon, it had been kept under cover, whereas with the Regent, a man of sceptical and free-thinking mind, it became open and public. Speculation, financial scandals — of course, but this was the period in England of the South Sea Bubble, a collapse almost as extraordinary as John Law's in France. During this period the great Powers were discovering credit and the colonies; they lacked financial experience; their 'dream palaces' melted away. Michelet's argument is that the Regent, Philip of Orleans, was a liberal with advanced ideas, who did his best to make an outworn financial system more just, and an anti-clerical who dealt kindly with Jansenists and members of the Reformed religion. Saint-Simon, an intimate of the Regent, confirms this view: 'He dearly loved freedom, and as much for others as for himself. One day he commended England to me in this regard, where there exists neither exile nor *lettres de cachet*, and where the King can forbid entrance only to his palace, and cannot hold any man imprisoned...' That the Regent nearly came to grief over his mistresses, that he failed in his reforms, Michelet does not deny, yet he dates from the Regency the emancipation of minds.

Philip of Orleans was agreeable, congenial, intelligent, with infinite grace of manners, a natural eloquence and a memory 'which made him seem well informed on government matters and regarding every sort of art and mechanics'. Like most sensual people, he was extremely lazy. It was one of his weaknesses to believe that he resembled Henry IV in every particular, and 'cultivated this resemblance no less in the vices of that great prince than in his virtues'. In the number of his mistresses Philip carried off the honours, having had over a hundred. 'Like Henry IV, he was by nature kindly, humane, and compassionate.' Ever since the rows in the royal family, slander had relegated him to solitude, which had matured him, and such obloquy made his position even more difficult when the time came for him to assume power. This royal duke was Regent Designate, even though Philip V, King of Spain, was more closely related to the infant king (because Philip V, when he accepted the Spanish throne, had renounced all his rights in France). Louis XIV, however, because of his dislike for the Duke of Orleans, his nephew-son-in-law, had established in his will a Regency Council, over which Orleans was to preside and in which were to be included Madame de Montespan's two legitimized bastards, the Duke of Maine and the Count of Toulouse. It was traditional, when a king died, that the *Parlement* should annul his will, in return for which those who benefited by the operation promised that body to let it share in the exercise of power and recognized its right of remonstrance. Thus it was that Philip became sole regent. It was a second tradition to disregard this promise; but *Parlement* had a short memory.

The regency was a reaction against many aspects of the Great Century. Louis XIV had ruled as an absolute king, with a few clerks; the Regent set up seven councils of ten members each, and highly valued the advice of the aristocracy. Louis XIV had protected the Jesuits; the Regent protected their enemies. Louis XIV had exalted his illegitimate children; the Regent humbled them and stripped them of their standing as princes of the blood. At Versailles Louis XIV had boarded ten thousand voracious families; the Regent eliminated most of the expenses of the court. In foreign affairs his adviser was the Abbé Dubois, 'that rascally Dubois', a weasel-faced diplomat, the master of his own weak master, that Dubois who had 'servile and low' beginnings, but wanted the cardinal's hat and got it. As England's man he succeeded in convincing the Regent of the dangers of the Spanish alliance; might not Philip V of Spain one day revoke his agreement and covet the throne of France? George of Hanover and Philip of Orleans, 'both of them usurpers', as Dubois cynically put it, were better suited to understand each other. As for Saint-Simon, he thought that England, wealthy, strong on the seas and jealous of France ever since the day when more than half that country had been English, would always be a formidable enemy. It was necessary he told the Regent, while seeking an agreement with her, to remember that she detested the French navy, yearned after France's colonies and was fortifying the Anglo-Norman islands under French noses; hence she should be dealt with honourably but cautiously, the fleet should be strengthened and an alliance made with Spain. Dubois carried the day, and an English-French-Dutch pact made war with Spain inevitable. The Regent's liberalism gave him no pain at the thought; George the Protestant and Orleans the freethinker came to an understanding against his Catholic Majesty. Here was a new policy, satisfactory to advanced minds for ideological reasons, though extremely dangerous for the country since the British navy was going to wipe out the Spanish fleet. What was to become of the French colonies when the English would be wholly masters of the ocean? But the Regent and Dubois gave little heed to the colonies or the future.

And yet the colonies or, as people called them, 'the Islands', were in fashion. Coffee from the Isle of Bourbon, Martinique and Saint-Domingo (Haiti) briskly cheered men's spirits. In Canada the *Coureurs des Bois* were exploring the Great Lakes area, and it was said that lovely Indian girls showed them no cruelty. The colonial epic seemed to partake at once of the Lives of the Saints and the courtly novel; while the Franciscans or the Jesuits brought the Gospel to the Algonquins and the Iroquois, the French colonists, unswayed by racial prejudice, took native women as their wives. La Salle, first to journey down the Mississippi River, had discovered the region which was later to be the heart of America, the Middle West, and the English had fearfully watched him turn their American flank by this operation. When, at the river's mouth, a French company founded Louisiana (Louis's land) and the town of New Orleans, both the British and the Spanish tried to cut off the new settlement.

These undertakings were given a new lease of life by a foreign banker, John Law, 'A Scotsman of I know not what birth, a great gambler and a great schemer, who had amassed big profits in various countries where he had resided . . . He was mentioned to the Duke of Orleans as a weighty man in matters of banking, trade, currency movements, money and finance; this made the Regent curious to meet him. He granted Law several interviews and he was so pleased that he referred to him as a man from whom he could gain light . . .'[1] What he did gain was something very different.

In no sense was Law a swindler. Like the majority of great financial

[1] SAINT-SIMON.

charlatans, he inspired confidence through the modesty of his demeanour and the mildness of his manners. A bold and ingenious banker, he had one idea which is basic to the modern concept of credit: to create apparent resources by printing money. 'The workings of trade', he wrote, 'revolve wholly about money. The more you have, the more people you can keep employed. Credit will take the place of money and will have the same results . . .' That this is a practicable procedure, if the covering security is adequate, has been proved by experience. In 1716 Law set up a General Bank to discount commercial paper, and in 1718 it became the Royal Bank with the State as its sole shareholder. His error lay in using as backing for the bank's notes shares in a company of the Indies, which was the heir of Louisiana and of the concessions made to Colbert's *Grandes Compagnies*. A nation's credit cannot be established upon a fluctuating basis; the Regent, however, vacillating when taxes were at issue because his government was weak, welcomed to his bosom a man who brought him funds without annoying anyone. At the outset came success beyond belief, values soared, and Law went up like a balloon. His advertising was flamboyant and ingenious: Indians bedecked with gold were paraded through Paris; engravings were distributed showing mountains of silver and cliffs of emeralds in Louisiana. But powerful enemies lay in wait for Law's downfall — the English, who feared the thought of renewed French colonial activity, the revenue collectors who saw a threat to their concessions and their profits. The public was bullish, the financiers, bearish; for several months speculation was unbridled and enormous fortunes piled up. 'Mother-shares' were split into 'daughter' and 'grand-daughter' shares; in order to buy 'grand-daughters', you had to have four 'mothers' and one 'daughter'. Street cleaners, lackeys and lords won millions; a whole encampment was built up around the rue Quincampoix where the bank had its offices. Fair speculatresses were on the look out for the newly rich, to ease them of some of their burdens. Law, chased by these women, resisted valiantly; he loved his own wife and also happened to be decent, despite malicious rumours. 'A duchess', wrote the Princess Palatine, 'has kissed Law's hand in public. Now if the duchesses so behave, where must not other women kiss him? . . .' Law sought in good faith to recruit settlers for America and to transform his Utopia into real wealth; he cannot be held culpable for all the speculators' follies. But when the crash came, as it had to come, the system was swept away with the fools. Suddenly owners of shares and bank-notes stampeded the bank in panic to get their money back. At first Law kept his wickets open wide; his friends had him made controller-general, tried to strengthen him, but he himself knew he was 'a trembling acrobat on the last rung of the ladder.'[1] He tried to put up a fight; in order to save his own currency, he outlawed the circulation of gold and silver. Still values tumbled. Now there was 'slaughter' near the bank's doors; on October 10th, 1720, the bank was put out of business through the influence of the farmers-general. Law fled, and he took nothing with him. 'I went forth naked', said he. 'I could not even save my coat.' He died in Venice (1729), 'a sorry beggar, timidly making excuses'; and this epitaph was composed for him:

> Here lies that Scot, now world-renowned,
>   Reckoner without peer;
> By rules, in algebra quite sound,
>   He sickened France for many a year.

This failure shook the country. Here was no matter of one financier's downfall; the State was involved in this business; the Regent had patronized it, the future Regent (the Duke of Bourbon) had grown rich on it. Not merely a few Parisian speculators, but a round million families throughout the country held the bank's notes. This was inevitable since these bills had become an enforced currency. When, after Law's flight, the revenue contractors and farmers-general regained control of finances and had determined to have a house cleaning and not to redeem bills to which they refused 'visas', ruin threatened every household. On the ground floor of the Louvre a thousand clerks were installed to carry out this huge operation — a star chamber for ordinary folk; the great disentangled themselves, the poor lost everything, and even endorsed bills were not paid. Serious discontent and disaffection followed, for a single big scandal weakens a regime more than hundreds of little ones, and the weakening of a regime already weak is perilous. Whig England was strong enough to withstand the South Sea Bubble; the collapse of Law's system made the monarchy totter. It took a hundred years and Bonaparte's genius to make it possible for anyone to dare suggest anew a bank of issue.

France had other reasons for wrath. In Marseilles and throughout Provence the plague was working dreadful havoc; only a sanitary cordon, pitiless but effective, protected Paris against it. Obscene pamphlets appeared dealing with the Regent's court and his private life; he was accused of being the incestuous lover of his eldest daughter, the charmingly silly Duchess of Berry. Was there any truth in it? The looseness

---

[1] JULES MICHELET.

of morals lent colour to every calumny. The Regent's intimate suppers were subtle debauches; he made designs for engravings of *Daphnis et Chloë* and it was said that he had the daughter he loved too well pose for these sketches. When she died at twenty-four after a secret confinement, the rumour grew. Then the Regent wavered between other ladies, Sabran and Parabère, the latter a 'black little raven' with knowing wiles.

As for his adviser Dubois, he thought only of his cardinal's hat, and he was not asleep these days. In order to win it, he was ready to exhaust the credit of the State and to turn France's policy inside out. This ambition forced him to come to terms with Spain and the Vatican; hence he wooed the Jesuits by supporting their bull in the *Parlement*, and arranged a Spanish marriage for the young king — a new Anne of Austria to seal the alliance. The Infanta came to the court of France there to receive her education. What did England, whose agent Dubois so long had been, think of this *volte-face*? As always, that country was ready to sacrifice appearances for realities; what she wanted was the Spanish trade and no competition therein from France. Throwing French interests to the winds, Dubois set up a Spanish-English-French alliance. At last he had his hat. But no sooner had he got it than he died; he had heaped upon himself every species of labour, baseness and anxiety of spirit to win a dignity which death at once snatched from him. The Regent soon followed in his footsteps. Long apoplectic, his doctors had warned him against sensual indulgence, but he preferred his pleasures to his life because life bored him. One December day in 1723, his head tumbled upon the shoulder of a pretty woman who had accompanied him before the King's council; he died as he had lived, a libertine.

Monsieur le Duc (the Duke of Bourbon, later Prince of Condé) who succeeded him was of even less worth. He was in thrall to the Marquise de Prie, daughter of a tax collector, wife of 'a starveling ambassador', in features a heavenly creature, 'of a sinuous and retiring, then suddenly bold, demeanour', a regular sibyl. The King was of age (at thirteen!) and hence the Duke of Bourbon was not a regent but prime minister. He governed ill, gave rise to outbreaks and instituted persecutions. Madame de Prie induced him to ship the Infanta, Louis XV's betrothed, back to Spain and to choose for the young king a princess unburdened with any dowry — Maria Leszczynska, daughter of the dethroned King of Poland, who possessed neither beauty nor means but was honest and good. Three explanations can be given for the change: Madame de Prie hoped to dominate a queen who would owe her everything; it was urgently necessary to marry the King off, lest were he left to his childhood companions, he become another Henry III; Maria, already twenty-two years old, could at once supply the crown with heirs whom the young Infanta, ten years her junior, would have delayed too long. As for the Church, it looked favourably upon a Catholic queen fully as devout as the Infanta. The Duke of Bourbon, however, could hope for nothing, as he had come to power only through the will and good offices of Fleury, the King's tutor; when he sought therefore to get rid of Fleury, the latter exploded and threatened to leave the court. The King, who could not do without his tutor, wept and sought refuge on his commode, then dismissed the Duke of Bourbon, who received orders to live at the Castle of Chantilly. Madame de Prie, exiled to her lands at Courbemine, there poisoned herself out of sheer boredom during the following year.

During the course of this minority, the licentiousness and weakness of those who ruled had taught those they governed disrespect and contempt. Literature had become frivolous and partisan. Marivaux's imaginative comedy gave France a poetic theatre which anticipated de Musset's, but Lesage had not Molière's power. Sacred eloquence burst into final flame with Massillon, the orator who had begun Louis XIV's funeral oration with the sentence, 'God alone is great, my brethren . . .' Fontenelle vulgarized ideas without vulgarity; Voltaire was at his beginnings; but the great figure of the period was Montesquieu, whose *Lettres Persanes*, published in 1721, an amusing but lively satire on the happenings at court, sounded the note of the Revolution without that young magistrate's ever suspecting it.

The Regency, though brief and seemingly rather empty, was big with consequence. After Louis XIV's reign, it was a breathing spell but also an abdication. Its frivolousness and spirit of speculation begat want of respect and of religion; the role of women — and not the best women — became greater; the government of France lost any feeling for the national interest. It had given up the effort of holding its own on the sea and had compromised the future of a colonial empire for which La Salle had opened such wonderful vistas. Why did not the country's scorn and discontent bring a new Fronde to birth? Because the monarchy had inherited so great a prestige from Louis XIV that any rebellion would have seemed scandalous. And yet the idol was shattered. Pamphleteers and rhymesters had made opposition fashionable; that which under the Grand Monarch would have been blasphemy was now becoming strong-mindedness. The whole business came to birth in a handful of ditties.

CHAPTER VI

HOW, UNDER THE REIGN OF LOUIS XV, FRANCE LOST HER SELF-RESPECT

IN 1726 Louis XV was a handsome young man, frail and gloomy, with the pretty face of a girl, unfeeling and cold. In his fearfulness, his lassitude, his sometimes cruel teasing, he recalled to mind Louis XIII. None of his tutors had taught him his duties as a sovereign; Cardinal Fleury had won his affection by favouring his laziness and by taking part in childish games. During the days of the Fronde, Louis XIV had been schooled by misfortune; Louis XV as a child had known only cringing and flattery. The moment he had to rule, he turned everything over to Fleury, who, Saint-Simon tells us, had not 'the slightest notion of anything when he took the helm of all things'. Michelet describes the Cardinal as an 'agreeable nobody', patient, pliant and smiling. The fact is that he governed better than most ministers. Fleury preferred good sense to beautiful thoughts and he excelled at 'saving candle ends' — a happy fault in a court where so many others were burning them at both ends. His inexperience was counterbalanced by the sound tradition of the government departments, trained by Colbert and Louvois. He was well advised and, as early as 1738, the eternal deficit had been covered. For an 'agreeable nobody', here was a most honourable achievement.

In foreign affairs the pacifist Fleury encouraged understanding with England, whose prime minister, Robert Walpole, shared his horror of war; neither could spare his country this ordeal, but they delayed it and struggled to contain its evils within limits. The spindly cardinal and the thick-set squire shared a dislike for vainglory and a healthy conception of the national interest. Neither the one nor the other laid claim to grand ideas, which helped them to have good ones, since the human mind, naturally weak, sees more clearly that which is close at hand. Had it been possible for Europe to be guaranteed peace, these two men would have done it, but inherited ideological or dynastic quarrels kept up the temperature of a sick continent. In France the leading spirits were traditionally anti-Austrian; now an opportunity arose to 'humble the House of Austria'. The Emperor, Charles VI, who had only daughters, passionately desired to leave his throne to the Archduchess Maria Theresa, but he could accomplish this only by having this Pragmatic Sanction approved by the other Powers. Fleury evaded the issue and was blamed by public opinion which accused him of weakness; the war party included in its ranks the military, the court and the men of letters.

The death of the King of Poland, Augustus II, in 1733 made the danger more threatening, for eastern Europe was undergoing a rapid transformation. When Peter the Great had rebuilt Russia into a great Power, he had insistently offered France an alliance. Through loyalty to old friends — Poland, Sweden and Turkey — the French Government had turned a deaf ear. In vexation Russia had then come to an agreement with Austria, and now the two countries were jointly endangering Poland. As candidate for the Polish throne both were supporting the Elector of Saxony, who would have been wholly loyal to the two empires, whereas the candidate of Polish independence was Stanislas Leszczynski, Louis XV's father-in-law. As was natural, the Queen of France supported her father; the King helped her through pride, having been humiliated at his marriage to a 'demoiselle' no longer the daughter of a king; French opinion was in favour of intervention because it was not fond of Austria; as for Fleury, he had the misfortune to understand that France, even if she wanted to, *could* not defend Poland against the Austrians and the Russians because geography has no feelings. But public opinion does. To satisfy the fanatical (who took no part in it), a small French expedition was shipped off to Danzig, fought heroically and was finally captured by the Russians. Only one road remained open — to attack Austria — and this was the country's choice. Fleury did what he could to make this war short and inoffensive. By the Treaty of Vienna (1738) he agreed to acknowledge Maria Theresa's rights to the throne on condition that she would marry Francis, Duke of Lorraine, and that Stanislas Leszczynski, king without a kingdom, would be given Lorraine, which at his death would revert to France. Here was one of the finest compromises in diplomatic history. Austria was satisfied, the father-in-law once again had a kingdom and France acquired a wholly French area.

But brief are the triumphs of wisdom. In England, peace-loving Walpole ultimately found himself being dragged into war. Mercantile nationalism was growing and the city of London wanted to fight Spain in order to despoil that country of the trade with South America; William Pitt cast scorn on Walpole's shameful weakness. 'So be it', said Walpole. 'It will be your war and I wish you joy of it . . .' He resigned and, by his departure, ended the first Anglo-French *entente*. Contrary to Walpole's principle, his successor involved himself in European affairs.

The Emperor, Charles VI, had died in 1740, and his legacy had awakened the greed of others. Frederick II, King of Prussia, a Machiavellian prince, unburdened by religious or chivalrous principles or by respect for engagements into which he had entered, laid claim to the rich province of Silesia. What rights had he to it? 'Fresh troops, a well-filled treasury, and a covetous soul.' Yet he passed for an enlightened ruler; he had succeeded in endearing himself to the writers of France (Voltaire in particular); he had the support of a ruling class as passionate as it was ill informed. Even Michelet, writing in the nineteenth century, still took the Prussian side in his business; by 1871 he would have been of a different opinion. Frederick was the aggressor, but Austria received the blame. An irresistible current drew France towards the Prussian alliance and war. Fleury, weakened by age (he was eighty-eight in 1742) refrained from interfering. An octogenarian can still be stubborn, but not unshakable. Louis XV would have preferred to see France an onlooker — his government had no quarrel with Austria — but opinion waxed eloquent, pressing, violent. The marshals and the mistresses were for war, and the King was told that England was becoming dangerous and that by beating Austria down with the support of the 'liberal' King of Prussia, France would be striking a blow at England. Finally the King yielded. It was more than a crime; it was a mistake and the beginning of a long series of wars which would give England mastery of the seas and Prussia dominion over Germany.

Maria Theresa did not lose her composure. She negotiated for the support of London; whereupon Frederick II, weighing the combined strength of Austria and England, abandoned France, which had compromised herself in his behalf. In exchange for Silesia, he betrayed his allies. Cut off in Bohemia, the French armies with great difficulty beat their retreat; in 1743 Fleury died of old age and grief. Carteret, Walpole's successor and an open enemy of France, organized against her a Hanoverian army which joined the Austrian forces. Then took place one of those French resurgences which from century to century shine over the pages of Europe's history. Eyes were opened. Marshal de Noailles advised carrying the war into Flanders, England's sensitive point; the King, spurred on by a warlike mistress, left to join the armies and fell seriously ill at Metz. Thereupon the country rallied about him and nicknamed him the 'well-beloved'. Voltaire praised him:

> Il sait aimer, il sait combattre;
> Il dépêche en ce beau séjour

Un brevet, digne d'Henri Quatre,
Signé: Louis, Mars et l'Amour.

[He knows how to love, he knows how to fight; in his fine dwelling he
dispatched a commission worthy of Henry IV, signed: Louis, Mars and
Love.]

On May 11th, 1745, in Louis XV's presence, Maurice de Saxe won the
victory of Fontenoy over the English, Dutch and Hanoverians; the
French army entered the Low Countries, taking Antwerp and Berg-op-
Zoom. Meanwhile Frederick II with total cynicism threw his weight on
one side, then on the other, was faithless, retracted, made his own
arrangements. England, mistress of the seas, threatened the French
colonies and even the shores of Brittany. An understanding must be
reached and this war, which should never have been begun, brought to
an end. The Peace of Aix-la-Chapelle (1748) pleased no one save
Frederick, who kept Silesia; in Paris the market-women acquired the
habit of saying 'as foolish as the peace'. As had long been the case whenever a war between France and England came to a close, each handed
back its conquests because the other held precious forfeits; in order to
obtain the withdrawal of the French troops who were in control of
Flanders, the English government had to evacuate Cape Breton Island
which commanded the approaches to Canada. Both in India and America,
Anglo-French disputes were left unsettled. No one of the great European
countries accepted the map of the world. All the old systems of alliances
were dying; France and Austria were asking themselves whether their
traditional hostility was still justified by a real opposition of interests,
or whether, on the contrary, Prussia's growth did not constitute for both
a common and fearsome danger. France and England were beginning
to understand, each for its own account, that they would never know a
lasting peace so long as the question of which should command the seas and
the colonies remained unsettled between them.

At home, the distinguishing mark of this first part of Louis XV's reign
was that the opposition, which thought itself liberal, defended reactionary
ideas, and that the Government, which was called reactionary, was actually progressive. Public opinion, founded on the Paris *salons*, was becoming more and more powerful, but its intentions had more merit than its
information. The War of the Austrian Succession had created a fresh
deficit and the Government proposed to meet it by taxing all fortunes,
including those of the privileged, with a levy of 5 per cent. The *Parlement*

refused to record this capital levy, which it would itself have had to pay like all the rest of the country, and denounced it as a 'monstrous exaction'. In a partisan spirit the literary men and the public lauded the *Parlement* for its resistance! Blame was levelled at the court's expenses, whereas it should have been at the foolishness of courts in general. The religious situation was similar; the Jansenist quarrel had been revived by a pontifical bull (*Unigenitus*) which condemned one hundred and one propositions in Quesnel's book as tainted with belief in efficient grace; the Church refused the Sacraments to those who did not accept the bull. The Gallican and Jansenist *Parlement* sustained the 'appellants', and Jansenism became a political party. Atheists, who certainly did not care a penny about grace, took its part. The strange thing was that the *Parlements*, so hotly supported by liberal writers, were the same tribunals which condemned blasphemers to death; nothing could have been more inconsistent, but in the midst of passions, everything is good as long as it feeds hatred.

The King's public and private life added to the general confusion. Louis was not a fool — 'He gave orders like a master and discussed matters like a minister', said Argenson. But generally, being born tired, he let 'the well-oiled wheels turn'. France did not forgive him the countless affairs she had tolerated in Henry IV; victories alone excuse scandals, and debauchery is not love. Louis's gallantries became more degraded with the passage of time. (The Queen had always bored him; he had given her ten children 'without addressing a word to her'. She protested gently, 'Always going to bed, always being brought to bed!') Starting in 1732 he took on, in the order of their ages, the three Nesle sisters — Madame de Mailly, Madame de Vintimille and Madame de la Tournelle, whom he made the Duchess of Châteauroux. They strove mightily to make a hero of him, but it was a hopeless task. After them a woman of the middle class, Madame Lenormand d'Étoiles, née Poisson, from adolescence trained for the part by a far-sighted tutor who saw in her a 'morsel fit for a king', became official mistress. 'She had been taught everything save morals, which would have stood in her way.'[1] The King made her Marquise de Pompadour, and she governed him, France and all Europe for twenty years. She snared him by means of pleasure, employed writers and artists for his distraction — Voltaire, Helvétius, Crébillon, Nattier, La Tour, Boucher, Van Loo, Bouchardon — and, when she herself was no longer fit for love, did not hesitate to turn herself

[1] SAINTE-BEUVE.

238

into a pander. The Parc-aux-Cerfs was not as bad as it was painted by the pamphleteers, yet the King did maintain there a small house for his secret pleasures, and it is a fact that Madame de Pompadour agreed to run it for him with her usual obliging efficiency. Hence her epitaph:

Ci-gît qui fut vingt ans pucelle,
Quinze ans catin, sept ans maquerelle.
[Here lies one for twenty years a maid,
Fifteen a whore, and seven a procuress.]

When she died in 1764, her place was taken by a 'nobody', Jeanne Bécu, otherwise Vaubernier, a pretty prostitute who did not give a fig for politics, but whose advancement scandalized the high-born women. In order to achieve the court and 'presentation' there, Jeanne had succeeded in having herself married to the Count du Barry, brother of one of her lovers who, had he not been already a husband, would himself gladly have obliged her.

The King's costly excesses were judged with legitimate harshness by a people overwhelmed with taxes and wars. In order to reach Versailles from Fontainebleau without crossing Paris, where he feared a bad reception, as early as 1750 Louis XV had built the 'Route de la Révolte', and here was a sign of the times. The penknife blow administered in 1747 by Damiens, a half-mad serving-man, astonished no one except the King: 'Why try to kill me?' he asked. 'I have done no one any harm.' But he had done the French a great harm by disillusioning them.

The misunderstanding between him and his people extended to foreign affairs; in the colonies, despite the Peace of Aix-la-Chapelle, the Anglo-French war went on. How, indeed could the Governments have stopped it? In bad weather it took two months to get to New York, six to Calcutta. The order to cease fire stopped nothing. In America the French governors were straining every muscle to join Louisiana and Canada, the Mississippi to the Saint Lawrence, by cutting behind the British colonies, which thus would have found themselves without a hinterland, encircled by the Alleghenies and the sea. In the midst of official peace, the struggle had broken out in the Ohio Valley, and the French, having driven out the colonials, had there built Fort Duquesne. Despite this advantage, the French position in Canada was far from being secure. Since the days of Charles II, the English colonies along the coast had constituted a homogeneous and well-populated area, numbering abour one million two hundred thousand inhabitants, whereas the French settlers scarcely exceeded sixty thousand. The English, a people among whom merchants were powerful, passionately clung to their markets, and to preserve them they were ready to make sacrifices to which France would never have consented, since French trade had no voice in council.

Not only were the colonials fighting in contempt of treaties in every corner of the globe, but on the sea, where two competent French naval ministers, Rouhier and Machault, had built France a new fleet, a worried British admiralty, without declaration of war, gave chase to French men-of-war. Louis XV remained content with sending notes, a procedure which, through seven thousand years of recorded history, ever since men have coveted the goods of others, has delighted and heartened aggressors. In point of fact a new Hundred Years War had begun with the accession of William of Orange to the English throne; the stakes were no longer the Angevin empire or the Anglo-French empire, but the empire of the world. That prize would belong to whichever of the two adversaries gained the mastery of the seas. Now for her to bend all her powers to the reconstruction of a navy, France needed peace on the Continent; on the other hand all England needed, traditionally, was one allied soldier there. Half a score of past experiences had proved that British naval and colonial victories were futile as long as France could occupy Flanders, for in every such case, when the moment came for a settlement, the colonies had to be handed back in order to obtain the evacuation of Antwerp. The only thing that remained, then, was to pick the soldier. Until 1748 England had lavished her subsidies upon Austria, but now Frederick II was asking less money than Maria Theresa, and he was a better strategist. England reversed her alliances.

At the same time France reversed hers. From the days of Francis I, the hatred of Austria had been the beginning of wisdom for a king of France, and it remained lively in the minds of most Frenchmen. Was it still wise? Did it serve the country's interests? There was reason to doubt it. What advantage did France win from new Prussian victories? Did there not lurk in Prussian success a threat to Germanic liberties and to the Europe of the treaties of Westphalia? It has been asserted that this reversal of alliances was a woman's achievement; that Frederick II, a woman-hater, had by his insults estranged at once Maria Theresa, the Czarina Elizabeth and Madame de Pompadour, whom he called 'Mademoiselle Poisson', or else 'Petticoat II', whereas the Empress of Austria always alluded to her in her letters as 'Madame, my very dear sister'. Perhaps the Pompadour's goodwill helped the Austrian sovereign, but the reversal of alliances had deeper causes. Bernis, the new French foreign minister, understood the Prussian danger. Unhappily the country did not support him. Defeats at sea, the loss of Canada and of India troubled public opinion scarcely at all; too sadly does a Frenchman remember Voltaire's phrase about a 'few acres of snow'. Frederick of Prussia's victory at Rosbach was greeted in France almost with joy. To heap praises on the enemy was in the manner of a Fronde; faced with a 'tyrannical' French Government, men wished to believe that the 'enlightened' monarch of Sans-Souci represented freedom. He was freedom's worst enemy, and the Bourbons were saints in comparison with the Hohenzollerns; but when the general opinion reasons ill, there is nothing more vain than to try to set it straight.

After Rosbach, Bernis was greatly discouraged. The King and the court did not react. 'I seem', said Bernis, 'to be the minister of foreign affairs for Limbo'; in vain did he point out the danger 'to God and his saints', meaning Louis XV and his close friends. He aroused them scarcely for a brief moment: 'Then the lethargy returned; great mournful eyes looked upon him, and that was all.' French fighting men were still gallant, of course, but everywhere there was disorder: 'It was needful to change our ways, and such a task, which requires centuries in another country, would be accomplished within a year in ours', if only someone would undertake to set the French to rights. Bernis, however, did not himself yearn for that job; on the contrary, with deliberate purpose he made way for Choiseul, friend of Madame de Pompadour and the *philosophes* and the most brilliant of French ambassadors. Choiseul had one policy — that of the Family Compact with Spain; this was a treaty of mutual assistance which, by uniting the two fleets, was to establish some sort of balance of maritime power. Yet on the world's oceans England was too strong even for this combination; the war turned out as badly for France at sea as it did for Austria on land. In 1763 the Peace of Paris had to be signed, and it was one of the saddest in French history. It cost France her empire and created England's. In this Seven Years War France had lost Canada, all the territory east of the Mississippi, India (apart from five trading factories), Senegal and the Grenadine (Windward) Islands. Frederick II retained Silesia. It must be granted, to Choiseul's credit, that immediately after the defeat he worked his hardest to rebuild a fleet, and also that it was he who annexed not only Lorraine (a legacy which came to France upon the death of Stanislas Leszczynski) but also Corsica, an island to become one of the most loyal of French provinces.

The reorganization of the army and the navy cost dearly: money was needed, and the only means of getting it was to take it where you could find it, from the privileged. Naturally they resisted vigorously: the clergy asserted that 'even among peoples plunged in the darkness of idolatry', religious property was respected. To move in that direction required the help of the *Parlements*, and Choiseul thought he had them in his pocket by obtaining from the King the expulsion of the Jesuits. This action won him the admiration of the *philosophes*, but in the *Parlement*, purse outweighed conscience. Opposition to the taxes remained lively, especially in Brittany, where the struggle of La Chalotais, a local parlementarian, against d'Aiguillon, the governor of the province, became almost a philosophical argument. 'It is of the essence of a law that it be accepted . . . The right to accept is the nation's right.' And this right could be exercised, Chalotais claimed, 'during the periods between sessions of the States General', only by the *Parlements*. Here was a highly debatable doctrine, especially since the *Parlements* of that day were not representative. In 1759 a certain Monsieur de Silhouette became controller-general of finances. He was held to be a thinker, and Voltaire wrote, 'I say that God has sent Monsieur de Silhouette to our assistance'. This divine messenger suggested a number of taxes, 'even on the air one breathes', aroused an outcry and disappeared after four months in office, leaving his name to the French language to designate a passing shadow. 'The eagle has changed into a goose', Voltaire philosophically remarked. The deficit, none the less, remained a deficit.

In 1770 Choiseul received a *lettre de cachet* exiling him to his estate at Chanteloup; his policy of revenge on England and of building up naval armaments worried the King. Before his downfall, Choiseul had had time to arrange for the Dauphin's marriage to one of Maria Theresa's daughters, the Archduchess Marie Antoinette, which strengthened his pro-Austrian policy. To the French, Choiseul's dismissal seemed unjust, and at Chanteloup he and his family had the sympathy of their friends lavished upon them. The coalition which had overthrown this minister was composed of the Chancellor Maupeou, the Abbé Terray, Controller of the Finances, and Madame du Barry, the King's mistress. Maupeou succeeded in making Louis XV understand that the aggressive power of the magistracy was becoming a national danger; it is essential to repeat once more that the French *Parlements* were at that time privileged and hereditary courts of justice and not elected assemblies. Their activities were harmful: they prevented the levying of taxes; they were a bulwark of intolerance and torture; they banded together throughout the kingdom under the leadership of the *Parlement* of Paris, to oppose the crown's decrees. 'This astonishing anarchy', as even Voltaire admitted, 'could not continue. The crown had to regain its authority, or the *Parlements* emerge triumphant.' The hereditary magistrates constituted a new feudality which perpetuated the privileges enjoyed by the old. They badly needed harsh treatment; in 1771 Maupeou suppressed the *Parlements*, abolished the sale of offices, established new and simpler courts — which were dubbed Maupeou *Parlements* — and made justice free of charge, at least in principle. Meanwhile the Controller Terray, a pitiless and therefore rather capable minister of finances, 'who possessed something of Sully's and Colbert's good sense', 'reduced the arrears on government obligations, postponed the repayment of borrowed funds which had reached maturity, converted the *tontines* [a special kind of government bond] into life annuities, increased the salt tax, and made trade in grain subject to strict regulation'; he reformed pension abuses and established the 5 per cent tax (on capital) and real-estate taxes. These were wise measures, but the Maupeou *Parlements* were treated with contempt, and the Abbé Terray's taxes, which were indispensable, gave rise to endless protest. 'People say that the Abbé Terray is without Faith, that he strips us of Hope and reduces us to Charity.' Public opinion, completely misguided, defended the tax collectors and contractors against the State; poor Terray, when the King asked him what he thought of the festivities at Versailles, answered: 'Oh, Sire, priceless!' [The French word, *impayable*, likewise meant that they could not be paid for.] In 1774, Louis, who had become the Little-Loved, died and was regretted by no one. And yet during the last years of his reign Choiseul, Maupeou and Terray had done good work; a sovereign with wisdom could still rescue the regime. Louis XVI was crowned. Would he be a god, or a cypher? He was an honest blockhead.

CHAPTER VII

HOW, DURING THE EIGHTEENTH CENTURY, THE *PHILOSOPHES* BECAME A POLITICAL FORCE

'WE had kindred spirits during Louis XIV's reign', said a *philosophe* of Louis XV's time, and it was true that scepticism in religious matters had been avowed as early as the seventeenth century by such freethinkers as Pierre Bayle. In 1692 Bayle had published the first instalments of a 'Dictionary', prefiguring the great *Encyclopédie*; cunningly, in notes and articles seemingly inoffensive, Bayle showed reason and faith to be incompatible, established the right of free-thought and sought to separate morals from religion. But if the eighteenth century had already arrived during the last days of the seventeenth, the seventeenth survived into the early years of its successor. In 1715 and thereabouts, Catholic and absolutist thought still continued all-powerful; if in the France of Louis XIV there were unbelievers, they were few and forced to silence or to secrecy. Hence it is a proper question to ask why, between 1715 and 1750, a new political and religious philosophy was so rapidly elaborated.

A number of reasons spring to mind. First, after the majestic restraint of the age of Louis XIV, France felt the need for relaxation. Greatness of feeling had ceased to be fashionable; tragedy was dying; comedy was becoming sprightly, and painting lubricious. The most serious subjects had to be put within the reach of the ladies, and the most far-fetched gallantry was mingled with astronomy. The general tone, the public taste, the subjects dealt with — everything was changing, political philosophy like all the rest. Secondly, England's influence was growing. In 1688, she had undergone a peaceful revolution, and was on the whole very satisfied with the results; the French could observe there the operation of wholly new institutions. 'Here is a country', Voltaire enviously remarked, 'where a man can think freely and nobly, without being hindered by any servile fear.' The French third estate, emboldened by the wealth won by its fathers and by the intelligence of its sons, wanted to free itself of the last vestiges of feudalism; the English furnished an example of the road to be followed. Finally, the French men of letters of the eighteenth century were playing a major role. Yet they still confronted two exasperating forms of opposition: pride of class which, among certain members of the nobility, went as far as an offensive scorn even for a commoner with genius, and ecclesiastical censure the medieval harshness of which no longer corresponded either to men's customs or to their feelings. Voltaire, a young writer who had won admiration and been made much of, was none the less thrashed by the servants of the Chevalier de Rohan-Chabot and thrown into the Bastille. Such experiences linger long in the memory; in consequence he went into an English exile (1726-29) and found there an altogether different society. The English Churches had learned tolerance: 'An Englishman goes to Heaven by the road of his choice ... Were there in England but one religion, there would be fear of despotism; were there two, they would be at each others' throats; but there are a score and more and they live at peace.' In England, Locke could define the laws of human reason as freely as Newton the laws of gravity. In that land the people were consulted concerning their taxes. From his British journey Voltaire garnered a volume — the *Lettres Anglaises* — in which, by describing England, he implicitly criticized the French system; Montesquieu likewise found a model society in the England which had achieved the revolution of 1688. Of course in all this there was a certain optimism, and the real England was not as perfect as these visitors would have had it, yet it is beyond denial that the English had found a way to combine order and freedom. Quite naturally the French came to the conclusion that what was possible on the other side of the Channel was possible on their side as well.

Their faith in reason became all the more confident because the human mind had, during the course of a century, won several handsome victories. Newton had shown that the earth, the complex movements of the heavenly bodies and falling objects were all linked together by a few simple laws. Reason had carried the day in analytical geometry and mathematical optics; why should it fail in politics and metaphysics? Spinoza had already expressed his *Ethics* in theorems; and if reason had not up to that time founded any perfect societies, was this not attributable to the fact that it was not at liberty to govern men's actions, that it was in bondage to superstitions and traditions? It would be enough to break those bonds, to sweep away the 'Gothic' trash which still cluttered thought and custom, for man to march on from progress to progress. Bad laws made unhappy societies; let us have good laws, and all would be for the best in the world's finest of kingdoms. It would be enough to replace the existing traditional customs with simple and natural rules. 'Would you know', announced Diderot, 'the history in brief of almost all our troubles? Here it is. There once existed a natural man; into this man was introduced an artificial man, and there sprang up in the cave a civil war which lasts for life . . .' Suppress the artificial man, meaning the man of tradition and superstition, and you re-establish peace within the cave.

What the men of the eighteenth century did not see, because they were vexed by certain absurd and offensive survivals, is that traditions are not *all* fetters, that many of them constitute the very framework of a society, that every society rests upon the legitimacy of some government, which amounts to saying that it rests upon a myth, and that nothing is more difficult or more dangerous than passing from one myth to another. The English succeeded in this enterprise, because the transition in that country was extremely slow and because they preserved side by side new myths and old. In France, although the absolute monarchy, the prejudices of the aristocracy and the inequitable system of taxation were justly condemned by 'the progress of enlightenment', what was needed, while putting the house in order, was to preserve its structure as long as the nation had no other roof under which to lay its head. Montesquieu clearly saw the danger; his *Esprit des Lois* points out that the value of laws is relative, depending upon climate, circumstances, popular habits, relative wealth; Voltaire also, when at his best, had some sense of history. But the other writers of the day quite honestly believed that reason, operating in the mind's vacuum, could on bare ground construct the ideal constitution. Their weakness, when we compare them to the English (and later to the American) political thinkers, was that they had never played any part in public affairs, even of a local character. Their strength was that this very lack of experience made them attractive to the French who, themselves stripped of every right of participation in government, had never been able to build anything except in the abstract. If, like the English, they had possessed practical means for changing institutions, they would have paid heed to the nature and the effects of such changes. But no first-hand knowledge had warned them 'about the obstacles which existing facts can lay in the way of even the most desirable reforms'. The sphere of public business 'to them was not only ill-understood but beyond their ken'.[1] So they listened to the writers, who alone laid the terms of the debate before the public; and thus when the French had to act, they carried over 'into politics all the habits of literature'[2] — habits little suited to action.

[1] ALEXIS DE TOCQUEVILLE. [2] Ibid.

Above all between 1750 and 1770 was the influence of the *philosophes* most profound throughout the land. Two cliques then divided the court and the King's mind: that of the Queen, the Dauphin and the King's daughters, which was ultramontane and reactionary; and that of the Marquise de Pompadour, Argenson, Choiseul and Malesherbes, which was 'philosophical'. Madame de Pompadour, a middle-class woman detested by the nobility and a royal mistress branded by the clergy, needed the support of public opinion and hence of the literary men; the latter hoped that the Marquise would help them fight 'superstition', which annoyed her as much as it did them. And support them she did. This was the time when the court, by protecting Voltaire, assured his election to the Academy (1746); when the *salons* over which presided such women of small virtue as Madame du Deffand, Madame d'Épinay and Mademoiselle de Lespinasse, moulded opinion; when, as we shall see, ministers protected the *Encyclopédie* against their own police. Had Louis XV been a Frederick II, or even a Francis I, perhaps an alliance might then have been cemented between the monarchy and the *philosophes* against the arrogance of the aristocracy and religious intolerance. But Louis XV was weak and lazy; he allowed the *Parlement* to hang and rack the unbelievers. Voltaire had to remind men that people, were they Protestants, Jews or freethinkers, had a right to justice. In the famous cases of Calas and the Chevalier de la Barre, he attacked the fanatics, as well as the government which backed the fanatics. The monarchy had lost its opportunity to enlist the *philosophes* in the defence of the throne.

Quite the opposite: thanks to the *Encyclopédie*, the *philosophes* enlisted the whole country in the defence of their own ideas. At the beginning the *Encyclopédie* was no more than a business venture, launched by the booksellers; but finally Diderot, who coupled a stormy genius with the solid virtues of a managing editor, was entrusted with the direction of the enterprise. He took as collaborators Montesquieu, Voltaire, d'Alembert, a whole constellation of stars of the first magnitude. At first the censorship saw in this scheme no more than a dictionary, but soon perspicacious minds realized that for the picture of the world inherited from the Middle Ages, the *Encyclopédie* was striving to substitute another, that of Newton. The universe of the Encyclopaedists was no longer created by God to test man; authority was no longer the foundation of truth; progress consisted in bringing man back to nature. All this doctrine was fairly well hidden under a veneer of commonplace information, but a knowing reader was well able to winnow it from the chaff. Politically, the *Encyclopédie* taught that kings, if they were to make their subjects happy, must be free to make new laws founded on reason; that inequalities of status were the worst of all evils; that education consisted in leading men back to natural wisdom. The influence of this work was enormous. Even though its price was nine hundred and eighty *livres*, and it ran to twenty-seven volumes, it attracted four thousand three hundred subscribers. The nobility at court and the provincial middle class — all France's *élite* — had the *Encyclopédie* available to it; sets were to be found in castle libraries and in the homes of more than a few country priests. Several times the *Parlement* and the clergy became aroused; the King had copies confiscated, but the Chief of Police and the Director of Booksellers' Censorship were themselves partisans of the Encyclopaedists; indeed on the eve of a raid this Director, Malesherbes, offered to hide the proofs in his own office for Diderot. Whenever the King sought information, whether on the formula for gunpowder or that for lip rouge, Madame de Pompadour had a copy of the forbidden work brought for his consultation. The King would find what he was looking for and regret the suppression. In her reception rooms the Marquise used to entertain certain of the Encyclopaedists; she wanted to make Louis XV the king of the *philosophes*, but she failed. 'That is not the fashion in France', he replied with regretful stubbornness. Yet the very essence of fashion is change.

It would be a mistake to suppose that the Encyclopaedists were a one-minded team. Buffon, a great naturalist and useful collaborator, but always 'ill at ease with his peers', quickly withdrew. The academician d'Alembert adhered only long enough to prove his sympathy with the group. The atheists, Holbach and La Mettrie, never saw eye to eye with Voltaire, a conservative deist; Voltaire described himself as anti-clerical and anti-Catholic, but in politics his morality was the morality of action, realism and opportunism, wherein he got along quite well with Diderot, another stalwart French bourgeois. Far more than Voltaire, Rousseau was annoyed at the irreligion of most of the Encyclopaedists; he represented a reaction against the rationalism and free ways of the century's early decades. Nor did he have the same admiration as Diderot or Voltaire for the 'progress of enlightenment'; he was turning his back not merely on tradition but on civilization. Rousseau believed not in reason, but in the feelings and emotions, and he made their outpouring into virtues. Politically he wanted a society based on a *Social Contract* by which men of goodwill would pledge themselves to live in accordance with natural morality. He could not be at his ease with the Encyclopaedists because 'they were men of science, and he the opposite'. But he strongly moved people's hearts. Nothing becomes more quickly tiresome than libertinage; its very ease makes it monotonous, and women regretted the days of great passions. Rousseau presented them with the *Nouvelle Héloïse*, substituting the man of feeling for the man of spirit in the heroic hierarchy, and thus changed the manners and customs of his day.

From 1750 to 1789 the Encyclopaedists' rationalist revolution and Rousseau's sentimental revolution progressed side by side; new sciences were coming to birth; in the *salons* there gathered not only men of letters and philosophers but also economists. Of the latter the 'physio-crats', of whom François Quesnay and Dupont de Nemours were the apostles, were then in fashion. They created the science of the production of wealth and thought that the part this science should play (like New-tonian science) was the discovery of natural laws. Of these they found three: Property, Security, Liberty. The role of government was, through the suppression of barriers, to give property and liberty free play in producing their happy effects. 'Leave things to themselves.' The Intendant Turgot, a *philosophe* office-holder, attended the meetings of this group and made available to it his experience as a technician. Disturbed at the scarcity of cereals which was then common in France, he laid the blame on the restrictions imposed on trading in grain; the farmers no longer produced, he said, because they were not free to sell. Turgot was none too fond of Quesnay's and his friends' 'sectarian air', but he became their great hope. 'If only Turgot were minister . . .' they would say. And that, as we shall see, is what he one day became.

Art in the eighteenth century followed the same line of development as literature. The painters were weary of the grandeur of the Great Century. Since far-fetched gallantry had succeeded passion, since love was a comedy, why should painting not have created for it a fairy stage setting? Watteau was above all a decorative painter, and his enchanted world lies half-way between the theatre and life; his lovers dwell in ethereal gardens which make you think of Shakespeare. Well do we know that the delightful illusion cannot last, and thence comes a pleasur-able sadness. Fragonard likewise joined dissoluteness and melancholy, and thus preserved a certain greatness. Boucher rounded out the move-ment of reaction against Largillière and Rigaud; in his world nothing is serious: 'His lovers are shepherds, but incapable of watching a flock'; his cupids are not gods but chubby pink babies. And then the public, just as it had tired of Louis XIV's style, grew bored with the graces of the Pompadour's. To Rousseau's sentimental reaction there corresponded a sentimental painting. Diderot as an art critic hoped that painting might become moral; Greuze fulfilled his hope, illustrated touching nothings and was saved from platitude only by the unconscious sensuality of even his most virtuous young girls. Chardin, one of the greatest — and most French — of French painters, marks the appearance in art of the very lowest middle class. In his paintings are to be found the harmony, the peace and the honesty of simple people's lives; he knew how to attribute an infinite value to the folds of a white cloth, to the soft reflections of a copper basin. Madame de Pompadour and Madame Geoffrin encouraged artists: Nattier, La Tour and Boucher painted the former; Chardin and Hubert Robert the latter.

The newsmongers continued their meetings at the Luxembourg, the Tuileries and the Palais Royal, but under Louis XV the *salons* played the greater role in the shaping of public opinion. France is the only country where social gatherings ever became historical institutions. Why? Because ever since the courts of love, the French had liked women's conversation and society. During the eighteenth century several houses became famous 'bourses' for ideas; there the *philosophes* met men and women of the world and celebrated foreigners. The two most renowned *salons* were those of Madame Geoffrin and of the Marquise du Deffand; these women were natural rivals, an aggressive imperialism being one trait common to all foundresses of such establishments. Madame Geoffrin, a rich bourgeoise, wife of a director of the Saint-Gobain cut-glass works, inherited a portion of Madame de Tencin's faithful; the Wednesdays at her domain on the rue Saint Honoré attracted Fontenelle, Montesquieu, d'Alembert, Galiani. The *Encyclopédie* constituted itself a party at her house. 'Maman' (that was her pet name) reached the summit of her glory when she made a trip across Europe to pay a visit to her 'son' Stanislas-Augustus, King of Poland, and was received as a sovereign of the mind, not only by this prince but by the Empress, Maria Theresa. Madame Geoffrin was a domineering friend, a little in the style of Proust's Madame Verdurin; her rival, Madame du Deffand, was less kindly but more intelligent. Being 'neither ardent nor romantic', all her life she fought off boredom. While young, she had had a brief affair with the Regent; at a ripe age she had another interminable one with Hénault, a presiding judge in the *Parlement*, whom she never loved; old and blind, she finally discovered love and desperately attached herself to the Englishman, Horace Walpole. All this constituted a rather sad life thronged with a world of faithful followers; Voltaire was a fixture of her establishment, Madame du Deffand stirring him up against the *philosophes*, at whom she poked as much fun as she did at the clergy. There was a certain nihilism in this old dowager, but her positive achievement lay in serving as a link between Englishmen and Frenchmen. Under Louis XV, the philosophical *salons* represented a likeable and tolerated opposition; under Louis XVI, with Madame Necker, they became the antechamber to power.

During the eighteenth century as during the thirteenth, French civilization was a European civilization; in every country the aristocracy spoke French, and this fashion long continued in Russia, in Sweden, in the Balkans and even in lands where German was the native tongue. In Tolstoy's historical novels, Russian characters converse among themselves in French. The French writers of the eighteenth century were read by the *élite* everywhere, whom they supplied with fresh ideas. Voltaire paid a protracted visit to Frederick II and Diderot corresponded with the Great Catherine; such cultivated Americans as Thomas Jefferson owned a French library. It is true that many of the elements in the 'philosophy' of the Encyclopaedists came to them from England; Locke's influence on the American Revolution was greater than Montesquieu's. But in many a European country, English ideas were spread only under their Frenchified forms; an economic doctrine became clearer, more readily assimilable, when it had been refined by Voltaire's mind. Be it a matter of trade in cereals, the plurality of worlds or final causes, a French writer was at hand to put the subject within the reach of all intelligent readers, whether in the form of dialogue or fable. Just as in the sterner days of medieval philosophy, France showed her inclination for universality.

CHAPTER VIII

HOW, UNDER LOUIS XVI, GOOD WILL GAVE BIRTH TO WEAKNESS

IN an absolute monarchy, the King's personality counts for everything. The worth of the regime and that of the sovereign are one: under Henry IV absolutism had seemed legitimate, under Louis XVI it seemed intolerable. Not that the King was worthless — far from it. He was constantly anxious to do well; he was devout and chaste, and he loved his people, nor was he a fool, either. He knew some history, geography and English, but government and politics did not attract him. More Leszczynski and Saxe than Bourbon, heavy in mind and body, with a tendency to fatness, he was actively concerned with only two things — hunting and the work of a locksmith. 'His Indecision' asked advice of everyone: 'How must I act? . . .' 'Act the King', was the reply once transmitted to him by Rivarol. Like all timid men, whenever he was driven into a corner, he hurled forth angry remarks which were deeply wounding; more frequently he dozed, worn out from riding and hammering at his anvil. Choiseul had married him off at sixteen to the Archduchess Marie Antoinette, in order to seal the Austrian alliance. The wedding festivities in Paris had been spoiled by a panic, and henceforth an aura of trouble surrounded this young couple. Marie Antoinette possessed grace and dignity; her imperial mother had commanded her to please and, working through her husband, to influence French policy, and so she tried, long without success, to win over this doltish adolescent. Her husband seemed terrified by the realities of love, so she fell back on feminine friendships — the weak and charming Lamballe, later the dangerous Polignac — and on her young brother-in-law, the Count of Artois. After she had become queen, she wished to continue 'to afford herself the sweets of private life'[1] which wounded those not admitted to her intimacy; from this sprang gossip and slander. At the very outset of the reign, this gracious woman, most worthy of being loved, had implacable enemies. When she emerged from her enchanted hamlet, she discovered the spitefulness of the outer world, and her reaction was that of wounded pride, indignation at the meanness, resentment at the insults.

[1] MADAME CAMPAN.

252

The King forgave too much, the Queen too little. When she had to admit to herself the weakness of 'her poor man', she became gloomy: 'You know the person with whom I have to deal', she wrote Mercy d'Argenteau (her mother's ambassador); 'the moment you think him persuaded, a word, an objection raised, makes him change his mind without his even suspecting it himself . . .' The household and the reign continued, seemingly normal, but there very quickly took place, under the ermine and beflowered velvet, a royal divorce and a national divorce.

Louis XVI belonged to the pious and humanitarian breed of Bourbons as had his father and the Duke of Burgundy; 'I should like to be loved', he said on his accession to the throne. But how make the kingdom happy? The King seems to have had faith in the possibility of regenerating the nobility: a fatherly monarchy, the liberties — that is to say, the continued privileges — of the three orders, *Parlements*, the States General; he hoped to preserve or infuse new life into all the ancient constitution of the realm. However, without being aware of it, he thus placed himself in complete disagreement with the *philosophes*, and even with Choiseul or Maupeou, who would have liked to start something new and discipline the privileged classes. Together with all his generation, Louis XVI had an instinctive faith in the excellence of human nature; when he chose his first cabinet, he summoned into it several of the fashionable reformers. At its head he had placed Maurepas, an aged, frivolous and sceptical man of state who was a bad choice for such a moment; yet he chose such colleagues for him as Malesherbes, the protector of the Encyclopaedists, and Turgot, the hope of all bold spirits — that Turgot whose hands Voltaire kissed with tears in his eyes. The sovereign and his minister met: 'It is not to the King that I give my devotion', said Turgot, 'but to the man of honour.' 'In him you will not be deceived', replied Louis XVI. Turgot left the meeting with deep emotion and wrote the King a fine letter detailing his programme: 'No bankruptcy, no increase in taxes, no loans . . .' Hence, increased production and curtailed expense. Production was to be encouraged by freedom of trade in cereals; as for reducing expenditures, 'I shall have to struggle against the natural kindness, against the generosity of Your Majesty and of the persons dearest to him'. This was an allusion to the young queen. Turgot reduced his own stipend from one hundred and forty-two thousand to eighty-two thousand *livres*, a righteous but ineffectual gesture. Voltaire praised the minister's first decrees: 'I have just read Monsieur Turgot's masterpiece. It seems to me that here is a new Heaven and a new earth.' Abroad, enthusiasm was lively: 'When a new King of France who sought the good', wrote Goethe, 'showed the best intentions of himself limiting his own authority, in order to do away with numerous abuses, achieve the finest results, and rule only for the sake of order and of justice, the most pleasant hope spread all over the world, and trusting youth believed it could assure itself of a magnificent future . . .' The intentions were subject to no doubt; it remained to be seen how action would suit them.

Had Turgot been kept in power by a strong king, he might perhaps have accomplished the needed reforms and spared France a revolution; in the Limousin, his thirteen years of work transformed the province. But he was to remain minister for only twenty-one months, and he was impeded in his work by three powerful forces: the Queen, because he supervised her expenditures and because she wanted her friend Choiseul, the ally of Austria, to be minister; the bankers and tax collectors, because he threatened their profits; and the masses, because they had been aroused by agents who led them to believe that the free trade in grains was impoverishing them. The skilful propaganda of the monopolists insinuated that this flour war was a new pact of famine. Thereupon the King, because he was worried and mawkishly sentimental, called back the members of the *Parlement*; it was sheer folly, yet in vain did Turgot strive against it. Condorcet wrote to him: 'It is said that the old *Parlement* will return unconditionally, which means with all its insolences, pretensions and prejudices.' Scarcely had it been recalled when indeed the *Parlement* began to block all reforms. In January 1776 Turgot hoped to do away with statute labour, have the cost of road building borne by the landowners and make the privileged classes subject to taxation: 'Taxes, which should be in proportion to wealth, among us are rather levies from which men free themselves by wealth . . .' He would also have liked to suppress the wardenship of the guilds and the freedoms of the corporations, because 'the right to work is a natural right'. Thus he succeeded in arousing against him 'the lords and the grocers'. The unfriendly *Parlement* no longer registered the minister's decrees except when forced to by a 'bed of justice', and once more acquired, through resisting reforms, an unwarranted popularity. The jeering public intoned: 'Monsieur de Malesherbes does everything: Monsieur Turgot muddles everything; Monsieur de Maurepas laughs at everything!' The King, faithful to his fixed and ill-fated notion of making himself beloved, remarked sadly: 'Monsieur Turgot causes no one to love him.' Louis XVI did not approve the decrees relating to the privileged: 'But surely they have not forfeited esteem', he naively protested. The *salons* announced that 'Turgot is disintegrating'. The minister then made a final attempt and spoke frankly to the King: 'Sire, you are lacking in experience; I know that at twenty-two and given your position, you have not the resources which the habit of living with equals supplies to private citizens in their judgment of men; but shall you have more experience in a week, in a month? . . . In truth, Sire, I no longer understand you . . .' He was ordered to resign his office; the Turgot experiment had come to naught. It was a serious business, but Versailles and France scarcely suspected it.

There were external as well as internal reasons for this failure; in order to set the finances to rights, Turgot needed peace; but in order to be re-venged on the English, Vergennes needed a war. Ever since 1768 Choiseul had been rubbing his hands over the warning signals of the American Revolution. He had rebuilt the French fleet, which by 1771 already numbered sixty-four ships of the line and forty-five frigates. Vergennes, Choiseul's successor, was in 1776 confronted with a *fait accompli* in America; should he support the rebel colonies? Yes, but without going as far as war, by secretly supplying them with arms through such intermediaries as Beaumarchais. After the Declaration of Independence, Franklin came to Paris, where his embassy was abetted by his prestige. Everything conspired in his favour – his fame as a scientist, his reputation for wisdom, the simplicity of his apparel, his brilliance in conversation. Poor Richard's philosophy was at one with that of the French middle class. His experiments with lightning were known to all: 'We have beheld him disarming tyrants and gods', was the inscription below his portrait by Carmontelle, and in his behalf Turgot even ventured into Latin: '*Eripuit caelo fulmen sceptrumque tyrannis*' ('From heaven has he snatched the bolt and from tyrants the sceptre'). The Academy of Sciences elected him one of its members, and he regularly attended the sessions; he met Voltaire, and the two illustrious old men embraced before a rapturous audience. In vain did the English embassy seek to create the impression that Franklin was unpopular in his own country, and a refugee more than an ambassador; both at court and in town there was talk only of the 'great Franklin'.

The Franklin legend answered the intellectual and sentimental needs of the French public: those were the days of the *Nouvelle Héloïse* and the Trianon dairy farm, the days when the simple rustic life was all the rage. Truth to tell, there was nothing rustic about Franklin, and he was far more sharp than simple; but he was beautifully able to play the part which was assigned to him. The moment he became aware of the success of his fur headgear and his spectacles, he wore them everywhere. Having inadvertently received a delegation without his wig and observed the tremendous effect of this accidental carelessness, he made a law out of this chance happening and did away with wigs. The Parisians believed him to be a Quaker; he was careful not to deny it. The fashion was for the ancient republics; it seemed as though the Americans were contemporaries of Cato and Fabius. Theóretically, the King of France was an absolute monarch; in fact he was dependent upon a public opinion, that of small groups which, in Paris and Versailles, without rights, without arms and without votes, imposed their ideas upon ministers; now these groups were precisely the people who made Franklin their idol. The young nobles admired him, just as they praised to the skies Voltaire and Rousseau. In this France, with ideas buzzing everywhere, there was talk 'of independence in army camps, of democracy in castles, of philosophy at balls, and of virtue in boudoirs'. America became the very promise of an expected and hoped-for freedom. 'New England had more sages than Greece.' The Continental Congress was the Roman Senate. Every young man wanted to fight for the insurgents. Grimm tells us of the enthusiasm which induced young people to leave fathers, mothers and brothers in order to rush to the aid of an Eskimo or a Hottentot if only it were in the name of freedom. Not alone reasons of state but the state of French reason governed Vergennes's actions.

At first the French troops in America were volunteers, for Vergennes did not want to plunge into this adventure without knowing what the insurgents might be able to accomplish. Then, in 1777, Burgoyne's surrender bred confidence; in December, Louis XVI recognized the independence of the United States and signed a treaty of alliance. France went into the war in the most disinterested way possible and hoped for nothing for herself in case of victory. The new Finance Minister, Necker, was faced with supplying funds for a war; he was a Geneva banker and an honest man, who had managed his own affairs competently, which was not sufficient assurance that he would manage well the business of France. But he had a wife whose *salon* gathered together *philosophes* and physiocrats, and at her table on Fridays there were served two dinners, one for those who abstained and one for those who ate meat, which was symbolic. This *salon* aroused a 'neckromania' and transformed the banker into controller-general. In order to support Vergennes's American policy, Necker did what Turgot was unwilling to do — he borrowed, and the popularity of the American cause ensured the success of his loans. In five years, from 1776 to 1781, he increased the debt by almost six hundred million *livres*. In 1781, when he began to be attacked (because he did nothing new), he published his celebrated *Compte Rendu*, the first official document on the financial situation ever to have been made public in France. Its success was incredible; all classes of society, from stone masons to marquises, read it. Unfortunately the *Compte Rendu* was extremely inaccurate and proclaimed an excess of receipts over expenditures amounting to ten million *livres*, when in truth there was a deficit of fifty millions. Necker reassured the country when his duty should have been to arouse it.

Nevertheless, Vergennes, by means of a skilful Continental policy, was imposing a European peace on Austria and Prussia. In 1780-81, Rochambeau's army and Admiral de Grasse's fleet made certain an American victory and the surrender at Yorktown. England was ceasing to be the 'tyrant of the seas'; France seemed to the world the protectress of freedom, and never had she been greater. The debt, however, had reached a milliard *livres*, an enormous amount for those days. America had won its liberty; Spain had acquired the Mississippi and Florida; 'France retained glory and ruin', as Michelet put it. Yet this is not altogether accurate: France had recovered the right to fortify Dunkirk, the ownership of Senegal and, in the Far East, an opening wedge of influence in Annam. Above all, Vergennes, Rochambeau and Lafayette had erected the foundations of a Franco-American friendship which was ultimately to become one of the country's most precious possessions.

At the moment of victory, Necker had already fallen from office – like Turgot, driven out by the hatred of the court. The financial problem seemed no longer open to solution; anyone seeking to cut down expenses was hated at Versailles; anyone trying to meet expenses through financial reform found the *Parlements* arrayed against him. These bodies insisted on Necker's departure and won their point because neither Maurepas nor the King wanted to take on a fight. The Queen and the 'Countess Jules' (de Polignac), after an interval, obtained the appointment of their man Calonne to the Finance Ministry. It is said that Figaro's witticism referred to him: 'The post required a man versed in figures; it was given to a dancer.' (*'Il fallait un calculateur, ce fut un danseur qui l'obtint.'*) Was this official as incompetent as legend has so long had us believe? Not in the least; on the contrary, he was the only controller-general ever to have set down in writing a complete plan of reform, and such was surely the reason why so cheerful and likeable a fellow was surrounded

I

by such violent hatred. Between 1781 and 1786 he sought to expand the country's economic activity; it is true that during the same period he continued the policy of borrowing — eight hundred millions more — what could he do? The privileged classes defended themselves with might and main; a man of finance was helpless against them; it was an author who launched the real attack.

Like Figaro, Beaumarchais was a Jack-of-all-trades; he knew intimately the great lords, their superficiality, their self-indulgence, and he painted their portraits. For a long time the King forbade any performance of the *Mariage de Figaro*, and today we wonder why: if this exquisite comedy, half Shakespearean in quality, could constitute a danger to the privileged, it was only because they had already sunk very low. The suppression brought it about that, when the *Mariage* was finally allowed on the stage, the public found a hidden allusion in every sentence. It was said that the Countess Almaviva called to mind the Queen and her indiscretions. 'Slander, Madame . . .' Marie Antoinette had been its appointed victim; even her good qualities were of disservice to her — she liked to live simply and take part in pleasures shared by all, she even attended the Opera ball. In another queen, this would have won people's hearts; but Marie Antoinette's enemies turned it into a crime. When at last she had children and the long-awaited dauphin, their legitimacy was denied. She had an innocent liking for trifling jokes and masquerades; advantage was taken of this to produce the astounding Necklace Case which, in the public mind, linked the Queen of France and Cardinal de Rohan to a swindle and did the monarchy as much damage as Calonne's financial policy. On a visit to Paris the Queen's brother, the Emperor Joseph II, had warned her against taking liberties which compromised her, but he likewise did her more harm than any other by persuading her to support in all circumstances the foreign policy of Austria. France got the impression that the *autrichienne* was dangerous to the country's security; she was held responsible for the deficit, though in fact the expenses of the court accounted for only 6 per cent of the total budget. But in Paris, as in London, lampoonists and pamphleteers went after her to their hearts' content. By contrast, the King was praised to the skies. He was referred to as 'that poor fellow!' and his 'sensibility' was regarded as a matter for pride.

In August 1785, convinced that with the systematic opposition of the *Parlements* other methods must be sought, Calonne decided to convene an assembly of notables — which malicious tongues, by an Anglo-French play on words, spoke of as the assembly of the *not able* – numbering a hundred and forty persons. Henry IV had successfully made use of this institution in an earlier day. This step was in line with the return to the monarchy's traditional past then being favoured by a sentimental reaction; Lafayette, who was one of the notables, wrote to Washington that the King and Calonne deserved the country's gratitude for having chosen this road. From it he hoped for great reforms. The assembly met in February 1787 and Calonne opened it with a revolutionary speech: 'Only in the abolition of abuses lies the means to answer our needs. The abuses which we are today concerned with wiping out for the public health are those of widest extent, enjoying the most protection, those having the deepest roots and the most spreading branches.' He set forth six proposals which corresponded to Lafayette's wishes: the establishment of provincial assemblies; a land tax in kind; a tax on the goods of the clergy; a reform of the poll-tax; freedom of trade in cereals; and the replacement of statute labour by a money quit-rent. But towards Easter, 1787, the privileged groups, enraged by this assault upon their ancient rights, won the dismissal of Calonne, and Loménie de Brienne, Archbishop of Toulouse, became first minister. This unbelieving prelate, free-thinking and frivolous, had less ability than Calonne, and the notables broke up without having done anything except add to men's confusion of mind. You would not suspect it from reading Lafayette's letters; he flattered himself on the 'excellent job' done and expected wonders from the provincial assemblies: 'Liberal ideas', he wrote, 'gallop from one end of the kingdom to the other', and he remarked with satisfaction that the Queen did not dare come to Paris for fear of being ill received. 'There is', he said, 'a strange contrast between the King's despotic power, the courtiers' conniving and servility, and the extraordinary freedom of language and of criticism spread throughout all classes. . . .'

Between Brienne and the *Parlements* a battle was joined which resembled the Fronde; in this conflict it was Brienne who represented a relative liberalism, but public opinion reserved its approval for the *Parlements*, spoke out against taxes (indispensable none the less), and showed itself more active in the provinces than in Paris. Normandy, Brittany and Dauphiné once again demanded their States General, long since suppressed. At Rennes there was a kind of uprising; a deputation of Breton gentlemen came to Paris, used insolent language and were thrown into the Bastille. In Dauphiné, where an alliance had been formed between the third estate and the nobility (something similar to the British Commons), a gathering of the three orders took place at Vizille, under the chairmanship of Mounier, royal judge at Grenoble, a man of talent and moderation. The Vizille Declaration proposed the taking of reasonable steps: no taxes or subsidies which had not been approved by the States General; double representation of the third estate and voting by individuals (not by orders), which would allow the third estate to have a majority. As early as August 1788 Loménie de Brienne announced that the States General would be convened on May 1st, 1789; he was planning an appeal to the third estate against the privileged and the *Parlement*. But public opinion was already tired of Brienne. The Treasury was literally empty; no one wanted to pay, everyone wanted to be paid. The King, seeing no means of escape from actual bankruptcy, summoned Monsieur Necker, who possessed the art of creating an illusion that he would extract more from the taxes and less from each taxpayer. The magician's return gave rise to the liveliest hopes; Loménie de Brienne's disappearance was celebrated at Paris by great demonstrations of joy in which the mob insulted 'Madame Deficit' (the Queen) and dragged in the gutter an effigy of Madame de Polignac. The Breton gentlemen imprisoned in the Bastille managed to have festive lights strung on the flat roof of that building — an act eloquent of the harshness of the regime! This comic-opera prison, however, had become a political symbol.

Necker could not do the impossible, but his popularity was a source of strength and he began generously by turning over to the Treasury two million *livres* taken from his personal funds. This gave the notaries confidence and they brought him six million *livres*; then the financiers and creditors took heart. State securities went up again. By virtue of expedients, Necker was able to hold on until the opening of the States General. The King, who did not like this arrogant 'sleight-of-hand artist', had promised to 'follow him in everything'; the minister, who had the optimism of conceit, told him: 'All will end well.' But he had to meet difficulties other than financial. In Paris the winter was severe; people were cold and hungry. The *Parlement* claimed that the convocation of the States General should be subject to the regulations of 1614! Necker took no notice and on January 1st, as 'France's New Year's Day Gift', announced the convocation of the States General with double representation for the third estate. But he did not speak of individual voting, and thus everything was still unsettled.

CHAPTER IX

HOW, IN 1789, FRANCE WITHOUT KNOWING IT WAS ON THE VERGE OF REVOLUTION

A REVOLUTION, which is a change in the managing class, can be brought on by a breakdown of the managers — excessive injustice, destitution and misery, military defeat. But certain revolutions are set in motion by the abdication of an *élite* which no longer believes in itself or its rights. In 1788 France was still the most powerful State in Europe, with a population of twenty-six millions (16 per cent of all those inhabiting the Continent) at a time when Great Britain had barely twelve millions and Prussia eight. She had just won the American war; her military and naval prestige had never stood higher — the victories of the revolutionary armies would be due not only to the fine energy of the Committee of Public Safety, but to the nation's latent power and to the tools of war inherited from the *ancien régime*. Throughout Europe was to be found the influence of the French *philosophes* and artists. Thus no one could justly have said that the French monarchy in 1789 had come to grief abroad. At home, was that monarchy oppressing the country? By law it remained absolute; in actuality, the liberals had held power for fifteen years. Malesherbes, Turgot, Calonne, Necker, Loménie de Brienne were certainly not tyrants. Yet France boiled with unrest and her Government had lost its reputation. Why?

First of all because the kingdom's ancient (unwritten) constitution no longer worked. The King could summon the States General; true enough, but since 1614 he had never done so. *Parlement* could require respect for the unwritten laws; quite so, but *Parlement* had become the bulwark of privilege. The nation was not hostile to the monarchy, far from it; it had been the monarchy which of old had reformed abuses and tamed the feudal lords; it had been the monarchy which had created France's unity and which, after the wars of religion and again after the Fronde, had bound up her wounds. The country banked all its hope on the King, but with the condition that the King should take the country's side. The country was ready to endow the sovereign with all the powers necessary to establish 'that government which will always be the most popular in France, the government of people of intelligence and men of good sense',[1]

[1] ALEXIS DE TOCQUEVILLE.

but the King was expected to bring the privileged into line and to protect the people against the organs of administration. These agencies were unpopular; feudalism had left parishes and villages more freedom than did the royal *intendants*. The *gabelle* (salt monopoly), the taxes, the poll-tax served as excuses for a constant spying which the French peasant, jealous of privacy in his own business, regarded with horror. All Frenchmen heartily cried 'Long live the King!' but they acclaimed the protector king and not the exploiter king.

Feudal survivals were no longer tolerable to public opinion. Freedom from taxation had earlier been granted to the nobility in return for its military services, but the lord had long since given up the military defence of his domains; since he had taken to dwelling at Versailles, he had even ceased to manage them. In 1789 the wealthy and powerful nobles no longer lived on their lands; those who did so were poor, despised by the *intendants*. In England the great peers, the country's political leaders, worked with the bourgeoisie; in France many bourgeois were richer than ordinary gentlemen; they had read the same books and been given the same training; the two classes shared the same vocabulary and talked their fill of 'sensibility' and 'virtue'; but in spite of this likeness in their ways of thinking, there continued between them a deep social inequality which was no longer accepted. The noble, even if he were enlightened, remained supercilious. 'It was not despotism', said Rivarol, 'which annoyed the country, but the prejudices of the nobility.' The *Mariage de Figaro* had displayed the unconscious insolence then characteristic of a great lord, even a likeable great lord. Count Almaviva retained few local privileges: a judge who hardly ever judged any more, a dovecot, a few hunting and fishing rights, a little sentimental poaching. But he was free of taxation, and this immunity rightly seemed scandalous. 'By destroying a part of the institutions of the Middle Ages, men had made a hundred times more odious those which they allowed to remain.'[1] The proof of this lies in the fact that the only provinces devoted to the Old Regime were those where there survived a real feudalism; everywhere else an impulse was afoot against a nobility which continued to enjoy privileges while it was no longer expected to perform its corresponding duties.

The religious framework was shattered, no less than the political. The mass of the people remained loyal to their churches and to their pastors, but these themselves were tainted with the prevalent irreligion. Many of

[1] ALEXIS DE TOCQUEVILLE.

the great lords loathed fanaticism: 'Voltaire captivated our minds', said one of them, 'Rousseau touched our hearts; we felt a secret relish at seeing them attack an old scaffolding which seemed to us ridiculous and pathetic.' The Church was not only exempt from the greater part of taxes, but levied a tithe on harvests. And to what purpose? What did she do in return? Of course she maintained the churches and bore teaching costs but the real work was done by mud-spattered, ill-paid parish priests, while the bishops and court abbés, who performed no spiritual ministry, drew upon vast revenues and lived lives often little edifying. Cardinal de Rohan, Archbishop Loménie de Brienne and others of the sort scandalized the faithful — though unfortunately they created more talk about themselves than some modest and devout prelate. The lower clergy was shocked at the injustices and subscribed to the *Encyclopédie*. The country people remained Catholic but, while devoted to their faith, they showed themselves hostile to the clergy's political privileges, and above all to intolerance.

France in 1788 wished great changes not because the country was in misery but because it was, on the whole, fairly well off. Relative prosperity gave birth to ingratitude towards those very institutions which had brought that prosperity into being; they were held to be shameful survivals, and it was not realized that they were also pillars and flying buttresses. Necker, whenever some wise man showed him the danger which lurked in destroying the results of a glorious past, would reply: 'We must rely on men's virtue.' Arthur Young, the British traveller and observer, had a very different reaction — one wholly British. 'I shall never conceive', he wrote, 'that men would stake this rich heritage on a cast of the dice, at the risk of being damned as the most unbridled adventurers who have ever committed a horror upon mankind . . .' No one troubled himself over what would be the reaction of the mobs were the barriers suddenly to be let down; no one pictured such reactions to himself, because France, since the Fronde, had known no great upheavals. Men believed that they saw in the American Revolution the pattern of all revolutions; there lay the example of a free society which with seeming ease had shaped itself by virtue of abstract principles. Lafayette and his friends, young officer noblemen returned from the American campaigns, had erected at the very heart of the managing classes a centre of propaganda for the new ideas; George Washington's moderation hid from them the danger of political catastrophe. Lafayette sincerely believed that France could imitate America without serious disturbances. He advised the Governor of

Dauphiné, who sought his advice on education, to begin French history with 1787. So little did he expect a bloody revolution that he complained rather of the softness of the French: 'French affairs', he wrote to Washington, 'are the harder to resolve because the people of that country seem in no way ready to turn to extreme measures. *Liberty or death* is not a fashionable motto on this side of the Atlantic.' A few years later this motto was to become so thoroughly fashionable that Lafayette himself could escape death only by losing his liberty.

Thus an enlightened minority believed it could keep any revolutionary movement under control; it failed to understand the extent to which Washington's case (that of a moderate who brought to a close the revolution he had himself begun) was historically out of the ordinary. By means of books, pamphlets, intellectual groups, the new ideas had won over the bourgeoisie; already political clubs, such as the 'Boston' or the 'Americans', had opened in Paris. In the secondary schools young men nurtured on the ideas of Rousseau were coming to maturity: at the Collège Louis-le-Grand, Robespierre and Camille Desmoulins; at the *collège* at Troyes, Danton and Buzot; among the Oratorians at Soissons, Saint-Just. Foreign influences were secretly working in the same direction; England, which ever since Yorktown had wanted to be revenged on France, encouraged anything which might weaken the French monarchy. In those days all Europe was politically amoral; 'Governments looked upon revolutions in neighbouring States as no more than private crises; they appraised them according to their own interests; they spurred them on or calmed them down on the basis of whether they thought their advantage lay in supporting or weakening the State in question.'[1] Vergennes fought in Geneva the democracy he helped in America: 'The rebels I am driving out of Geneva', he said, 'are the agents of England, whereas the American rebels have been our friends for many a year. I have dealt with the one and the other, not with an eye to their political system but with an eye to their attitudes towards France. Such is my reason of state.' Now the English reason of state, based on the same line of thought, did not fear revolution in France, even hoped for it. By such cynical performances as the partition of Poland, the European sovereigns opened the way to a revolution which, 'in order to upset their thrones and overturn their empires, had only to apply against them their own methods and follow their own example'.

As for the French, few among them in 1789 wished for a constitutional

[1] ALBERT SOREL.

monarchy of the Anglo-Saxon sort. The King, they thought, should hold his privileged ones in check, and public opinion should hold the King in check. But how would this judgment be expressed or imposed? Except for a few great thinkers like Montesquieu, and later Mirabeau, the *philosophes* had not attentively studied the system of guarantees which protected English or American liberties; Voltaire had known them only superficially. The French economists lauded absolute monarchy to the skies. 'The position of France', said one of them, 'is infinitely better than that of England, for here we can carry out reforms which may change the whole state of the country in an instant, whereas among the English such reforms can always be thwarted by the political parties.' They did not think that monarchy sprang from divine right, but they accepted it and, for the reform of France, relied upon a democratic despotism. They could imagine nothing but bureaucracy and centralization; they did not see that American freedom had its origin in the town meeting and in free local institutions. The word *republican* they never used, save in the Latin sense of 'the public thing'. They wasted no time on the jury, on *habeas corpus*, the secret ballot, the very cornerstones of the Anglo-Saxon system. When Lafayette reported the play of words on the Assembly of Notables — *not able* — he little knew to what extent the thrust was deserved.

Taine taught that a classical and abstract spirit, having elaborated for a universal man the doctrine of the social contract, drew men's minds in a continuous movement towards the destruction of the *ancien régime*. This description, however brilliant, does not correspond with the facts. The directions the Revolution was to take were not at all clearly defined in 1788; here was nothing similar to the Russian Revolution, which was carried out by unbending doctrinaire minds toward a precise end. The French of Louis XVI's day had a mind to repair the house, not to tear it down. They had a dread of intolerance and social inequality, but they continued to respect their sovereign. Yet why did a revolution against the remains of feudalism take place in France, where the nobility had lost all power, rather than in Hungary, Poland, Austria or Prussia, where the aristocracy remained medieval? Precisely because it did so remain. Because, 'in this French land, by dint of urbanity, of epicureanism, of flabbiness, all who were wealthy, great by birth, landlords, men of fashion had become wholly spineless';[1] because the nobility had no strength left, or even the will to defend itself; because that nobility lived a tamed life at Versailles and had cut itself off from the nation; because, with Paris

[1] ALEXIS DE TOCQUEVILLE.

the nation's nerve centre, a Parisian uprising could carry the regime away with it; because, all effective public life having ceased since Louis XIV, the French were able to tumble, without foreseeing it, into a sanguinary revolution which those who began it had never wanted.

What exactly did they want? They wanted what they had once had — a king meting out justice who could restore order. Several times during their history had they seen, after great troubles, meetings of the States General which gave utterance to aspirations, and then kings carrying out those aspirations. Of such sort had been the reforms of l'Hôpital, Sully and Richelieu after 1614, and even (without any States General) of Colbert after the Fronde. The monarchy could continue only if the King were an arbiter. In this sense, the revocation of the Edict of Nantes had 'marked the beginning of the monarchy's decline'. This institution had 'to be moderate or not be'. But it had also to be energetic towards the factious: Louis XI had brought to heel the appanaged dynasties; Henry IV, the religious parties; Richelieu, the political parties; Mazarin, the princes of the blood; Louis XIV, the *Parlements*. It was expected that Louis XVI would bring to heel the last of the privileged. The third estate had acquired wealth, culture and power; it hoped for equal rights and careers open to talent; it also demanded the removal of the barriers which prevented a capitalist liberalism from taking the place of a medieval economy. One *élite*, the middle class, was seeking in France to supplant another, the aristocracy, which had overlooked its duties as a managerial group in order to devote itself to pleasure and cultivation; it was no longer ready to use force in its own defence. It was lost.

The financial disorder which, by leading to the convocation of the States General, started the Revolution, was not the cause of the trouble, but one of the symptoms of the disease. Making up the deficit was out of the question only because it was impossible to tax the wealth of the aristocracy and clergy. This refusal on the part of the privileged, the attitude of the *Parlements* which sustained this rebellion against the State, and the just displeasure of public opinion at the unconcern of the public authorities were what made thorough changes necessary. Over these changes the King of France could preside, as British sovereigns several times have done in the course of history. It was his task to guarantee, without violence, the transfer of power from one class to another. Had Louis XVI chosen this position, the monarchy would have been saved. But the King could likewise make himself the champion of the threatened classes; in that case, he would perish with them.

BOOK FOUR

THE FRENCH REVOLUTION

CHAPTER I

HOW THE REVOLUTION BEGAN

THE French Revolution began not in tumult but idyllically: when, on January 1st, 1789, Necker announced that the King was summoning the States General and granting the third estate double representation, the news was greeted with affectionate enthusiasm, and His Majesty's kindness caused 'torrents of tears' to be shed. But ideas were far less clear than feelings were lively. Would the voting be by orders or by heads? The minister had given no indication. Were the vote to be by orders, all the effects of double representation would be cancelled. And what meaning could be attached to consulting the voters in a country without political education? For want of candidates and creeds, the electors were being asked to draw up statements of policy by means of memoranda. Pamphlets supplied them with advice; of these the most celebrated was that written by the Abbé Sieyès, a soured clergyman with a cold, moderate outlook, '*What is the third estate? Every-thing. What has it been until now? Nothing. What does it seek to be? Something.*' This brochure had a quick success, reaching a sale of thirty thousand copies. Its title was restrained, since 'everything' was satisfied to be 'something'; the Abbé's advice was not to attack the privileged with too much violence, for this 'would risk plunging France into a frightful predicament'; to bear in mind the general interest; to reform taxes and punishments. He maintained, however, the historically false thesis of the two Frances: the people's France springing from the aboriginal Celts, and the oppressors' France, heir to the Frankish invaders. In most of the provinces fervour for the monarchy seemed untouched: 'The King has given us freedom to complain. What a precious benefaction! How much thanks must we give to a monarch whose tender concern seeks to ask questions of his subjects!' The rhetoric of the day remained classic, and in it Cicero and Rousseau had each his share.

The court refrained from campaigning, but individuals, particularly the Duke of Orleans, a demagogic prince of the blood, had fewer scruples. Some of the electoral gatherings of the clergy were stormy, the poor and mud-spattered priests attacking the prelates with their fine carriages. In Provence, Count Mirabeau, a speaker of genius and a profound political thinker, was pushed aside by the nobility because he had led a scandalous life and because his violence aroused fears. Everything about him seemed immoderate — his enormous head, his clothes, his voice, his passions, his features — 'My ugliness likewise is a power', he used to say. At that time, no Frenchman had a more intelligent knowledge of history; none better understood the workings of the British monarchy. But his cynicism worried people: 'The deficit is the nation's treasure', said Mirabeau, and the witticism cut too deep, since it gave offence. Spurned by his own estate, which was dismayed at his past and which he annoyed by his talk of 'necessary sacrifices', Mirabeau offered himself to the voters of the third: 'Granted that I'm a mad dog; all the more reason for electing me; despotism and privileges will die by my fangs.' He was elected by Aix and by Marseilles, and he was to be the greatest orator of the States General.

The declaration of the third estate was devised as follows: Each parish compiled memoranda (*cahiers*) which were brought to the assembly of the bailiwick, and this body worked out a collective memorandum. The grievances were much the same throughout France. The peasants complained of the poll-tax, the salt tax, the tithe, the exclusive rights of the lords to hunt pigeons and rabbits (which destroyed crops); the bourgeois asked for a constitution, a representative assembly, or at least the periodical meeting of the States General. All wished for the suppression of feudal rights and privileges; the right to vote taxes and to control their expenditure; the abolition of censorship. With these things accomplished, the French monarchy's golden age would begin. 'Here is the happy moment at which reason and mankind, regaining their birthright, bring forth freedom, the golden age so long desired.' The nation was preparing itself to make a new contract with its king, the old one having been torn up 'by mutual consent'.

The deputies chosen were of high moral and intellectual quality. About 50 per cent were lawyers, the rest being great nobles, businessmen, priests; there were more men of law than administrators. 'But it was the legal experts who had created the modern monarchy, modern France; it was they who had regularized and formulated the royal Revolution; they would formulate and regularize the Revolution of the middle class.'[1] Ill assorted by the very nature of the three orders, this assembly seemed homogeneous in culture; throughout France, education had been clerical and Latin; Robespierre and Mirabeau were both of them readers of

[1] JEAN JAURÈS.

Seneca and Plutarch; Rousseau had more disciples among the deputies than Montesquieu. Where now was the States General to meet? Paris, then much excited, would have been risky; the King chose Versailles, which was no less perilous. 'His Majesty was determined to gather together around his own dwelling the States General of the kingdom, not in any way to embarrass their deliberations, but to preserve for them the character dearest to their hearts — that of counsellors and friends.' The real reason was that Louis XVI cherished his hunting and did not want to journey away from his favourite forests. His advisers should have told him that the nearness of Paris would inflame the assembly and the capital, that the deputies would find it very hard to secure lodging in Versailles, that court life there would be at once a humiliation and a scandal to the third estate. An uneasiness made itself felt straightway; beginning with the royal opening session (May 5th), the third estate, which was obliged to wear black, found itself penned up in a special enclosure, while prelates' robes and nobles' many-coloured clothing blazed around the King. None the less, everyone cried 'Long live the King!' and many deputies were prepared to be enthusiastic. A speech from the throne, however, which was most vague and which discussed neither the vote by individuals nor the frequency at which the States General was to be summoned, disappointed and chilled. 'A general restlessness, an exaggerated desire for change have captured men's minds', said the King, 'and they would end by leading opinion wholly astray were they not promptly given proper direction by a meeting of wise and moderate views.' With a few warm words, the sovereign or his ministers might have been able to win and dominate this assembly still without leadership; yet Necker was as spiritless as the King. He undertook to explain to the States General that the deficit did not exist and that he, Necker, by his skill as a conjurer, would suffice to bring the budget back into balance. If this is the case, thought his listeners, why on earth was it necessary to convene all these deputies of the nation? 'There is no one at the helm', said Mirabeau with asperity. In order to explain this absence of pilots, a legend took shape: the King and Necker, patriots both, would have liked to speak up, to state their views, but the Queen, the Count of Artois and the court prevented them. But it mattered little: the third estate had five hundred deputies; the nobility one hundred and eighty-eight; the clergy two hundred and forty-seven. Voting by head would give the country a popular constitution. Envoys were exchanged between one order and another; the third invited the members of the two privileged chambers to

unite with it in verifying credentials. From May 15th on, a dozen democratic priests responded to this invitation; together with these, the deputies
of the third estate proclaimed themselves the National Assembly.

This illegal assembly expected to be dissolved from the very beginning;
it was not. The deputies, made bold, decided that taxes would continue
to be levied as long as the National Assembly should sit, but the moment
it broke up, all gathering of taxes which had not been freely approved by
it should cease throughout the kingdom. 'No taxation without representation.' In a word, the Assembly demanded that France should have a
charter. This constituted a seizure of power, and it aroused intense excitement among the nobility and the clergy. Each of these two orders
numbered in its ranks liberals and irreconcilable conservatives; among the
clergy the liberals won the day: six prelates and one hundred and forty-
three priests joined forces with the Assembly, which welcomed them with
deep feeling; clergymen and laymen wept with joy. The opposition prelates and the nobility entreated the King to put a stop to this usurpation; a
royal session was announced for the twenty-third and, during the inter-
vening time, the hall where the Assembly had been meeting was closed.
The deputies rushed to the 'Jeu de Paume', a large, unfurnished exercise
hall or indoor tennis court. Standing upon a table the astronomer Bailly,
a liberal respected for his age and admired for his knowledge, presided;
the Assembly swore 'never to separate and to meet in any place where
circumstances might require until such time as the Constitution should
be established on solid foundations'. On June 23rd the royal session took
place; in an altered voice, Louis XVI announced that the States General
would deliberate by orders and that it could discuss taxes but not privileges. Thus, contrary to its historic mission, the French monarchy took
up against the people the defence of the feudality. Nobility and clergy
marched out behind the King. The third estate remained, in dejected
silence. Then it was that the Grand Master of Ceremonies, the Marquis
de Dreux-Brézé, appeared to give the deputies of the third estate the order
to withdraw, and Mirabeau answered with his resounding sentence: 'Sir,
go tell your master that we are here by the will of the people and that
we shall leave here only at the point of the bayonet!' The exact words are
under dispute, but not their meaning. For the first time the King of
France had been treated by the third estate not as its protector but as its
adversary. 'They want to stay?' said Louis XVI. 'Well, damn it! Let
them': an expression, perhaps, of his natural pliancy, but also of his
military weakness. He was not even certain of his French guards, who

said 'that they were third estate'. But his equivocal consent was interpreted as an act of the real will of a monarch whom the Assembly refused to believe hostile.

The court had yielded; the nobility capitulated. The Assembly seemed triumphant, and people turned to it. The King himself 'commanded' the three orders to meet; already optimists were saying that the revolution was over and that it had not cost a drop of blood. Mirabeau praised such moderation and the great changes which had been wrought merely by the collaboration of patriotic intentions. 'History', he said, 'has too often recounted the actions of nothing more than wild animals, among which at great intervals we can pick out some heroes; now we are allowed to hope that we are beginning the history of man.' It would have been possible to look upon the constitutional monarchy as an accomplished fact had the King in all good faith accepted the Assembly, since the Assembly itself accepted the King. Unfortunately on July 11th the court party of resistance won him over, and a little later Necker was dismissed. Breteuil, Broglie, Foulon – those who were called 'the Queen's Party' – were victorious. On July 12th, when the capital learned of Necker's dismissal, that minister's bust veiled in crêpe was paraded through the streets – in those days a banker could still be a popular hero. He was no more than a symbol, but what is more important than a symbol? The new ministers were not intransigent and would surely have sought a compromise; they were not given time to do so. Foreign regiments, dispatched to preserve order, were showered with stones on the Place Louis XV and invaded the Tuileries gardens; the people of Paris feared a *coup d'état* and the city bristled with rumours: 'The troops are going to butcher the patriots! . . . The brigands are marching on Paris! . . .' Bread was scarce; supplies for more than three days were lacking; there were one hundred and twenty thousand paupers, who were told that the court opposed the Assembly's helping them. Brochures and pamphlets abounded: 'Thirteen appeared today, sixteen yesterday, ninety-two last week.'[1] These called for the withdrawal of the troops and adjured the soldiers not to forget their duties as citizens. The Palais Royal gardens, under the protection of the Duke of Orleans, who cherished vague and sinister hopes, had become an open-air club. There a youthful attorney without briefs, Camille Desmoulins, 'a young rascal of genius',[2] in whom were mingled in some part 'Figaro, Gavroche and Bixiou', blended in his speeches 'Homer, Cicero, and the Café Procope'.[3] On this July 12th, he

[1] ARTHUR YOUNG.   [2] MICHELET.   [3] SAINTE-BEUVE.

clambered upon a chair and cried out: 'To arms!' Out of a horse-chestnut leaf he had fashioned himself a green cockade; from then on every passer-by had to wear one if he wished to avoid insults and kicks on the shins; the dictatorship of the mob was beginning. Crowds stripped the gunsmiths' shops, sought to break into the arsenals, carried away from the Invalides twenty-eight thousand muskets and five cannon; then, learning that the powder supplies had been taken to the Bastille, all turned their steps towards that fortress.

The taking of the Bastille is one of those events about which it is not easy or even fair to write objectively; if you limit yourself to describing the bare action, as does Taine, the heroic attack is nothing more than a bloody riot. If we are to understand the part played by this event in French history, we must consider, as we have done with Necker, less what the Bastille really was than what it was symbolically. Its crenellated towers in the very centre of Paris seemed like a dark shadow of feudalism; the *lettres de cachet*, its mysterious imprisonments, added to its sinister repute. Even the *cahiers* of the Paris nobility called for its removal; yet Monsieur de Launay, its governor, was bound in duty to defend the Bastille which had been entrusted to him. He did so with restraint and invited a number of the assailants to come to see with their own eyes that he had not taken any warlike measures, and fired only at the last extremity. In the crowd which dragged the cannon before the fortress's walls there were, as in every crowd, heroes, monsters and idle fools. The heroes must have been numerous, because the besiegers' losses were heavy; the monsters must have been cruel, because, after the Bastille was taken, its governor and other soldiers were slaughtered while defenceless. Launay's head and that of Flesselles, the provost of the merchants, were borne through the streets of Paris. Sadism, always latent, was on the increase. The effect of the fall of the Bastille was stupendous: suddenly the people knew its strength. July 14th, 1789, had been the first of those great revolutionary 'days', brief dramas which, during a few hours of Parisian rioting, would each time change the face of France.

The King, on July 14th, had been hunting all day, and then, tired, had gone to bed; on the morning of the fifteenth the Duke of Liancourt awakened him to tell him the news. 'Is this a rebellion?' asked Louis XVI. 'No, Sire, it is a revolution.' The King's promise to withdraw the troops meant that the monarchy was giving up its own defence. At first the Assembly was appalled; it was by majority middle class, opposed to violence. Bursting forth, the members trod in the footsteps of the Paris crowds which were now flooding towards the Bastille in order to level it. The astronomer Bailly, hero of the 'Jeu de Paume', was named mayor of Paris, and Lafayette, hero of Yorktown, was put in command of the National Guard. On July 17th, Louis came to Paris and went to the Hôtel de Ville, where he received the tricolour cockade, and so accepted the Revolution, but without intelligence or warmth, so that he gained no advantage from his gesture. 'His doltish, stupid face made one pity him', said the priest, Lindet. The Paris Commune, which had just been born, at first tried to maintain a legal link with the Old Regime, but anarchy was getting the upper hand with incredible speed. Without trial, the mob hanged the minister Foulon 'from the lamp-post' and slaughtered his son-in-law, Berthier de Sauvigny; the law was falling asleep; the human beast had been unleashed. The royal administration was discredited, ousted, while the revolutionary administration did not yet exist. In the provinces, the municipalities at first struggled to guarantee an orderly and peaceful transition, but there two fears soon brought forth what was called the 'great dread': one, legitimate, the fear of hunger, because grain was no longer in circulation; the other, imaginary, was the fear of 'brigands'. Who were these brigands? No one could have told you. Whole villages went into hiding; in order to fight off the brigands, 'federations' of towns and cities were formed. 'A horrible anarchy', the Venetian Ambassador said, 'is the first aspect of the regeneration it is desired to bestow on France . . . There no longer exist either executive power, laws, magistrates, or police. . . .' Castles and tax offices were set on fire by the people, though persons had not yet begun to be molested. Fury was being spent on the local bastilles, the crenellated battlements of privilege; here was another *Jacquerie*, another peasant uprising, such as had been so frequent in French history. What could be done to calm down the provinces? Speaking before the Assembly on the night of August 4th, the Viscount de Noailles, one of Lafayette's companions in America, asserted that the sole cause of this agitation was the retention of feudal rights, and that the sole means to bring it to an end was their abolition. The Assembly rapturously applauded this young noble in this adherence to the gospel of the third estate; the deputies wept, embracing one another. In the enthusiasm of the occasion, each individual wished to forfeit something — hunting privileges, aristocratic monopolies. The third estate declared itself deeply touched by this 'orgy of generosity' on the part of the privileged. 'What a nation! What a glory! What an honour to be French!' And truly the Fourth of August was an evening of union and love of which the nation could be proud. On August 11th, Cardinal La Rochefoucauld and the Archbishop of Paris relinquished their tithes without indemnity; this was the reform which finally won the peasants over to the Revolution.

Never had a regime so speedily committed suicide; in April the monarchy appeared all-powerful; in August almost nothing remained of the old institutions, and the country seemed delighted. The Count of Ségur wrote: 'The middle classes, the peasants, even the women seem somehow spirited, proud, heartened. A people bent under the yoke once again walks erect.' All at once there existed in France only equal citizens, endowed with inalienable rights. On August 26th, the Assembly defined these rights in its *Declaration of the Rights of Man and of the Citizen*, 'for all men, for all times, for all countries'. This declaration was essentially republican, although no one was yet talking about a republic; even the third estate believed that the King alone could preserve a union of provinces so diverse. The nation had become sovereign, but the Government remained monarchical, even by divine right: 'Louis, by the grace of God and by the constitutional law of the State, King of the French . . .' Was France then moving in the direction of an English-style monarchy? This form of government, however, presupposed a tradition, parties, a responsible cabinet. Only such truly great men as Montesquieu and Mirabeau had understood the theory of the separation of powers. As early as 1789, Mirabeau had said: 'I want a free but monarchical constitution.' In order to bolster the executive, he suggested giving the King a right of temporary veto: 'The representatives', said Mirabeau, 'can constitute an aristocracy dangerous to freedom. It is against this aristocracy that the veto is needed. The representatives would likewise have their veto, which would lie in the refusal to vote taxes.' At once the demagogues aroused the people against those who favoured two chambers and the royal veto; the Duke of Orleans had the Palais Royal swarming with his agents and parasites. Did Paris lack flour? The agitators warned the city and made it apprehensive: 'The King will say, "*Veto*", and you will have no bread.' This outlandish word *veto* worried the citizens just as formerly the word *deficit* had alarmed the *philosophes*. Already the Revolution's second crew was at work. 'The radical bourgeoisie was lining up against the moderates.'[1] Marat, a fanatical, disillusioned and sickly doctor, who had written a pamphlet on the vices of the English constitution, attacked 'the traitors, the bicameralists', and summoned the

[1] JEAN JAURÈS.

poor to battle. This second crew possessed resources and troops. It wanted its Day — October 5th, 1789.

What would be its purpose? To go to Versailles in order to hurl Mounier, that wealthy bourgeois from Dauphiné who was President of the Assembly, 'out of his seat of office, and Antoinette out of the throne'. Its justification was that the Flanders Regiment, said to be loyal to the King, had just arrived at court and that during a banquet of the body-guards, the soldiers had decorated themselves with black cockades. The band had played: 'Oh Richard, oh my King, the whole world has left you!...' and a counter-revolutionary frenzy had seized the court. At once several thousand women were recruited to march on Versailles, and there were men disguised in skirts mingled among them; the court would never dare order the use of firearms against such a procession. Despite Lafayette, at whom the crowd screamed, 'To Versailles or to the lamp-post!' the National Guard joined forces with this invasion. At the castle, Lafayette found its defenders hesitant; he heard women talk of kill-ing the Queen; he entered entirely alone and was ill received by the court nobility among whom he numbered so many relatives. 'Here is Crom-well!' was the cry of greeting. To which he replied, 'Cromwell would not have come in unaccompanied', which was true enough. Soon the palace was overrun and several soldiers killed; the King must promise to live at Paris and the Assembly must agree to follow him there. This was folly on the part of the legislature, because it thus placed itself under the thumb of the mob, and the mob is not the people. In the parade which in triumph brought back from Versailles 'the baker, his wife, and the baker's little man', the bleeding heads of the slaughtered guards were born aloft on pikes, and amid this gruesome carnival the King entered the Tuileries castle. There he was the prisoner of the Paris Commune, but still had the support of the people, who wished merely to sever him from the influence of the court and the Queen. Thenceforth the National Assembly met in Paris; the King came in state to attend the session of February 4th, 1790, in order to announce his acceptance of the principles of the Revolution and to promise that he 'would promptly prepare the mind and heart of his young son for the new order of things which circumstances had brought about'. Once again on that day you might have thought that the Revolution was over and that, like its American counterpart, it would give birth to a liberal regime. 'But', said Mirabeau, 'when you undertake to run a revolution, the difficulty is not to make it go; it is to hold it in check'.

We can readily understand how out of this brief period Michelet fashioned an epic. The oath of the 'Jeu de Paume'; the upsetting within a few days of so ancient an order; the birth of the tricolour, since linked to so much that is glorious; the people's artillerymen threatening a lowering fortress in the July sunshine; the young nobility forswearing its privileges during a memorable night — such ideas and dreams strike the imagination, and it is natural that in their day they should have awakened noble feelings and great hopes. On the other hand, Taine, and many foreign observers, put their emphasis on the injustice and violence of the mobs, on the massacre of an innocent garrison, on the intrigues of the Duke of Orleans's agents, on the anarchy in the provinces, and came to the conclusion that, 'however bad a government may be, there is something worse, and that is the abolition of Government'. The truth seems to be that a group of most worthy deputies came to Versailles with a programme of reasonable reforms; that the lack of energy and decision on the Government's part made it possible for other, more brutal, forces to carry the day; and that the 'Eighty-Niners' had been led to commit acts they themselves had not foreseen, which were contrary to their own principles.

CHAPTER II

HOW THE ASSEMBLY FASHIONED A CONSTITUTION

I N Paris the Assembly met in the riding school of the Tuileries. 'They are in the riding school', people said, 'but the horsemen will be at the Palais Royal.' And indeed the riding masters, the fanatics, daily thronged the galleries, chalking up the mistakes. On the floor, men of talent were not lacking; to the Left, Barnave, romantic Buzot, handsome Pétion, Alexander Lameth, veteran of the American War of Independence and Robespierre, the Arras lawyer; in the Centre the great liberal lords such as Clermont-Tonnerre and Liancourt, or democratic priests like the Abbé Grégoire; on the Right, a number of excellent men, but of so little influence they rarely attended; towering above them all, Mirabeau. He was the greatest speaker in the whole Assembly, but his reputation as a man who could be bought and as a voluptuary brought him into disrepute. After the October 'days', the Count de la Marck asked him to prepare a memorandum for the King, and Mirabeau drew up a document of wonderful sanity, advising the sovereign to leave Paris and appeal to France: 'The provinces want laws.' But, Mirabeau added, the King should not cross the national frontiers: 'A king, who is the only safeguard of his people, does not flee before his people.' Above all the King should not stand *against* the Revolution: 'It is sure that a great revolution is *needed*, that the nation has rights, that it is on the road to recovering them all', but 'the inseparability of monarch and people lodged in the hearts of all Frenchmen'. He added: 'Do what you can in order that the people at the castle may know me to be more disposed towards them than against them.' To which the Queen very foolishly replied: 'Never shall we be in such sorry state, I think, as to be reduced to the painful extremity of having recourse to Mirabeau.' A little later she understood better, indeed so well that Mirabeau came to think: 'The King has only one man, and that is his wife.' Of Louis XVI he said: 'Imagine some ivory balls slippery with oil which you vainly seek to hold together.' In July 1790 he had an interview with the sovereigns in which he made the mistake of accepting the court's offer to pay his debts, but his devotion was genuine: 'He accepted their allowances in order to govern them and not to be governed by them.'[1] He had a fine gift for phrases: 'I am the man for re-establishing order, not for re-establishing the old order.' Mirabeau and Lafayette working together would at that time have been able to govern France, Lafayette supplying the National Guard and Mirabeau the Assembly, but Lafayette liked praise more than power; Mirabeau's reputation frightened him off and he paid no attention to his overtures.

The Constituent Assembly had had no political experience; it wanted, as Gouverneur Morris, the minister from the United States, put it, 'An American Constitution with a king instead of a president', without reflecting 'that they have not American Citizens to support that Constitution'. Besides, they lacked the solid political education which had been imparted by the town meeting. The Assembly was unaware of the need for rules; it tolerated disorder in its meetings; it laid itself open to pressure from the galleries; it forbade the King to choose his ministers from among its members — an insane decision which deprived France of a Mirabeau cabinet. In short the Assembly wanted parliamentarianism without any of the conditions which make parliaments possible. Moreover, the real power lay outside the Assembly: a society called the Jacobins moulded public opinion. It met in Paris at the Convent of the Jacobins on the rue Saint Honoré and soon had many affiliated groups in the provinces which, in each commune, dominated, persuaded and ruled. It was this group of incorruptibles which asserted what it called the unity of the nation, which was really only the unity of a party. The Jacobin orators talked largely about the people, but in their view this people existed only in the consciousness of patriots. 'On this earth, virtue is in a minority', Robespierre was later to say. What was coming to the top, then, was not a democracy, but the 'doctrine of the small number of elect'.

In 1790 the Jacobins still accepted the monarchy, and the Constitution created by the Assembly was monarchical. Thanks to Mirabeau, the King had been given the veto power; he could use it against any measure during the lives of three legislatures, or for six years; but since he had no power to dissolve the Assembly, this body, in case of a difference, had only to refuse him funds in order to bring him to terms. Moreover, the bureaucrats, thenceforward almost all to be elected, were no longer dependent on him; he was 'without men and without money'. The Assembly had likewise defended itself against the royal army by forbidding it to come closer than some thirty miles to the legislative body. Suffrage was not

[1] LOUIS MADELIN.

280

universal; only active citizens voted, meaning those who paid taxes; the Revolution leaned upon the power of the people, but the Constitution was for the middle class. On the administrative level, the Assembly had broken the old provincial framework and had created eighty-three 'departments' in order to put an end to localism and separatism. These departments, in turn, were to be divided into districts and cantons; and finally the basic cell was the commune, which named its municipal government, maintained its national guard and collected the taxes. Judgeships were elective at all levels. Mirabeau had severe strictures for this system which, said he, left the government powerless and, for want of a central administration, guaranteed omnipotence to popular groups dominated by an active minority. 'The kingdom's disorganization', said he, 'could not have been better contrived.'

While this radical transformation was being carried out the country seemed curiously calm. The heedless and frivolous aristocracy lived as it always had; in Paris the tea parties were charming, and the political *salons* prattled wittily and declaimed with fervour. The patriots gathered at Madame Bailly's or Madame Necker's. At the cafés — de Valois, de Foy, de la Régence — were held the Revolution's 'permanent sessions'. In the theatres, appallingly bad plays devoted to civic virtue were performed; Molière was looked upon as an aristocrat; in Marseilles the *Mariage de Figaro* was barred because it 'was reminiscent of anti-social distinctions'. Fashion, eagerly followed, was turning patriotic and revolutionary: women wore Liberty hats, Constitution jewellery, and ribbons the colour of which was described as 'Foulon's blood!' A student from Bordeaux wrote to his father: 'You must surely have heard with joy about this charming little decree which knocks out all those coats-of-arms, all those vain ornaments created to flatter the hopes of our wretched aristocrats ...' The bourgeoisie was relishing its day in the sun: pupils at an art school abused pencils too hard for their taste by calling them 'feudal'. The shoemaker hoped that he would one day surely see his son a marshal of France, and he said so to his noble customers, who took no offence; this hope kept up his faith and his good spirits. When the King journeyed to the Assembly, the crowd would hail him. 'I have been deceived', said he; 'I am still King of the French.'

The King of the French lacked money as much as formerly did the King of France. 'Bankruptcy stood at the door.' Now the Church owned three milliard *livres* in property; Talleyrand, a bishop and turncoat grandee, crippled, freethinking and brilliant, suggested placing this property at the disposal of the State. Even the most patriotic of the clergy protested long and loud; had they not given up the tithe and thus contributed their share of sacrifice? Moreover, many of their holdings were in trust, originally established as pious foundations. Nevertheless, on April 10th, 1790, ecclesiastical properties were declared the property of the nation. Necker, the Finance Minister, was rather embarrassed by this gift; what would he do with these holdings? Offer them for sale? That would have threatened a serious depreciation in land values. The municipalities, with Paris in the van, agreed to buy them and to pay for them in bonds; then paper money was issued, secured by this property of the nation. These were the assignats. 'Whoever had any in his pocket became, despite himself, a defender of the Revolution',[1] for if there were ever a return to the Old Regime, the confiscation would be annulled and the assignats would lose all value. Thus the nationalization of the property of the clergy created in France a powerful coalition of interests; it also produced a good deal of discontent first among the despoiled prelates, then among the many faithful who were scandalized at what had happened. It was becoming difficult to believe in an idyllic revolution; disorder was spreading and it was hard to quell it because the army seemed none too reliable.

How could it have been? Among the officers there were some who, seeing an opportunity for advancement through demagogy, became informers against their comrades; others, unable to accomplish anything and discouraged at the lack of discipline among the troops, resigned. Regiments placed their commanding officers under arrest. The best minds in the Assembly saw the danger of 'this military democracy, a variety of political monster which has always ended by devouring the empires which have produced it'.[2] In order to rebuild the unity of the army and the nation, it was decided to ask the regiments to send delegations to a Festival of Federation which was to take place in Paris, on the Champ de Mars, on the anniversary of the fall of the Bastille. This notion of federation, American in origin, was then the rage. All France was promised representation. In Paris, prostitutes, Franciscan friars and masons laboured together on the construction of tiers and grassy terraces before the altar of the Fatherland: 'Hearty fishwives pushed barrows filled by ladies with the vapours.' Lafayette, who had a sentimental liking for symbolic gestures, came to dig for two hours: 'What a general! and how he is loved!' But Mirabeau murmured, 'Clowning Caesar . . .' and the

[1] ROBERT LINDET.   [2] La Tour du Pin, quoted by LOUIS MADELIN.

Queen, 'I clearly see that Monsieur de Lafayette wishes to save us, but who will save us from Monsieur de Lafayette?' It proved a fine festival, splendidly arranged. Talleyrand said the Mass; Lafayette swore, in the name of the federated, to support the Constitution; then the King himself gave his oath amid much applause. The Queen displayed her son; feeling hearts were touched. It rained in torrents; but what did that matter? The rain was 'the tears of the aristocracy'. Once again Frenchmen loved one another; once more the Revolution was over.

A portion of the nobility, however, did not accept these changes and left France; there were several waves of emigration — 'that of pride, that of apprehension, that of fear'. Emigration became an offence in February 1792; in itself it was in no way reprehensible, but it became so when the *émigrés*, banded together along the banks of the Rhine, or collected around the Count of Artois at Turin, and asked the sovereigns of Europe to support the French counter-revolution. Of course many other factions before them (the Burgundians, the Huguenots, the Ligue) had appealed to foreigners, but such surrendering of principle is always dangerous and subject to blame, and it was natural for the patriots to be exasperated at the machinations of the *émigrés*. For a long while the threat they constituted was empty, because the Governments of Europe could not reach any agreement. Russia, the new Continental power, had its eye on Sweden, Poland and Turkey, in order to secure itself windows towards the West; Russia hoped to see Prussia and Austria embark on a French campaign which would give it a free hand. But Austria and Prussia understood this game and abstained from all commitments; the Count of Artois, advocate of intervention, was preaching in the desert. Queen Marie Antoinette suggested to her brother the Emperor that he make a small frontier demonstration, but he showed little fraternal eagerness and said (like Mirabeau) that at least he must wait until the King should have left Paris.

Louis XVI, a most honourable man, would probably have remained loyal to the new Constitution if an insoluble problem of conscience had not arisen to face him. The confiscation of the property of the clergy had made necessary the creation of a budget for religious worship. Now if bishops and pastors were to be paid by the State, they became government employees. Should they not thereafter be elected by their parishes and dioceses? Such was the Assembly's decision, under pressure from the Jansenists and the *philosophes*. It has been said that three Latin words killed the monarchy: *veto*, *deficit* and *unigenitus*. And it is true enough that the Jansenists, those Protestants within the Catholic fold, had not yet forgiven the Bourbons for the bull *Unigenitus*. They spurred on the advocates of revolution in the Church. 'The service of the altars is a public function', urged Mirabeau, and even some of the faithful supported him, pointing to religious tradition. What was the Pope in the early days of Christianity? A plain bishop of Rome. The first Christians had elected their bishops. Why not revert to this custom? Perhaps the Pope himself would have yielded, through fear of witnessing the birth of a separatist Gallican Church, had the Assembly not made two mistakes: it carved the dioceses out afresh to make them coincide with the new departments, a 'geometrical and lay' operation which was beyond its competence; and it demanded of priests an oath of loyalty to the nation, that is, to the King and the Constitution. All the bishops save four refused to swear and a great number of pastors followed their example; from thenceforward there were in France two kinds of priest: constitutional or sworn (*assermenté*) priests and refractory priests. Pope Pius VI condemned the civil constitution of the clergy; what would the King do? He was devout and more anxious for his eternal salvation than for his throne; after much heart-searching he made up his mind. This intervention by the Assembly in the spiritual realm had deeply upset him and produced in him an abrupt change of attitude: he ceased thinking that it would be possible for him to accept the Revolution and co-operate with it.

As for France, or at least the greater part of France, it would have liked, in the first months of 1791, a return to a calmer political life. Already in many sections people no longer voted; unemployment was general and complaints bitter. In March 1791, Mirabeau died, 'shocked at the idea that he had contributed only to a vast demolition'. Before dying, he said to Talleyrand, 'I carry away with me the last shreds of the monarchy'. And indeed the compromise he had wished was becoming difficult. The King looked upon himself as greatly sinful because he had agreed to the civil constitution of the clergy and was terrified at the approach of the day when he would have to fulfil his Easter duty. He dreamed of leaving Paris, where he no longer felt free to act in accordance with his conscience. Why not go to Metz, where he could rejoin Bouillé's loyal army? Perhaps that army would suffice to re-establish him in his past greatness, without recourse to foreigners. On June 21st he fled with the Queen and the Children of France; at once the alarm was sounded in Paris. At Varennes, Louis XVI was recognized, arrested and brought back to Paris through mobs hurling insults at him; thereafter he was to be the enemy of the people. When he arrived at the Tuileries, he learned that the Assembly had decided to hold him prisoner there and that he was suspended; he had lost the prestige so long preserved in spite of his weakness; the spell was broken. The Bourbon, to disillusioned subjects, seemed a poor fellow; the violent spoke of him as a 'fat pig' soon to have his throat slit. But the monarchical tradition had been so powerful that not a single member of the Assembly yet dared to proclaim the dethronement, so that, in order to avoid having to pass judgment on the flight to Varennes, a fiction was accepted: the King had not fled, he had been kidnapped.

Such was not the reaction of the political clubs. At the Jacobins', certain citizens asked that the King be considered as having abdicated; this motion led to a split, and the moderates departed to found the Club des Feuillants. To the Left of the Jacobins, the Cordeliers' Club, the Society of the Rights of Man and of the Citizen, became republican immediately after Varennes. New men were participants in this group — Danton, Camille Desmoulins, Marat, Hébert — who expressed themselves as favouring the 'suppression of the royal automaton'. The Assembly resisted. Sieyès asserted himself in support of the monarchical regime 'because it ends in a point', which was a reason more aesthetic than political. Barnave, a young, romantically handsome deputy of the third estate, who had been sent to Varennes as one of the Assembly's commissioners to bring Louis XVI back to Paris, had been moved by the misfortunes of the royal family and defended it: 'I have grown much older lately', he said. The Assembly itself had grown older. Once the vanguard and brains of the Revolution, it was now outflanked and left behind. Many of its members said in discouragement that the Constitution could not work if authority were not strengthened: Rivarol poked fun at those people who, 'having been firebrands, now come to volunteer as firemen'. At last, on September 4th, the Constitution was completed. The King came before the Assembly publicly to accept it. The people delightedly believed in a reconciliation. The goal of the Revolution has been reached', said the King. 'Let the nation resume its happy nature.' But not so easily can one disband the passions. On the twenty-fifth, having finished its labours, the Assembly broke up. It had decided beforehand that none of its members could participate in the new Assembly — a decision which merely deprived the country of the experience that had been gained. 'There remained for us', said Malouet, 'only one great mistake to make, and we did not fail to make it.'

CHAPTER III

HOW THE MONARCHY PERISHED

THE new Assembly, called the Legislative, had to be made up of new men since the members of the Constituent Assembly had excluded themselves from election to it. The Right of the Old Regime had disappeared; the Right in the Legislative was made up of moderate Jacobins, the Feuillants. That fact alone allows us to measure the speed with which yesterday's revolutionary was becoming the reactionary of tomorrow. The Feuillants remained what they had always been, constitutional monarchists; in the eyes of the Cordeliers they were already counter-revolutionaries. In the Centre sat the deputies who called themselves 'independent' and who were in fact undecided. To the Left were those later called the Girondists, because the Bordeaux (Gironde) deputies (Guadet, Vergniaud) played a great part among them. Two men dominated them: Jacques Brissot, a writer blessed 'with as much wit as want of foresight', who had lived in England and America and who was thought to be a diplomat because he had been a traveller; and Pierre Vergniaud, a day-dreaming, melancholy lawyer, who escaped from a disappointing universe through rebellion, the call to arms and the conjuring up of antiquity. The Girondins were suckled on Demosthenes and Plutarch. Orators rather than men of action, capable of knightly enthusiasm, but also of unfeeling hardness, they would almost all of them have given their lives 'to have made a fine speech'. Their own eloquence carried them away. 'In the last analysis, a brilliant political general staff — except that there was not to be found among them a single statesman.'[1] At the extreme Left were to be found a few representatives of the Cordeliers, but the real leadership of this group — Robespierre, Marat and Danton — were outside the Assembly.

Danton, the son of Champagne peasants, had come to Paris to finish his legal studies, had married his coffee-house keeper's daughter and had quickly captivated his neighbourhood, the district of the Cordeliers; like Mirabeau he was powerful and ugly, pitted with smallpox. 'Nature has given me for my portion', he said, 'an athletic frame and the rough features of Freedom.' This intelligent Porthos had passions as vigorous

[1] ALBERT SOREL.

as his features. He loved Paris, living and his wife; from time to time he needed an interval for retreat and love. As early as 1788, while attorney to the King's council, he had said, 'Don't you see the avalanche coming?' He had realistically thrown himself into the Revolution, in the success of which he believed; he was not resolutely hostile to the monarchy or to property or to the Church. Perhaps he was venal, but, like Mirabeau, in order to govern and not in order to be governed. 'A man like me is beyond price', he would say. Both the witticism and the attitude would have inspired Robespierre with horror. This diminutive Arras lawyer seemed as sad as Danton was jovial. At school, Robespierre had been a glutton for work, and a visit to Rousseau had been a formative influence, but if Maximilien used the language of the *Social Contract*, he had none of Jean-Jacques' genuine sensibility. His green, near-sighted eyes, his head like 'an angry cat's', his icy, pontifical manner, his intellectual arrogance, his faith in his own infallibility repelled the best of his contemporaries. But the weak were attracted. 'Robespierre will go far', said Mirabeau; 'he believes everything he says.' Danton loved love; Robespierre loved only himself. Danton loved battle; Robespierre, base flattery. Danton was too easy to reach; Robespierre was incorruptible. Danton was on terms of intimacy with all his friends; Robespierre showed intimacy only towards the people; and the people admired Robespierre's virtues – his continence, his honesty – all the more in that they were then rarely practised. Danton supported Robespierre, and Robespierre leaned upon this strength because he needed it, but he was annoyed by 'the Titan's aggressiveness', and was already planning to dispense with him.

The King came before the Legislative Assembly and was applauded; he spoke of restoring order in the army and preparing French defences. This theme must have pleased the Girondists, many of whom wished to declare war against feudal Europe; were not the Revolution's worst enemies the Coblenz *émigrés* and the Emperor of Austria? A campaign against the Queen's own brother would make it possible to put French policy on a war footing, to treat the *émigrés* and refractory priests severely, and to oblige the King to take sides. The internal situation continued to be bad; bread was lacking and the assignats were sinking in value; a state of siege is one of the expedients of weak governments. The King, or at least his War Minister, the Count of Narbonne-Lara, was not inimical to the idea of a war; he hoped thereby to get the army in hand and save the monarchy through a victory; whereas the Queen, at the bottom of her heart, perhaps hoped to save it by a defeat. The renowned Condorcet, mathematician and philosopher, the oracle of the Assembly, though doctrinally a pacifist, had become a partisan of war through benevolence. Only Robespierre feared war. 'We should be betrayed, thus defeated', he said. 'Or else, were we to be the victors, the triumphant general would become the new enemy of the people.' He was right (as later would be proved by Bonaparte) but this danger lay in the future, and the Assembly did not believe in it. In Austria a new and younger emperor, Francis II, asked nothing better than to take up the Girondist challenge; in a conflict with France the European princes saw a double advantage — 'defending their thrones and weakening a rival'.[1] The war party abroad was not lacking in excuses: French difficulties with the Elector of Trier on the subject of émigrés; support given to the Belgian revolutionaries, the seizure of the Papal States in Avignon. Meddling in French internal affairs, the Emperor of Austria denounced the Jacobin Club and denied that the King was free, expressing himself in simmering notes. After a short honeymoon, Louis XVI had indeed come into conflict with the Legislative Assembly; he had refused his sanction to certain measures voted against the émigrés and the priests, and a violent propaganda had been set in motion against the veto. Paris was hungry, and 'Monsieur Veto' was accused of starving the Parisians while awaiting their slaughter by his friends beyond the Rhine.

At this moment the court committed the ultimate mistake: it dismissed Narbonne, the only one of its ministers who had the ear of the Assembly. In a resounding speech, Vergniaud threatened the Tuileries: 'Terror and dread have often sallied forth from that palace; let them today enter it in the name of the law. Let all those who dwell there know that the King alone is inviolable, that the law will, without distinction of persons, overtake all the guilty sheltered there, and that there is not a single head which, once convicted of crime, can escape its blade . . .' So great was Vergniaud's success that the whole cabinet had to resign. Under a normal parliamentary regime, the King would have summoned Brissot, Vergniaud and Isnard to form a government, but the absurd provision in the Constitution which prevented his choosing ministers from the Assembly remained in force; the task was to discover who could represent the Girondists at the Tuileries. This matter was settled during a luncheon at the home of Roland, a political friend of the Girondists then in his sixties, a former inspector of factories, a Cato who wore shoes without buckles,

[1] ALBERT GUÉRARD.

'honest in the worst sense of the word', austere and pure with all the spitefulness of his virtues. Roland would have amounted to nothing had it not been for his wife, Manon, who was pretty and ambitious, violent and passionate, capable of love and hatred, but not of judgment. Open-hearted and gushing, Madame Roland was of the lower middle class and a true daughter of the eighteenth century, having from childhood carried Plutarch to church in place of a prayer book. At the age of twelve she had wept because she was neither a Spartan nor a Roman. Then had come for her, as for so many others, the hour of the divine Rousseau. When, in 1780, she had met Roland – he, a collaborator on the *Encyclopédie* – she had believed that by marrying this Lyons greybeard she would enter a sacred society. It was she who undertook to thrust her local bigwig upon Paris; by her charm and her political fervour, she had attracted to her *salon* the handsome young Girondists, and she had won great influence with them because she was vehement. She loathed Marie Antoinette with the implacable hatred of one woman for another. Once her husband had been selected for the Ministry of the Interior, she became the real cabinet officer, and even the soul of the cabinet, whose members she invited to lunch with the party leaders of the Assembly. Dumouriez, a scheming and likeable soldier, became minister of foreign affairs. 'He was', said Manon Roland, 'a very witty rake who poked fun at everything except his own interests and glory.' And he thought he would win that glory by making war on Austria, for which reason he greatly pleased the Jacobins. On April 20th, 1792, war was declared; the King of Prussia immediately joined forces with the Emperor.

The French army was in no state to sustain a war; numerous officers had fled the country and many of those who remained were no longer respected by their troops. The National Guardsmen were neither trained nor equipped. France had only eighty thousand men to put in her front lines, while Prussia alone had twice as many. Moreover, the campaign began with a rout. The effect in France was complex: the Queen's party grew bolder and hoped for the downfall of the revolutionaries; the Jacobins, feeling themselves in danger, took violent steps: the disbanding of the King's guard, the deportation of the refractory clergy, an encampment of 'federated' guards at the gates of Paris. The King refused his approval of the two latter measures and dismissed his Girondist cabinet. Lafayette, who was in command of one of the armies, came back to Paris, seemingly on the side of the court, and, momentarily, the Assembly gave way. The Jacobins felt that they needed a 'Day' to frighten Louis XVI and to force him to call back the right ministers. This Day of June 20th was, like all the party's stratagems, worked out in Madame Roland's *salon* and then carried out by the gangs which, on such occasions, controlled the streets—those of Santerre the brewer and Legendre the butcher. Under pretext of planting a Liberty Tree on the balcony of the Feuillants' clubrooms, a mob armed with pikes and sabres overflowed the riding-school hall and the Tuileries. What remained of the monarchy foundered in tragic buffoonery; the King, astoundingly calm and courageous, refused to reconsider his veto despite being elbowed and ridiculed by a crowd more chaffing than ferocious. He said he was a good patriot and donned a red cap; then one fellow wanted to see just how far 'Veto' would go and handed a glass of red wine to the King, who drank it. Up went the cry, 'The King drinks!' At last Pétion, handsome Pétion, Paris's new mayor and popular for the time being, extricated the sovereign. He and his queen were safe for the time being, but the last shreds of the royal purple had been torn away.

The reaction against these shameful events was lively enough. When Lafayette appeared before the Assembly to protest in the army's name, the Feuillants applauded him, and the Centre, thinking that he would act, seemed ready to join the Right in his support; the Jacobins reviled him as 'a rascal, a traitor, and an enemy of the Fatherland'. The court, which should have propped itself on him, held its grievances dearer than its welfare: 'Better to perish', exclaimed the Queen, 'than to be saved by Monsieur de Lafayette and the Constitutionals!' It was human but quite absurd. Meanwhile the danger of a reaction which might sweep away the whole fabric of the Revolution temporarily drew the Girondists and Robespierre together. The Left was awaiting the arrival of the federated National Guards, especially those from the south, who were the most fervent, for a decisive Day. In the Assembly there was open talk of the King's dethronement without anyone's daring to utter the word *republic*. The climate was so fickle that one day Lamourette, the Bishop of Lyons, made an appeal for French unity in the face of foreign danger and all the deputies embraced each other in 'an incredible rapture'. Such was the 'kiss of Lamourette', on the morrow forgotten. On July 11th the Assembly proclaimed '*the Fatherland in danger*'; this formula was to permit the conscription of men and the gathering of arms. On July 14th, at the Festival of Federation, Pétion, Mayor of Paris, was cheered at the King's expense; the Queen's eyes were filled with tears. Throughout the city there had been erected platforms decked with the tricolour; a plank stretched between two drums served as a table where recruiters were accepting voluntary enlistments. They proved numerous, and the popular enthusiasm was mixed with an energetic frenzy against the court, whose secret intrigues with the enemy had become known. It is beyond doubt that the Queen was in communication with the Emperor, her nephew; the 'betrayal of the Tuileries' had been provoked by acts of violence, but it was not to be denied. Outside France, Louis XVI's brothers, Provence and Artois, behaved as though they wanted to ruin him. From Coblenz there was issued a manifesto, insulting to the French, under the signature of the Duke of Brunswick, who was in command of the Prussians, Austrians, Hessians and *émigrés*, although it was done against that general's judgment. Were the royal family not respected, France was threatened with military execution and Paris with 'total destruction'. It would have been impossible to have compromised the sovereigns more adroitly; since the King's defenders had had the impudence to threaten Paris, the people of Paris decided to rid themselves of the King.

Morris, the American, sarcastically summed up the 'Brunswick' Manifesto and showed how this stupid document was to forge unity among all patriots by saying to them: 'Be all against me, for I am against you all; and make a good Resistance, for there is no longer any Hope . . .' The reply was, 'To arms, citizens!' and everywhere men sang a new anthem, the *Marseillaise*, written at Strasbourg for the Army of the Rhine by Rouget de Lisle, but brought to Paris by the six hundred *Fédérés* who had come on foot from Marseilles. These good patriots had been eagerly awaited to help the Parisians overthrow the monarchy; for many men, and among them Danton, Camille Desmoulins, Marat and Fabre d'Eglantine, had come to believe that if they were to defeat the kings of Europe, they must not be under the command of one of them. The war demanded national unity, establishment of the Republic and a strong government. Paris felt the outbreak coming. The hesitant Assembly, monarchist in spite of everything, marked time, but alongside the Paris Commune there had been set up an 'insurrectional commune' of which Danton and his Cordelier boon companions were the instigators. This commune planned a Day for August 10th which was to settle Louis XVI's fate. On the day before, in order to paralyse resistance, Mandat, who was in command of the National Guard and would have protected the King, was arrested and then put to death. Some National and Swiss Guardsmen and certain gentlemen declared their readiness to defend the

Tuileries, but when the rioters attacked, many of these defenders went over to the people. Rœderer, the Attorney General, advised the King to take refuge in the midst of the Assembly; the Queen protested, preferring to die on the spot, but Louis XVI said, 'Let us go!' Vergniaud, who was in the chair, received the royal family: 'Sire,' said he, 'you can count on the firmness of the National Assembly; its members have sworn to die in support of the right of the people and the constituted authorities.' Their actions were not as resolute as his words; the Assembly watched the progress of the insurrection and governed its conduct by events. When the Tuileries had been captured and the Swiss Guard slaughtered, the Assembly voted not for dethronement, but the 'suspension' of the King until a national convention should have reached its decision. The Assembly had decided to confine the King in the Luxembourg Palace; the Commune insisted that he be taken to the Tower of the Temple, where he would be under the people's guard.

Meanwhile some government was necessary. Since August 10th, two-thirds of the deputies, in fear of their lives, no longer dared attend the Assembly. The Commune was triumphant; the Revolution was entering a new stage — the party of legality was beaten; the party of violence was prevailing. Robespierre would have liked a genuine dictatorship by the Commune; Danton let the Assembly languish on. What did he care? He knew he was master. An executive council of six members had been chosen, in which nominally Danton was merely Minister of Justice; in fact, he was everything. What was he after? His opponents maintain that when Danton appeared, 'flaming and flaunting his revolutionary enthusiasm . . . the vehement tribune of the people . . . the uncompromising leader of the masses',[1] it was only a mask; that Danton was in financial straits and that he was getting money from England and the Duke of Orleans, to whose profit he had promised to restore the monarchy. 'In Paris he was the man of the working-class districts, the defender of the proletariat . . . At Arcis-sur-Aube, his native village, he was acquiring land, a wife, woods, some two hundred and fifty acres of fields.'[2] However this may have been, he held the Girondists in the palm of his hand and imposed his will upon them: the Convention must be chosen by universal suffrage; suspects and relatives of émigrés must be ferreted out; a revolutionary tribunal must be set up. At the hands of this tribunal, Danton himself was one day to perish.

After August 10th, Marat urged the slaughter of the nobles and the

[1] MATHIEZ.　　　　　[2] PIERRE GAXOTTE.

priests; for the country must be terrified. 'A crowd of people sunk in debt and crime' were hired for this task; they were paid six francs a day plus what wine they wanted. On September 2nd the Commune, under threat from the Assembly, frightened at the advance of the *émigrés* and Prussians, started the performance; killing went on in all the prisons. Who judged? Whoever called himself a judge. Who carried out the sentences? Whoever liked blood. The September massacres were an outbreak of collective sadism; they were the work not of the people of Paris but of a handful of murderers. More than twelve hundred prisoners died amid scenes of horror and depravity; among them was the Princess de Lamballe, friend of Marie Antoinette. The Assembly, feeling the knife at its throat, dared not intervene; the Commune approved; public opinion remained curiously indifferent and cynical. 'The murders continue', wrote Gouverneur Morris; 'the weather is pleasant.' Danton, who could have put a stop to this butchery, let it go on, talked of necessary justice; only a few months would suffice to make him sadly repentant. His excuse was the pressure of those days: half Europe was marching against France; many officers were deserting; Paris, prey to siege fever, was athirst for terror.

Brunswick, having captured Longwy and Verdun, marched on the capital through the narrow valleys of the Argonne. But he ran into Dumouriez and Kellermann, and above all clashed at Valmy (September 20th, 1792) with the artillery of the old French army, the best in Europe. Kellermann's infantry held firm and, almost without a fight, Brunswick withdrew. In this brief burst of cannon fire the fate of France and of Europe had been settled. The invaders began a general retreat; the French Revolution had for the first time revealed its military strength; Goethe, who was present at Valmy, said that a new era was beginning. With Alsace as his point of departure, Custine penetrated into Germany as far as Mainz and Frankfort, while in the north Dumouriez also made ready to take the offensive. With surprise the Austrians and Germans watched these new French armies, mobile and fast moving because they lacked everything and lived on the country by requisitioning instead of carrying with them their own supplies. The new ideas followed the flag: the population of the Rhineland woke to the notion of freedom. 'Unite yourselves to France', said the scientist Georg Forster, 'a nation of twenty-five million men powerful enough to upset thrones like houses of cards . . . Awaken from your slumber! Take courage and become free Germans, friends and brothers of the French!' Yet on the very day of Valmy, the

Legislative Assembly disbanded; it had in fact yielded power to Danton a month earlier. On September 20th, the first deputies of the National Convention were gathering at the Tuileries, and on the twenty-first, the Convention met in the riding-school, taking the place of the now defunct Assembly.

CHAPTER IV

HOW THE COMMITTEE OF PUBLIC SAFETY
AROSE FROM THE CONVENTION

OUTSIDE Paris the elections to the Convention had taken place
amid calm and what was very nearly indifference. In the provinces the word *republic* had obtained little currency, yet no
man dared call himself a royalist. The winning deputies seemed to have
three dominant ideas: to sustain the abolition of privileges, to avoid a
counter-revolution which would involve reprisals, to protect property;
the provinces remained conservative. As a whole, the Convention was
middle class, elected in opposition to the September massacres, but in
Paris the Commune had triumphed. In the new legislature, the Girondists
sat on the Right; once more the old advanced party had become — without
changing its programme — the moderate group. Out of seven hundred
and fifty members, there were some hundred and sixty-five Girondists.
Facing them, on the Left, sat the Mountain. Danton dominated it, flanked
by his assistants, Camille Desmoulins and Fabre d'Eglantine. Robespierre,
icy and correct, awaited his hour; near him sat the hardest and the most
intelligent of the fanatics — Saint-Just. 'That which constitutes a republic',
said he, 'is the destruction of everything which opposes it', a strange way
to define life in terms of nothingness. At the Mountain's summit, Jean
Paul Marat, alone in his bodily filth and stench, a sick man who was
cynical and often cruel, had this much to be said for him: that he knew
the depths of misery and spoke of them with pity. Of all these men, he
was the best able to comprehend a social revolution. The Mountain had
a programme — the public welfare, a state of siege, purification, dictatorship. Between the Gironde and the Mountain there extended a third
group, the party which waited and was prudent, saying little. This was
the *Plaine*, or the Swamp (*Marais*). The deputies of the Plain watched
the Gironde and the Mountain, ready to slit each other's throats; some
already thought that upon the dead bodies they would one day build a
government. Yet to the left of the Mountaineers sat the section of the
Rabid (*Enragés*) who wanted the common ownership of goods, which
would have been well within the logic of the Mountain's revolution.
At first it looked as though the Gironde was going to run the Assembly;

Pétion was elected president by two hundred and thirty-five votes out of two hundred and sixty-three voting. Then the question of the regime had to be settled: 'Nothing new this Day', Morris sarcastically observed, 'except that the Convention has met and declared they will have no King in France. . . .' The people of Paris greeted the decree with cries of 'Long live the Republic!' but that term had not yet passed the lips of the deputies; it was only after this popular manifestation that the Assembly decided the Republic would be one and indivisible. Thus it was announced *what* the Republic would be before anyone had ever said that it would be. Now, the Convention could decree unity and indivisibility, but it could not achieve them, for it was itself split, not into parties but into factions. Madame Roland and her friends hated Danton; the Gironde, guilty of so many disorders, was becoming the party of order and could see salvation only in the establishment of a departmental guard which would undertake to protect the Assembly against the Commune. The Girondists, cultivated and liberal bourgeois, feared the people and respected principle; the Mountain casually paid its respects to principle and relied upon the people to carry out the Revolution. 'The aristocracy of the rich upon the ruins of the feudal aristocracy — ' said Robespierre, 'I do not see how the people, which must be the end of all political institutions, makes any vast gain by this sort of arrangement.' He called for and foretold the reign of real equality — not that Robespierre and his associates were not themselves, by birth and upbringing, bourgeois, but they thought that by thus setting the popular Commune against the Girondists, they would have a better chance of eliminating promptly the King, the nobles and the priests.

'The souls of the men who made up this assembly were always agitated and passionate, clouded, often narrow and possessed by the blindest of fanaticisms, that of reason infatuated with itself. And yet their actions were ordered in accordance with a law they held in common: this assembly, in which rivalry gnawed so many lesser souls, showed in the defence of the fatherland a great collective soul, wholly compounded of sacrifice, constancy and faith. It was an emanation of the very soul of France.'[1] This soul had good reasons to be moved, for the armies of the Republic were victorious; in the north, in the east, people were offering themselves to France. What answer should be given them? Must Dumouriez's conquests be repudiated? Or might they be accepted at the risk of making him into a Caesar? The General came to Paris between

[1] ALBERT SOREL.

two victories, laid a propitiatory offering of red roses at Madame Roland's feet and was authorized to liberate Belgium, at that time Austrian territory. Thus the Convention reverted to Richelieu's policy. 'France's history was grasping unto itself that Revolution destined to break it asunder.' Even Danton took Dumouriez to his bosom. The occupation of Belgium was easy and brilliant; at Jemappes, to the tune of the *Marseillaise*, the Austrians were ousted; on November 15th the French were at Brussels, on the twenty-eighth at Liège. To the Brussels' magistrates who brought him the keys of their city, Dumouriez said: 'Citizens, keep your keys yourselves, and hold them fast.' Here was a symbolic gesture; Dumouriez hoped, not to annex territory, but to build up around France a zone of security, a belt of independent and friendly countries: Holland, Belgium, Savoy, the Rhenish States. The Convention announced that it would grant 'brotherhood and assistance to all people who sought their freedom'. Many of the Mountaineers adopted the thesis of the natural frontiers — the Pyrenees, the Alps and the Rhine. 'France's boundaries are shown by nature. There should lie the limits of our Republic, and no power will be able to prevent our reaching them.' Here was an announcement that Holland would be invaded and therefore assurance of English enmity. Indeed England began to concern itself with Louis XVI's fate on the day the French arrived at Antwerp. It had become difficult, however, to bring the war to a close. 'We must', said old Roland with artless and cruel frankness, 'make the millions of men we have under arms keep on marching as far as their feet will carry them, or else they will come back to slit our throats.' From the decree of December 15th, 1792: 'We do not want to dominate or enslave any people . . . but every revolution needs a provisional power . . . which in some fashion causes the levelling to be systematically done . . . Such power can belong only to the French in those countries whither the pursuit of France's enemies has drawn her armies . . .' The instructions given to the generals were to abolish the tithe and feudal rights everywhere they went, to break the existing authorities and to bring about the election of provisional administrations from which enemies of the Republic would be excluded. 'War on castles, peace to cottages!' Defensive war was becoming ideological war, in which the dissemination of the Revolution's principles would be greatly helpful to the armies.

Was it necessary to try the King? The Gironde did not want to; it feared dividing France, arousing provincial opinion, and cutting itself in two. Even Danton was careful: 'Without being convinced that the King is entirely blameless, I find it only just, I believe it useful to get him out of the situation in which he now is.' The 1791 Constitution had declared the King's person inviolable, to which some replied that since August 10th he had become a simple citizen. In that case, answered those who opposed his trial, he was responsible only for his acts since August 10th and lay within the jurisdiction, not of the Convention sitting as a high court of justice, but of the ordinary tribunals. Saint-Just and Robespierre, on the other hand, wanted the King's trial and death. To their minds he was not a man under indictment to be judged but an enemy to be killed. Over and above this, they thought by means of this death to dig an unbridgeable gulf between the Gironde and the Old Regime. Buzot, and Danton himself, hoped to save 'Louis Capet'. But the discovery, in the Tuileries strong-room, of compromising correspondence which proved, it was said, that those near the King had plotted against the Revolution, and that he had been aware of it, forced the Girondists to yield. Already Robespierre was accusing them of royalist reservations, and Marat was insisting upon a roll-call vote, which meant justice subject to the blackmail of fear. Thenceforth the verdict was beyond doubt. Brave attorneys — Malesherbes, Tronchet, De Sèze — undertook to defend the King, and he, during his questioning, showed much calm and dignity. The basis of his defence was the denial of ever having acted against his principles. De Sèze pleaded the inviolability of the sovereign. The pressure brought to bear on the deputies was so strong that Madame Roland, although personally hostile to the royal pair, was wholly outraged. 'What charming freedom we enjoy in Paris!' she exclaimed. She had been nauseated by the September massacres: 'You know my enthusiasm for the Revolution; well then, I was ashamed. Our Revolution has been sullied by rascals; it has become ghastly.' Attacked by Marat she said: 'I doubt whether more dreadful things have been published against Antoinette, to whom I am likened and whose names are bestowed upon me.' O great Nemesis! When the vote was taken concerning the punishment to be inflicted on the King, there were seven hundred and twenty-one ballots cast; a majority required three hundred and sixty-one. Death was the vote of three hundred and eighty-seven deputies, among them that of Philip Equality, formerly Duke of Orleans, cousin of Louis XVI. All this took place on January 16th, 1793; on the twenty-first, the King's head fell; from the scaffold he cried: 'People, I die innocent!' That day Paris lay gloomy; eyes were lowered. The religion of divine right, the memory of Saint Louis and of Henry IV awakened in men's minds a feeling of guilt. The regicides, slowly becoming aware of their awful responsibility, understood that thenceforth they must maintain the Revolution or perish. Danton had himself voted for death, reluctantly. Robespierre had wanted something beyond expiation; he had wrought it.

The Gironde, in the matter of the King, had been weak; it had allowed first the trial and then the execution to be forced upon it. It was to atone for its weakness, because on January 21st, 1793, a pitiless skein of circumstances began to uncoil. Europe, alarmed at the theory of natural frontiers and the war of propaganda, seized the excuse supplied by this 'heinous crime' (the killing of the King) to unite against France. This formidable coalition allowed the Mountain to set up the Revolutionary Tribunal and the Committee of Public Safety. 'It is wholly necessary to establish briefly the despotism of freedom in order to crush the despotism of Kings.' The Vendée, shocked at the fate of its 'martyr king', rose, and civil war was used to justify the establishment in every commune of revolutionary committees. Dumouriez talked of marching on Paris and wiping out the clubs and thus compromised his friends the Girondists — in vain, since he did not act. When, in April 1793, a nine-member Committee of Public Safety was created, no Girondist had a seat on it, Danton was its head. And the Gironde was at that moment all the more powerless because it was split, the internal difficulties of the Roland household having had their repercussions on the party. Dumouriez's treason was the final blow for the Gironde. Having sought to involve his army against the Commune and having failed, the General went over to the enemy. The Gironde had had nothing to do with this, but he had been its man; it bore the burden of his sin. Belgium was lost; the Vendée was in rebellion; the English fleet was at Toulon; these military reversals made inevitable the Gironde's political defeat.

The greater part of the country was showing itself weary of the Revolution; from this the Mountain concluded, not that they should yield to the country, but that they must force it to revolutionary action. A violent campaign was started against the Girondists. When Marat denounced them in the provinces as 'traitors', the Gironde had him indicted for incitement to murder; thereupon the Commune had him acquitted amid manifestations of delirious joy. And so, when Paris defied the Gironde, the Gironde threatened Paris. In many large cities (Lyons, Nantes, Bordeaux) it still held power; so it dreamed of urging the departments to insurrection. Isnard, a Girondist, foretold terrible reprisals, were the Commune ever to dare touch the party's national representation: 'Paris would be annihilated; yes, the whole of France would wreak vengeance for such a criminal attempt, and soon men would wonder on which bank of the Seine Paris had stood . . .' But such talk never stops violent men; it merely exasperates them. The Commune, knowing itself the stronger because it was impossible in the midst of war to recruit at short notice an army with which to march on Paris, decided to defy the Gironde and to produce a Day. On June 2nd, eighty thousand men surrounded the Assembly. Hanriot, the new commander of the National Guard, had brought along sixty cannon. Robespierre called for the indictment of twenty-two Girondist deputies. The encircled Assembly tried to leave its meeting place in order to prove that it was free; Hanriot roughly issued the command, 'Cannoneers, stand by your guns!' The Convention shrank back, wandered about, then returned to its hall where, on a motion by Couthon, Marat slowly, cruelly, enjoying their terror, read out the list of the Twenty-Two. They were the greatest names of the Revolution — Frankenstein's monster was turning upon his creators. The Girondists had run the Revolution in the days when it lived on rhetoric; now that it was fighting with its back to the wall, it needed men of action.

The threat of provincial reaction, which had not saved the Girondists, became more real after their fall; a number of them had succeeded in making good their flight and become leaders of local uprisings. Buzot, Madame Roland's Saint-Preux and Nemours in one, stirred up Normandy and raised a small army there; the Vendée had already rebelled: Lyons, Marseilles and Bordeaux seemed inclined to; in all, two-thirds of the departments were rising against the Convention. This movement for the decentralization of France was called *federalism*; and had the Girondists been strong men, they might have played a strong game and perhaps won. But they had more high-flown sentiments than they had force of will, and an uprising in time of war was offensive to a nation of patriots; the French were either monarchists or revolutionaries, but not Girondists. In Paris hard and energetic men took power. Even Danton seemed too spineless towards the Girondists and was eliminated on July 10th through a clever stratagem of Robespierre's. The latter wholly dominated a second Committee of Public Safety, the 'great committee', on which relentless leaders thrust events. The army in Normandy was defeated; Lyons, which had revolted, was retaken, and there were those who wanted to destroy the city and deprive it even of its name; Toulon, where the insurgents had called in the English, was recaptured after a brilliant siege during which a young artillery officer, Captain Napoleon Bonaparte, rendered distinguished service. In the Vendée, the success of the royalist insurgents (*chouans*) dismayed the local republicans, tainted as they were with federalism, and caused them heartily to desire reconciliation with the Convention. This body presented them with an excuse for such a compromise in the new Constitution of 1793, one of history's greatest swindles. Never was a people offered more guarantees against the dictatorship of a man or of an assembly: a legislature elected for one year only; laws subject to popular referendum; an executive council of twenty-four members, half of which must be newly elected each year; the Constitution itself to be submitted to the people in a plebiscite. Never did freedom seem better safeguarded and never was there less freedom; for the moment this most punctilious Constitution had been approved by the nation, but it 'was deemed too beautiful to risk spoiling it by putting it to use'.[1]

But this conjurer's trick, and the promise, which of course was not kept, of a fresh election, gave minds time to calm down. Federalism, defeated with arms, died out in men's hearts. Marat's assassination — he was killed in his bath by Charlotte Corday, a young girl from Caen — afforded excuse for harsh measures; from then on the Jacobin minority could rule under the banner of patriotism, and the regime of Public Safety was far more absolute than the monarchy had ever been. At the top was the Committee itself, constituting the executive; police matters were the jurisdiction of the Committee of General Safety, but the 'great' Committee controlled everything. Its ten members exercised a collective dictatorship. This group said it would remain in power 'until peace came'; it was illegal, tyrannical, but it was a magnificent war government. Never has a minister worked harder or better than Carnot, who moulded the armies of the Republic, or Jeanbon Saint-André, who built its navy. Without discussion the Convention approved all the Committee's decrees. In the armies, throughout the countryside, commissioners or accredited representatives watched over suspects and purged administrative agencies. The war required all the nation's strength; fourteen armies, seven hundred and fifty-two thousand men, had been raised in the nation's defence. This general mobilization was a novelty, but the French were far from complaining. Soldiers' letters showed the enthusiasm of the troops: 'So,

[1] Louis Madelin.

mother dear, we shall be well satisfied when we see this Republic we love so much blossoming in spite of its enemies . . .' The greater part of these soldiers were mere children, enlisted in levies, but someone had had the capital idea of mingling them with veterans, thus establishing the mixed brigades (two battalions of volunteers, one battalion of veterans) which were to win so much glory during the wars of the Revolution and of the Empire. Carnot, forging the sword which would one day be Napoleon's, deserves only our admiration, but the labours of the Committee of Public Safety had other, more sinister, aspects.

CHAPTER V

HOW THE TERROR BROUGHT ON THE REACTION OF THERMIDOR

IN explanation of the Terror, a number of reasons have been alleged — Marat's assassination, royalist plots and, above all, the military reverses of the summer of 1793. The Committee's members were, said Mathiez, 'acting in legitimate self-defence. They were not only defending their own ideas, their persons or their goods. They were at the same time defending the fatherland'. Is it certain that the Terror really saved the Republic? The guillotining of such patriot generals as Custine, Beauharnais, Biron and De Flers was at once a crime and a mistake. There was a time, however, when cruelty was accounted as strength of character. Said Saint-Just: 'The government of the Republic owes only death to the enemies of the people.' This was mere rhetoric, but it killed all the same. In September 1793, the 'sections' (local popular assemblies) requested that the Convention place 'the Terror on the order of the day'. Soon the search was not merely for the guilty but for suspects, and those considered suspect were various: nobles and their relatives, unless they had publicly displayed their loyalty to the Revolution; all suspended officials; all those who had emigrated, even when they had returned to the country within the set time limit; all those who had spoken a hostile word about the Revolution; all those who had done nothing in its behalf. Such a range allowed the condemnation of anyone who was displeasing or a nuisance.

The guillotine, a new device, speeded up the slaughter through the simplicity of its operation. Even though the September massacres had 'emptied the prisons', there were about two thousand eight hundred heads severed in Paris and fourteen thousand in the provinces; other forms of execution (by drowning and the firing squad) accounted for further victims, many of those who perished coming from the ranks of France's most valuable citizens. Except in a few isolated cases, the accusations had no foundation — 'From August 10th to 9 Thermidor, there was not a single royalist plot.'[1] But the Government, without means to assure a supply of food, provoked resentment. 'The time has come', said

[1] AULARD.

303

Madame Roland, 'which was foretold, when the people would ask for bread and they would be given corpses.' Then it was that informing became an act of civic duty, the guillotine an altar of virtue. For fourteen months the Revolutionary Tribunal sat without recess; Fouquier-Tinville, the public prosecutor, a frightful man with pale lips and a low forehead, a failure in private life, called for heads, and they fell with bloody monotony. The indictments varied little — a royalist plotter, an agent of Pitt or Coburg. Thus perished Marie Antoinette; her sister-in-law, Madame Elizabeth; Madame Roland, who sighed as she was about to die: 'O Liberty, what crimes are committed in thy name . . .'; the scientist Bailly, so popular three years earlier; the poet André Chénier, who, accused and slandered by Camille Desmoulins, had thought 'that it is beneath a man of honour to take up his pen against a man who can be answered only by denials'. Meanwhile, Madame Roland's elderly husband had committed suicide, as did also her friend Buzot, and Pétion, and the wise Condorcet. 'So many talents', wrote the liberal-minded Benjamin Constant, 'slaughtered by the most cowardly and stupid of men.' Even though heads might fall 'like roofing-slates', Paris seemed calm: 'There are days when we do not seem at war any more than in the midst of a revolution.' The Tuileries gardens were well kept up, and in the streets elegant carriages were still to be seen. In the provinces, at Cambrai, at Arras, at Lyons, local dictators fired away, put to the sword, guillotined. At Nantes, Carrier drowned two thousand persons. Some of these proconsuls were sadistic fools; others, honest enough, thought they were acting 'for the welfare of posterity'. France let them have their way, but already a small number among the first leaders of the Revolution were reacting.

Danton and Camille Desmoulins had both been appalled at the trial and death of the Girondists; Danton, their opponent but not their enemy, wept. 'I shall not be able to save them!' he exclaimed. After his first wife's death, he had married a young girl of sixteen and sought escape in withdrawal and love; he went boating on the Aube and described himself as surfeited with mankind. Camille Desmoulins, who had had Brissot and Pétion as witnesses of his marriage, said with horror: 'It is I who have killed them', and indeed his pamphlet, *Histoire des Brissotins*, had helped to undo them; he was so filled with remorse that he wanted to enlist in the army and have himself killed in his turn. Danton dissuaded him from this scheme; he had more efficacious and indeed more courageous ways to make amends for the crime: 'Look', he said to him. 'The Seine is running red with blood. Oh, there's too much blood being shed! Go back to your post and ask for clemency. I shall support you.' From that day forth, Desmoulins, in his paper *Le vieux Cordelier*, supported the idea of such a 'committee of clemency' as Danton wanted to see formed. And thus arose the faction of the Forbearing (*Indulgents*), in opposition to that of the Rabid (*Enragés*) led by the horrible Hébert, who had 'made a career of all extremism, that of the guillotine and that of the altar'. Thanks to his inspiration, the Commune extolled the cult of Reason and the Supreme Being; in the Cathedral of Notre Dame it held a ceremony wherein a Goddess of Reason, all too present in the flesh, was worshipped. Imitated in the provinces, these parodies of religion turned into orgies. At the same time, the Commune having voted a 'general maximum', meaning a price limit, articles of daily use disappeared; soap, bread and sugar could be found only on the black market. Women lined up in queues before the shops of the merchants who, raging at the regulations, told them: 'Here's some maximum! If you don't like it, do the other thing!'

Robespierre watched both Forbearing and Rabid factions with disgust; Robespierre admired only Robespierre. His negative virtues are not to be denied; he scorned money and hated women with the mad fury of some chaste men, angered by femininity itself. His misogyny had contributed to the fates of Manon Roland and Lucile Desmoulins, wife of Camille. At once a pedant and a dandy, at once a '*sans-culotte*' (a rabid revolutionary, against all court dress) and a wearer of silken breeches, 'a precious poetaster turned hangman',[1] he entertained the fearful certitude of the man who believes he has a mission. In perfect good faith he confused his personal enemies with the enemies of France; he knew himself to be so incorruptible that he denied himself no crime. Perhaps his hardness is to be explained by his total lack of contact with the ordinary daily life of humanity. 'That fellow', Danton used to say, 'isn't even capable of cooking an egg.' But Robespierre was capable of commanding and organizing: when he took power, he found all Europe lined up against France and two-thirds of France against the Committee; in six months he had re-established order. He urged the total obliteration of the individual for the benefit of the fatherland and of religion: 'There dwelt within him', said Thibaudeau, 'something of Mahomet and of Cromwell.' And this Mahomet was ambitious to be Allah. Saint-Just, who idolized him, wrote to him. 'You whom I know, like God, through

[1] TAINE.

305

prodigies alone . . .' Robespierre set about beating down the factions because they disturbed the monstrous egoism of his system; now should he begin with the decapitation of the *Indulgents* or the *Enragés*? He chose Hébert as his first victim because Danton, the stronger of the two, could help him to destroy Hébert (who at once, thanks to Fouquier-Tinville, became 'an agent of Pitt and Coburg'). Once Hébert was dead, it was Danton's turn. He could have shown fight and sold his skin dearly, but this debauchee was weary of life and at heart harrowed with remorse. 'I prefer', he said, 'to be guillotined rather than to guillotine . . . Besides, mankind bores me.' It was nearly a suicide. 'Does a man', he asked, when friends advised him to flee, 'carry off his country on the soles of his shoes?' Arrested on March 31st, 1794, he remarked: 'It was about this season of the year when I caused the Revolutionary Tribunal to be set up; I ask forgiveness of God and of men.' When he was sentenced to death, he cried out: 'Infamous Robespierre, the scaffold claims you! . . . You'll follow me!' In the tumbrel: 'Come now, Danton, no faintheartedness!' On the scaffold he gave orders to the executioner: 'Show my head to the people; it's worth looking at.' His mistakes, his achievements, his remorse had been those of a giant.

With Hébert and Danton dead, Robespierre was the master of France. The Committee's technicians kept in the background behind the dictator in whom triumphed terror and virtue, 'virtue without which terror is baneful, terror without which virtue is powerless'. Strong as he was, he saw an enemy in every man who did not bow low enough; before the Revolutionary Tribunal he called for heads and ever more heads. Bishops, monks, atheists, royalists, republicans, the virgins of Verdun and tax collectors — all were thrown to the guillotine. In the dismal tumbrels, little girls and men of eighty were seen passing by; whole families paid for the flight of one or two *émigrés*. The aged wife of Marshal de Noailles was executed on 4 Thermidor, together with her daughter-in-law, the Duchess of Ayen, and her grand-daughter, the Viscountess de Noailles; her brother-in-law and sister-in-law (the Marshal and the Duchess of Mouchy) had gone to the scaffold only a few weeks before. At about that time Chateaubriand learned in England that the Revolutionary Tribunal had just consigned to their fates 'Malesherbes, his daughter the Presidente de Rosanbo, and his grandchildren, the Count and Countess of Chateaubriand, all dying at the same hour on the same scaffold'. Everyone who thought for himself, everyone who retained some moral courage, was in prison; more than ten thousand innocent people were under indictment, that is to say, already condemned. Meanwhile, Robespierre, with great ceremony, celebrated the feast of the Supreme Being on the Champ de Mars; 'Were God not to exist, it would be necessary to invent Him'; Robespierre had contrived to replace him. The chorus from the opera sang, 'Father of the Universe, supreme intelligence . . .' and Robespierre read a sermon. During this weird ceremony, you might briefly have wondered whether he were the priest or the idol. The Convention, no longer able to protest, murmured; Fouché, who, although a graduate of a college run by the Oratorian Fathers, was making his career in atheism, spoke to the Jacobins about Robespierre and the Supreme Being in veiled and hostile language. From that day forth Robespierre swore he would ruin Fouché, thus forcing Fouché to defend himself; but it was dangerous to push Fouché into manœuvring, all the more dangerous because he was going to find allies in the Assembly. Ever since Robespierre had insisted upon the right to indict deputies without the Convention's consent, that body had trembled; from cowardice it had allowed France to be beheaded; now it was ready, from cowardice, to behead Robespierre. There was nothing to justify the Terror any longer. The armies of the Republic, especially that of Sambre-et-Meuse, were winning victory upon victory. Saint-Just, feeling that danger was the Committee's great source of strength, asked Barère no longer to 'puff them up', but Barère only acclaimed these victories the more vigorously. Even the Committee of Public Safety itself was weary of the Incorruptible.

These victories, which 'pursued Robespierre like the Furies', were attributable to the Committee's efforts, but likewise to the quality of the troops. The Republic had more than eight hundred thousand trained men, and these were well-armed men since a huge effort had been made to produce guns, cannon and powder. The brains of the scientists had laboured alongside the people's will-to-work; the semaphore helped communication between the Government and the armies; during the Battle of Fleurus, a captive balloon allowed observation of enemy movements. Above all, morale was at its highest pitch. France then had the greatest army in Europe; the troops knew it, felt it. They were buttressed by a vivid faith in the excellence of the principles they defended, and in every land they found hidden allies in the enemies of the feudal monarchies. Moreover, they were admirably led; Carnot had at once protected the good generals of the Old Regime who were loyal towards the new and furthered the rapid promotion of young commanders such as Hoche,

Marceau and Kléber; to all he gave instructions in which may be found the seeds of the Napoleonic strategy: 'Act *en masse* and offensively; at every opportunity engage in bayonet combat; give battle on a large scale and pursue the enemy until he is wholly destroyed; live off the enemy . . .' Delegates sent by the Convention accompanied the armies to watch over and urge on the generals. By the spring of 1794, France had acquired tremendous military prestige, so that Europe was amazed at the strength of a country going through a revolution, yet Europe's moral anarchy contributed to French success. Prussia and Austria, allied against the Revolution, were rivals in Poland and kept an eye on, instead of helping, each other. Austria hesitated to summon a Prussian army into Flanders; by contrast, the French general Pichegru led one hundred and sixty thousand men to the French general Jourdan, who had two hundred and thirty thousand. At Fleurus the Sambre-et-Meuse army crushed the enemy, thus giving all Belgium to the French, who entered Antwerp on July 23rd. Such were the Volunteers of the Year II of the Republic.

Robespierre was all-powerful, and he was undone. For he lost all sense of proportion. The law of 22 Prairial (June 10th, 1794) which, by depriving them of their parliamentary immunity, threatened the lives of all the deputies in the Convention, gave the most cowardly among them courage to do for their own salvation that which they had not dared do for the salvation of the country. Fouché, cunning and treacherous, had been at work on the Assembly, and particularly on the Plain; in the Committee of Public Safety, Carnot and his friends, threatened by Saint-Just, were turning against Robespierre. Executions continued at an increasing rate; the widows and orphans left behind constituted a whole people of enemies; in Paris the shops put up their shutters when the tumbrels went by. Here is a minor yet significant detail: Tallien, an influential member of the Convention, wanted to save from death Thérése Cabarrus, formerly the Marquise de Fontenay, who had been his prisoner, had become his mistress and was about to appear before the Revolutionary Tribunal. Now aware that a wave of hatred was rising against him, Robespierre took the offensive. On 8 Thermidor (July 26th, 1794) in a stupid speech before the Convention, he called for a purge of the Committee of General Safety and the Committee of Public Safety. This purging of the purgers was disturbing. During the night a handful of men succeeded in rousing the 'Swamp Frogs'. The next day, 9 Thermidor, Saint-Just came before the Convention to make a speech, which was skilful enough, suggesting that measures be taken so that the Government 'without losing anything of its revolutionary energy', could not 'tend towards the arbitrary, support oppression, or usurp the powers of the nation's representatives'. This meant putting an end to Robespierre's dictatorship. Tallien interrupted Saint-Just: 'I ask', he said, 'that the curtain be torn asunder.' The Convention at once declared itself in permanent session. Robespierre tried to take the floor; he was greeted with yells of 'Down with the tyrant!' and was refused the right to speak. There followed a scene of confusion during which the hatred which the Swamp had so long swallowed grew bold and broke out into unanimous croaking on the part of the Frogs. At last someone cried: 'Put his arrest to the vote!' Robespierre in confusion retorted: 'And I call for death.' He was answered: 'A thousand times have you deserved it.' A few loyal friends, his brother among them, came and stood at his side. At the President's orders, some policemen arrested the two Robespierres, Couthon, Le Bas and Saint-Just.

The drama's second act took place in the Hôtel de Ville. The Paris Commune, the moment it had heard of Robespierre's arrest, had decided to revolt and to 'free the Convention of oppression', which meant arresting the members inimical to Robespierre. It had also given the prisons orders to refuse to receive him, and had him brought before itself at the Hôtel de Ville. At this moment the Incorruptible could have set up a revolutionary Government, hostile to the Convention, and gambled on the consequences, but he hesitated, refused to sign a call to arms, perhaps because he had legal qualms, and then consented, too late. Had he wanted to fight, would he have had Paris with him? It seems unlikely. All the local assemblies of the middle-class neighbourhoods were tired of the Terror. Barras, appointed commander of the armed forces, gave proof of energy and marched against the Hôtel de Ville. There a policeman shattered Robespierre's jaw with a pistol shot. The next day he was guillotined together with his companions, before a vast multitude which applauded and cried out, 'Down with the tyrants, long live the Republic!' This was the same crowd which, a few months earlier, had booed his victims.

Tallien and Barras, who a few months earlier had been so happy to be among the terrorists, were hailed as the conquerors of the Terror. On 7 Thermidor it would have been difficult to find in all Paris a hundred men with the courage to condemn the excesses; on the eleventh Robespierre had not a friend left. Suddenly tongues were loosed; a hundred thousand suspects emerged from their hiding-places; now the accusers were accused, and the guillotiners guillotined. Fouquier-Tinville and the jurymen of the Revolutionary Tribunal suffered the fate of their own victims, and then the tumbrels ceased carting their daily contingent to death. Hastily Paris changed. The surviving Girondists came back; hope transformed the *salons*; the theatres presented anti-Jacobin plays. Gilded youth affected the green collar of the Vendée insurgents; had its hair dressed 'à la victime' and sported heavy sticks with which the 'dandies' and the 'incredibles' belaboured the Jacobins. Thérése Cabarrus, who became Citizeness Tallien, a pretty *merveilleuse*, as the affected ladies of the day were called, though she was a woman not without kindliness and brains, was queen of the day; gratitude and irony united to nickname her 'Our Lady of Thermidor'. Marat's cult became a crime; busts in his likeness were smashed, and the ex-Jacobins, now hunted down, complained of being oppressed by the aristocracy. The Thermidor revolt, however, was a reaction of small bourgeois, of employees and clerks, not of aristocrats. Its leaders were not royalists. To mock the Revolution and its principles was regarded as elegant and witty, but to cry 'Long live the King!' seemed premature. And why a King? The wish of the new governing classes was to continue to govern.

CHAPTER VI

HOW THE DIRECTORY PREPARED THE WAY
FOR THE CONSULATE AND EMPIRE

THE members of the Convention had fashioned Thermidor out of their fear; the people had not interfered because they were hungry. Five days earlier a decree had established maximum wages; 'Damn the maximum!' cried the people. But once Robespierre was dead and the maximum wiped out, prices shot up; food and clothing were to be found only on the black market, and the English blockade was making the famine worse. Shoes which were worth five *livres* in 1790 cost two hundred in 1795 and two thousand in 1797. The workers, who had lost the right to act collectively and had not obtained the right to vote, were incensed; to the challenge of the sentries, 'Who goes there?' they replied, 'A hollow belly'. Their destitution seemed to them all the more insupportable because the new rich, the profiteers of the Revolution, paraded their luxury, their parties and their wives — clad in diaphanous but ruinously expensive dresses — through the streets of Paris. The hollow bellies saw the gilded bellies growing fatter — bellies which were also 'rotten'. The sale of the nation's holdings had brought with it milliards in profits, and on the ruins of a society the newly rich danced. Alongside them there was another happy class — the farmers. 'The peasant alone is satisfied . . . he alone is successful: he has bought almost all the pastures, fields, and vineyards belonging to the estates of *émigrés* . . .' Despite the high prices, the peasant was sure of eating his fill, and by supplying the black market he was growing rich. Thus he became more and more conservative and hoped for a strong Government which would restore order in France.

But the enriched peasants and the 'Jacobins with feathered nests' were agreed in demanding that this Government should not molest the positions they had won; they wanted to bring the Revolution to an end, yet they did not want to lose its dividends. They would give up nothing, nor would they tolerate reprisals. Naturally such was not the state of mind of the former monarchists, of the plundered nobles, of the gilded youth which wore the red ribbon about its neck, 'victim style'. The royalists wanted and expected a return to the Old Regime, the punishment of the terrorists, the restitution of confiscated properties; the young fops sought to stir up the people of Paris against the Convention. They would display a piece of white bread and say: 'Not everyone who wants a piece can have this; this is bread for deputies.' They would have liked to raise the cry, 'Bread or the King!' But the workers of Paris showed little enthusiasm for the King. In the provinces such campaigns had more success; armed partisans—the Companions of Jehu, the Companions of the Sun—brought about a White reign of terror in the Midi and in Lyons. The prisons filled with republicans; then the counter-revolutionaries broke into them and slaughtered the prisoners as cruelly as the men of September. Ferocious were the words of incitement: 'If you have no arms, if you have no guns, dig up the bones of your fathers and make use of them to wipe out these brigands!' The blood thus spilled did not serve the cause of the King in exile; France understood that 'the Bourbon princes were more likely to start a State inquisition than to grant a civil Edict of Nantes'.[1] Persecution and exile are evil counsellors. Among the *émigrés*, thirst for reprisals was stronger than love of country; on the Right, excited and cruel fools talked of having eight hundred thousand Frenchmen put to death; the new King, Louis XVIII (Louis XVII had died in the Temple) proclaimed from Verona that the monarchy would return as absolute, that liberties would be suppressed and the revolutionaries purged. Had it not been for royalist stupidity, a restoration might perhaps have been possible, but this stubbornness gave courage to the Frogs of the old Swamp. They had to keep themselves in command or perish.

The people of Paris would have liked the stillborn Constitution of 1793 to be put into effect, but Tallien, Barras and the Thermidorians had passed the Constitution of the Year III, which better served their interests since it was republican without being democratic. Just as, in case of serious illness, a family will seek the advice of some famous consultant, they had thought of asking Sieyès to formulate this document, since he was a constitutional expert and technician, but when Sieyès responded only in sibylline fashion, a Commission of Eleven had, without him, proposed a novel and fantastic arrangement. The executive would be a Directory of five members, elected by the Chambers, with one director to be replaced annually; two assemblies — the Five Hundred and the Ancients — were to represent 'Imagination and Reason'. The system would be one of qualified electors; in other words, in order to be a voter, one had to be a property owner. This, of course, favoured the peasants

[1] ALBERT SOREL.

at the expense of the workers. No machinery was provided to resolve any conflict between the executive and the legislature; on the other hand, in order to afford the Directors greater prestige, they were covered with plumes and embroidery. This was not to contribute to their greater respect. When it was submitted for popular approval, this Constitution of the Year III, 'that virgin with eleven fathers', was approved, although an additional article, providing that two-thirds of the new Assembly must be chosen from among the members of the Convention, was accepted only by a narrow margin and there were millions of abstentions. By means of this amendment the Jacobins kept themselves in office, because they knew that otherwise the popular suffrage would turn them out. France, while disapproving, let it pass; the country was disgusted and, above all, tired out. 'The nation', said Mallet du Pan, 'seems as exhausted as some frenzied person who has been bled, and undergone a strict diet.'

The country's obvious aversion to the two-thirds clause revived royalist hopes, and in Paris the young swells organized demonstrations against the Convention. This body, seeing itself in danger, entrusted its defence to Barras, who ever since Thermidor was reputed a thunderbolt of war and carried a large sword slung from his belt. Barras thought that against White Terrorists the best champions would be the former Red Terrorists, who knew that their lives were at stake; he had thousands of republicans released from prison and gave them arms. The royalists spoke with scorn of this holy battalion of 'guillotine-lickers', but the revolutionary defences took shape. Barras determined to entrust the command to Jacobin officers; among others he summoned a diminutive Corsican brigadier-general, Bonaparte, who, after having distinguished himself as an artilleryman at the Siege of Toulon, had compromised himself on Robespierre's behalf and was about to depart for Turkey with a military mission. Bonaparte's later glory has caused his part during these Vendémiaire days to be overestimated; the cannon he had Murat bring up did not play a decisive role in the Convention's victory, but the young Corsican's forcefulness was noticed. He was praised by name from the rostrum of the Convention, was made second-in-command of the Army of the Interior, and became one of Barras's close friends; it was at his house that the General met one of Barras's ex-mistresses, Josephine de Beauharnais, a charming and daring creole from Martinique, whom he would shortly marry. The Day of 13 Vendémiaire guaranteed the safety of the regicides, but the Convention was at the end of its career. The American Morris, for the last time looking at this spineless body, said: 'I continue to think that they will fall under the domination of a single despot.' On 4 Brumaire of Year IV (October 26th, 1795) the Convention declared its sessions at an end and broke up to the cries of 'Long live the Republic!'

The Directory took power. The 'Five Sires' elected by the Assembly were five regicides; Viscount Paul de Barras was a dissolute and sadistic rake, filled with contempt for men and convinced of the possibility of ruling them by means of their passions; the four others were reputed austere republicans. It is important to point out that the handful of dissipated men of pleasure which has given the Directory its reputation did not constitute the France or even the Paris of that day. A people of decent men and women wanted order, honesty and unity; they were the ones who, a little later, would constitute the backers of the Consulate. The dominant feeling was a desire to rebuild; people were weary of utter poverty and hatred. The country was bankrupt. The assignats 'were going completely to the devil'. The purchasing power of money, the lack of daily necessities — these were the two major worries of the day. The Jacobins, who were blamed for so many misfortunes, continued unpopular, but the royalists fidgeted in a vacuum, as though politics had ceased to interest the French. Office-holders had to swear hatred for royalty and the Constitution of 1793; they swore; events had taught them the value of oaths. Babeuf's communist conspiracy was discovered, and the plotters were arrested and guillotined without any popular agitation in their support. But this apathy could suddenly give place to a tempest. At first the 'masquerade at the Luxembourg Palace', with the five Directors in plumed hats, laces and silken breeches and stockings, had provoked laughter; it was soon to cause outcries. Only war still afforded some prestige to the Government. 'We should be lost if we were to have peace.' Consequently the Directory fell back on an old dream of Charles VIII's, the conquest of Italy. Weak at home, it made vast plans abroad — to strike at Austria in Italy and at England in Ireland. But who would command these expeditions? Jacobin generals were needed, good soldiers and honest men. Hoche was chosen for Ireland, Bonaparte for Italy; 'General Vendémiaire' had a right to Barras's gratitude, and the Director thought he could be sure of him since he had just installed one of his former mistresses, Josephine de Beauharnais, in the young Corsican's bed.

None yet realized the measure of the slender general with a Roman profile, whose burning love for a somewhat lively creole made the Directors smile. The son of a Corsican patriot, educated at the École de

Brienne, a fine officer, this 'skinny mathematician' had for ten years, in shadow and in silence, made himself ready for the highest destiny. At Brienne his teachers recorded: 'Wholly tending towards self-esteem, ambitious, aspiring to everything, liking solitude.' Their diagnosis was right. While the majority of the men of his day were carried away by their own eloquence, this youth went straight to the point; he was constantly studying, asking questions, checking information. He had a taste for detail, liked to read reports and inventories and had a contempt for men, whom he looked upon as objects, not as beings, 'as things, and not as fellows'.[1] He wrote well, in a quick-moving style in which Plutarch and Rousseau were mingled. 'With no other stopping places than the throne or the scaffold',[2] he subordinated everything to his ambition and his person. He was a born despot, knew how to master wills, and wanted none round him except those bent to his purpose: 'I should not know what to do with them if they did not have a certain mediocrity of character or of mind.' Among the generals, 'he liked to bestow glory only on those who could not carry it'. The moment he reached the Army of Italy, he dominated those magnificent soldiers of fortune, Augereau, Lannes, Murat, Masséna, and made them 'almost afraid'. To troops ill nourished and in rags, he pointed to rich territories to be occupied and cities filled with works of art. He presented the Directory, which had expected him to furnish a diversion, with a whole harvest of victories — Montenotte, Dego, Millesimo, Lodi. By a lightning campaign, Italy was conquered within a month: 'Soldiers, you have in two weeks won six victories, taken twenty-one battle flags, fifty-five pieces of cannon and several strong places, conquered the richest portion of Piedmont; you have made fifteen thousand men prisoners, killed or wounded more than ten thousand . . . But, soldiers, you have done nothing, since there remains something for you to do! . . .' Though a trifle worried at his triumphs, the Directors, elated at the silver and gold he was tossing them, wrote to him, 'You are the hero of all France'. It was true. For two years, in the horror of slaughters, corruption and famine, France had forgotten the taste of glory; now she was rapturously rediscovering it. Paris baptized Josephine 'Our Lady of Victories'. Even Italy, happy at seeing her Austrian occupation forces driven out, greeted the French soldiers as liberators, and Bonaparte, succeeding where the kings of France had failed, was soon, through the victories of Arcole and Rivoli, to conquer the peninsula.

[1] MADAME DE STAËL.   [2] TAINE.

The men of the Convention had, in 1795, been forced on the nation by law; with the first free elections, those of 1797, all – or almost all – of them were defeated. France had chosen as her representatives 'decent folk' hostile to the Directory, and some of them even royalists. The religious question had played an important part in this election: 'Will the churches be reopened? Will the bells ring? . . .' 'Roman superstition' and peace won a majority in the councils. But the remaining Jacobins did not want peace; it would hasten the day when accounts would have to be settled. Those who called for war to a finish said that England, in case of a compromise, would never leave France in peaceful possession of the left bank of the Rhine and of Italy; they fulminated against the 'party for the former boundaries' and caused addresses to be dispatched from the armies protesting against the enemies of the Republic. Bonaparte, who still supported the Directory, let it have Augereau, a masterful general who invaded and subdued the new assembly. Barthélemy and a number of exiles were shipped in iron cages to Guiana, where many of them died; this was the *coup d'état* of Fructidor (September 1797). Whatever men of virtue and honour there were in France had again to go into hiding; the war party had triumphed.

The Government itself had shown the soldiers how to treat the councils and had shown them, too, that the civil power could not stand in their way; Barras soon was regretting he had put the Jacobins back in the saddle, for they opened up a campaign against the morals of the Directors. In the midst of general destitution, the wealth and profligacy of the 'rotten bellies' aroused indignation. One man alone had then an unsullied prestige in France – Bonaparte. He had played his hand well. Having helped the Directors to re-instate the Jacobins, his instincts had told him that this return to excesses, these deportations, these untoward purges were going to frighten the French, who now wanted the re-establishment of order, freedom of worship and security. Before Fructidor he had opposed the peace party; after Fructidor, he supported it and himself signed, against the orders of the Directory, the Treaty of Campo-Formio. He did not care a rap now for the Directors; he felt them to be at his mercy and he wanted power; but a little more patience was needed. Meanwhile, Paris awaited her General; his sayings were quoted, as reported by officers of the Army of Italy; his ideas were scrutinized. They were reassuring; Bonaparte was for reconciliation, for moderation. Suddenly it was learned that he was in Paris, at Josephine's house; rue Chantereine, where they lived, was renamed rue de la Victoire. A born politician, he operated with marvellous skill and aroused curiosity by his modesty. When he appeared in public at a reception given by the Directory, he combined an altogether military brusqueness and stiffness with a charm which became irresistible in winning over the Institute of which he wished to become a member. Then he once more became invisible, and this well-timed withdrawal drew to him those who feared a Cromwell — or a Monk. He said he had only one ambition — to lead an expedition into Egypt, take Malta, Alexandria, perhaps India, away from England. Here was a traditional scheme of French diplomacy; Choiseul had given it shape and Talleyrand approved it. Throughout his youth, Bonaparte had been obsessed by the East; in the days of his poverty, he had thought of enlisting in the Turkish army. In 1798 he wished to disappear for a time, return laden with new glories, and, if circumstances then favoured him, take power.

The Egyptian expedition succeeded, at least to the extent that Bonaparte was able to land, despite Nelson, free Egypt of the Mamelukes, and proceed as far as the Levant; but then Nelson destroyed the French fleet near Aboukir, and the Army of Egypt, blockaded, no longer could obtain supplies. Already Bonaparte, ever a man of big ideas, was talking of coming home via Constantinople and Vienna. He soon learned, however, that at home everything was not well with the Directory. Internally, elections were going against the Government, and, after the Fructidor swing to the Left, the Directors had suddenly swung Right and wanted to clean out the Jacobins as they had cleaned out the royalists. This see-saw set all parties against them; and in occupied countries uprisings were beginning to take place against the armies of the Republic. The Revolution had been the champion of nationalism; now it was turning against it. The Austrians and Russians were entering Milan; the English were preparing to land in Holland; the Swiss were rebelling against the French; Jourdan had fallen back across the Rhine. Bonaparte's decision was made; he must return. Indeed, although he did not yet know it, the Directory was calling him back. At the risk of being censured, he left the Army of Egypt to Kléber and outwitted the English patrols; he arrived in France at the moment that Sieyès, newly a member of the Directory who regarded the Thermidorians' vacillations as dangerous and outmoded, 'was seeking a sword' for a *coup d'état*. Sieyès had thought first of Hoche and then of Joubert. These two heroes now being dead, there remained Bonaparte — less sure but more brilliant.

The hour of the middle party had struck, as it always does in France, as had happened after the Fronde and after the Wars of Religion. People were tired of the Directors, of executive weakness, of hateful laws, of unjust banishments. Neither Jacobins nor royalists — such was the feeling of the country. Sieyès, Fouché and Talleyrand — 'a trio of priests' — as political sleight-of-hand artists had only to make use of this feeling to produce a quick change. Of the plotters, the one who hesitated the most to employ the army against the representatives of the people was the General; Bonaparte had the wisdom to foresee that he who is put in power by the bayonet can be driven from it by the same weapon. He wanted a vote of the assemblies. Since Sieyès had already made sure of the co-operation of the Ancients, there remained only the Five Hundred. Sieyès decided to call a meeting at Saint-Cloud, in order to get them away from the people of Paris; Lucien Bonaparte, Napoleon's brother, who was chairman of this body, gave his approval to the move. The manœuvre took place on two days: 18 Brumaire at Paris and 19 Brumaire at Saint-Cloud, and the second day almost turned out badly. The Jacobins, whom Sieyès wanted to eliminate, were men used to political battles and versed in the art of defending themselves. Bonaparte, in a state of nerves and easily disconcerted by a hostile audience, lost his head and almost fainted when he heard himself greeted by the Five Hundred with cries of 'Down with the Dictator! It's illegal!' The grenadiers no longer knew whether they should obey him or arrest him. Lucien Bonaparte saved the situation; as president of the Five Hundred he had the legal right to call for the support of the troops against any deputy who might disturb that body's deliberations. He made use of this right. A roll of the drums and Joachim Murat brought in the grenadiers, who cleared the assembly room. The *coup d'état* had succeeded. By means of a handful of deputies, recruited among the fugitives, Lucien had a motion passed whereby three consuls would succeed the Directory. The two Directors who had conceived the stratagem had taken as their associate the general who had made it possible — it was now Bonaparte, Sieyès and Roger Ducos; but the public heard only one name. No one disputed the legality of the new regime: France had not been raped; she had yielded.

CHAPTER VII

HOW THE FIRST CONSUL REBUILT
FRANCE'S UNITY

THE French of that day did not look upon 18 Brumaire as an attempt to destroy their freedom. They had had so little of it for many years. Whether the Government called itself a Directory or a Consulate was all one in the Parisians' eyes; a few departments protested, feebly and unsuccessfully. The middle class, its confidence renewed, bid up the 'consolidated thirds' (government bonds) from eleven to twenty francs. The royalists hoped that Napoleon would be a Monk, the republicans that he would be a Washington. Modest and conciliatory, he dressed in civilian clothes to underline the fact that he did not rule as a general, and he showed himself strangely deferential to the great oracle Sieyès, whose share in the Government maintained the fiction of revolutionary continuity. Did the Revolution in fact continue? Bonaparte himself did not know the answer: 'The Revolution', he would say, 'must learn to anticipate nothing.' Throughout this whole period, 'he marched by slow stages'. And here was the reason for his success. France was desperately ill; after five years of fever, she had fallen into a natural prostration; her wounds must be dressed, her finances restored, her spirits calmed; government had to be at a venture.

Meanwhile, Sieyès was drawing up in solemn secrecy another constitution, that of the Year VIII. Its text, which was awaited as the artist's masterpiece, was outlandish and anti-democratic. 'Power should come from above, confidence from below.' The people no longer elected representatives, but eligible persons, from among whom a Proclaimes-Elector chose those elected. A legislative body voted the laws; a Tribunate had the right to discuss them; a conservative Senate acted as supreme court to uphold the Constitution. The deliberative assembly was not the assembly that voted, and one day it would suffice to suppress the Tribunate to put an end to all discussion. Bonaparte, to whom Sieyès offered the post of Proclaimer-Elector, replied that he preferred to be nothing rather than ridiculous, and that he would not accept a post of 'fattening pig, the fleshless shadow of an idle king'. Therefore Sieyès created a First Consul, the real head of the executive power, who naturally was Bonaparte; Sieyès and Roger Ducos faded into the background, and the First Consul, whose dominant idea was to 'create fusion', meaning the unity of the French, chose as his assistants Cambacérès, who had been chairman of the Committee of Public Safety, yet always a moderate, and Lebrun, a man of the Old Regime, but in no way an aristocrat. Contrasting labels, identical realities: here was the secret of unity.

This Constitution of the Year VIII, become dictatorial through the installation of a First Consul, was overwhelmingly approved in the plebiscite. The people were eager for internal peace and the former revolutionary *élite* was ready to accept anything as long as the personnel of the Convention retained its grasp on the helm. 'The ignorant class', cynically remarked a former member of the Convention, 'no longer exercises any influence either on the legislature or on the Government; everything is done for the people and in the name of the people; nothing is done by it and at its ill-considered dictation.' In other words, France had changed aristocracies; there was no longer any question of democracy. When the new consuls entered office, on December 25th, 1799, they announced: 'Citizens, the Revolution is anchored to the principles which began it. It is completed . . .' Here was exactly what Mirabeau had vainly said ten years earlier. It now remained to pacify the Vendée and above all to reorganize finances, for on the evening of 19 Brumaire, the Directory had not a franc to its name. In this Bonaparte showed his extraordinary gifts for administrative organization as well as his contempt for the most elementary liberties. In the eyes of the French, he alone was the government; constitutions, proclamations mentioned but one name, contained but one clause — Bonaparte. The assemblies were often made up of talented men, but never possessed the slightest authority. The press was muzzled by a decree suppressing any paper which might publish articles contrary to 'the social covenant, the sovereignty of the people, and the glory of the armies'. This budding despotism was strengthened by total administrative centralization; prefects, under-prefects, mayors — all were chosen by the Government. Paris was made an exceptional case and placed under the surveillance of a prefect of police. Many former revolutionaries disapproved these steps; all accepted them because they retained their stipends, because the nation wanted order and because the officials were well chosen. Only much later did the danger of so strong and uncontrolled a power become manifest; for the present the moderation of the tyrant tempered the effects of tyranny.

With Bonaparte everything was calculated. If, at the beginning of the

Consulate, he took up his residence at the Tuileries, it was to indicate at once the continuity of power and to show the royalists that, as far as the Bourbons were concerned, he would not be the temporary caretaker of a palace which awaited them. He found a sour pleasure in occupying the dwelling of kings: 'Come, my little creole', said he to Josephine, 'sleep in the bed of your masters!' But to Bourrienne, his secretary, he remarked: 'It is not the whole thing to be at the Tuileries; the trick is to stay there.' Better than anyone else he knew how extraordinary had been his luck and how much he remained at the mercy of chance. To last, he must please the French, and Bonaparte always believed that they preferred glory to freedom. The Republic? 'It's a will-o'-the-wisp with which the French became infatuated, but which will pass away like so many others. They require glory, the satisfaction of their vanity, but about freedom they know nothing.' Nevertheless he still paid respect to the externals of the Revolution; he made people address him as 'Citizen Consul'; he furnished the Tuileries with statues of Scipio, Brutus, Washington, Mirabeau; but Alexander and Caesar were there, too. Talleyrand helped to rally round him the great names of the Old Regime — Ligne, Noailles, La Rochefoucauld. 'Only those people', Bonaparte would say, 'know how to be servants.' At the same time he continued to appear at the Institute, then very much to the Left, and to assure the ideologues of his friendship: 'I belong to no coterie; I belong to the great coterie of all the French. No more factions; I don't want any and I won't allow any.' To the prefects he said: 'Welcome all Frenchmen, whatever party they may have belonged to. Rally all hearts to a common feeling, love of the fatherland. Judge men not by the vain and trifling accusations of parties, but on a sure knowledge of their trustworthiness and their ability ...' After so many perils, misfortunes and uncertainties, this policy was the only one which could succeed. Following spasms of violence, the moderate party always swells; at this moment it was France and it acknowledged Bonaparte as its leader.

But what the country expected above all from the First Consul was peace abroad; he himself wanted it because it alone would allow him to continue his task of internal pacification, because he knew that one single defeat would suffice to overthrow a regime as new as his and finally because, as a *coup d'état* general, he feared similar adventures on the part of other generals. A Moreau, a Desaix, a Hoche, were he to be victorious on the field of battle, could become a dangerous rival. And Bonaparte could brook no rival: 'That would be to wound me where I am most sensitive . . . It would be like telling a passionate lover that you have slept with his mistress . . . My mistress is power; I have done too much to win her to let anyone steal her from me . . .' And thus, for reasons of home policy, Bonaparte wanted peace. Austria and England refused him his wish, not believing that he could hold off all Europe. Moreover France had invaded Belgium, where England by tradition and strategy did not tolerate her presence. In the spring of 1800, Austria resumed hostilities. Bonaparte insisted upon going to the front so that no one else might gather the prestige of victory, but he could not be in command himself because he was the chief of the executive power, and so he made Berthier nominal commander. Actually the orders were Bonaparte's. At Marengo he fought one of those battles which seal an ambitious man's fate — and almost lost the day. When noon came, he had lost; only Desaix's arrival saved him, and Desaix's death left him the glory. Surely Bonaparte had been born under a lucky star. His return to Paris was triumphal, for he had bestowed peace on a country which had suffered severely from war. More and more he was the idol of France.

These early days of the Consulate were, like the advent of Henry IV, or like Louis XIV's reign after the Fronde, one of the golden ages of France: one of those happy times that see the rebirth, after years of disorder and misery, of unity and prosperity. Bonaparte had become the 'providential man'. And now what would he do with his prestige? Re-establish the monarchy? Why should he pull the chestnuts out of the fire for a king in exile? No, he wanted the national reconciliation to be wrought by him and for him. It was a difficult task, for to the revolutionaries he must say: 'You will keep your heads and your jobs, but you must forswear your hates; you shall allow the Catholics to practise their religion in peace.' And to those who had been proscribed: 'Your churches will be reopened; the list of *émigrés* will be torn up; but you shall forswear all vengeance against the men of the Revolution — yes, even against the regicides.' The principles of the Revolution had to be maintained; the social transformation had to be established, while at the same time the link with the past was forged anew. It was a superhuman undertaking, fit for a superman.

At Milan he had attended a *Te Deum* in the cathedral; the news had created a great stir and had infused fresh life in Bourbon hopes. It should rather have aroused their fears, for Bonaparte's scheme was to rob the Bourbons of their Catholic backing, not at one and the same time to re-establish the Bourbons and Catholicism. To Louis XVIII, who had

had a conciliatory message transmitted to him, he replied: 'You should have no wish to return to France; you would have to march in over a hundred thousand dead bodies.' Disturbed and undeceived, the royalists (especially the Vendéeans), since they saw in him the only obstacle to a restoration, coldly decided to assassinate him. Pistol shots and explosive devices followed in quick succession. Bonaparte at first mistook the authors of these attempts; he blamed, not the royalists with whom he was flirting, but the republicans. By means of deportation, he rid himself of 'Robespierre's remains', meaning the incorrigible revolutionaries, the simon-pure Jacobins. But the plots continued. He began to believe that if he wished to put an end to them, he would have to make his power hereditary. Were the Consul to be without heir presumptive, the royalists would have some reason to say: 'With him gone, our turn will come.' However, Josephine, who was six years her husband's senior, gave no sign of pregnancy, so that already Bonaparte's brothers had their eye on the succession. One of them, Louis, received orders to marry Hortense de Beauharnais, Josephine's daughter; perhaps if this pair, married without regard to their own wishes, had a son, the child would be an acceptable heir. But this solution, however sentimentally pleasing to Bonaparte, had no legal validity. The political mind has a horror of the void; fear of a vacuum was to lead France to the hereditary empire. Victory is nothing if it does not bring peace, and this Bonaparte obtained in two stages. In 1801 he signed the Peace of Lunéville with Austria, an excellent treaty for France since it obtained for her the left bank of the Rhine and a protective zone fashioned out of friendly republics. To the Belgian delegates the First Consul said: 'Ever since the Treaty of Campo-Formio, the Belgians are as much French as the Normans, the Alsatians, the people of Languedoc or Burgundy. In the wars which followed this treaty, our armies suffered a few reverses; but even had the enemy set up his headquarters in the Faubourg Saint-Antoine, the French people would never have yielded its rights or given up the union with Belgium . . .' It was handsomely spoken, but would England accept the idea of a French Belgium? In order to force the British to do so, Bonaparte dreamed of setting up a 'Continental blockade' which would close the European markets to the English merchants. The only trouble was that for this policy to succeed, it was necessary that all the ports of Europe be closed — there could be no Continental blockade without a Continental empire. Here were dangerous wheels within wheels. The Czar, Paul I, who passionately admired Bonaparte, seemed ready to help and to bring with him Denmark, Sweden and Prussia in a league to defend the freedom of the seas. This scheme was coming to a head when the Czar was assassinated during a revolution which Bonaparte blamed on English intrigue, but which was more likely the work of the threatened Russian commercial interests. No longer able to rely on Russia, Bonaparte temporarily gave up his great plan and had to sign the Peace of Amiens with England (1802). This compromise settlement recognized *de facto* conquests, but each of the two signatories had mental reservations. England, which promised to evacuate Malta, had no intention of doing so; and Bonaparte did not give up his dream of a Continental blockade.

He now felt himself powerful enough to impose religious peace on France. The Treaty of Amiens had been signed on March 26th; on April 8th the Concordat was voted, and on the 18th, Easter Sunday, a solemn *Te Deum* was sung in Notre Dame to celebrate at once the re-establishment of peace and the restoration of religion. On the porch of the cathedral, with bells ringing in full peal, the Archbishop and thirty bishops greeted the First Consul, who, clad in red garments which supplied an excellent foil for the sulphureous pallor of his handsome countenance, was conveyed beneath a canopy. As they walked in his train, many of his officers disapproved 'this mummery'. That evening, when asked for his impressions, General Delmas said: 'There lacked only the hundred thousand men who got themselves killed to do away with all that.' In the streets the people sang, 'On Sundays shall we celebrate — Alleluia!' Bonaparte was not a believing Catholic, but a deist and a political Catholic; the tradition of Philip the Fair was more natural to him than that of Saint Louis. Army murmurings over the Concordat gave him pause; he was not yet strong enough to talk about making his power hereditary. And the former members of the Convention were on the watch. Bonaparte decided not to ask for hereditary transmission, but a life consulate; in 1801 a crushing majority (three million and a half against eight thousand) granted it to him. Thibaudeau, a regicide member of the Convention, cleverly summed up the situation in a letter to Bonaparte: 'The men of the Revolution, no longer able to oppose the counter-revolution, will help you carry it out, because you are henceforth their only guarantee.' It was a cynical declaration of support – and a warning.

More sure of himself than ever after this plebiscite, Bonaparte amended the Constitution, gave himself the right to choose his successor and broadened his prerogatives at the expense of the assemblies, the latter yielding without a murmur: the grenadiers frightened them and genius held them spellbound. Never had France been governed by a man with such a creative imagination. Peace entranced the country; prosperity was returning. For France is naturally rich; she requires only wise policies, unity and self-confidence to restore a good financial situation. The First Consul made a provincial tour to encourage the manufacturers of Lyons, Rouen, Elbeuf; he inspected the works at the basins of Le Havre, built up the canal network. 'What with the Bank of France, the Great Book of the Public Debt, the establishment of chambers of commerce, here was his chicken-in-the-pot period, when that side of his nature ruled.'[1] He presided in person over meetings at the Council of State where jurists worked out a new civil code which unified France's laws and would serve as a model for other nations. Everything he constructed bore the imprint of his clear, geometrical mind. He organized education as though it were the training of an army. In all France's secondary schools, the same Latin passage was being translated at the same hour; the military drum would summon the pupils to recitations — and it was still rolling in 1900, in the *lycées* of the Third Republic. Bonaparte created the Order of the Legion of Honour, thus affording himself a tool similar to that which the orders of knighthood had been for the kings of France. Like Louis XIV, he thought that men must be busied with questions of precedence and etiquette in order to deprive them of the leisure needed to criticize the Government. At the Tuileries, a court was being born; dress swords and silk stockings were replacing boots and sabres; Josephine had her ladies-in-waiting, with highly authentic pedigrees. Bonaparte was invested with fresh dignities; he was President of the Italian Republic, Protector of Switzerland and of the Germanic Confederation. Aiming high and far, he considered colonizing Louisiana, which included the whole American Middle West; he dispatched an expedition to Saint-Domingue (Haiti) with the threefold purpose of ridding himself of certain doubtful military men, of recapturing that island, which France had lost, and of preparing to invade America. Only the first of these ends was accomplished; General Leclerc (Pauline Bonaparte's husband) and a great portion of his army died of yellow fever in Saint-Domingue. With Bonaparte's consent, Talleyrand then sold Louisiana to the United States; for fifteen million dollars he gave that country the opportunity to become a giant Power. For France, this constituted a huge sacrifice and the final renunciation of that American empire about which Champlain and the Cavalier

[1] JACQUES BAINVILLE.

de la Salle had dreamed, but war with England loomed, and it would have been impossible to defend this distant colony against the British fleet. The generous was also the practical solution.

At first England had seemed to accept the Treaty of Amiens. Addison, the Prime Minister, called himself a lover of peace; British trade wanted peace; and the British aristocrats were happy to return to Paris, astounded at finding along the Champs-Élysées Greek goddesses, naked under their gauze dresses, instead of bloody heads. But the two countries promptly began to accuse each other of bad faith; the English allowed their press to attack Bonaparte and he in turn accused them of plotting his assassination, wherein he was not mistaken. He charged them with having failed to evacuate Malta; to which the English replied that Bonaparte, in contempt of the Treaty of Amiens, was coercing Switzerland, separating the Valais from it in order to guarantee himself passage over the Simplon, annexing Piedmont and reorganizing Germany; and in all this they were right. The *Moniteur Public* published, in connection with a 'commercial' mission to the East under Colonel Sebastian, a report brimming with charges and threats. From it the British learned that the First Consul was not giving up his ambitions either in Egypt or in India; their determination to keep Malta despite the treaty was thus rendered all the stronger. Bonaparte was not ready to go to war, but he could not yield on Malta without losing face. During the course of a violent interview, he told Lord Whitworth, Great Britain's Ambassador to Paris, that he could easily destroy Britain on her own island — which was to betray ignorance of a country so dangerous to provoke. 'The English want war', he said, 'but if they are the first to draw the sword, I shall be the last to put it in the scabbard.' From that moment he prepared for the invasion of England; not only did he gather a great army at Boulogne, but he undertook to build first a fleet and then a barge flotilla. Was not the impossible his speciality? With his usual calmness and obstinacy, John Bull did not become excited. Nannies threatened English children with 'Boney'll get you'; the cartoonists depicted his tyrant's head on a trident: 'Ha! My wee Boney, now what do you think of John Bull?' Volunteers enlisted by hundreds of thousands; for lack of guns, the British Government equipped them with pikes. Pitt replaced Addington — which meant that the war would be offensive and not defensive. Everywhere the English fleet firmly held the seas, seized shipping and colonies. 'I do not say', grumbled the First Lord of the Admiralty, 'that the French cannot come. I merely say that they cannot come by water.'

Because of his excessive historical imagination, Bonaparte wanted to be emperor, and once again he encountered the opposition of the former Jacobins and the republican people of France. The French, however, were anxious to retain the natural frontiers won by the Revolution — the Rhine and Belgium; one man alone could hold them, and England was resolved to beat that man down. Unwittingly, she was to raise him to the heights, for Fouché and his *agents provocateurs* were drawing Downing Street into a trap. There was no lack of prospective assassins; what with republicans, military men and the Vendée insurgents, the possibilities were all too many. The bravest of the Vendée men, Georges Cadoudal, known simply as Georges, was landed in France by the British; meanwhile the hostile or jealous generals — Moreau, Pichegru — were plotting. 'The air was full of daggers.' Before acting, Georges awaited only the arrival of a prince of the House of Bourbon who, once Bonaparte had been slain, would guarantee interim rule. Which prince? The police hesitated. Bonaparte determined to forestall the attempt at eliminating him by seizing a Bourbon and having him shot. The kidnapping and execution of the young Duke d'Enghien, who was innocent of participation in any plot, was Bonaparte's only political crime, but it was a premeditated crime. By it he expected to achieve two results: to frighten the royalists and to supply the regicides, those who had 'voted', with the certainty that Bonaparte, now become one of their number, would not make the empire into a counter-revolution. Having received this bloody pledge, the Senate, which was filled with ex-members of the Convention, no longer hesitated and offered the imperial throne. 'I came to make a king', said Georges Cadoudal as he died, 'and I have made an emperor ...' English complicity had been proved through the seizure of a clumsy British agent's papers, and this strengthened Bonaparte's position. From then on his ambitions admitted of realization; after all, the monarchy would have been more repellent than an empire which, to men steeped in Roman history, seemed the normal sequel to the consulate. Napoleon wanted to be consecrated in Notre Dame and by the Pope; obsessed by the tenuousness of his regime, he sought to link it to traditional institutions and to become emperor by divine right. Since Pius VII needed the Conqueror of Europe, he promised to be present; upon his arrival he discovered that Josephine, whom he was to consecrate as empress, had not been married by the Church. And so, on the night before the consecration, he had to perform a secret wedding at the Louvre. On December 2nd, 1804, Napoleon I became

Emperor of the French. With a steady imperial hand, he took the crown from the hands of the Pope and himself, symbolically, placed it upon his own head; then he swore upon the Gospel to preserve equality, liberty, the rights of property and the integrity of the Republic's territory. And it was indeed to save the essence of the Revolution and to defend its natural borders that the nation had chosen him. The French seem capricious, but they know what they want.

CHAPTER VIII

HOW THE EMPEROR CONQUERED EUROPE

APOLEON had received from the Pope the crown of Charlemagne; did he dream of rebuilding Charlemagne's empire? Many people thought so. He took a curious pleasure in his residence at Aix-la-Chapelle; he rushed to Milan to seek the crown of Lombardy. He wanted to have a court; he wheedled and coaxed the former aristocracy; he created dukes and princes, and made kings of his brothers. Yet he was too intelligent not to view this performance with a certain irony: 'Ah, Joseph!' said he on the day of the Consecration, 'if our father were to see us!' Later, at Saint Helena, he explained: 'I felt my isolation. And so, on all sides, I let go anchors of safety to the bottom of the sea.' This sea was the French people's past, and he sought to plumb its depths. Once, while reviewing troops, he sat upon the throne of Dagobert. Alas! objects cannot communicate the greatness for which they were the stage setting, and 'time respects nothing built without it'. All the same there remained within Napoleon something of the Corsican subaltern, of the Jacobin and of the cynic; Rousseau, Machiavelli and Plutarch vied for his heart. Some of his aphorisms were those of a revolutionary: 'A throne is merely a plank adorned with velvet.' If at the Tuileries he seemed to imitate Versailles, it was because 'you are much more sure to engross men with absurdities than with sensible ideas'. If he made great hereditary nobles out of his marshals, if he forced them to come to his receptions dressed as courtiers, it was because he feared too robust an army. He treated his nobility as Louis XIV had treated his, and nipped its feudalism in the bud. Basically, Napoleon believed only in force: 'In order to govern you must be a soldier; you can rule only with spurs and boots.' Thus he alone in his palace amid his grandees would wear a uniform. To repeat, everything he did was done for a reason; he possessed a mind quick and spacious, intellectual clarity, no illusions about mankind, a great skill at winning men without flattering them. His only weakness (a very serious one) was too vivid an imagination. In immediate action, on the battlefield, before the Council of State, he was admirable; the moment he began making great schemes for the future, he let himself be carried away. Could he rein himself in? 'You can give a first impetus to events', he said, 'afterwards they carry you along with them.'

By 1805, matters had him in their train. He had wanted peace, at least for a time long enough to reorganize France and build her a great navy. But England had sworn his downfall; the creation of the French Empire had frightened the sovereigns of Europe, and had determined them to join forces with Pitt. By 1804 the Third Coalition (it was Napoleon who thus baptized it, for he counted back to 1792, thus binding himself to the wars of the Revolution) had been formed — England, Austria, Russia, Sweden and Naples. Its object was to reduce France to her former frontiers, although care was taken not to state this openly; Europe had learned to know the reactions of the French when their national honour was at stake. Talk was prudently limited to the disquieting ambitions of the Emperor and the necessity of putting an end to his conquests. To Napoleon's mind the situation was clear: he had to conquer England or be crushed by her. No compromise was possible. Then, since the English were unbending on the subject of European hegemony, could he conquer them at home? Many historians have thought that the Boulogne camp was only a pretence and that Napoleon knew the operation was impossible. But that is false. He thought that if the navy could for three days — or even for one — afford him mastery of the Channel, and if he could take two hundred thousand men across, he would soon be reviewing his troops in Saint James's Park. He imagined that the London 'rabble' would greet the French as liberators, happy, as had formerly been the American rebels, to shake off the yoke of George III. That on this point Napoleon was mistaken, that the English militiamen would have put up an excellent fight, that to have supplied his army with munitions would have been difficult if not impossible — all this we know today. But the Emperor did not believe it. He thought that London must be taken and the knot of the coalitions severed there, after which Europe would be his and Charlemagne's empire would be reborn.

The plan came to grief. However great was Napoleon's genius, he could not, out of nothing, create ships or admirals, and the Revolution had bequeathed him a navy which was all too weak and which the Battle of Aboukir had made even weaker. All the French fleets were watched and bottled up by British fleets; Nelson lay outside Toulon, Cornwallis outside Brest. The Emperor had ordered Villeneuve, who commanded a Franco-Spanish fleet, to go to the Antilles, to pretend there to join battle, thus drawing the English into that area, and then to rush back under full sail towards the Channel so as to guarantee him the few hours of mastery which would be necessary and sufficient. But in August 1805 Napoleon learned that Villeneuve, instead of moving towards Boulogne, had taken refuge in the port of Cadiz. Hesitation? Timidity? Perhaps. Such were the feelings of the Emperor who thereafter always spoke of 'the ignominious Villeneuve', and would exclaim: 'What an army! What a navy!' But it is possible also that Villeneuve, seeing himself inferior in the number and quality of his vessels, had feared with reason to lose the only large squadron remaining to his country. The season, however, was growing late. Austria now seemed ready, and were there too long a delay, Russia might join forces with her. Abruptly Napoleon made up his mind and dictated orders for a Continental campaign. Everything was provided for in these orders, even the day of the entry into Vienna. But he firmly intended to return, 'once the Continent was pacified, to labour on the ocean for peace at sea', which was his way of saying that he would wage a naval war. As for England, she had no plans except to hold, to hold and to hold, in order one day to beat down the 'tyrant'.

Never was Napoleon more admired and worshipped by his soldiers than during this brief and dazzling campaign; as they saw it, the victories of the Revolution were continuing and its ideas were triumphing in him. The Emperor asked them to 'break this hateful House of Austria', to 'break the league which England's hatred and England's gold have spun'. They recognized the distant echo of the Committee of Public Safety. But what impressed the army was that, thanks to the genius of its general, it was victorious without fighting, it won battles 'with its legs'. Napoleon made pawns move on the chess-board and forced an Austrian army of one hundred thousand men to surrender without a fight at Ulm. Soon the Grand Army's invincibility would be an article of faith: 'When the Austrian generals were in the middle and Napoleon around them, it was said that the Austrians were surrounded; when Napoleon was in the middle and the Austrians around him, it was said that the Austrian flank had been turned.' But the day after Ulm, he received terrible news. Villeneuve, who had not fought when it was needful, had left Cadiz when there was no need, and the French and Spanish fleets had been annihilated by Nelson at Trafalgar (October 21st, 1805). England was undoubtedly becoming mistress of the seas; Napoleon saw that he could no longer defeat her except by closing the Continent to her. For this purpose it did not suffice to have entered Vienna; there remained a Russian danger and a Prussian danger. With the Czar he would have liked to have come to an understanding, for an alliance would have been more valuable than a victory. But the Russians made the mistake of attacking at Austerlitz before the Prussians were ready, and on a terrain the Emperor knew well. 'That army is mine', he said. He drew them out on to frozen ponds and then broke the ice with cannon shot; it was December 2nd, the anniversary of his coming to power and of his coronation. He flung out one of his flashing orders of the day: 'Soldiers, I am satisfied with you... You need only say, "I was at the Battle of Austerlitz" to receive the reply, "Here is a brave man".'

After this victory, what were his demands? From Russia, to the great scandal of his generals, he asked nothing, for more than anything else he was covetous of the Czar's friendship. To Prussia, which, by attacking his communications, might have sealed his downfall, he offered Hanover, the property of the crown of England. From Austria, against the advice of Talleyrand, who vainly urged moderation, he extracted both the German Empire and Italy. This was the end of the Holy Roman Empire, incompatible with the new empire of Charlemagne. Following Richelieu's classic policy, he made Germany into *the Germanies*; he set up the Confederation of the Rhine, of which he was to be the president, which included sixteen kings and ruling princes. In Italy he drove the Bourbons from Naples, and on this throne installed his eldest brother, Joseph, a mild, likeable man little suited to govern. Louis Bonaparte (Hortense's honorary husband) became King of Holland. Jerome (whom the Emperor had forced to declare void his marriage of love to an American, Miss Patterson) married the Princess Catherine of Württemberg. Elisa, the eldest of the three Bonaparte sisters, was Princess of Lucca and Piombino, later Grand Duchess of Tuscany. The princely heir to the throne of Baden had as his wife one of Josephine's nieces, Stéphanie de Beauharnais, and Eugène, the Empress's son, was son-in-law to the King of Bavaria. What was Napoleon's purpose in thus turning Europe inside out? Why did he offer the slightly ridiculous spectacle of a family of 'new made kings'? Did he not see that he was stirring up everywhere black clouds of jealousy and resentment? He knew it better than anyone; he was well aware of the shakiness of what he had built; he clearly appraised the deficiencies of all these Bonapartes to whom he handed out kingdoms, 'but events were dragging him along with them'. He used his own people because he recognized the strength of the family clan in Corsica; with them, who were nothing without him, he believed he could count on a minimum of loyalty, whereas real princes would always betray him. Oh! If only he could let go more reliable anchors! If England, herself

... Pitt had just died; perhaps Fox would prove more tractable. But Great Britain's foreign policy does not depend upon the party in power, and, for that matter, Fox in his turn died in September 1806. With him the race of giants finally died out in England; the dwarfs were going to show how, leaning on a tradition, they could have a strength of their own.

When he had tried to come to terms with London, Napoleon had offered the English Hanover in exchange for Sicily; this was the same German kingdom he had already given to Prussia. The Prussian patriots, with beautiful Queen Louise at their head, found in this act of bad faith an excuse for rebellion against the conqueror. Prussia sent the Emperor an ultimatum, at which he rejoiced; since he must prove his strength, he welcomed so auspicious an opportunity. Once more Prussia, Russia and Austria were going to have themselves drubbed like the Curiatii, one by one. The campaign was as brilliant as that of Austerlitz; at Jena and Auerstedt, Prussia was crushed, and the Emperor entered Potsdam. He sent back to Paris three hundred and forty battle flags and the sword of Frederick the Great. In Berlin, during June 1806, he issued the decrees which forbade the importation of British goods and which even excluded from European ports all neutral vessels that had touched at a British port. He wanted much more, however; he wanted the Russian alliance and a European federation against England; he wanted 'to proceed to the conquest of the sea by the powers of the land'. It was to bring about this great scheme that he delayed in eastern Prussia and Poland. In this latter country, he did not conquer, he 'liberated' — or at least the Poles hoped so. In Warsaw a bedroom plot placed in Caesar's bed a young Polish beauty of twenty, Marie Walewska, the guileless wife of an old man. From this liaison there would be born, at Walewice Castle and under the benevolent eye of Count Walewski, an imperial bastard who, half a century later, would be the minister of foreign affairs of Hortense's son. Marie Walewska had sacrificed herself (without too much repugnance) on the Emperor's bed for the cause of her country's independence. But in vain. How could he have re-established Poland when he was eager for the Russian alliance? There Napoleon had his first encounter with snow and the spring thaws; 'In Poland', he said, 'God has created a fifth element — mud.' At last he was able to join battle. This was at Eylau (June 1807), a murderous engagement for that day and one which, despite the victory, saddened the Emperor like a bad omen; he long recalled that blood-stained burial ground. Finally, in June 1807, after the victory of Friedland, Napoleon had his peace and his alliance. At Tilsit, he met Alexander I, the youthful and enthusiastic Emperor of Russia, who seemed won over and almost under the spell of this wonderful mind. Never had Napoleon been more radiant or more charming; he had wanted victory over the Russians only in order to obtain a reconciliation with them. Now he thought he possessed what he had so long pursued, the consolidation of his whole venture; the anchor seemed to be holding. Napoleon spoke of repudiating Josephine and marrying one of the Czar's sisters; he offered Alexander advantageous arrangements in Sweden and Turkey, in return for which Alexander pledged himself to close his ports to the English. As for Prussia, she would lose her Polish provinces, which would go to a phantom Poland called the Grand Duchy of Warsaw, and all her provinces west of the Elbe, which would constitute a kingdom of Westphalia, would be given to Jerome Bonaparte. Moreover, Frederick William was required to observe the Continental blockade and to pay a hundred million in war indemnities, an enormous sum beyond his power to produce, and this, as was pointed out, would make it possible 'to occupy Prussia in a permanent way'. Here was a turn of speech which Europe would not be hearing for the last time.

And so England found herself once more in splendid isolation; it did not seem to trouble her. His Majesty's ministers displayed 'no inclination whatever to turn the other cheek'.[1] Quite the opposite, on the excuse that the French were making ready to invade Holstein and seize the Danish fleet (which was not the case), the English decided to do it themselves, landed on the Continent, bombarded Copenhagen and carried off fifteen Danish men-of-war plus some thirty smaller ships. This aggression in peace-time was morally reprehensible, but it proved that England was not dead or about to die. To paralyse her; what ports remained open on the Continent must be closed to her; especially in Spain and in Portugal Napoleon saw himself doomed to become 'the head customs officer of Europe',[2] an arduous and thankless task. In Portugal he had a try at military blackmail and sent Junot there with thirty thousand men, but when Junot reached Lisbon, the court and the fleet had set sail for Brazil. Nevertheless, the Continental blockade produced results; many English factories closed down; had England not been England, one might have thought that she would yield. But the Continent suffered also; it lacked sugar, coffee and spices, and Napoleon had to break his own blockade in order to import greatcoats and footgear for his soldiers.

[1] ARTHUR BRYANT.   [2] JACQUES BAINVILLE

The Spanish question was a most delicate one. King Charles IV called himself Napoleon's ally, but his Prime Minister, Godoy (whose omnipotence was partly explained by the fact that he was the Queen's lover), was betraying his king and negotiating with the English. Would it not be more prudent to place a Bonaparte — or perhaps Murat, Napoleon's brother-in-law, the Emperor having given him his sister Caroline in marriage — on the Spanish throne? Of course there must be a decent excuse for breaking the alliance. Charles IV did not get on with his son, the Prince of the Asturias, and the son hated Godoy. Suddenly in 1808, while the Emperor remained undecided, the Spanish people took the matter in hand; an uprising broke out in the town of Aranjuez; the terrified king abdicated in favour of his son (who became Ferdinand VII), and then retracted his abdication. Napoleon had the idea that this throne was becoming vacant and that he could risk anything. He enticed the father and the son to Bayonne, under colour of negotiating the issue, and then held them prisoner. Talleyrand was given the job of housing them, keeping them busy and entertaining them at Valençay: 'You might bring Madame Talleyrand there with five or six ladies. Were the Prince of the Asturias to attach himself to some pretty woman, no harm at all would be done ...' This was not a role to trouble Talleyrand, but there remained the Spanish people. How would they react to this little melodrama? The Emperor, with ill-founded optimism, was sure the Spaniards would welcome it. Spain was suffering under an authoritarian clergy, a greedy nobility and backward laws; he would emancipate it; he would make them cry: 'Down with the Inquisition!' He said: 'You will see, they will look on me as the liberator of Spain', and he recalled his reception in Italy at the time of Arcole and Rivoli. He forgot that Spain was not Italy and that the Empire was not the Revolution. Hastily a royal 'transfer' was decreed among the Bonapartes; Joseph was promoted to be King of Spain while Murat became King of Naples. For a moment Napoleon could have thought that the conquest of Europe was completed; on her thrones he saw only relatives, friends or slaves.

The relatives grumbled; the friends betrayed; the slaves plotted. Against this 'parvenu of glory', the sovereigns, even those among whom no love was lost, came to agree; an underground Holy Alliance took shape. Hampered in their trade, ill fed, the peoples of Europe no longer looked upon France as a liberator. The Emperor knew, or felt, that his hold was not firm and that, were he to suffer 'the least trouble' in France, several Powers would at once leave him in the lurch. Hence 'troubles' must be warded off. Now there existed in the country no assembly save one where men could speak out – the Tribunate. Quietly, by a decree of the Senate, the Emperor did away with the Tribunate. The Senate and the Legislative Body seemed submissive, and would be so as long as success continued, but Napoleon, crystal clear when he was dealing with Frenchmen, estimated this devotion at its true value. Who really liked him? The people? They were weary of conscription. Napoleon pretended to disregard losses in human life: 'I have an income of one hundred thousand men', he would say; and, after a murderous battle, 'One night in Paris will make all that good'. Nevertheless, he divined the country's weariness: 'What will they say when I die? They will say, "Phew! Thank Heaven!"' Who loved him? His marshals? Rather than knights of the round table, they were conspirators. His ministers? Talleyrand and Fouché, his diplomat and his policeman, were already covering themselves against his ultimate downfall. His women? Neither his mistresses nor his empresses were ever fond enough of him to remain faithful to him.

In 1808 the lack of an heir made the Empire even more shaky. He had again spoken of the idea of adopting one of the sons of Louis Bonaparte and Hortense, but Joseph and Jerome had cried to high heaven. Should he seek a divorce to obtain a legitimate child? Despite Josephine's tears, he was thinking of it more seriously since the birth of several bastards had proved to him that he could have sons. But to make such an abandonment acceptable would have required a brilliant match. The Czar, to whom he had made overtures, had replied in an evasive fashion that the Dowager Empress disapproved such a plan, and Napoleon had not been able to be angry since the Russian alliance was his only hope.

Now, believing that Spain was won, he urged Alexander to hold another interview with him. Had he not beguiled this young enthusiast at Tilsit? He would beguile him again. The Constantinople question should be settled; thereafter the two emperors could together get the better of England. She should first be worn down by multiple attacks at widely scattered points; then a fleet would hurl an army into Egypt; another would circumnavigate Africa in order to threaten India from the sea; meanwhile the Russian and French armies, crossing Turkey, would threaten it by land. This succession of unforeseen blows would end by triumphing over British tenacity; England would yield, would recognize the conquests of the two emperors, who would divide the world . . . Thus did the great realist yield to the pleasure of dreaming. But between Caesar and Rabelais's Picrochole there lies no more than a single defeat.

CHAPTER IX

HOW THE EMPEROR LOST EUROPE

T HE first crack appeared in Spain. When the Spanish people, angered at the outrage committed against Ferdinand VII, had risen and had welcomed Joseph Bonaparte at Madrid with a riot, the Emperor had not taken seriously this rebellion without an army. Were there guns behind every bush? Perhaps so, but an outbreak, even with guns, is not a war. Marshal Bessières and General Dupont de l'Estang were instructed to bring this guerrilla uprising to a rapid conclusion. This, thought the Emperor, would at most be a police operation. When he learned that these partisans had, at Bailén, won the surrender of General Count Dupont and seventeen thousand soldiers, he fell into one of his towering rages. Never, since Villeneuve at Trafalgar, had any of his lieutenants done him such disservice, and the consequences were serious. Joseph had to fall back: 'It requires vast means to pacify Spain', wrote this pessimistic Bonaparte, 'this country and this people resemble no other ... There remains not a single Spaniard adhering to my cause...' And why should there have been?

Here the English found the opening they had so long looked for. British policy against a conqueror is always the same: hold the seas, seize the islands and other colonies, let the enemy lengthen his lines of communication on land, then attack him at a point on the periphery where supplies can be shipped by water and where England finds allies she can furnish with arms and money. When, in 1808, Spanish insurgents appeared in London, they were received with admiration and affection: 'Every nation fighting the common enemy of mankind is a friend.' English armies landed in Spain and in Portugal; they had been wonderfully trained by Sir John Moore to make use of a novel tactic capable of stopping Napoleon's soldiers. As in the days of the archers of Crécy, the British army, small but excellent, was offering a fresh answer to the problem of land warfare. Sir Arthur Wellesley forced Junot to capitulate at Cintra; a new Continental front had been opened, and the presence of the Emperor himself in Spain had become necessary.

But other events, fully as serious, kept him elsewhere. At Rome he had come into conflict with the Pope, who, as a temporal sovereign, was not applying the Continental blockade; Pius VII could not yield on this point, because the duty of the sovereign pontiff lies in keeping contact with the Catholics of the entire world. A military occupation of Rome, since it roused the indignation of the Spanish clergy, made Joseph's situation even worse. Austria, so frequently humbled by Napoleon, was watching with passionate interest the Spanish revolt and the English intervention, and had put forty thousand men under arms. At all costs Vienna must be prevented from going to war, and the only way to do this was to persuade the Czar to threaten Austria. Consequently at the Erfurt meeting (September 1808) Napoleon brought all his weapons into play: he flattered, wheedled, enticed, became annoyed, stamped on his hat, calmed down when he saw that the Czar remained impassive, made advances to Goethe, displayed Talma and the Comédie Française, strove to please and deserved to succeed. But the atmosphere was no longer that of Tilsit; already in the air at Erfurt there was a hint of the odour of death. Talleyrand, who was negotiating for the Emperor, secretly advised the Czar *not* to bring any pressure on Austria and *not* to give his sister in marriage to Napoleon; these rebuffs, said he, might stop the Emperor on his path of conquest. Perhaps it was true, but if Talleyrand thus did France a service, he did his master none, and Alexander became more and more evasive in his interviews with Napoleon. Who knew how much longer the incredible adventure would last?

The Emperor's story began to resemble the classic myth of Sisyphus; he would resolutely push his boulder up, only to see it each time roll back down the slope. He rushed to Spain, where he found a country sullen, passionately aroused and in full rebellion; from Paris he was warned that in his absence Talleyrand and Fouché were plotting against him; he dashed to Paris, hurled thunderbolts at these malcontents, but dared not punish them. Napoleon calmed a worried public opinion: 'There will be no more wars.' And at this moment Austria, well stocked with British gold, attacked. Again victory must be quickly won, because Prussia, and perhaps Russia, would fly to the aid of a successful Austria. Once again he rolled his stone up to Vienna; Wagram (July 1809) was a handsome victory, but Wagram did not give France the same joy as Austerlitz. 'We victors now know that we are mortal.' Bad news came: Portugal was lost, Spain tottering. In Rome the Pope had been arrested and deported, and in all Europe the Catholics muttered. Napoleon would jettison one plan for the sake of something better; in place of crushing Austria, he was going to try to draw her into his team. Russia was turning tail and the spectre of another alliance beckoned him. At the bottom of his heart he knew well that he was not and never would be a member of the sovereigns' International: 'They have all agreed to meet at my grave, but as yet they dare not gather there.' Nevertheless he clung to a hope that by marriage he might insinuate himself into this narrow, closed circle. Since he could not have the Grand Duchess, why should he not take the Archduchess? Thus would he link the interests of a powerful State, Austria, 'to the established order of things in France'. Finally he obtained the daughter of the Caesars, Marie Louise, a plump, fresh princess of eighteen. Josephine was cast aside. His delusion was to believe that the father-in-law would consider himself bound to the son-in-law; on Metternich's advice, Francis II had sacrificed his Iphigenia in order to gain time; when the hour should strike, he would not scruple to dethrone the husband and take back the daughter. But Napoleon was intoxicated at entering the Habsburg family; this snobbishness was his weakness. He had begun by becoming the embodiment of the Revolution; he ended by introducing Marie Antoinette's niece into his conjugal bed. At least this august broodmare finally gave him — and within a year — an heir to his thrones who, in remembrance of the Holy German Empire, received at birth the title of King of Rome.

The Austrian marriage did not put the Emperor's affairs to rights; nothing could do so as long as England remained hostile and undefeated. Napoleon continued to set a date when, of necessity, the blockade would bring the surrender of his island foes, but the set hour would come and England would not collapse. Her king was mad, her regent frivolous, her ministers second rate; it mattered little, for her instincts and her virtues sustained her. Europe, on the contrary, weary of this blockade which ruined business and made men hungry, protested; during the summer of 1811, Russia allowed one hundred and fifty British vessels under the American flag to enter her ports. Napoleon could not tolerate this defiance of his system; he let Alexander know that if the Berlin decrees were not obeyed, war would follow. Alexander no longer feared him; he had observed the campaigns of Wellesley (now become Lord Wellington) in Portugal and Spain: the refusal to join battle, the wearing out of the French forces — Du Guesclin's old strategy against the English made the English successful against Bonaparte, and it would be still more effective in Russia, where 'General Winter' would take command. If necessary, Alexander could withdraw as far as Kamchatka. Napoleon had been warned against the severity of the Russian climate, but he paid no heed: 'All Europe has the same climate', he said, which might be called the climatology of despots. In theory Prussia and Austria were to be his allies against Russia, but secretly these two Powers informed the Czar that, the very moment the monster weakened, they would become Russia's allies against France.

The Russian campaign began in May 1812 and it was exactly as Alexander had wanted; Napoleon harvested only victories, and all these victories were useless. First he thought the Czar would yield before the threat of invasion by an army of six hundred thousand men, but the threat proved vain; then he thought this would happen if the French armies were to occupy Smolensk, but they found Smolensk abandoned; finally he hoped for the end when these armies reached Moscow. 'Within a month we shall be in Moscow; in six weeks we shall have peace', said Napoleon. He took Moscow; in no time the city was in flames; 'This', he remarked with sadness, 'forebodes us very ill.' So he, he the victor, made offers of peace. Alexander gave no reply. What was Napoleon to do? Remain in Moscow? There he was substantially cut off from Paris; Cossacks were harassing his rear; winter was on the way, which would make his return difficult. For a long time he waited — for too long a time, since he took to the road in the bad season, with an army inadequately equipped against the cold. This Russian retreat was a tragedy but also a miracle. We can hardly understand how Napoleon could succeed without fresh supplies in his withdrawal from a land of ice, where a horde of enemies harried him; the snow, the frozen and treacherous rivers, and the Cossacks gnawed at the world's finest army. There remained of this *Grande Armée* only sick men in rags. On December 5th the Emperor left his troops hastily to start off by sleigh for Paris, where the bad news might provoke a revolution.

The victim lay ready for the dogs of prey: nationalism and counter-revolution joined forces throughout Europe to undo the work of the French Revolution. In Prussia the patriots prevailed, hoped to unite all Germany under their standards and sought a Russian alliance. Austria? Napoleon clung to his family and dynastic hope; he contemplated leaving the regency to Marie Louise in order to soften the heart of the Emperor, Francis II; but Prince Metternich, the all-powerful minister, was unequivocally his foe. England? He knew he could not be at peace with her so long as he kept Belgium, and he could not give up the left bank of the Rhine without losing all his prestige in France. 'My position is difficult. Were I to make an agreement hurtful to honour, I should founder.' His position was worse than difficult, it was desperate, for he could no longer win his game, and if he began to make some concessions, all would be demanded of him. In 1813 Prussia declared war against him. Vainly was he the victor at Lützen and Bautzen; already Metternich was making ready the defection of Austria; this time a coalition of the kings against the usurper would really take place, and it would try to sever him from France. As far as his ministers and his marshals were concerned, the thing was done, for most of them viewed the adventure as 'in process of liquidation' and thought of their own line of retreat. Napoleon's only chance of salvation lay in the fact that the nations opposing him did not agree on their political ends; Berlin wanted the unification of Germany, which made Vienna and Moscow fearful. Thus after their victory at Leipzig, where a hundred thousand Frenchmen struggled against three hundred thousand enemies, the Allies would have been satisfied to leave Napoleon France's natural frontiers, the Rhine, the Alps and the Pyrenees. Surely they must have had a very deep respect for his talents as a general. But he refused. Moreover, England had not approved of these proposals and would not have ratified them. As an artist as well as a sovereign, Napoleon knew he was lost and wanted to end handsomely: 'If I happen to be killed,' said he, 'my inheritance will not devolve upon the King of Rome. As matters stand, only a Bourbon can succeed me.' His keen intelligence was rediscovering its realism in defeat.

'A year ago, all Europe was marching with us; today all Europe is marching against us . . .' Six hundred thousand Russians, Austrians, Germans and English invaded France from all sides; never had the Emperor shown himself a greater general than in this campaign of France, but no longer would people help or serve him. The country seemed war-weary; the soldiers (the 'Marie Louises') were children; and the marshals had ceased carrying out orders. Nevertheless, Napoleon still won victories. By means of movements as precise and as ingenious as those which in earlier days had brought him to Ulm and Austerlitz, he everywhere confronted his enemies, defeated the Austrians, pursued the Prussians, put Champaubert and Montmirail in the same category as Wagram and Rivoli. At the end, he was personally directing the artillery fire. But 'victory', as he himself had said, 'belongs to the big battalions'. Phlegmatic and pitiless, Blücher was tightening the circle and hastening towards Paris. Marie Louise and the infant King of Rome were already on their way to Blois. Finding the road to Fontainebleau open, Napoleon went there and was shortly visited by a delegation of marshals, headed by Ney, which had come to ask for his abdication. 'There is no longer any salvation for France,' they said, 'except in a return of the Bourbons; Louis XVIII would be well treated by the kings of Europe.' Above all they hoped that the marshals of France would be well treated by Louis XVIII. Napoleon made one final effort to win them over: 'We shall fight!' They remained icy. From Caulaincourt's *Mémoires* we know that he tried to kill himself, but even the poison betrayed him, and so he resigned himself to unconditional abdication. He had long known that any hope of a regency was an idle dream; the very regicides wanted the Bourbons — on condition that they lost nothing by it. Thus, upon the staircase of the Palace of Fontainebleau, in a scene composed by a great artist, he bid farewell to the Old Guard: 'If I have consented to outlive you, it is to do further service to your glory. I want to put in writing the great things we have done together . . .' When he embraced the Eagle, the aged veterans wept openly; they alone had loved him; they alone remained loyal to him. Marie Louise had gone to meet the Emperor of Austria; her choice had been made.

It is noteworthy that the Allies, when they held at their mercy the man who for fifteen years had so greatly troubled them, far from treating him as a war criminal, sought for him a bearable place of exile and even a diminutive sovereignty. They decided to make him master of the Island of Elba, lying in the Mediterranean south of Corsica, which amounted, as people said, to bestowing on Caesar the kingdom of Sancho Panza. Moreover, it is also noteworthy that he accepted this, and even took an interest in it; at Fontainebleau he immediately asked for books about the island and began to inform himself on his new realm; you might have thought that here was Lieutenant Bonaparte studying the fortifications of Toulon. None the less he still remained the nervous intellectual, unable to endure contact with a hostile crowd; just as he had been at Saint-Cloud on 18 Brumaire, so was he on his journey to his island, with Allied officers as escort amid the jibes of those who came to see him pass. Mobs are rarely steadfast. In Paris the Count of Artois, and even the enemy sovereigns, had been welcomed with indecent enthusiasm. 'The moment it was certain that the lion was chained,' said Madame de Chateaubriand, 'sufficient words could not be found to damn him for whom incense had so lately been burned. Everyone, as he went to greet the foreigners, acted as though he were freshly returned from Coblenz. Handkerchiefs and petticoats became white flags. The blue and the red were trampled under foot, and the most rabid were those who had been the most Bonapartist . . .' At Malmaison, the Empress Josephine and her daughter, Queen Hortense, gave a dinner in honour of the Emperor of Russia; Hortense was soon to pay court to Louis XVIII and win from him the title of Duchess of Saint-Leu. Everywhere men shouted, 'Long live the King!' and austere Madame de Chateaubriand added: 'We women would cry "Off with our heads!" were we to hear our neighbours do so.' Meanwhile the Senate, the Emperor's appointees, solemnly voted for the return of the 'freely chosen' king and outlined a proposed constitution which the Count of Artois publicly accepted, while secretly urging his brother to have none of it. Talleyrand, at whose house on the rue Saint-Florentin the Emperor Alexander was staying, ran the show. An armistice was signed, relegating France to her 1790 frontiers; the new map of Europe was to be drawn by a congress which would gather in Vienna. The great adventure seemed to be over. But the French Revolution continued, and the triumphant royalists were soon to be made aware of it.

CHAPTER X

HOW THE EMPEROR OVERTHREW THE KING
AND THE CONSEQUENCES THEREOF

ALLEYRAND had wanted the Bourbons to come back because the Bourbons represented a principle, but he 'was not a little distrustful of the Bourbons' principles'.[1] The useful principle was legitimacy; the dangerous principles, absolutism and divine right. A real legitimacy could come about only through France's acceptance of the monarchy; what then must he do to make monarchy acceptable? He must reassure the French. Because the Bourbons brought with them peace, they profited from a prejudice in their favour; but, to win acceptance, they had still to set at rest the minds of the peasants, the army, the bureaucrats, the purchasers of the nation's holdings – all those whose livelihoods depended on the triumphs of the Revolution. Talleyrand explained to the King the conditions required to win the well-being and love of 'his peoples' – a guarantee of individual freedom, freedom for the press and freedom of conscience; an independent and irremovable judiciary; no extraordinary or administrative tribunals; responsible ministers; no laws decreed without the agreement of the Legislature and the Executive. Louis XVIII was ready to grant the kingdom such a constitution and to bind the monarchy by an inviolable charter, but he wanted to concede the charter, not to submit himself to it. If he represented a principle, he thought, it was because he was the legitimate king; hence he could not be 'called' by a senate or even by the nation. He was the king because he was the king. In his own eyes, he had never ceased (since his nephew's death) to be Louis, by the grace of God King of France and of Navarre. When he 'granted' the Charter, that document ended with these words: 'Given at Paris, in the year of Grace 1814, and of our reign the nineteenth.' Hence from the very moment of this first governmental act, everyone was dissatisfied. On the Right, the rabid royalists – 'Louis XIV's light infantry' – scolded: 'Why the Charter? There is only one constitution: *What the King wants, the law wants.*' In the army, the officers on half-pay criticized everything; the soldiers regretted the tricolour, the 'little shaveling', and the grey frock-coat;

[1] HENRY HOUSSAYE.

344

in every barracks they sang, *'He will come back . . .'* From the Left, Carnot reminded the King that public opinion is a power, and that no legitimacy would hold were France not there to support it. Louis XVIII understood and approved Talleyrand's profound analysis, but the *émigrés*, who thought themselves the only good Frenchmen and were the only ones to think so, extolled royal absolutism, the division of the kingdom into provinces, restitution of the national holdings, suppression of the Concordat, the privileges of the nobility and the clergy — in a word, the counter-revolution. They worried the people as much as they did the army.

The opposition was unaware, and wrongfully unaware of the work, painful but useful — indeed admirable — done by the King and Talleyrand in foreign affairs. It was out of the question to obtain an advantageous peace treaty for a defeated France from sovereigns she had made deeply uneasy for twenty-five years; thanks to Alexander's intelligence and Talleyrand's skill the treaty was as little bad as it possibly could have been. The Czar would even have been willing to concede a line of fortresses along the north-east frontier (from Nieuport to Speyer, by way of Mons) but his German allies would have none of it. They wanted to keep the invasion routes open. Nevertheless, in order to preserve what was essential, Talleyrand was dexterous enough to trap the sovereigns in their own principles; if they maintained the legitimacy of their own thrones, he told them, they must also recognize that of the kingdom of France. For a time, of course, they held the power and could impose solutions, but 'power passes; the hatreds it engenders are lasting'. He persuaded them that France should pay no indemnity and even — an astounding concession — that she should keep the works of art carried off by Napoleon. When, in October 1814, the Congress gathered at Vienna, you might for a moment have thought you once again beheld the old Europe, freed of its fears, going on with the dance. The faithless Empress, Marie Louise, entertained the enemies of her captive husband; the court of Vienna had supplied her with the Count of Neipperg, a proved Don Juan, as 'gentleman in waiting'; already she had taken him as lover, and a little later, in order the better to separate her from Napoleon, he was to furnish her with adulterous offspring. Metternich was seeking to surround France with buffer States: an enlarged Holland, a Rhineland, at England's suggestion, entrusted to Prussia. How did it happen that Britain, having so long refused France the Rhine, was willing to give it to Prussia? By sheer mistake; who then thought of the Prussian danger?

Similarly the Austrians were regaining northern Italy, and who then thought of Italian nationalism? The Vienna diplomats would have been astonished indeed to hear talk of a principle of nationality; their principle was legitimacy, and nothing mattered less to them than the wishes of the various populations. Delighted with their labours, they were still dancing when, on March 7th, 1815, after a great fancy-dress party, they suddenly learned by courier from the King of Sardinia that Napoleon had landed in France and was marching on Paris.

Why had he come back? Had he been preparing for his return ever since his arrival at Elba? It is most unlikely. At first he had devoted himself, with all his usual diligence, to his tiny kingdom. 'I am a dead man', he would say. But he had been hoping that the Empress and the King of Rome would join him, whereas it was Marie Walewska who came, with his other son. She was now a widow and free, and hoped to share a glorious exile. Tremendously disappointed, Napoleon shipped off mother and bastard, spurning these proffered affections. But have we any reason to think that Walewska herself would have remained faithful? She at once married a second husband, the Count of Ornano, and died in childbirth. Napoleon suffered a further disappointment: the terms of the Treaty of Fontainebleau were not being observed, the pension therein promised had not been paid, and his funds were running out. From France messengers arrived who told Napoleon that the republicans and Bonapartists were plotting against Louis XVIII, and that, if he did not hasten, someone else might well overthrow the monarchy. This fear made up his mind for him, and he arranged for his departure with all the attention to detail of a chief of staff; a proclamation was printed on the Island of Elba: 'The eagle, with the national colours, will soar from belfry to belfry, even to the towers of Notre Dame . . .' With him he had only about a thousand men and could not rely on force; his weapons were the memory of fifteen victorious years, and the help of the army and the people. Yet this conspiracy of glory was powerful; in Paris the old war-horses, when they met each other, would mutter: 'Do you believe in Jesus Christ?' 'Yes, and in His resurrection . . ' And Fouché said: 'The spring will bring Bonaparte back to us, with the swallows and the violets.' Of a sudden the telegraph announced 'the landing of the Man'.

On March 1st, 1815, he was at the Gulf of Genoa; his plan was to reach Grenoble by way of the Alps, thus avoiding Provence, which he knew to be royalist. To the first soldiers sent to arrest him, he bared his breast: 'If there is one among you who would kill his Emperor, here I am . . .' Neither the men nor even the officers dared carry out the King's orders; all about them they felt the presence of countrymen and townsmen, already surfeited with reaction, and favourable to the Empire. Grenoble opened its gates, and then Lyons; whole regiments had attached themselves to the Emperor and constituted a small army; he had now enough men to take Paris. Was there reason to believe Paris would be defended? Chateaubriand advised Louis XVIII to await the usurper at the Tuileries, Charter in hand, but Louis XVIII seemed to have little feeling for the beauty of this tableau. 'You would like me', he said, 'to sit upon the curule chair [as the Roman senators did, awaiting the Barbarians] I don't feel like it . . .' There remained Marshal Ney, who had sworn to meet Napoleon and bring him back in an iron cage. He left and soon became aware that none of his soldiers were obeying him; the Emperor wrote to tell him that he would greet him as he did the day after the Battle of the Moskova. Ney, won over, joined forces with him. And thus fell the last hurdle. On March 20th, the Emperor slept at the Tuileries; Louis XVIII and his ministers had fled to take up residence in the Belgian city of Ghent, and a new emigration followed after them.

Far more than a military achievement, the restoration of the Empire had been a people's movement. If it was to last, guarantees had to be given to the liberals without at the same time arousing the royalists. Napoleon tried to keep the royalist functionaries at their posts, the greater part of them formerly having been his own men, but he took Carnot into his cabinet and entrusted to Benjamin Constant, only yesterday his enemy and opponent, the drafting of an act to be added to the constitutions of the Empire; thus did Napoleon himself bow to the fashion of the day and forswear autocracy. Benjamin Constant retained the principle of imperial heredity, but provided for free elections, ministerial responsibility to the chambers, freedom of the press and of worship and the abolition of provosts' courts. Naturally he satisfied no one — the true Bonapartists wanted an imperial dictatorship, essential to their regime; the Jacobins demanded universal suffrage; and the royalists worshipped legitimacy. A plebiscite, however, approved the new Constitution, by a million and a half 'yeas' to four thousand eight hundred and two 'nays'; the majority had abstained from voting. Napoleon wanted to make out of his taking the oath to this new Constitution a ceremony reminiscent of the Frankish warriors and Charlemagne's Fields of May; the Carolingian Empire had always obsessed him. His brothers and he appeared in Roman garb, which was not wholly inappropriate, but the masquerade was displeasing and gave rise to anger. The public knew that the Allied sovereigns had formed a new coalition against the Empire, that, in a joint meeting at Vienna, they had outlawed Napoleon, and that in Belgium the last French army was going to have its last chance.

Between March and June the Emperor had gathered together five hundred thousand men; the Allies had a million. A defensive strategy was doomed to defeat — Napoleon took the offensive. Never were his plans more brilliantly laid than at Waterloo (June 18th, 1815), but his lieutenants gave him clumsy service, and he himself, on the day of the battle, seemed without strength of spirit or moral energy. By the stubbornness of his defence, Wellington broke the heroic assaults of the Old Guard; on the evening of Waterloo, the last French army ebbed back on Paris, beaten. Now all France insisted upon abdication; in Paris a provisional government was formed under the chairmanship of the everlasting Fouché, who was labouring on behalf of the Bourbons. Napoleon went first to Malmaison, to the home of his step-daughter Hortense (Josephine was dead), and then reached the port of Rochefort and the Island of Aix. From there he could surely have broken through the blockade and sought asylum in America, where admirers were preparing him a refuge; he preferred to give himself up to the English. 'Royal Highness,' he wrote to the Prince Regent of Britain, 'exposed to the factions which split my country and to the hostility of Europe's great Powers, I have brought my political career to its end. I come, like Themistocles, to sit at the hearth of the British people. I put myself under the protection of its laws, a protection I beseech of Your Royal Highness, as being that of the most powerful, the most constant, and the most generous of my enemies.'

Thus had the 'heroic comedian' succeeded in carrying off 'a fine exit'.[1] Fontainebleau, the Island of Elba, the attempt at suicide, and the Sancho Panza kingdom would have added up to an inglorious finale; the appeal to England's generosity, the internment at Saint Helena, death on that distant bit of rock would make the Emperor into a martyr. In June 1815 many Frenchmen hated Napoleon because they blamed him for the country's losses and defeats; very soon, thanks to distance, to dislike of the Bourbons, to resentment against the English, to great memories and to the greatness of things recounted about his captivity, hate would give place to pity and then to regret. The army would never

[1] JACQUES BAINVILLE.

cease to recall the small hat and the grey frock-coat behind which it had 'crossed the Alps and the Rhine', conquered all the kings of Europe and carried the tricolour as far as Moscow. The people were to link Bonaparte's memory to that of the Revolution. Thus the Bonapartists and the Jacobins, forced together, formed the kernel of a great opposition party, and finally, in 1830, the Emperor's shadow ended by sweeping out the Bourbons.

CHAPTER XI

HOW THE REVOLUTION AND THE EMPIRE
HAD TRANSFORMED FRANCE

JUST as the breakdown of an atom unleashes a chain of reactions the sum of which constitutes a terrifying force, so the events, apparently limited and subject to control, which took place in Paris and Versailles in 1789 brought about in France and through the entire world a chain of explosions the end of which we have not yet seen. The most important and the best of the French Revolution's effects was that it wrote into the legal code that social equality which, during the eighteenth century, was only slowly penetrating men's behaviour. Feudalism had been doomed ever since the Hundred Years War, the establishment of standing armies, and the creation of a royal artillery; during the lengthy anarchy which had followed the collapse of the Roman Empire, the nobility had rendered great services, but from the moment when there had come into being firmly established national monarchies, capable of guaranteeing the administration and policing of large States, the feudal nobility had become useless and impotent. From sheer momentum, however, it had long retained its privileges and its arrogance. The monarchy, which at the start had found its support among the privileged, would always have hesitated to force upon them any absolute equality with the other classes; for lack of a bold reforming king, a shock treatment was required. Within a few days the Revolution swept away all privileges; thereafter there could be no further question of tax exemption or of careers open to the nobility alone. The Empire was to continue this relative equality; even the Restoration would not dare touch it except with infinite caution. The effects of this were little by little to be felt the world over, and it has been truly remarked that the taking of the Bastille is the most important event in English history.

To the Revolution's credit we must also record the secularization of European society. Like the nobility, the Church had rendered the most signal services; unlike the nobility, it was still useful. But it could be more useful and even stronger if it were to renounce those political and financial privileges which offended the faithful themselves. After centuries of domination, the Church had reached the point of sacrificing, in many respects, its spiritual authority to its temporal prestige; too often had the Church called upon the secular arm to protect it against heresy or unbelief. The French Revolution made ready the way for the laicization of the State: freedom of worship, the emancipation of the Jews, the suppression of courts with jurisdiction over matters of faith — these were triumphs of the Revolution, and they added to the security and well-being of a great multitude of men. Thus the Catholic Church lost a portion of its goods and its political power, but these losses made of that Church a more sincere and more respected religious force. We shall later see how the last explosion of this chain in France — the separation of the Church from the State — was followed by a remarkable rebirth of Catholic influence.

Another happy effect of the Revolution was the consummation of France's unity. The kingdom had been made up of provinces united to the crown at different periods; they were unequally taxed, governed by different laws and customs and cut apart by tariffs. 'France was not a State; here rather was a union of several States lying side by side but not amalgamated. Chance and the events of centuries past had brought about this whole. The Revolution destroyed all these little nations and made out of them a new one. There was no more Normandy, Brittany, Burgundy; there was one France . . . France exhibits to the world the spectacle of a nation of more than thirty million inhabitants, bounded by natural frontiers, constituted of only one single class of citizens, governed by one single law, one single procedure, and one single order.'[1] Unfortunately the period which elapsed between the destruction of the old world and the shaping of a new one was anarchical; following the artificial and tyrannous order imposed by the Terror came the corruption of Thermidor. The principles of 1789 had been admirable; their consequences in 1798 seemed catastrophic; and hence many French people wished for the return of the monarchy. The outcome was 18 Brumaire and a new kind of despotism; the Committee of Public Safety had prepared the way for Bonaparte's dictatorship. By crushing all the forces of resistance, it had allowed only one power to remain — that of the army. Napoleon was not the Revolution in arms; he was the army seizing the Revolution, but he preserved many of its triumphs.

Napoleon believed in equality and did not believe in liberty; he praised the Revolution for having destroyed the monarchy and feudalism, because his own advancement had been made possible only by this destruction.

[1] NAPOLEON.

He sincerely wanted 'careers open to talent', but this did not prevent his founding a nobility and a Legion of Honour; he believed it impossible to govern men without appealing to their vanity or their ambition, but the path to honour should be toil and bravery, not birth. Under the Empire, all citizens had an equal right to public employment, an equal duty to contribute to the public expenditures. Nothing could have been more democratic than the way Napoleon selected his marshals. He had a right to say, 'I have organized the Revolution'. His weakness lay in not understanding that freedom was an essential element in the Revolution. As a matter of fact (and he said it several times) he believed that the French esteemed equality, and above all honour, much more greatly than they did liberty. He had saved them from anarchy; he had gathered in for them a great harvest of glory; he did not consider that he owed them anything else. The French, in the last resort, were of another opinion.

The Revolution had swept clean, destroying those institutions which it regarded as superannuated; Napoleon's task was to rebuild the State within the new framework required by revolutionary principles. He was admirably equipped for this job, having both a taste and a talent for centralization. The system of autonomous communes set up in 1790 had been a total failure; Napoleon did away with all local autonomy. He had the departments run by prefects, the *arrondissements* by sub-prefects and the communes by mayors, all of his own choice. Here was a return to the *intendants* (or 'comptrollers') of the monarchy, and Napoleon clearly saw this: 'My prefects were emperors on a small scale.' To his mind, these dictatorial institutions were temporary weapons of war, and he intended, on the return of peace, to make them more flexible. But no French government has yet found the means to create strong local institutions, such as exist in England or the United States. Thanks to Napoleon, the central institutions were at least vastly bettered. For the collection of taxes the Emperor had five or six thousand officials where the monarchy had had two hundred thousand; the taxes paid by a farmer were four times less than under the Old Regime, while the yield to the State was twice as great. The legal codes and judiciary had been elaborated under the Emperor's direction. In the realm of education, he founded the University of France, which supervised all teaching, elementary, secondary and higher; even the seminaries for the clergy were put under its authority. With the Church, he made the 1802 Concordat. In a word, he gave France her modern shape, which continued until 1939 much as he had moulded it.

Since he had no faith in freedom, he gave little impetus to arts and letters, which are always stunted in a climate of despotism; in this connection, Louis XIV had been far less tyrannical than he. It must likewise be conceded that ages of revolution and war are little propitious to artists. Poetry is 'emotion recollected in tranquillity'; when tranquillity is lacking, the emotion leaves its mark but finds no expression; rather is it in the course of the years following great upheavals that are born the works inspired by them. During the Revolution and the Empire, many writers were to be found in France, but few geniuses. The most talented were guillotined (like André Chénier) or found asylum with the opposition (Madame de Staël, Benjamin Constant). After having backed the Emperor's designs in his *Genius of Christianity* days, Chateaubriand was alienated by the assassination of the Duke of Enghien and dwelt in hostile seclusion. Art was imperial, pompous, allegorical and not without greatness. The Revolution had encouraged neo-classicism, and David's Romans had filled the Romans of the Convention with enthusiasm; the Empire continued this tradition, erected triumphal arches in imitation of the Caesars, built commemorative columns and commissioned David to paint the 'Coronation'. The technique of French artists and artisans remained impeccable. Ornamental detail called to mind the Egyptian campaign, abounded in the imperial bees, in eagles, in caryatids, in laurel wreaths. The N, the master's initial, was everywhere, and sealed this age made in his likeness.

The Revolution and the Empire are two aspects of one same event — the end of the Old Regime. Bonaparte's dictatorship was the inevitable outcome of governmental anarchy after Thermidor. The great historian Guglielmo Ferrero thinks that France and the world would have been better off had it been possible for legitimacy to have been spared and had the French monarchy itself (as did the English) watched over the transition from feudalism to democracy, from privilege to equal rights. After all, he points out, the violence of the Revolution caused a great panic throughout Europe and twenty-five years of war. A novel concept, conscription, marked the beginnings of 'total war', and we today have witnessed its baneful spread. The eighteenth century had striven to establish a law of peoples, a law of nations; the beginning of the twentieth has seen contempt for the law of peoples and for any international law whatever. From excellent principles — liberty, equality, fraternity — has come (says Ferrero) modern totalitarianism, which is a backward step for mankind. What Ferrero fails to point out is that, even had she wanted to, France could not have taken England's road, because her past was a different past. In 1815 Talleyrand and Louis XVIII had the wisdom to understand that no equilibrium was possible for the country so long as it failed to reconcile the social victories of the Revolution with a principle of legitimacy. Would this principle be the monarchy? A new Bonapartism? A Republic ruled by a majority? All France's history in the nineteenth century was that of three parties in quest of a legitimacy.

The Revolution and the Empire constituted one of the most highly dramatic sequences of events in history; from it the French have preserved a love of glory and a feeling for greatness. Other peoples have acquired the habit of following happenings in France just as formerly the ancient world interested itself in Greek affairs. This has given birth among Frenchmen to a lasting sentiment of kinship with the Emperor. Napoleon knew this well: 'After all,' he said at Saint Helena, 'a French historian will most surely have to grapple with the Empire; and if he has any generosity, he will surely have to grant me something, have to make allowance for me, and his task will be easy, for the facts speak, they shine forth like the sun. I have sealed the chasm of anarchy and I have unravelled chaos . . . I have aroused all ambitions, rewarded all merits, and pushed back the frontiers of glory! All this is indeed something!' It was this complex gratitude, this blending of revolutionary and imperial memories, this will to keep intact at once the rights of the citizen and the nation's dignity, which, after 1815, were to explain the united action against the Bourbons on the part of Bonapartists and republicans, and, later, the amazing adventure of the Second Empire.

BOOK FIVE

YEARS OF WAVERING

CHAPTER I

WHY THE RESTORATION DID NOT LAST

THE Emperor's defeat made necessary a second Restoration; in Paris a provisional Government, organized by the eternal Fouché – a man so constant in his inconstancy – called in Louis XVIII. The senators and generals of the Empire and the revolutionaries in their well-feathered nests were all ready once again to cry, 'Long live the King!' provided that the monarchy would refrain from disturbing them in the enjoyment of what they had acquired. What mattered to them was not the regime but the jobs. At first Louis XVIII accepted everything except the tricolour cockade. Talleyrand, upon whom England and Austria insisted, and who after all, had served his country well at the Congress of Vienna, was entrusted with choosing the cabinet. That the King should accept the backing of 'Vice and Crime', of Talleyrand and Fouché, made Chateaubriand indignant, but Louis had tasted exile and, no matter what the price, did not want to go 'off on a fresh journey'. Apart from his age and his infirmities, he was not a bad sovereign. People said of him: 'The King is partly an old woman, partly a capon, partly a son of France, and partly a pedant.' All this was true. Louis XVIII, son of France, believed in his rights, but he wanted a quiet reign, loved peace, classical tags, and risqué stories, and understood that he could retain his throne only by accepting the ideas of his subjects. Absolute monarchy seemed to him desirable, but out of the question; from this arose his firm intention of abiding by the Charter. As early as July 13th the voters had cast their ballots, the voting age had been lowered from thirty to twenty-one, and censorship had been abolished. The cabinet wanted to show that it was liberal. Could it do so?

With Louis XVIII by himself, France would probably have come to a reasonable understanding. She would not have loved him, because he had been brought in by defeat, but she would have tolerated him because he embodied peace. But with him had returned the *émigrés*, the formerly privileged, who had 'learned nothing and forgotten nothing', did not recognize the new society and wanted France to return to the days before 1789. After twenty-five years of exile and of hardship, they were athirst for vengeance; at their head, the King's own brother, the Count of

Artois, prided himself on being, with Lafayette, the only Frenchman who had not changed in a quarter-century. At the Pavillon de Marsan, he surrounded himself with his own court, fanatical and reactionary, eager for reprisals; his sons, the dukes of Angoulême and Berry, their wives, courtesans and bodyguards all talked treason the livelong day, and in their eyes a traitor was anyone who had fought for France. Everywhere, but especially in the south, the 'White Terror' reigned; in country regions, on the excuse of punishing Bonapartists, houses were plundered. The Ghent runaways were calling for the chastisement of the generals of the *Grande Armée*: 'We are going marshal hunting', gleefully remarked the Duke of Berry. With certain honourable exceptions, the clergy approved these excesses; the Congregation, a secret laymen's association dedicated to the defence of religion, lauded the un-Christian violences of the Pavillon de Marsan. Sighed Louis XVIII, 'They are relentless!' *They* consisted of his brother and his nephews, of women become savage because they had been afraid, of *émigrés* who since the Charter viewed the King as a crowned Jacobin, wanted to replace the Convention's guillotine with the Old Regime's gallows, and took delight in the horrible catch phrase, 'It is time to put a stop to clemency'. *They* were the rabid Rightists who dug deeper instead of filling up the bloody trenches of the Revolution.

Talleyrand and Fouché, having complacently lent a hand in the proscription of their friends, were themselves soon banished. Talleyrand had first made it his business to exile Fouché, who departed for Dresden in disguise; 'the Limper' had hoped, 'by throwing Fouché to the wolves, for a time to sate their appetites',[1] but ever since Vienna the Emperor of Russia had detested him, and he was soon replaced as Prime Minister by the Duke of Richelieu, heart and soul an *émigré*, who had left the country in 1789 and returned in 1814; he had remained a patriot while abroad, had proved a good administrator, honest and tolerant, and was an intimate friend of the Czar, who had made this Frenchman, during his days of exile, governor of the Crimea. Furious at having been played false, Talleyrand ironically remarked: 'The Duke of Richelieu? I don't know him very well; I merely know that of all Frenchmen he has the best acquaintance with the Crimea.' As a matter of fact, the Duke of Richelieu was at that moment the best possible choice, and therefore he did not last. He was barely given time to sign a peace which reduced France to her 1790 frontiers. Before parting company, the three sovereigns

[1] DUFF COOPER.

of Austria, Prussia and Russia, under the influence of the mystic Alexander, had united themselves into a Holy Alliance out of which they wished to construct a sort of League of Christian Nations; Louis XVIII agreed to join, but the English regent refused. The sovereigns pledged themselves to protect religion, peace and justice. Alexander meant what he said; the others looked to the Holy Alliance much more for the alliance than for holiness.

The 1815 voters — there were very few of them, less than a hundred thousand qualified to vote in the whole country — were aristocrats and wealthy bourgeois seeking above all to thrust aside the men of the Revolution and Empire. They sent to Paris a legislature made up of *émigrés* and squireens as vindictive as they were ignorant. Louis XVIII dubbed this assembly, which was too counter-revolutionary for his taste, the 'Nonesuch Chamber'. Out of four hundred and two members, it included three hundred and fifty *ultras*, rabid royalists who wanted a purge, discriminatory laws, the re-establishment of privileges — in a word, total reaction. 'If you have not lived through 1815, you do not know what hatred is.' The Revolutionary Tribunal was coming back, but under other names; the sons of the victims had become the hangmen; provosts' courts condemned admirable Frenchmen to death or to banishment. To France's horror and the joy of a few women of the world, Marshal Ney was put to death. Later on Guizot excellently defined the reasons why these punishments were unjust: 'The Emperor Napoleon had been long and brilliantly in power, accepted and highly regarded by France and Europe, sustained by the devotion of a great number of men, both the army and the people. Notions of right and duty, feelings of respect and loyalty were confused and conflicting in many hearts. It was as though two true and natural Governments there confronted each other, and many minds could easily, and without bad will, have been none too lucid in their choice. Without any improper indulgence, Louis XVIII and his advisers might, in their own turn, have allowed for this moral confusion . . .' The King should have pardoned Ney and built 'out of royalty a duke to stay this tide of blood'. He probably wanted to, for all his utterances about the rabid were caustic: 'If these gentlemen had full freedom', he said, 'they would end by purging me as well.' The White Terror was a perfect example of what not to do if you wanted to give France good government, but Louis XVIII, who would have loved to carry on the tradition of Henry IV, was too old and too weary to hold in check the *tricoteuses des salons*.

Luckily he got support and advice from a handful of moderate royalists who, thanks to the strictness of their precepts and the dogmatic tone of their judgments, were christened the 'Doctrinaires'. Among the wise men who thought that Restoration should not become Reaction were Pasquier, Sainte-Aulaire, Royer-Collard and their friend Decazes, who was prefect of police, a dogmatic and intelligent lawyer, and a great favourite of Louis XVIII; he was to be Richelieu's successor. Decazes hoped to reconcile Frenchmen of both camps; Royer-Collard and his associates thought that the Revolution had been more social than political, and that a scheme was needed whereby the society born of this Revolution, with its rights and its interests, could reconcile itself to the monarchy. They hated the tyranny of assemblies as much as that of a Bonaparte. 'The people is powerless', they used to say, 'against the powers which emanate from the people.' Hence they felt it necessary to maintain, over and above the elected Chambers, a hereditary monarchy and divine right. To the Left of the Doctrinaires were the 'Independents', such as the Duke of Broglie and Lafayette, liberals loyal to eighteenth-century principles, to whom, for want of being able to express themselves more openly, adhered former Bonapartists, former Jacobins and peasants frightened by the return of the nobles and the spectre of feudal privileges. The Charbonnerie (literally, 'charcoal yard'), a secret society, hatched underground plots against the regime; 'carbonarism' had been born in the forests of Italy, where patriots had long dwelt as charcoal burners; it was international and aimed 'at all tyrants'.

This Restoration France was hard to govern: the officers on half-pay and the patriots regretted the Emperor; the people and, above all, the bourgeoisie wanted to preserve the social equality established by the Revolution; the country as a whole remained attached to the tricolour and dreamed with mingled weariness and pride of twenty-five years of glory. Nevertheless, the French were ready to put up with the monarchy because they had suffered far too much, and a wise government would have taken pains not to arouse them: Stendhal's Julien Sorel, had he been better dealt with, would have resigned himself to hypocrisy and social success. But if Louis XVIII and Decazes were capable of prudence and even of courage; if in September 1816 the King and his minister dared dissolve the 'Nonesuch Chamber', the royalists of the majority indeed proved themselves 'more royalist than the King'. They could not bear seeing skilful administrators, trained by the Revolution and the Empire, retained for technical reasons in jobs that they themselves coveted.

Chateaubriand thundered against the Jacobin faction which, said he, hung on to all the offices: 'It has invented a new jargon to achieve its ends . . . As it formerly referred to *the aristocrats*, it now refers to *the ultras* . . . So, then, we are the ultras, we, the sad heirs of those aristocrats whose ashes lie at Picpus . . . To dissolve the only assembly which, since 1789, has displayed purely royalist feelings, is in my opinion, an odd way of saving the monarchy . . .' Odd? Perhaps, but it was the only one. For the first time since 1815, the people of Paris cried 'Long live the King!' And it was written: 'France breathes the Charter triumphs, and the King reigns.'

He was not to reign long. Unfortunately for France, the policy of reconciliation he so ardently desired became impossible when, in 1820, Louvel, 'a little weasel-faced mongrel, a snarling lone wolf', assassinated the Duke of Berry, nephew of the King and the great hope of the ultras, who at once hurled accusations at Decazes: 'Those who have assassinated His Lordship the Duke of Berry', they said, 'are those who have rewarded treason and punished loyalty; those who have bestowed governmental office on the enemies of the Bourbons and the hirelings of Bonaparte!' This was absurd reasoning, since no one had more to fear from the effects of this crime than Decazes, but it was a clever, perfidious and dangerous attack. Faced with his family's rage and tears, Louis XVIII could not retain Decazes in power. Chateaubriand, a splendid writer but an unscrupulous partisan, gloated over the crime: 'Our tears, our sighs, our sobbing have astounded an unwary minister; his feet have slipped in blood and he has fallen.' The Duke of Richelieu came back, this time with the ultras' support, which condemned him to follow their policy; intolerable discriminatory laws suspended the freedom of the press and individual liberty. A committee including Lafayette, Casimir Périer and Laffitte was established to collect funds and help citizens under prosecution; a new electoral law created an aristocracy of money which was entitled to a double vote. Paris bestirred itself in protest; the cry of 'Long live the Charter' became sedition. An absolutist and clerical propaganda was launched by the leaders of the 'priest party', Jules de Polignac and Mathieu de Montmorency. All the talk now was about 'good books' and 'good studies', and *good* meant reactionary. When, seven months after her husband's death, the Duchess of Berry brought into the world the Duke of Bordeaux, who was called 'the Miraculous Child', the royalists' excitement became so outrageous that in honesty Richelieu had to resign. The Count of Artois, the King's brother and heir to the throne, had openly opposed him despite his given word: 'What did you expect?' the King asked Richelieu. 'He plotted against Louis XVI, he has plotted against me, he will plot against his very self.' He knew his man.

This time power had to be given to the ultras willy-nilly. At least Louis XVIII chose one who seemed the least dangerous among them — Villèle, a man retiring to the point of dullness and an able administrator. Internally this was a painful period of official candidacies, mass purges and stampedes by the ultras for sinecures, to which the liberal answer was a campaign to 'restore the people their voice', as well as conspiracies which the Government repressed, often with cruel harshness. Four young sergeants were executed at La Rochelle after having been found guilty by a jury chosen from among their political enemies. Yet despite these shameful injustices, the ministry remained in office because it had some success in foreign affairs; France, humiliated by the 1815 defeats, was joyful at having a new part to play in the congresses of the Holy Alliance. For the sovereigns, the European problem was this: how to combat the disease of liberalism. And, in particular: how to intervene in Spain to save Ferdinand VII from the Cortes in rebellion? Chateaubriand, who had been given the portfolio of foreign affairs, succeeded in having this task entrusted to the French army; it seemed a paradox indeed that the Government of a country exhausted by twenty-five years of warfare should seek the honour of fighting on behalf of the Holy Alliance; and this Spanish war was iniquitous; its only object was to impose despotism. The liberals were revolted; the doctrinaires said that here was the death of the French monarchy; both were mistaken. The French love glory, and the Duke of Angoulême's victories strengthened the regime; thereafter the army accepted the white banner without aversion. The electors of 1823 were able to send to Paris a chamber much the same as its predecessor.

In 1824 Louis XVIII died and the Count of Artois became Charles X. The change cut deep: 'Louis XVIII was a moderate of the Old Regime and an eighteenth-century freethinker; Charles X was an *émigré* to the fingertips and a submissive bigot.'[1] From then on the ultras had the King of their hearts' choice, and, spurred on by his new master, Villèle went so far backwards into the past that he annoyed the most ardent royalists. When a law labelled 'On Sacrilege' made the theft of sacred vessels subject to the same penalty as parricide — the hand to be severed and the

[1] GUIZOT.

head sliced off — when there was talk of returning to the clergy the functions of public registry offices, when it was desired to restore primogeniture, even Chateaubriand protested against the foolhardiness of those who aspired to govern as though it were still the year 800, whereas everything pointed to vast changes in human societies. He depicted the world of the future: 'In the Kentucky wilderness there will pass along iron highways wagons, as if it were enchanted, moving without horses, and at extraordinary speed carrying vast weights as well as five or six hundred travellers. The isthmus which unites to each other the two Americas will burst its barriers in order to allow ships passage from one ocean to the other . . .' These changes and a thousand others, he pointed out, must bring as their consequence the spread of enlightenment among society's lower classes, making them unmanageable for any power not basing itself upon reason. He predicted that if the monarchy continued to make mistakes, a republic would follow it. When Villèle, having muzzled the press, wanted to make it impossible to publish hostile pamphlets by virtue of a law ironically called that 'of justice and of love', royalists, liberals, Bonapartists and republicans united in protest. The pamphlets, indeed, could easily be supplied by foreign presses, so that as Casimir Périer remarked: 'It would be equally effective to present a bill with this as its purport: Printing is abolished in France to the profit of Belgium.' The French Academy presented the King with a petition of protest drawn up by Chateaubriand, Lacretelle and Villemain. A milliard-franc indemnity, granted to *émigrés* whose properties had been confiscated, annoyed the majority of the nation; owners who had been deprived of their lands by the Revolution were being indemnified by incomes having a capitalized value twenty times as great as the total 1790 revenues. In Paris the ministers were booed, and in the provinces they were beaten at the polls; in 1828 Villèle had to resign. 'You are forsaking Monsieur de Villèle,' the Dauphin told the King, 'that amounts to your taking the first step down from your throne.'

With Martignac, Charles X made a last stab at liberalism. It could not succeed because the cabinet lacked the King's confidence; he was still the 1789 Count of Artois and had no faith in the Charter which he had sworn to respect. Thenceforth the regime was doomed to failure. In 1815 France had accepted a compromise founded upon the monarchy and upon the Charter, because she thought she thus reconciled legitimacy and national sovereignty. But when the country realized that the King was still in touch with Villèle, gave Martignac no support and was laying plans for a return to the Old Regime, the 1789 opposition — unanimous and bold — was reborn. A young journalist, Adolphe Thiers, remarked: 'We must lock the Bourbons up in the Charter; so hemmed in, they will explode.' This learned ambitious little man from the south, the author of a ten-volume *History of the Revolution*, had with the support of Talleyrand and the banker Laffitte, established an opposition paper, the *National*, which the liberal public eagerly gobbled up. When Charles X dismissed Martignac and summoned Jules de Polignac to take over the government, the nation felt that a *coup d'état* was being prepared against what freedom still remained. Polignac was the son of Marie Antoinette's friend, a decent enough fellow, but an unintelligent visionary, an absolutist, 'in a mystical way, vague and crafty',[1] who in 1815 had refused to swear allegiance to the Charter. Even if Polignac had had all the family charm, nobility and courage, his obstinacy, his narrow-mindedness, the naivety of his monarchist faith could in all France satisfy only a handful of fanatics. 'Poor Jules,' said Chateaubriand, 'he is so limited.' Polignac swore that he would have respect for freedom. 'I am so sorry', retorted Michaud, the historian of the Crusades. 'Why?' 'Because, since your only supporters are the men who want *coups d'état*, if you don't pull them off, you will have no one left on your side.' Asked the *Journal des Débats*: 'Will they tear up this Charter which created Louis XVIII's immortality and his successor's power? Let them remember well that the Charter is now an authority against which all the efforts of despotism will shatter themselves.'

When the Chamber met on March 2nd, two hundred and twenty-one deputies voted an address, respectful but firm, expressing to the King the nation's anxiety. Charles X replied by dissolving the Chamber. This was stark folly. The success of the liberals in the elections which would follow was certain; Polignac and Charles X alone seemed to have no suspicion of it. 'These fellows do not know what a King is,' said their newspaper, 'now they do know; a breath has scattered them like straw.' Imagination is the mistress of illusions: the royal breath had scattered nothing whatever. Polignac showed himself resolute, 'but he did not know the object of his resolution'. When the elections brought the opposition up to two hundred and seventy (as against one hundred and forty-five supporters of the cabinet), the King could still have saved his throne by changing ministers. In the *National*, Thiers published the formula for constitutional royalty: 'The King reigns and does not govern.' To

[1] GUIZOT.

reign is to be willing to be the reflected image of the country. 'The King is the country-made man.' Charles X did not believe in parliamentary rules: 'Louis XVI was lost through concessions', he said. 'I have but one choice, to drive or be driven.' He did neither. The Charter authorized him to issue Ordinances; he signed four such, drawn up by Polignac, but greatly exceeding the powers assigned to the sovereign by the Charter. One suspended the freedom of the press, another dissolved the Chamber and the two last changed the balloting procedure; these Ordinances were unconstitutional, unpopular and intolerable. Since the King possessed no armed force to back him in his illegality, the monarchy was committing suicide. 'Still another Government', said Chateaubriand, 'hurling itself down from the towers of Notre Dame.'

The Ordinances aroused Paris just as Necker's dismissal had in 1789. On July 26th, 1830, the journalists published a protest drawn up by Thiers, that ambitious journalist whose superiority of intelligence dominated the opposition. The cry went up at the Palais Royal, 'Long live the Charter! Down with the Ministry!' The King instructed Marshal Marmont to re-establish order in Paris. It was a silly choice. On the twenty-seventh, barricades were raised; the troops attacked them; a parliamentary quarrel was turning into a popular revolution. On July 28th, a group of students, young men from the École Polytechnique, and workmen unfurled the tricolour flag and set it waving from atop the towers of Notre Dame. Paris had retained the tradition of street fighting, and soon the whole eastern end of the city was in the hands of the insurgents, while the King sat passively at Saint-Cloud and Marshal Marmont, in command of the soldiery, received neither orders nor supplies. On the twenty-ninth he was utterly outflanked, and Charles X, surrounded in his covert, had to sign the withdrawal of the Ordinances. But it was too late; the French people wanted no more of this regime. In three days, the 'Three Glorious Days', Paris had driven forth the King who had forsworn the Charter. The cloth was cut indeed; it remained to sew it together. Who could bring the country unity? Lafayette as president of a republic? He was almost 'as shy of responsibility as he was amorous of popularity'; he took far more delight in negotiating for the people and in the name of the people than in aspiring to rule it. Thiers had other schemes, which he laid before a meeting of the liberal leaders at the home of the banker, Laffitte: 'Charles X can never come back to Paris; he has shed the blood of the people. The Republic would lay us open to dreadful division, and it would embroil us with all Europe. The Duke of Orleans is a prince devoted to the cause of the Revolution . . . The Duke of Orleans was present at Jemappes [Dumouriez's great victory]. The Duke of Orleans has borne the tricolour standard under fire; he alone can bear it still, and we want no other flag. The Duke of Orleans has spoken: he accepts the Charter as we have always wished it. It would be from the French people that he would accept the crown . . .' Would the Duke take the throne? No one doubted that he would; he was devoured by ambition. Would he be acceptable? Thiers and his associates worked out a formula to appease the victors of July. The Chambers — therefore the nation — would offer the Duke the title of Lieutenant-General of the Realm. Charles X tried to abdicate in favour of his grandson, the Duke of Bordeaux; he thought that the Duke of Orleans would govern as a regent and that the monarchists would unanimously rally 'around the ruins of the throne'. This might not have been an impossible solution, but the Duke of Orleans wanted to be king, and through Lafayette, who was his protector, he procured a popular manifestation in order to frighten Charles X. It was effective, and the King, together with his family, set sail for England.

There remained the task of getting the insurgents, largely republicans and Bonapartists, to welcome a new monarchy. The Duke of Orleans rode on horseback to the Hôtel de Ville with a rather unfriendly reception from the crowds, which cried as he passed by: 'Long live liberty! Down with the Bourbons!' Lafayette, however, with his instinct for spectacular gestures, placed in his hands a tricolour flag, led him out on to the balcony, and embraced him. Everyone applauded and the game was won. At the beginning of August, the Chamber decided that the Duke of Orleans and his male descendants in the order of primogeniture would be, no longer Kings of France, but *Kings of the French*. The Duke took the name of Louis-Philippe I; he had five sons, all strong and handsome — Orleans, Nemours, Joinville, Aumale and Montpensier; the dynasty's safety seemed assured. Those most surprised of all were the insurgents, who had thought they were making a republic and had brought to birth a bourgeois monarchy; the Palais Bourbon had defeated the Hôtel de Ville.

And so the Restoration had come to naught. The monarchy survived, but it was weakened, stripped of the prestige of legitimacy, beholden to the uprising which had created it, battered by those who grieved for the Revolution and those who wept for the Emperor. Was this failure inevitable? Could the 'bloody ditch' dug by the Terror never be filled and levelled over? *Never* is a word which politicians should never use, but the experience of the Restoration had showed that this ditch still held Frenchmen apart. Of course it is easy to say that if Louis XVIII had been able to force acceptance of his will to reconciliation, if the ultras had been more reasonable, if Charles X had respected the Charter, then between 1815 and 1830 the monarchy would have taken fresh root. The trouble is that the problem lay in governing, not the France that should have been, but the France that was, the France still trembling from the impact of the Revolution on the Old Regime, France in a turmoil of passions. That was not easy, and the victory of Thiers and his friends bore with it heavy responsibilities. 'I also am victorious', Royer-Collard sadly remarked on the evening of July 29th.

CHAPTER II

WHY THE JULY MONARCHY DID NOT LAST

THERE was no more King of France; there was a King of the French. He had not been crowned at Reims but at the Palais Bourbon. He had not spent his young days at court but with the armies and in garrets. Having wooed the Jacobin Club and fought bravely at Valmy, he had become an *émigré* despite himself, a man suspect to the revolutionaries because he was a Bourbon, hated by the royalists because his father had been a regicide, earning his living as best he could in Switzerland and America. His marriage to Marie Amélie of Naples and the Two Sicilies, conservative in religion and in her feeling for legitimacy, and his protest against the murder of d'Enghien, had ultimately won him a half-pardon from the royal family. Exile and harsh poverty had made him prudent, astute and free of illusions, 'except on his own account'. He wanted to be, and he thought he was, the happy-medium king, the incarnation of compromise between the Revolution and the monarchy. He was proud of his lack of pride, played at being good-natured and charmed people with his princely good-fellowship. At the Palais Royal, which was his home, he set up no Versailles ceremonial; he called workmen 'my friends', and the National Guardsmen 'my comrades', A cartoon showed Lafayette saying to him; 'Sire: come, come! Please put on your hat!' The bourgeois king strolled about the streets, an umbrella under his arm; when idlers gathered beneath his windows and called out his name, he would appear on a balcony, surrounded by his numerous family, would brandish the tricolour and sing the *Marseillaise*. And the Parisians were tickled by this obliging compliancy.

But if Louis-Philippe played up to the people, it was because he was resolved to govern; if he was willing to be a citizen king, it was because he wanted to be a king. He had been raised to the throne less because of the Revolution than because of fear of the Revolution, and many of his advisers would cheerfully have forgotten the July days; the Duke of Broglie would have liked the King to take the name of Philip VII, to emphasize the continuity of the regime. 'There has been no revolution,' said Casimir Périer, 'there has merely been a change in the person of the Head of the State.' Actually, Louis-Philippe was far less democratic than his easy manners would have led you to think; he would never have tolerated in France an English parliamentary system, under which the King reigns and does not govern. Authoritarian and even stubborn, he expected to choose his ministers and truly preside over his council. 'I am the driver of this coach', he said, which was not very different from Louis XIII's remark about being 'owner of the shop'. He had a policy of his own, which was conservative and favoured peace; being against all flourishes, bold strokes and adventures, he wanted to be the Napoleon of peace and set at rest the thrones which had shivered over the July Revolution. 'The monarchy in accordance with the Charter,' he said, 'nothing more, nothing less.' And yet he agreed to amend that Charter, and in a slightly more liberal direction.

The new king's intentions were good, but he was in a false position. In the minds of the legitimists and of his own wife, he was a usurper; he had pilfered the throne from the Duke of Bordeaux, whose protector the royal family had made him. He had the simple-minded and modest ambition to marry off his sons to 'legitimate' princesses. Those who, like Chateaubriand, averred a romantic attachment to a dynasty which, after all, they had never supported till the day it fell, had a fine chance to shower the Palais Royal with shame and scorn; from the point of view of the Faubourg Saint-Germain, any noble family which adhered to this 'base regime' acted treasonably. As for the July fighters, the workmen, the republican students, the Bonapartist officers, they had revolted out of a spirit of adventure. In case of absolute necessity, they would have accepted a chauvinistic monarchy, but their reason for having produced the Three Glorious Days was to obtain glory, to tear up the 1815 treaties, to regain the country's natural boundaries. 'The sight of the tricolour flag was what aroused the people, and it certainly would be easier to push Paris towards the Rhine than towards Saint-Cloud.' The mystics of July were growing sad — as happens after every revolution — at seeing the politicians busy getting or keeping jobs. 'How pitiful it is to see how many people fasten tricolour cockades to their stewpots', wrote Victor Hugo. The extremists were asking who had consulted the French on the choice of a King of the French — half of an already dissolved Chamber, which represented, when it was in full session, a hundred thousand voters, had transformed a lieutenant-general into a sovereign. By what right? Like the monarchists, the republicans viewed this likeable fellow as a usurper.

Who did support him? The July Monarchy in fact leaned upon a new oligarchy, that of the middle classes, that of the businessmen and consular judges, newly-rich bankers and industrialists, so proud of being invited to the palace and already eyeing the peerage. Of course the new regime was going to broaden the franchise — two hundred instead of one hundred thousand of Balzac's bourgeois were to run France — but the vote was not to be conferred on all citizens, or on all 'qualified' ones, meaning educated citizens with formal diplomas, or even on all the National Guardsmen — those citizen-soldiers who were the bulwark of the regime. Even Guizot, a relatively liberal Protestant historian, was opposed to universal suffrage. 'The middle class', he said, 'makes public opinion and should govern society. The nobleman is outside that society; he does not know it well enough. The people have not time to think, and express only desires and complaints. The middle class is in a position to be reasonable and liberal . . .' In a word, class government — that was the notion of the so-called 'Resistance' party, which was in fact the party of the established order, of Guizot and Casimir Périer. This resistance was of a wholly conservative sort: resistance to change. It was under fire from the dissatisfied of the Left and of the Right, as is so readily apparent in Stendhal's *Lucien Leuwen*. Thiers, one of the men who had wrought the 1830 revolution, inclined to adhere to the Resistance. 'There are people', wrote Victor Hugo at that time, 'who think that they are very advanced, but who are still living in 1688. And yet it is a long while since 1789.' Against the Resistance was aligned the 'Movement', reformist and liberal, under the leadership of Lafayette, Laffitte and Odilon Barrot, this last 'the most solemn of the uncertain and the most pensive of the empty-headed'. To the Right of both there were a few legitimists; to their Left, the hotheaded crowds of Paris; between them, the middle party, the everlasting Swamp, by turns powerless and all-powerful; above 'the Castle'; around them, the thirty million French who fed, enriched and defended France, but had no voice in the councils. This surely was an unstable equilibrium.

The regime's first days were troublesome; revolutions are diseases with a short incubation period and a most lengthy convalescence. A people which has just witnessed the triumph of an uprising is tempted to turn to force every time it is discontented. Now the people of Paris are not readily contented; the July fighters had had all the demands, with none of the rewards, of victors. The medals given them bore the legend, *Bestowed by the King*; was it not they, rather, who had bestowed on him a kingdom? Charles X's ministers had been placed under arrest; the more violent demanded their lives, but General Daumesnil, a wooden-legged hero in command of the fortress of Vincennes, refused to hand them over to the mob. Ultimately the King and the Government succeeded in saving them, but not without hubbub in the streets. Said Guizot: 'With regard to blood, France wants nothing done unprofitably. All revolutions have shed blood in anger, not by necessity; three months, six months later, the blood shed has turned against them; let us not today slip into the rut we avoided even in the thick of the fight . . .' Passions, however, continued red-hot; in reaction against the clericalism which had triumphed beyond bounds during Charles X's day, there appeared an aggressive anti-clericalism. Because a Mass had been celebrated there on the anniversary of the Duke of Berry's assassination, the Church of Saint-Germain-l'Auxerrois was broken into and plundered, and the Archbishop's palace was pillaged. Even though Louis-Philippe had called upon the Movement party and Jacques Laffitte, a radical banker with a winning tongue, to form a Government, riots spattered Paris and a number of provincial cities with blood. After the July Revolution, Poland and Italy had risen; the French people would have liked to help these insurgents, but the Government refused to give provocation to the sovereigns of Europe. Whence arose fresh trouble. All Paris was singing one of Béranger's songs: 'It is Poland and her faithful people, who so oft for us hath fought . . .' Timidly Laffitte made a beginning of reform; for municipal elections, he added to the rolls those holding certain academic degrees, over and above those already having the franchise because they paid certain minimum taxes; for other elections, he lowered that minimum, but even though his measure doubled the electorate, it did not enfranchise the masses. And the masses were annoyed by the establishment of a new National Guard, which was to be made up of all Frenchmen paying direct taxes and capable of buying their own equipment. These provisos kept out the people and made the armed forces, like the vote, a bourgeois privilege. And so no one was pleased with the Government: its prudence annoyed the Movement and its weakness incensed the Resistance. It was 'government by surrender'.

The conquest of Algeria, begun during the last days of Charles X's reign, continued gloriously; it displeased England, which was jealous of anything happening in Africa and, to keep the British Government quiet, it was essential to avoid other conflicts with its policy. The situation in Belgium, however, threatened to prove dangerous; the Belgians had revolted against the Dutch and asked the French for protection. Should

annexation be attempted, thus restoring the frontiers of the Revolution?
The King would thereby have gained prestige, but England had always
stood out against this solution. A great power at Antwerp! — never
would she accept that. Louis-Philippe had the courage and wisdom to
arrange with England that Belgium should be made an independent
nation and to refuse, on behalf of his second son, the Duke of Nemours,
the crown the Belgians proffered him. A Coburg, Leopold I, became
King of the Belgians and son-in-law to the King of the French; his
late wife had been heiress to the throne of England, and now he married
Louis-Philippe's eldest daughter. This policy of good sense kept France
out of war, but every Frenchman agreed with Chateaubriand: 'I cannot
resign myself to the yoke of a chicken-hearted monarchy which allows
France to be humiliated.' A golden-mean regime, backed at once by the
shopkeepers and the bankers, exasperated both the aristocrats and the
proletariat. 'I doubt', Chateaubriand also wrote, 'whether Liberty will
long be satisfied with this beef stew of a home-loving monarchy; the
French made Liberty serve her apprenticeship in a battle camp, and she
has retained, among their descendants, a taste and love for her early
days . . .' As was to be expected, however, the elections, which expressed
the voice of a class and not of the country, indicated benign contentment
with the provender.

Strengthened by this vote, the King called upon the Resistance, with
Casimir Périer as its leader, to form a cabinet. A banker succeeded a
banker, but Périer was as gruff as Laffitte was jolly. 'He had been created
by God for times of disturbance and violence. The passion of his soul, ever
serious, was reflected in his features, his attitude, his glance, his tone of
voice . . . He induced a certain dread in his partisans as in his opponents . . .'[1]
He selected a fighting cabinet. 'France', he said, 'has wanted royalty
to be national; she has not wanted royalty to be powerless.' The
country felt his iron hand, and the opposition cried out to heaven. There
were riots which were soon quelled without special legislation. 'The
general law must suffice for everything', remarked Casimir Périer. At
the very moment when this prudent strength seemed about to triumph,
the cholera, which, like other perils, M. Périer had fearlessly fought, finished
him off (1832). A new ministry (Soult, Thiers, Broglie, Guizot), as
must happen to all golden-mean governments, continued at odds with
both Right and Left. On the Right a legitimist insurrection seemed
possible when the Duchess of Berry, mother of the young Duke of

[1] GUIZOT.

Bordeaux, landed in France and attempted to incite those loyal to the senior branch of the Bourbons to rebellion in the Vendée and elsewhere. She was arrested and imprisoned in the citadel of Blaye, and there the august widow was discovered to be pregnant, which exploded any influence she may have had. In vain did she claim a secret marriage. The first 'Miraculous Child' had delighted the monarchists; the second confounded them. But no sooner had the Government disposed of insurrection on the Right, than the funeral of a liberal general served as excuse for a republican uprising, which ended in the slaughter of the Cloître Saint-Merri and the rue Transnonain. In 1834, Lyons, and then again Paris, rose in arms; in 1835 and 1836, attempts were made against the King's person. Nevertheless, despite the violence of both oppositions, the July Monarchy continued to rule, partly thanks to the talents of such men as Thiers and Guizot, partly through corruption and favouritism. Out of four hundred and fifty deputies, one hundred and ninety-three had government jobs; they paid for their promotions with their votes. As for the electorate, that new privileged caste, they received grants-in-aid for their businesses, employment for their relatives and even favours from the courts of justice. 'What is the Chamber?' people would ask. 'A great bazaar, where everyone barters his conscience for a job.' To honest minds, the scandalous holding of public office by elected deputies became as important a matter as electoral reform, for whoever is a dependant on power cannot control it.

It has been remarked that the July Monarchy's only problem was to know whether France should be governed by M. Thiers or by M. Guizot, and it is true that 'these two great ambitions attended by two great talents' represented the two policies of the regime. At first Thiers and Guizot served together, '*duumvirs*' in the livery of order. Both of them were 'gentlemen', historians, gallant fellows, and in case of need they were able to work together, but their personal traits set them against each other. Guizot, a Protestant of ascetic habits and irreproachable private life, remained loyal to the doctrinaire party, its doctrine being conservatism based on the middle class and peace based on agreement between France and England. Thiers who was from Marseilles, slight in stature, charming and sprightly, and who supplied Balzac with a model for his Rastignac, had married the daughter of his wealthy mistress, Madame Dosne, and the 'astuteness of this bourgeoise united to the southern craftiness' of Thiers had together pushed the man, before his fortieth birthday, into the French Academy and the premiership. Paris was amused by this little dwarf of a genius who believed himself to be a 'civilian Napoleon'; a current jest was that some day Thiers would have his statue on the Place Vendôme between the Emperor's legs. Yet Paris likewise admired Thiers when, with his furious energy, he completed the Arc de Triomphe, adorned the Place de la Concorde with an obelisk, proceeded on horseback at Bugeaud's side to suppress a riot and held England in check. With stubborn constancy, Guizot remained faithful to the doctrinaires' essential ideas; Thiers, far less steadfast, broke with the Left after having served as its guiding light, relied for support on the mass of the politically inactive and flirted with the conservatives. He at first advocated a Continental policy directed against England, and then turned savagely against Austria and Metternich when the latter rejected his request for an archduchess for the Duke of Orleans. As for Louis-Philippe who was expert in the game of divide and rule, he watched 'with amused interest' the quarrel between the parliamentary leaders and took advantage of it to build up the sovereign's authority — dangerous successes, since each one of them added to his own responsibility.

Towards 1838, the regime's position seemed fairly strong; it had lasted, and that was a great merit. It was backed by the mass of the peasants, because it afforded them peace, prosperity and good roads. Guizot had bettered primary education, and Thiers had done as much for the public monuments. Lastly the Algerian war had added to the prestige of the King's sons, since they had fought in it with distinction. The Duke of Orleans, heir to the throne, had the reputation of being a liberal, and those who wasted no love on the father could await with confidence the reign of the son. On the debit side, the Carlists (legitimists) remained hostile, and the Bonapartists, cheered by the public acclaim which greeted the solemn return of the Emperor's ashes and by the sentimental rebirth of the Napoleonic legend fostered by poets and song writers, clung to their hopes. The Duke of Reichstadt (ex-King of Rome) was dead; the new pretender, son of Hortense and perhaps of Louis Bonaparte, a bold and romantic young man, was merely Napoleon's nephew; nevertheless the Bonaparte name was enough to afford him an unquestionable prestige: 'It is a great deal to be at once a national glory, a revolutionary pledge, and a principle of authority.' Twice, first at Strasbourg, then at Boulogne, Louis Napoleon tried to excite the French into revolt; after the second attempt, he was interned in the fort at Ham. But even if this Bonaparte was for the moment defeated, the tradition of the cockaded Empire still made hearts beat more quickly. Intoxicated with history, Thiers would gladly have involved France in fresh adventures and shown resistance to England, which in Syria was supporting the Ottoman Empire against its vassal the Pasha of Egypt, Mehemet Ali. But the King wanted peace at any price; he would willingly have subscribed to the saying of Alphonse Karr: 'M. Thiers plays at heads or tails with France's fate, and the coin is already spun.' Louis-Philippe had no use for such games of chance; he put Guizot in Thiers's place, because, like him, Guizot loved peace and the English and said: 'The Syrian question is not an occasion for legitimate war; I hold this to be obvious.' Anglo-French friendship was back on a firm basis, and the two countries' sovereigns exchanged cordial visits. Thereupon the King was more bitterly attacked than ever; the bourgeoisie, which owed him everything, poked fun at him, and his love of peace passed for cowardice. Because his head was shaped like a pear (*poire*), a parody of a popular Latin hymn, calling attention to this, became all the rage (*Adoremus in aeternum sanctum Phillipiorum . . .*'). Cartoonists and journalists vied in attempts to alienate the nation from its Government. 'Now at last it is realized', wrote Heinrich Heine, 'that there is something even more lamentable than government by mistresses and that more honour is to be discovered in the boudoir of an elegant lady than in a banker's counting-house . . .' Thus some sighed for Madame de Pompadour, others for Robespierre, all for Bonaparte, and the most moderate of kings was, naturally enough, the least loved.

Louis-Philippe made no great effort to win affection. Thanks to the limited suffrage, he had the voters on his side, and thanks to subsidies and gifts, the Chamber. With Guizot, a minister after his own heart, he in fact wielded personal power. Guizot remained the embodiment of the middle way, wise, realistic, without any yearning for false grandeur and without the least streak of bombast. He was intelligent, noble-hearted and disinterested; he was blamed for having said to the French, 'Get rich', but the phrase had been taken out of its context. What he sought to do was to give France an oligarchical government on the British pattern yet however persistent an Anglophile he may have been, he was not blind, and would describe England as 'a great country which has great faults'. Such as she was, though, he admired her as the 'bulwark of liberty' and wanted to live with her in 'cordial understanding' (*entente cordiale*). The French public, at that time violently anti-English, regarded any agreement as surrender. The case of Pritchard, a British missionary and consul, who had been arrested by French bluejackets at Tahiti because of advice he had given Queen Pomaré, and for whom England demanded an indemnity, very nearly led to a declaration of war. The British Government had been churlish and offensive; to the applause of the Chamber, Lamartine announced that France wanted peace, but a worthy peace, a French peace and not an English peace, and the country was all for Lamartine. Firmly resolved not to go to war over Queen Pomaré, the King and Guizot granted the Pritchard indemnity, and were accused of being arrant cowards. Dissatisfaction grew when England induced Guizot to make a white peace with the Sultan of Morocco; Marshal Bugeaud had just defeated the Moroccans at the Battle of Isly, and the English watched with anxiety France winning a more and more extensive grip on North Africa. The cabinet won with a majority of only eight votes, and the King asked Guizot to remain in power. Louis-Philippe had always been authoritarian; as he grew older, he became stubborn, and he was now seventy. His eldest son, the Duke of Orleans, had been killed in 1842 in a carriage accident, and his grandson, the Count of Paris, the heir to the throne, was only four. The King's second son, Nemours, who would probably be regent, was not a liberal; the dynasty's future no longer seemed quite so secure.

Yet at that moment Europe needed to have a firm and prudent government in France. Germany and Italy had aspirations to unity, and Austria, that unity's principal obstacle, seemed to the liberals the most oppressive power on the Continent. The Italian revolutionaries appealed to France for help; Guizot and the King refused to become embroiled with Austria, and they were right, but under the bitter attacks of the opposition, they had recourse to badly chosen weapons of defence. Corruption was constantly on the increase. The Minister of Public Works sold a salt-mine concession for one hundred thousand francs, with a former minister of war acting as go-between. Actresses bargained for privileges with deputies, and the gossip sheets supplied the public with tales of scandal. Balzac is full of such characteristic details, and they were true; many Frenchmen were moved by them to feelings of disgust and sadness. Now the opposition was penetrating into circles which had hitherto seemed by their very nature conservative. Among the Catholics, who had been so keenly legitimist in Charles X's day, there was a growing liberal party the leaders of which — Lamennais, Montalembert and Lacordaire — wanted to bring clergy and people closer and bring about 'separation between the throne and the altar'. Meanwhile, in its struggle with the university, the higher clergy was arousing anti-clericalism. The bishops reproached the university for producing atheists; the lectures of

Michelet and Edgar Quinet at the university condemned the Jesuits and the Inquisition. The danger of these quarrels lay in the fact that a portion of the bourgeoisie sent its children to the university for their education, while another part preferred the religious establishments, so that thus it was possible for young Frenchmen to learn disunity with their ABC's. On all sides there was bitterness and a desire for change.

In 1794, at the time of Thermidor, the country, weary of the Revolution's violence, had dreamed of a restoration; in 1845, weary of material corruption, it recalled only the revolutionaries' idealism. Thiers and Mignet had begun their historical rehabilitation: Lamartine's *Histoire des Girondins* completed it. At the outset of his career, it would have been difficult to conceive a less 'advanced' writer than this gentleman vine-grower, diplomatic official and dynastic poet. But a blend of ambition and deep feeling utterly changed him. 'Presumably', he said, 'a wave of terror would set me adrift.' Yet Lamartine felt the revolution surging up and awaited it with cheerful anguish. In 1846 Louis-Philippe, by insisting that princely marriages should once more unite the Houses of France and Spain, had displeased England and shattered the *Entente Cordiale*. Palmerston, who was pursuing a radical policy in Europe, was by no means pleased to find Guizot's conservatism blocking his path. Now during that period, English opposition seemed a fatal blow to any French regime; Palmerston found it easy to stir up the liberals, and even Thiers, against the Government by calling upon French sympathies for the European revolution. To come to terms with Austria, prudent though it might be, struck at the country's oldest instincts. 'The day on which the King signed the Spanish marriage,' said Lamartine, 'he signed, I believe, the ultimate, almost certain abdication of his dynasty ... The King is crazy, M. Guizot is inflated with vanity, M. Thiers is a weather-cock, opinion is a girl of the streets, the nation is a doddering old fool in a play. The argument of the comedy will be tragic for many ...' Lamartine had no fear of the tragedy so long as he was its protagonist; his book on the Girondists ended with an encomium of the Terror; of course it had had its innocent victims, but 'from their blood had sprung forth eternal truths'.

The *Histoire des Girondins* was a howling success; its revolutionary romanticism consoled its readers for the depths of Louis-Philippe's prosaic rule. Those were the days of reformist banquets at which, while the dessert was consumed, orators demanded universal suffrage. Cobden, who had just completed a stay in Paris, had taught the French the technique of agitation for reform which had succeeded so wonderfully in 1832 in England; throughout the kingdom dinners and speeches multiplied. At Mâcon, Lamartine said: 'Be sure that this royalty will fall, not in blood but caught in its own trap. And after having had the revolution of freedom and the counter-revolution of glory, you will have the revolution of the public conscience and the revolution of contempt.' Through his hatred of Guizot, even Thiers was turning to the Left and hoped for an outcome which he none the less knew was perilous: 'If anything could delight me, it would be the lasting humiliation of these ministers of counter-revolution. They are like some leaky ship you watch gradually sinking into the water.' In a truly constitutional monarchy the danger would not have been great; the King would have shifted cabinets and carried out electoral reform; but Louis-Philippe governed, and it was he who was the butt of the oppositions. A monarchist opposition declared itself in favour of reform in order to avoid revolution; a socialist and republican opposition hoped that the agitation for reform would lead to revolution. In February, Guizot forbade attendance at a reformist banquet in Paris, and Lamartine determined to go to the appointed place despite the ban: 'Were the Place de la Concorde deserted, were all the other deputies to shirk their duties, I should go to the banquet alone with my shadow behind me.' His shadow added nothing, for he could hardly have rid himself of it. But it was a poet's shadow and it was for poets that the French then felt they hungered. The other deputies did not go; students and workers filled the Place and made a bonfire of the Tuileries' chairs (February 21st, 1848). On the twenty-second, processions filed through the streets crying, 'Down with Guizot! Long live Reform!' During the night a few barricades were thrown up in working-class quarters: when the National Guardsmen were summoned, they too cried out, 'Long live Reform!' This middle-class hostility meant serious business for a middle-class regime.

Now worried, the King suddenly became constitutional, dismissed Guizot and summoned a reformist, Molé; people thought that everything was settled, and the vast majority of the French rejoiced. But on the evening of the twenty-third, during the course of a demonstration in front of Guizot's house on the Boulevard des Capucines, one of the demonstrators let off a pistol and the soldiery answered by firing a salvo. Some twenty persons were killed, both men and women; five of the bodies, loaded on a cart, were hauled through the city surrounded by torches. The mob cried out for vengeance; Molé refused to form a Government; the King called in Thiers (who, at the beginning of the uprising, had shown his dislike for Guizot by placing illuminations in his windows) and then Odilon Barrot, giving command of the army to Marshal Bugeaud, a man very unpopular with the Parisians. Because they were willing to serve the regime, the populace now hooted the same Thiers and Barrot it had yesterday acclaimed. Tired and demoralized, the troops gave way. Thiers advised the King to retire to Saint-Cloud and there to assemble soldiers for the retaking of Paris — siege warfare would be better than street fighting. Louis-Philippe tried to go out on horseback but, being ill received by the National Guardsmen, returned to the château and under his sons' pressure abdicated in favour of his grandson the Count of Paris. Here was what such men as Victor Hugo had hoped for, since they would have liked to save the throne and looked to great things from the regency of the young Duchess of Orleans (Helen of Mecklenburg) who was an intelligent and liberal princess. On the advice of her friends, the Duchess went to the Palais Bourbon with her two children; she was welcomed there by the deputies, but an armed mob broke into the hall. Ledru-Rollin, a socialist deputy, proposed the formation of a provisional Government and was seconded by Lamartine, who read a list of names which the people accepted by acclamation: Dupont de l'Eure, an elderly figurehead; Arago, a moderate scientist; Lamartine, poet; Ledru-Rollin, Marie, Crémieux, Garnier-Pagès. Meanwhile, at the Hôtel de Ville, the socialists were likewise forming a Government. The struggles between the Assembly and the Commune which had stained the First Republic with blood must at all costs be avoided. In haste the Palais Bourbon Government took in a few of the Hôtel de Ville men: Louis Blanc, an intelligent little fellow, without political experience, who had written l'Organisation du Travail, a book in which he had defended the right to work, equal wages, State purchase of industries and their management by collective councils; Marrast, Flocon and the working man Albert, a personage of mythical renown, dignified, quiet and moderate. The July Monarchy was gone.

It had died for 'lack of *panache*'. Accustomed by the Revolution and the Empire to harvests of glory, France had found this regime — peace-loving to the point of complacency — both dull and ridiculous. 'France is bored' was the phrase heard on all sides. That boredom had been wholesome, but was suffered with ill grace; the nation believed it had been humiliated. The middle class had little by little become, 'for the rest of the country, a small aristocracy, corrupt and vulgar, by which it seemed

shameful to let oneself be ruled'.[1] All that was young and intelligent had
cut itself loose from the dynasty. Up to the time of the Duke of Orleans's
death, men like Hugo had founded their hopes on him; his death had left
no one for their devotion. Guizot, an estimable character, pursued a policy
which he believed was realistic and which took no account of the reality
of idealism. Foolishly England had demanded of this Government, which
was so friendly towards her, a series of surrenders that were to precipitate
its downfall. The whole crew of journalists and pamphleteers had created
in the public mind an image of a vulgar and ridiculous creature to supplant that of the most intelligent of kings. Corruption had brought about
the opposition of the worthiest, and the ambition of others had profited
thereby. A power the origin of which was not legitimate could have sustained itself only through glory or through virtue; it had merely displayed
common sense, and that was not enough. Louis-Philippe had afforded
France some of the happiest years in her history, but the French do not
live on happiness. In 1848 Paris was reopening the path to adventures;
it remained to be seen whether the provinces would follow.

[1] DE TOCQUEVILLE.

CHAPTER III

HOW FRANCE THOUGHT AND FELT
BETWEEN 1815 AND 1848

THE 1848 revolution, said Lamartine, even though he had foretold it, 'surprised, everyone'. By this he meant that it had been
more sudden and quick than he had thought it would be. He had
expected a shower, not a thunderbolt out of an azure sky. The explanation of this phenomenon was latent electricity and the high tension of
public opinion. Ever since 1789 France had resembled a plucked elastic
cord which vibrates from right to left, unable to come to rest. The
Revolution had stripped the monarchy and aristocracy of power and given
it to the bourgeoisie; Bonaparte, during the period of the Consulate, had
vainly tried to bring the country into equilibrium and to reconcile the
two halves of France; the Restoration represented a 'Right' phase of
oscillation, with the Ordinances as its point of furthest stretch; the 1830
revolution had been a 'Left' phase, followed by the wonted return to
the Right. This constant restlessness had for sixty years kept the nation
in a feverish state which was unhealthy, but which, thanks to the excitement it induced, made healthiness seem dull and insipid. The French
had heard so many eloquent voices, thrown up so many barricades, sung
so many *Marseillaises*, so often crossed 'the Alps and the Rhine' that
'their souls sang in brazen clarions' and they no longer wanted to do
without the smell of powder and glory. After each revolution, they went
through a short period of weariness and then, the minute they were
rested, re-entered a blazing period of exaltation. France could have discovered a flat happiness in a present which was not without its charms;
she preferred to dream of the past or the future; she listened to history
and the poets. Politics, like literature and feelings, were romantic in
those days.

We have seen how, under Rousseau's influence, a reaction had taken
place in France against classical rationalism and libertinism in morals,
towards passionate love and a vague religious feeling. A whole pre-
romantic French literature extends from the *Confessions* to *Paul et Vir-
ginie*, from Madame de Staël to Chateaubriand. What are its characteristics and what is romanticism? There are few words more difficult to

define. In his *Lettres de Dupuis et Cotonet*, Alfred de Musset poked fun at everything that can be said about it. Before everything else, romanticism is a revolt — Shelley and Byron in England, Goethe and Schiller in Germany, Stendhal in France all regarded romanticism as 'the right and the duty of a generation to express a new sensibility through a new form of art', and regarded classicism as 'a host of regulations which seek to impose upon living sensibility forms of art dictated by the sensibility of bygone generations'. After having read the Baron d'Holbach's *Système de la Nature*, a pure product of the Age of Illumination, Goethe could not keep from laughing. During the eighteenth century the *philosophes* had told men: 'You are a rational creature, made to understand what other men understand.' The man of the nineteenth century, lyric man, thought that individual feeling is, as much as and more than universal reason, the criterion of truth. To defend and re-establish Christianity, Chateaubriand appealed, not to the rational intelligence, but to the heart.

The transition from one school to the other had not been a sudden one; the same writer could be at once a man of the eighteenth and a man of the nineteenth century. Rousseau belongs to the eighteenth in his *Social Contract* and to the nineteenth in his *Confessions*. The favourite author of Byron, prince of the romantic, was Voltaire, prince of the classical; Stendhal avowed the philosophy of the eighteenth century with the passion of the nineteenth. All the same, 1815 was a milestone, and the generation which was then reaching adolescence had many characteristics in common. It had fought and it had suffered; it had formed great hopes and it had been disappointed. All thinking youth suffered from an 'illness of the century' (*mal du siècle*). Werther is Childe Harold's brother, and he in turn is the model for de Musset's heroes. After such stupendous happenings, the Children of the Century awaited a great renewal and believed that no part of the classic tradition should survive. In painting, Géricault and later Delacroix are among the romantics of French art; in literature, Stendhal sacrificed Racine to Shakespeare and had no thought that his admirers a century hence would love both Racine and Shakespeare. Hugo clapped a Liberty cap on the old dictionary, pulled the Alexandrine about and tore it apart, and tried to write Shakespearean dramas. Literary 'Days' (such as the first performance of *Hernani*) followed upon the revolutionary 'Days'. The new writers did not all belong to the same political faction; Stendhal, who was against the monarchy and against religion, in his *Le Rouge et le Noir* sympathetically analyses the feelings of a young plebeian who, still deeply moved by the Napoleonic epic, finds himself shattered by the vanity of reborn privilege and the religious tyranny of the congregation. Hugo and Lamartine, on the other hand, during their younger days tried to fit themselves into the world of the Restoration: since success in that age required one to be royalist and Christian, the Children of the Age attempted to find a moral justification for this attitude in a sentimental return to the past. But only a quarter of a century later Lamartine, and then Hugo, both sounding boards of opinion, became republicans — after they had paid their court to the July Monarchy.

What we must realize is that all the parties, even those of classical tradition, in that age showed the marks of romanticism; Joseph de Maistre was a romantic monarchist, just as Chateaubriand was a romantic Catholic. The classicist accepts the real; the romanticist escapes from it. This escape took various forms — escape in space, or exoticism; escape in time, or an obsession with history. The nineteenth century loved history and sought inspiration from it. It was in Germany that this movement began, at the moment when that land had been invaded by the armies of the Revolution; in order to counter revolutionary propaganda, all aimed at the future, Germany sought refuge in her heroic age. Then France herself, after 1815, plunged back into her tradition. And throughout Europe the nineteenth-century taste for history made nationalisms more violent and bitter. Historical novels were all the fashion: Hugo, Alfred de Vigny and Dumas the elder followed the example of Sir Walter Scott; France produced a whole generation of historians — Guizot, Thiers, Augustin Thierry, Edgar Quinet, Michelet. Lamartine and Thiers employed history to kindle popular passion. Like the great romantic artists, such as Victor Hugo and Gustave Doré, Michelet distorted and glorified those who sat for his portraits, but the pictures he displays to his readers are so fine that in their minds they remain the very image of France. From him several generations of French people were to take their ideas about the monarchy and the Revolution, even though, while he believed he was depicting the history of France, what he really depicted was the soul of Jules Michelet. But he gave lasting shape to the memories and the desires of French men and women.

Michelet shows us to what extent the historian can invade and expropriate history; yet this was not merely a characteristic of Michelet but a characteristic of the period. A classical writer labours to abstract himself from his work; a romantic writer boldly thrusts himself upon the scene. He no longer describes *the* passions but *his* passions. His private life spills over into his plays and novels and is known to the public; Victor Hugo's finest poems were confessions, just as were Byron's; Lamartine's famous 'Lac' conjures up an episode from the poet's own experience of love. To this of course you may reply that Alceste utters to Célimène feelings which were the same as Molière's for his own wife. True enough, for there never was a wholly impersonal art, but the classicist transfers and hides his passions, whereas the romantic unfurls his like a banner. The classicist seeks to be in tune with a public of mannered people; the romantic defies the public, and by his scorn triumphs over it. Towards 1830 the artist and the bourgeois stood in opposing camps, but the opposition was superficial, and the French romantic remained a bourgeois in his way of life, which derived in part from the social, almost priestly, character of literature in France.

Balzac was the great historian of manners for the first half of this century. All France files through his *Comédie Humaine*: the provinces with their political intrigues, their haughty down-at-heel aristocrats, their misers of genius, their local muses, their passions simmering in silence; Paris, with its gossip sheets, its ladies of easy virtue, its bankers, its wonderful and dangerous women of the world, its merchants, its judges, its doctors, its thieves. As a Catholic and a monarchist, Balzac believed that he was demonstrating the need for moral and political traditions by displaying the excesses to which the passions will sink when the individual is left to his own resources. He makes it clear to us that Louis-Philippe's reign was not an age of moral greatness. There was no deep faith, religious or political, merely a frenzied race for jobs, power and wealth. The industrial revolution was in full swing with its attendant *laisser-faire*, which is likewise social irresponsibility; it was the age of Crevel, a new-rich trader, a captain in the National Guard, a rake and a sybarite. This bourgeoisie, especially in textiles and banking, was taking the form of a new feudalism; in these large families, directorships were handed down from father to son, and the well-to-do of Louis-Philippe's reign believed as naively as formerly did the aristocracy in their rights as a governing class. This captainship of industry by divine right had its virtues: it was hard-working, sometimes even charitable, but its charity remained condescending and amounted to an ill-concealed basic egoism. England during the same period was no more generous; Dickens's and Disraeli's arraignments are as harsh as Balzac's, but in London appearances were better preserved than in Paris.

Even the Catholic Church had gone through its romantic crisis. During the eighteenth century, it had been weakened among the higher circles at court and in the cities by the arguments and taunts of the *philosophes*, yet even during the Revolution it had maintained its prestige in the country districts. Bonaparte the politician and Chateaubriand the poet had restored Catholicism to favour among thinking people. Whereupon Bonald, Maistre and Charles X's excesses had compromised it afresh; their aggressive clericalism had awakened an ever potential anti-clericalism which had come to a head in the sack of the Archbishop's palace. Even among the bourgeoisie, nominally Christian but still intellectually Voltairean, there were those who wished that Catholicism might become liberal. After 1830, priests and laymen — such men as Lamennais, Lacordaire, Montalembert and Ozanam — strove to make the Church in France integral with the new world. Alexis de Tocqueville hoped to reconcile 'the spirit of freedom and the spirit of religion'. The prediction of the socialism of the future indited in his *Mémoires d'Outre-Tombe* by the aged Chateaubriand, a Catholic of the finest sort, though long an unbeliever, is linked to this movement. To the young men who visited Lamennais at his La Chesnaie estate, it seemed possible to be at once 'a penitent Catholic and an impenitent liberal'. Condemned by the Pope, Lamennais was unable to remain in the Church; reconciling the principles of the Revolution and the doctrines of the Church was not an easy business. For a long time to come, the educational question was to remain a source of conflict between Church and State. The reactionary spirit of the congregation was to continue its struggles against the popular Christianity of La Chesnaie, but the movement had lasting effects, and social Catholicism opened the way to a 'Christian democracy', the influence of which is today greater than ever in France.

At the moment when the July Monarchy crumbled, historical romanticism had petered out. Minds were still seeking escape, but rather in the future than in the past, and towards this future two roads lay open, roads, moreover, which criss-crossed and merged. Rapid advances in the experimental sciences and the development of industry brought about a rebirth of faith in progress, in the upward and continuous movement of mankind towards happiness; Renan wrote, although he did not publish, a book called *L'Avenir de la Science*, and in every French village there blossomed forth a *Café du Progrès*. To this romanticism of science there was joined a romanticism of the people. Disgusted at bourgeois rapacity, generous spirits like George Sand were troubled at seeing so much misery side by side with such great wealth and expected a new France to arise from the working classes. The great romantics Lamartine and Hugo, after their conservative beginnings, were moving in the direction of the democratic parties; this was the moment when Victor Hugo, prompted by his mistress, Juliette Drouet, began thinking of a great novel of the people, which he was only to write at a later date (*Les Misérables*). Lamartine was about to plunge into the Revolution and drown in it both his happiness and his abilities. It was the day of great systems and great hopes: Fourier, Cabet, Saint-Simon and Proudhon were elaborating various forms of socialism and communism. Saint-Simon, a descendant of the great writer of memoirs, had a remarkable mind and greatly influenced the thinking of Auguste Comte and Augustin Thierry. He founded an 'industrialist' school which held that social institutions should have as their purpose the betterment of the poorest class's lot, but that the reform of the State should be entrusted to the industrialists, because they were experienced in large undertakings. Saint-Simon believed in free trade and in well-being achieved through the development of techniques and means of communication. The Second Empire was to live in this faith. To the Saint-Simon industrialists as to the romantic writers, the coming revolution appeared as a lyric outburst. 'What are we creating, gentlemen', Lamartine was to say to the students immediately after the Days of February, 'what is our country creating today, if not the most sublime poetry?'

To which a young man armed with a gun replied: 'Enough of words!' The writers who spoke so often about the people knew that people only slightly. Since the French Revolution, the people had changed; it cherished the memory of twenty-five years during which, rioting in the streets of Paris or fighting for the Empire, it had altered the world. In 1789 the people had been made up of artisans or peasants, and factory workers were few; between 1815 and 1848 the industrial revolution had created a proletariat. The number of steam engines had grown from twenty to five thousand; France's working-class population exceeded six million. The average wage was absurdly low (1.78 francs for a thirteen-hour day); workers did not own the right to strike; they were housed in dirty hovels. The golden mean was golden only for the bourgeois; proletarians starved to death. Thus the proletariat was at once more abjectly poor, more concentrated and more aware of its own strength than in 1789 — conditions highly favourable to fermentation. To its mind, political revolution was merely a means; it wanted that social revolution which would at last guarantee its rights: the right to work, the right to bread, the right to defend its own interests. In 1830 it had once more let itself be killed for freedom; it had been cheated and was seeking a new alliance. Those who served as its advisers – Barbès, a wealthy bourgeois communist, and Auguste Blanqui, 'the Locked-up One' – were not comfortable geniuses like Hugo and Lamartine; they spent their lives in conspiracies and prisons and had both been condemned to death and then pardoned. Their demand was not for a parliamentary republic, but for seizure by force and the dictatorship of the proletariat.

'The real nature of the revolution of 1848 lay in the conflict between the working people and the middle class.' It was overalls against frock-coats; caps against hats. In clothing and in speech, the classes were then sharply distinguished; no popular press existed, and therefore reading did not make for a common vocabulary: the romantic writers did not speak the same language as the roughs on the Pont au Change. When they came face to face, the bourgeois and the workers, often without being aware of it, mistook each other's meaning. But those bourgeois who had taken part in the February Days, either through ambition or through contempt for the regime, showed a prudent respect for this people of Paris which made and unmade revolutions. How could you close your eyes to the social revolution when the Hôtel de Ville and the Police Prefecture were in the hands of armed workers in red sashes? George Sand wrote: 'Great and good People, thou art heroic by thy nature . . . mild as Force itself! . . . Thou wilt rule, O People; rule in brotherhood . . .' And Lamartine: 'Affection, affection, always affection for the people, and the people in return will lend you their hearts.' That remained to be seen. Before granting their love, these men and women, remembering the tricks of 1830, were going to keep a sharp eye on their representatives; this time they were not going to have any lieutenant-general of the realm fobbed off on them. Nevertheless, there remained a common capital of memories and victories with which to knit together the two groups and preserve France. When anyone spoke to them of Valmy or of Austerlitz, of the taking of the Bastille or the Three Glorious Days, both trembled and acknowledged each other as brothers and companions-at-arms. And this was amply shown on the day when a proletarian in rags, and with tears in his eyes, threw his arms about Lamartine.

CHAPTER IV

WHY THE SECOND REPUBLIC DID NOT LAST

T HE Palais Bourbon Government had moved over to the Hôtel de Ville, but between the two groups and their papers there continued to be a deep fissure; the *National* men (Palais Bourbon) wanted a political revolution, the Republic, prompt elections and the tricolour; the *Réforme* men (Hôtel de Ville) demanded a social revolution, delayed elections (to gain time in which to carry out their plans before the conservative provinces could make themselves felt), and the red flag. Lamartine was the republicans' great man, Louis Blanc the socialists'; Ledru-Rollin wavered between the two. All three were men of good-will, but without experience in public affairs. Agreement was reached on three points: freedom of the press with abolition of the stamp tax (which brought the price of papers down to a penny), freedom of assembly (which promoted a rebirth of clubs) and the right of every citizen to belong to the National Guard (which shifted the equilibrium of power in Paris and seemed to strip the bourgeoisie of any possibility of governing by armed force).

The opening days were riotous; delegation after delegation invaded the Hôtel de Ville. Workmen armed with guns demanded the right to work and minimum wages; it was necessary to promise them the establishment of national workshops to afford labour for the unemployed. Louis Blanc, whose ideas had won the day, was given the task of drawing up the decree. Groups of picturesque and voluble foreigners came begging the support of the new French Government for the oppressed liberals of all Europe. The communists, of both the Cabet and the Barbès varieties, pawed the ground in their impatience. Lamartine, Minister of Foreign Affairs, replied to everyone in speeches which were harmonious, noble and flowing; as someone said: 'This is no man, it is a lyre.' None the less he it was who saved the tricolour flag, which the extremists accused of being a compromise in which the king's colour, white, remained. One of the things he said in this connection brought applause from the crowd and has remained famous: 'The red flag has merely made the circuit of the Champ de Mars, dragged in the people's blood; the tricolour flag has gone round the world, with the name, the glory, and the freedom of the Fatherland . . .'[1] To calm the demonstrators, Lamartine conceded a red rosette on the staff. To quiet the sovereigns, he promised that the French Republic would not spread propaganda abroad. To protect itself against the cries for vengeance, that sad aftermath of revolutions, the Government decreed the abolition of the death penalty for political offences; Lamartine himself helped Guizot to get across the frontier. The heads of the provisional Government were not cruel men; they were romantic and warmhearted; they wanted a France great and free; they believed in progress through brotherhood and science; but they knew nothing about the national economy and precious little about the French provinces. On April 9th they determined to hold elections open to universal suffrage. The enfranchised population suddenly swelled from two hundred and fifty thousand to nine million voters; it was a leap in the dark.

The extension of the franchise had frightened the bourgeois, but they were quickly reassured. In the elections of April 23rd, the masses appeared more conservative than had the qualified voters; in deciding upon universal suffrage, Paris had signed away its right to govern the country and had handed over that right to the provinces. A Paris uprising could contest the legitimacy of a Government based upon an electorate with property qualifications, but not of a Government holding a national majority. The Palais Bourbon had triumphed over the Hôtel de Ville; to have effected a social revolution, it would have been necessary, as Blanqui desired, to proclaim the dictatorship of the proletariat, but men's minds were still far from ready for that. With good grace or ill, they accepted the Republic; almost everywhere, peasants and gentry had together planted Liberty Trees; the National Guard (still a bourgeois organization) had attended in full regalia; and the village priest had blessed the poplar bedecked with ribbons. Generals, judges, bishops — citizens of every rank supported the new regime; the July Monarchy, hated by both Right and Left, found none to defend it. 'So much the worse for them; they have richly deserved it', said the legitimists. The greater number of the nine hundred representatives were republicans and moderates; the advanced republicans had only a hundred seats. In Paris, Blanqui, Barbès and Raspail were defeated. The French were willing to accept a political, not a social revolution. 'We had been counting on bad elections', said the *Réforme*, 'but the event, we must grant, has exceeded our expectations.'

[1] Certain texts have it as: 'with the name of glory and the freedom of the Fatherland' but this obscures the meaning.

At their first meeting the deputies named a committee of government from which Louis Blanc was excluded. 'The democrats prevailed, over both the reactionary and the demagogic.' That was the feeling of Lamartine's friends; such ungracious words were not calculated to please the friends of Louis Blanc.

The workers of Paris were discontented, not that they had this time been swindled of the Republic, but because they had been swindled of the *Sociale*. They had, however, won two measures: the creation of a 'Government Committee for Labour', which met at the Luxembourg under the chairmanship of Louis Blanc, talked a great deal and did little or nothing; and the national workshops. The latter, intended to give the unemployed some occupation and to prove the feasibility of a collective economy, had been organized by the Minister of Commerce, Marie de Saint-Georges, otherwise known as Marie, who opposed them; he had therefore taken great pains to make sure they would fail. The labourers in these shops (fourteen thousand in March, one hundred thousand in June) were employed on perfectly useless earthworks. Unable to take any interest in such idle toil, they spent their time tossing pennies or founding political clubs which would soon want their Day. On May 15th, under the leadership of those two veterans of Paris uprisings, Barbès and Blanqui, they broke into the Palais Bourbon, declared the Assembly dissolved and proclaimed a socialist Government composed of Louis Blanc, Barbès, Blanqui and the workman, Albert. The legal Government, however, sounded a general alarm, the National Guardsmen from the prosperous quarters freed the Assembly, and Barbès and Albert were arrested at the Hôtel de Ville — thus putting an end to the first escapade. Thereupon it seemed urgent to do away with the national workshops, a breeding-ground for disturbances, an 'organized strike costing one hundred and seventy thousand francs a day'. On June 21st, the workshops were disbanded and the workmen were urged to enlist in the army or find jobs outside Paris. It was most likely that so radical a step would bring about another riot; the people of Paris, deeply disappointed, exasperated at seeing its victory again frittered away, was going to try yet another Day. Wittingly the Government took its chances; the political revolution was challenging the social.

For some time past, Cavaignac, the Minister of War, had had his battle plan against the 'Reds'. His scheme was to withdraw from the working-class neighbourhood in the east and to concentrate his soldiers in the west, to wait until the revolt was ready to break out, then to attack. On June

23rd, some thousands of working people gathered before the Bastille column, knelt in remembrance of the first martyrs in 1789 and, crying out, 'Liberty or death!' retired behind barricades and demanded the re-establishment of the national workshops. The Assembly declared a state of siege and gave plenary powers to General Cavaignac. He had available about twenty thousand regular army troops, the National Guard from the western parts of the city (well fed to the point of bursting) and the militia. After February 1848, however, the workmen had also been issued with National Guard weapons. The battle, the sorry battle, was fierce and lasted for four days; the army fought with discipline, the bourgeois National Guard with fury. 'The fanaticism of the interested counterbalanced the exaltation of the needy.'[1] The rioters slaughtered General Bréa, and the Archbishop of Paris, Monseigneur Affre, was killed by a bullet while trying to make a plea for civil peace. In all there were several thousand dead. Cavaignac's victory was complete, and he demanded from the Government the most severe reprisals. Thousands of the insurgents were deported, in mass and without trial, the socialist party was broken, and its papers were suppressed. Here was a misguided fury to provoke other furies, a new trench of blood, but this time between the workers and the bourgeoisie. 'The cotton cap', wrote Flaubert, 'proved itself no less ghastly than the red cap.' And Louis-Philippe, recalling that he had been overthrown by a few corpses, said bitterly: 'The Republic is lucky . . . it is able to fire upon the people.' Four months had sufficed to weave the shroud of the February Revolution.

The Assembly decreed that General Cavaignac had deserved well of the fatherland; rather had he deserved well of the bourgeoisie. He was a republican beyond reproach, and everyone thought that he would be elected President — that is, everyone except Lamartine, who thought he himself had a chance, and who insisted that the election should be by universal suffrage. Such was the American method; experience was to show it was perilous in France. Lamartine won his point; it was decided that the legislative power would be entrusted to an assembly of seven hundred and fifty members and the executive power to a citizen elected for four years by the people and not eligible for re-election. No one thought of excluding members of families that had reigned over France. Jules Grévy, a young lawyer and republican deputy, had suggested a president of the council elected by the Assembly who would at the same time be head of the State. His proposal was rejected. 'I am well aware',

[1] GUSTAVE FLAUBERT.

asserted Lamartine during the course of this debate, 'that the multitudes have their moments of aberration; that there are names which attract the crowd just as a red rag will lure unreasoning animals. I know this, and more than anyone I dread it . . .' He dreaded it but took the risk, because he clung to the hope that he would by this means be elected President of the Republic. 'If the choice of the President lies with the people, and does not take place for the next two months, I shall be chosen, you may be sure. But some entertain the erroneous idea of having him chosen by the House. I shall combat this foible.' By six hundred to two hundred, the Assembly decided that the presidential election would be by universal suffrage and that the President would be answerable to the High Court were he to violate the Constitution. But since the President had the armed forces at his disposal, he in fact became the master; the Constitution contained the germs of the disease which was to kill it.

Who were the possible candidates? In order to be elected by a parliamentary assembly to the presidency of the State, a man must have given proof of political capacity and assurances of loyalty to the regime; election by plebiscite requires only an extended popularity. Lamartine thought he possessed it; Cavaignac had it among the bourgeois, but not among the workers and peasants; a third candidate was looming on the horizon. He was Louis Napoleon Bonaparte. This son of Hortense de Beauharnais and (perhaps) of Louis Bonaparte, who had become imperial pretender upon the death of the Duke of Reichstadt, had never wavered in his faith in the powers of his magic name. In youth he had been liberal and even *carbonaro*; when his first vain attempts at a *coup d'état* had landed him in jail, he had written much and worked hard during his confinement. Indeed, he had built up a complex system, which he called Bonapartism, and in which order and revolution, socialism and prosperity, liberalism and authority were mingled. In London, where he had long dwelt, he had made such friends as Benjamin Disraeli and Lady Blessington; rich Britons (among them, his mistress, Miss Howard) and bankers from the city had helped him financially, gambling on his future. From the dawning of the February Days, a little group of faithfuls had tried to launch the new Bonaparte. Prudently and wisely he had shown himself little; he was waiting for 'illusions to fade', but in the June by-elections, he was the victor in four departments. 'I believe', he had said, 'that from time to time men are created whom I should describe as providential, into whose hands are committed the fates of their countries. I believe myself to be one of these men . . .' Along the boulevards people sang, '*Po-lé-on, nous l'aurons!'* ('Napoleon, we'll have him!') He continued to keep very much in the shade, through skill, or lack of it, merely sputtering before the Assembly, and thus calming the members' fears. 'What an idiot! He is sunk', said Ledru-Rollin, after listening to him. But the Other One had also gone to pieces on the rostrum, and for all that had carried off the 18 Brumaire.

When Louis Napoleon at last ventured to place himself in nomination for the presidency of the Republic, a united front of republicans and royalists should at once have been forged against this potential Caesar. But the royalist leaders, who constituted what was called the Committee of the Rue de Poitiers (Thiers, Berryer, Montalembert and other 'old fossils'), knew that a royalist candidate had no immediate chance. Cavaignac, whom they would gladly have supported, refused because of his extreme republicanism to make any commitments to the party of order, and so they turned to Louis Napoleon who, being ready to make any promises because he was resolved to keep none, thus won the support of Thiers and his associates. 'He's a simpleton', they said; he was no such thing, however, and they were handing him the majority of France. That majority was in a mood for adventures; the peasants and the middle class had been dismayed by the events of June; an additional tax of forty-five *centimes* had irritated the countryside. Ever since the business of the workshops, labour had been sulking at the Republic; now it rediscovered deep in its heart an old background of Bonapartism, and knew that this new Bonaparte called himself a socialist. On the streets they sang:

> Voulez-vous du micmac?
> Choisissez Cavaignac.
> Voulez-vous d' la canaill'?
> Choisissez M'sieur Raspail.
> Voulez-vous un coquin?
> Choisissez Ledru-Rollin.
> Mais voulez-vous du bon?
> Choisissez Napoléon.

When the votes had been counted, Prince Louis Napoleon had five and a half million, Cavaignac a million and a half, Ledru-Rollin, the socialist candidate, three hundred and seventy thousand and Lamartine less than eight thousand. 'Lamartine had strangled with his own hands that Republic of which he loved to call himself the father.'

Those whom the gods would destroy . . . The Constituent Assembly had attained madness; it had allowed an ambitious prince, bearing a formidable name, to become head of the executive power, which meant master of the police and the army, and at the same time it gave him this power without any chance of re-election. This was equivalent to making all the arrangements for a *coup d'état*. But Louis Napoleon, silent and close-mouthed, still trod warily. He solemnly swore as an honourable man to respect the Constitution, formed a cabinet under the chairman-ship of the everlasting Odilon Barrot, and undertook, by travelling about the country, to solidify his popularity. On May 13th, 1849, were held the elections for the Legislative Assembly which was to replace the Con-stituent Assembly. This time the 'reactionaries' won sweepingly over the moderate democrats, who returned seventy members, and the 'Reds' of the Mountain, who obtained one hundred and eighty seats. The rue de Poitiers had brought about the election of some four hundred and fifty deputies, almost all Orleanists and legitimists, with a handful of Bonapartists. Seemingly this meant the country's return to monarchy, yet since those loyal to the Count of Chambord, ex-Duke of Bordeaux, in the senior Bourbon line, could not reach an understanding with the faithful followers of the Count of Paris, in the junior line, the methodical dreamer in the Élysée Palace could quietly and cynically complete his plans. To make use of the monarchists to crush the Republic, and then to disarm the monarchists in order to impose the Empire, seemed a rash manœuvre, but to a man who has no one in his way, everything is easy. Thiers, confident, sure of his majority, of the rue de Poitiers and above all of himself, gave the President paternal advice: he urged 'democratic sim-plicity'. Louis Napoleon listened, thanked him and secretly had imperial liveries designed for the Élysée footmen. Vieil-Castel, a keener observer than Thiers because he was more detached, wrote: 'I acknowledge that the President has one great quality: he is brave; and one great political virtue: he does not say much.'

The republicans clumsily bared their flank to the enemy on the watch. To please the Catholics, who, under a system of universal suffrage, represented a great power, the President had organized an expedition on behalf of the Pope against Mazzini's Roman Republic; demonstrators of the Left, aroused by a speech of Ledru-Rollin, marched upon the Palais Bourbon crying that the Constitution had been violated. A cavalry charge easily halted them, but the Assembly took advantage of this excuse to withdraw liberties that had been granted — freedom of press and assembly. Sick at heart, the people of Paris remained passive. A law on education, called the Falloux Law (the Count of Falloux was Minister of Public Instruction) set up a *de facto* alliance between the Church and the University (1850). As Montalembert, who had long since abandoned liberalism, put it: 'We must have our own Rome expedition, here at home.' In other words, the republicans must be swept out of education as they were cleaned out of Rome, or at least they must be controlled. Then it was that conflict between the school teacher and the village priest grew bitter, a conflict which was to divide small French communities for more than half a century. Under the July Monarchy, the Church had been conciliatory; in 1848, she had blessed Liberty Trees. Now she rallied to the party of order, which was really that of the established order, while the bourgeoisie, once Voltairean and liberal, now, because it had been afraid, was reverting to a political Catholicism. What you had was an alliance between the congregation and the happy medium; Thiers had even gone so far as to suggest that the bishops appoint all school teachers! The Catholics viewed him as even more Catholic than they were themselves and left this choice to the prefects. Lastly, in this rush towards reaction, universal suffrage was reduced, in clever and oblique fashion, by means of a law which required three years of residence for voters, a qualification which had to be proved by reference to the rolls for direct taxation. This amounted to the restoration of the property qualification; thus were three million voters, almost all working men, deprived of their rights. In less than two years, the political victories of 1848 had been lost to the French people; Louis Napoleon and his royalist majority had succeeded in creating the Republic without the republicans. Now the task was to discard the monarchists.

During the 1850 long vacation, each party made preparations for the *coup d'état*. Thiers went to see the Orleans princes at Claremont House; the legitimists called on the Count of Chambord at Wiesbaden; there was much talk of fusion between the royalist groups; as always, it came to nothing. Meanwhile the Prince-President held military reviews, and the troops who cried 'Long live the Emperor!' were those most commended. Slowly but surely the Executive was making the Assembly impotent. The *coup d'état* technique is simple; in key posts you must have your own men. The Prince removed Odilon Barrot from the presidency of the Council, although the latter had a faithful majority in the Assembly. That body let things slide; it was committing suicide. For Changarnier, a monarchist general who was sure to protect the Legislature, the Prince substituted General Magnan, who was wholly devoted to his person. During the sad debate which followed, Thiers, who now realized the truth — but too late — said: 'The Empire is made.' The Prince-President could only agree to the continuance of the Republic if he were to obtain a change in the Constitution allowing him to be re-elected; lacking this, he was forced to turn to a *coup d'état*. But how get an amendment when it required three-quarters of the deputies to pass it, and when the parties all wanted different changes? France, wrote the Spanish Ambassador, 'is full of monarchists powerless to set up a monarchy and sighing under the burden of a republic which has no republicans to defend it . . .' He could see no way out except revolution or dictatorship, the torch or the sword, the Mountain or the Empire.

The odds were on the Empire. The other parties were split and, over-suspicious, cancelled one another out. The Prince-President, master of the machinery of power and aided by tried conspirators, could act with greater secrecy; none are more loyal than adventurers when the adventure involves profit, and in this one, the booty was France. Who could stand in his way? The Assembly was not even able to agree to a proposal made by its own treasurers, giving it the right to post in army barracks a regulation concerning the requisition of troops by the legislative power. 'The Assembly', wrote Vieil-Castel, 'allowed itself the pleasure of plotting against Louis Napoleon. The impatient and the rabid talked of sending him off to Vincennes. It would require, they said, merely a wave of the hand, and no one would even notice it.' Perhaps, but at least some action was required, and they did not even give any thought to reaching agreement among themselves. The republicans voted against the scheme because they feared a *coup d'état* on the part of a monarchist Assembly, and the Bonapartists because they were themselves determined to carry one out against that Assembly. 'There is no danger', naively remarked a democrat, Michel de Bourges, 'and I am willing to add that if there were a danger, there is also an invisible sentinel who watches over us; that sentinel is the people.' He was mistaken. Indeed, who was ready to give his life for the Second Republic? Not the bourgeois, for they were monarchists; not the workers, for why should they protect an Assembly which ordered the troops to open fire on them and which had deprived them of the right to vote? Not the army, for Louis Napoleon and his associates, who were far from being children, had taken their precautions in that department.

The strength of every army, and also the chink in its armour, is that it obeys orders; capture the source from which orders flow and you are master of the whole stream. Louis Napoleon was sure of the commander of the troops, Magnan; he still needed a minister of war devoted to his service. He sent to Algeria for General de Saint-Arnaud, a man whose courage was as great as his scruples were few. He was merely a brigadier, so a brief expedition into Berber territory was organized to supply an excuse for making him into a divisional general. Magnan and Saint-Arnaud openly told certain selected officers: 'We shall soon need you, but you will have orders written and signed by us; in case of failure, no government could possibly hold you answerable.' There remained the Prefecture of Police, another post of command; the President installed there a man on whom he could rely, Maupas. Morny, the Prince's half-brother (born of Queen Hortense's affair with Flahaut, and hence Talleyrand's natural grandson) a witty, charming and wholly amoral adventurer, was to be the leader of the conspiracy. By the autumn of 1851, all arrangements had been made and the *coup d'état* was in readiness. Saint-Arnaud, however, wanted to wait until the Assembly should be in session; were the deputies scattered about in their constituencies, they could organize a Gironde and some sort of federalism. In Paris, Maupas would have them arrested in their beds; that would make it possible to deal with them later on, while at the same time avoiding any danger of fatalities — which are always to be regretted. 'No further harshness is needed once people are in jail.' Then also, December 2nd, anniversary of Austerlitz and the coronation, was, for the Bonapartists, the auspicious day above all others; it was chosen.

On the evening of December 1st, Louis Napoleon and Morny displayed the greatest calm; the Prince received guests at the Élysée and no emotion betrayed him. When the last of those invited had left, he opened the file labelled *Rubicon*; with him the memory of Caesar was an obsession. At dawn the troops occupied positions mastering all Paris. When the inhabitants of that city left their homes the next morning, they found two proclamations plastered on the walls; one was an appeal to the people announcing that the object of these activities was to foil the Assembly's treacherous plans, and the other was an appeal to the soldiery: 'I count upon you, not to break the law, but to obtain respect for the country's first law — national sovereignty . . .' Many of the representatives had been put under arrest; Thiers had shown so little heroism that he was set free the very next day — to the great indignation of the Bonapartists. Others still at liberty gathered together at the *Mairie* of the twentieth *arrondissement*; Hugo, Carnot, Arago, Jules Favre and Michel de Bourges set up a resistance committee. At the meeting-place of the Assembly, its president, Dupin, yielded without a struggle before a show of bayonets. 'We are in the right', said he, 'but these gentlemen have the power. Let us go.' Here was Mirabeau in reverse. The soldiers were in a joking mood: 'Would you dare arrest a representative of the people?' 'You bet!' The Austrian Ambassador found that Paris reminded him of Lisbon in the days of the *pronunciamentos*; and the 'overalls' approved of the *coup d'état*. 'Why should we defend your twenty-five francs a day?' workmen asked the deputies, whose honorarium seemed to them excessive. One of the representatives, Dr. Baudin, is reputed to have answered: 'You are going to see how a man dies for twenty-five francs a day.' He fell, struck by three bullets. The retort is probably apocryphal, but the bravery was real. A liberal and bourgeois opposition had taken shape on December 4th; it was beaten down, without serious strife, by General Magnan. In Paris there were three hundred and eighty persons killed,[1] many by firing squads without a trial; in all France there were twenty-six thousand arrests. The regime was never able to cleanse itself of these bloodstained and tyrannical beginnings. In 1830 power had lain with the bourgeoisie; in 1848 with the people; in 1851 it lay with the army. With the troops behind it, the victorious gang thought it might act as it chose; just as in the days of the White Terror, ultras asked the Prince to veil the Statues of Mercy and Pity, to be a man of bronze, 'unbending and just', and to 'journey across the age, the blade of repression in his hand'. Yet Morny's grandfather had already remarked to Louis Napoleon's uncle: 'Sire, you can do everything with bayonets except sit upon them.'

All who remained loyal to the Republic were brutally eliminated, and local vengeances came to repression's aid. 'One half of France is informing on the other', wrote George Sand. In every department a mixed commission settled the suspects' fates, not by trial, but by administrative 'decisions'. Some were temporarily expelled from France, others were permanently exiled, yet others were transported to Algeria, and the most ill-fated were shipped off to Cayenne. Decisions were not subject to appeal, and the accused were not apprised of the charges against them. Any member of a secret society could be deported, and the republican party was held to be a secret society. The injustice and extent of this persecution, however, created a republican opposition; the writers in exile

[1] Horace de Vieil-Castel said two thousand, but this was merely a rumour.

waged a war on Louis Napoleon which weakened his position abroad and eventually did so in France. First in Brussels and then on Jersey and Guernsey, Victor Hugo wrote *Les Châtiments* and *Napoléon le petit*; he had played his part in creating the uncle's magic legend, he would now bear witness to the base legend of the nephew. In both instances he painted his figures a trifle larger than nature; nevertheless, poets fashion the world anew — or at least they fashion the image men have of that world.

The tyrannical steps which had followed the *coup d'état* were unforgivable; the Prince's breach of his oath, beyond denial; but to accuse him of having strangled the Republic would be very wide of the mark. The Second Republic would have died anyway. In all likelihood, what the *coup d'état* had stifled was a rebirth of the monarchy. Taine somewhat heretically wrote: 'Monsieur Bonaparte is no worse than the others. The Assembly hated the Republic more than he did, and, had it been able, it would have violated its oath just as he did in order to plant Henry V or the Orleans princes on the throne . . .' The first 1848 elections had shown that the country would have accepted a moderate Republic, while at the same time the majority in France had shown itself hostile to the social and democratic Republic. The inner crisis started by the 1789 Revolution was not yet over; the Jacobin Republic retained its few fanatics, but had no more strength; the monarchists had been made impotent by the conflict between the two branches of the Bourbon family. The democratic dictatorship of a Bonaparte became, for the second time, a provisional solution. It was confirmed by a plebiscite. At first the Government wanted to have the citizens vote publicly, inscribing their yeas or nays upon a register; public outcry led to its granting a secret ballot. What did it have to lose? Opponents were few; Montalembert surrendered. 'To vote against Louis Napoleon is to summon a red dictatorship to take the place of the dictatorship of a Prince who, during the last three years, has rendered matchless services to order and Catholicism.' And said Taine: 'Which is worse, a presidency in the Russian style, or the *Jacquerie* of the secret societies? . . . On both sides I see only scorn for law and brutal violence.' There were seven million four hundred thousand yeas and six hundred and fifty thousand nays. A *Te Deum* was sung in Notre Dame Cathedral. 'The people who a month ago asserted that Louis Napoleon was a congenital idiot are now proclaiming him to be a great man.' Twenty years later these same people would once again find him an idiot, but twenty years constitute a life span for a regime. Thiers was right, the Empire was made.

CHAPTER V

WHY THE SECOND EMPIRE DID NOT LAST: THE AUTHORITARIAN EMPIRE

THE sequence of events leading from the Second Republic to the Second Empire was roughly parallel to that which, at the century's beginning, had led from the Directory to the First Empire. The Constitution of January 1852 created in fact, if not in name, a consul in the Bonapartist sense of the word, meaning a dictator. This 'president', elected for ten years, held the executive power and had the sole right to make treaties and war; he proposed all legislation and appointed all officials; neither he nor his ministers were responsible to the Chambers. Said the Prince: 'I am quite willing to be baptized in the waters of universal suffrage, but I do not intend to live out my life with wet feet.' Three major bodies were to assist the President: the Council of State, which framed the laws; the Legislative Body (elective, but selected from a list of official candidates) which voted the laws; and the Senate, which was made up of one hundred and fifty members appointed for life by the President and acting as watchdogs of the Constitution — watchdogs who in fact watched very little. No provision was made for the case of a conflict between the President and the Legislative Body. 'I view as a serious evil', said Montalembert, the Catholic orator and one of the few courageous men in this Assembly, 'the annihilation of all control and the debasement of the only elective body existing in the French Government...' The 1852 Constitution applied in full rigour the Bonapartist doctrine that despotism, in order to win acceptance, must present itself as a people's dictatorship and a temporary expedient. 'Freedom', as Louis Napoleon put it, 'has never helped in the establishment of a lasting political structure; freedom crowns such a structure when time has made it strong.' Surely he had never read the history of the United States. No more than that of the Second Republic was the 1852 Constitution practicable. 'A Constitution which does not afford a State the means of change does not afford it the means to maintain itself.'[1]

The emperor was already beginning to hatch out of the prince-presidential shell; the eagle was replacing the republican pike on flagstaffs, and people called it the 'Eagle's first flight'. Whenever the President travelled

[1] BURKE.

through the provinces, Persigny, more Bonapartist than this Bonaparte, had his claque cry out: 'Long live the Emperor!' The Prince lectured the masses on the excellences of a Government which would keep France as she had been 'after regeneration by the 1789 Revolution and organization by the Empire'. Soon he was able to announce: 'The burst of enthusiasm which has made itself felt throughout France in favour of restoring the Empire forces on the President the duty of consulting the Senate with regard to this matter.' The outcome of this consultation was a foregone conclusion; the Senate ordered a plebiscite on the re-establishment of the imperial dignity in the person of Louis Napoleon Bonaparte, and seven million eight hundred and thirty-nine thousand yeas made the Prince-President into the Emperor Napoleon III. (The King of Rome had been Napoleon II, just as the Dauphin of the Temple had been Louis XVII.) There were two hundred and fifty-three thousand nays and two million abstentions, particularly in the provinces which had remained monarchical. The only fear which might have held the French back from so dangerous a course would have been that of a fresh crop of Napoleonic wars, but Napoleon III had reassured them. 'The Empire means peace', he kept repeating, and not without meaning what he said. Of course a man bearing his name should, he thought, do great deeds; but if Napoleon I had brought France victories, Napoleon III would bring her peace, prosperity, industrial progress, the welfare of her people and perhaps, later on, freedom. 'I grant that, like the Emperor, I have many conquests to make. Like him, I want to win over to civilization the hostile parties. I want to win over to religion, morality, and comfort that portion of the population – still so numerous – which . . . in the very bosom of the earth's most fertile soil, can barely obtain the prime necessities . . .' His Government was to be that of cheap bread, great public works, holidays and leisure. He would have sincerely liked to be a good tyrant; sadly enough, there are no good tyrants.

At the time of his becoming emperor, Napoleon III was almost forty-five years old; he was a large, heavy man, not without dignity. His long moustache and goatee lent him a most novel appearance, in its day much imitated; his grey eyes seemed lustreless, without a spark, but on occasion they could flash like lightning. In France he had long seemed out of place; having lived there only as a child and later as a prisoner, he had no French friends outside his little band of faithful followers. A cosmopolitan prince, he spoke 'German like a Swiss, English like a Frenchman, and French like a German', with the cautious slowness of a man who is not very sure of his words. He was silent, a good listener, courteous and gentle mannered, and he possessed a curious charm which attracted women as much as it did men. 'At first glance', said one visitor, 'I took him for an opium addict. Not a bit of it; he himself is the drug, and you quickly come under its influence.' He was not lacking in humour; when his cousin, Prince Napoleon, had the temerity to say to him: 'The Emperor? But you are like him in nothing', he replied: 'You are wrong, my dear fellow; like him, I am saddled with his family.' Within limits, he had a certain degree of culture, with a liking for history, political theory and the art of war. Twenty years of conspiracies, schemes and captivity had packed his brain with a whole world of illusions. 'Scratch the Emperor', observed Guizot, 'and you will find the political refugee.' His shyness sometimes made him curt, but he was resolved to be popular and worried those whose task it was to guard him because of his mania for shaking hands. 'We saw to it that he shook only the hands of police-men.' His projects were generous, but always confused, except in con-spiracy, where he had displayed a kind of genius; his extraordinary career made him fatalistic and superstitious. His youth in Italy among the *carbonari* had taught him the strength of European nationalism; there-fore he defended the right of peoples to determine their own destinies, which was to make of this despotic sovereign an unexpected champion of liberal Europe. His dream was a European federation. At heart he felt himself a disciple of Saint-Simon; his stay in England had led him better to understand working people's aspirations, and he was even more a humanitarian than an authoritarian. 'My friends', he would say, 'are working in the shops.' But having been elected by the bourgeoisie, he was never able to build the socialist Empire which was certainly what he wanted. All in all, the man was interesting, the sovereign troublesome.

His isolation from the country made him the tool of those around him, and they were not of a reassuring species. Since the Empire was to be hereditary and the Emperor was not married, the heir-designate was Jerome Bonaparte, and after him, his son Prince Napoleon, nicknamed 'Plonplon', who was thirty years old, an intelligent fellow with a curious bent of mind, an anti-clerical and therefore frightening to the conservatives without being attractive to the republicans. Jerome's daughter, the Princess Matilda, a friend of Sainte-Beuve, Renan and the Goncourts, served as a link between the intellectuals and the Empire. Napoleon III's illegitimate half-brother and companion in adventure, Morny, a dandified businessman, gaudily paraded his birth and planted a hydrangea (in French, *hortensia*, an allusion to their mother, Queen Hortense) on his coat of arms, taking for his motto, *Tace et memento*. He certainly remembered, but he did not remain silent. In 1853, the Emperor married a young Spanish girl, Eugénie de Montijo, and it was a love match; Napoleon liked women, but until then he had never liked one woman very long. With little confidence in the dynasty, the courts of Europe had not been lavish in their offers of princesses; there was no Marie Louise available for this new Bonaparte, an adventurer at whom the sovereigns looked down their noses. 'He is not', as people put it, 'the son of his father, and everyone is the son of his mother.' When he announced his marriage, he reminded the French that Josephine herself had not been of royal lineage; he informed the Council of Ministers: 'I am not asking your advice, gentlemen; I am informing you of what I have decided to do.' He asserted that he would be able 'to impose himself on the old Europe' and that the epithet 'upstart' became glorious 'when you are given your start by the free suffrage of a great people'. Eugénie was startlingly beautiful, with red hair and blue eyes and shoulders transparently white. Her mother had been a friend of Mérimée's and Stendhal's, and she herself recalled having sat, while still a little girl, on M. Beyle's knees, though she had certainly acquired none of his brilliance. She knew very little, but knew that little in four languages and uttered it with fiery conviction. It was said of her that she began by being the futile woman and ended by being the fatal woman — a harsh witticism, but by and large a true one.

At the beginning of the reign, Eugénie's political influence was nil; the Empress limited herself to setting the fashion in a court where the old French nobility was seldom to be seen, but which was not lacking in graciousness. At the Tuileries, the Empress and her ladies displayed their handsome shoulders in crinoline gowns which were recorded for posterity by the artist Winterhalter; at Compiègne, Mérimée and the Emperor created a pleasant atmosphere, half frivolous and half cultivated. Masked balls, plays, charades and a parlour game consisting of dictation passages strewn with grammatical traps afforded entertainment by turns; writers, scientists and artists were made welcome at court. Pasteur and Leverrier there rehearsed their discoveries; Gounod played the piano and sang. Napoleon did not long continue faithful to his lovely Spaniard, and famous adventuresses, such as La Castiglione, to the great advantage of foreign Governments, made this too-easy conquest. 'He chases the first petticoat he sees', said his cousin, Princess

Matilda. Thus it came to pass that, in order to avoid jealous scenes, the Emperor began occasionally to yield to the Empress's influence; she was an ultramontane Catholic and championed the Vatican against modern Italy. A son, the Prince Imperial, was born to her in 1856, and the mother's anxiety for the child's future often had a baneful influence over French policy. This family of imperial upstarts and its amateurish court gave neither France nor the rest of the world any feeling of security; at Compiègne, policy 'seemed improvised like charades'. All the changes France had been subject to since 1789 had left their imprint on that policy. 'I am socialist,' the Emperor would say, 'the Empress is a legitimist, Morny is for the House of Orleans, Prince Napoleon is a republican; only Persigny is a Bonapartist, and he is mad.' Persigny, Minister of the Interior, had shared in the Emperor's earliest conspiracies, and Napoleon III was loyal to him out of gratitude; the Empress hated him because he had opposed her marriage.

Well intentioned but poorly counselled, Napoleon III began at a disadvantage. The Empire, which strove to combine a popular vote (the plebiscite) with hereditary power, was a hybrid regime; it had won the affections of the French in Napoleon I's time because France was then emerging from a frightful upheaval; exhausted by internal strife, bled white by the Terror, the country cried aloud for a peacemaker. Such was not the case in 1852. Throughout Europe, men's minds were generally turning towards parliamentary government and freedom of thought. In France, the middle-class businessmen and peasants, terrified at socialism ever since the June Days of 1848, as well as at the sudden revelation of the strength of the working class, had wanted a sword and voted for the Empire. Through disgust and discouragement the workers had remained passive. But with few exceptions, the country's best minds and the student population were never reconciled to the regime; the *coup d'état* was regarded as a crime; even the Empress herself remarked: 'It will be a millstone round his neck all his life.' Rebuffed by those whom he would have liked to allure, the Emperor could rely only on the interests which had created him and, like the Saint-Simonians, seek social progress through material prosperity. As we shall see, he succeeded fairly well, but prosperity has never compensated for freedom.

The early days of the regime were rather brilliant. In foreign policy, reasonable French people had feared that his theories might lead the Emperor to take a warlike attitude; would he demand the abrogation of the 1815 treaties, insist upon the natural frontiers, fly to the aid of oppressed national groups? Quite the opposite – he did everything he could to reassure the rest of Europe. Not that he renounced his great forebear's ambitions; but he knew that he must prevent the formation of a coalition in order to have any chance of achieving them, and that to do this he must remain on friendly terms with England, whose hatred had overthrown the First Empire. Now the British Government of that day was resolved to defend the Ottoman Empire against Russia; Napoleon III proposed an alliance against the Czar. The ensuing conflict meant to him a means of increasing his prestige by winning England to his cause, by appeasing the French liberals – who were the enemies of autocratic Russia and the friends of Poland – and, finally, by pleasing the Catholics, since the excuse for French intervention was the protection of the Holy Places. The Crimean War was far from easy, and at first the other side was victorious. 'This new Empire', wrote Victor Hugo, 'begins with 1812.' The campaign, however, ended in the fall of Sevastopol and a total Franco-British victory; the Zouaves at Malakoff and MacMahon with his famous, 'Here I am, here I stay', won their places amid the legendary heroes of the French army. The peace conference was held at Paris, thus confirming France's new-born prestige; the French Minister of Foreign Affairs, Napoleon I's illegitimate son, Count Walewski, presided. France obtained no material advantage, but she had at last broken the league of the sovereigns against the Revolution and had even, she believed, gained the friendship of England and of Prussia. As Austria was from then on isolated, Napoleon III's schemes for the liberation of Italy had entered the realm of the possible. Unfortunately, despite his illusions, he really possessed the friendship of neither England nor Prussia. Yet on the morrow of the Crimean War, having humbled Russia, France's only rival on the Continent, he could believe himself Europe's most potent sovereign.

France's internal prosperity seemed to match her apparent success abroad; the early achievements of authoritarian regimes often seem propitious, some years being required to make clear the dangers inherent in the lack of freedom. Napoleon III was sincerely concerned about the welfare of poor people; under his reign, charitable associations, day nurseries and mutual-aid societies grew in number; in many of the larger cities, working-class quarters were erected which were unbeautiful but an improvement on the hovels they replaced. Today such paternalism would seem offensive; then it was thought effective. Napoleon was even considering the establishment of workmen's retirement pensions; in 1864 he finally did away with the ban on workers' associations and acknowledged the right to strike. The conditions under which labour lived were still dreadful; the working day was twelve hours; in *l'Assommoir* and *Germinal*, Zola showed his readers the ravages of alcohol and promiscuity. Yet we must grant that the Empire did more to cure these evils than had the regimes before it, and it was able to do this because France's financial position was excellent. Never before had the country grown rich so quickly. Up to that time, private banks (Rothschild, Hottinguer, Mallet) had underwritten state loans and managed portfolios; a new breed of financiers — Pereire, Fould and later Germain — had the idea of turning to the public at large and soliciting that public's savings for investment. Thus were established the Crédit Mobilier (which did not succeed), the Crédit Foncier and, ultimately, the Crédit Industriel et Commercial, the Crédit Lyonnais and the Société Générale. First the lower middle class and then the peasants acquired the habit of investing in securities, and by this means large-scale, corporate capitalism developed.

Savings canalized by these banks, paid for France's economic development; the State encouraged railway construction and granted the systems a guarantee of the interest on their indebtedness. In 1842, France possessed only 336 miles of track (as against about 3600 in the United States and 1650 in England); in 1860 she had 5918; in 1870, 11,000. Transatlantic navigation companies were organized. Everywhere the regime fostered industrial concentration; iron and coal mines were given as concessions to powerful corporations. The managers of banks, transport companies and mines were chosen from among a small number of families; a capitalist oligarchy, in good part Protestant or Jewish, gradually replaced the numberless family businesses of an older France and thereby confirmed the socialists in their regard for Marx's teaching, which had foretold this centralization. In conformity with Saint-Simon's notions, great public works were undertaken to beautify the city of Paris, where poverty-stricken enclaves lay side by side with shiny newness; that city's prefect, Haussmann, a ruthless and arrogant man but a wonderful administrator, took on the task of supplying the capital with those broad avenues which the increased traffic and the tourists brought in by the new railways made imperative. The Emperor in person had laid out the plan to transform the Paris of the Old Regime into the city of today. Certain writers found fault with the rectilinear boulevards. 'This is Philadelphia; it is Paris no longer', wrote Théophile Gautier; he had never seen Philadelphia, and the Parisians of today are grateful to Haussmann for having spared their city congestion without having deprived it of its beauty. In 1855, a World's Fair attracted five million visitors who marvelled at France's industrial power. Technically, and from the point of view of national wealth, the Empire had imposing results to its credit. Its Council of State and its prefects were beyond dispute efficient, they were all too skilled at repression, but they were zealous administrators.

Yet, in spite of the success of its prosperity policy, the Empire was not a stable regime; it lacked that mysterious virtue, legitimacy. The adventurer seemed successful, but he remained none the less an adventurer; a muzzled public opinion was not convinced. A government which knows it is recognized as legitimate by the majority in the country has no fear of freedom; the imperial Government was so little sure of itself that it would not even allow the publication of the debates in a wholly domesticated Legislative Body. The newspapers, subject to censorship and to prior admonition, were cautious and pro-Government; even private conversations were subject to police surveillance: 'Only the Government speaks, and no one believes what it says.' The public got along as best it could; books by authors in exile (Victor Hugo, Edgar Quinet, Émile Deschanel, Louis Blanc) came in as contraband and won all the more readers because they were forbidden. The Orleans monarchists and the legitimists, although unable to agree among themselves and unite under one banner, joined in their fault-finding and constituted a so-called liberal group, extraordinary because of the abilities of such leaders as Thiers, Guizot, Montalembert, Dupanloup and Berryer. The French Academy was the stronghold of this intellectual Fronde; solemn addresses before it supplied opportunity for slightly veiled attacks against the Empire. 'Let's elect Lacordaire', said Victor Cousin, 'since we can't elect the Pope as a joke on the Empire.' However a few writers, such as Sainte-Beuve, Mérimée and Nisard, had attached themselves to the regime, allured by the Empress and the Princess Matilda; Sainte-Beuve went into the Imperial Senate, and the students clamorously upbraided him for it. As for the republicans, those who were not living in exile sought refuge in seclusion; whenever the exiles started plotting (which they did without skill and in vain, for they had lost contact with France and were fighting battles long out of date), new deportations at once afflicted their friends inside the country. When, in 1857, elections took place to renew the Legislative Body, the lack of all freedom of the press or of assembly, and the shameless placarding of official candidacies, discouraged the opposition. The requirement that every deputy should swear a personal oath to the Emperor kept out most of the republicans; between 1857 and 1863 the opposition in the Legislative Body consisted of only five members, among these being Émile Ollivier — whom many regarded as a new Thiers — Jules Favre and Ernest Picard. In 1859 Napoleon III felt strong enough to grant a full and absolute amnesty; Victor Hugo and Louis Blanc refused it; said Hugo: 'Until the end I shall share freedom's exile. When she returns, I shall return.'

The whole opposition was weak, and the Emperor could have overlooked a handful of malcontents had he not alienated two powerful conservative groups which until that time had supported him. A new phase in imperial policy was precipitated by a plot organized by the Italian *carbonari*, who could not forgive the Emperor Napoleon III for having forgotten the commitments of their 'brother', Louis Napoleon Bonaparte. In his youthful days he had espoused the cause of Italian independence, but once he had come to power, he had reversed his opinions and dispatched the Rome expedition in defence of the Pope's temporal power. In 1858 Orsini and three other Italian patriots hurled bombs at the Emperor's carriage, killing or wounding more than a hundred persons. This attempted assassination was followed by very harsh repressive measures, but it had surprising results in that it modified Napoleon III's Italian policy in the direction which Orsini desired. From his cell, the condemned man had written the Emperor beseeching him to give the Italians their freedom; were he to do this, his name would be loved and respected; were he not, the attempts would continue. In both the Empress and the Emperor this letter aroused fear and compassion; there was some question of a pardon for Orsini, who had suddenly become a hero; then the hero was guillotined, but the cause for which he died triumphed. The Emperor had a secret interview with Cavour, Minister of the King of Piedmont (and Castiglione's uncle); it was agreed that France would help the Italians to drive out the Austrians and, in return for its help, would obtain Savoy and the County of Nice.

This nationality policy, a favourite fancy of the Emperor's, seemed generous since France was going to help people of the same race, held apart by force, to unite; in fact it was fraught with danger. To establish new major States in Europe was to pave the way for fresh wars and, as far as France was concerned, to set up rivals, perhaps even enemies; for gratitude is never a collective virtue. The Italian war began in 1859; the Austrian army was defeated by the French at Magenta and Solferino.

All Italy, and especially the Romagna, rose against the Pope, whereupon the Empress and the French clerical party protested. Napoleon III hesitated and temporized; and when, counter to his expectations, Prussia took sides against Italy, he signed an armistice with Austria — thus alienating the Italians — and then advised the Pope to yield — which alienated the French clergy. Ultramontane and liberal Catholics, hitherto split, joined forces to demand that the Emperor protect the Pope. Napoleon III could not refuse Rome to Italy; was he not the champion of the principle of nationality? Ultimately he begrudgingly defended the Holy See; Pius IX, however, had already turned to the French legitimists and had accepted their offer of volunteers, the papal Zouaves, who hoisted the white banner of the monarchy. Thereupon, through a plebiscite, King Victor Emmanuel created Italian unity and seized the greater part of the Papal States; the Emperor had lost the Church's support without having won Italy's friendship and had succeeded in dissatisfying both liberals and clericals — a grave source of weakness in a France where the Church was more powerful than ever.

A second cause of discontent on the part of French conservatives was Napoleon III's free-trade policy. In this connection, as in the matter of nationalism, he was sincere and sought the State's welfare. Having lived in England in the days of the great debate over protection, and having observed the victory of free trade and the prosperity which followed, he was determined to push France towards international free trade. The French industrialists, however, protested. Secretly and without consulting them, the Emperor in 1860 negotiated a treaty with Great Britain which eliminated all embargoes, lowered all tariffs and, in return, obtained concessions for certain French products such as wine. There followed a general and most unjust outcry from all French industry; the manufacturers thought they were ruined and cursed the Government. Thus under attack from both clericals and capitalists, Napoleon was inclined to draw nearer to the mass of the people and the republicans — a tendency in the Bonapartist tradition and corresponding to the Emperor's personal preference. Thus began that new regime which was called the Liberal Empire.

CHAPTER VI

HOW THE EMPIRE BECAME LIBERAL AND HOW THE WAR OF 1870 BROUGHT ON ITS COLLAPSE

AFTER 1860 the Emperor and the Empire were on the decline. The Emperor, worn out by sensual excesses, was beset by a chronic and painful bladder complaint; the Empire faced growing opposition. The clericals embittered by the Roman question, accused the Emperor of having abandoned the Vatican; *l'Univers*, the Catholic publicist Veuillot's paper, was suppressed. When the clergy showed its hostility, the Government turned to repressive measures; it was forbidden to gather money for the Pope; the bishops' pastoral letters were made subject to a stamp tax and to prior examination by the authorities if they were of a political nature. Thereupon the Empress protested and the Emperor said to her: 'Eugénie, you surely forget two things — that you are a Frenchwoman and that you have married a Bonaparte.' By a seemingly paradoxical shift, the monarchist and clerical Right loudly clamoured for freedom of opinion, which could, at that moment, be serviceable to it. Thiers allied himself with the clericals, partly through ambition and partly through patriotism; he feared the long-range effects of the Emperor's ideas on nationalism and judged that it was necessary to win back parliamentary liberties. This task could only be effected by stages: first, the Legislative Body obtained the right annually to vote an address in reply to the speech from the throne; ministers without portfolio were appointed to defend the Government's policy; then publication of the debates was authorized. The Union Libérale, a conservative parliamentary group, together with the republicans obtained two million votes in the election of 1863, and this was doing well for opponents of the Government in a country where there existed neither freedom of the press nor freedom of assembly and where official candidacies were thick as flies.

Napoleon had been able to disregard the republican opposition; he could not without peril alienate the conservatives who had created him. Prince Napoleon would have preferred the Empire to veer towards Jacobinism and lean upon the workers: a great realist, Napoleon III knew himself to be a prisoner of the bourgeoisie. Since the middle class's taste for parliamentarianism was reawakening, concessions were in order; in the new Legislative Body, Thiers was able to champion 'the necessary liberties'. His audience was all the greater because spiritual liberties then seemed under threat from Pius IX's *Syllabus*, which condemned as 'monstrous' the nineteenth century's essential principles, declared the Church superior to the State, required for it a monopoly in education, admitted neither freedom of worship for non-Catholics nor freedom of the press, and in general reverted to the teaching of the most absolutist popes in the Middle Ages. There was a certain degree of challenge in this attitude, as well as the desire to create a difficult situation for Napoleon III; but liberal Catholicism was the principal victim of the new Vatican policy, and popular Christianity received a blow from which it did not recover for a quarter of a century. As for the Emperor, he was always enthralled by vast and complex schemes; as early as 1861 he had taken it into his head to revive his prestige among the clericals and in military circles by intervention in Mexico, where two factions, one anti-clerical (that of the dictator, Juarez) and the other Catholic, were vying for power. Mexico reputedly possessed fabulous riches; the financiers who had risked some of their capital there, wanted to install a European emperor — the Habsburg, Maximilian, brother of Austria's Emperor, Franz Joseph. Napoleon III had been won over; in his youth he had studied a plan for an inter-oceanic canal in Nicaragua, and he hoped above all that by founding under his own protection a Catholic Latin empire, he would combat throughout the whole world the influence of Protestant and Anglo-Saxon liberalism.

This 'grand scheme of the reign' was dangerous, not because Maximilian, a man of good character, was other than a desirable sovereign, but because the Mexicans had no use for an emperor, least of all a European emperor. In this adventure French troops suffered futile losses, and France wasted strength of which she was to have only too great need in a Europe where the Italian precedent had awakened all hopes and raised all questions anew. She was unable to force Maximilian down Mexican throats; Juarez retained his power in such regions as were not occupied by French troops, and Maximilian himself had neither money nor an army. In 1865, the United States, having regained freedom of action through Northern victory in the Civil War, reaffirmed the Monroe Doctrine, which suffered no interference by European Powers on the American continent. It supplied Juarez with arms. Napoleon III had to recall Bazaine; Juarez seized the unfortunate Maximilian and had him shot, while his wife, Carlotta, rushed as a suppliant to Saint-Cloud, where she threw herself on the floor before the Emperor, then dashed to implore the Pope in Rome and, having obtained nothing, finally went mad. Such was the appalling balance sheet of an operation to which the French public not improperly ascribed motives of personal profit and which brought on further internal troubles. France was heartily weary of the Emperor's great notions. 'It's all very well to study the life of Caesar, but for God's sake, Sire, study it during the leisure which would be afforded you by a thorough and certain peace.' The need for rest was general; in the Legislative Body, an alliance was being arranged between Bonapartists tired of personal power and liberals tired of sterile opposition. Émile Ollivier had broken with the Left, Louis Buffet with the authoritarian imperialists; between those who wanted to overthrow the Empire and those who wanted it dictatorial, a third party was coming into being.

Meanwhile, with cynical genius, Bismarck played on Napoleon III's illusions. His nationality policy had embroiled the French Emperor with Austria because of the support he had lent the Italians in their efforts towards national unity, and it had embroiled him with Russia because he favoured a free Poland; it led him to accept, in contempt of the law, Prussia's annexation of the Danish provinces of Schleswig and Holstein. The Emperor was not alarmed at seeing Prussia become the centre of a North German Confederation since he imprudently believed that thereafter Germany would look for French support. When in 1865 Bismarck asked him for an interview at Biarritz and, with seeming frankness, announced that he was going to declare war against Austria in order to expel her from the Germanic Confederation, that he was going to revise the German Constitution and make an alliance with Italy, and that, in return for French neutrality, he would gladly permit France to gain certain territorial compensations, once again Napoleon was seduced. He thought that here was a means of making good his Mexican reverses by tearing up the 1815 treaties. Crafty Bismarck had been careful not to put anything in writing. His war against Austria in 1866 was a triumph won within a few weeks, which for the first time displayed the scientific and industrial nature of modern warfare: quick mobilization, superior weapons and the systematic use of railways led to Prussia's lightning victory, and she speedily set up the Confederation of North Germany. The only risk Bismarck had run was the mobilization of the French army along the Rhine at a moment when German strength was concentrated in Austria; by forceful pressure at that critical instant, Napoleon III could have won concessions for France. But such an opportunity comes only once; when Napoleon claimed his reward, it was too late. He asked for Mainz, at least; Bismarck made mock of this 'innkeeper's note'. Belgium? Bismarck quickly informed England, which loyal to her traditional phobias (the 'Antwerp pistol'), screamed to high heaven and turned against Napoleon III. Luxemburg? All Germany protested against the yielding of an area considered Germanic. Meanwhile, Italy made an alliance with the victors in order to obtain Venezia. And so the 1815 treaties had been scrapped and the principal of nationality had triumphed over the principle of legitimacy, but to the advantage of Prussia.

Nothing fails like failure. Against an Empire victorious in the Crimea and Italy, the opposition had been powerless; disaster in Mexico and diplomatic defeats in Europe shifted the equilibrium of internal forces; annoyed and humiliated, the country began to support such members of parliament as were inimical to the regime. Although it was forbidden in France, Hugo's *Châtiments* was surreptitiously circulated and rekindled men's hatred. As the waves of public opinion broke over the head of an emperor weary and ill, he little by little gave ground. The right of questioning members of the Government from the floor was restored to the Chambers; Thiers told the ministers: 'There is no mistake left for you to make.' In a public speech, Napoleon himself referred to 'black specks which darken the horizon'. Sainte-Beuve, hitherto in disrepute because of his acceptance of the *status quo*, found new prestige by defending freedom of thought in the Senate against an ultramontane offensive. Aroused by Garbaldian attacks on the Pope, the clericals called for a second Rome expedition and for a purge of France's teaching personnel. Yielding to the Right, Napoleon undertook once again to defend the Pope's temporal power, and then, yielding to the liberals, lessened the severity of the press laws. Henri Rochefort, Marquis of Rochefort-Luçay, took advantage of this to establish *La Lanterne*, a weekly sheet which was disrespectful and witty. The first number included the famous gibe: 'France numbers thirty-six million subjects, without counting its subjects for complaint', as well as this *Dialogue in a Café*: (A customer asks for a newspaper.) 'Waiter! *La France!*' — 'As soon as it's free, sir.' — 'I shall have to wait a long time.' Here was no work of genius, but each Thursday a hundred thousand copies of *La Lanterne* amused Parisians at the regime's expense. A committee was set up to gather funds for a monument to Victor

Baudin, one of the victims of the *coup d'état*. Those who contributed were prosecuted, and their trial afforded an opportunity to a young lawyer, Gambetta, to attack the Empire with such eloquence that he became one of the heroes of the younger generation. His peroration delighted Paris. 'For seventeen years now', said he to those in authority, 'you have been France's absolute masters ... We do not seek to discover what use you have made of her treasures, of her blood, of her honour, and of her glory ... What best condemns you, because it is evidence of your own remorse, is the thing which you have never dared to say: "We shall celebrate the Second of December as a national holiday." Well, that anniversary you have not yourselves wanted we shall take over to our own use. Each year it will be the anniversary of our dead until that day when the country, having resumed mastery, will require your expiation ...' Thenceforward the republicans had a leader. 'This Gambetta', remarked the Emperor, who believed that every man had his price, 'really has a great deal of talent. Is there no way in which we can calm him down? There was no way. The Government had become so feeble that he had great difficulty in getting Marshal Niel's military legislation passed by the Chamber, even though this was absolutely essential because of the recently demonstrated superiority of the German army. In its fury, political partisanship even forgot the lasting interests of the country.

Could the Emperor have fallen back on the working people? He could not. In 1851 the workers had allowed the *coup d'état* to come off because of their hatred for the middle-class republic; but for the last ten years they had been keeping their distance. At the urging of Proudhon, they had joined together in mutual-aid societies; then international socialism, as defined by Marx and Lassalle, had filled them with the greatest hopes. The Emperor had given them a few vague reforms; Marx promised them the social revolution. In 1789, he told them, the bourgeoisie had triumphed over feudalism; one day the proletariat would overcome the bourgeoisie; and after this last revolution, society would no longer be divided into classes, since the means of production would belong to the workers. In 1863, while a number of French working men were on a visit to London, the International had been established; in 1866 and 1867 it had held congresses and had called for the nationalization of transportation systems, mines, forests and telegraphs. The number of individual memberships was small and the total of dues tiny, but in France labour organizations adhered to the International as groups; 'white overalls' sang the *Marseillaise* along the boulevards. In his *Germinal*, Zola has portrayed the role of the International in the strikes of that day, which were often bloody. Many of the bourgeoisie began to speak with terror of world revolution; the imperial Government feared it, employing troops against the strikers; and the socialist workers, as the middle-class liberals had already done, severed their ties with the regime. On every occasion the opposition openly showed its resentment towards the Emperor, and he no longer dared retaliate; he was branded as a Caligula or a Heliogabalus; people referred to 'the Spanish woman' as they had formerly to the Austrian. During the distribution of prizes awarded after the annual secondary-school competition young Cavaignac refused to receive his academic laurels from the hands of the Prince Imperial and, when the Empress complained, the Emperor replied: 'Sooner or later, Louis must surely come to know the opposition.' This placid resignation encouraged attack: the 'Badinguet' family had as many songs written about it as had formerly Louis-Philippe's.

The 1869 elections reflected the disaffection of the French people; government candidates harvested four and a half million votes; those of the opposition, four million three hundred thousand. If you take into account the official pressure in favour of the former, here was a triumph for the latter. Rochefort had been elected to a Paris seat (in the by-elections); Gambetta, who had stood as an 'irreconcilable', became deputy for Belleville. Even the country districts were affected by the Government. The middle party could now round up one hundred and sixteen votes — in conjunction with Thiers and his monarchist associates, a majority. 'At the Tuileries', said Mérimée, 'there was nervousness. The feeling was like that aroused by Mozart's music when the Commendatore is about to appear ...' Against the advice of the Mamelukes of the authoritarian Empire, the Emperor decided that he must surrender and amended the Constitution; the 1870 *Senatus consultum* was to be, for the Second Empire, what the Additional Act had been for the First; henceforth the Legislative Body would, like the Emperor, be able to initiate laws, and the budget would be voted item by item. Ministers would be responsible to the Chambers, but the Emperor would have the right to appeal from them to the people. The Empress and the Mamelukes opposed this plan, but vainly; the Emperor was secretly bargaining with the middle party, and on January 2nd, 1870, Émile Ollivier was entrusted with the selection of a cabinet. Napoleon III should have summoned Thiers, who had had more experience, but Thiers would have insisted on curbing the Emperor's power to that of a constitutional sovereign; Émile

Ollivier, who was more pliant, was also younger, and this seemed fitting if there were to be a completely new deal. 'We shall afford the Emperor a happy old age', was the way Ollivier put it; he meant what he said, and his ministry was at first well received; the Academy, an opposition stronghold, elected the Prime Minister to Lamartine's seat. Yet the pessimists remarked that freedom would finally crown the structure 'at that moment when its foundations gave way', and Gambetta remained unreconciled. 'Between the 1848 Republic and the Republic of the Future, you are merely a bridge', said he to the Government, 'and it is we who shall pass over it.'

In conformity with the Empire's principles, these liberal reforms were submitted to a plebiscite in May 1870. The republicans had tried to oppose this procedure; one of them, Jules Grévy, had said that if the principle of an appeal to the people were maintained, the Assembly would be powerless and the citizen would be handed over to the Executive, which, on a question *framed as the Government chose*, would put the citizen between 'the abyss and the acceptance of the accomplished fact'. Crémieux established an anti-plebiscite committee, but the Government frightened the press by law suits, prosecuted republicans for conspiracy and easily carried the day. The question set before the electors was ambiguous, because those who had drawn it up had adroitly confused two problems in it — the problem of the regime and the problem of reforms. There were seven million three hundred and fifty-eight thousand yeas, and one million five hundred and seventy-one thousand nays; Paris and the large cities of the south were the only opposition citadels; all the country districts were in favour of the Empire. After the results had been made known, Gambetta sadly remarked: 'The Empire is stronger than ever.' Internally, this was true, but in foreign affairs all the storm warnings were out. Bismarck, now certain of France's isolation, because England feared her and Austria reprehended her, and certain also of the strength of the German army, had been deliberately seeking an excuse for war ever since 1866. 'I was sure', he wrote later, 'that we must have a German-French war in order to achieve the organization of Germany.' What opposition could the French Empire afford this pitiless realist? A sovereign worn out and vacillating, perhaps generous, but mentally confused and put in the falsest of positions by his nationality principle; an unpopular Government, the butt of the newspapers and of youth; an intelligent but dangerously optimistic Prime Minister who asserted that never had the continuance of peace in Europe been more certain; an army which, despite

Marshal Niel's legislation, continued to be neglected. On June 30th, 1870, the Legislative Body sustained Ollivier against Thiers's advice and voted a reduction in the number of standing troops. Flying in the face of the evidence, France was gambling on peace.

Germany was gambling on war. In 1868, Queen Isabella II having been overthrown, the Spanish crown was offered to Prince Leopold of Hohenzollern-Sigmaringen, brother of the Rumanian Prince Regent (later King Carol I) and a relative of the King of Prussia. In the French Parliament the reaction was unanimously hostile; speakers recalled the Empire of Charles V, feared a France caught in a vice were German might allowed to penetrate Spain, and the breakdown of the balance of power in Europe. 'Rarely have we seen such agreement reigning among the organs of the various parties', wrote Francis Magnard in *Figaro*.[1] Jules Simon, Thiers and Gambetta were at one with the Empire's journalists in their protests against this intolerable proposal. To the great surprise of everyone, the Hohenzollern candidacy was withdrawn on July 12th; here was peace with honour. Said Ollivier to Thiers, who was urging prudence 'Rest easy. We have peace in our grasp; we shall not let it slip away.' Then personal vanity came into play: the Empress, Ollivier and the Minister for Foreign Affairs, the Duke of Gramont, each sought personal triumph. The refusal of the Spanish crown had not emanated from the King of Prussia but from Leopold's father; against Thiers's advice, Gramont had the absurd idea of demanding that William I should forbid the Prince to reverse his decision. This vexed the King, and he informed the French Ambassador, Benedetti, that he considered the matter closed and, when Benedetti grew insistent, he refused to receive him. The German reply was in no way offensive, but in it Bismarck saw an opportunity to start the war he had wanted; he shortened the telegram, which King William had forwarded him from Ems in order to keep him informed, thus giving it an abrupt and peremptory tone which was not characteristic of the original text. When Bismarck showed this revised version to his generals, Moltke and Roon, he made no secret of the fact that he expected it to lead to war; the generals approved. 'It is in our interest', said they, 'to precipitate the conflict.' Both Gramont and Ollivier charged at the red rag which Bismarck dangled before them; Gramont referred to 'a slap in the face which had just been given him' Before the Legislative Body Ollivier proclaimed war and requested credits. Thiers alone protested; Ollivier replied that he accepted this

---

[1] Quoted by ALBERT GUÉRARD.

responsibility 'with a light heart'. In the streets of Paris, the crowds cried out, 'Hurrah for the war! On to Berlin!' From Gavroche the street urchin to the Prince Imperial, all youth was singing the *Marseillaise*; but in the provinces, seventy-one prefects out of eighty-seven said that the war was accepted only with hesitation and regret. Never had an international cataclysm been set in motion on a flimsier excuse.

Germany had prepared for war. France had to improvise. Niel had suggested a plan of organization and mobilization which had not been put into effect. A French reservist in the north had to journey far south to reach his mobilization point — or else it might be far west — only subsequently to have to travel east in order to reach the front, and from this arose frightful confusion in transport. The infantry weapon (the Chassepot rifle) was good, but the artillery's guns were inferior to the enemy's, and the supply services were less than nothing. Food, ammunition, ambulances — everything was lacking. This did not prevent Marshal Lebœuf from saying: 'We are ready, more than ready ... Were the war to last a year, we should not have to buy so much as a button for a pair of leggings ...' But the greatest German superiority lay in the quality of the men in command. The army leaders of the Second Empire had been trained in campaigns which were either easy (Italy), colonial (Algeria) or positional (Crimea); they were utterly ignorant of how to wage a war of movement. Some of them did not even know how to read a map. Moltke, a great general, had behind him, as head of the civil government, a man of genius, Bismarck. Napoleon III, who wanted to take active command of the army even though he had 'a stone as big as a pigeon's egg' in his bladder, left behind him in Paris only the unfortunate Empress and an unpopular Government. The soldiers and the officers fought bravely, but what could they do without leadership? From the very beginning the campaign was disastrous. In two days the Germans had won two victories, had broken across the frontier and had invaded Alsace and Lorraine; excitement throughout the country reached so high a pitch that on August 12th the Emperor had to transfer command to Marshal Bazaine, of Mexican fame. Bazaine, weak and irresolute, retreated and let slip the last fleeting opportunities for victory, allowing the enemy to cut off the army of Lorraine at Metz. There remained the armies of Alsace and of Châlons; MacMahon, who commanded them, wanted to fall back towards Paris; the Empress as regent informed him that if he abandoned Bazaine, revolution would follow. He accepted certain defeat, was surrounded at Sedan on September 2nd, and surrendered.

The war was barely a month old; it was lost and the Emperor was held captive. Shortly afterwards he sought asylum in England.

Thus began the baneful period of German hegemony in Europe. For the second time the Empire, a monarchy by popular vote, left France invaded and at the mercy of her enemies; for the second time a Bonapartist regime, lacking deep roots, had been swept away in a few hours by the wind of defeat. Although he was without the least evil intention, the man who had personified this regime bore a heavy share of responsibility; the Emperor's ideas, sometimes brilliant, sometimes generous, often imprudent and then chimerical, had greatly helped in handing Europe over to Prussia. Nevertheless, some of the best of Frenchmen remained faithful to him. 'Despite the idle and stupid outcries of the populace', wrote Louis Pasteur, 'and all the cowardly betrayals of these latter days, the Emperor can await with confidence the judgment of posterity.' Posterity has condemned the repressive harshness which followed after the *coup d'état*, the crushing of liberty, the wars for prestige. Yet it has acknowledged that the Emperor's social ideas were in advance of his day, and that the parliamentary leaders shared responsibility with the sovereign for the war of 1870. The truth of the matter was that France, between 1850 and 1870, had lost much of its demographic, industrial and military importance. This did not mean that the country had to abdicate, but it did call for wise diplomacy and an effort as dogged as Richelieu's to prevent the erection of a German bloc. The great mistake made by Napoleon III and his subjects was their forgetfulness of the traditional conditions for France's survival.

CHAPTER VII

HOW ROMANTICISM WAS SUPERSEDED

IN France, the first half of the nineteenth century had been a marvellous age for literature, as richly endowed with writers of genius as the Renaissance or the early years of classicism; with the Second Empire began a twilight of the Gods. Victor Hugo, who had not accepted the *coup d'état*, lived in exile until the end of the regime, first on Jersey and then on Guernsey; as a writer, this was his salvation, for exile rescued him from politics and afforded him the leisure to compose such great works as *Les Misérables*. But his absence deprived the romantic school of its most brilliant leader. As for Lamartine, his political downfall had made him into a needy writer condemned to producing potboilers; finally he accepted a pension from Napoleon III, who, with that generosity which was natural to him, offered it unconditionally to one of his most steadfast opponents. Even had it retained its leaders, romanticism was due for a change; its feeling of freshness had worn off, needs were different, readers had lost their faith. The French of 1852 had seen so many regimes crumble that they had become cynical and thought everything was humbug; before 1830, some among them had believed in the throne and the altar; before 1848, in the people and progress. Restoration and revolution had been equally disappointing. What was left? Science? Industry? Here many pinned their hopes, and the school of Saint-Simon had brilliantly graduated from the theoretical to the practical level, but others had bitterly observed the mediocrity of those who made the wheels of business turn, the stupidity of accepted notions; expecting nothing further from the world of reality, these sought asylum in the perfection of art.

Romanticism had been an escape into the past, into the future, into exoticism and the fantastic; all these paths were now well trodden and therefore closed: only one remained open to the artists — escape into technique. In the contrived paradises of art, human conventions preserved a certain value; if the poet could not help suffering or despising his own day, at least he could inject some order and beauty into the evocation of his unhappiness. The creation of perfect forms without other purpose than to create forms served Baudelaire, Flaubert and the Parnassian poets as a solution. Flaubert, born a romantic and at heart remaining

a romantic, a fanatical devotee of Hugo, Goethe and Byron, nevertheless understood that romanticism was a mistake, a flight from reality,
and he wrote the most anti-romantic of all novels, *Madame Bovary*,
'which is to romanticism what *Don Quixote* had been to the romances
of chivalry'.[1] Flaubert sought to depict meanness and mediocrity, Voltaireanism debased in Homais, Christianity debased in the Abbé Bournisien, science debased in Charles Bovary, love debased in Rodolphe and
Léon. What else remained?

The romantic poet had had a fondness for confessions, but his confessions had been glorious; his loves may have been unhappy, they
remained none the less heroic. Baudelaire, on the other hand, took man's
misery into account; to that rhetoric of love which was Emma Bovary's
downfall, he contrasted a realistic view of sin and vice; he was more
Christian than the Catholic and monarchist choirboys of 1815. He reminds us of Racine; he points the way to Rimbaud, Verlaine and Mauriac;
his choice lay with 'awareness in the midst of evil' and — ultimate escape —
with death: 'Oh, death! old captain, the time has come! Let us weigh
anchor!' Leconte de Lisle, leader of the Parnassian school, issued an
identical summons:

> And thou, divine death, made to encompass all and all erase,
>   Welcome us the living to thy star-decked breast,
> Free us of time, of number, and of space,
>   Restore to us what daily life has troubled — rest.

Yet this nihilism remained verbal; Leconte de Lisle and his Parnassian
followers were to come to satisfactory terms with their despair, and most
of them, as Thibaudet put it, died in the harness of the civil service.
They talked a lot about death; they had not the least desire to seek
him out.

Under the Second Empire the bulk of the bourgeoisie found escape
in pleasure; the regime allowed little political freedom, so to the devil
with politics! Never had Paris been more frivolous or more brilliant.
The theatre was having a rebirth — realistic and middle-class comedies
by Émile Augier; moralizing and middle-class comedies by Alexander
Dumas *fils*; middle-class comic sketches by Labiche, which for fifty
years were to delight audiences at the Palais Royal; and finally dazzling
operetta by Meilhac and Halévy, set to the music of Offenbach. The
whole world rushed to Paris to be entertained by all this sparkle and

[1] THIBAUDET.

gaiety. No longer were the French provinces cut off from the capital; thanks to the railways, every provincial bourgeois yearly came to spend his few days in Paris and make the rounds of the theatres; no longer would a play run for fifteen or twenty performances, as in Molière's day, but for a hundred. New cafés opened, adorned with padded red plush, illuminated with gilt chandeliers; Garnier's opera house, which has a beauty of its own, symbolized the wealth of the day and its liking for the new rococo. There Gounod and Ambroise Thomas had their triumphs. Famous courtesans made conquests which even included the Emperor; La Païva built herself a palace on the Champs Élysées, and the gossips said: 'All it lacks is a pavement for her to walk her beat.' Scandal mongering — 'very Parisian' — was a gold mine for the newspapers; Villemessant dedicated the *Figaro* to the memory of Beaumarchais, Jean Jacques Weiss put the *Débats* under Voltaire's patronage. Never were talented journalists more numerous. The spirit of the Boulevards — quick, light in touch, superficial — became famous throughout Europe, while at the same time spreading the false impression that France was a flighty country. Offenbach's music and Meilhac and Halévy's librettos impertinently poked fun at everything which other ages had treated with respect. The bacchanal in *Orphée aux Enfers*, the quadrille in *La Vie Parisienne*, the parodies in *La Belle Hélène* swept away gods and men in the wild gyrations of a frenzied dance. In Victorian England, where appearances, at least, were kept austere, the yellow-backed French novel was tucked away to avoid scandal; the English journeyed to Paris to have their fling, and then found fault with Paris for the pleasures they had gone there to enjoy.

But the Boulevards were not France; never had that country brought forth a more vigorous generation of critics, essayists and historians. In 1863 Littré published his *Dictionnaire de la Langue Française*, a major work for the excellence of the examples he culled to illustrate usages and for its scientific philological knowledge. Sainte-Beuve was the critical sovereign, and his Monday essays made and unmade reputations; he painted for the French a vast gallery of literary and historical portraits in which were mingled the learning of a scholar and the analytical subtlety of a novelist. More than any other, Sainte-Beuve, the prime champion of the romantics, did his share to preserve France's liking for and tradition of the great classics. A generation of historians infinitely better informed and more methodical than that of 1830 tried to extract from the flux of events ideas of more general import. After his discovery of American democracy, Alexis de Tocqueville wrote *l'Ancien Régime et la Révolution*, a book of substance in which Taine was to find basic material for his *O igines de la France contemporaine*. Taine and Renan and Fustel de Coulanges were preparing themselves to make history more intelligible through their great works of synthesis. In 1863 Renan published his *Life of Jesus*; it shocked many people, but the Emperor none the less retained him in the chair of History at the Collège de France. Meanwhile, Michelet continued his tempestuous writings in which flashed forth, beneath the thunderheads of an excessive lyricism, marvellous lightning flashes; and Prévost-Paradol, journalist, historian and one of the Second Empire's most intelligent men, wrote prophetic books on the effects of the doctrine of nationalities. Germany in those days had learned historians but none capable of uniting learning and style as did Tocqueville or Renan.

During the days of the liberal Empire, reaction against romanticism produced realism; the romantic wanted escape, the realist came back to earth and often wallowed in it. Hugo, Dumas, Sand, Eugène Sue and above all Balzac had tried to fashion worlds: 'Their motto was that of their leader, competition with the facts of life; and those facts were symbolized by the public registry office. Towards 1850 this competition abated. As regards the registry office, the novelists had changed from being its competitors to being its employees. Realism had arrived.'[1] The Goncourts were the first masters of this school (*Manette Salomon, Charles Demailly*), since Flaubert belonged to the transition and was above all schools; but Flaubert's disciples, Maupassant and Daudet, were realists. As for Zola, he was the heir at once of realism, of Balzac's ideas on reshaping the world and of the Darwinian scientific apparatus. He set himself the task of writing the natural and social history of a family under the Second Empire, with a genealogical tree and a full account of hereditary influences the whole to take up thirty-two volumes; he wanted the novel to be a scientific experiment (in naturalism) — which is obviously fanciful. But the war of 1870 and the later decay of the Great Families were to lend some semblance of the laboratory to this study in the disintegration of a class. Zola was likewise one of the first to praise the realistic painters at a time when Courbet and Manet were acutely disturbing both public and critics. Their vigorous, sometimes brutal, art annoyed the newly rich of the Second Empire — as sentimental in their tastes as they were cynical in their business dealings. Manet, who rightly believed that he was continuing the great tradition of Velasquez and Goya, became the object of a very

[1] Thibaudet.

423

real persecution; his *Déjeuner sur l'herbe* and his *Olympia* were considered shocking. Courbet sought to create a democratic art, and his *Enterrement à Ornans* was an attempt to translate Zola into painting, but his strong and sensual nudes were beautiful in their own right, above all schools. In the musical world, Charles Gounod readily triumphed — and for good reason. At the same time, however, the great Hector Berlioz, crushed by the critics, died in 1869 without any acknowledgment of his genius.

The 1871 defeat reduced to silence those writers who had rallied to the Empire; Mérimée, one of France's best prose stylists, died conscious of the decadence of a society he had loved. Prévost-Paradol committed suicide. France, jolted back to serious-mindedness by disaster, was above all to give heed to writers who could enlighten her on the causes of her unhappiness. Taine, through his *Origines de la France contemporaine*, and Renan, through his *Réforme intellectuelle et morale de la France*, became the diagnosticians of the political disease which for almost a century had weakened the country. They themselves turned to the scholars in their quest for analogies and for advice — Berthelot's influence on Renan is well known. As for the aged Hugo, who returned from exile the moment the regime collapsed, he was to know the glory of being a political patriarch under the Third Republic, during a period when literature was far removed from everything he had loved. The Empire's downfall brought no intellectual disaster in its wake. Far from it. The 1815 defeat had given birth to the Children of the Century and a literature of escape; by contrast, the 1871 defeat invigorated the best men and brought them back to reality.

CHAPTER VIII

CONCLUSION

THE years between 1815 and 1870 were distinguished in France by the instability and multiplicity of her regimes; while swearing his oath to Louis-Philippe, Talleyrand said with a smile: 'Well, well, Sire, this is my thirteenth . . .' Men who had so often given and then withdrawn their allegiance could not have faith in the legitimacy of any power; yet power has value only through legitimacy, which means the almost unanimous adhesion of those governed; the minute this is lacking, there ensue anarchy, unsettled minds, civil strife. The French Revolution had stripped the kings of their majesty; thereafter, where in France did legitimacy lie? Did it remain an attribute of the senior branch of the Bourbons? Some still believed this, and in 1870 there were many unrepentant monarchists who wanted to restore Henry V to the French throne; but in the national memory, the shadow of Charles X darkened his family's prestige. The people of Paris proudly remembered that they had twice overthrown this branch of the Bourbons; the republicans feared that it continued to head the party of reaction and vengeance. What of the junior branch? It possessed no sort of legitimacy, having neither heredity nor popular loyalty on its side. The Empire? Napoleon III in his exile was still hopeful and said: 'I alone can unravel the situation', but Bonapartism in its wish to be at once hereditary and Jacobin implied such contradictions that that regime would never again be possible. The Republic? Here lay the logical solution, since universal suffrage had been established and accepted. Yet in the eyes of many aristocrats and members of the middle class, it was intermingled with the Terror and with disorder. Thus any regime would divide the French; the bloody ditch was still unfilled.

Where did the country's power really lie? An alliance had been cemented between what remained of the old aristocracy, the upper bourgeoisie and the large landed proprietors; these 'notables' had in fact run the country under Louis-Philippe, and they had discovered men of worth to represent them in office. The Duke of Broglie, Guizot and Thiers had shown themselves the match of the best ministers under the Old Regime. During the days of the Second Empire this team had disappeared from the public eye and Napoleon III's coterie had reigned supreme; financiers and speculators but men of action also, had shared in the great adventure. Pereire, Fould, d'Eichtal and Mallet, while making their own fortunes, had enriched France; by digging the Suez Canal, de Lesseps had brought his country world renown. For a long time Louis-Philippe's prudent bankers had warily watched a generation they thought too bold; then they had joined forces with it. After the fall of the Empire, the alliance of wealth and birth presented a substantially united front. Some regretted Louis-Philippe, others Napoleon III, and a few Charles X, but all dreamed the same dreams for the future. They saw confronting them a vast and mysterious force — universal suffrage. What would emerge from it, and what did the French people desire in 1870? In 1848 the mass of the peasants had shown itself conservative; until the very end, the Empire had won heavy majorities. The Church remained powerful. The Notables had some reason to hope that the voters would once again entrust them with the country's government.

But another current was beginning to flow. The enrichment of the country had not been limited to a few families of merchant princes; a great body of small industrialists, of small traders, conscious of their success, were demanding consideration. In every provincial city, the professors, doctors, lawyers, notaries, chemists and veterinary surgeons constituted a liberal group thirsting for equality, richly endowed with talent, which some day might well challenge the pre-eminence of the Notables. The urban population was growing at the expense of the rural; it was above all made up of workers who had not won from the Second Empire the same advantages as the bourgeoisie. Nurtured on a respect for economic liberalism, Napoleon III had abandoned the working class to the inter-play of the law of supply and demand, and this had operated to the employers' profit because the employees were unorganized. Hence there came about a rebirth of republicanism and socialism, the populace of the great cities finding as mouthpieces such lawyers as Gambetta or Grévy. The Church's influence, which in the country districts operated to the advantage of the Notables, was weaker in the cities; ever since Darwin, a conflict had brought science and religion into opposition, and a new Voltaireanism was engendering a new anti-clericalism. Flaubert, in the persons of his chemist Homais, and his Abbé Bournisien, depicted the more petty aspects of anti-clericalism and clericalism under the Second Empire. Republicanism, socialism and anti-clericalism were just means to continue the Revolution, or to protect its conquests.

At the moment when the Empire crumbled, France's foreign policy was far more important than her domestic policy. Within a few years the map of Europe had changed; France no longer held first place – a sad fact for the French, but one which every reasonable and honest statesman had to take into account. For this phenomenon there were several reasons. The Empire's enemies blamed its inefficiency, the decadence into which it had allowed the army to sink, the immorality of the regime. Although he was a republican, Freycinet would have none of this explanation: 'We must not, through ignorance, excessive humility, or party spirit, allow it to be said by those around us that France has been unworthy of herself. Those who assert this are embittered by misfortune or blinded by passion.' The Emperor's most serious mistake had been his defence of the principle of nationality; in the name of this abstract idea he had, with his own hands, brought into the world great countries to rival France; thenceforward there was to be in Europe not merely, as under the Old Regime, an Austria, but a Germany unified, powerful and aggressive. France, with twenty-five million inhabitants, had once been able to recruit armies which held all Europe in check, but her neighbours' rate of population growth had been more rapid than her own. From 1870 on, France was to remain a great Power, but she would no longer be the first Power on the Continent. The mistakes of the Empire had made this situation clear to everyone; they had not created it.

If the 'time of wavering' had produced a France militarily less potent, it none the less left her wealthy and prosperous; never had she grown richer than under the July Monarchy and the Second Empire. This prosperity was in part linked to the industrial revolution of the nineteenth century; the enrichment of England, Germany and Belgium was coeval with that of France; it was likewise due to the interest governments then took in the development of industry, of means of communication and of city planning. In their day these great public works brought scandal in their wake; they made it possible for men to accumulate fortunes far too rapidly, but they afforded later generations indispensable tools, and if, under the Second Empire, the Boulevards were spendthrift, the lower middle class, the provincials and the country people proved themselves loyal to the thrifty traditions of the French peasant. In 1870, the 'old stocking' was stuffed with gold. This was to be demonstrated when the provisional Government, in order to free France of foreign soldiery, had to borrow, and its loans were oversubscribed, fourteen times as much being offered as the amount needed. The man with savings, were he of the upper or lower middle class, shopkeeper or farmer, was then becoming all-powerful. For a long time Governments which had come to power through universal suffrage were not to last long unless they were approved by the restricted suffrage of those who held the purse strings and took their advice from the bankers. Until the 1939 war, radical or socialist Governments in France were to be stopped short by the 'wall of money'.

BOOK SIX

THE THIRD REPUBLIC

CHAPTER I

THE GOVERNMENT OF NATIONAL DEFENCE

GOVERNMENT survives serious military defeat only if it is both old and strong. The Second Empire was still bent on adventure, and Sedan killed it. It was not a revolution, but a collapse — there was no bloodshed and no one tried to breathe new life into the Empire. The moment the Legislative Body had listened on September 3rd to the reading of Napoleon III's telegram, 'The army is defeated and captured; I myself am a prisoner', Jules Favre, in the name of the Left, moved for dethronement; but no party wished to inaugurate the new regime and thus assume responsibility for an arduous peace. On the fourth, Thiers suggested, 'seeing that the throne was vacant', the naming of a Government Committee of National Defence. The people of Paris, who wanted a republic, swarmed into the galleries; firmly Gambetta called upon this crowd to respect freedom of debate, the very first condition of popular emancipation: 'It is in the name of the fatherland as in the name of political freedom — two things I shall never dissociate — that I adjure you to be calm.' The deposition of Napoleon III and the dynasty was announced, but the mob continued to clamour for the republic; in order to clear the Palais Bourbon, Jules Favre, the leader of the Left, cried out: 'This is not the right place to proclaim the Republic', and, with Gambetta, he drew the demonstrators off towards the Hôtel de Ville — a skilful move, for the tradition of the Hôtel de Ville was mandatory on any Parisian crowd. There a revolutionary party was already drawing up its list — Blanqui, Félix Pyat, Flourens. But the crowd yelled, 'The Paris deputies!' and the latter formed the Government Committee of National Defence. In it Jules Favre and Jules Simon represented the moderate bourgeoisie, Crémieux and Garnier-Pagès the memories of 1848 and Gambetta radicalism. Thiers, who preferred to await a regularly elected government, had refused to serve, but had done so without hostility and in words of great dignity, which left the way open to an appeal to his experience and prestige: 'I cannot approve of any violence, but I cannot forget that we are facing the enemy and that he is near Paris.' He persuaded the Empire's Legislative Body to disperse without resistance; the Empress had already left the Tuileries.

431

Thus once again Paris had decided on the country's behalf; the prestige of the capital was such that the Government did not feel it could leave the city, even though it was threatened with imminent siege. Crémieux was sent as a delegate to Tours to organize provincial resistance; General Trochu, in command of the Army of Paris, became head of the Government, which thus indicated its dedication to military resistance. Jules Favre was Vice-President and Minister of Foreign Affairs; Gambetta, Minister of the Interior. A manifesto addressed to the Powers asserted that France would not yield an inch of her territory or a stone of her fortresses. A proclamation announced elections, but how could the country be consulted? A portion of it was occupied by the Germans; many voters were with the colours; and a political battle in the face of the enemy would risk a breakdown in solidarity. Already the country's unity seemed tenuous. Some men, Thiers among them, thought that France would obtain better peace terms by negotiating at once, without continuing a war she could not win; others, like Gambetta, were inspired anew with the Jacobin spirit of 1792 and argued that the Republic would be invincible. On September 12th, the Government entrusted Thiers with a mission to London, Vienna and Saint Petersburg; he was to sound the attitude of the Powers towards France. Jules Favre met Bismarck at Ferrières, in the Rothschild castle, to discuss an armistice with an eye to an election. Bismarck required as prior condition the surrender of Strasbourg, Phalsbourg and Toul, and the occupation of the Paris forts; and as a condition for peace, the ceding of Alsace and Lorraine. The provisional Government refused to accept this shameful capitulation. Gambetta telegraphed the prefects: 'Paris, incensed, swears to hold out to the finish. The departments must rise!' On September 19th, Paris was surrounded.

At Tours a group of fine men did its best to recruit armies, but it lacked a leader; Crémieux was too old to act as a quickening force. Suddenly, on October 7th, came the astounding news: 'Gambetta, having left Paris in a balloon, has arrived at Amiens and is hastening towards Tours.' At once the streets of that city filled; the renown of this young tribune, his eloquence, and the drama of his flight moved everyone to hope for a change in luck. Gambetta's selections were excellent. For the War Office he chose a young engineer, Charles de Freycinet, who worked wonders; under the impulse of new and enthusiastic men, France expected to see once again the miracle of Du Guesclin and Joan of Arc. Since in all Tours there was only one general staff map, fifteen thousand photographic copies of it were rushed through; two regiments and a battery of artillery were raised and equipped daily, weapons were manufactured in France or purchased abroad, and six hundred thousand men were placed under arms and organized in their respective units. The disaster at Sedan and the besieging of Metz having stripped the army of leadership, new generals were improvised. D'Aurelle de Paladines, Chanzy and Faidherbe proved themselves worthy of their commands. Very shortly the Army of the Loire was in a condition to resume the offensive. On the day (October 11th) when Gambetta had taken up his tasks, Paris, tightly blockaded, could communicate with Tours only by means of balloons and carrier pigeons; Bazaine was shut up in Metz; throughout the rest of the country you could not have found over forty thousand soldiers and a hundred pieces of artillery. Nevertheless, Gambetta did not despair of saving the capital. Trochu would make a sortie and would effect a junction with the Army of the Loire; the German lines would be broken. 'I shall return with an army', Gambetta had told Jules Favre, 'and if I have the glory of delivering Paris, I shall ask no more of fate.'

Historians have not given enough heed to the magnitude of the Tours delegation's efforts, which were comparable to those of the Committee of Public Safety. These efforts failed, but for reasons unconnected with the activities of Gambetta and his associates. On October 29th, 1870, Metz surrendered; Bazaine handed over to the Germans the Empire's last and best army and — what was much more serious — freed the Army of Prince Frederick Charles, which was very shortly to prove a threat to the new Army of the Loire. At the same time Gambetta learned that Thiers's trip across Europe had been a total failure; neither England nor Russia understood that Thiers, in foretelling the dangers of a German hegemony, spoke as a historian and a prophet. At that moment, intervention by England and Russia would have avoided a century of misfortunes. With his back to the wall, Gambetta issued a proclamation which was to become famous: 'Frenchmen! raise your souls and wills to the height of the terrible perils which lay hands upon the fatherland; it is still up to us to make ill fortune weary and to show the whole world what it means to be a great people resolved not to perish . . .' Yet if the delegation wanted to act, it must do so before the arrival of Prince Frederick Charles. As once Joan of Arc had done, Gambetta ordered the retaking of Orleans and won the day at Coulmiers. Here was a surprise for all Europe, anxiety for Germany, a vast hope for France. Everywhere buildings were dressed with flags and fireworks let off; already people saw the blockade of Paris broken and Bismarck forced to a compromise peace. Gambetta no longer shared these illusions; he knew too well his own weakness and Trochu's. In fighting a hopeless fight for honour's sake, however he remained in the tradition of chivalry.

In the last analysis, victory rests with the 'big battalions'. Had France then found support abroad, her heroic efforts would have saved her, as formerly Spain had been freed from Napoleon through England's intervention. In her isolation France was doomed. Provincial resistance, campaigns by militia and sharpshooters, the Garibaldian epic — all of these gave rise to wonderful feats, but the outcome did not remain in doubt. A sortie by Trochu came to nothing; the Army of the Loire had to retreat and then was cut in two; the Tours delegation had to withdraw to Bordeaux. 'I shall defy the storm', said Gambetta; 'never has despair come close to my soul.' He had the notion of a campaign in the east (Bourbaki's army) in order to cut the German lines of communication; in the north he urged Faidherbe on. In Paris certain influential members of the Government were growing weary of this resistance and now shared Thiers's belief that it would stiffen the enemy's demands. The siege was becoming a heavy burden; as always the Parisians showed their mettle, but they were starving and prices were going up. They were eating dogs and rats and the animals in the zoo. The joy of being able freely to declaim the *Châtiments* and acclaim a Victor Hugo back from exile was wearing thin. Bombardment had begun. The discontented, daily growing in number, complained of Gambetta's dictatorial decisions. At Lille, he found the people disheartened: 'No weakness!' said he. 'If we do not despair, we shall save France. When this happy day shall dawn, you will see that, however possessed I may be by a patriotic passion which finds foreign invasion intolerable, I am at heart inspired by a republican faith which views dictatorship with horror.' He meant what he said, but Thiers — no less a patriot — still thought that by negotiating sooner, at least Lorraine could have been saved.

On January 18th, 1871, the German Empire was proclaimed at Versailles, in the Hall of Mirrors. Bismarck had triumphed over Richelieu; the Treaties of Westphalia were torn into shreds. This triumph was not to be lasting, but at the moment Germany seemed to be master of Europe. Paris was at the end of her resources; a last sortie had failed; on January 28th an armistice was signed at Versailles between Jules Favre and Bismarck. A national Assembly was to meet at Bordeaux; there Gambetta received a dispatch from the Government: 'Carry out the terms of the armistice and summon the voters for February 8th.' The Bordeaux delegation was astounded and annoyed – even more so when it discovered that Jules Favre, through weakness or negligence, had agreed to exclude the Army of the East from the armistice and had neglected to inform Gambetta of this fact. This army of eighty thousand men, thus cornered into surrender, preferred to cross into Switzerland, where it was greeted with a warmth and a friendship which deserved and aroused France's gratitude. The Government's pledges to Gambetta had not been honoured; it had been agreed that if at some time Paris had to capitulate, the rest of France would continue the struggle; Ferry had written to Gambetta: 'I swear to you . . . We shall bequeath you France to defend, beyond the Loire, beyond the Garonne, in Toulon or in Cherbourg, as though Paris did not exist . . .' The Government explained that the need to summon a constituent assembly and the impossibility of doing so without German agreement had dictated this painful *volte-face*.

The strife between Jules Simon, who came to Bordeaux as representative of the Paris government, and Gambetta was violent; not only did Gambetta refuse to forgive his colleagues for the nature of the armistice, but he disagreed with them over the elections. He wanted to deny eligibility to all Frenchmen who, between 1851 and 1870, had been ministers, senators or prefects under the Empire. Jules Simon regarded this exclusion as arbitrary, oppressive and counter to the rights of citizens. Bismarck, delighted at seeing the French quarrel, telegraphed Gambetta that such a provision would be contrary to the terms of the armistice; in haste Jules Simon summoned to Bordeaux Pelletan, Arago and Garnier-Pagès, thus obtaining a majority. Gambetta handed in his resignation, no longer being, as he put it, in communion of ideas or hopes with the Government. In his *Mémoires,* Freycinet claims that his chief could have put up a resistance: 'His popularity at Bordeaux was vast, and he had been many times implored to assume dictatorship.' An enthusiastic crowd cheered him below the windows of his dwelling, but would the remainder of the country have supported him? For the majority of the French, the man of the hour was Thiers. He had foreseen how disastrous this war would be, had done everything to prevent it and then to bring it to a close. He continued to assert that negotiation would have been more fruitful after Sedan, denied the effectiveness of provincial resistance and now described Gambetta as a 'raving idiot'. Others, on the contrary, thought that Gambetta had saved the country's honour and were grateful to him for never having despaired of the Republic. Moltke himself, the head of the German armies, wrote: 'We must render justice to this country's powerful resources and to the patriotism of the French. After having beheld the whole French army taken prisoner, France was, in this brief interval, able to put into the field a new army . . . larger than that which had been destroyed.' And Von der Goltz: 'History must acknowledge in Gambetta two undeniable merits which will adorn his memory. The first was to have restored to France a feeling of her strength immediately after she had fallen so low; the second was that he cleared the way for a moral renewal.' The struggle between Thiers and Gambetta had been none other than that between the chanson de geste and the fabliau; it was the perennial French struggle.

CHAPTER II

HOW FRANCE BECAME A REPUBLIC

THE elections of February 1871 were held without preparation, and so the country was taken unawares; it wanted no more Bonapartists, who were responsible for the war and hence for the defeat; nor did it want any republicans, whom it regarded as the advocates of a resistance the majority considered idle. It voted for the old monarchist candidates, for 'France's ancient nobility', in order to cast its vote for peace. The conservative majority was increased by this feeling, yet it was, in fact, a very real feeling throughout the country. Out of six hundred and fifty deputies, four hundred were legitimists or Orleanists. 'Country squireens, old chaps who had not been outside their châteaux since 1830',[1] greeted one another in Bordeaux, along the *Allées de Tourny*, and incensed the Bordeaux crowds by crying: 'Long live the King!' They already thought the restoration an accomplished fact. 'France has but to speak; it is God's hour', the Count of Chambord wrote to them. 'We are people restored to health after having been given up by all the doctors', wrote the Duchess de Noailles; 'we need to convince ourselves of our health, and shout at the top of our voices.' After such an electoral defeat, the republicans likewise felt the need of convincing themselves that they were not dead, and bellowed their scorn for 'an assembly of rustics'.

Why did not this monarchist majority set up a monarchy? First, because it was divided. The two branches of the royal family had reached no agreement; the two pretenders, the Count of Chambord (legitimate branch) and the Count of Paris (Orleans branch) worked against each other. Secondly, the monarchist party did not want to saddle itself with the defeat; in 1815 the Bourbons had already once come in with the foreigner's baggage trains; they had no wish that the King's first act in 1871 should be to sign a calamitous treaty. Hence the Assembly adjourned the question of the form of government; yet as someone had to govern, it appointed a 'head of the provisional government of the French Republic' who could be no one else but Monsieur Thiers. This little old fellow, with his conspicuous forelock, then possessed tremendous prestige;

[1] DANIEL HALÉVY.

437

described at the outset of his political life as a Balzacian adventurer, then as a venturesome cabinet minister, a historian in the tradition of Caesar, 'who had dreamed of making history and had made it', he had just, despite his advanced years, dashed all over Europe to plead his country's cause. He seemed at once a patriot and the embodiment of common sense. This great bourgeois had become the 'idol of the average bourgeois'.[1] Multiple candidatures still being allowed, he had, in February 1871, been elected by twenty-six departments, and of this he was legitimately proud. 'France would not understand', he said, 'were I not at this juncture to be its first man.' And he was. France was to have reason to congratulate herself on her choice. The task he undertook was vast and thankless; Thiers, his intelligence in full flower, knew himself able to succeed in this political feat, and he certainly took it for granted that his part would not be temporary. To the monarchist he said: 'The monarchy is something to think about two years hence'; to the republicans he secretly promised the republic; at the bottom of his heart, he was all for Adolphe Thiers. Admirably familiar with France's past, he deplored her having abandoned the 'healthful routine' which constitutes a people's very bone-structure, but he also knew that history cannot run in reverse and he thought the Republic would be 'the regime which would least divide us', especially if he were to be its president. 'I am', he remarked one day, 'a monarchist who practises the Republic.'

The peace negotiations were painful; Thiers and Jules Favre braved Bismarck, who insisted upon an indemnity of six milliard francs, the occupation of a portion of France until that sum should be paid, and the annexation of Alsace and Lorraine. Thiers succeeded in having the amount reduced by one milliard and saved Belfort, but on his way home he wept. He loved his country and knew that France would not resign herself to the loss of two of her most French provinces, and that these spoils would be the cause of wars to come. When, at Bordeaux, the deputies from Alsace and Lorraine made their dignified protests and announced: 'We proclaim inviolable for ever the right of Alsatians and Lorrainers to remain members of the French nation. And we swear, as much for ourselves as for our constituents, our children, and their descendants, to lay claim to it for ever and by every means, in the very face of all usurpers', when Hugo, Edgar Quinet and Clemenceau gave this protest their support, Thiers knew that the right was on their side. But might was in the saddle, and Thiers said to the Assembly: 'Have the

[1] MAURICE RECLUS.

courage of your convictions: it is either war or peace.' The treaty was ratified by five hundred and forty-six votes against one hundred and seven. Not only the deputies of the lost provinces but Hugo and Gambetta withdrew. 'I wait', said the latter, 'until republican France finds herself once more.' He had not long to wait. Meanwhile Thiers promised the monarchists to undertake nothing which would prejudice the ultimate form of government: 'If you want to reorganize, merely do nothing which will divide you ... I swear before the country not to draw up in connection with the report on constitutional questions any proposal without your knowledge, for this would truly be treason on my part ...' This patriotic truce was then called the Pact of Bordeaux. On March 11th the Assembly resolved to adjourn until the twentieth, at Versailles.

One of the terms of the treaty of peace was a symbolic German entry into Paris; this triumphal march along the Champs Elysées (March 1st) was brief, but it sufficed to raise Parisian indignation to fever pitch. The Germans filed down an empty, silent avenue, draped with black flags. The city was incensed. Patriotic Paris would have none of the treaty; republican Paris would have none of the Assembly; Paris, the capital, would not tolerate the Government's decision to establish itself at Versailles. Did the monarchist Right, people asked, want to obliterate even the memory of 1789? The Assembly was to meet on March 20th; on the eighteenth, revolution broke out in Paris. Its immediate cause was an attempt to take away from the National Guard the cannon which had been given them during the siege; the underlying cause was the old communal and Jacobin tradition. Revolutionaries and patriots were united in their anger; the troops sent to Montmartre to recapture the guns fraternized with the crowd, which shot two generals, Thomas and Lecomte. A central committee, the elements of which had come together during the siege, took charge of the uprising; it included district mayors, Guard officers, workmen of the Blanqui persuasion, Jacobins ashamed of defeat. This committee had no definite programme, except opposition to the defeatist and reactionary Versailles Government. Here was civil war, and Thiers was well aware of it; he had written the history of such conflicts, and he knew that troops left in contact with a rebellion are always contaminated by it. Hence his strategy was to abandon Paris to the insurgents, to gather loyal forces outside the city and to attack only in full strength. He himself withdrew his Government to Versailles. This plan brought him victory, but only after two months of terror for which both parties must be held responsible. Versailles lined up 'federated' prisoners before firing squads; whereupon the Commune seized hostages, among them the Archbishop of Paris and the Presiding Judge of the Court of Appeals, who were both shot prior to the final defeat of the Commune.

Its defeat was inevitable because the provinces did not support the capital. At the outbreak of the insurrection, in the republican south, Lyons and Marseilles began to be anxious and wondered whether the monarchist Assembly would try, in Paris, to crush the Republic. Daniel Halévy says that Thiers then made promises to freemasonry and that the provincial radicals sacrificed Paris in return for being guaranteed the Republic. The monarchists got wind of these negotiations and demanded an explanation; Thiers, who scorned the country gentlemen's party, answered them sarcastically: 'Before you attack me, wait a few weeks. Then your capacity and courage will be equal to events.' Thiers's own capacity and courage were beyond doubt, but when he triumphed over the rebellion, he showed a want of generosity; having promised honest, legal trials, he allowed the slaughter of prisoners by the Versailles troops. A torrent of blood was shed; repression produced seventeen thousand dead plus arrests and deportations without number. No defeat in the war of 1870 cost France so many lives; this cruelty left lasting hatreds behind it, and every year the people of Paris came to do honour to the victims of the 'men from Versailles' along the Wall of the 'Federated'. From the June Days of 1848 and the days of the Commune dates that 'secession of the proletariat'[1] from which France has so greatly suffered and which has made her political life so different from that of England or the United States. Thiers, however, emerged even stronger from this 'appalling victory'; he had shown the conservative majority not only that the Republic was not the Revolution, but that it could subdue a revolution. Through the defeat of the Commune, he had been freed of the extreme Left; all he needed to do, to remain in power, was to rid himself of the extreme Right.

But before any political steps could be taken internally, the important thing was to rid the country of the Germans. The final treaty had been signed at Frankfort on May 10th; there remained, to bring the occupation to a close, payment of the war indemnity. This was done by degrees. For his first loan, Thiers asked two milliard francs; he obtained five. On June 29th he reviewed the army on the green at Longchamp; it was a magnificent procession, and the crowd gave an ovation to the 'great little

[1] GOGUEL.

man' with his escort of cuirassed cavalry. Once again France astounded Europe, not only by the speed of her recovery but by her changeableness. By-elections took place in July 1871. Everything seemed to indicate a monarchist success; all the talk was of fusion; the Duchess of Chartres was received at the President's home. Yet the same electorate which in 1870 had given seven million yeas to Napoleon III and, in January 1871, a crushing majority to the royalists, on July 2nd of the same year elected only republicans. How explain this? The country was regaining self-possession; there was no longer any question of immediate resistance; on the matter of an ultimate *revanche*, all Frenchmen were agreed. Thus Gambetta was no longer frightening, and he himself, taking his cue from the polls, had offered Thiers an alliance. 'The future belongs to the wisest', Thiers had said. 'The Republic will be conservative or it will not be at all.' 'We then must be the wisest', Gambetta had replied. 'That won't be very hard.' Reassured, France severed herself from a class she distrusted; thereafter the republican party had two leaders, 'one a Whig, the other a Tory ... thenceforward the door was closed against monarchist plottings'. Gambetta became the head of an 'opportunist' party and supported Thiers. Their alliance enraged the Right.

For a long time the monarchists had believed that the only obstacle to a restoration lay in the rivalry between the two branches of the House of Bourbon; this hurdle, however, did not seem insurmountable. The Count of Chambord had no direct heir; suppose he were to reign and have the Count of Paris as his successor. The Orleanists agreed to this solution. There then arose a second obstacle. Thiers, who had the support of the opportunists, had succeeded, despite the Pact of Bordeaux, in having his title of Head (*Chef*, which he called 'suitable for a cook') changed to that of President of the Republic, and he now spoke of a 'loyal trial of republican institutions'. The excellence of his administration had added even more to Thiers's prestige; he had effected the passage of a law on army recruitment which was to remain until the war of 1914 the charter of the French military establishment, and he had inspired such confidence that in 1872 a loan of three milliard francs had been subscribed fourteen times over, twenty-seven billion being offered by the Germans themselves. This had allowed him to pay off the balance of the indemnity and to become the 'liberator of the national territory'. But the danger over, this was soon forgotten. Because Thiers had done his job too well, the Assembly wanted to get along without him.

The Right fearfully heard Gambetta speak of the coming to power of 'new social strata'. Did he mean that the 'day of the Notables' was over, and did Thiers approve this? A message in which the President said: 'The Republic exists; it is the country's legitimate government', struck the monarchists with final panic. They decided to eliminate Thiers. In this manœuvre they had, from 1873 on, the support of the Bonapartists, who had lost their leadership with the death of Napoleon III. The moderate centre joined forces with them after the election in Paris of Thiers's candidate's opponent, a radical deputy named Désiré Barodet. Was this the promised conservatism? The monarchists had finally unearthed a leader, the Duke of Broglie, son of Louis-Philippe's minister and grandson of Madame de Staël. He challenged Thiers, and on May 24th, 1873, out-voted him. When he signed his resignation, the President did not believe it would be accepted. 'They have no one', he said. But a victorious party always finds someone. That same day, during an evening session, Marshal MacMahon was elected President of the Republic. Thiers was persuaded that this honest soldier had had no part in the plot and would not be willing to serve as his successor; on the first particular he was right — MacMahon was chosen President of the Republic without having been consulted — and he was almost right on the second: at first MacMahon refused. But the royalists divulged their secret to him: with Thiers's downfall, there was hope of the King's return, and what prestige would attach to the great soldier who would make way for the House of France! MacMahon, a sentimental monarchist, yielded. Halévy recounts that when he arrived at the Élysée Palace, his first words were: 'Where are the regulations?'

The rub was that there were no regulations, that is, no Constitution. MacMahon fell back on another military turn of speech. 'I regard the post at which you have placed me as that of a sentinel who guards the continued integrity of your sovereign power.' The Duke of Broglie, now head of the government, was fully resolved to set up the monarchy and to do it legally. But there remained a third obstacle — the most formidable of all — and that was the monarch. The Count of Chambord, 'the miraculous child', posthumous son of the Duke of Berry, was a Bourbon romantic; his feeling for the monarchy was that of Chateaubriand, and moreover he practised the virtues which Chateaubriand remained content to praise. Believing that his only strength lay in the principle of legitimacy, without which he was 'merely a large man with a game leg', he refused to come to terms with any assembly. The symbol to which he passionately clung was the white flag. Now all his partisans knew that the army would not accept this, 'that the very rifles would go off by themselves', that even the Vendée stood ready to rally to the tricolour, so covered with glory was it. Vainly did messenger after messenger seek him out. At the very moment when it was believed that the monarchy was an accomplished fact, the Count of Chambord proved inflexible: 'I am being asked to sacrifice my honour . . . It is the fashion to contrast the firmness of Henry V to the cleverness of Henry IV. I claim that in this respect I do not yield him anything; but I should like to know what lesson he would have taught anyone unwary enough to have dared to urge him to forswear the standard of Arques and Ivry . . . I want to remain wholly what I am . . . My person is nothing; my principle is everything . . .' Henry V was unwilling to be the 'legitimate king of the Revolution'. These handsome feelings cost him the throne (October 1873).

The monarchists read this pronouncement with despair; it delighted the Bonapartists and republicans. 'None will deny', said Thiers, 'that the founder of the French Republic is *Monsieur le Comte de Chambord.*' There remained for the Right what the Duke of Broglie called the line of retreat: the continuance of Marshal MacMahon's powers by personal right. Broglie hoped to make the Marshal independent of the Assembly and create in him a sort of regent, a lieutenant-general of the realm, who would retain office until the moment when a more tractable pretender made the restoration possible. The Count of Paris was of the same opinion: 'Since we cannot establish the monarchy, we must organize a constitutional Government with an executive power placed above party strife.' What the Count of Paris feared above all was the Empire; to avert this solution, Orleanists and republicans were united. Towards the end of 1873, the Count of Chambord requested a secret meeting with the Marshal-President and offered to present himself before the Assembly, there to be acclaimed sovereign. MacMahon, punctilious about the 'regulations', refused to see him. 'I thought', Chambord remarked bitterly, 'I was dealing with a Constable of France; I found only a police captain.' On November 19th, the term of the Marshal's personal mandate was fixed for seven years. There followed a period of confusion, during which continued the policy described as that 'of moral order', but which was neither moral nor conducive to order. It consisted in bullying the Left press, purging republican bureaucrats and singing 'Save Rome and France — in the name of the Sacred Heart . . .' By annoying a great many of the French, the aggressive clericalism of the Moral Order led to the recrudescence of a militant anti-clericalism. On May 15th, 1874, the Duke of Broglie made public a scheme for a Constitution — a non-responsible President of the Republic, responsible ministers, two Chambers, the right to dissolve Parliament with the agreement of the Senate. This was the British monarchy without its monarch. De Broglie was defeated, and a committee of thirty, named by the Assembly, spent the remainder of the year in seeking to reach agreement between the parties and in drawing up a Constitution.

For the firm establishment of the Republic, an alliance was needed between Gambetta and the moderate monarchists; Gambetta himself proposed this difficult union: 'The Republic is the inevitable thing', he said to the men of the centre, 'and you should accept it, not as party members, not as men of feeling, but as men truly wise in politics . . .' The need of a settlement was clear to the mind of every reasonable citizen; once again Bismarck was showing hostility towards France because that country was recovering too quickly to suit his taste. The Assembly must at all costs avoid letting itself be trapped into a fresh war without having afforded the nation a stable government. Monsieur de Laboulaye, chairman of the Assembly's constitutional committee, begged his colleagues to act. 'Europe is watching you, France implores you, and we supplicate you, we say to you, "Do not burden yourselves with any such responsibility! Do not leave us in the unknown; in short, have pity on this unhappy country!" ' Despite the pathos of this speech, any vote was blocked by the extreme Left which, through loyalty to the memories of the Revolution, wanted no second chamber and had paradoxically made alliance with the unrepentant monarchists. At last Henri Wallon, a historian and a member of the Institute and the Assembly, offered this amendment: 'The President of the Republic is elected by a majority vote by the Senate and the Chamber of Deputies meeting as a National Assembly. He is appointed for seven years and is open to re-election.' This time it was no longer a question of Marshal MacMahon, but of all his ultimate successors. The article was approved by three hundred and fifty-three votes against three hundred and fifty-two. The Republic had been established by a margin of one vote, and by a slip, for this wording settled the method of electing the president of a Republic the very principle of which the Assembly had not yet accepted.

The constitutional law of 1875 founded the Third Republic; since it had been framed by monarchists, it was so designed as to allow the King an opportunity to return. Thence came the President's long term of office, as well as his right to dissolve the Chamber with the consent of the Senate. Having learned its lesson from the events of December 2nd, the Assembly had wisely avoided having the President elected by the people, which in France would have been dangerous. In substance the President played the part of a constitutional monarch; he had no veto power, which safeguarded him against lasting quarrels with the nation. The Senate, chosen at second remove by colleges in which the delegates of the municipal councils were dominant, was to be, thought Gambetta, 'the grand council of the communes of France', and, the conservatives believed, a moderating factor. The senators were elected for nine years and renewed a third at a time, but the Right, to make sure it would hold a majority, had succeeded in carrying a provision that the Assembly would name seventy-five permanent — that is, life — senators. It assumed that these seats would go to conservatives, but at the last moment a coalition of Bonapartists and republicans won for the latter fifty-seven of these permanent seats. Thus did the political skill of the Left assert itself; it was still without a majority in the country, but it was obvious that Gambetta's 'new strata' would demand their share in government with increasing authority. Universal suffrage had put up with the Notables during a time of confusion, and in this it had shown its wisdom, for all in all the Notables had, from the administrative and economic point of view, provided good government. 'Within a few years the finances had been reorganized: the 1875 budget had been met, with a surplus of a hundred millions; government obligations had advanced 10 per cent in five years; savings-bank deposits had increased 27 per cent. Coal production was up 60 per cent; iron production, 26 per cent; cast iron, 23 per cent. Eighteen thousand kilometres [11,000 miles] of railway track had been built between 1871 and 1875; foreign trade had expanded 21 per cent; harbour activity had almost doubled. The Paris Exhibition of 1878 was a brilliant indication of France's rebirth.'[1] Yet man does not live by bread alone and prosperity does not take the place of freedom. In the eyes of Frenchmen, Governments of 'moral order' are never more than temporary expedients; Thiers and the Duke of Broglie had finished their work; the future seemed to belong to Gambetta.

[1] ROBERT LACOUR-GAYET

CHAPTER III

HOW THE REPUBLIC TURNED REPUBLICAN

THE Republic had been established by monarchists; it was now a question of whether it would be operated by republicans. Thiers persistently believed that in France the latter had only a million and a half voters on their side, out of about eight millions, but this was a mistake based upon too literal a study of the voting record. Thiers took no account of the floating vote which makes up all majorities; from the day when the Republic had taken command, the floating vote went over to the Republic. Meanwhile the Right held on to President MacMahon, who thought that his 'orders' were to keep the radicals at a distance, and who governed through business cabinets. The situation required much prudence on the part of the Left; in this Gambetta was not lacking. More and more the opportunist statesman was hatching out of the flaming radical. Why should he have aroused fear among the urban or rural lower middle class? He had talked about 'new strata', not 'new classes', and being first of all a patriot, he weighed the German danger. Finding an excuse in a law passed during March 1875, which enlarged the French army, Bismarck was again beginning his threats; there were those who said that, in fear of a war to recoup French losses, he was contemplating a preventive war. This was not proved, but an alarmed England and Russia intervened with the Iron Chancellor, and he yielded. Gambetta met the Prince of Wales, dreamed of a Russian alliance and announced that Germany would one day be crushed between the Latins and the Slavs. Thanks to him, the republicans appeared to the country as conservative patriots; it was now the Right which seemed ready to risk adventures. The Left accused it of wanting (as did formerly Napoleon III) to put the Pope back on a temporal throne; anti-clericalism was growing. The French peasants remained good Catholics, but they feared a feudal reaction, and to their minds the Church remained the Castle's natural ally.

1876 was an election year; in the Senate the Right retained the majority, though it was smaller; the Chamber had a republican — but moderate — majority. It was still possible for men of the Centre, such great Catholic bourgeois as Armand Dufaure, to rule with the backing of a coalition. On many matters, the Duke of Broglie could agree with Thiers, Jules

Grévy, Jules Ferry and Challemel-Lacour, men in the same cultural tradition. The stumbling block was the anti-clericalism of the Left, in whose eyes the principles of 1789 were like the creed of a lay religion which was fearful of the Church's spiritual competition. Vainly did the Prime Minister, Jules Simon, 'an Israelite with the temperament of a Roman cardinal, subtle, ingratiating, and catlike', affirm: 'I am deeply republican, deeply conservative'; such sayings as Gambetta's 'Clericalism — that is the enemy', or Ferry's 'No enemies to the Left', made the Right bristle. Its hostile attitude in turn pushed the Left Centre towards the radicals; after Jules Simon had agreed to one or two votes in the Chamber which ran counter to the Marshal's principles, on May 16th, 1877, that old soldier in effect cashiered the minister. 'We can no longer march together', he said to Jules Simon. 'I prefer to be overthrown rather than to remain under Monsieur Gambetta's orders.' As he saw it, it was a question of hierarchy.

It is usual to speak of 'The Sixteenth of May' as a *coup d'état*; the description is unjustified, but this interference of the President in the relationship between the Legislature and the Executive was certainly contrary to the Constitution; to the Chambers alone belonged the upsetting of cabinets. As for the President, he had the right to ask the Senate for the dissolution of the Chamber. The deputies, on the advice of their President, Jules Grévy, understood what was transpiring and vigorously girded themselves for battle. 'Remain within the law', Grévy told the members; 'remain there wisely, firmly, and confidently . . .' A manifesto was drawn up and signed by three hundred and sixty-three republican deputies. The Senate granted the Marshal dissolution, but by only a narrow majority. 'We leave three hundred and sixty-three,' said Gambetta, 'we shall come back four hundred.' The Duke of Broglie presided over an interim cabinet and made the preparations for the election. It was a thankless job. We have seen under the Restoration, at the time of the two hundred and twenty-one, how the French act in such instances. This Chamber had just been elected; why should the voters suddenly have changed their parties at a president's orders? The Left banded together for republican defence; so firm was their unity that, Thiers having died, the people of Paris afforded a spectacular and emotional funeral to the conqueror of the Commune; a few weeks earlier Gambetta had made the Chamber acclaim the 'liberator of the territory', the same man who had once before called him a 'raving idiot'. By contrast the coalition of the Right was crumbling. The monarchists feared the Bonapartists; the liberal Orleanists thought Louis Veuillot's challenge impolitic: 'Clericalism, there lies salvation!' Taine found fault with the Marshal. 'It's his charge at Reichshofen all over again — after the day has been lost. The elections will return him a Chamber as radical or more so. There will be nothing left for him but to resign. I see Gambetta President of the Republic within four months...' In October 1877, despite shameless pressure by the Government and official candidatures, three hundred and twenty-six republicans were elected; they had not come back four hundred, but they retained a majority of one hundred and nineteen votes. What would the Marshal do? Gambetta had told him: 'When France has made heard her sovereign voice, you will have to submit or resign.' MacMahon, for his part, remembered the heroic saying of his youth: 'Here I am, here I stay.' He tried to stay, and submitted, but against the grain. When they took office, Gambetta counselled his republican associates to be moderate: 'Above all I dread the intoxication of success . . . I ask my party to call a halt . . .' This was wise prudence, for the majority of the party of Movement over that of the Established Order was slighter in the country than it was in the Chamber; unhappily this prudence was not imitated by the beaten Notables. Had the latter now accepted the Republic with good grace, France could, like England, have found a constructive opposition; but in 1877 the ditch still yawned wide, and the French Right still dreamed of fanciful returns to power.

The Republic of the dukes was dead; that of the republicans began under happy auspices. The country was prosperous; in 1878 a World Fair, which showed France more beautiful than ever, proved to the world that 'the Republic will be Athenian'. From this point of view, the war had not interrupted the normal progress of letters and the arts. The same writers — Hugo, Taine, Renan, Flaubert and Zola — continued at work, with a little more seriousness, and a sorrowful seriousness, springing from the misfortunes of the fatherland. The academic painters of the Second Empire continued to be popular, but already Manet, Monet and Renoir were silently at work and were preparing, for the very morning after defeat, the most brilliant of rebirths. The Notables had bequeathed to the new strata a brilliant financial situation; their regime had been honourable and their management patriarchal. A balanced budget had been re-established from the proceeds of indirect taxes alone, and it had been possible to increase the army appropriations as Gambetta had asked. At the Congress of Berlin, in 1878, Bismarck offered France Tunisia, not without the base ulterior motive of embroiling the French with Italy and drawing France's attention away from the Rhine. Bismarck, however, miscalculated, and through his stratagem consolidated France's colonial empire. The Republic grew ever stronger; the 1878 elections stripped the Right of its last citadel, its majority in the Senate. The Marshal's position was becoming difficult; the Government having decided to relieve of their commands nine generals known to be inimical to the regime, MacMahon refused his signature and handed in his resignation. He left the presidency with lowered prestige; he had shown himself a partisan and, by appealing to the country in a situation where the country's judgment was not the least in doubt, he had made difficult any future exercise of the right of dissolution. Jules Grévy, his successor at the Élysée, had a clear mind, composure and cultivation. A man of the upper middle class with liberal views, a man of letters who knew Horace, Racine and Lamartine by heart, he was also a cautious jurist, a 'sly peasant' who clung to his cash, and an old man of seventy-six who was rather weary and suspicious of adventures. As first magistrate of the Republic, he wanted to be no more than 'the family lawyer', a legal and constitutional adviser and 'the brake on the chariot of State'.

Gambetta had led the republicans in their victorious fight; Grévy should have offered him the premiership; but Grévy did not like Gambetta's impetuosity and he feared his prestige. 'It is still too soon', he said. Grévy called in Waddington, and then Freycinet, Gambetta's former deputy at Tours, and sidetracked the latter with the presidency of the Chamber. The obligation to the radicals had none the less to be met in some measure; in order to establish in the eyes of Europe the ties with the Revolution, the *Marseillaise* became the national anthem and the Fourteenth of July (celebrated for the first time in 1880) France's national holiday. Until that time religious and lay schools had competed on an equal footing; but now Jules Ferry, a doctrinaire of the Left, introduced an educational code whose famous Article VII deprived unauthorized congregations of the right to teach. This measure struck at the Jesuits, the Marists and the Dominicans. Ferry, who believed in the efficacy of a lay morality, suppressed religious instruction in the State schools and, by creating the 'godless school', drew upon himself unrelenting wrath. As had happened under Louis XV, the Jesuits were driven from their religious houses (March 1880), while judges resigned rather than carry out these decrees. In the secondary schools, the philosophy course assumed great importance; middle-class boys were brought up on the metaphysics of Kant, as one can discover by reading Barrès's *Le*

Déracinés. Others sought asylum in religious establishments, of which many continued to function. Primary normal schools were set up to train teachers; these were to become centres of laicism and radicalism. In 1880 there were also established the first secondary schools for girls — a great novelty, since the teaching of young women had been the last inviolate citadel of Catholicism. The conflict which thus set the Church against the State was unfortunate, since in France the Church was a powerful force; it retained spiritual strength, and by means of its missionaries, it had done more than the State to spread French culture throughout the world. Yet the State, Ferry thought, had a duty to insist that the Church should recognize the freedom of the mind; the fact that Monseigneur Dupanloup believed himself obliged to resign from the French Academy because Littré, a positivist, had been elected to it, was a dangerous sign of intolerance. The religious schools did not disappear, but between them and the university there began a rivalry the dangerous results of which were to become fully obvious during the days of the Dreyfus Case.

Gambetta remained at once the prodigy and the problem child of the Republic. To those doctrinaires Grévy and Ferry, he was displeasing for his untidiness, his affair with Léonie Léon, his tardily developed taste for society and above all for his success. The moment he was cheered by a crowd, there was a cry of dictatorship; the President of the Republic and the Senate feared simultaneous voting for a list of names as well as multiple candidacies because there was danger that each election might turn into a plebiscite on Gambetta. Grévy, a pacifist, found fault with Gambetta's references to history's 'great reparations' and to 'imminent justice'; it was feared that by such talk he would arouse Bismarck's suspicions, since the German wanted France to forget any idea of a return engagement and absorb herself in colonial ventures. Yet when Jules Ferry, who assumed responsibility for the espousal of such ventures, was hotly attacked by the partisans of *revanche*, Gambetta, always generous-minded, lent him his support. After the 1881 elections, which confirmed the republican majority, Grévy finally decided to let Gambetta form a cabinet and hang himself. The sly old notary of the Élysée succeeded. The country expected that Gambetta's ministry, about which there had so long been talk, would be a great government 'of all the talents', in which the leaders of the republican majority would be united. Nothing of the sort took place; one by one the great ones refused to participate; one was opposed to simultaneous voting for a list of candidates; another to the colonial policy. As a matter of fact, all of them scented a reversal and wanted to keep themselves on the available list. When Gambetta finally announced the formation of his cabinet, the public was stunned at reading the unknown names. Here was a ministry of clerks and personal friends. The Left was astonished at finding General de Mirabel named chief of the army general staff and the journalist, Jean Jacques Weiss, director of political affairs at the foreign office. Within a few weeks the great ministry was out of office on the issue of simultaneous voting. A few months later Gambetta died, at the age of forty-four, from the result of an 'accident' and an illness. He had been unjustly dealt with by the Republic he had created, saved and knit together; the statesmanlike qualities he had displayed with so much brilliance and wisdom would have been serviceable indeed during the crises which were soon to place the regime in jeopardy. But of all crimes, pre-eminent ability is that which men least forgive.

Gambetta's death removed much of the romantic warmth from French politics; from time to time a Jacobin born after or before his season called for the election of the judges, the separation of the Church from the State, income tax. However, the moment the Left began pressing it, the Centre, by a see-saw which was for fifty years to become the pattern of French political life, drew over to the Right and blocked major reform. In foreign affairs, the debate was between those who, like Ferry, sought to build a colonial empire, and those who, like Clemenceau, were obsessed by Germany and the Rhine; neither side saw that their plans were complementary. In 1882 the *revanchards* triumphed and prevented France from pursuing, side by side with England, a policy of intervention in Egypt. In 1885, when Ferry wanted to root out piracy in Tonkin, or, to put it more frankly, to make Tonkin into a French colony, Clemenceau feverishly denounced him, had him voted out of office, trampled on his prostrate form and had the 'Tonkinese' booed in the streets of Paris. On that day, Ferry, a devoted servant of his country, saw his political career ruined; he was accused of making Indo-China into another Mexico, where France's army would fritter itself away. 'We no longer know you, nor wish to know you', Clemenceau shouted at him. These violent altercations created a spirit of anxiety and distrust which harmed the Republic and cleared the way for those who might be tempted to overthrow it. The 1885 elections proved calamitous to the republicans; on the first ballot, one hundred and seventy-six conservatives of doubtful loyalty were elected as against only one hundred and twenty-seven republicans;

on the second, the republicans, by means of alliances, were able to re-establish their majority, but a storm signal had shown that the regime could find itself in danger. In Gambetta's time, the republicans had succeeded in making themselves masters of the Republic. Would they succeed in remaining so?

This was devoutly to be desired, for the Republic remained the regime which least split the French people; in ten years it had accomplished useful tasks and had given to the country statesmen as remarkable as those of earlier administrations. Gambetta, Ferry and Challemel-Lacour were not unworthy of Thiers, Guizot and Royer-Collard. Not only had the Republic been financially adroit, it had rebuilt the army and enlarged the colonial empire in Tunisia and Tonkin. The Indo-China expedition, at first so unpopular, had in the end aroused the popular imagination, and Admiral Courbet and Commander Rivière had become national heroes. Little by little the shock of defeat was wearing off and France was re-gaining confidence in herself; yet despite such good reasons for optimism, many foreign observers in 1886 considered the regime very weak. The still numerous monarchists and Bonapartists clung to their dreams; the Church, which felt itself under threat, was hostile; many republicans, sickened at the pettiness of political daily life, sighed for the heroism of past battles. 'How beautiful', they would sigh, 'was the Republic under the Empire!' Ever since Gambetta's death, the masses had been seeking a hero, or at least a leader. The best the republican party could offer them was Ferry the Tonkinese, discredited unfairly but beyond repair, and Grévy, an unpopular, pettifogging lawyer. France, unaware of her good fortune, had not that wholehearted respect for her institutions which forges a regime's legitimacy.

CHAPTER IV

HOW THREE CRISES PUT THE REPUBLIC IN JEOPARDY

THE nation was ready for adventure; all it lacked was an adventurer, and Freycinet unintentionally dug up one when he took General Boulanger into his cabinet as Minister of War. He was a youthful general of forty-nine, a former Rightist turned republican through ambition and convenience, recommended by Clemenceau, his fellow-pupil at the Nantes lycée. At first Boulanger seemed to his colleagues harmless and decorative, but he had an instinct for flashy self-advertisement. A law of June 1886 had forbidden entry into the country to the head of any family which had reigned in France and had banned the holding of any office or commission by other members of such families. The intention of those who had framed this legislation was not that the law should apply to princes already in active army service. Boulanger, exceeding the designs of the legislators, struck from the active list the Duke of Aumale, a general commanding a division, and the Duke of Chartres, Colonel of the Seventh Chasseurs. This action aroused much talk and attracted attention to Boulanger; and since he had introduced into the army a series of dramatic reforms, since he concerned himself about the troops' food and lodging, since he was reputed to side with the simple soldier against the army administrators and since he was 'elegant and soldierly', he became popular. At a July the Fourteenth military review, his fair beard and his black horse were cheered, and Paulus, a creator of popular songs, launched 'En r'venant d'la R'vue ...' (Coming Home from the Review . . .) in which he turned the handsome general into an embodiment of the French army. Rochefort, that marquis of the extreme Left, took the General under his wing, Boulanger assuming the demeanour of a patriotic demagogue. The moment was propitious for chauvinism; France again had good reason to be worried over the foreign situation. Italy and England seemed estranged by what had happened in Egypt and Tunisia. Bismarck, on the watch for an opportunity to crush a France too strong for his fancy, in April 1887 played up the Schnaebelé Case (that of a French superintendent of police, lured across the border by a German colleague, and then arrested as a spy),

an incident which could have led to war had it not been for the prudence
of Grévy, who handled his case with the skill of a master in the law.
Their uneasiness led the French to seek out a soldier; Boulanger became
the symbol of *revanche*, the man who 'made Bismarck falter':

> See him over there! He smiles as he goes by
> He has just set free Lorraine and all Alsace . . .

Boulanger had set free nothing whatsoever; Ferry laughed at him as
a 'music-hall Saint-Arnaud' and Grévy as a 'demagogue general'; but
the League of Patriots, founded by Déroulède, clasped him to its bosom;
Clemenceau and Rochefort gave him wholehearted support. Here was all
that the crowds needed; Boulanger become their idol, 'Boulangism' a
system of political philosophy, and 'La Boulange' a political party. The
President and Parliament were disturbed, tried to understand this phenomenon. What was making the pot boil so furiously? a threatened
Caesarism? A Bonaparte without a victory to his name? The great sooth-
sayers of the Republic won over the support of the moderate Right (thanks
to the Prince of Wales, who had been enlightened about Boulanger by
his friend, General de Galliffet) in order to form a ministry without
Boulanger, who was appointed to the command of the Thirteenth Corps
at Clermont-Ferrand, thus forcing him either to leave Paris or to declare
himself an open rebel. A vast concourse poured into the railway station;
women lay down on the tracks to prevent the train from leaving; but
basically Boulanger was a man of discipline, timid, afraid of his own
adventure. He reported for his new duty. Yet events were to afford him
a fresh opportunity. In 1887 a republican scandal was uncovered; Daniel
Wilson, President Grévy's son-in-law, had made use of his influence to
traffic in the sale of posts and decorations. The President, a most upright
man, was unaware of these goings-on, but family loyalty exercised
rather too great an influence on his public actions. 'One of his brothers
had been made a general, another, Governor of Algeria, and it was a
popular jest that unfortunately no brother of Grévy's was a priest, for he
would certainly have been made a cardinal.'[1] Grévy made the mistake
of trying to defend Daniel Wilson; Paulus, who made an unmade kings,
sang: 'Oh, what bad luck to have a son-in-law . . .' The Boulangists who,
until then, had had no platform, cried out for constitutional revision and
denounced the misdeeds of parliamentarianism. Grévy, abandoned by

[1] D. W. BROGAN.

everyone, had to hand in his resignation; this was a crisis of the first magnitude.

It was urgently necessary to elect a new president. Who would he be? Ferry? Major opposition to the Tonkinese would have meant risking the overthrow of the Republic. A powerful party declared itself in favour of what young Maurice Barrès called 'summoning the soldier', meaning Boulanger; this 'revisionist' party demanded that the President be directly elected by the nation and that the cabinet owe allegiance only to the head of the State, all of which was demagogic Caesarism. With sneering cynicism Clemenceau said that 'the most stupid' fellow they could find must be sent to the Élysée and suggested the name of Sadi Carnot – an unfair sally, since Sadi Carnot was far from stupid. As a minister, he had given proof of courage and technical knowledge, but Clemenceau found amusing his slightly ridiculous polish, 'in the style of Georges Ohnet's heroes'. Sadi Carnot was a product of the École Polytechnique; the great Carnot was one of his ancestors, and he possessed all the republican and middle-class virtues. His square-cut beard was impeccably trimmed, his manners were beyond reproach, his speeches were colourless. One might have questioned whether he would have the vitality the situation demanded. The cabinet was clumsy enough to put Boulanger on the retired list, thus giving him the right to run as a candidate for the Chamber; this he did not fail to do and was duly elected for Dordogne and Nord. The Right had supported him on an extremely vague policy: 'Dissolution, a Constituent Assembly, Revision', while a few deluded revisionist radicals had joined forces with this anti-republican movement. A bad speaker, Boulanger was far from formidable on the floor of the Chamber, but nothing stood in the way of his manufacturing his Day in Paris; as against 'parliamentary corruption', the mob worshipped him without knowing him, or rather because it did not know him. The Right, already cured of its fit of reasonableness, supported him because it innocently hoped that he would be the Monk of a deceased monarchy, or at least that he would beat down the Republic. And thus did it once again spoil its opportunity to establish itself in the regime and become a worthy conservative opposition. The Boulange had become 'the union of the malcontents'.

In January 1889 Boulanger was elected deputy for Paris by two hundred and forty-six thousand votes. 'To the Élysée!' his friends cried out to him; the crowd would have borne him there like Sudanese fanatics in their Mahdi's train. The police and the army were hesitant; the collective hysteria was such that everyone thought Boulanger master of France. Everyone, that is, except Boulanger; he, himself, had no faith in this wild escapade. By temporizing he gave the republicans time to pull themselves together; already Clemenceau, who had done so much to make him, was disgusted with him. When the General appeared in the Chamber, Charles Floquet, the Premier, hurled at him his famous, if laughable, remark: 'At your age, Sir, Napoleon was dead!' This queer reproach upset Boulanger. In consequence of another scolding from Floquet, who taunted him with having slipped 'from sacristies to the halls of government', he fought a duel with the head of the cabinet. The ministry ordered the dissolution of the League of Patriots and made adjustments in the procedure of the High Court, the function of which was to try crimes against the safety of the State. These steps alarmed Boulanger; he thought he was to be arrested and feared separation from his mistress, Marguerite de Bonnemains, whom he loved more than anything else, more even than power. On May 1st, 1889, the General took the train for Brussels; he was fleeing like 'some clerk short in his accounts'. The bubble burst; Boulangism was finished; vainly did his adherents follow him to London, Jersey and Brussels, begging him to return; his only concern was his tubercular and emotional Marguerite de Bonnemains. When she died in 1891, the General committed suicide on her grave. Said Clemenceau: 'He died as he lived, a young second lieutenant', and the journalist Séverine remarked: 'He began like Caesar, continued like Catiline, and ended like Romeo.' In 1889 the Government, having learned its lesson from the Boulanger business, had done away with those multiple candidatures which left the door open to a plebiscite by bits and pieces and had substituted balloting by districts for simultaneous balloting for a number of names. The regime was saved. Congratulations were in order, for heaven alone knows where the foolish Boulanger adventure might have dragged France.

It was becoming an established custom to inaugurate a World Fair in Paris every eleven years; that of 1889 was remarkable in more ways than one. It coincided with the hundredth anniversary of the French Revolution; it displayed the principles of that Revolution as accepted by the entire world; it made it possible for thousands of foreign visitors to see with their own eyes how firmly established was the Republic, despite the recent jolts it had suffered; and it afforded them a lofty notion of France's genius. The astonishing Eiffel Tower was the accomplishment of a great engineer whose labours had transformed the building of bridges and viaducts and who was also to become the founder of aerodynamics and make possible the construction of aeroplanes. The success of the exhibition, the country's justifiable pride and, in addition, the fear of socialism which was springing up to the Left of radicalism, finally led the most reasonable elements in the established order to rally round the regime. Ever since the sixteenth of May, these people had been sulking and sneering at the Government, to France's great hurt; they had successively hoped to see MacMahon, then Boulanger, re-establish the monarchy. Now the best of them were awakening from such dreams. But there remained one barrier preventing a consolidation — the Church. The alliance of throne and altar had been more than a figure of speech; the Vatican, for centuries linked to the House of France, had continued under Pius IX to support the Bourbons. Pope Leo XIII, however, a pontiff of high genius, thought that the Church's role should never be to combat a country's lawful government; the Church can fight hostile legislation, not a Constitution. The Church is eternal; it outlasts dynasties and regimes: it had sacrificed of old the Merovingians to Pepin, it could surely sacrifice the Count of Paris to Sadi Carnot. The Pope instructed Cardinal Lavigerie, Archbishop of Algiers, to put out feelers on the subject of reconciliation, but for a long time it was doubtful whether such a notion would succeed. Among the fanatical monarchists and Bonapartists, it had become perversely fashionable to hate the 'slut', which was their name for the Republic. A pontifical encyclical supplied wise directives from the Holy See to the Church of France and its faithful: a bishop might support a republican candidate provided that that candidate offered guarantees of religious freedom. This attitude permitted the establishment of a Catholic republican party, which caused the parliamentary majority to shift towards the Centre. The Republic was becoming moderate.

After Boulangism, the Republic took on a new aspect; its leaders had realized that Boulanger's unbelievable success had arisen not from his tawny beard and his black horse but from the Schnaebelé incident and Bismarck's attacks. Boulanger himself was nothing, and the matter was closed, but the portent was significant; thenceforward any government which wished to last in France had first of all to assert its concern for the nation's security and dignity. Freycinet's prestige, then quite considerable, came from his having supplied the army with an excellent rifle, the Lebel, and a new explosive, melinite. The moment the French Republic appeared more stable, stronger and more tolerant, foreign friendships began to be cemented; Gambetta had always had the idea that France's natural allies were England and Russia. England, still estranged over colonial rivalries, was not ready, but Russia, perturbed at the formation of a Triple Alliance (Germany-Austria-Italy) was gradually drawing closer to France; the French fleet was welcomed at Kronstadt; the Russian Admiral, Avellan, came to Paris and was given an ovation. Between czarist Russia and republican France the ideological breach was broad, but the loans which Russia floated in France were well received; the French were ready to pay a high price for the joy of being no longer isolated; as for the banks, they were paid their commissions and disposed of the securities; they had nothing to lose.

In 1893 a financial scandal shook the columns of the Palais Bourbon. The Panama business did not harm the Republic as much as Law's downfall had the monarchy, but it wielded a lasting influence over the country's affairs. Ferdinand de Lesseps was a great engineer who had pierced the Isthmus of Suez and of whom France was justly proud; when he had announced his intention of digging a canal across Panama, the French public had backed him with its savings. But Lesseps had been mistaken in his belief that a Panama canal could be built without locks; the task was far more burdensome than he had foreseen, and into the bargain yellow fever was ravaging his employees. In order to muzzle criticism, the Panama Company paid money to the newspapers, and in order to obtain the right to issue a milliard and a half in bonds, it bought votes in the Chamber. This had occurred in 1888 and for a long time, although the Panama Company was in the tightest of straits, successive ministers succeeded in keeping undisclosed the stratagems to which they had lent themselves. The bond-holders still hoped that the Government would come to their rescue; de Lesseps's name inspired so much respect that no one dared demand an investigation. In 1892 the Rightist press, especially a fanatically anti-Semitic paper, La Libre Parole, saw a political weapon in this business and exploded the bombshell. Baron Reinach, who had acted as intermediary between the company and the members of Parliament, committed suicide; Baïhaut, the Minister of Public Works, who was honest enough to make a clean breast of it, was the only politician found guilty. But a whole generation of public men was bespattered; Floquet, Clemenceau and a score of others were compromised and had for long years to withdraw from public life. This had two major consequences: a youthful team, that of Poincaré and of Barthou, made its début in office far sooner than it would normally have done; and because radicalism had been struck in its very leadership, the Republic was by circumstance forced back somewhat more to the Right.

From 1893 to 1898 France was ruled by moderate ministers, and it looked as though the Third Republic was going to resume the middle-class tradition of Guizot and Louis-Philippe; her political leaders were products of the great schools — the Polytechnique, the Normale — or of the Bar. Twenty years afford a regime a certain stability, and already great republican families were growing up whose roots and branches penetrated all the Government departments. The new Notables differed so little from the old that when an anarchist assassinated Carnot in 1894, he was succeeded in the presidency by Casimir Périer, the grandson of the July Monarchy's reactionary minister. A whole series of anarchist attempts at assassination culminated in this presidential murder. The terrified Chamber countered with discriminatory laws which the opposition christened 'villainous legislation'. A socialist party was growing and it had remarkable leaders: Jules Guesde, a theoretician of Marxism; Millerand, Viviani and Jaurès, all three great speakers. Already that seesaw movement was emerging which so long proved the Republic's source of energy; between the Left (radical, then socialist) and the Right (whether Republican Union or Democratic Alliance) there stood an opportunist Centre which, by alternately throwing its weight to Right and Left, assured equilibrium to the regime. After six months, President Casimir Périer resigned, because he found the presidency lacking in means for action. It looked as though the Élysée was becoming a risky address — MacMahon and Grévy had resigned, Carnot had been assassinated. Félix Faure (who followed Casimir Périer) was not to finish his seven years either. Meanwhile, the conservative Republic of Méline, Ribot and Hanotaux continued along its accustomed way. The Russian alliance, wildly acclaimed by the French people, added to the regime's prestige. When Czar Nicholas II came to Paris on a visit to a 'friendly and allied' nation, he was given an enthusiastic welcome.

A third crisis, thanks to the political unintelligence of the Right, first shook the Republic to its very depths and then brought into office various elements of the Left. This was the Dreyfus Case, so famous that in the end it was referred to simply as 'The Case'. It began in 1894 and at first seemed merely a matter for the courts to settle. A memorandum found in the waste-paper basket of Schwarzkoppen, the German military attaché, and handed over to the army's Intelligence Service, seemed to prove that a general-staff officer was acting treasonably. Because of a likeness in hand-writing, but also because of latent anti-Semitism, suspicion fastened upon Captain Alfred Dreyfus; he was condemned by a court-martial, stripped of his rank and shipped to Devil's Island. His family, who knew him to be innocent, investigated further and, in 1897, accused a Major Walsin-Esterhazy of having written the memorandum. Colonel Picquart of the Intelligence Service had himself arrived at the conviction that Dreyfus was innocent and advised his superiors to tell the truth. Stubbornness, pride and prejudice won over justice, and even prudence. Not only did Colonel Henry refuse to admit Dreyfus's innocence, he even forged documents to prove his guilt. Esterhazy was acquitted before a court-martial. Émile Zola, who had written and published a famous letter, *J'accuse* . . . in which he denounced this injustice, was prosecuted and condemned. France then split into two camps, for and against Dreyfus, and the Right made the mistake of identifying itself with the anti-Dreyfus group. It thought thus to defend the army and the Church, but, quite on the contrary, it compromised both by associating them with a bad cause. Two 'Leagues' glowered at each other — that of the Rights of Man and that of the French Fatherland. Friends in fact and in spirit, such as Lemaître and Anatole France, Lavisse and Rambaud, found them-selves on opposite sides of the barricade. Clemenceau and Jaurès — radi-calism and socialism — out of concern for justice had taken up the cudgels for Dreyfus, but they speedily realized the political advantage which could accrue to the Left from The Case. No longer was it merely a question of knowing whether a Jewish officer was or was not guilty, but rather whether the army and the government could, by appealing to reasons of state, deprive citizens of their rights.

The League of the French Fatherland rapidly assumed the factious appearance of the League of the Guises; monks belonging to it incited disloyal generals. In 1899 Félix Faure's sudden death was a most severe blow to the anti-Dreyfus faction which he had favoured; his successor, Loubet, heard himself booed by those whom Anatole France dubbed the 'troublemakers'. Déroulède wanted to try a *coup d'etat* and order the troops to make an assault on the Élysée; he failed. So great was the scandal of the forgeries that a review of the trial was imperative. Loubet thought the moment opportune for crushing the enemies of the regime; he called in Waldeck-Rousseau, a man of the upper middle class, an oppor-tunist, but brave, who succeeded in gathering into his cabinet General de Galliffet, the conqueror of the Commune, and the socialist Millerand, bogy of the bourgeoisie. Jaurès was able to make his party understand that the Republic was in danger and that its duty was to man the guns; the whole Left joined forces around Waldeck-Rousseau. The Court of Appeals, with all its sections sitting jointly, reversed the 1894 decision and remanded Dreyfus to the Rennes court-martial. This second decision, so eagerly awaited, was nonsense. Dreyfus was found guilty by five votes to two, but with extenuating circumstances. The decision enraged the Dreyfus faction. When, to calm the high feelings, Loubet offered Dreyfus his pardon, Dreyfus's adherents hoped that he would refuse, but Dreyfus and his family accepted. Galliffet announced: 'The incident is closed.' But it was not. In 1906 the second decision was to be annulled by the Court of Appeal, Dreyfus was to be restored to his rank and then promoted and decorated, and Picquart was to be made a general and Minister of War.

But this did not constitute the true Dreyfus revolution. Dreyfus had long since ceased to interest his partisans, who had reached the conclusion that, had he been a member of the court-martial, he would have found himself guilty as a matter of discipline. Charles Péguy, who had so ardently championed justice in the Cahiers de la Quinzaine, sadly measured the gap which, after the victory, separated the idealists from the politicians in the party. The politicians rejoiced at the votes they had won back, at the atonement they had obtained; the idealists grieved for the purity of their struggle. Waldeck-Rousseau and his successor, Émile Combes, above all strove to prevent the recurrence of such offensives against the Republic; unruly soldiers and rebellious monks had for several years dominated the Government. There was no need to go outside the monarchy's own arsenal to discover weapons with which to hold the religious orders in check, yet a law was voted to expel all those not 'authorized'. It became an excuse for pillage by unscrupulous liquidators, and the 'milliard-franc' resources of the religious houses melted away in a golden haze. Combes, a politician from the provinces, utterly impervious to seduction by Paris society, determined to have done with the regime's hidden enemies. An over-zealous Minister of War made use of a detestable means to purge the army: he had files prepared on all army officers by certain of their colleagues and encouraged tale-bearing. From this there resulted a deep split in the French army, promotion governed by political and not by military considerations, and a dangerous uneasiness which would finally be healed in 1914 by the terrible jeopardy in which the country found itself. These long-range consequences of The

Case were regrettable, but, taking everything into account, the French Republic emerged from this third and most serious crisis with honour. It has been said that in no other country would such an injustice as the Dreyfus Case have been possible, but that in no other country would that injustice, once committed, have been fought with so much courage or redressed with so much generosity.

HOW COLONIAL RIVALRY BETWEEN FRANCE AND ENGLAND ENDED BY GIVING BIRTH TO THE *ENTENTE CORDIALE*

THE creation of a French colonial empire continued to be a Franco-British issue. During the eighteenth century, it had been possible to conceive that France, by joining Canada to Louisiana, would assure herself a large part of the North American continent; she had interests in the Antilles, Africa and India; her imperial hopes were reasonably well founded. The Treaty of Paris (1763), Napoleon's naval defeats and finally the 1814 treaties had settled the question in England's favour; always threatened in Europe, France could not, as Great Britain had done, devote the better portion of her resources to the building of a fleet. Now mastery of the seas, or the benevolence of those who possess that mastery, is one of the prerequisites for maintaining a colonial empire. France retained only scattered fragments of what had once been hers; then, towards 1830, the conquest of Algeria afforded her a fine stretch of territory, near home, which was very quickly assimilated to such a degree that it was made into three French departments. After 1870, Bismarck had thought that if he could implant in the French hopes of a new empire, he would succeed in deflecting them from their desire to get even with him, and would embroil them with England. Here was the reason for assigning Tunisia to France (1878). A little later on, by withholding intervention in Egypt (as a result of pressure brought by Clemenceau), France allowed England to win preponderance in a country where French culture was a long-standing tradition. However, the French mortgage on Egypt was not legally wiped out, and the consequent rivalry remained a cause of friction between France and England.

It is to the Third Republic's honour that it brilliantly succeeded where the monarchy and the Empire had failed and that it created a magnificent French colonial empire. The treaties of 1814 had left France a few West African ports; they were points of departure for expeditions and exploring parties which, thanks to men like Savorgnan de Brazza and Faidherbe, gave France Senegal and the Niger as far as Lake Chad and the basin of the Nile; the Foureau-Lamy expedition across the Sahara linked

Mediterranean and tropical Africa. In 1892 Dahomey was conquered; in 1895 the island of Madagascar. Cochin-China, Annam and the Protectorate of Cambodia had been added to Tonkin in Indo-China, and these constituted a prosperous area where Gallieni and Lyautey served their apprenticeships as empire builders. In the Indian Ocean, on the Red Sea and in the South Pacific, France acquired such strategic ports as Djibouti and such rich colonies as New Caledonia. Several of these possessions had been won almost without the country's knowledge and despite parliamentary opposition; the evacuation of Tonkin had been defeated by a margin of only four votes. A handful of brave and disinterested men — officers, missionaries, civilian administrators, great cabinet ministers: Ferry, Eugène Étienne, Gabriel Hanotaux — had presented the Republic with this empire, the importance of which the public long failed to recognize. Through the example given by Brazza and Gallieni, there grew up a school of administrators which tried to live on good terms with the indigenous peoples; the loyalty of these natives soon became so deep-rooted that France was able to recruit among them a great proportion of the troops it required to police the empire. And thus, contrary to what Bismarck had foreseen and hoped, France's military strength was not deflected but increased by the development of the empire.

To make up for his miscalculation, it was imperative for Bismarck to succeed in the scheme to create bad feeling between France and England by using Africa, 'a continent created by Providence to vex the Foreign Office'. The two countries' imperial ambitions did, indeed, risk creating antipathy between them. The English wanted to build a railway from the Cape to Cairo, and for this they needed the Sudan: certain French colonial officials thought that French neglect in Egypt could partly be repaired were French expeditions to succeed in cutting Africa in two horizontally and penetrating to the Nile, to the rear of areas occupied by the British; here in short was an African repetition of the French operation which had failed in America and had brought on the Seven Years War — occupation of the hinterland. The results came near being equally tragic. Major Marchand's expedition, after having crossed the Continent, suddenly encountered General Kitchener's far more numerous force at Fashoda, a village in the Sudan. The British Government demanded the withdrawal of Marchand's troops; the French national pride flared up; for some days war was in the offing, and both fleets were mobilized (1898). The French Ministry of Foreign Affairs, however, was then in the hands of Delcassé, who clearly saw the absurdity of a conflict between France and England while Europe's supreme danger lay in Germany's growing strength; he had the courage (and in the then excited state of public opinion, it was a high order of courage) to say to himself: 'Perhaps, by yielding on this painful yet relatively trifling issue of Fashoda, might it be possible to initiate a general settlement of all Franco-British differences?'

In his labours for such a reconciliation, after 1902, Delcassé was abetted by King Edward VII, who was moved both by his sentimental affection for France, where he had spent a portion of his youth, and by a legitimate fear of his nephew Emperor William II's ambitions. The King could have accomplished nothing without the support of the cabinet, but, like him, Lord Lansdowne was worried over Germany's maritime plans; England had always been hostile to any European Power which might undertake to build a great fleet. Throughout all her history, her search had been for a soldier on the Continent. In the days of Louis XIV and Napoleon, she had sought one against France, and this long rivalry had left much distrust in men's minds, but in 1904 the power equilibrium had shifted and agreement seemed possible. England wanted the winding up of any French claim on Egypt; France, greatly bothered in Algeria by the raids of Moroccan robber bands, wanted to have a free hand in Morocco. On these foundations Delcassé and Lord Lansdowne built up an understanding called the *Entente Cordiale*. Here was no alliance, and French public opinion still showed considerable restiveness, but William II himself undertook to tighten these bonds. When he beheld Russia, France's ally, defeated in Manchuria by Japan, the Kaiser thought himself master of the world; his landing at Tangier rudely asserted that Germany was not without an eye for Morocco; for some months he succeeded in intimidating the French Government, and Delcassé, disowned by his colleagues, had to resign in June 1905. But a policy of Franco-German *rapprochement* had no future; the lost provinces and Germany's boundless ambitions were insurmountable obstacles. The 1906 international conference at Algeciras recognized France's rights in Morocco; England supported France with all her weight, and Theodore Roosevelt's pressure constrained Germany to yield; from that moment, perspicacious Frenchmen knew that they dwelt under a constant threat of war.

From 1906 to 1914, it seemed as though France were living on two levels: that of patriotism and that of dissension. On the one hand the conquest of Morocco was the occasion of great deeds, and General Lyautey, a disciple of Gallieni, proved that the great traditions of French colonial policy would be preserved. Under cover of a treaty granting a French protectorate, he sought the support of the Sultan and the great caïds and in a very short time accomplished miracles of organization; respectful of the natives' faith and way of life, Lyautey built his modern towns outside the ancient cities of Fez, Rabat and Marrakesh. He transformed the port of Casablanca, established a phosphate industry, revived the local arts and crafts and made Morocco into one of the most prosperous countries in the world. Meanwhile, great ambassadors (Barrère and the brothers Cambon), with an eye to a war unfortunately all too probable, gathered for France a whole retinue of allies; yet while these faithful servants of their country plied their trade to the best of their ability, internal policy was unstable. Clemenceau, pro-English, had to share power with Caillaux, advocate of reconciliation with Germany. The latter, who was trying to introduce income tax in France, thus aroused against him the representatives of the Established Order; as for Clemenceau, opposed by aggressive socialists and a powerful General Confederation of Labour (C.G.T.), which stirred up a series of strikes extending as far as government employees, he wanted to re-establish the State's authority and thus drew upon himself the hatred of the extreme Left. In 1909 Clemenceau fell from power. Germany, more and more irritable and irritating, provoked incident after incident (Agadir, Casablanca) and, as was to be expected, made Caillaux's policy impossible. Towards 1912 the country began to understand the immediacy of the threat; how could France have reached a lasting agreement with a nation which regarded every concession as a new point of departure? This was the reason for selecting as President of the Republic a patriotic Lorrainer and nationalist, Poincaré; Barthou, Poincaré's colleague for a quarter of a century, suggested re-establishing three-year compulsory military service (at that time the training period was only two years). Thus political uneasiness still engrossed all minds when suddenly there came the first thunder clap, giving notice of the great conflict (June 1914).

Ever since Algeciras, Germany had realized that it would not have the support of its sole ally, Austria-Hungary, in any colonial enterprise; it was already aware that, despite the Triple Alliance, Italy would lend no support in any case. By brilliant diplomacy, however, France had succeeded in combining the Russian alliance with British friendship and in cementing a Triple Entente. Hence if Germany wished to start and win a European war, it must be over a question involving Austria. The Austro-Hungarian Government was interested almost exclusively in

Balkan problems and in the repression of its Slav subjects. A young Serb's successful attempt at Sarajevo against the life of the Austrian Archduke and heir-apparent at once struck the Germans as an excellent excuse for the war of liquidation which they believed inevitable. In France, the Government was so far from conceiving the seriousness of the situation that the President of the Republic, Poincaré, and Viviani, the Prime Minister, were in Russia at the moment when an Austrian ultimatum was sent to Serbia. When Schoen, the German Ambassador, paid a visit to the French Foreign Office in order to announce that if Serbia did not yield, the consequences of her refusal would be 'beyond calculation', the advice given Serbia by France and England was so temperate that the Serbian response amounted to an acceptance of the ultimatum's terms, painful as they were, save on one minor point. But the Germanic Powers' will to war was so strong that they refused to accept even this single reservation, or, later, to participate in a European conference or bring the dispute before the Hague Tribunal. On July 25th, 1914, Austria declared war against Serbia. This unleashed an automatic sequence of mobilizations. Austria began it; then came Russia, then Germany, then France. Russia was bound to support Serbia, France was Russia's ally; England had the strongest of reasons for action, and the invasion of Belgium supplied the British Government with the emotional excuse necessary to win over public opinion. The German socialists, contrary to the promises they had made Jaurès, had done nothing to stand in the way of mobilization, and, on July 31st, Jaurès himself was assassinated by an insane fanatic. Very fortunately the 'holy union' of the French took place the moment mobilization was ordered. Ever since the Revolution, France had been searching for an equilibrium which she could not succeed in finding, and for a regime the legitimacy of which would not be disputed. The country had been terribly divided, but since 1870, distrust of Germany, the desire for *revanche*, the need for a new pact with glory had all been strong sentiments, shared by men of all parties. The moderate Poincaré on this score agreed with the radical Clemenceau; the socialist Jaurès, though he would have done anything to prevent war, was a man to wage it passionately were it to become unavoidable. In 1914, without a complaint, without a single incident, the French citizens accepted the places meted out to them in the armed forces and, confronting the enemy, forgot their own quarrels. Many of them knew and the rest felt that the civilization they were about to defend was one of the loveliest and the happiest in all the world.

CHAPTER VI

HOW HAPPILY FRANCE LIVED BEFORE THE
1914 WAR

TOWARDS 1910 France seemed as prosperous as any European country could be during threatening and anxious days. The Case had been her last serious internal crisis: thereafter the regime had been accepted by the greater number of the French. The party of the Established Order retained its geographical positions, and France's 1914 electoral map was not very different from that of 1877; the Notables, however, seemed at last to have abandoned their dangerous dreams of social reaction.[1] City and country liked the republican holidays, the military review on the Fourteenth of July, the *Marseillaise* on school prize days. Deputies and senators behaved like benevolent patrons in their constituencies; the great republican families constituted an oligarchy which occasionally mingled with the old aristocracies. This republican nobility was open to men of talent, and in Paris, a provincial politician, if he showed some ability, was taken under the wing of the elect and by them transformed into a statesman. The superimposed layers in the pyramid of power were less clearly defined than in the days of the kings. The President of the Republic, without authority if he did not have a strong character, was at the summit only in the eyes of the law; in actual fact, on his same level were to be found the 'consular' figures — former premiers and the leaders of the main sectors in the population. The administrative hierarchies — the Treasury, the Council of State, the Diplomatic Corps, the army and navy — kept their doors ajar to welcome a little new blood, but tended to recruit from hallowed families. The great schools — the Polytechnique and Normale — knit political groups together through a fellowship based on identical modes of thinking and social customs.

The power of this oligarchy was mitigated by the activity of the provinces, which continued to be the primary source of all political strength. A deputy or a senator could not become a minister and dominate Paris unless he retained the confidence and loyalty of an electoral fief. Democratic and anti-clerical freemasonry was potent, and there the lower middle class counted for more than the upper. The Case and the legisla-

[1] GOGUEL.

tion against the religious Orders had somewhat bettered the position of the University at the expense of the great monastic houses, but the latter survived, some of them behind transparent masks, and successfully prepared candidates for the Polytechnique and the military academy at Saint-Cyr. The Catholic Church remained one of the greatest moral and political forces in the country; little by little it had rooted out the Voltaireanism of Flaubert's bourgeoisie, but its opposition to the regime was less ardent and the separation of the Church from the State, while it had impoverished the priests, had also brought them closer to the people. Reconciliation was becoming a reality. France's general level of culture, particularly in the literary field, was higher than that of most other countries. In every town and every village there existed a small society, avid for books and ideas, subscribing either to the *Revue des Deux Mondes* or to more 'advanced' literary journals (*Revue de Paris, Mercure de France, Nouvelle Revue Française*). This chosen few yearly journeyed to Paris, there to come in contact with the season's new productions, to replenish its stock of ideas, to see in the big theatres along the Boulevards the latest plays by Donnay, Bataille, Bernstein, Flers and Caillavet or, in the *avant-garde* theatres like the Vieux-Colombier, Shakespeare, Claudel or Vildrac. The Republic was still Athenian.

The purchasing power of the masses remained inadequate, and wages were too low, but the position of working people had been improved. Under a strong General Confederation of Labour were grouped various individual unions, and the right to strike was unchallenged, except in the public services (Briand had stopped short a railway strike by calling the railway workers to the colours). The working day had been shortened from twelve to ten hours. The majority of the population remained rural, but the split between country and city had grown less. Although many important inventions of the day had been made by Frenchmen, industry had developed less quickly in France than in the United States, Germany or England. Why? Partly because coal was less abundant in France, and her iron ores were of lower grade. Likewise because the French bourgeoisie proved less enterprising, more conservative, less easily won over to collective action. Finally, because the market was limited and because, since customs tariffs protected agriculture, living remained relatively expensive and exports were limited. Nevertheless, the country exported luxury goods — wines, dresses, silks, laces, gloves, perfumes, as well as works of art and books. Throughout the entire world, French art and craftsmanship retained a prestige without compare; France's great vineyards, her celebrated dressmaking establishments, even her cheeses bore names which had become commonplace along the banks of the Missouri or the Amazon. The country's beauty and the delights of living there attracted to Paris, to the watering places and to all France many foreign tourists whose spending assured a healthy balance of trade. The reputation of French art schools drew to Montparnasse English and American artists, enchanted by a life free of puritanical repressions. Early in the twentieth century, French heavy industry seemed to have taken a new lease of life, thanks partly to the discovery of processes which made possible the refinement of the iron of Lorraine, partly to agreements between the French iron masters and the Saar coal mines, partly to the development of water power to make up for the lack of coal and finally to the development of a new industry, that of the motor-car, in which French engineers had been among the first to interest themselves. In 1913 France was producing forty-five thousand motor-cars a year – a large number for that day.

In relation to the other great Powers, France in 1914 still seemed a country of handicrafts, of small businesses and small properties; but concentration was far advanced in banking, where large corporations with many branches (Crédit Lyonnais, Société Générale, Comptoir d'Escompte etc.) were becoming all-powerful, and in retail trade, where department stores were increasing their total business at the expense of the small shopkeepers. That French industry was then far from negligible was proved by the 1914 war; mass production of weapons showed the country's resources. The Third Republic had continued the task of equipping the nation set in motion by the Second Empire; it had set up factories in provincial centres hitherto purely agricultural (Michelin at Clermont-Ferrand, blast furnaces at Caen, chemical and electro-metallurgical industries in areas with water power, the industrialized dairies of the Charentes). As for nineteenth-century French agriculture, it had been outstripped by that of England and Germany, which had both achieved higher yields per acre. This was attributable to the smallness of the areas tilled by each farmer, which made it difficult to use expensive agricultural machinery, and to the fact that, being less scientific, French agriculture likewise used fewer fertilizers. However, at the beginning of the twentieth century, necessity forced farmers to be more progressive. The countrysides were becoming depopulated by the exodus to the cities, fear of the inheritance laws, birth control and the weakening of the religious influence. Lack of man-power forced many small owners to sell out or to join forces; rural co-operatives purchased machinery. Because of the protective tariff, wheat remained the most remunerative crop, but grape vines, mulberry trees and sugar beet yielded the country a more genuine profit. The wiping out of a great number of vineyards by phylloxera had its political consequences, for only those landowners wealthy enough to buy American plants had been able to replant their vines, and hence the wine-producing regions of the south-west gradually moved towards the Left.

The Third Republic's financial position had never been disastrous; without being easy, it had still made possible the conquest of a colonial empire and an expansion of the economy. But a struggle had arisen between the need for higher production and the desire for fiscal justice, which led in 1907 to the passage of the first income-tax plan. There is a certain piquancy in the fact that the Republic thus went back to that personal tax against which the 1789 Revolution had been directed, but with a change in the class benefiting from the exemptions. At first the tax rate was very low and it was accepted without a murmur, but in wartime military expenditures were to unbalance the budget, require new turns of the treasury's screw and disproportionately increase the debt. The danger arose from the fact that French policy was not, and could not be, cut to fit French economic resources; during the period when France had dominated Europe, she had likewise had the largest population on that continent. In 1914, if it wanted to maintain a powerful army and navy (which were necessary for survival), the country was forced to live beyond its means. Little by little the confidence of the thrifty crumbled and, as on the eve of the Revolution, the financial problem was to become a political problem which, between the two world wars, would gnaw away at the Republic as it had gnawed at the monarchy. But before the 1914 war, reasons for worry seemed few; the currency had long been stable in its relation to the pound and the dollar, which were respectively worth twenty-five and five francs. The French peasant and *petit bourgeois* saved up a little gold (the symbolic 'stocking') and bought Government securities; each family planned the lives of its children from the cradle to the grave; dowries, contracts and wills were still, as in Balzac's day, a favourite subject for novelists. The middle class, high and low, continued legalistic, economical and prudent.

André Siegfried, one of the keenest gatherers of the fauna and flora of French bourgeois family life during those early years of the twentieth century, has recorded the part played by the word *petit* (small) in its vocabulary. His observations no longer hold true after the two world wars, but in 1914 the small bourgeois carried out his small economies, and was satisfied with a small income, a small house and a small garden. His shops were called, *Au Gagne-Petit*, *Au Petit Saint Thomas*, *Au Pauvre Diable*, *Au Bon Marché*; his newspapers, the *Petit Parisien*, the *Petit Journal*, the *Petite Gironde*, the *Petit Marseillais*. Far more than a desire for luxury and comfort, he had a liking for moderation, for modesty, and he achieved greatness only in three of his characteristics. His feeling for family solidarity sometimes led him to sacrifice his small income, so dearly won, to save the honour of a distant cousin who bore his name, or to keep in the family some bit of land or town house; his total devotion to his country in war-time made him unhesitatingly accept the heavy burden of compulsory military service; and finally there was his respect for culture. Many a farmer or small merchant subjected himself to continued self-denial in order to afford his children a higher education. Men of letters and scientists were more honoured in France than in any other nation; a theatrical opening, the publication of a book, an election to the French Academy, occasionally even a grammatical controversy were in that country regarded as great events. At times this interest was of a gossipy and superficial nature, but respect for things of the mind remained one of France's constant and finest characteristics.

The Third Republic furnished literary history with a list of names as brilliant as any emanating from any other period; immediately after the war of 1870, Taine and Renan, both overwhelmed by the defeat, laboured to supply France with moral goals. In his *Origines de la France contemporaine*, Taine sought to show the republicans that they must be careful not to break all links with the Old Regime, whose failings he admitted, but which none the less remained the foundation on which they must build. In his *Réforme intellectuelle et morale*, Renan prophesied that Germany and Russia would one day be two giants which would threaten Europe's freedoms. Renan accepted the Republic, but with a grain of salt; he was Prospero watching Caliban take charge of the kingdom; he awaited, without fear but without great hope, catastrophe or a gradual disappearance in the mire. Maurras, a poet and a partisan, tried to breathe new life into the monarchical idea by establishing the *Action Française*. Anatole France was Renan's disciple as far as the graceful effortlessness of his style and his ironic scepticism were concerned; while Maurice Barrès was the inheritor of Chateaubriand's 'cello and his beautifully singing sentences. The Dreyfus Case had torn both of them from their aesthete's games and each in his opposing camp won listeners for his special pleading. Zola and his followers had continued the line of Balzac, but with more scientific pretentiousness. Naturalism, or realism, had made the mistake of seeking reality principally in sordidness, whence there arose among the poets a burning desire for escape which first produced the Parnassians (Leconte de Lisle), then the symbolists (Mallarmé) and finally Paul Valéry, a great poet and writer of classic prose, whose work was to dominate his time. It is noteworthy that the greatest writers of the Third Republic, André Gide, Claudel and Valéry, although known before 1914, achieved fame only after 1920. Charles Péguy, the very embodiment of the French people, a Christian socialist and patriot, had during the days of The Case published his magnificent *Cahiers*; he was killed at the outset of the 1914 war.

Towards the end of the century, one philosopher had a profound influence on French thought, literature and art. Henri Bergson probed the mechanism of the memory, the immediate data of consciousness, the wellsprings of morality and religion. He denied being anti-intellectual, or even anti-Cartesian, but in point of fact he taught that the intelligence, a useful instrument, does not suffice for man, and he defined the intuition, or apprehension — no longer analytical but immediate — of reality. Leibnitz had already warned men against the error of taking the chaff of words for the grain of things. Bergson asked the philosopher, and above all the artist, to tear away those labels which are words and to seek, beneath this verbal knowledge, underlying reality. This teaching was to inspire a French novelist as great as Balzac, Stendhal and Flaubert — Marcel Proust. In 1913 he published the first volume of his lengthy work, *A la recherche du temps perdu*. Proust's themes — wholly Bergsonian — are the nature of time, memory and art, time being subject to 'recapture' by the involuntary memory and under the form of eternity, which is 'likewise that of art'.[1] Proust (like Stendhal and Baudelaire) demonstrated that French classicism and the perfection of its form can join forces with originality of thought and boldness of representation. The influence of women in French society continued to be important; during the days of the Dreyfus Case, the rival *salons* of Madame de Loynes, a passionately reactionary courtesan, silent partner in the *Action Française*, and of Madame Arman de Caillavet, where Anatole France and Jean Jaurès held forth, had served each week as headquarters for the general staffs of the two camps.

In art a fine school of painters sought out, as Bergson advised, the

[1] SANTAYANA.

underlying reality beneath the stereotyped; these were the impressionists — Monet, Renoir, Sisley, Pissaro. Helped by scientific research in the components of light and in pure tones, but above all led on by their own genius, they produced canvases more brilliant, more luminous, and more beautiful than those of the traditional painters, then lording it over the academies and the exhibition halls (Bouguereau, Carolus Duran, Bonnat). Manet and Degas, although differing greatly from the impressionists, like them breathed new life into French painting. Cézanne was the first master of those who, weary of the breakdown of form, were by contrast to return to pictures solidly built and architecturally designed. Seurat, whose use of stippling was merely a technical device, was himself a great devotee of structure. Under the Third Republic, French painters made France the world centre of their art; all the world's museums wrangled to obtain the canvases of her masters, long neglected in their own country. At the same time, Fauré, Debussy, Ravel, Dukas and Duparc thrust to the fore a new school of French music, at once traditional in its taste for measure and original in its style of composition and its harmonies. Finally, in the sciences, Berthelot, Pasteur, Henri Poincaré, Hadamard and Painlevé had built for their country the world over a position equalling that which it held in the arts, while Becquerel and Pierre and Marie Curie were already beginning the great discoveries of the atomic era.

Thus the France of 1914 had no reason to be envious of Louis XIV's France, or of the France of the Renaissance; never had the country had greater renown or a more justifiable prestige; it even seemed to be acquiring, once the Dreyfus Case was over, that stability which it had so long lacked. Accepted by all save the little *Action Française* group, republican institutions were achieving legitimacy. And yet this land, so seemingly prosperous, dwelt on the edge of an abyss. Few Frenchmen suspected it; ever since 1870, they had been aware of the existence of a German peril, but they had not adequately appraised the revolutionary population changes which had come about in Europe during the nineteenth century. Between 1800 and 1914 England had quintupled her population; Germany and Italy had tripled theirs; despite intensive immigration, the French population had not even doubled. France contained only about one-tenth of the people of Europe, whereas she had been drawn by her memories, by her traditions and by her will to survive into assuming a full half of Europe's responsibilities. The load was too heavy and the danger was appalling.

CHAPTER VII

HOW THE 1914 WAR WAS WON

NEVERTHELESS, France, in August 1914, was confident; the troops marched off singing the *Marseillaise*. The desire for *revanche*, lulled between 1889 and 1905, had been aroused ever since Germany had renewed her blackmail. The *Entente Cordiale* had awakened great hopes; Russia, it was thought, would draw off to the east such a number of divisions that the balance of strength would be re-established. The French knew that almost the entire globe was on their side, at heart or in fact. The Russians and the Serbians had been the first to go to war; Belgium was to pull England in; Italy remained neutral, and one could hope that she would join the Allies; Japan would take care of the Far East. It did not seem as though Germany and Austria could stand up against this giant coalition. Joffre's plan, which was offensive, involved an invasion of Alsace during the first days of the war, and for a week France thought that it would succeed. She was stunned and desperate when she learned that the German army in Belgium was sweeping everything before it, that Liège and Namur had fallen, that the French army had just been defeated at Charleroi and was in full retreat. The secretiveness of the Government added to the national anxiety; after a month of painful uncertainty, there suddenly burst forth, 'like a clap of thunder', the astounding communiqué which announced that 'from the Somme to the Vosges', the line remained unchanged. This fine specimen of understatement revealed the extent of the disaster: the roads to Paris and to the Channel both lay open to the Germans.

What had happened? Simply this, that the Germans, taking their chances with a Russian invasion, had concentrated on the French frontier a larger army than the French general staff had thought possible; that German machine-guns and heavy artillery had proved superior; that the purely offensive fighting tactics advocated for some years in France had brought about useless losses. The fine courage of the army was not enough against a well-fortified enemy with frightful firing power. For a few days there was a reasonable fear that the 1914 war would end, like that of 1870, within a few weeks and in disaster. But the Germans, instead of pushing towards Calais or Paris, followed the conventional rules of the game and pursued the French army; in this pursuit they too quickly lengthened their lines of communication and had difficulty with their ammunition supplies. Finally the Russian advance, more speedy than the German high command had foreseen, led it at the most critical juncture to take several divisions away from Von Kluck, who was in command of the invasion. Joffre, a thoughtful and level-headed Catalonian, had had the moral courage to continue the retreat until the moment when he thought the circumstances favourable for a final stand; at last, in early September, he saw the German army engaged on the Marne along the arc of a circle formed by the French army, and threatened on its left wing by the Paris garrison, which Gallieni had painstakingly prepared for such a manœuvre. Joffre decided it was time to join battle. By every means at hand, even by requisitioning the taxicabs of Paris, Gallieni brought up his troops against the rear of the German army. Foch, halted in the marshes of Saint-Gond, dispatched his stirring telegram: 'My left is broken, my right is weakening; the situation is excellent: I am attacking.' Von Kluck, fearing he would be outflanked and cut off from his bases, drew back. Paris and France were saved.

The victory of the Marne was one of those amazing recoveries France has had all through her history; it made impossible any lightning victory on the part of the Germans, but it did not free all France's territory. The weeks which followed were called the Race to the Sea, because each of the adversaries strained every effort to reach the shores of the Channel as quickly as possible and thus cover its flank. The Belgians, French and English succeeded in holding the Germans before Ypres; Antwerp had fallen, but the French Channel ports remained in the hands of the Allies, which made possible the supplying and reinforcing of the British army. On both sides, the troops dug trenches, protected by barbed wire, and two lines, a few hundred yards apart, followed a course which extended from the Belgian coast to the Swiss frontier, constituting an enormous bulge in which were held captive Flanders, Artois, a portion of Picardy and Champagne and all the provinces of the north-east; once again in the history of the struggle between defensive tactics and shock tactics, defence had won the day. For months and years the opponents were to seek means to break through this barrier and resume a war of movement; that this break-through could not be accomplished by means then known was demonstrated by the Allies' fruitless and murderous offensives in Champagne and Artois. Winston Churchill, the most brilliant of the English ministers, suggested a novel solution — an attack on the Dardanelles. Turkey had become Germany's ally; breaking this Eastern front would make it possible to help Russia and try conclusions in the East. This campaign might have succeeded; it came to nothing because it was not pressed with enough obstinacy, and after heavy losses the Allies abandoned the Gallipoli Peninsula. Meanwhile the Austro-German armies had crushed Serbia, and Briand had effected at Salonika the opening of a new Eastern front, a step which later was to have its happy outcome.

In order to prevent the Germans from moving their reserves from one front to the other, according to the exigencies of the moment, Joffre in 1916 won acceptance for the idea of a general Allied offensive. The Germans decided to forestall this. William II's line of reasoning was that England formed the soul of the coalition, that Russia was already paralysed and that if the French army, England's sword, were broken, the war would be over. Hence such a point of attack must be chosen as would force the French command to use all its forces, up to the last battalion, in defence. Along the French front there were two key positions — Belfort and Verdun. Verdun was selected, and the attack began with extreme violence in February 1916. Joffre entrusted the defence to General Pétain, who, starting as a colonel at the outbreak of the war, had in less than two years become commander of an army group. The main difficulty was to supply the heroic army of Verdun in its narrow salient, the approaches to which were commanded by the German artillery. Pétain organized his supply trains, counter-attacked, and after assaults without number, the German attacks began to lose their force; the battle of Verdun was as costly to the Germans as the 1915 offensive had been to the Allies. These, in their turn, launched a new offensive in Champagne, under the command of General Nivelle, who had replaced Joffre because the Allied Governments blamed the hero of the Marne for the stagnation into which the war had fallen; it was disaster. The magnitude of the losses in comparison to the trifling ground gained showed, as had the Battle of Verdun, that the defensive still had the upper hand.

This superiority of armour was more profitable to the Germans, whose positional situation continued advantageous, than to the Allies whose territories had been invaded. The countries which had taken sides with the Triple Entente — Italy (1915) and Rumania (1916) — found themselves in no better position than France. On the seas, the German submarine campaign, so perilous for an England dependent on her merchant fleet for her supplies, had been temporarily slackened because of diplo-

matic notes from the United States. However, a naval engagement, the
Battle of Jutland, did not result, as might have been hoped, in the destruction of the German fleet. The year 1916 ended in deep discouragement for the Allies. It was true that the British army had then reached
a total of one million two hundred thousand perfectly equipped men,
and that the French army still numbered, with the Belgians, two million
six hundred thousand men. But no one could see any means to victory.
The Battle of Champagne had demonstrated that barbed wire, machine-
gun fire and artillery barrages left an attacker little hope. The French
army was dissatisfied with the leave system and was sapped by the
country's dull weariness. In 1917 serious mutinies broke out in sixteen
army corps; Nivelle was replaced by Pétain, who undertook personally
to visit many of the regiments, improved the soldiers' diet and re-established discipline with a minimum of severity. On September 15, 1916 the
English used for the first time on the Somme a weapon until then kept
secret, the assault vehicle (tank), which was ultimately to shift the balance
of power in favour of the offensive. Invented in England, this vehicle
was a shield, mounted on caterpillar tracks, capable of covering infantry
and, in theory, of moving over any sort of terrain. On the Somme a deep
penetration was effected, but the British command was not yet ready to
exploit its success and this first attempt was merely a trial, without lasting
effect. Tanks were again used in 1917 at Cambrai with greater success but
once more without lasting success.

Allied disasters continued to pile up. The imperial Russian Government
collapsed; Kerensky's pro-Allied Government was replaced by Lenin's,
and in order to devote himself entirely to the internal revolution, Lenin
negotiated an armistice with the Germans. In April 1917 submarine
warfare had caused Allied shipping losses of a million tons — a drain it
could not long stand. It is true that the resumption of attacks without
warning against merchant vessels had led to an event of major importance — American entry into the war on the Allied side — but the United
States had no army, and no one yet knew its wonderful capacity of
improvisation. In actual fact, the United States' decision to go to war
meant the turning-point in the Allied fortunes; the three combined navies
were at last able to master the submarine danger in the Atlantic; the greatest
minefield ever attempted was laid between Norway and Scotland.
A bold operation carried out by the British navy closed the Belgian ports
which had served as bases for small submarines. The construction of tanks
was pressed with feverish activity in France and in England, while in

America a large expeditionary force was being trained. In France, all those who urged a compromise peace were subdued by Clemenceau; he had had his unpopular hour at the time of the Panama scandal, but he had always been the man who wanted *revanche* and the English alliance. Little by little he thrust aside Briand, who himself had waged the war with intelligence and bravery, but who would at that moment gladly have listened to the offers of a separate peace made by Austria. With the help of the forceful Georges Mandel, Clemenceau rebuilt for France her spirit of Public Safety; radicalism, Jacobinism and chauvinism — the traditional combination was once again coming to the fore.

Everywhere along the front in 1918, the soldiers in battle spied Clemenceau's old felt hat and listened to his mocking voice; the stubbornness of this old man then proved its usefulness to France, for Germany, in order to force the issue, was making a desperate effort. The Russian armistice had restored to her a slight superiority in numbers on the Western front, and the Allied defence was badly co-ordinated. Haig and Pétain were respectively in command of the British and French armies, but were not subject to the authority of a single command. The German general Ludendorff took advantage of this situation and, in March 1918, attacked the hinge of the two armies, hoping to spring it and force the British back towards the sea. He almost succeeded and got as far as the gates of Amiens. Thereupon an inter-Allied command was established which was entrusted to General (later Marshal) Foch, Haig and Pétain both being placed under his orders. It was a good choice. Not only was Foch a strategist who thoroughly knew his trade — he had written *Principes de la Guerre* and was steeped in real experience — but he also had a heart impervious to fear which believed victory possible and was resolved to win it. The early days of his command were difficult; he had to deal with fresh offensives, both on the French and on the English fronts (the Battle of the Lys, and the Battle of the Chemin des Dames). Ludendorff thrust a deep salient towards Paris, which extended as far as Château-Thierry, but he thus exposed his flank. And Allied power was on the increase. Already American divisions were arriving and General Pershing, who had at first, as was natural, wished to build an independent American army, had ultimately, because of imminent danger, agreed to amalgamation. Thus Foch was daily strengthened by fresh reserves, whereas Ludendorff had none remaining to him.

In July 1918 hope changed camps. On the fifteenth, Ludendorff made an attack in Champagne which was stopped by Gouraud's army's elastic defence; on the eighteenth, Foch launched a counter-attack from Villers-Cotterêts, under Mangin's command, with a heavy tank contingent, which inflicted a serious defeat on the Germans. Once again the lance had pierced the armour. Foch pressed his attacks all along the line in an endlessly renewed series of jabs and surprises. Haig, Pétain and Pershing each in turn moved forward. In the East, also, the Salonika front was becoming active; Franchet d'Esperey was very soon to force the Bulgarians to sue for peace, opening the road to Vienna for the Allies. At the end of October, Turkey withdrew from the war. For some time, the German high command, knowing that Foch was preparing a great offensive which would carry his armies into Germany, had been negotiating with President Wilson, who had transmitted to it his Fourteen Points. On November 4th, Austria capitulated. A revolution broke out in Germany and the Emperor, William II, fled into Holland. On November 11th, an armistice was signed at Rethondes, in the Compiègne forest, the Germans accepting all the conditions laid down by Foch.

It was a great victory for the Allies, and especially for France, which until the very end had played the chief part in the coalition and exercised supreme command. Of course France knew that she could not alone have won a war against Germany, as much for lack of sufficient troops as for the size of her industrial plant; the time had passed when she raised and equipped the largest armies on the Continent. If, at the beginning of the war, Russia had not engaged sixty German divisions, the Battle of the Marne could not have been a victory; without the British fleet and army, France could not have held out for four years; without the American divisions, France and England might perhaps have been victorious, but only after long and deadly years of struggle; without American industrial production, defeat would have been inevitable. But if France had needed her allies (and she was the first to acknowledge it), she had, through the bravery of her armies and the prestige of Foch and Clemenceau, none the less won a glorious place in the world's opinion. She was in an excellent position for the coming peace conference, and no one thought that this could be held anywhere but in Paris, which had become what Vienna had been after the Napoleonic wars — the place where the new Europe would be hammered out. The President of the United States and the Prime Ministers of Great Britain, Italy and Japan assembled there to discuss with Clemenceau the future order of Europe.

The Congress of Vienna had based its decisions on the principle of legitimacy; those of the Paris Conference were based on nationality.

Napoleon III was triumphant over Talleyrand, sentimentality over experience. President Wilson believed in the right of peoples to self-determination; in order to avoid a break, Lloyd George and Clemenceau, more sceptical, accepted a doctrine contrary to the whole diplomatic tradition of both their countries. The Treaty of Westphalia had left a strong France confronting a divided Germany; the Treaty of Versailles left a strong Germany confronting a Balkanized Europe. The carving up of Austria-Hungary left Germany master of central Europe, without anything to counterbalance her. The danger would have been less had this Germany been truly disarmed, had the German high command been dissolved, had reparations absorbed the country's excess resources. But disarmament was sabotaged, the high command was never even disturbed, reparations were paid only at the beginning, and then with American money. Thus France, bled white by her terrific losses, once again found herself at grips with a Germany which had lost almost none of her war potential and which, from 1920 on, was to gird herself for a new war. It is true that France had finally won back Alsace and Lorraine, that she acquired mandates over Syria, Togoland and the Cameroons, but on the essential point — security — she had no guarantee whatever. Clemenceau had requested the left bank of the Rhine, to deprive Germany at once of a starting-point and of an industrial region without which it would be difficult for her to wage a war. Wilson and Lloyd George refused. They offered to substitute for this annexation a treaty of guarantees. But this treaty was not ratified by the United States Congress, and Great Britain refused to involve herself alone. At least it was to be hoped that Wilson would provide support to a strongly organized League of Nations, which would serve as guardian over the treaties. Wilson having been eliminated by the American elections of 1920, the United States did not enter the League. The victory had been magnificent; nothing encouraged the hope that it would be lasting.

CHAPTER VIII

HOW, BETWEEN 1919 AND 1939, VICTORY CRUMBLED INTO DUST

FOR France, the major problem continued to be that of security. From the beginning of her national existence, she had suffered Teutonic invasions, and in the course of the previous fifty years alone she had twice been attacked by Germany. After a victorious war, she had a right to expect that steps would be taken against this danger. Yet her allies had not allowed her to take them herself and had refused to take them in common; there was great disillusionment in France, and deep discouragement. Clemenceau, the country's idol in 1918, was defeated in 1920 when he stood as candidate for the presidency of the Republic against Deschanel, the heir of a great republican name but without personal prestige. A new and dangerous voting method had brought to the Palais Bourbon a 'horizon-blue' Chamber, a National Bloc and an aggressive return of the Notables. Patriotic sentiment had favoured the war veterans, and fear of communism had hurt all the parties of the Left. The Russian Revolution inspired great hopes among the European proletariats, but great fears in the parliamentary States. Soon the socialist party was cut in two; the partisans of the dictatorship of the proletariat and immediate revolution founded the French communist party; the others continued to back a unified socialist party with Léon Blum as its leader, a talented speaker and writer who abided by parliamentary discipline. The labour unions also split into the C.G.T. (socialist in allegiance) and the C.G.T.U. (Unitary [One-Party] General Federation of Labour), communist in tendency.

The fears of the middle class were increased by an odious financial situation. Until 1914 budgetary deficits had been constant but not worrying. In 1920 the expenses of war and of pensions to its victims and to fatherless families had created a vast debt which the payment of damages to war victims was to increase by eighty milliard francs. All the north and north-east of the country had to be reconstructed. 'Germany will pay!' Klotz, the Finance Minister, had exclaimed, and because it was the enemy who would foot the bills, the indemnities had been over-generous. However, to make Germany pay soon seemed an insoluble problem. The total reparations had been swollen beyond any reasonable figure by the demands of Lloyd George, who had included pensions in it. Resolved not to pay, Germany played bankrupt and set to work to devaluate her own currency, which freed her of her internal debt. At the same time, from England and the United States, she obtained privately financed loans, so that her financial position, seemingly desperate, was in fact better than that of victorious France. That country had to set aside, for the payment of her war debts, the greater part of the sums received as reparations. This whole system, ingeniously worked out by the German bankers, pumped gold out of the United States and brought it into the Reich in the form of American credits, then into France and other countries under the name of reparations, then back to the United States under the guise of war-debt payments. It was a useless and exasperating circuit for all the interested parties except Germany, which ingeniously deflected a portion of the current and used it to build new cities and war plants.

Meanwhile France had to find money or go bankrupt. Millerand, a former socialist who had become the hope of the conservatives, had, as early as 1920, replaced Deschanel — seriously ill — as President of the Republic. In 1922 he summoned Poincaré, one of his predecessors, to the premiership, and Poincaré tried to make Germany pay by occupying the Ruhr. Here was the best means at hand, even the sole means, but it injured powerful interests. A campaign was organized against 'warmonger Poincaré' and at the very moment when the strong hand was beginning to yield results, the electorate repudiated Poincaré, just as the deputies had repudiated Clemenceau. In the 1924 elections Millerand, who had supported Poincaré and had thus assumed a position incompatible with the President's traditional and functional neutrality, was ousted by the Chamber, which refused to have any dealings with the ministers he chose. Power returned, as before 1914, to the radicals. Doumergue, radical and Protestant, was elected President of the Republic; the Ruhr was evacuated; Caillaux, father of the income tax, became Minister of Finances. He crashed into the 'wall of money'.

The income tax, accepted and respected in England, had not produced the expected results in France. The first reason was that, in the days of the monarchy, the country's tradition had been one of secrecy in business affairs and horror of arbitrary power in the Treasury, a feeling unknown in England where, for centuries, there had been free consent to taxation. The second reason was that, because French capital was more thinly spread than elsewhere, legislation which threatened it affected more quickly a majority of the voters and aroused political reactions. For that reason, the radical party, then brilliantly and honourably led by Édouard Herriot, found itself forced to waver between the socialists, with whom it would emotionally have preferred an alliance, and the moderates, whose support it needed to secure loans. 'Their hearts on the Left, their pocketbooks on the Right', wrote André Siegfried. In 1926, when the country's credit was melting away because of the flight of gold and the pound sterling had risen to two hundred and twenty-five francs, Poincaré had to be recalled, a new 'family lawyer', who, not by any brilliant measures, but by the confidence he inspired among people with savings, brought the franc up to 20 per cent of its pre-war value. A franc worth twopence: here was the measure of France's vast losses during the course of the war, losses intensified by the flight of capital – a most reprehensible practice which stultified the high income-tax rates. In the 1928 elections, thanks to Poincaré's prestige, the moderate party triumphed. Tardieu, an intelligent and disillusioned member of the upper middle class, was to be the political leader of this Chamber, and he left foreign affairs to Briand, the last hope in Europe for peace-loving and liberal men.

Aristide Briand, a man of compromise and insight, a great, imperturbable artist of diplomacy and the rostrum, had had, ever since 1918, a deep desire to re-establish true peace in Europe. He had placed his skill and his eloquence at the service of the League of Nations, but the Geneva organization was warped by the absence of the United States and Great Britain's mental reservations. In 1924 Herriot had vainly proposed a sensible protocol which would have put 'teeth in the pact'; he had come to grief before Ramsay MacDonald's opposition. Briand had sought by other means to induce England to guarantee French security. Assisted by his personal friendship with Austen Chamberlain and Stresemann, he succeeded in negotiating the Locarno Pact (1925) under which France, Germany, Poland, Italy and Great Britain mutually guaranteed one another against any aggression. Thus England seemed to be protecting Germany against any ultimate aggression on France's part; Briand, however, knew that such an eventuality was inconceivable, and, by this roundabout means, he had drawn England out of her post-war isolationism. As a matter of fact, at the only moment when it might have been serviceable (March 1936), the Locarno Pact failed to function. Yet Briand took this gamble, as he later took his chances with a European

Federation and the Kellogg Pact. During Chancellor Bruning's tenure of office — he was a Catholic and relatively moderate — Briand still hoped for direct reconciliation with Germany. In this he failed. His long labour on behalf of peace, however honourable and necessary, had not won him the gratitude of Parliament. When in 1931 he ran as a candidate for the presidency of the Republic, he was defeated by Paul Doumer. Not long after, Briand died, the last champion of a Europe in jeopardy.

On the surface, nothing in France had changed. Institutions seemed to be functioning normally; the Chamber held its sessions, the electors cast their votes, the soldiery went through its manoeuvres, the police kept order. But in many minds the parliamentary system had suffered serious blows; the attacks against the institutions of the Third Republic came from both the Left and the Right. On the Left, the Third International argued for the one-party system and the dictatorship of the proletariat; on the Right the perilous example of Italian fascism aroused culpable hopes among French reactionaries, whether monarchists or totalitarians. Once again the Right harped on the unhappy theme that 'things couldn't be worse', and it started campaigns, as foolish as they were reprehensible, to discredit the republican men of state. These redoubled in violence when the Stavisky Affair came into the light of day, a far less serious business than the Panama scandal, but one which proved the corruption of some politicians and a few judges. The incident should have been brought to a rapid conclusion in the courts, but the law was not efficient; parliamentary committees seized upon the case and suddenly, as in the days of Dreyfus, France found herself split in two. In Paris, disorders, at first sporadic, quickly turned into an uprising, and on February 6th, 1934, the Palais Bourbon was literally besieged by the mob; the troops had to open fire to defend the Concorde bridge. There were a few dead. Such a thing had not happened since the time of the Commune. What did these demonstrators want? They cried: 'Down with the thieves!' but those behind them wanted to overthrow the Republic. The success of the totalitarian regimes had turned many heads, and the incompetence of the cabinet had helped the conspirators. The ban on playing Shakespeare's *Coriolanus* at the Comédie Française, 'because it was an anti-democratic play', and the nomination of the head of the Sûreté as director of that theatre, quickly assumed an atmosphere of scandal and farce. But the comedy had its victims; was the Third Republic, like the July Monarchy, to founder in ridicule, bespattered with blood?

It was saved, first of all by the socialists who, by calling a general strike, avowedly to defend the Republic, showed to good purpose that the working people of Paris would not abandon the capital to gangs of would-be fascists, and then by President Lebrun's summoning his predecessor, Gaston Doumergue, whom he asked to form a ministry of reconciliation. Doumergue, as President of the Republic, had done very well and, through his amiability and adroitness, had exercised more influence than any other head of the State for many long years. A 'great ministry' was formed, a cabinet of republican union, which ranged from Édouard Herriot (radical) to André Tardieu (moderate), and in which Chéron and Pétain participated. Doumergue was accepted by the Left because he had himself been a man of the Left, yet every honest partisan of parliamentary government could not help being upset at seeing the President of the Republic agree that a cabinet which had always held a majority in both Chambers should be overthrown by an uprising. At once the Doumergue ministry was confronted with a revival of the Stavisky Affair; a magistrate named Prince, who had had a hand in the case, was found dead on the railway tracks near Dijon; was it suicide or assassination? The Left said suicide, and the Right assassination, and once again passions flared up. Doumergue had long thought that France was becoming impossible to govern; ministries fell every three months because, he said, the executive power was defenceless, because the right of dissolution was too difficult to exercise, because the parties were too numerous and too little organized, and finally because the deputies had the right of initiative with regard to expenditure. Doumergue, who wanted to amend the Constitution in order to bring it closer to British practice, which he considered better, determined to convene a National Assembly for this purpose. However, the prestige of the former President was already crumbling; he had insisted on speaking directly to the country on the radio, but this means, effective as it was in America, was still offensive to the French legislators. Here, it was repeated, was Bonaparte's 'appeal to the people'. The public was tired of hearing Doumergue 'call himself the Just'.[1] The Right press, breaking the truce, unjustly belaboured the radicals in the cabinet, and they resigned. In November 1934 Doumergue himself, under attack from all sides, had to step down. The French were still at loggerheads.

Now these domestic divisions were all the more dangerous as the power and aggressiveness of the European fascist States increased; not only was Mussolini absolute master of Italy, but in Germany an anti-Semitic

[1] D. W. BROGAN.

agitator 'of mystical brutality', Adolf Hitler, had come to power in 1933 and openly spoke of building 'the greater Germany'. A fanatically inspired younger generation made up his following. Hitler's bible, *Mein Kampf*, asserted that France's final destruction was the goal, friendship with England the means. Those who governed France hesitated to take any steps, for what sure allies had they? In 1933 Mussolini had suggested a pact of the four great Powers (Britain, France, Italy, Germany), which would have been a Locarno without Poland. This proposal had come to nothing; but Poland, worried, had drawn away from France. What would Italy do next? In 1935 Mussolini threatened Ethiopia; were a war to break out between these two countries, both members of the League of Nations, what should France's attitude be? An unhappy fate had willed that the English and French Governments should be at odds. For fifteen years, France had been in despair because England had refused to use her power in defence of collective security, and in 1935 she had been deeply distressed to learn that England had separately signed a new naval treaty with Hitler's Germany. She was astounded when suddenly a strong movement of public opinion (set going by Anthony Eden) forced the British Government, in the case of Italy and Ethiopia, to back collective security and a recourse to sanctions. Without doubt the League of Nations had the right to support one of its members, but they were availing themselves of that right very late in the day and at a time when the political outcome would be to push Italy into Germany's arms. Up to that time, Europe had had one stroke of luck — the two dictators had no liking for each other; each took offence at the other's arrogance. After the Ethiopian business, they came to terms in order to demand revision of the 1919 treaties. Whereas before 1914 France had every year seen an increase in the number and the strength of her friends, about 1936 she began to see an increase in the number of her enemies and in the weakness of her friends. When, in March 1936 Hitler, in disregard of the Versailles Treaty, decided to militarize the left bank of the Rhine, England, bound under the Locarno Treaty, should have joined France in protest. But English public opinion, and, curiously enough, especially the opinion in liberal and advanced circles, maintained that Germany had a right to equality and that France's claims to security were unreasonable. In France, an interim cabinet, which was conducting a general election, did not think it had the authority needed to start a war. From that day forth, Germany knew that she could defy her late conquerors with impunity.

In this hour of peril, France was unfortunately busier about her domestic politics than foreign affairs. The uprising of the Sixth of February had united all the parties of the Left in a legitimate fear of violent and reactionary fascism. Until that time, the communists and the socialists, the socialists and the radicals, had rigorously opposed each other. Between the radicals and the communists, there existed no doctrinal link whatever, but nothing unites men so successfully as a common enemy. The Sixth of February welded the three great Left parties into a Popular Front, which won a brilliant victory at the polls. The hope of the socialists and of their leader, Léon Blum, a man of good faith, of great culture and of courage, was to achieve a legal and peaceable social revolution, analogous in its principles and its projects to the American New Deal. To this there were many obstacles. The 1936 victory had not been a socialist victory but a victory of the Popular Front, and Léon Blum had a majority in the Chamber only if the three parties held together; the communists wanted to push Léon Blum further and faster than he wanted to go; the radicals served as a brake, and were assisted in this by the Senate, which remained more moderate than the Popular Front. Immediately after the election, the communists organized a series of strikes, which included the workers' occupation of the factories ('sit-down strikes') in order to force the Government's hand and win the immediate enactment of a programme which (in Blum's mind) was to extend over the next four years. Blum informed the communists that he had no intention of being a Kerensky, adding that if his task was made impossible, his successor would not be a Lenin. He was able to effect a few useful reforms, but like all Governments of the Left, ran up against the 'wall of money'. In September 1936 the franc had to be devalued. When the Government requested plenary powers (meaning the right to legislate by decree), the Senate refused them. The old campaigners of radicalism replaced the socialists at the helm.

Since March 1936 Hitler had known that he could venture everything; thenceforward his preparations for war were carried on more openly. German air power first equalled and then surpassed that of the Allies, while only such isolated voices as that of Winston Churchill gave warning of the terrible danger. A civil war had broken out in Spain, in which Germany and Italy aided the elements tending towards fascism and tried out new methods of warfare, while France and England sought refuge in self-deceit by their policy of non-intervention. This policy, repudiated by the communists, had helped to shatter the Popular Front.

In Great Britain, the Chamberlain cabinet, despite the warnings of Eden, who resigned, still hoped to appease Hitler. The Prime Minister naively believed that if Germany were given satisfaction on some points, she would then be willing to co-operate in maintaining the order of Europe. Hitler played upon this desire for peace, which he sensed was no less ardent in France. Germany, he said, wanted no conquests; she merely wanted to protect her blood brothers. With this excuse, he swallowed province after province; Europe, weary of conflict, resigned itself to the event. Isolated, terrified and powerless, the victim was devoured, and at once the Government of the Reich selected a fresh prey for the season to come. Thus the German armies, in March 1938, entered Austria, and in October of the same year, Czechoslovakia. This latter operation should have led to war, for Paris had a treaty of alliance with Prague, but the French Government sacrificed everything on the altar of its agreement with England, and England refused to become involved, alleging the traditional reasons — her inability to consider hypothetical cases, the need to consult with the Dominions. At Munich (September 1938), Czechoslovakia was carved up. The diplomacy of the Western Powers lost all prestige in the East; the Munich decisions had been reached without Russian agreement, and because of this mistake, Russia was irretrievably alienated. France, bled white between 1914 and 1918, and feeling her military and economic exhaustion, still remained blind to the imminence of the danger and the folly of such compromises. On their return from Munich, the ministers were greeted with rapture, and Chamberlain was given a reception at the Hôtel de Ville as harbinger of peace.

During March 1939, in contempt of the Munich agreements, Hitler invaded and annexed all Czechoslovakia. Such perfidy overwhelmed Neville Chamberlain who, abruptly changing his tactics, offered Poland, appointed victim of the next aggression, a treaty of mutual assistance, France was already bound to Poland; this new British attitude strengthened those among the French who, seeing that war was inevitable, devoted all their thought to preparing for it. Daladier, the radical Premier, reacted vigorously against a new series of sit-down strikes and re-established the authority of the State. He answered Mussolini, who was making his organized demonstrators scream 'Nice! Savoy! Tunis! Corsica!', by a trip to Corsica and Tunisia, the success of which warmed the hearts of French patriots. Anxiety gnawed deep. A Russo-German agreement caused consternation among the British and French ministers; the disparity in power between the two camps seemed formidable, but the wish for appeasement had been followed by a desperate resolution, a will to have done with compromises followed by fresh blackmail. France and England had tried everything — and perhaps too much — to keep the peace; they had failed because they had clashed with a demoniacal will and an extravagant pride. When, without declaration of war, Germany invaded Poland, Danzig was her excuse, the conquest of Europe her real goal. After England, France addressed an ultimatum to Hitler, and on September 3rd, 1939, at five in the afternoon, she began her second world war. More than any other which France has waged in the long course of her history, this was a war of principles and ideals. The issue was whether violence and cynicism or international law would dominate the world.

CHAPTER IX

THE SECOND WORLD WAR: FIRST PHASE

IN the Second World War, France's position was vastly more perilous than in the first. In 1914 she had had a great part of Europe on her side; in 1939, Italy was hostile, Russia temporarily had her hands tied by her non-aggression pact with Germany, Belgium sought to remain neutral. On whom could France still count? Great Britain and Poland. Great Britain showed that she meant business, and everything encouraged the hope that the Dominions would assist her, but England had long before warned the French Government that her contribution, in case of war, would above all be in sea and air power; on land she had promised only thirty-two divisions within three years, meaning ten or so during the first, most critical, year. Poland contributed her bravery and her patriotism, but her army, compared to the German army, had insufficient equipment; obviously she could not play the part which in 1914 had been played by Russia. As for France, she had lost the best of her youth between 1914 and 1918; hence she lacked man-power and, because of Italy's connections with Germany, she was forced to leave troops in North Africa and Syria, whereas in 1914 it had been possible to bring the colonial army back to the home country. Finally, the position of the United States was less favourable to the French than during the First World War. Not only was there no question, in 1939, of that country's entering the war, but its neutrality law was to make more difficult the buying and shipping of war supplies.

And yet these supplies would have been indispensable to French success. France and England lacked tanks, anti-tank and anti-aircraft guns, and planes; in large-scale British manœuvres on the eve of war, searchlight companies and anti-aircraft batteries had of necessity been represented by dummies. After a few months of war, the German air force would number about fifteen hundred fighter planes and three thousand five hundred bombers; the French air force, five hundred and eighty fighter planes, many of them antiquated, and ninety-six bombers; the British air force in France, one hundred and thirty fighters and five hundred bombers.[1] Some people placed their faith in the Maginot Line, a

[1] HENRY BIDOU.

system of reinforced concrete structures with underground galleries and pillboxes which shut off the eastern frontier; this line was strong and was defended by crack troops, but it did not cover the north-east or the north, and it was not difficult to outflank it by crossing Luxembourg and Belgium, the classic pattern of German invasions. The Germans for their part had built a Siegfried Line (or West Wall) composed of casemates echeloned in depth and systems of barbed wire. It would have been possible, in September 1939, to launch a frontal attack against the Siegfried Line while the Germans were busy in Poland, but experimental offensives in the Saar yielded small results. Material means as well as the offensive spirit were lacking. This war was far from inspiring the French with the same enthusiasm as that of 1914; many of the working people were disturbed at seeing Russia in the opposite camp, and some of the middle class had a secret sympathy for fascism. The army was doing its duty, but in England as in France, public opinion refused to believe that the fight would be to the death, while in America the anti-fascist liberals blamed the Allies for their lukewarmness.

Meanwhile Germany carried on her Polish campaign at top speed. By means of co-ordinated tank and plane attacks, a tactic which, if not new, was here at least applied massively for the first time, the Germans, in a few weeks, despite heroic resistance, crushed the Polish army, which after the early days of October 1939 no longer required the attention of the main body of Germany's forces. The 1939-40 winter passed quietly enough. In the north the French and British armies, stretched along the frontier, laboured to build a fortified line, which could not possibly be as solid as the Maginot, but which it was nevertheless hoped would be strengthened by reinforced concrete strongpoints and barbed-wire barriers. In the spring of 1940, this line was far from finished; the casemates lacked guns and the frontier was still perilously vulnerable. Great Britain still believed that she could bring Germany to terms through the blockade; Germany's answer was a submarine counter-blockade. At first the submarines were ineffective; the English and French navies sank a number of them. Round about February the Germans laid magnetic mines in the Channel; the idea was that they would be attracted by passing ships and would wipe out the British merchant fleet, but an answer to this, a very simple device, was at once worked out. The English blockade seemed to be succeeding better than the German counter-blockade. At that time Germany could obtain from Russia a great part of the metals and oil she needed; her weak points were petrol and iron. For her petrol, she could employ synthetics, the output of the Rumanian wells and a portion of the Baku production; for iron she was dependent upon Sweden, whose ore reached her via the Norwegian port of Narvik.

In the spring of 1940 a profound uneasiness was current in France and England; both parliaments were complaining of the management of the war. Paul Reynaud, who had been reproaching Daladier for his lack of initiative, defeated him in the Chamber, and became Premier. Earlier in April the Allies thought they would 'cut the iron route' by planting mines along the coast of Norway and Germany thereupon moved into Denmark and Norway. She quickly occupied the harbours and airports, but did not send an expedition in force, and it seemed as though an Allied counter-attack would be feasible. It was tried. General Béthouart and his Alpine Chasseurs, supported by an English fleet, recaptured Narvik, but in the light of German air superiority, the British cabinet judged the operation too risky, and Norway was abandoned. Already German armoured divisions were massed along the borders of Belgium and Holland, and an attack was to be expected. It took place on the morning of May 10th, Germany violating the neutrality of Belgium, the Netherlands and Luxembourg. General Gamelin ordered the Groupe d'Armées du Nord to move forward, its left stretching as far as Holland and its main body coming to a halt along the Dyle. Sedan was the pivot for this movement. The Belgians gave cover from Antwerp to Namur. Thus the Allied armies emerged from behind their reinforced concrete shell and ventured into open country. But Hitler's plan was not to attack frontally; the basic task of the German armour was to cross the Ardennes and the Meuse, to break through the front at Sedan, and then to dash for the sea, clinging to the river basins of the Somme and the Aisne. This movement was to sever the Allied army group in Belgium from its bases. It succeeded because the numerical superiority of the German air force was crushing; because German tactics, a combination of dive-bombing and tank attacks, produced the effect of surprise and made it possible to push the fighting into the undefended rear; because the sector attacked was not fortified in depth; and because supplies were lacking, especially anti-tank guns. 'Even Joan of Arc couldn't have stopped tanks with a pea-shooter', as one American correspondent put it.

By the fifth day of the offensive, a gap thirty miles wide had been torn in the French front, at the spot where the Ninth Army had been stationed. Through this hole poured the German armoured divisions on their race to the sea. The road to Paris lay open; from Belgium there surged back a tidal wave of refugees, driven from home by the bombardments, their fear of the Nazis and the rumours spread by German agents. This flight psychosis infected the inhabitants of northern France; soon there were millions of men, women and children on the roads, accompanied by push-carts, cars and beasts of burden, which made the movements of the Allied armies difficult or wellnigh impossible. For them the only hope was first of all to stop the breach at Sedan. Then the First Army Group, turning back from Belgium, and armies hastily assembled in the south would both simultaneously attack the long corridor thrust forward by the German armoured forces. Caught in a vice and cut off from their fuel supplies, the *Panzer Divisionen* would have been crushed. General Gamelin wanted to fight such an engagement. On May 20th he was relieved by General Weygand, who faced a tragic situation. The Germans had reached the sea; Weygand could no longer communicate with his northern armies except by going to them in person by plane. At once he gave General Billotte, General Gort and the Belgians orders to attack southward. To sever the German corridor, it was only necessary to make a thrust of some twenty-five miles. Weygand's manœuvre, wholly logical and required by the geography of the situation, did not succeed because General Billotte, who was supposed to co-ordinate it, was killed in a car accident; because the flood of refugees brought the armies to a standstill; and because the First Army Group was in great disorder, being cut off from its supplies, and this sudden *volte-face* was at the moment too difficult for it to execute.

Disastrous events piled up. On the twenty-seventh, the King of the Belgians surrendered; on the twenty-eighth, General Gort began embarking his troops at Dunkirk. General Weygand, realizing that it was impossible to fight the battle he had planned, gave orders to defend the Dunkirk bridgehead and to save by sea everything that could possibly be saved. This action was made glorious by the heroism of English and French sailors and the thousands of British civilians who brought to Dunkirk everything in England that would float, and by the voluntary sacrifice of the French divisions which, under the command of General de la Laurencie, defended the bridgehead until the last troops had been embarked. Two hundred and sixty thousand British and ninety thousand French were taken over to England. Hitler, however, was able to proclaim that in this brief campaign he had taken one million two hundred thousand prisoners, Dutch, Belgian, English and French. There remained to General Weygand only forty-three divisions to defend the Somme and the Aisne, and more than ever they lacked anti-tank guns. An attempt was made to replace these with seventy-fives. Wise instructions were issued to the troops regarding defence in depth, but the disproportion between the forces engaged left little hope. It was inevitable that along a line so weakly held, the enemy would break through at one point or another. A German column dashed towards the Seine; Paris was lost. General Weygand warned the Premier that it might be necessary to ask for an armistice; the armies were not only worn out, they were scattered. There were countless acts of individual bravery; many units, for honour's sake, dearly defended river crossings. But the enemy's total mastery of the air made it impossible for a general command to function; the aeroplane was dominant in this new warfare. On the night between June 10th and 11th Mussolini declared war on France; as the French Ambassador François-Poncet expressed it, it was 'a stab in the back', a description later repeated by President Roosevelt.

The French Government decided not to defend Paris, in order to save the city from destruction, and fell back to Tours. But where would it go next, since Tours was already under bombardment? Some argued in favour of the 'Breton redoubt', which could be covered by the fleets; but what a target this would have been for the German bombers! Others proposed continuing the war in Algeria, but North Africa had no factories, no great surplus of foodstuffs and no aviation fuel. At that moment England lacked the means to re-equip its own army and could not have assisted France; the United States alone would have been in a position to furnish supplies for this new base of operations, and its hands were tied by its own neutrality law. Those who favoured the Government's moving on to Africa hoped that the Germans and Italians would not be able to reach that far, and in any case thought that even another defeat would be preferable to surrender; those opposing it said that the enemy must not be offered an excuse to invade the French Empire, that the air force there would be impotent, that the colonial cities would be destroyed, and that thus France would sacrifice her last hope. On June 13th, Paul Reynaud asked Churchill, who was at Tours, what England's reactions would be were France to find herself forced to sign a separate peace. Churchill replied: 'We shall not heap reproaches on an unfortunate ally. And if we are victorious, we assume the unconditional obligation to raise France from her ruins.' Yet he could not make this obligation an official communication without consulting his cabinet. The French Council of Ministers remained deeply divided; all agreed in thinking that neither the fleet nor the air force should fall into German hands to be used against England. The army chiefs would have nothing to do with a capitulation in open country and wanted to ask for an armistice. Reynaud won his point that before a decision was reached, a final appeal be made to President Roosevelt; of course it could not succeed, since, for one thing, the President had no right to take sides with France without Congressional approval, which he could not then have obtained, and, for another, America had neither tanks nor planes to give. On June 14th, the Government decided to leave for Bordeaux.

During the night between the fifteenth and the sixteenth the American answer arrived – a refusal. Then came the reply from England, which was in two parts. First, the cabinet, although refusing to ratify Churchill's words at Tours, still conceded that France might make overtures to obtain an armistice, on condition that the French fleet first be conveyed to British ports. This proposal, for reasons still obscure, was not communicated under this form to the French ministers, who hence were unable to express their views on this grave matter.[1] Second, the British note proposed an alternative, which was the establishment of an 'indissoluble Franco-British union'. The citizens of each of these two countries would at once acquire citizenship in the other; there would be but one war cabinet and one sole command. Here was a bold and majestic idea; it had its virtues, but it came at a moment when French minds were in no way prepared for it and had not, in the confusion at Bordeaux, time to study it. Its rejection was 'instinctive and spontaneous'.[1] Nevertheless, this rejection did not imply an acceptance of the armistice. No vote on this question had taken place. Paul Reynaud, now seeing, as he said, that he was in a minority, 'no longer considered himself qualified to intervene in London in order that France might be freed of her obligations'. He handed in his resignation and told the President of the Republic that, if he desired to follow the current in favour of an armistice, he should call in Marshal Pétain. Harsh judgments have been hurled at almost all the men who took part in this debate. Historians should take into account the situation of the country at that moment, the millions of refugees on the roads, entire armies disintegrating, the number of prisoners growing hourly. 'Had they been hard as flint,' said Monsieur Lebrun, the President of the Republic, 'men who lived in that atmosphere of confusion and horror could not have remained calm and serene.'

An armistice was signed on the twenty-second and went into effect on

[1] ALBERT KAMMERER.

the night between the twenty-fifth and twenty-sixth. Whatever opinion one may have regarding the very principle of this transaction, certain of its stipulations were inadmissible, especially the delivery to the Nazis of the liberal Germans who had sought refuge in France, and of the German aviators captured by the British. As for the fleet, the principal subject of the Franco-British debate, it was neither handed over to Germany nor sent to English ports, but each unit received formal orders to scuttle its ships rather than let them fall into the hands of a foreign Power (Admiral Darlan's order of June 24th). Were the armistice to place the fleet at Germany's mercy, the ships should at once either be taken to the United States or scuttled. This order remained binding even if contrary orders were later received, and even if they were signed by Darlan. These measures were at least a guarantee that Germany would not be able to use the French fleet against Great Britain.

Under the armistice, France was divided into two zones, one called 'free' into which the Germans at first did not penetrate, and the other called 'occupied', far greater in extent. The Government of the free zone established itself at Vichy, a famous spa, whose numerous hotels housed the various ministries. On July 10th, the National Assembly, under the presidency of M. Jeanneney, granted full powers to Marshal Pétain and made him the head of the French State. On June 18th General de Gaulle had issued his famous appeal from London, and on the twenty-eighth Mr. Churchill had recognized him as the 'leader of the Free French'. No attempt would be made to revive France's Legislative Body under the form set up by the 1875 Constitution until 1944, and the attempt then failed.

Thus the Third Republic had died. Although it had sadly faded away during an evening of defeat, it had, for the greater part of its existence been a fortunate and glorious regime. Between 1875 and 1914, it had so strengthened France that, during the course of the First World War, the Allies had, by common agreement, entrusted the high command to French generals and chosen Paris for the seat and Clemenceau for the chairman of the Peace Conference. Before 1914 the Third Republic's diplomats had surrounded France with a cluster of matchless alliances and had succeeded in reconciling Russia and Great Britain to France's advantage. The Republic's colonial administrators had built for it a fine empire and had so thoroughly won over the loyalty of the native peoples that during the 1914-18 war, it had been possible to use on the European continent almost the entire colonial army. France's literature, painting, science, music and luxury industries under this regime had shone with unquestionable brilliance. In 1918, France, one of the principal victors, had seemed to rank among the greatest Powers of Europe and the world. Why did she lose this position between 1919 and 1939?

We must grant that, even in 1919, despite its splendid victory, the country had been hard hit. It had — taking the size of its population into account — suffered heavier losses than any other. If during the four war years patriotism had filled the ditch which ever since the Revolution had separated the Right from the Left in France, the memory of this long feud remained lively in men's minds. The French conservatives had been unable to form a governmental party, respectful of existing institutions, on the British type; just as formerly they had centred their hopes on the restoration of regimes faded beyond repair, so, in the February Days of 1934, they had vaguely nourished the absurd dream of some sort of fascism — an attitude all the more deplorable that it was the doing of a handful of agitators, with no mandate behind them, at a time when there existed among the French bourgeoisie elements worthy of forming a republican Centre. The Movement party itself had lacked cohesion, especially in financial matters. The French had never lacked military courage — even the brief campaign of 1940 was the occasion of heroic feats — but civic courage and fiscal courage had long since grown weak. Too many French people no longer had confidence in their Government. During the last years of the regime, the franc had again slumped. From five francs, its 1914 equivalent, the dollar had gone up to almost fifty francs, although it had itself been devalued by forty per cent; this currency depreciation had increased the burden of war-time purchases abroad. The opposition of those with savings had ceased to act as a brake on the political parties because the war and the German experience had shown that a country can live without money and, seemingly with impunity, become totally bankrupt. But the currency collapse had brought with it the ruin of the lower middle class, both rural and urban, which had been the mainstay of radicalism; now this class was pushed towards the extremist parties of Right and Left. Moderation and prudence, the virtues of the Third Republic, had become anachronisms. France which in an earlier day had financed the development of new countries, had not enough capital to modernize its own equipment, or enough faith in the future to take great risks. During the time of the New Deal, America had been able to accept a shortening of working hours because it had a production potential far greater than the country's needs and because it was not under any imminent threat of war; France had not had the years of respite needed to work out a new economy.

Ever since the nation's birth, France's traditional mission had been to constitute on the European continent the advance guard of freedom; in the days when she had been the strongest State on that continent, she had been able to fulfil this mission by herself, and the armies of the Revolution had long held a balance in Europe. In 1918 she had been able to win only with the support of powerful allies, and it must not be forgotten that had Russia not kept sixty German divisions engaged on her front in 1914, the war would then have ended in as prompt a defeat as that of 1940. France's allies, however, made the mistake of rebuilding Germany between the two wars and making her into the greatest Power in Europe, and in 1939 the Third Republic had not had energetic backing. For various reasons, the positions of Belgium, Russia, Italy, Yugoslavia and Rumania were no longer what they were in 1914 and, by agreement with the French Government, England's military support was becoming more circumscribed. Under these conditions, there was little hope of winning the war except through a return to the 1918 line-up – the creation of a great British army, the intervention of the United States and Russia's return to the anti-German coalition. Once these changes had taken place, the same causes were to produce the same effects. As long as France remained isolated, or inadequately assisted, her defeat was inevitable, and this was no longer a consequence of the mistakes of the Third Republic, but of the unequal distribution of forces. The 1875 Constitution, unjustly censured, had not prevented the 1918 victory. Of course, had she been better prepared, France would have had more planes and more tanks, and she would have held out longer; but whatever her political regime had been she would not have been able, without her natural allies, to gather enough strength to conquer Germany. The moment the coalition of the previous conflict once again came into being, France regained her place in the world.

CHAPTER X

THE SECOND WORLD WAR: SECOND PHASE

FROM the signing of the armistice to the Allied landings, the French war drama was played on several planes. France could be liberated only by the establishment of an anti-German coalition and that coalition's victory; she was to be saved by the tenacity of England, by Russia's entrance into the war, by the intervention of the United States and by her own resistance elements working as a team with the Allies. On the internal level, the so-called Vichy Government was subject to constant enemy pressure. As long as the French could hope that Marshal Pétain was playing a waiting game, the majority respected him; each time the Government spoke of collaborating with the enemy, the regime became unpopular. The forces of the occupation, already detested as such, little by little infuriated the French by the cruelty of the Gestapo, by the execution of hostages, by deportations and by anti-Semitic persecutions. By way of internal resistance, a secret army and information network had been set up immediately after the armistice. By harassing the enemy, by transmitting information to the Allies, by abetting the escape of English and American aviators, later by force of arms, the French Resistance contributed to the ultimate victory. Then there were the Free French, the first name given by General de Gaulle to his London organization, which he later called the Fighting French. Having the British radio at his disposal, he heartened the French and thus gained manifest prestige among them. He kept French troops in the war alongside the English, won the adherence of several French colonies (Chad, the Cameroons, etc.) and, in 1943, was to become the head of a provisional Government. Finally, there was North Africa. There the armistice had permitted the continued existence of a French army, which clandestinely preserved its weapons and watched over its fitness. An autonomous North African resistance movement got in touch with the Americans and made possible their 1942 landings, the first step towards liberation.

On the world plane, the sequence of events is well known. After the defeat of the Franco-British armies, a German invasion of England was to be expected. But Hitler did not have the equipment necessary for this operation, that amphibious equipment which the Americans were later to build and use with so much success. Moreover, Germany could not essay this difficult undertaking until the British air force had been neutralized. This is what she tried to do between August and November, 1940. The attempt failed. The pilots of the Royal Air Force, although only one-quarter as numerous as those of the Luftwaffe, inflicted such losses on the latter that Goering put a stop to the Battle of Britain. England's victory in the air restored hope to many Frenchmen. There followed a long and painful period of British defeats; in Yugoslavia, in Greece and in Crete the Germans triumphed with lightning speed. In the desert, between Tripolitania and Alexandria, the Italian divisions were reinforced by Marshal Rommel's *Afrika Korps*; for a few weeks there was reason to fear that the Axis Powers would reach Suez. At Vichy, the advocates of collaboration regained the ground which they had lost as a result of the Battle of Britain; but in June 1941 Hitler made the arrant blunder of attacking Russia. By this mistake, as much political as military, he reinforced the Resistance in France, since he thus unified the working class against him. America was not yet a belligerent, but Roosevelt openly supported Germany's enemies and assisted them.

In December 1941 the United States entered the war, as the outcome of the Japanese attack on Pearl Harbour and Germany's declaration of war. Forced to conduct a campaign on two fronts, America determined to launch its first principal effort against Germany. What device would be used to free Europe? In 1942 neither America nor Britain possessed the forces necessary to land in France. The Germans had erected along the Atlantic coast a fortified line whose strength the Allies perhaps overestimated, but which had inflicted dreadful losses on the Canadians during their heroic Dieppe raid. The plan jointly worked out by the British and the Americans was to take North Africa as a landing stage and, operating from this base, to attack the 'soft under-belly of Europe'. Roosevelt and his advisers had long thought that it was important to procure themselves friends in North Africa; American consuls and vice-consuls had been installed there, and they had established contact with a small group of French military men and civilians who were prepared to help them. There was reason to hope that when the day came, the French army of North Africa, still a considerable force, not only would not seriously oppose a landing, but would join forces with the Allies. General Giraud agreed to place himself at the head of this movement. He had wished that the landing should take place in southern France, where the people of the French Resistance could lend it support, but the Americans considered this operation too extended for their still limited means, and on November 8th, 1942, landed in Algeria and Morocco. At first there was some confusion. Admiral Darlan, who happened to be at Algiers and whom a portion of the armed forces viewed as their only legal commander, was hoisted to power through a compromise which astonished and offended American public opinion; but the Allies hoped thus to consolidate their position in North Africa, at first precarious, and the French army did line up at their side. Indeed this army played an important part in the Tunisian campaign. Under Lend-Lease, President Roosevelt had agreed to re-arm new French divisions (General Béthouart's mission to Washington), and thus there took shape in 1943 the French expeditionary corps which, under General Juin's command, was to play a part in the Italian campaign.

Meanwhile, the French political situation was laboriously shifting in Algeria. When Admiral Darlan was assassinated on December 24th, 1942, in American eyes General Giraud had become the guardian of French interests in North Africa. But Britain, which had made analogous commitments to General de Gaulle, would not allow him to be sacrificed. During the Casablanca Conference (January 1943), Roosevelt and Churchill brought the two generals together and asked them to work with each other for the liberation of France. Immediately after the victory in Tunisia there began lengthy and troublesome negotiations. General Giraud proposed that, when they returned to France, a Tréveneuc Law be put in force, under which power reverted to the departmental general councils until the National Assembly could be convened. General de Gaulle and his followers wanted more radical changes. They secured the formation at Algiers of a Committee of National Liberation (later the Provisional Government of the French Republic) and the inclusion of representatives of the Resistance, come from France, in a Consultative Assembly, which consisted of these as well as a certain number of deputies and senators who had succeeded in escaping. General Giraud and General de Gaulle were to be alternately chairmen of the committee. In actuality, this committee was so constituted that from the outset the majority in it belonged to General de Gaulle, and thus General Giraud and his friends were little by little eliminated. The Algiers Government prepared numerous laws supposedly to be applied upon the Government's return to France, especially one to purge collaborationists through special new courts of justice, one on the ineligibility of those members of Parliament who had voted full powers to Pétain in July 1940 (including some ninety per cent of the senators and deputies), and one on the control of the press.

At the end of 1943 the time was ripe to begin the reconquest of the continent of Europe, where, in every occupied country, resistance movements awaited the Allies. The need to cover landings with an umbrella of planes made it necessary to progress by stages; from Tunisia, Eisenhower, the Commander-in-Chief, moved on to Sicily, then from Sicily to Italy, where the French army, under General Juin's command, played an important part. Would it be best to continue in this direction and wage a wholly Mediterranean war, with fresh landings in the Balkans? Some were of this opinion, but Roosevelt and Stalin prevailed at the Teheran Conference (November 1943), and it was decided that the principal attack against fortress Europe should be launched in France, with the British Isles as its springboard. Appointed Commander-in-Chief of the Allied armies, General Eisenhower, as supreme Commander of the Allied forces, employed bomber squadrons to crush German industry. Meanwhile preparations were made in minute detail for a landing in Normandy, including prefabricated harbours and underwater pipelines to lay across the Channel. The scheme was to cut off the Cotentin peninsula and make a quick seizure of the port of Cherbourg. Unfortunately, in order to 'seal off' the terrain of the attack and hold off any German reinforcements, it was necessary to destroy the bridges and railways, thus wreaking terrible damage in France and the destruction of certain Norman towns and of monuments which could never be replaced, such as the Town Hall of Rouen. The landing took place on June 6th, 1944, and was wholly successful; the Cotentin and Cherbourg were occupied. The whole German Seventh Army, cornered between the British, the Americans and the Seine, was wiped out. It had been demonstrated that the German command, from the moment it lost mastery of the air, could no more extricate itself from a desperate situation than the French army had been able to in 1940. By the middle of August 1944 General Patton's armoured forces were rolling towards Paris without meeting any serious obstacles along the way.

If we are to understand events in Paris, we must know the nature of the diverse elements making up the Resistance; this movement, after as well as before the Allied landings, had greatly helped the liberators, but although it was at one against the forces of occupation, it was not homogeneous. It was made up of several groups with various political allegiances (the National Front, the Liberation, the Combat, the Franc-Tireur, etc.), and a non-political military organization, the A.S. (Secret Army, also called the Organization of Army Resistance). 'The men of the Resistance all want an uprising against the foreign Power and order; almost all, a revolution against Vichy's power and order; a lesser number, revolution against the power and order of the Third Republic; an even smaller number, revolution against the existing socio-economic power and order.'[1] Several French traditions were here mingled, but they were temporarily united by a common object. Some fought like the knighthood of every age; others, like Jacobins to save and re-establish the Republic; still others, like the insurgents of the June Days, to establish a socialist democracy; all were in agreement before everything else to free the soil of the fatherland. The Allies had parachuted weapons to the F.F.I. (French Forces of the Interior) and the F.T.P. (Franc-Tireurs and Partisans), the latter being communists; in May 1943 all these movements had been unified, and a Council of National Resistance had been set up, first under the chairmanship of 'Max' (Jean Moulin), then, after he had been executed by the Germans, of Georges Bidault. A general delegate (Parodi) represented the Algiers Committee of National Liberation in this council.

The Germans' approaching departure was to raise in Paris the grave question of the transmission of power, for a capital cannot remain without a Government, and the 'French State' had faded away after a few days of idle negotiation. Under advice from Washington, Marshal Pétain and Laval had sought to hand power back to Parliament, but this procedure was at once displeasing to the Germans, to the Resistance and to the Algiers Government. It came to nothing, and Marshal Pétain, against his will, was dragged off to Germany. What was to succeed him? The Third or the Fourth Republic? The Resistance's extreme Left, by starting an uprising in Paris as early as August 19th, attempted to tip the scales in favour of revolution. A truce made with the German General, Dietrich von Choltitz, was disavowed by the Parisian Committee of Liberation and broken on the twenty-first. Meanwhile, radio messages had been sent, announcing that the capital was liberating itself and requesting Allied troops to come as soon as they could to the movement's support, to prevent the still possible destruction of Paris. General Eisenhower wanted the first division entering Paris to be a French division and had the Second Armoured Division (Leclerc's) moved into the vanguard. On Thursday, the twenty-fourth, the first French tanks arrived, and on the

[1] ADRIEN DANSETTE.

following day General von Choltitz signed the formal capitulation. Not only for France, but for the whole world, the liberation of Paris was a symbol of victory. In South America, in the United States, in England, happy crowds celebrated this triumph of the Spirit. In Paris, on August 26th, General de Gaulle was acclaimed from the Arc de Triomphe to Notre Dame, yet on the very porch of that church there burst out a volley of which we have not yet a full explanation. A break between the General and the internal Resistance seemed out of the question to everyone while the war was still raging and in the presence of the Allied armies; moreover, an instinctive patriotism then held together the great majority of the French, although a potential ideological conflict remained.

On August 15th a potent Allied army, which included the First French Army under General de Lattre de Tassigny, had landed in southern France; it moved up the valley of the Rhône to effect a junction, on the eastern frontier, with the forces which had pushed through from Normandy, and it met with little opposition. Germany was at the end of her tether. South of the Loire there remained no troops of occupation apart from a south-western pocket (Bordeaux, Saint-Nazaire). Eisenhower well knew that this pocket could easily be reduced whenever he wished, and concentrated his strength in the north-west in order to cross the Rhine and the Siegfried Line. Meanwhile Montgomery's army of British and Canadians freed the north of France and Belgium; a hundred days after the Normandy landings, the Allied armies from Ostend to the Swiss frontier were ready for the invasion of Germany.

Nevertheless, the campaign lasted the whole winter. In December a German counter-offensive, against an ill-defended sector in the Ardennes, seemed for a while to place Namur, Liège and Sedan in jeopardy; then, in the south, Strasbourg, threatened anew, was saved by French troops from cruel reprisals. This last convulsion of Hitler's armies had no permanent effect; the Allies crossed the Rhine; Germany was invaded. In April the Americans and the Russians met on the Elbe. Hitler committed suicide, and on May 7th, 1945, in a small red school building at Reims, the enemy signed an unconditional surrender.

Japan remained to be vanquished. French naval units, especially the cruiser *Richelieu*, participated in this last campaign, which in its turn ended on September 2nd, with the capitulation of the enemy. The Second World War was over.

CHAPTER XI

FRANCE AFTER LIBERATION

THIS period has not yet sufficiently emerged from the passions it aroused for a historian to be able to study it objectively; and yet we must indicate the main outlines of the picture. What was the country's legal government in 1944? Vichy's 'French State', repudiated since November 1942 by the majority of Frenchmen, had been dissolved by the Germans. No real force any longer supported this regime, disavowed even by those who in good faith had first regarded it as the legitimate heir of the Third Republic. Was it possible to re-establish this Third Republic and its institutions? Obviously, Parliament could have been convened, minus those of its members who had committed grievous faults; the National Assembly could have been called together; the 1875 Constitution could have been modified if it was considered necessary and a regular President of the Republic could thereupon have been chosen. This procedure would have had the advantage of removing France from an interim status, of avoiding useless discussion and of assuring the Government of the collaboration of men who had experience in public affairs. It was not followed, partly because the country, which had suffered greatly, held a grudge against those whom it considered responsible for its misfortunes and seemed to want 'something new'; and mostly because the men who, either at London and Algiers, or in the internal Resistance, had taken over command in dangerous circumstances thought they had a right to retain it. Hence it was decided that the French Republic would be administered by a provisional Government, that a Constituent Assembly would be chosen, and that the new Constitution would be ratified by a plebiscite.

It was still necessary to agree on the make-up of the provisional Government. A great majority wanted at that time to confer the presidency on General de Gaulle. The Algiers ministers had moved to Paris the moment the capital had been liberated, but they had to take into account the desires of the Resistance. A compromise ensued: new men who came out of the National Council of Resistance and who had proved their worth in action (Bidault, Teitgen) entered the Government and worked with the Algiers contingent. First of all the war had to be brought to a close, then a Constituent Assembly had to be elected; the decisions reached on voting procedure exercised a controlling influence over these elections. The balloting method whereby each *arrondissement* voted for a single representative was replaced by voting for a list, with proportional representation. The result was to promote the establishment of big parties and to give them mastery over their elected candidates, they being, thanks to this new procedure, no longer directly dependent upon the electorate. The Algiers Government had decreed that all deputies and senators who had voted full powers in 1940 should be ineligible, and thus a great part of the Third Republic's politicians found themselves left out. This was a very hard blow to the Radical party, many of whose men, thus banned, were personally popular in their constituencies. What was more, the vote had been given to women, which the Radicals believed would augment the influence of the Catholic Church. The results of the first ballots showed that three great parties, about equal in size, dominated the new France—the Communist party, the United Socialist party and a new party, called the Popular Republican Movement (M.R.P.), a Catholic organization with a social programme, not far removed from the old Christian Democrats. The Radicals, the Moderates and the Independents shared the rest of the votes; the Right had scarcely dared show its face.

The problems to be solved were vast. Not only did a Constitution have to be elaborated, but the currency had to be saved, food supplies assured and transport reorganized. The ravages of war had turned the country upside down; there were fewer French people than in 1939, the losses having been in several categories: there were the soldiers killed on the field of battle; there were the victims of the occupation, both those shot and those deported (two-thirds of the latter not having returned); there was the abnormally high death-rate, the consequence of a starvation diet; and there were the civilian victims of the bombardments prior to liberation.[1] Almost two million dwellings had been damaged, five hundred thousand of these beyond repair. Almost all bridges, railway stations and dams had to be rebuilt. A housing crisis prevailed in all the large cities, and especially in Paris, into which flowed the refugees from the devastated areas. Ever since the war of 1914 rentals had been legally

[1] Figures supplied in 1947 by the Ministry of Veterans and War Victims: Fighters in the Armed Forces, 149,954 dead; Deported, 150,000; Civilian Victims, 188,000; Shot by Firing Squads, 30,000; War Prisoners Dead During Captivity, 38,000; F.F.I., 24,400; Others Missing, 37,000. This amounts to a total of 620,000 French people, a figure including only the war's direct victims; several hundred thousand *indirect* victims would have to be added to make it complete.

held down to such a low figure that no landlord could build, or even maintain existing buildings. Many factories had been stripped of their machinery. Clothing, household utensils, furniture—everything was lacking. The two 'paps of France', field crops and animal husbandry, had in part been dried up by the lack of fertilizers, agricultural machinery, fodder and man-power. Half the vineyards had to be replanted. In 1939 France produced 87 per cent of the food she consumed (her imports being oils, coffee, cocoa and sugar); in 1945, she produced barely 65 per cent. Hence it was necessary to buy abroad, but here arose a problem of currency and ship chartering. Payments made to the Germans as occupation costs (three hundred milliard francs) and war expenditures had brought on considerable inflation; the value of the franc in relation to the dollar, during the war fixed at fifty to one, had to be officially lowered to one hundred and twenty to one, and it was much lower still on the black market. Lend-Lease was continued by the United States until the end of hostilities, but when it ceased, it was necessary to fall back on credits. The purchasing power of the franc had dropped from 100 in 1913 to 18.2 in 1926 and to 1.8 in September 1946. Budgetary expenditures for the fiscal year 1946 were in the neighbourhood of 600 milliard francs as against 5 milliards in 1913; military disbursements amounted to 72 per cent in 1945 and 38 per cent in 1946 (a peace year) of the total budgetary receipts. The 1946 deficit stood at 215 milliards; public charges represented about 30 per cent of the national income.

The Government of France was thus an infinitely hazardous enterprise. Abroad it was requisite to maintain within the ranks of the great nations a country which remained worthy of this position, but which could no longer, on the military level, keep up with richer and more prolific lands. At home it was requisite to rebuild an economy which even in 1939 had been inadequate because of insufficient equipment. In France seven million farmers barely fed forty million French; in the United States, eight and a half million farmers fed one hundred and twenty-six million Americans and produced an exportable surplus. Hence the yield per man in America was three or four times that in France. Why? Through a better use of machinery? Partly so; but this mechanization of agriculture and industry had been made possible in the United States only by the abundance of that country's energy sources — coal, oil, natural gas, water power. France had to import 38 per cent of her energy, and even with these imports, it was as though each American had at his disposal one hundred and seventy robots, while each Frenchman had only twenty-four. Thus the French problem was above all a problem of industrial equipment. Many food-stuffs imported by France, a part of the raw materials for her textile industry and some of her oils could be produced on her own soil, but to accomplish that would require a far-sighted Government, having the courage and intelligence to make a continuous effort of organization.

Poor in man-power, poor in energy and poor in raw materials, France still possessed no less precious resources and values that were hers alone: the intelligence of a population which had through many generations produced and then produced again ingenious scientists, skilful diplomatists and clever artisans; the toil of her workers and her peasants; a tradition of taste inherited from centuries of cultivation which, by letting her craftsmen live in an atmosphere of beauty, afforded them an opportunity to surpass those of other lands; the graciousness of her cities and of her countryside; the charm of her social life. France's prestige abroad still rested on the dramatic character of her history, on her heroic battles for freedom, on her marvellous powers of recuperation; and also on her writers, her artists, her architects. What was needed, to give the country the means for yet another rebirth, was to export her taste and her culture and to attract foreign visitors to her shores. But how was such a pro-gramme to be carried out immediately after a conflict that had left the nation profoundly divided and that, in many cases, led political parties to subordinate economy and culture to ideology? France's problems were becoming first and foremost political problems.

The political equilibrium was not stable; from the very first months, conflict had arisen between General de Gaulle and the Constituent Assembly. Not that the General opposed the policy of planning and nationalization desired by the Communists and Socialists and accepted by the M.R.P. (*Mouvement Républicain Populaire*). Mines, banks, insurance companies and a few large industries were nationalized, with indemnities in Government securities for the dispossessed owners. But the General, more concerned with France's greatness and her place in the world than with finance and economics, clashed with the Assembly on the question of military credits and handed in his resignation on January 21st, 1946. His successor as head of the provisional Government was for a short time Félix Gouin, a Socialist. Meanwhile the proposed Constitution was taking shape; the majority in the Assembly, following the tradition of the French Revolution, wanted to have the country governed by a single all-powerful chamber. This scheme was rejected by the electorate, and on May 5th, 1946, the M.R.P., which had advocated this rejection, became the first party in France. Its leader, Georges Bidault, presided over the new provisional Government. The second Constituent Assembly revised the proposed Constitution in accordance with the desires of the electorate and created a Council of the Republic, a second chamber which was far from possessing the same powers as the Senate under the Third Republic. In the second referendum on the Constitution, General de Gaulle advised another vote of nay; he considered the President's powers inadequate. The yeas carried it by a very small margin; the Fourth Republic was born.

The new Assembly, elected for five years, numbered 168 Communists, 93 Socialists, 160 M.R.P., 59 members of the Left Group, R.G.R. (Radicals and the like), 82 miscellaneous and 12 Mohammedans. Hence the Communists had become the largest party. Only a few votes were lacking to the Communists and Socialists in order to give them together an absolute majority of Marxist allegiance. But the Socialists were divided, some wishing to create a proletarian front with the Communists, others closer to the political liberalism of the Radicals, while still loyal to a planned economy. 'The line of demarcation', someone wrote, 'cuts through the heart of every Socialist.' It having been impossible to form a coalition ministry, Léon Blum, a respected veteran of the Third Republic, agreed to set up an interim cabinet composed principally of Socialists, and to see to it that the Constitution got under way. He governed — and very ably — until first the Council and then the President of the Republic had been elected. Meeting at Versailles in accordance with tradition, the Congress elected to the presidency for a seven-year term (January 16th, 1947) a Socialist, Vincent Auriol, a man of good sense and good faith, much beloved by all the parties. Since Léon Blum refused to remain in power, the Socialist Paul Ramadier was entrusted with constituting a quadripartite Government — Communist, Socialist, M.R.P. and R.G.R. (*Rassemblement des Gauches Républicains*). Édouard Herriot was elected president of the Assembly. Thus the foremost posts in the Fourth Republic went to the veterans of the Third. Outside the Chambers, General de Gaulle continued to urge revision of the Constitution, a presidential administration; and in April 1947, in order to push this campaign, established the Rally of the French People, to which he hoped to see all the anti-Communist French adhere, and which, he said, was above parties.

In May 1947 France's position as a whole appeared better than might have been hoped by those foreigners who, at the moment of liberation, had seen the country in disarray, drained of its substance. The food situation certainly left much to be desired, reconstruction seemed slow to the war victims, special courts were still functioning and men were far from that reconciliation which Bonaparte had so wisely imposed after no less violent internal troubles. Nevertheless, the French had laboured valiantly. Order had long since been restored in the rural areas (much disturbed in 1944-45); the transport system had been put in repair and the bridges rebuilt; the railways were running normally; once again most of the articles of daily life were to be found in the shop windows. A bad harvest had shortened bread supplies, meat was still lacking, fuel supplies were far from being certain for the coming winter. But if France's position was compared with that of other countries, and above all to what a 1944 observer might have feared, it had to be recognized that the country by and large was healthy and that France was slowly recovering her balance.

BOOK SEVEN

THE FOURTH AND FIFTH REPUBLIC

CHAPTER I

FRANCE SINCE 1947

THE Fourth Republic made its bow in circumstances of considerable difficulty. The reason for this was partly that it found itself faced by a situation which would have endangered any regime, partly that its Constitution was badly drafted. Those who created it had hesitated between a presidential form of government, modelled on that of the United States, and a government by Assembly. The result was a mixture of the worst features in both systems. The President of the Republic had power to nominate the President of the Council, whose *investiture*, however, had to be carried by a constitutional majority of the National Assembly (one-half of the total votes, *plus* one). Such an absolute majority was not easy to obtain. The first Ministry was a three-headed affair, consisting of the M.R.P. (*Mouvement Républicain Populaire*) or Catholic Republicans, the Socialists and the Communists. This alliance was a direct result of the Resistance, in which the three groups had worked hand in hand. But a lasting *entente* with the Communists was impossible, because they continued to pursue their party tactics which aimed at placing their own people in all the key positions with the object of clearing the way to revolution. Outside Parliament, General de Gaulle, who no longer occupied a position of power, embarked on a campaign of speeches and public meetings. The Communists accused him of plotting dictatorship, and demanded the setting up of Vigilance Committees. The result of this was to drive the *Rassemblement du Peuple Français* more and more towards the Right, though much against its will. Having begun as a movement directed against all parties, it now became, in its turn, a party.

The end of the year 1947 saw a complete rupture between the Communists and the two other groups in the Government coalition. Up till then, the Communist party had supported the freezing of prices and wages. But now it made a complete turn round and gave its backing to a policy of wage-claims and strikes. This was bound to have some success, for the French people were discontented. The price of coal had risen by 76 per cent as a result of the withdrawal of the Government subsidy; that of sugar by 50 per cent. A whole series of strikes, accompanied by violence, began in December. Gangs of miners moved about the Nord department, stopping trains, and demanding that the factories be closed. Very soon there were disturbances all over France. For a while it seemed not impossible that the Fourth Republic would be overturned.

The Government, however, won the day. Léon Blum had advised the formation of a new group of parties: *The Third Force*, which should have as its object 'to rally all republicans, those who refuse to submit to the dictatorship of a political party, those who set their faces against seeking help against such a danger in a system based on personal power'.

It soon began to look as though an impossible task was facing the Governments of *The Third Force*. They were composed of disparate elements which were at odds on all the more important issues. The only way to drive this ill-assorted team without risking a spill was to make sure that it should never move forward at all. There has been much criticism of the 'stick-in-the-mud' methods of the first leaders of the Fourth Republic. That they should have had to be adopted at a time when there was so much to be done was certainly regrettable, but no sooner did an energetic President of the Council attempt to act, than he was overthrown.

Nevertheless, a considerable amount of work was going on behind the scenes. Frenchmen are always more ready to dilate upon the mistakes of their rulers than to praise their achievements. The programme of national rehabilitation known as the Monnet Plan, assisted by American aid (the Marshall Plan) was brilliantly successful. Those who find fault with the Fourth Republic should remember that it had to grapple with problems caused by widespread destruction, that the country found itself faced not only by the necessity of reconstructing roads, harbours, bridges, railway tracks and stations, but had, in addition, to find new sources of power and to equip many factories on modern lines. Between 1948 and 1953 the production of electric current, in terms of kilowatt hours, moved from 23 to 42 milliards: the number of tons of motor-fuel handled by French refineries increased from 2,800,000 to 22 million, and deliveries of cement from 3,400,000 tons to 8 million. At the same time the motor-car industry showed a tremendous forward movement.

France was starting again from a very low pre-war level. The country had been subjected to enemy occupation. Above all, her population, after a long period of stagnation, had suddenly and rapidly taken an upward curve. This growth will be of immense value in the years to come, but its immediate effect has been to saddle the community with a far greater number of children than had been anticipated. A gigantic effort has been made to provide new schools. All things considered, it is only fair to admit that the work of the Fourth Republic, during its brief lifetime, was anything but negative.

As the date for the 1951 elections drew near, the problem of the existing electoral law had once again to be dealt with. Prior to the war, Frenchmen had voted by the method of *scrutin d'arrondissement*, with two ballots. In 1946 a system of proportional representation had been introduced. From the purely arithmetical standpoint this seemed fair enough, but life is more than a calculation of figures, and in fact proportional representation has never, anywhere in the world, produced majorities capable of carrying on a government. If, in 1951, it had been allowed free play, the two great opposition parties, the Communists and the Rassemblement (R.P.F.) would together have had a majority in the Assembly. But since they could never agree about anything, government would have become impossible.

A new method was devised: proportional representation *plus* 'inter-marriages'. It was agreed that the parties should have the right to conclude alliances among themselves. In Departments where this system obtained more than 50 per cent of the votes, all the seats would be credited so the 'allied' lists. In the others, the rules of proportional representation thould hold good. It was calculated that the new electoral law would reduce the number of Communists and R.P.F. elected, and this turned out to be the case. The Communists, with the same number of votes as before, had 50 per cent fewer seats. The R.P.F. captured 121. The Conservatives, who now called themselves Independents, gained ground.

It looked as though it would be easy to carry on the government with this new Assembly in which a Fourth Force, comprising the three parties of the former coalition, with the addition of the Independents, would have a comfortable majority. But very early in the session the dangerous question of the undenominational schools was unfortunately reopened. This in itself was quite enough to divide the M.R.P. (Catholic) from the Radicals and the Socialists. The latter found themselves once again in opposition.

The financial situation was growing rapidly worse. The deputies very considerably increased the public expenditure, but refused to vote the taxes required to meet it. The country was importing more and more, exporting less and less. Edgar Faure, the President of the Council, had to warn the House that the reserves of gold and specie were scarcely sufficient to meet three days of foreign payments. He very rightly demanded an increase in taxation, and was thrown out for his trouble.

Vincent Auriol called upon Antoine Pinay, an industrialist from the provinces, to form a government. Pinay had already been a minister, and the President had been favourably impressed by his sound common sense. He was accepted by the Assembly, but only because he was supported by a group of Gaullist deputies who had grown sick of voting with the Communists. He checked inflation by issuing a successful tax-free loan with a gold backing. When, however, he proposed to increase the duty on spirits, he in his turn was defeated. The Assembly, it seemed, was completely unable to resist the pressure exercised by vested interests. Since, too (as we shall see later), the war in Indo-China, and the fulfilment of certain international obligations, necessitated credits on an enormous scale the country's indebtedness was greatly increased.

At the end of 1953, the Congress (the National Assembly and the Council of the Republic) met at Versailles for the purpose of electing a new President of the Republic. M. Vincent Auriol had added to the prestige of that high office. Through seven difficult years he had never for long left the country without a government, and had acquitted himself with honour. The business of election went on for several days, and it was only at the thirteenth ballot that M. René Coty was chosen. He was a Senator from Normandy, a strong-minded and patriotic man, who was fated to find himself confronted by worse difficulties, both at home and in the French Union, than had beset any of his predecessors.

At the Brazzaville Conference of 1944 it had been decided that the word 'Empire' should no longer be used in speaking of the French overseas territories. These were now to be known as the *French Union*, and their inhabitants were given grounds for hoping that they would achieve, by successive stages, a position of independence *inside* the French political system. The word 'Empire' had become unpopular for several reasons. (a) It seemed right and proper to grant to the native populations which had furnished so many soldiers to the French military effort the right to play a part in the government of their own communities. (b) Both America and Russia, though each for different reasons, were taking a strong stand against what they called 'colonialism', and by doing so were awakening lively hopes. (c) The Asiatic and Arab peoples were becoming conscious of their strength.

But each national group within the French Union had its own particular problem which demanded its own particular solution. Algeria was a part of metropolitan France, administered by the Ministry of the Interior. Black Africa came under the Ministry of French Overseas Territories.

Morocco and Tunisia were Protectorates, the one with its Bey, the other with its Sultan, under the aegis of the Foreign Office. In Indo-China (or Vietnam) an Emperor had been established on the throne by France and recognized as a sovereign ruler though he was not accepted as such by the country at large. Laos and Cambodia were 'Associated States', as, indeed, was Indo-China, one part of which was in the hands of the Communists led by Ho-Chi-Minh. Reforms had been promised to all these peoples, but the successive governments, weighed down by the work involved in dealing with metropolitan problems, could not give their undivided attention to the difficulties of the French Union except when they produced an explosive situation.

In North Africa, a change had come over the picture with the formation of the Arab League, which was now encouraging the nationalists in the different countries. It found the soil well prepared. France had brought education to the new generations, and had herself instructed them in the love of liberty. Very soon, reforms, which had they been put forward at the right time might have satisfied the North African peoples, were now regarded as unsatisfactory. Rebel bands (in Tunis they were called the Fellaghas) were a standing threat to the security of the colonists and of such Moslems as had remained loyal to France. Their acts of violence, their assassinations, brought repressive measures in their train, and tempers rose on both sides. In Morocco the French authorities thought that calm could be restored by removing the Sultan Sidi Mohammed Ben Youssef, setting aside his two sons, and establishing Ben Arafa on the throne. They soon realized their mistake. Disorders increased and murderous attacks became more numerous.

In Indo-China it might have been possible in 1947 to negotiate with Ho-Chi-Minh, and that would certainly have been better than the long and terrible war in which France was to lose many brave soldiers and some of her best officers, to say nothing of the milliards of francs for which there was such a pressing need at home.

It was easy enough to foresee that the end of the Korean war, by liberating a mass of Chinese material, would lead to a recrudescence of the military operations in Indo-China. So long as General de Lattre de Tassigny was in command, the level of morale remained high. But he returned to France, where he died, and in any case even he could not have brought the war to a successful conclusion. Two-thirds of the country was controlled by the *Viets*, who had numerous, though not openly avowed, friends. The French Army fought bravely, and managed to gain ground at the cost of heavy losses, but this was almost immediately lost again as a result of 'infiltrations' against which no defensive system was proof. An increasing number of the politically minded at home were coming to realize the futility and dangers of the campaign, but the Americans insisted that the struggle should be continued. The disaster of Dien-Bien-Phu, in which a French garrison of twelve thousand first-rate fighting men was taken prisoner by the *Viets*, resulted in an active threat to the whole of the delta and to the town of Hanoi. In spite of much unavailing heroism, the game was lost.

The Indo-China affair brought about the fall of the Laniel Government. The President of the Republic called upon Pierre Mendès-France to form a new Ministry. The newcomer had a reputation for courage in both war and politics. As a member of General de Gaulle's Cabinet in 1945, he had put forward a programme of national austerity similar to the one that had brought financial salvation to Belgium. It was, however, turned down, and he had at once resigned, being unwilling to assume responsibility for a policy with which he did not agree. On June 17th, 1954, he delivered his investiture speech in the Assembly. 'A cease-fire in Indo-China,' he said, 'must be arranged as soon as possible,' and he went on to declare that his Government would bring about the desired result in four weeks. Either he would present his solution to the House on July 20th, or he would resign. He further stated that he would submit a programme of economic reforms, and a plan to deal with the problem of a European Army. In North Africa he would pursue a liberal policy. Finally, he would construct his Government without reference to arithmetic or party vetoes. He was given an overwhelming majority – 320 non-Communist votes plus 99 Communist. Only 43 deputies actively opposed him, though there was much whispered criticism in the lobbies. The feeling was general that the country needed rapid solutions, and even his secret adversaries dared not withhold their support.

A conference was just then in session at Geneva. Delegates from China were present, and it was on them that the issue of peace in Indo-China depended. Contact was established with them, and afterwards with the representatives of the Vietminh. On July 21st a cease-fire agreement was signed. Thus ended a conflict which had been a running sore in the body of France for a number of years. Parliament gave its approval, and then adjourned for the recess. A few days later, Mendès-France, accompanied by Marshal Juin, flew to Tunis, saw the Bey, and returned with a peace plan which would grant internal independence to Tunisia. It looked as though a second grave problem had been solved. Not everyone was satisfied, but the proposal was widely supported on the ground that it seemed to be the least bad of many possibilities. Meanwhile, at the Ministry of Finance and Economic Affairs, Edgar Faure was putting the finishing touches to an eighteen-months plan which was to produce excellent results.

On only one issue was France still deeply divided: the construction of Europe. Robert Schuman had succeeded, without much difficulty, in getting adopted his scheme for the creation of a European Coal and Steel Community, a supra-national organization with headquarters in Luxembourg. Many French 'Europeans' were hoping that the second stone in the edifice would take the form of a European Defence Community (E.D.C.). It was scarcely to be expected that German rearmament would be greeted with enthusiasm in a country which had so frequently been overrun by German armies; but the E.D.C. had the advantage of integrating the German armed forces into a collective body. Mendès-France was of the opinion that E.D.C. would not be ratified by the French Parliament, and in any case he was not very enthusiastic about it. He left the Assembly free to decide, and E.D.C. was buried without a debate. The 'Europeans' were very angry with him over this check to their plans. He declared that he had always remained faithful to the Atlantic Pact, and was perfectly willing that Germany should be admitted to membership of NATO, on condition that the British and Americans should leave their troops in Europe. But the supporters of E.D.C. were disappointed and bitter.

The 'style' of the Mendès-France administration, the rapidity with which it reached decisions, appeared to be popular in the country. It was less so in the Assembly, which had been brought to heel at a time of great anxiety. Many of the deputies were grateful to the President of the Council for having provided them with solutions which they would never have dared to press of their own accord. But in February 1955 a vote of confidence was taken on the Government's North African policy and resulted in a defeat for M. Mendès-France. Edgar Faure's investiture was approved by 369 votes to 210. There had been a modification of the Constitution. From that time on a simple majority was held to be sufficient for investiture, and only those deputies actually present in the House at the time were entitled to vote on a motion of confidence.

The Faure Government encountered serious difficulties in Algeria, where bands of terrorists were a constant danger to isolated farms, roads, and even towns. So far, Algeria had been free from troubles, but now the situation began to develop in an alarming manner, and reinforcements had to be sent. By this time a very large proportion of the French Army was in North Africa. In Morocco, Faure reinstated the former Sultan, Mohammed Ben Youssef, and restored a state of relative calm, if not of complete peace. The Sultan promised that the rights of the French settlers should be respected. It was agreed to open negotiations immediately after the elections with a view to establishing Moroccan independence.

The elections were due to be held in June or July 1956. But by the terms of the Constitution the President had the power to dissolve the Assembly if two successive governments were defeated within eighteen months on motions of confidence. The Assembly having given Edgar Faure a minority vote, he at once exercised this right. The two Radical leaders, Mendès-France and Faure, were by this time on bad terms, and the party found itself cut in two. The elections were put forward to January 2nd. The principal parties were: the Communists; the Republican Front (Socialists and Mendès-Radicals); the Faurists (R.G.R.); the Right Centre (Pinay); the Social Republicans (to whom General de Gaulle had refused the right to make use of his name); and a new party, the Poujadists, whose leader was a bookseller from Saint-Céré. The Poujadist party consisted of a number of small shopkeepers and manual workers, and was at first publicized as an anti-tax organization, though on the eve of the elections it embarked upon a violent demagogic campaign. The results of the voting brought surprise and disquiet. The Communists obtained 150 seats, and the Poujadists, 52. This meant that in the new Assembly one third of the members would be declared enemies of the regime. The Social-Republicans were reduced to a handful. Neither the Right Centre nor the Left Centre could command a majority. The Socialists formed a minority Government under Guy Mollet, and received the support of the Assembly for more than a year, because there were urgent questions awaiting settlement.

First and foremost was that of North Africa. In both Morocco and Tunisia it had been possible to negotiate with reigning sovereigns and responsible leaders, and these two states had in fact won complete independence, though at the same time retaining certain cultural links with France. In Algeria the problem was more complex. It had never in the past been a nation, and such unity as it had was entirely due to France. The French settlers were numerous, and had been established in the country for several generations. They felt strongly that in an independent

Algeria under the domination of the National Liberation Front (F.L.N.) there would be for them no security of tenure. The F.L.N., for its part, declared that no solution short of independence would be acceptable. Guy Mollet, after paying a visit to Algeria, decided to fight, and sent more than four hundred thousand men to reinforce the troops on the spot.

The international situation was still disturbed. Russia was trying to turn the Western position by arousing the Middle East and Africa. In Egypt, Colonel Nasser was dreaming of an Arab Empire extending from Pakistan to Morocco, of which he would be the head. He tried to strengthen his hand by nationalizing the Suez Canal. The British and the French, both seriously injured by this act of grab, prepared an expeditionary force, the object of which was to recover the Canal. From the military point of view, the operation seemed easy, but diplomatically it was impossible, because it was opposed by both Russia and the United States. Britain was deeply divided over the wisdom of the action, and it had to be abandoned. This failure, however, in no way affected the cordiality of Anglo-French relations, and in April 1957 Paris gave an enthusiastic welcome to Queen Elizabeth.

The idea of a united Europe was making headway. Two treaties — the Common Market and Euratom — have tightened the bonds between the six countries of Europe, and England seems inclined to join hands with this community. The Mollet Government had prepared both measures, but was overturned at the very moment when they were to be submitted to the Assembly. It was replaced by a Bourgès-Maunoury Cabinet largely composed of the same ministers, and later by one presided over by Felix Gaillard. The scandalous instability of these successive governments had the effect of persuading an ever increasing number of Frenchmen that a profound revision of the Constitution was indispensable and ought to be carried through with the least possible delay.

At the beginning of 1958 the situation of the regime seemed to be highly precarious. There was no coherent majority in the Assembly. In any given parliamentary group were to be found violent supporters and opponents of a policy of negotiation in Algeria, where there was a growing feeling of uneasiness alike in the Army and among the French settlers. When it was the turn of the Gaillard Government to be turned out, the French elements in Algeria feared that an administration favourable to autonomy might soon find itself in power. On May 13th, as the result of the revolutionary movement in Algiers, a mob seized the Government buildings. A Committee of Public Safety was set up and demanded the complete integration of Algeria with France. A number of generals were included in this Committee, and the Army of Algeria made it clear that it was prepared, if necessary, to seize supreme power in France with the object of forwarding this plan.

In Paris, M. Pflimlin, whose investiture had been voted by the Assembly, realized that he no longer had the means at his disposal for carrying on the government of the country. Neither the Army nor the police would have supported him. An appeal for discipline by the President of the Republic was ineffective. It looked as though civil war was a possibility, and might in fact break out at any moment. Many men of widely differing political views thought that in this state of confusion only one man had the necessary prestige to enable him to save the country from dismemberment: General de Gaulle. He had long remained outside the political arena, and had taken no part in the recent controversies. He was living quietly in retirement at Colombey-les-deux-Eglises. The reputation which he had gained during the war was still undiminished in the eyes of most French people. He enjoyed the respect of the Army, and it was to him that the soldiers now appealed. He issued a statement to the effect that he was prepared to devote himself to the service of his country, but would accept power only if it were offered him in accordance with the law of the land. M. Coty was ready to take steps to this end.

The leaders of the several political parties, and ex-President Vincent Auriol, established contact with General de Gaulle. They found a man of assured serenity whom prolonged meditation during the years of withdrawal from public life had humanized. His intentions seemed to them to be compatible with the survival of republican institutions. He offered to form a government and submit his investiture to the normal process of a vote in the Assembly. If this went in his favour, he would then adjourn Parliament and work out the details of a new Constitution in which increased power would be given to the executive. He procured the necessary vote at a session in which he showed that he possessed a high degree of parliamentary skill. Included in his list of ministers were several new men and two Presidents of the Council of the Fourth Republic (Guy Mollet and M. Pflimlin). The *Garde des Sceaux*, Michel Debré, produced a draft Constitution which was then amended by the Council of Ministers, and finally submitted to a Consultative Committee under the chairmanship of Paul Reynaud, and to the Council of State. In the text, as approved, the representatives of the people retained the right to overturn a government by a vote of censure, but the President of the Republic

– the keystone of the new State – was given the power to dissolve Parliament, and also to appeal to a Referendum. The Overseas Territories were to be allowed to choose between independence and integration.

General de Gaulle went in person to Madagascar, Black Africa, and to some of the big French cities, for the purpose of explaining the principles of the Constitution. The enthusiasm with which he was welcomed augured well for the final vote. The Referendum on the Constitution took place on September 28th, 1958. The exceptional number of votes cast was sufficient evidence of the tremendous interest aroused in France, Algeria and the Overseas Territories by this form of popular consultation. The Constitution was adopted by enormous majorities – 79.30 per cent in metropolitan France, and even more in Algeria and Black Africa. Only Guinea returned an answer of *No*, thereby opting for independence. For France, this vote of confidence given by emancipated populations was an act of homage and a powerful encouragement. No one could say what the future might hold, for institutions are man-made things. But the recovered sense of union showed every sign of ushering in a high period of hope and stability. On October 5th the Constitution was proclaimed. The Fifth Republic had started on its career.

The Parliamentary elections were held at the end of November 1958. They resulted in a big majority for the parties which had associated themselves with General de Gaulle. The Radicals, the Socialists and the Communists all lost a number of seats. The new Constitution entrusted the choice of a President to an enlarged electoral college. It was no longer with Parliament that the responsibility lay of choosing the Head of the State, but with delegates representing all the Communes of France. President Coty having tendered his resignation, General de Gaulle was regarded by an immense majority of the French people as the only possible successor. On December 21st, he was elected *Président de la République et de la Communauté*. A stable leadership seemed now to be assured for the next seven years. President de Gaulle appointed as his *Premier Ministre* (a new title for the Head of the Government) M. Michel Debré, who on January 15th, 1959, presented his Cabinet and his Programme to Parliament. He obtained 453 votes as against 56, with 27 abstentions.

A tour of the French Provinces made by General de Gaulle proved the extent of his popularity. The confidence of his fellow-countrymen found an echo in the attitude of foreign countries. Capital soon began to flow into France. The previous tendency was reversed. The country had been threatened with an insufficiency of currencies from abroad. Now in less than a year a reserve of two milliards of dollars was built up, and it became possible to repay earlier loans instead of asking for new ones. The strengthened financial position made practicable a more independent foreign policy. The French Government accepted the idea of a united Europe, of a Common Market, and of the Atlantic Community, though it insisted on playing a more important role in the latter.

The essential questions now confronting the Government were as follows:

(a) *Algeria.* In a speech delivered on September 16th, 1959, General de Gaulle made an offer of self-determination to the Algerians — that is to say, the right to choose their own future by a free vote. Guarantees were promised to the National Liberation Front enabling it to send representatives to Paris for the purpose of negotiating a cease-fire. The F.L.N. replied to the effect that the stipulated conditions did not permit of any such negotiation.

(b) *The Communauté.* The Council of the Community has had a number of sittings under the presidency of General de Gaulle. The countries composing it may be divided into two groups. On the one side are those who wish to retain their political links with France; on the other, those who demand independence, though they are, at the same time, anxious to keep their economic and cultural relations with France untouched. This choice is permitted by the Constitution. Guinea, at the time of the Referendum, chose independence.

(c) *Nuclear Armaments.* The French Government is of the opinion that the safety of France can be assured in two different ways: the destruction of all existing stocks of the atomic bomb (very unlikely), or her inclusion in the 'Atomic Club'. To this a number of objections have been made, economic on the one side (the intolerable burden of expenditure), political on the other (that the security of France is assured by NATO); but the Government has replied by pointing out that the defence of the nation should not depend exclusively on the goodwill of its partners.

(d) *The World Situation.* During the last months of 1959 there was a slackening of international tension. Mr Khrushchev's visit to the United States seemed to be opening the way to a Summit Conference. France is in favour of such a conference provided it is carefully prepared beforehand. French relations with Germany appear to be excellent, as also those with Italy. The French Government, much strengthened by its increased prestige, hopes to work in concert with its allies for the maintenance of peace.

The main facts of the population problem in France are generally known. First there is the very considerable rise in the birth-rate since the war.

What are the causes of this reversal? The most important would seem to be the new attitude of the State towards families. The allowances, benefits and priorities now available are an encouragement to parents. Also to be considered is the fact that the determination of the nineteenth-century *petit bourgeois* to leave his land to one son only so as to avoid splitting it up has become meaningless in a period like our own in which inheritance plays a very small part in the normal household budget. In these days, most people live on what they earn. For the same reason young people marry earlier and more adventurously. They depend less than formerly on the generosity of their parents. Child-bearing has become less painful, less dangerous and less onerous. The number of children per family oscillates round a figure of 2.3. A recent inquiry shows that the majority of young French couples hope to have three, which means a still greater increase in the birth-rate.

There is the fact that during the same period the death-rate has fallen. Improved hygiene has reduced infantile mortality. Antibiotics have made relatively harmless many diseases which were once fatal to the old. There has been immense progress in surgery. In short, the population of France, which in 1958 stood at around 44 million, looks like reaching 46 million by 1971.

In this mounting tide of population there are certain secondary waves or undulations which have to be considered. The war years (1939-45) naturally had a low birth-rate, and this deficiency will have an effect upon the immediate future. Between the years 1960 and 1962 there will be a marked diminution in the number of young men taking their places in the active life of the community. On the other hand, the ten very plentiful classes of children born between 1946 and 1956 will from now on be successively reaching the age at which the schools will absorb them — nursery, primary and secondary, technical colleges and institutions of higher education. It is essential therefore that plans should be made well in advance for dealing with a schools problem, a labour problem and a housing problem. The last of these is of capital importance, and presents great difficulties. Not only has the population increased: it is more and more drifting into the towns. New and innumerable arrivals from North Africa and the French countryside are invading Paris. Many have nowhere to live.

The rural population of France now amounts to about 12.5 million, 7.5 million of whom work on the land, that is to say $33\frac{1}{2}$ per cent of the active population as compared with 5 per cent in Great Britain and 20 per cent in Holland. But with every year that passes, the old peasant stock is becoming more and more urbanized. This drift to the towns exists in all countries. It is, however, more dangerous in France, where the young people are abandoning great tracts of land which will never again be cultivated after they have left. In what does the attraction of the towns consist? The prestige of the machine: the cinema, which opens the eyes of the countryman to pleasures of which he has previously known nothing: a lessening of the feeling that oppresses agricultural workers of being 'exiles' in their own country. What do they want? Additional machines that will enable them to farm the land more intelligently and with less man-power. Many a young fellow about to abandon the farm for the factory would remain on the land if he could have a tractor to drive. A tractor may not always be a good investment financially, but in terms of psychology it most certainly is. All the young farmer wants is to make French agriculture more scientific. But in order to do that he must be given a lead. Unfortunately there is a shortage of technical advisers. All the same, in the course of the last few years much valuable work has been done in this direction. 'Display areas' have been created which, farmed by the most modern methods, have produced yields that serve to instruct whole districts. In Lozère, a country of poor grassland, the production of pasture has been doubled. Certain villages from which the population had been draining have had to build new houses. But a great effort is still needed if French agriculture is to be properly equipped for the task of producing anything like enough to supply the needs of the market.

French industry is suffering from excessive production-costs. This is partly due to the financial burden occasioned by the 'welfare state'. Social security is more complete in France than anywhere else in the world: consequently it is a heavier charge on the community. Women and men are paid the same wages for the same work. A very equitable international agreement has suggested that this system should be generally applied, but only in France has this been done. Nevertheless, in certain fields French industry is competing successfully with that of other nations. It has equipped factories in Germany, Belgium, and even the United

States. France sells electrically driven locomotives all over the world, and compares favourably with Germany and Switzerland in the production of dye-stuffs. She ranks second as a supplier of iron ore, and leads Europe in the matter of aluminium.

Two new organizations, the *Plan* and the *Aménagement du Territoire*, have been set up for the purpose of looking ahead and preparing for the future. The latter is trying to decentralize French industry by directing it to the smaller towns, and even to rural areas, where both man-power and accommodation are less of a problem. In the Bordeaux region, for example, where too much attention has been given in the past to vine-growing and commerce, much benefit will be derived from the building up of the timber trade, and the establishment of oil refineries. Capital plays a greater part in France than elsewhere. A geographer (J.-F. Gravier) has written a book — *Paris and the French Desert* — in which he shows that Paris is constantly expanding, while the provinces are becoming emptier. Now, the overall costs of running a town multiply in relation to the growth of its population. In 1949 those of Paris worked out at 25,000 francs per head, as against 8,000 in Bordeaux, and 4,000 in a town of 3,000 inhabitants. To this must be added the many hours lost each day as a result of traffic congestion by men whose time is very valuable. It is essential that factories should be taken to areas which have a long-settled population, rather than that workers should be sucked into the 'great wens'.

If the cost of living in France is high, the main reason is that the State now absorbs 40 per cent of the national revenue compared with the 12 per cent which was the figure before 1914. Life is expensive because the cost of running the State machine is tremendous. Nevertheless there is a considerable amount of discontent in the ranks of the civil service. Many more people are in State employment now than before 1939, but they are relatively less well paid than formerly. Today's salaries make it impossible to maintain the standard of living that obtained in the period between the wars. This holds good of all the income groups, from the highest to the lowest. In the old days, senior officials could keep up appearances. At the present time a *Président du Cour d'Appel*, or a *Préfet*, has heavy responsibilities. True they are no heavier than those of his predecessors, but life has become more precarious. A colonel finds the education of his children a great strain. A university professor, if he happens to be a family man, cannot make ends meet. In the old days many French civil servants had private incomes, and wives who had brought them a dowry: nowadays the notion of a dowry is as much a thing of the past as an inheritance. The French press has changed in character since the war. The number of Paris newspapers has diminished, and only one of the survivors (*France-Soir*) can boast a circulation of over a million. All the same, these Paris papers exercise a great influence on the Government and on Parliament. In the rest of France, the provincial press has acquired an authority and a standing which it never had before 1939. *Ouest-France, La Voix du Nord, Paris-Normandie, Le Progrès* (Lyon), *Le Dauphiné libéré, La Nouvelle République du Centre-Ouest, Nice-Matin, Sud-Est*, and ten others, have between them several million readers. Their leading articles are widely quoted every morning on the radio. Though Paris attracts the vital elements of the country, national politics are decided not by the Parisian intellectuals, still less in the *salons* which were all-powerful in the days of Balzac, but by the many thousand villages and market towns where Frenchmen work, go fishing, play at *boules* and talk politics in the local café. It is by the schoolmaster, the postman, the lorry-driver, that ideas are spread. In the nineteenth century, revolutions were made in the Paris streets. Today, the Paris police force is large and strong. The State, weak where creative thought is concerned, is powerful in defence. It is provincial public opinion that directs the country at the polls.

French literature still leads the world, and enjoys an international popularity. The last of the 'giants' of the period between the two wars (Valéry, Gide, Claudel, Alain, Martin du Gard) have all died since the Liberation. But the generation that has followed theirs has a number of excellent writers to show: Mauriac, Romains, Cocteau, Montherlant, Giono, Émile Henriot, Sartre, Camus, Chardonne, and many others. The young men are rich in promise. They have been blamed for their tendency to dwell on the darker aspects of life, for their pessimism, and it is true that the earliest of the post-liberation novels and films did revel in piling on the horror. This was due to the many acts of violence that had marked the Occupation, to the hardships endured during a period of great difficulty, and also to the influence of certain American novelists. But this obsession with pessimism shows signs of weakening under pressure from a public that wants works of a wider scope, of a truer and more generous attitude to life.

The theatre, especially in Paris, retains its prestige. The acting, the perfection of the stage settings, the way in which the classic tradition still lives on — all these things continue to make a deep impression, not only on visiting foreigners but on the audiences of those countries that have been toured by the Comédie-Française and the Marigny Company. The visit of French actors to Moscow in 1954 assumed the proportions of an international incident, and proved to the Russian public that the art of the West has still much genuine beauty to offer. The French theatre has also deeply influenced both Canada and the United States. The taste for a certain kind of perfection is one of the things that France has never lost. The love of achieved form, the satisfaction of a job well done, whether it be that of a cook, a dressmaker, or a painter, has produced an atmosphere in which art thrives, with the result that writers and artists from many lands, and even simple tourists, are irresistibly drawn to France. There is at the present time a genuine renaissance of the theatre in many of the French provincial cities, at whose annual festivals the classical masterpieces are played to crowded and enthusiastic audiences drawn from every social class.

France has still much to give to mankind. The prestige of her literature and her art, the love felt by so many foreigners for 'la douce France', are very far from being extinguished. In the economic field the resources of the country are great, though they have not always been used to the best advantage. It seems that, for some time now, a serious effort has been made to organize the French, to persuade them to conquer an over-narrow individualism. If they have the wisdom to unite, if they can make the best of their reformed institutions, if the French community can combine order with liberty and prosperity, if peace can be maintained throughout the world, there should be no insurmountable obstacles to a wise and stable government preparing for France a future worthy of her past.

CHAPTER II

CONCLUSION

THERE is a free will for nations, and peoples, like individuals, build their own lives. France will be tomorrow what she chooses to be. But this freedom is exercised within the range of certain limits defined by what has gone before and by the means at hand. History does not ascertain the future; it studies the past and describes the hereditary factors at work. 'What do I care whether John the Fearless passed this way,' a physicist once said, 'since he will never pass here again? . . .' But his progeny will pass, and will find here the same earth, the same climate, the same national behaviour. Because France happens to lie at the western extremity of the European continent, she has throughout her history been threatened and invaded, and from this has sprung her desire for a strong authority, which she found first within the framework of the Roman Empire, found anew in Charlemagne, in Louis XIV, in Bonaparte, and which the prefects of the Third Republic gave her as had the *intendants* of the Old Regime. Because France dwelt on the fringe of the Mediterranean and the Atlantic worlds, of the Latin and the Germanic civilizations, she has, all through her national existence, had to adapt herself and work out new ways. Chivalry, courtesy, romantic love, Chartres and Versailles are French creations the influence of which has been universal.

Although England's neighbour and coeval, France has had a wholly different history. The English monarchy, established by conquest in 1066, was able very shortly to grant local freedoms; the French monarchy, at first infinitely precarious, had to build France bit by bit and had to struggle against local tyrannies. From this arose the French movement towards absolute monarchy. The double danger created by a girdle of external enemies and by feudalism at home made the French tolerant of centralized power; they long ago granted it permanent taxes; only at a very late date did they demand a representation which the English had enjoyed ever since Magna Carta. One of the first results of this centralization was the creation of a deep gap between the masses and an absentee select few, and from this came the Revolution's violence, bloody memories and, during the last hundred and fifty years, the great difficulty in achieving the country's unity, except in times of national peril. A second consequence has been to make England a nation naturally more respectful of law; sharing in government, the English willingly obeyed it. The French became rebellious because they had no other way in which to assert themselves, and they have remained so. In the seventeenth century, life at court, and the capital's spiritual dominance, gave birth to the classic spirit, a tradition of analysis, a liking for abstract terms, while at the same time lack of contact with the business of daily life stripped political thought of any practical temper and strengthened in France the spirit of party rather than the spirit of compromise. Ideological conflicts are far more perilous among the French than among the realistic Anglo-Saxons. In England and America we find no quarrels over institutions, over the power of the Church, over the free or laicized school. The rationalism of the universities had, even in the Middle Ages, contributed to making the French a people passionately dedicated to logic; the opposition, an indispensable wheel in the parliamentary machinery, has all too often been treated in France as a heresy.

Several times in the course of her history, France has seemed bankrupt, now by invasion, now by civil war. Often other peoples have thought that she was lost, but she has always driven out the invaders promptly, and always a middle party has finally rebuilt French unity long enough to make reconstruction possible. 'In all the ages of their history', writes an American historian, 'the French have given proof of an inexhaustible vigour, of a capacity quickly to raise themselves out of disaster, of a courage and persistence which the worst misfortunes have been unable to beat down. How many times in the course of the centuries have we not seen France, torn with internal strife or prostrate at the feet of her enemies, immediately astonish the world by her wonderful powers of recuperation? . . .' This was true after the Hundred Years War; it was true after the Wars of Religion; it was true in the years of the Consulate; it was true in Monsieur Thiers's time; it is still true in our own day. The Frenchman is no less stubborn than the Englishman, but he cannot be so in the same fashion. The Englishman does not admit that he can be beaten; the Frenchman has had the experience of defeat; he knows that his country from time to time runs the chance of being overwhelmed by a superior force. But he knows also that never has the conquest been of long duration and that each time the enemy has been driven forth. Once invaded, France pulls herself together; resistance is a classic phenomenon in her history. 'The land has been taken; hearts are beyond capture.' Her awakenings are as miraculous as her crises are troublesome.

This steadfast faith the French have in their own destiny, this certainty that France cannot perish, finds its explanation in the memories of a long and glorious history. The nation has the reflexes of a scion of illustrious ancestors who acknowledge *noblesse oblige*. If the Frenchman agrees less willingly than the Englishman, the German or the American to bow before administrative regulations, he does obey 'a kind of unwritten law which is imperiously forced upon him by a certain national ideal of perfection . . . This explains, despite the seeming confusion, the genuine order which in fact exists in French organization, the unity of national thought despite all divisions; the good sense despite the incoherence, as well as the respect for everything which embodies the collective ideal. This respect, this admiration for a great and noble action, for the quality of a piece of work, for everything which is beautiful or elegant, and above all for the skill of an orator or the power of an intellectual, is deeply felt by the Frenchman, in spite of his familiar tendency to scoff at that which he admires. Few peoples are capable of overthrowing so many ministries, always to summon the same ministers back to power, of ill-treating its great men so shamelessly, and of exalting them so highly. . .'[1] An age-old pride, natural in the heirs of a magic past, has up to this day strengthened the French in their trials and furthered difficult reconciliations among them when such were demanded by the country's welfare.

France's history, a lasting miracle, seems more dramatic than that of other countries. Like Greece in another age, it has the special privilege of deeply moving the people of the earth to the point where they take part in France's quarrels. The story of Joan of Arc, that of the kings of France, that of the French Revolution, that of the Marne, that of the Resistance, form a part of the heritage of all mankind. If England has preserved in the modern world Rome's imperial and judicial tradition, Paris has played, both in letters and in the arts, the role of Athens. No nation holds its language and its literature in greater respect than does France; she has created a language of precision which has made for clarity in thought, and from this she has gained an intellectual empire extending far beyond her physical borders. For five centuries, 'everything which was French was universal, and everything which was universal was French'.[2] France's writers in their influence have made themselves the evangelists of Western civilization, while their country constituted the military and moral vanguard of liberty for the continent of Europe. A difficult role. The vanguard is ever in danger and, when the main army

[1] DOCTEUR RENÉ LAFORGUE.   [2] ÉTIENNE GILSON.

follows it only after a space of three years, the vanguard is in danger of being overwhelmed. Being a Frenchman was and will remain a dangerous business; it is all the more honourable.

There are those who wonder whether this glorious past, and the sense of obligation which it has engendered, are not too heavy a burden for France to carry in a world which has been shaken to its foundations. 'The French,' they say, 'find themselves obliged by their traditions to maintain a standard of living which is really beyond their means. . .' This would be true if the influence of France is estimated wholly in terms of her military strength. We have seen, however, that it is, on the contrary, mainly intellectual and spiritual. If, at long last, an effective international organization comes into being, a very considerable part in it will be played by France, and, should this organization run on the rocks, she will undoubtedly find some way of achieving security in a closer union with her neighbours and her overseas territories. She will have to give more attention than she has given hitherto to the new disciplines imposed by a scientific age, but her earlier adaptations seem to augur well for her future successes. It is she, quite possibly, who may give birth, in pain and suffering, to solutions which will enable mankind to continue the human experiment.

[References to Kings and Emperors will be found under this general heading, listed in chronological order under the sub-heading of the countries.]